# ORDNANCE

CW00743375

# STREET ATLAS
# Nottinghamshire

## Contents

**IV** *Key to maps*

**VI** *Administrative boundaries*

**1** *Street maps*

**222** *Index explanation and abbreviations*

**223** *Index of towns, villages and rural localities*

**224** *Index of street names*

PHILIP'S

First edition published 1994 by

Ordnance Survey          and          Philip's
Romsey Road                             an imprint of Reed Consumer Books Limited
Maybush                                   Michelin House, 81 Fulham Road, London, SW3 6RB
Southampton SO9 4DH                and Auckland, Melbourne, Singapore and Toronto

ISBN 0-540-05858-0 (Philip's, hardback)
ISBN 0-540-05859-9 (Philip's, softback)
ISBN 0-319-00377-9 (Ordnance Survey, hardback)
ISBN 0-319-00378-7 (Ordnance Survey, softback)

To the best of the Publishers' knowledge, the information in this atlas was correct at the time of going to press. No responsibility can be accepted for any errors or their consequences.

The representation in this atlas of a road, track or path is no evidence of the existence of a right of way.

Printed and bound in Great Britain by
Butler & Tanner Ltd, Frome and London

## Key to map symbols

⊕ British Rail station

⊖ London transport station

🚂 Private railway station

🔴 Bus or coach station

Ⓗ Heliport

◆ Police station (may not be open 24 hours)

✚ Hospital with casualty facilities
(may not be open 24 hours)

☐ Post office

+ Place of worship

◼ Important building

P Parking

🔻174 Adjoining page indicator

⊠ No adjoining page

═══ Motorway or dual carriageway

A27(T) Main or through road (with Department
of Transport number)

╤ Gate or obstruction to traffic (restrictions
may not apply at all times or to all vehicles)

- - - - Footpath

— — — Bridleway

— — — Path

═══ Track

The representation in this
atlas of a road, track or path
is no evidence of the
existence of a right of way

| | | | |
|---|---|---|---|
| Amb Sta | Ambulance station | LC | Level crossing |
| Coll | College | Liby | Library |
| FB | Footbridge | Mus | Museum |
| F Sta | Fire station | Sch | School |
| Hospl | Hospital | TH | Town hall |

| 0 | | ¼ | | ½ | | ¾ | | 1 mile |
|---|---|---|---|---|---|---|---|---|
| 0 | 250m | 500m | 250m | 1 Kilometre | | | | |

**The scale of the maps is 3½ inches to 1 mile (1:18103)**

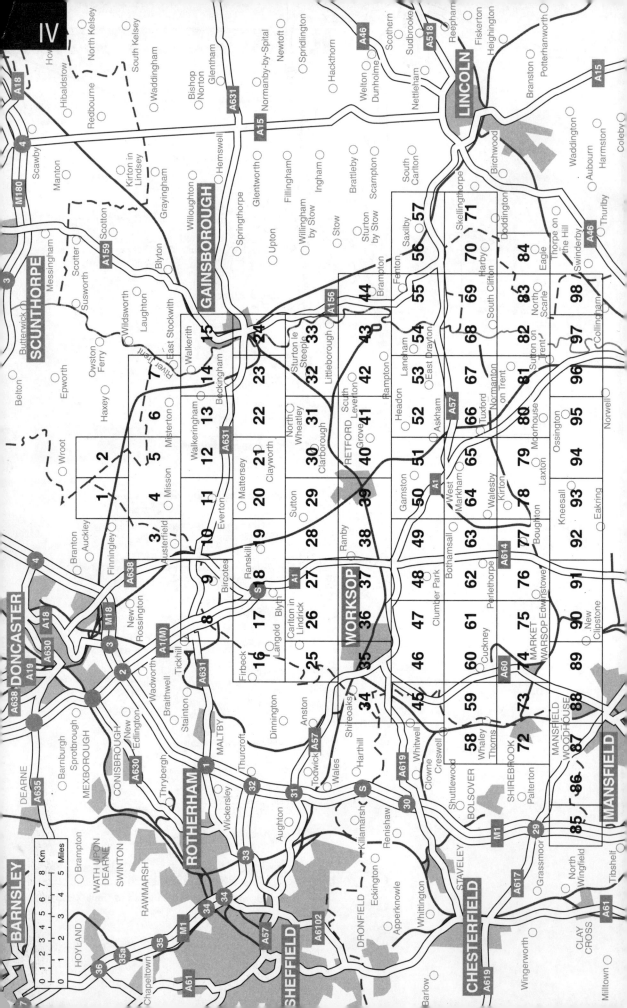

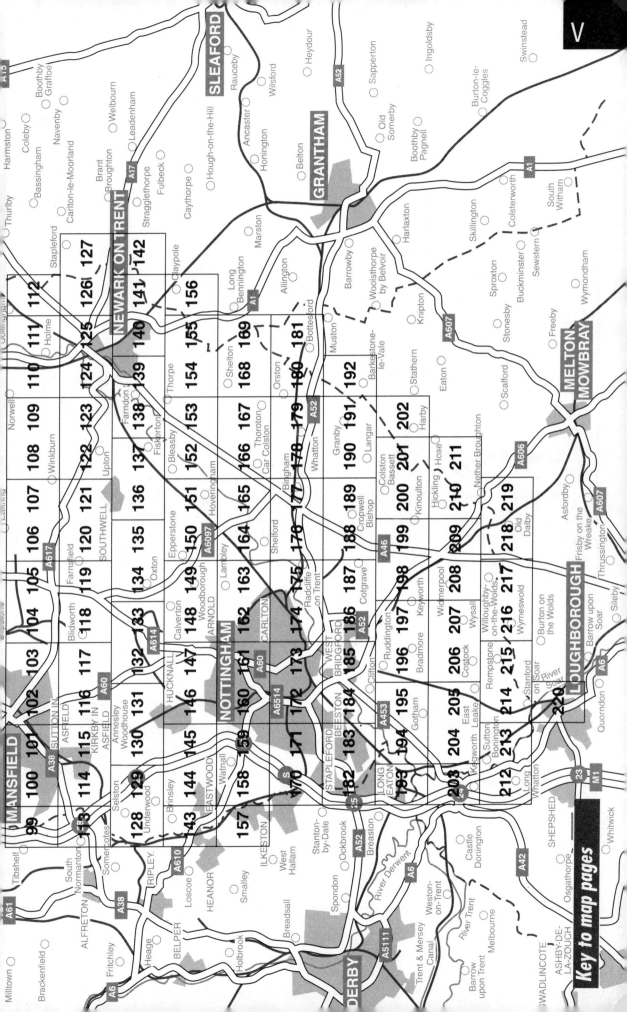

Key to map pages

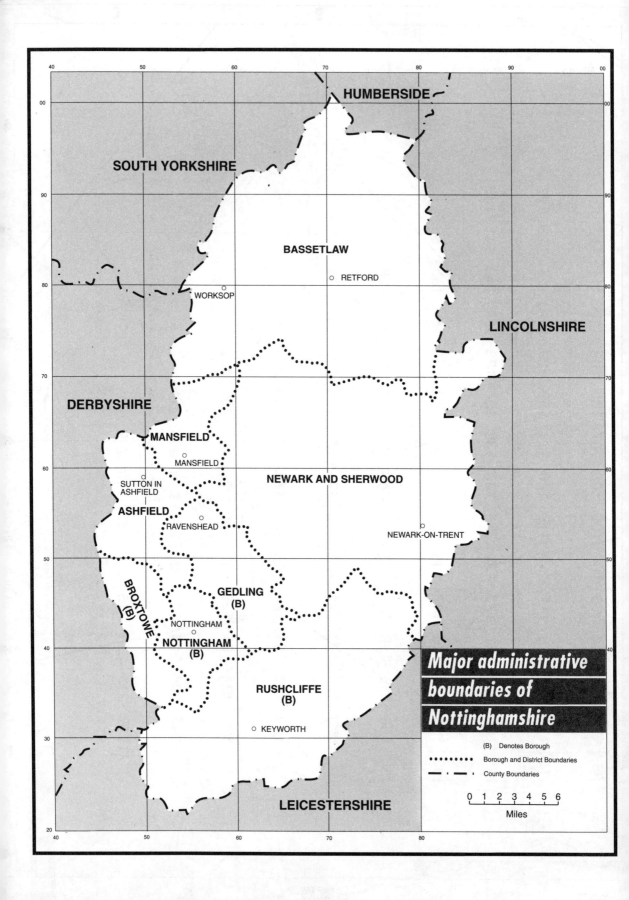

VI

**Major administrative boundaries of Nottinghamshire**

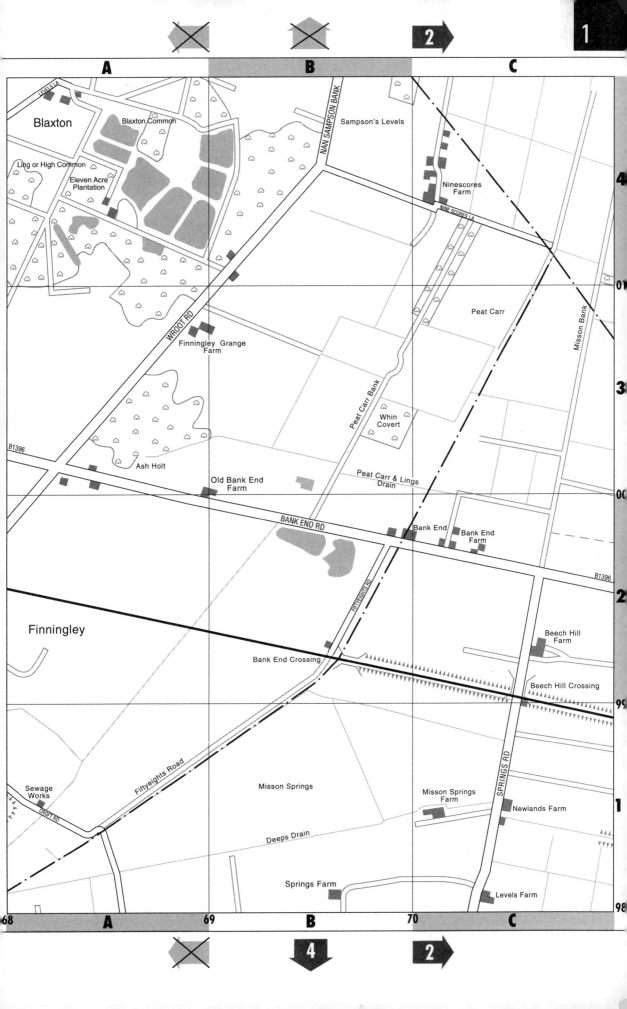

Blaxton

Blaxton Common

Sampson's Levels

NAN SAMPSON BANK

Ling or High Common

Eleven Acre Plantation

Ninescores Farm

NINE SCORES LA

WROOT RD

Peat Carr

Misson Bank

Finningley Grange Farm

Peat Carr Bank

B1396

Whin Covert

Ash Holt

Old Bank End Farm

Peat Carr & Lings Drain

BANK END RD

Bank End

Bank End Farm

B1396

Finningley

FIFTYEIGHTS RD

Beech Hill Farm

Bank End Crossing

Beech Hill Crossing

Sewage Works

CROFT RD

Fiftyeights Road

Misson Springs

SPRINGS RD

Misson Springs Farm

Newlands Farm

Deeps Drain

Springs Farm

Levels Farm

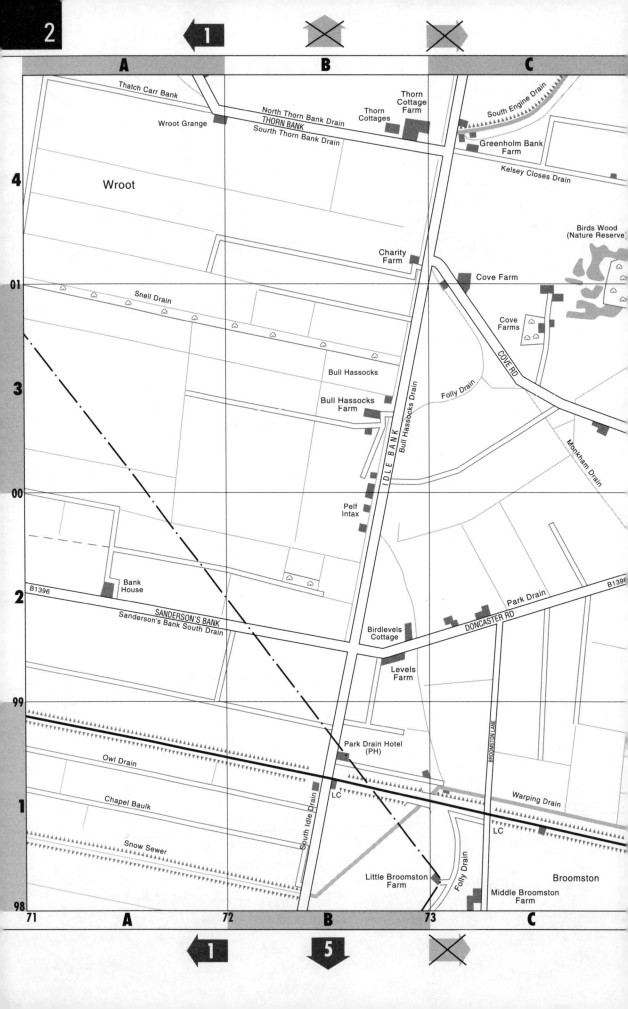

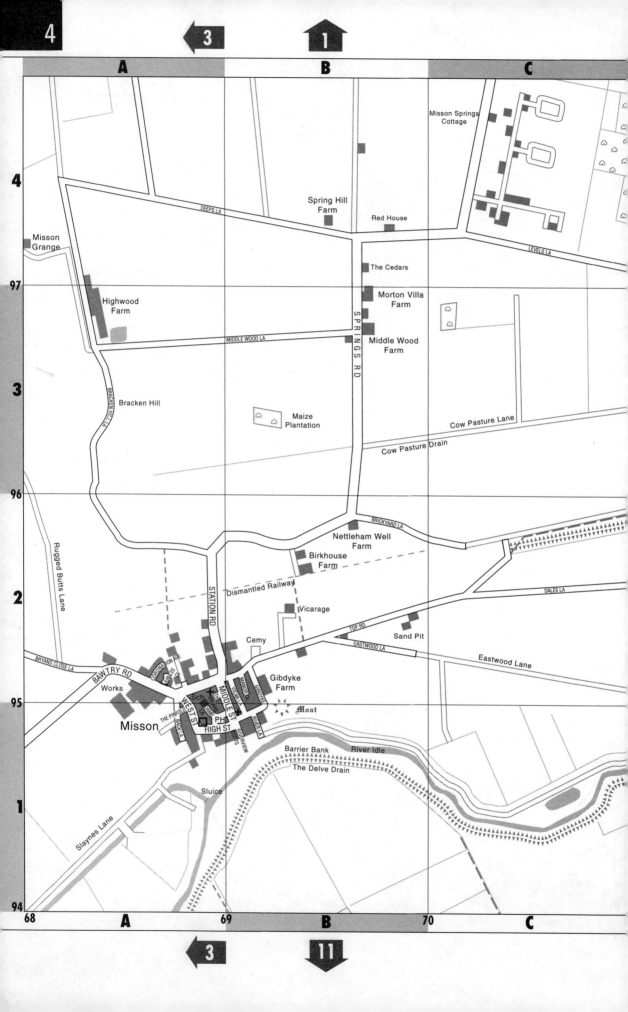

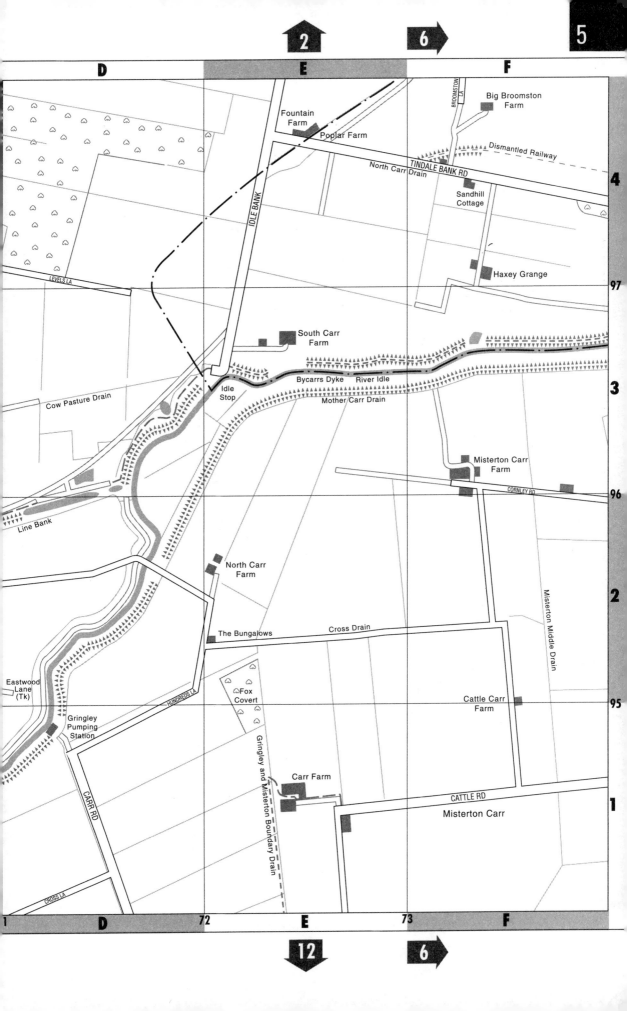

D
E
F

Fountain Farm

Poplar Farm

BROOMSTON LA

Big Broomston Farm

Dismantled Railway

TINDALE BANK RD

North Carr Drain

IDLE BANK

Sandhill Cottage

4

Haxey Grange

97

South Carr Farm

LEVELS LA

Bycarrs Dyke   River Idle

Idle Stop

Mother Carr Drain

Cow Pasture Drain

3

Misterton Carr Farm

CORNLEY RD

96

Line Bank

North Carr Farm

Misterton Middle Drain

2

The Bungalows

Cross Drain

Eastwood Lane (Tk)

Fox Covert

Cattle Carr Farm

95

Gringley Pumping Station

HUNDREDS LA

Gringley and Misterton Boundary Drain

Carr Farm

CARR RD

CATTLE RD

Misterton Carr

1

CROSS LA

5

A | B | C

**4**

Langholme

Langholme Wood

Haxey

Langholme

Langholme
Farm

Dismantled Railway

Langholme

Cornley
Farm

Cornley Lane

TINDALE BANK RD

Langholme
Manor

STATION RD

A161

LC

**97**

Hunter's
Hill

Richmond
Farm

North Carr

**3**

Mother Drain

River Idle

North Carr
Farm

Haxey Gate
Bridge

Haxey Gate Inn
(PH)

Haxey Gate Rd

NORTH CARR RD

Debdhill Farm

Mother Drain Bridge

**96**

Cornley
Farm

Cornley Carr
Farm

Debd Hill

Cornley

Debdhill Road

**2**

New Cemy

CORNLEY RD

Red House

White House
Farm

Haxey Rd

LAUREL AVE

PARK AVE

**95**

Sandholes Lane

Cattle Farm

CARR LA

CHURCH ST

Misterton

HIGH ST

STATION ST

A161

**1**

CATTLE RD

MINSTER RD

Cooper's
Bridge

GRINGLEY RD

Liby

WHARF RD

Wharf
Bridge

GROVE WOOD RD

Green's Yard

Chesterfield Canal

GROVE WOOD TERR

**94**

GRAVELHOLES LA

74 | A | 75 | B | 76 | C

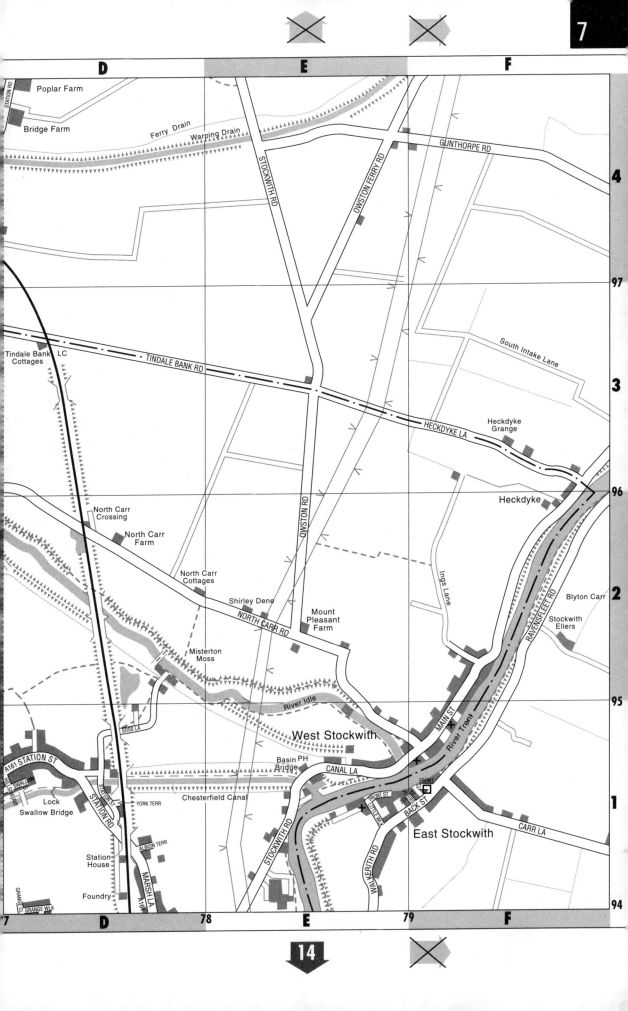

D    E    F

4

97

3

Poplar Farm

Bridge Farm

STATION RD

Ferry Drain

Warping Drain

STOCKWITH RD

OWSTON FERRY RD

GUNTHORPE RD

South Intake Lane

Tindale Bank Cottages    LC

TINDALE BANK RD

HECKDYKE LA

Heckdyke Grange

96

North Carr Crossing

North Carr Farm

North Carr Cottages

Shirley Dene

NORTH CARR RD

Mount Pleasant Farm

OWSTON RD

Ings Lane

Heckdyke

Blyton Carr

Stockwith Ellers

RAVENSFLEET RD

2

Misterton Moss

River Idle

West Stockwith

SOSS LA

River Trent

MAIN ST

95

A161 STATION ST

SWALLOW CL

HILLS LANE

Lock
Swallow Bridge

STATION RD

YORK TERR

Basin PH
Bridge

Chesterfield Canal

CANAL LA

STOCKWITH RD

FRONT ST

BACK ST

East Stockwith

CARR LA

1

FRONT ST
LITTLE WK

Station House

Foundry

ALBION TERR

MARSH LA
A16

GRANGE CL
GRANGE WLK

WALKERITH RD

94

7    D    78    E    79    F

# A B C

**Tickhill**

Sch

ESTBFIELD CL
A60 DONCASTER RD
WINNERY CL
RYE CROFT
HEATHER CL
HEATHFIELD DR
LANGDALE DR

DADSLEY RD

COMMON LA

Bracken Croft Lane

Sewage
Works

PAPER MILL LA

NORTH GATE
MANGHAM LA
AIREDALE AVE
MERRIL INGS
THE PADDOCK
CROFT DR
SCARBOROUGH CL
BEECH AVE
WALNUT AVE
ALDERSON DR
ALDERSON CL

WILSIC RD
MONK RD
ST MARY'S CRES

Tollbar
Bridge

Goole
Bridge

**4**

Sch

ST MARY'S MEWS
ST MARY'S RD
THE CLAY
VINE RD
NETTLE GTH
THE COURT
ORANGE CROFT
BROOM CL
NEWTON DR
SUNDERLAND CL

SUNDERLAND ST

Spital
Hill

Sandrock
Farm

STRIPE RD
Sandrock
Plantation
Sandrock
Park

Bog Hill
HIGH COMMON LA
SHEEPWASH LA
B6463

Warehouses

Schs

NEW RD
PINFOLD CL
PINFOLD
Lib
MARKET PL
ST MARY'S GATE
BRIDGE
CHURCH
A631
CASTLE GATE
LANCASTER CRES
LUMLEY DR

Tickhill
Spital

BAWTRY RD

**93**

CastleFolds
Farm

A60 WEST GATE

DAM RD
LINDRICK
LINDRICK
WATER LA

Tickhill
Castle

Little Black Lane

West Bank
Farm

Goole Dike or River Torne

Moorhouse
Farm

BLYTH RD

A631

**Harworth**

MOOR TOP RD
MOOR TOP
BAULK LA
SANDROCK RD
OXFORD
GREENWOOD AVE
RUTLAND RD
RUTLAND CRES
THOMPSON AVE
SMITH RD
AMANDA RD
CAMBRIDGE
WINDERMERE
MAYDRIVE
DORSET DR
DEVONSHIRE RD

**3**

Water Lane

Tickhill Low
Common

Sewage
Works

TICKHILL RD

Cemy

**92**

Bagley
Green

Bagley Dike

Rose
Cottage

COMMON LA
COMMON LA

BRIAR CT
THORNHILL RD
HOLLY CT
BRAMBLE WAY
KIRTON LA
CHURCH LANE
THE GREEN
THE GLEBE
WYTHY CL
SAXON CL
MAYFAIR CL
RUSSELL AVE
BAWTRY RD

Bagley Farm

MILL LA
BOWERS
SCROOBY RD

B6463

MAIN ST

PH

HILL RD

Sch

**2**

Dismtld Rly
Dismtld Rly

STYRRUP RD

BLYTH RD

SNAPE LA

**91**

Banks Carr Drain

Styrrup Carr

Industrial
Estate

BRUNEL CL

River Torne

Grange
Farm

Hall

SELBY RD

Conveyor

**1**

OAKLANDS DR

MAIN ST

PH

PINFOLD LA
PAGDIN DR
PINFOLD LA

**Styrrup**

B6463

Spoil Heap

STYRRUP LA

Styrrup Quarry
(disused)

A1(M)

**90**

**D** **E** **F**

Martin Beck Lane

High Common LA

Tickhill Grange Cottages

High Common Farm

Warehouses

Tickhill Grange

Martin Lane

Martin LA

INGHAM RD

HERMES CL

MARTIN LA

ST MARTIN'S AVE

MARTIN LA

4

CHESTNUT DR

YEW TREE DR CRES

ELM TREE DR

ASH TREE AVE

SYCAMORE CRES

TICKHILL RD

A631

93

BAWTRY RD

Swinnow Wood

Plumtree Farm Ind Est

PLUMTREE RD

Menagerie Wood

WEST WOOD ESTATE

Fish Pond Wood

3

Caravan Park

GRANGE VIEW

BROWSE DR

Recn Gd

BAWTRY RD

THORESBY

1 BALMORAL CT
2 SANDRINGHAM CT
3 STRATHMORE CT
4 WINDSOR CT
5 HARDWICK CT
6 BROOKSIDE WLK
7 HAREWOOD CT
8 CHATSWORTH CT
9 ARUNDEL WLK

Plumtree Farm

School

GALWAY AVE

GALWAY RD

GALWAY DR

Hawk's Nest

A614

Lady Holt Lane

92

WELBECK RD

LINDSEY RD

WHITBY RD

BEECH RD

FESTIVAL AVE

SANDYMOUNT WEST

BEVERLEY RD

SANDYMOUNT EAST

HOLDERNESS CL

WEST ST

DORCHESTER RD

EAST ST

WOODROVE

SWINNOW RD

Sch

Sch

WHITE HOUSE RD

NORFOLK DR

ESSEX RD

ESSEX DR

SUFFOLK AVE

SUFFOLK DR

CUMBERLAND CL

WESTMORLAND CT

White House Plantation

GIBBET HILL LA

A638

Hill RD

HILL TOP LA

Sch

F Sta

Liby

SHREWSBURY RD

GROSVENOR RD

CREWE

TALBOT RD

HAMPDEN RD

CHURCH RD

NORFOLK RD

DROVERSDALE RD

WATH SLACK RD

HOWARD RD

THE CRESCENT

THURCROFT

MICKTON

MILNE AVE

NORTH AVE

MILNE DR

MILNE DR

MILNE DR

SCROOBY RD

South Carr

Sowcarr

Gibbet Hill

GREAT NORTH RD

MILL LA

A638

2

P

CROPSLEY RD

Sports Ground

Droversdale Wood

Dismantled Railway

South Carr Farm

Riverside Farm

Spoil Heap

Ruins Plantation

Penny Acre

River Ryton

91

Colliery

Lords Wood

SNAPE LA

Works

Layland Plantation

Bawtry Lodge

Broom Hill

Triangle

Coronation Clump

The Holt

1

BLYTH RD

Sand Pit

Steer Bank Farm

Harworth Lodge

A614

Round Holt

Neale's Covert

90

2 **D** 63 **E** 64 **F**

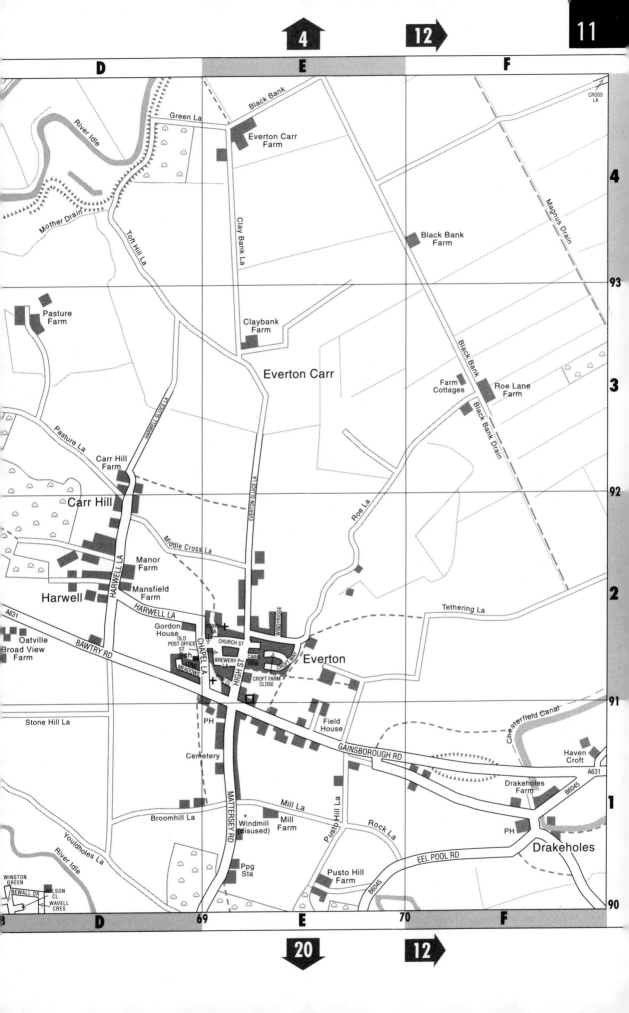

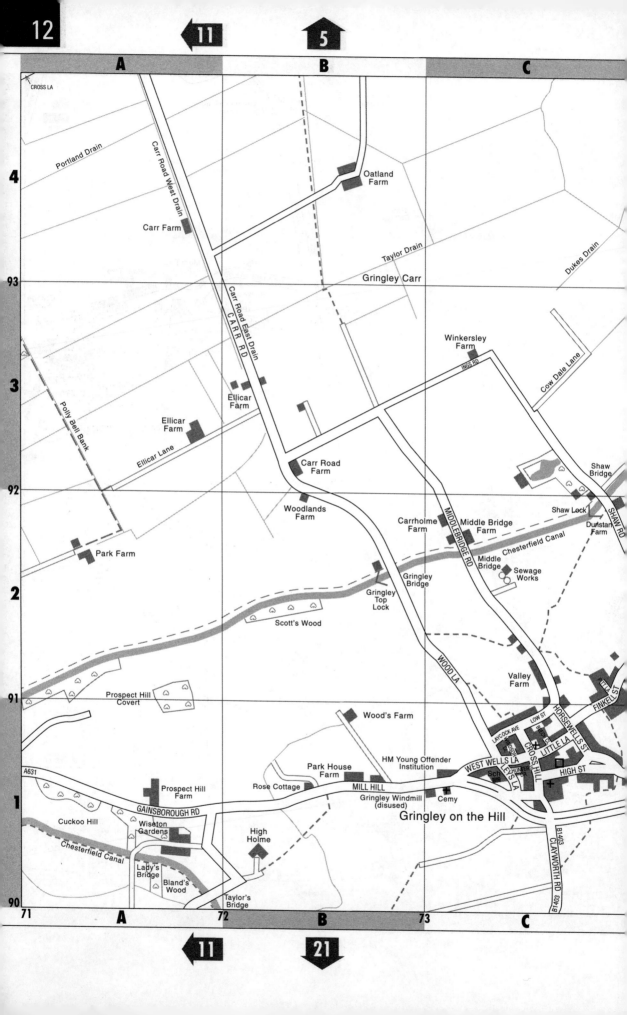

CROSS LA

Portland Drain

Carr Road West Drain

Carr Farm

93

Carr Road East Drain

C A R R   R D

Polly Bell Bank

Ellicar Farm

Ellicar Farm

Ellicar Lane

Oatland Farm

Taylor Drain

Gringley Carr

Dukes Drain

Winkersley Farm

INGS RD

Cow Dale Lane

Carr Road Farm

Shaw Bridge

Woodlands Farm

92

Park Farm

Carrholme Farm

MIDDLEBRIDGE RD

Middle Bridge Farm

Shaw Lock

SHAW RD

Dunstan Farm

Chesterfield Canal

Middle Bridge

Sewage Works

Gringley Bridge

Gringley Top Lock

Scott's Wood

WOOD LA

Valley Farm

91

Prospect Hill Covert

Wood's Farm

A631

Prospect Hill Farm

Park House Farm

Rose Cottage

HM Young Offender Institution

MILL HILL

LAYCOCK AVE

LOW ST

HORSEWELLS ST

FINKELL ST

WEST WELLS LA

CROSSHILL

LITTLE LA

HIGH ST

Sch

1

Cuckoo Hill

GAINSBOROUGH RD

Wiseton Gardens

High Holme

Gringley Windmill (disused)

Cemy

B1403

CLAYWORTH RD

B1403

Chesterfield Canal

Lady's Bridge

Bland's Wood

Taylor's Bridge

**Gringley on the Hill**

90

71

A

72

B

73

C

GROVE WOOD RD

Hodson's Bridge

Fountain Hill Farm

GRINGLEY RD

B1403

Gringley Road Farm

Sch

Tupcroft Road

Fountain Hill

FOUNTAIN HILL

Manor Cottage

Manor Farm

**4**

Smith's Bridge

Moor End Farm

Pear Tree Farm

**93**

FOUNTAIN HILL RD

Grange Farm

BRICKYARD LA

Brickmaker's Arms (PH)

NORTH MOOR RD

WEST MOOR RD

Leys Farm

CAVE'S LA

West Moor Farm

NORTH MOOR DR

MOORLAND WLK

Sch

West Moor

MILL BAULK RD

The Moor

SCHOOL HOUSE

HIGH ST

Chesterfield Canal

SOUTH MOOR RD

MOORLAND CL

**3**

BRICKENHOLE LA

South Moor Farm

**Walkeringham**

Church Farm

Highfield Farm Cottage

Highfield Farm

**92**

GRINGLEY RD

Lowfield Farm

MILL LA

Highfield House

WOODEN BECK HILL

Glebe Farm

**2**

SHAW RD

WALKERINGHAM RD

OAKS LA

HALL'S RD

BEACON HILL RD

B1403 GREEN

**091**

Bumblebee Lane

Beacon Hill

• Mast

Gringley Gorse

HIGH ST

Pit (dis)

**1**

A631

Grange Cottages

Gringley Grange

West Road

LANCASTER RD

Green Farm

Cross Keys (PH)

Sandy Furze Farm

Pear Tree Hill

Pear Tree Farm

Sandyfurze Bungalow

A631

MUTTON LA

**90**

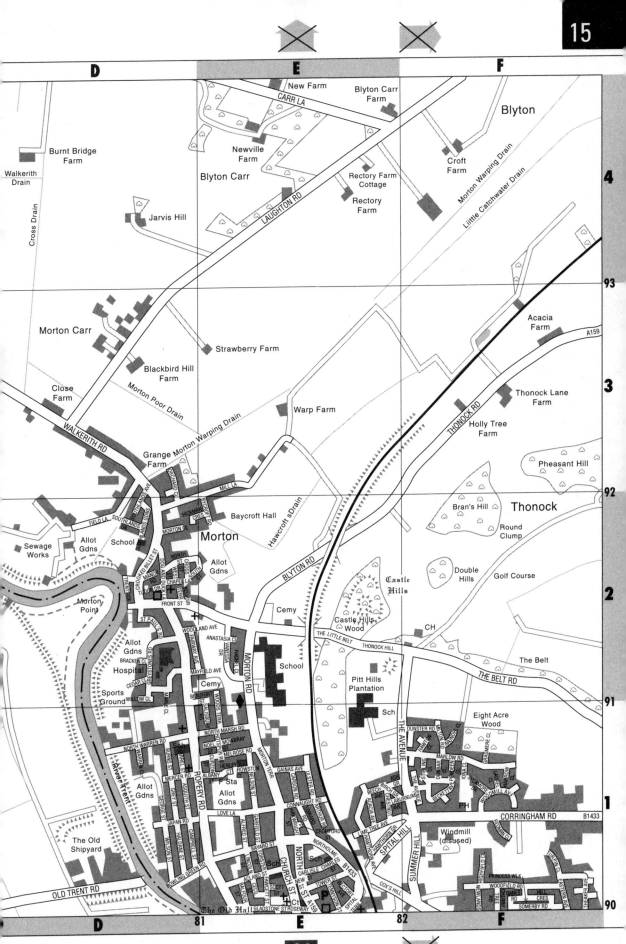

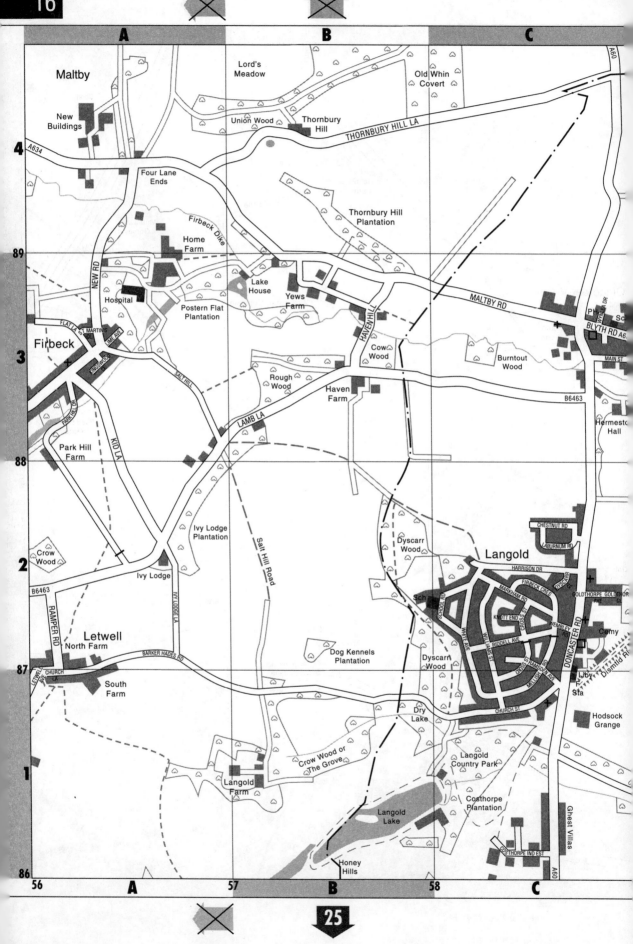

Maltby

New Buildings

Lord's Meadow

Old Whin Covert

Union Wood

Thornbury Hill

THORNBURY HILL LA

Four Lane Ends

Firbeck Dike

Thornbury Hill Plantation

Home Farm

A634

4

89

Hospital

Lake House

Yews Farm

MALTBY RD

PH

Sc

BLYTH RD A6..

Postern Flat Plantation

NEW RD

HAVEN HILL

Cow Wood

Burntout Wood

MAIN ST

Firbeck

FLAT LA ST MARTIN'S

LIME AVE

MOSS WOOD

3

SALT HILL

Rough Wood

Haven Farm

B6463

Hermeston Hall

PARKIN DR

KID LA

LAMB LA

88

Park Hill Farm

Ivy Lodge Plantation

Salt Hill Road

Dyscarr Wood

CHESTNUT RD

LABURNUM RD

Langold

HARRISON DR

Crow Wood

2

Ivy Lodge

IVY LODGE LA

Sch

FIRBECK CRES

DYSCARR

GOLDTHORPE

GOLDTHOR
AVE CL

B6463

RAMPER RD

MARKHAM RD

KNOTT END

CROSS ST

WEMBLEY RD

DONCASTER RD

Cemy

Letwell

North Farm

BARKER HADES RD

Dog Kennels Plantation

Dyscarr Wood

WHITE AVE

WILLIAMS ST

RIDDELL AVE

RAMSDEN AVE

MELLISH AVE

Dismtld Rd

87

LETWELL AVE

CHURCH LA

South Farm

CHURCH ST

Lby

R Sta

A60

Dry Lake

Hodsock Grange

1

Langold Farm

Crow Wood or The Grove

Langold Country Park

Costhorpe Plantation

Ghest Villas

COSTHORPE IND EST

Langold Lake

Honey Hills

86

56

A

57

B

58

C

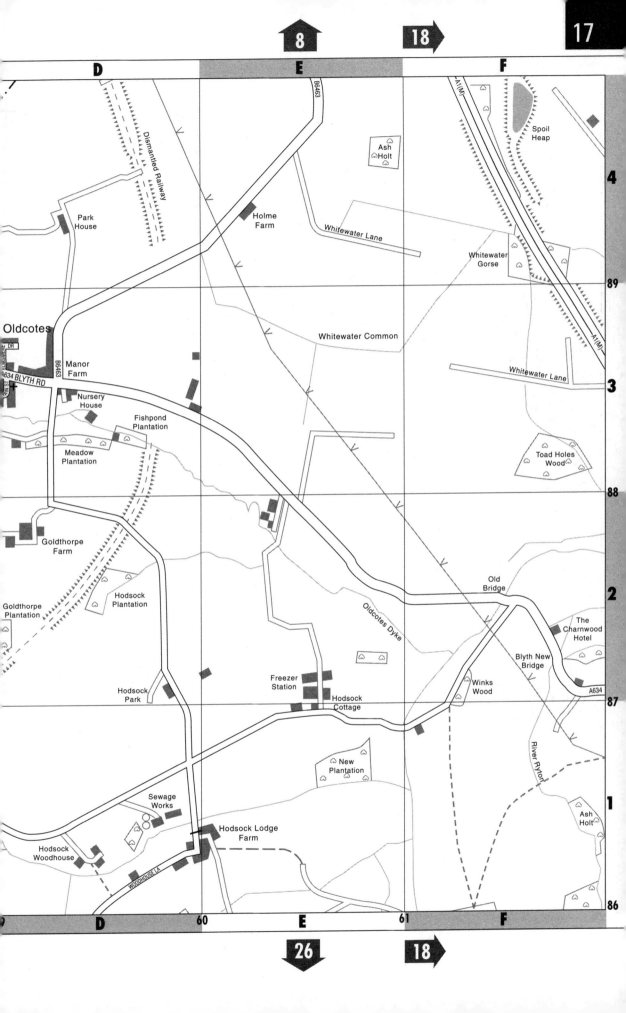

D     E     F

B6463

Dismantled Railway

Park
House

Holme
Farm

Ash
Holt

Spoil
Heap

A1(M)

Whitewater Lane

Whitewater
Gorse

**4**

**89**

Oldcotes

FLAXMORE DR

B6463

A634 BLYTH RD

Manor
Farm

Nursery
House

Fishpond
Plantation

Meadow
Plantation

Whitewater Common

Whitewater Lane

A1(M)

Toad Holes
Wood

**3**

Goldthorpe
Farm

Goldthorpe
Plantation

Hodsock
Plantation

Hodsock
Park

Freezer
Station

Hodsock
Cottage

Oldcotes Dyke

Old
Bridge

The
Charnwood
Hotel

Blyth New
Bridge

Winks
Wood

A634

**2**

**88**

**87**

New
Plantation

Sewage
Works

Hodsock Lodge
Farm

River Ryton

Ash
Holt

**1**

Hodsock
Woodhouse

WOODHOUSE LA

**86**

D     60     E     61     F

A B C

4

Nook Flatt Wood

Sunny Nook

Elm Cottage

Lodge

East Lodge

The Woodlands

Serlby

GREEN LA

A614

Kirk View

HARWORTH AVE

BLYTH RD

BAWTRY RD

THE WOODLANDS

The Laurels

Serlby Hall

Home Farm

CH

Serlby Park

89

A614

ROMAN BANK LA

Roman Bank Earthwork

Black Cat Plantation

Bishopfield House

3

A1(M)

WHITE LANES LA

B6045

Service Area

Blyth Wood

Serlby Park Golf Course

Roe Hill Plantation

Bishopfield Farm

BISHOPFIELD LA

A1(T)

Hodgkinson's Holt

Decoy Pond

88

Nornay

COMMON LA

Bridge Farm

River Ryton

Brecks Wood

Roman Bank La

South View

B6045

NORNAY CL

2

PRIORY CL

Blyth Hall

Inn
THE MALTINGS

B6045

The Grange

BLYTH RD

Blyth

PARK DR

SHEFFIELD RD

A634

MILL MEADOW VIEW

The Mantles

87

A634

HIGH ST

MARTIN'S RD

RETFORD RD

RYTON FIELDS

Mill Farm

B6045

A634

MOOR LA

Belmont

Double Acre

BAULK LA

WORKSOP RD

B6045

SHERWOOD CRES

BRIBER RD

SPA FIELDS
CRES

School

GRAVES MOOR LA

Sycamore La

1

BRIBER HILL

SPITAL RD

A1(T)

LONG BRECKS LA

A634

86

62

B6045

Spital Farm

A B 63 B 64 C

D
E
F

WINSTON GREEN
CUNNINGHAM CL
KEYES CL
KEYES RISE
KEYES CT

BROOMFIELD LA

Mattersey Grange

GREEN LA

A638

Mattersey Wood

Main Drain

4

Hollins Holt

BRECK LA

Lodge Farm

89

Scrooby Top House

Lodge Court

LC

B6045

RANSKILL RD

MATTERSEY RD

3

FOLLY NOOK LA

ARUNDEL DR

OAKS CL

Bridge House

STONEHILL CL

SOUTHFALL CL

SPINNEYMEAD

CHERRY TREE WALK

School

BISHOPFIELD LA

WHITTON CL

RAVENSHILL CL

88

STATION AVE

COMMON LA

Sewage Works

PH

High House Farm

B6045

STATION RD

LC

BLYTH RD

A638

BACK LA

**Ranskill**

Headlands La

+

2

Antcliff Plantation

GREAT NORTH RD

Cemy

INNERWOOD AVE

HUNTSMAN CL

The Poplars

PH

HOLDS LA

BLACKSMITH LA

87

BAULK LA

Daneshill Lakes
(Nature Reserve)

LOW ST

Moat Farm

Works

**Torworth**

DANESHILL RD

1

Torworth Crossing

Daneshill Piggery

Works

Daneshill Lakes
(Nature Reserve)

Torworth Grange

A638

86

D
66
E
67
F

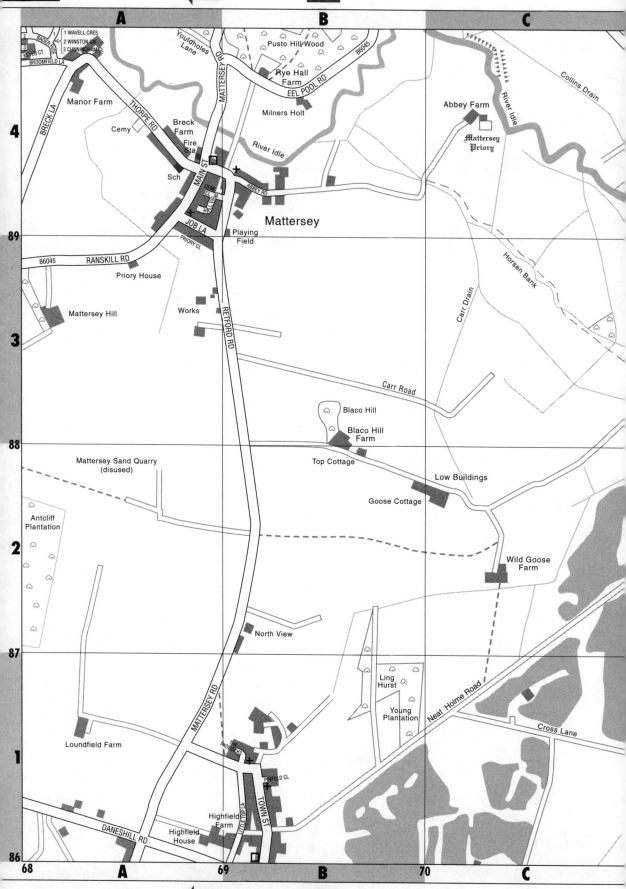

**A**  **B**  **C**

1 WAVELL CRES
2 WINSTON GN
3 CUNNINGHAM CL

K'S EYES CT
BADER RISE
BROOMFIELD LA

Youldholes Lane

Pusto Hill Wood

B6045

Collins Drain

Manor Farm

THORPE RD

BRECK LA

Rye Hall Farm

EEL POOL RD

Abbey Farm

River Idle

**4**

Cemy

Breck Farm

Fire Sta

Milners Holt

River Idle

Mattersey Priory

Sch

MAIN ST

MATTERSEY RD

ABBEY RD

DENE CL

HELMSLEY

Mattersey

JOB LA

PRIORY CL

**89**

Playing Field

B6045

RANSKILL RD

Priory House

Horsen Bank

Carr Drain

Mattersey Hill

Works

RETFORD RD

**3**

Carr Road

Blaco Hill

**88**

Mattersey Sand Quarry
(disused)

Blaco Hill Farm

Top Cottage

Low Buildings

Goose Cottage

Antcliff Plantation

**2**

Wild Goose Farm

North View

**87**

Ling Hurst

MATTERSEY RD

Young Plantation

Neat Holme Road

Loundfield Farm

THE PADDOCKS

Cross Lane

**1**

PINFOLD CL

Highfield Farm

LITTLE TOP LA

TOWN ST

DANESHILL RD

Highfield House

**86**

**68**  **A**  **69**  **B**  **70**  **C**

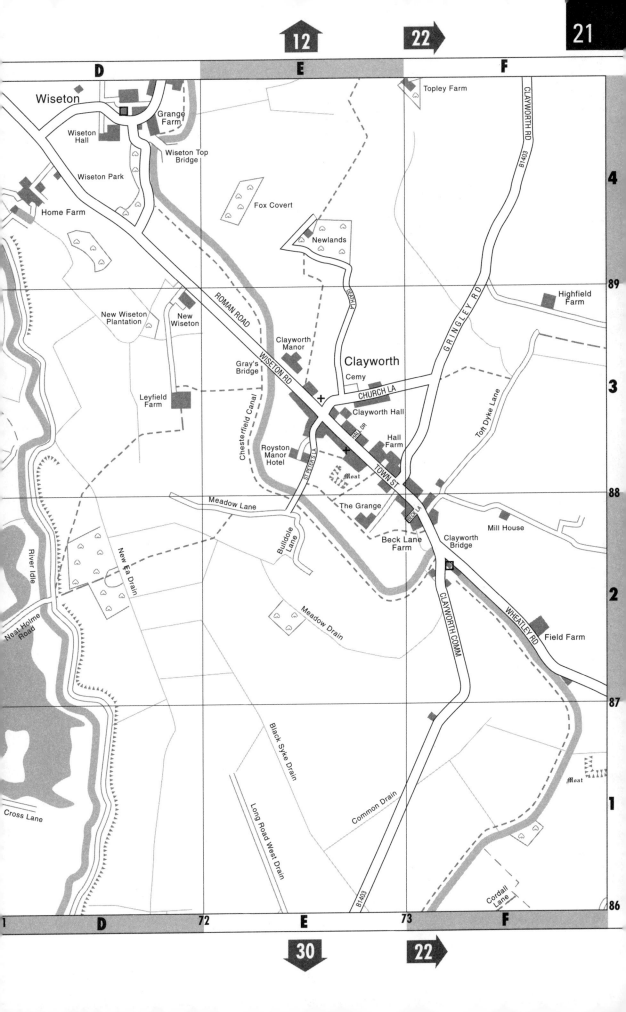

A    B    C

South Sandy-Furze
Farm

MUTTON LA

WOOD LA

Ash Lea

Wood
Farm

4

Beckingham
Wood

Tong's
Wood

89

Clayworth
Woodhouse

Dogholes
Wood

Saundby Park
Farm

3

Wheatley
Wood

88

Freeman's
Gorse

Hangman Lane

Wheatley Wood
Farm

Wheatley Wood
Farm

Wheatley
Grange

Walk Lane

2

LANCASTER RD

Lovers' Lane

87

Wheatley Rd

Northfield Leys Road

Trough Baulk Lane

WOOD LA

A620

North Point

1

Eastfield

Hayton Castle
Farm

Long
Plantation

Allot
Gdns

GAINSBOROUGH RD

HAUGHGATE HILL

Greenacres

86

A620

A620

74    A    75    B    76    C

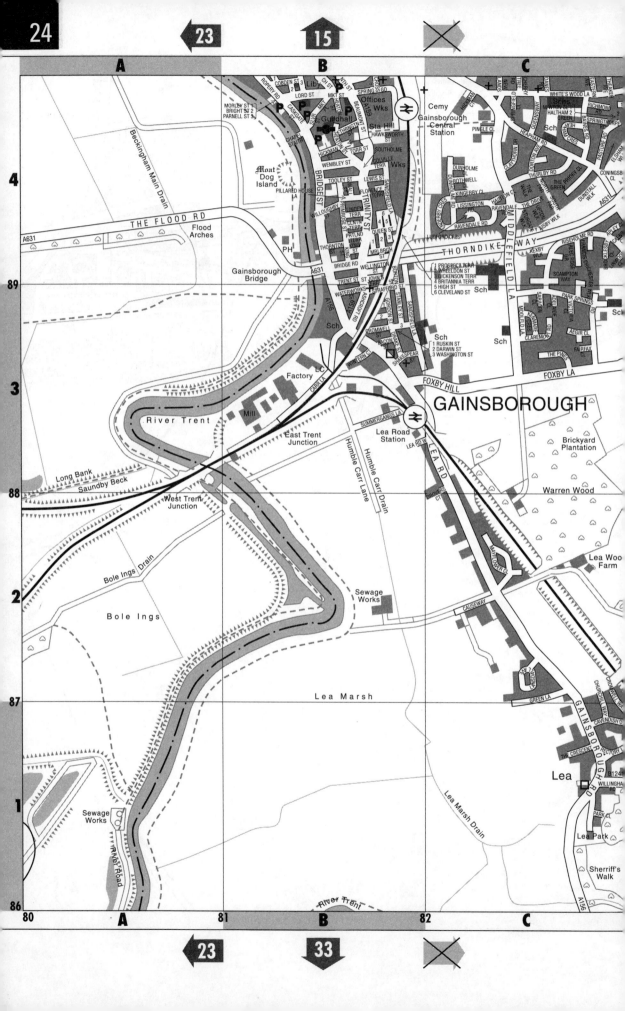

GAINSBOROUGH

River Trent

Lea

Miller Lands

Acorn Piece

Langold Holt

Woodland Farm

Buckwood Farm

ROTHERHAM BAULK

Costhorpe

WEST VIEW

Ingham Bungalows

Trading Estate

DONCASTER RD

PH

CHILTERN WAY 1
PENTLAND DR 2
HAMBLETON CT 3
LOWTHER SQ 4
CLEVELAND CL 5
BEVERLEY WLK 6
CHICHESTER WLK 7
CHEVIOT CT 8
MENDIP CT 9
CANTERBURY WLK 10
LICHFIELD WLK 11
COTSWOLD CT 12

LILAC GR

WILLOW AVE

LIME TREE AVE

SYCAMORE RD

BEECH GR

KNATON RD

STEWART RD

KINGSTON RD

LE BRUN SQ

OXFORD RD

Liby

QUEENS RD

Schs

WINDSOR GDNS

WINDSOR RD

CONWAY DR

LONG LA

ARUNDEL DR

WARWICK AVE

KENILWORTH DR

Green Lane

Castle Garden

Wallingwells Wood

Carlton in Lindrick

Carlton Wood

Wallingwells

Wallingwells Hall

Hollin Hills

CARLTON HALL LA

Wallingwells Park

Owlands Wood

The Lawns

Mus

Carlton Lake

CHURCH LA

Corn Mill Farm

The Ashes

Holme Wood

South Carlton

Field House Farm

The Bottoms

Owlands Wood Dyke

Holme House Farm

Hardwick Ashes

OWDAY LA

Woodsetts

Broom Farm

The Homestead

Owday Wood

Owday Plantation

Nab's Ashes Wood

Little Broom Wood

WORKSOP RD

Rough Piece

Whipman Wood

Cocked Hat Wood

Sand Hill Plantation

WOODSETTS LA

GATEFORD RD

Fox Covert

Ashes Wood

Dog Kennel Plantation

CARLTON RD

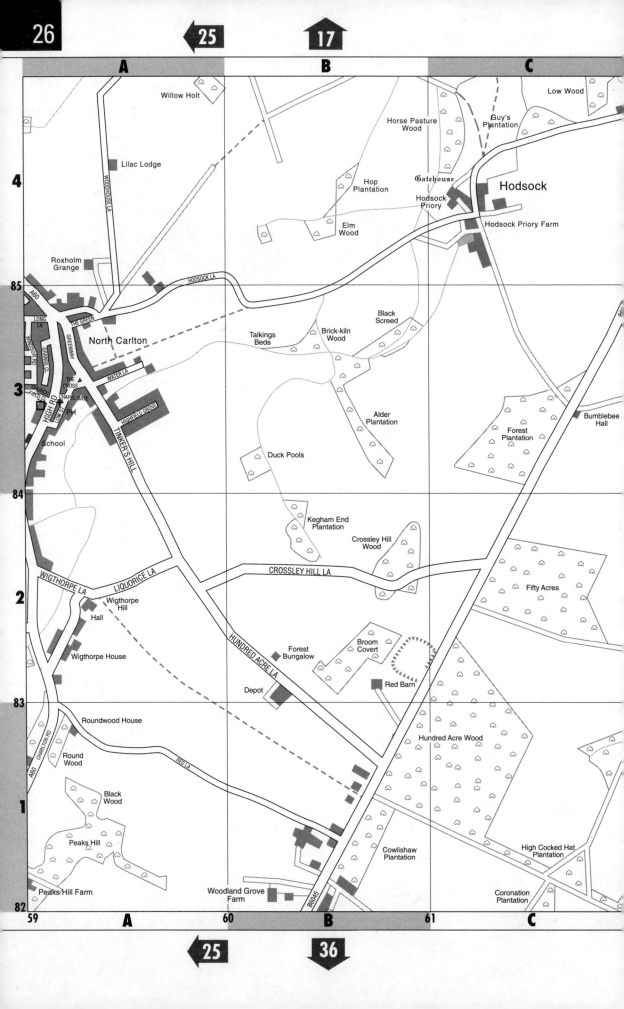

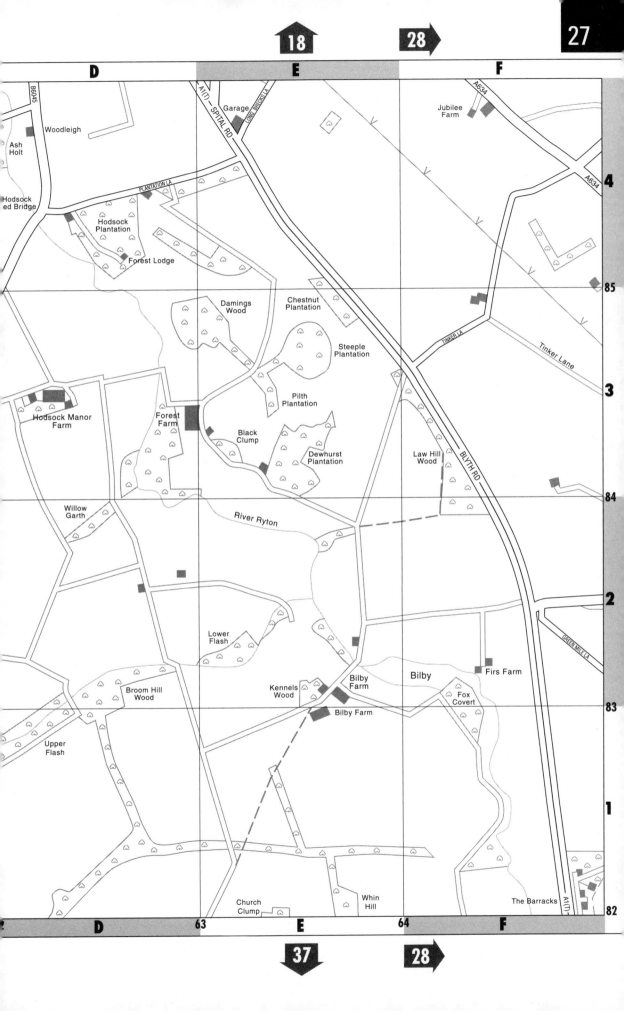

D E F

4

85

3

84

2

83

1

82

D E F
63 64

Woodleigh
Ash Holt
Hodsock ed Bridge
Garage
Jubilee Farm
PLANTATION LA
Hodsock Plantation
Forest Lodge
Damings Wood
Chestnut Plantation
Steeple Plantation
TINKER LA
Tinker Lane
Pilth Plantation
Hodsock Manor Farm
Forest Farm
Black Clump
Dewhurst Plantation
Law Hill Wood
BLYTH RD
Willow Garth
River Ryton
Lower Flash
Bilby
Firs Farm
Broom Hill Wood
Kennels Wood
Bilby Farm
Bilby Farm
Fox Covert
GREEN MILE LA
Upper Flash
Church Clump
Whin Hill
The Barracks

B6045
A1(T) — SPITAL RD
LONG BRECKS LA
A634
A634
A1(T)

A                    B                    C

4

A638

A634

College
Farm

The
Woodlands

San Diego

85

Main Drain

Daneshill Lake
(Nature Reserve)

Wind Pump

Grange
Farm

A634

Hotel

Ash
Holt

Sutton-cum-Lound

MIRE LA

EATON

TOWN ST

Tinker Lane

3

KENNEL DRN

GREAT NORTH RD

STATION RD

LC

SUTTON LA

Glebe
Farm

THE COPPIC

Barnby Moor

84

Ranby Cottage
Farm

Knives Hill
Plantation

Eleven Acre
Plantration

Barnby Fox
Covert

Barnby Moor
Bridge

A6

2

OLD LONDON RD

Forest
Lock

Lock

Ranby Hall
Farm

Low
Farm

Ranby Hall

83

Chesterfield Canal

Canal Cottage

Lock

Weir

Lock

GREEN MILE LA

Towing Path

Lock

Keepers
Cottage

1

Forest
Farm

Big
Clump

82

65                   A        66        B        67        C

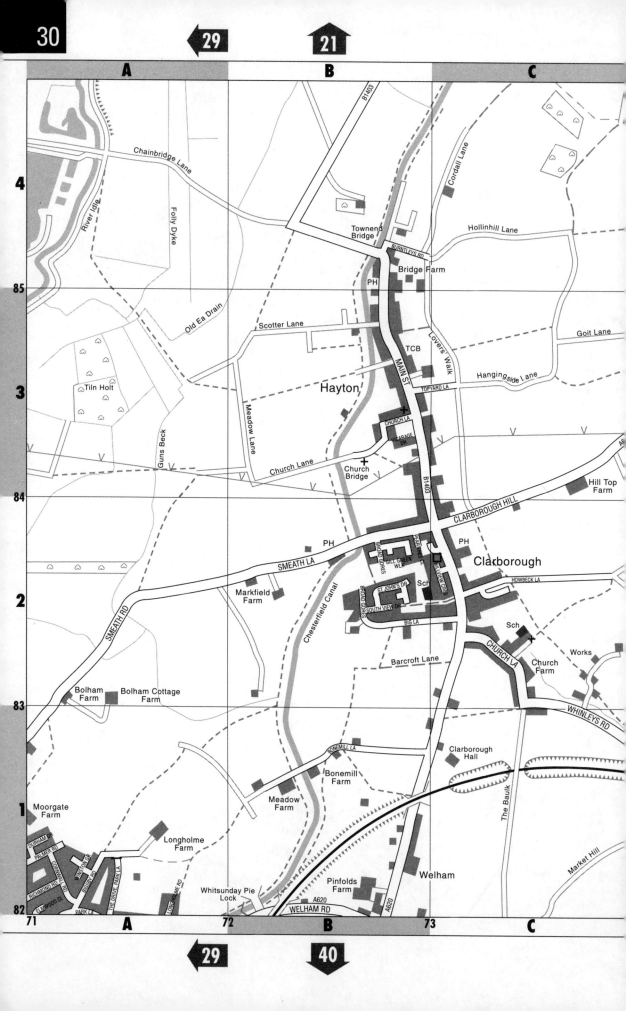

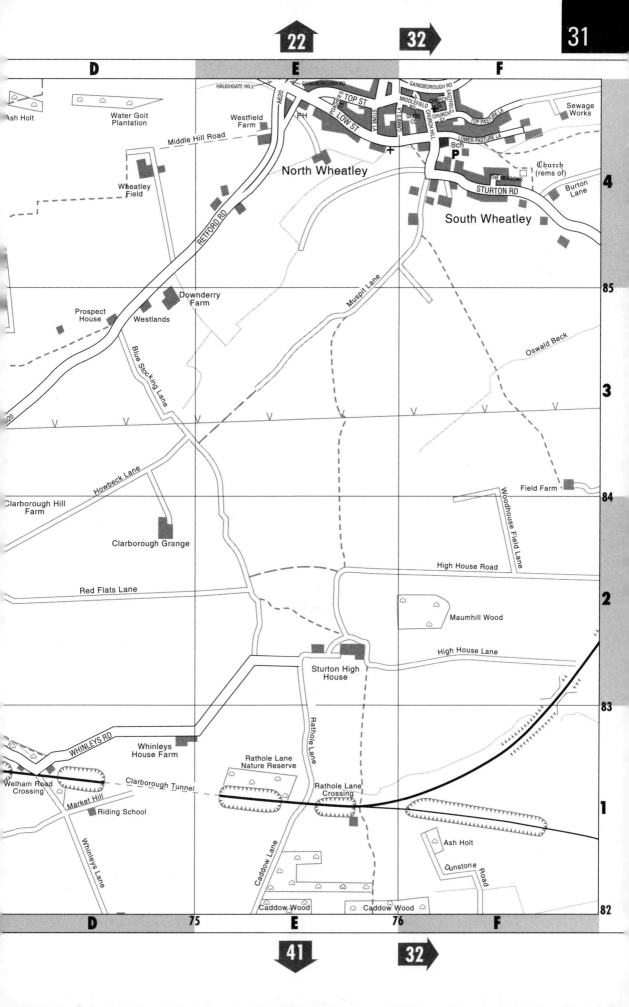

Ash Holt

Water Goit
Plantation

HAUGHGATE HILL

Middle Hill Road

Westfield
Farm

GAINSBOROUGH RD

TOP ST

POACHER'S LA

LOW ST

STONE LA

PH

A620

GAINSBOROUGH RD

MIDDLEFIELD
RD

CAMB'S LA

GLEBE
CL.

CHURCH HILL

CHURCH
ST

EASTFIELD

TOP PASTURE LA

LOWER PASTURE LA

Sewage
Works

Wheatley
Field

North Wheatley

RETFORD RD

Sch

P

THE MEADOWS

STURTON RD

South Wheatley

Church
(rems of)

Burton
Lane

4

Prospect
House

Downderry
Farm

Westlands

Muspit Lane

85

Blue Stocking Lane

Oswald Beck

A620

3

Howbeck Lane

Clarborough Hill
Farm

Field Farm

84

Clarborough Grange

Woodhouse Field Lane

High House Road

Red Flats Lane

Maumhill Wood

2

High House Lane

Sturton High
House

83

WHINLEYS RD

Whinleys
House Farm

Rathole Lane

Rathole Lane
Nature Reserve

Rathole Lane
Crossing

Welham Road
Crossing

Clarborough Tunnel

Market Hill

Riding School

Caddow Lane

Ash Holt

Dunstone Road

1

Whinleys Lane

Caddow Wood

Caddow Wood

82

31
23

A    B    C

Wheatley Beck

West Burton

Burton Lane

**4**

Oswald Beck

Footgap Lane

River Ro

Low Farm

West Burton
Power Station

**85**

WHEATLEY RD
ROMAN ROAD

Wood Lane

Woodland Farm

STATION RD

GAINSBOROUGH RD

WATKINS LA

COMMON LA

NORTH ST

North Street
Farm

Crow Tree
Farm

**3**

BROWN CT

CROSS ST

Sturton le Steeple

Manor Farm

FREEMAN'S LA

Freeman's Lane

BRICKINGS WAY

LOW HOLLAND LA

LITTLEBOROUGH R

**84**

PH

CHURCH ST

SPRING LA

Sch

LC

Springs Lane

Stud Farm

Low Holland
Farm

LEVERTON RD

Catchwater Drain

**2**

Fenton

THREE LEYS LA

Fenton Lane

**83**

Dog Holes Lane

The
Homestead

Grange Farm

The Old
Vicarage

KETLOCK HILL LA

**1**

Sturton Road
Farm

STURTON RD

NORTHSKILL

NORTHFIELD RD

ST
MARTINS
RD

Sch

FINGLE ST

HABBLESTHORPE RD

HABBLESTHORPE C

INFIELD

MARPLE LA

MILL CL

MANOR FARM
RISE

SOUTHGORE

MAIN ST

LA

STREET
LANE
RD

SCRIMSHIRE'S RD

**82**

Windmill

ASHWORTH
AV CRES

TOWNSIDE RD

77    A    78    B    79    C

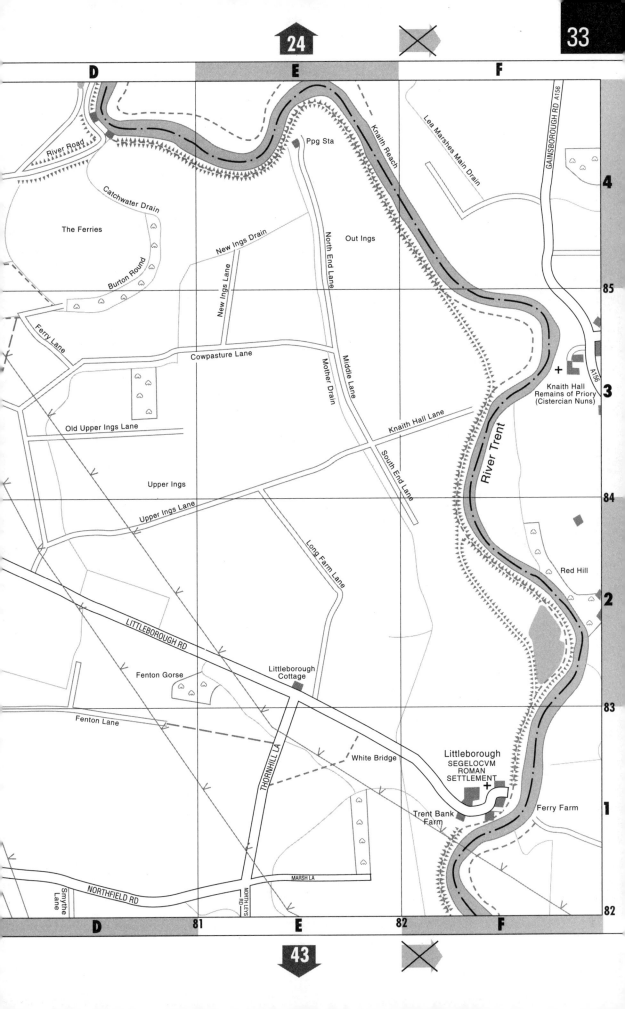

D      E      F

River Road

Catchwater Drain

The Ferries

Burton Round

Ferry Lane

New Ings Drain

New Ings Lane

Cowpasture Lane

Old Upper Ings Lane

Upper Ings

Upper Ings Lane

North End Lane

Mother Drain

Middle Lane

Ppg Sta

Out Ings

Knaith Reach

Lea Marshes Main Drain

GAINSBOROUGH RD A156

Knaith Hall Lane

South End Lane

Knaith Hall
Remains of Priory
(Cistercian Nuns)

River Trent

A156

Long Farm Lane

Red Hill

LITTLEBOROUGH RD

Fenton Gorse

Littleborough
Cottage

Fenton Lane

THORNHILL LA

White Bridge

Littleborough
SEGELOCVM
ROMAN
SETTLEMENT

Trent Bank
Farm

Ferry Farm

Smythe Lane

NORTHFIELD RD

NORTH LEYS RD

MARSH LA

4

85

3

84

2

83

1

82

D     81     E     82     F

**A**

Fan Field

Dismtd Rly

Fan Field Farm

Low Spring Wood

Quarry (dis)

**B**

Brancliffe Grange

Canal Feeder

Turnerwood Bridge

Broad Wood

Towing Path

Turnerwood

Chesterfield Canal (disused)

**C**

Potters Nook Bridge

Sch

CARTWRIGHT ST

GLENTHORN CL

SHIREOAKS COMM

Shireoaks Station

LEEDS RD

CORNWALL RD

YORK PL

WOODSIDE RD

WALNUT AVE

CHERRY T

AVE

LC

PEMBROKE

**4**

Old Spring Wood

**81**

BACK LA

BETHEL TERR

SHIREOAKS ROW

Allot Gdns

Colliery

**Shireoaks**

Hatfield Farm

SHIREOAKS RD

Bottom Farm

LITTLE LA

**Thorpe Salvin**

Moat

Bondhay Dyke

THORPE LA

Shireoaks Park

Ford

Lob Wells Wood

Top Farm

Netherthorpe

The Hall

**3**

Netherthorpe Airfield

Shireoaks Park Wood

Oak Wood

SPRING LA

Holme Carr Wood

Top Hall

COMMON RD

NETHER THORPE RD

WHITWELL RD

**80**

Thorpe Common

DUMB HALL LA

Scratts Wood

Holme Carr

Whitwell Road

**2**

Silver Birches

STEETLEY LA

Works

**79**

SCRATTA LA

Dumb Hall

Armstrong Quarry

Steetley Farm Cottages

Firbeck Farm

Firbeck House

Steetley House

Firbeck Common

**1**

FEATHERBED LA

**Darfoulds**

Firbeck Lane

Arrow Farm

A619

Harness Grove

A619

**78**

**53** **A** **54** **B** **55** **C**

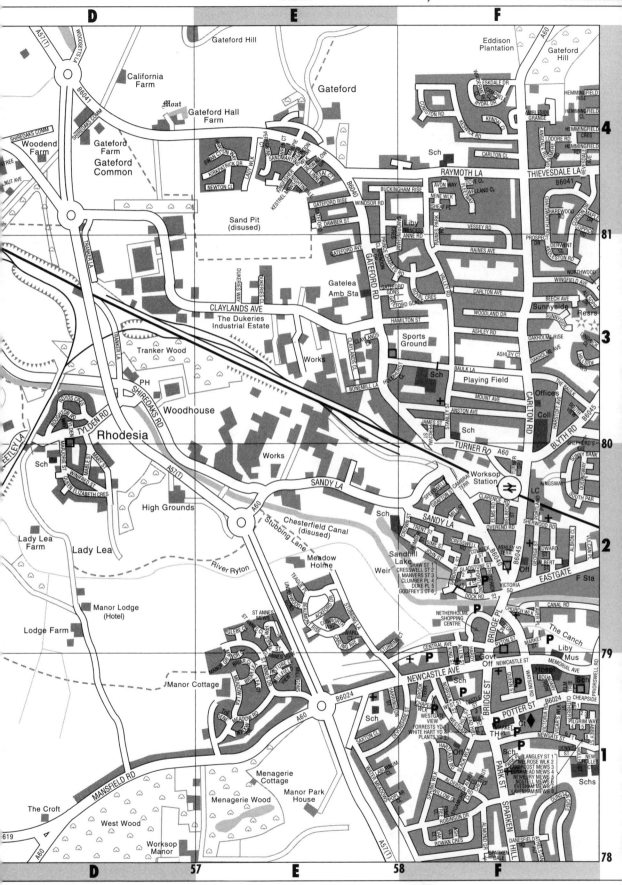

D E F

A  B  C

Long Plantation

Carlton Forest Farm

B6045

Thievesdale House

Thievesdale Wood

Thievesdale Lane

4

WESTERALE ROSEDALE BEDALE RINGS WHITIN DALE COVER DALE

THIEVESDALE LA
B6041 WESTMINSTER CL WINCHESTER CL WORCESTER CL CANTERBURY CL DURHAM CL STABLE CLOSE WHEAT CROFT FARM LA PADDOCKS

Runway (disused)

Forest Hill

81

Sch MAPLE DR WESTWAY GLOUCESTER RD ROCHESTER CL HEREFORD CL MERCIA CL CUMBRIA KENT CL RIDGEWAY LANCASTRIAN WAY ST DUNSTANS GREENACRE RD PROSPECT PREC

B6041 BLYTH RD

Club House

Rayton Angle

Rayton Angle Cottage

3

WINGFIELD AVE WESSEX CL PRIMROSE WAY VICCA CT SINGLETON LONGHURST MONTROSE CARINGTON UILLER BEMBRIDGE

Kilton Forest Golf Course

Hospital

HIGHLAND GR BLYTH GR B6045 KILTON HILL CHESTERTON DR COWPER GOLDSMITH CL GOLERIDGE RD OSBERTON VIEW BROWNING RD KIPLING CL TRUEMAN CT CARNOUSTIE

Gravel Pit Wood

80

SHEPHERD'S AVE SUNFIELD CL SUNNY BANK KEATS CRES KILTON CL KENNEDY CT SHAKESPEARE ST KILTON GLADE BURNS RD THACKERAY CL SCOTT CL PLANTATION RD NASH CL MACAULAY CL

Black Hill Clump

THE OVAL KINGSWAY Sch BYRON WAY MILTON DR HARDWICK GDNS BROOKE CL

Kilton Schs Works SOUTH PAR LONGFELLOW DR TENNYSON RD SITWELL RD

2

KILTON RD KILTON TERR CANAL TERR MASEFIELD PL DICKENS RD KILTON RD RAYTON SPUR DRAYONDALE MERRICK DR ROSSETTI GDNS

WORKSOP

Rayton Farm

HIGH HOE RD PRIORSWELL RD SHELLEY ST GARSIDE ST HOE DR HOE AV BEAN AV BRACEBRIDGE

RAYTON LA

Sewage Works

River Ryton

79

Bracebridge

Sch Cemetery LOWTOWN BRACEBRIDGE CT

B6079

CHEAPSIDE B6040 B6041 HOWARD ST HARDWICK CRES

Chesterfield Canal

1

Sch LOWTOWN VIEW TENBY CL TALBOT RD FURNIVAL ST VERNON ST CLINTON ST NETHERTON PL LINCOLN ST FEATHERSTONE RD HARDWICK RD RETFORD RD FOREST LA

Cemetery

NETHERTON RD LOWTOWN ST FURNIVAL ST RADFORD ST

Manton MANTON CRES COLLEGE ST NUKERIES CRES SHERWOOD ST HIGHFIELD JACOBS LA MANTON VILLAS

Manton Colliery

RICHMOND RD PELHAM ST SOUTH MOOR RD SOUTHBECK RISE SOUTH AVE KINGSTON RD

Sch Sch

Spoil Heap

B6040 A57(T) A57(T)

78

59  A  60  B  61  C

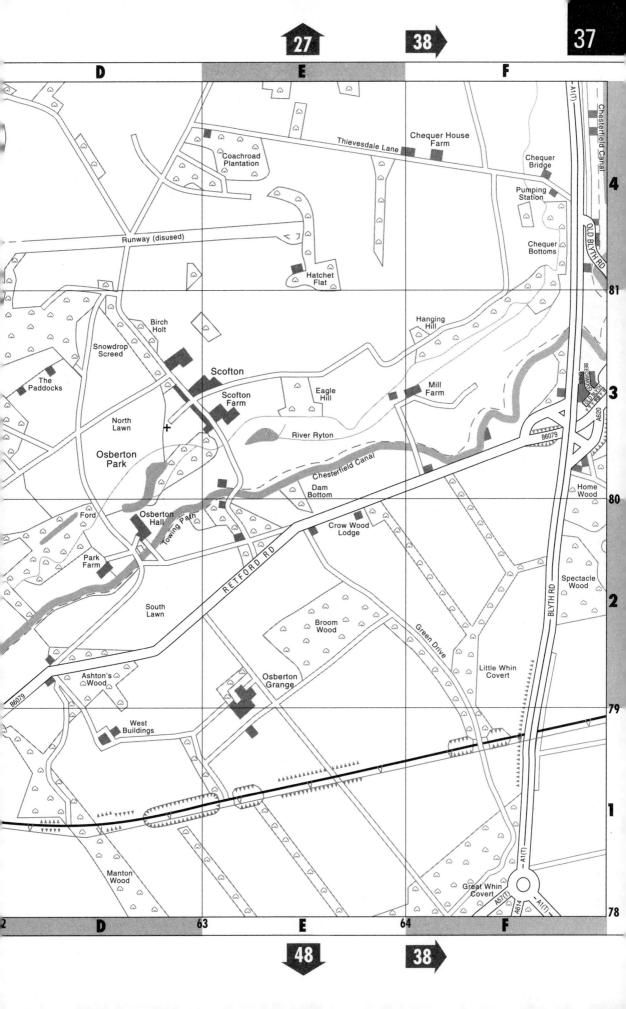

D E F

Chesterfield Canal

Thievesdale Lane

Chequer House Farm

Coachroad Plantation

Chequer Bridge

Pumping Station

OLD BLYTH RD

A1(T)

4

Runway (disused)

Chequer Bottoms

Hatchet Flat

81

Birch Holt

Snowdrop Screed

Hanging Hill

BEECHWOOD TREES

The Paddocks

Scofton

Scofton Farm

Eagle Hill

Mill Farm

OLD BLYTH RD

A620

3

North Lawn

River Ryton

A620

Osberton Park

Chesterfield Canal

Dam Bottom

B6079

Home Wood

80

Ford

Osberton Hall

Towing Path

Crow Wood Lodge

BLYTH RD

Park Farm

RETFORD RD

Spectacle Wood

2

South Lawn

Broom Wood

Green Drive

Little Whin Covert

Ashton's Wood

Osberton Grange

B6079

79

West Buildings

Manton Wood

Great Whin Covert

A1(T)

A57(T)

A614

A1(T)

1

78

37
28

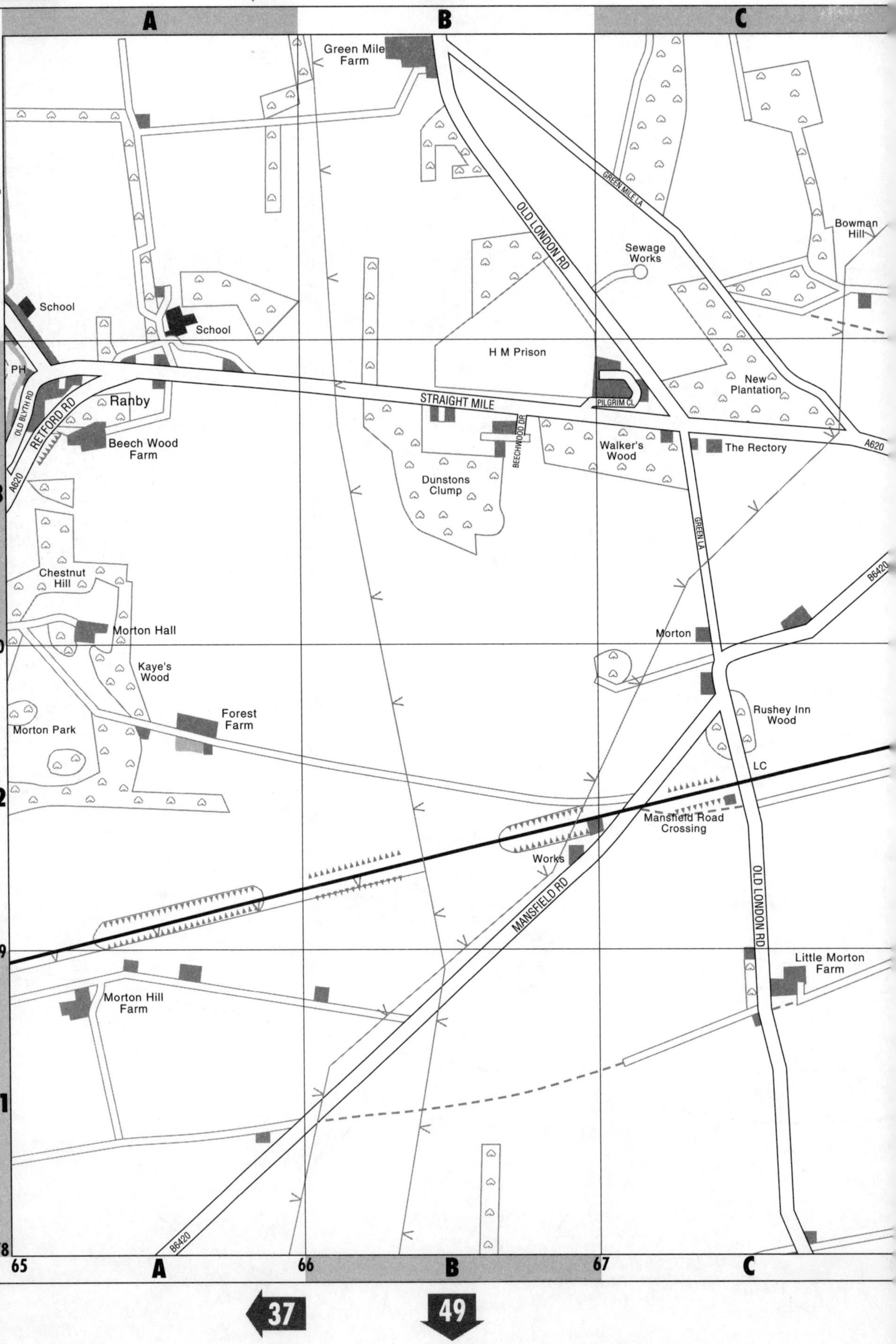

A      B      C

**4**

Green Mile Farm

OLD LONDON RD

GREEN MILE LA

Sewage Works

Bowman Hill

**81**

School

School

H M Prison

New Plantation

PH

Ranby

RETFORD RD

OLD BLYTH RD

A620

STRAIGHT MILE

PILGRIM CL

BEECHWOOD DR

Walker's Wood

The Rectory

A620

Beech Wood Farm

**3**

Dunstons Clump

Chestnut Hill

GREEN LA

B6420

Morton Hall

Morton

**80**

Kaye's Wood

Rushey Inn Wood

Morton Park

Forest Farm

LC

**2**

Mansfield Road Crossing

Works

MANSFIELD RD

OLD LONDON RD

**79**

Morton Hill Farm

Little Morton Farm

**1**

B6420

**78**

65      A      66      B      67      C

37
49

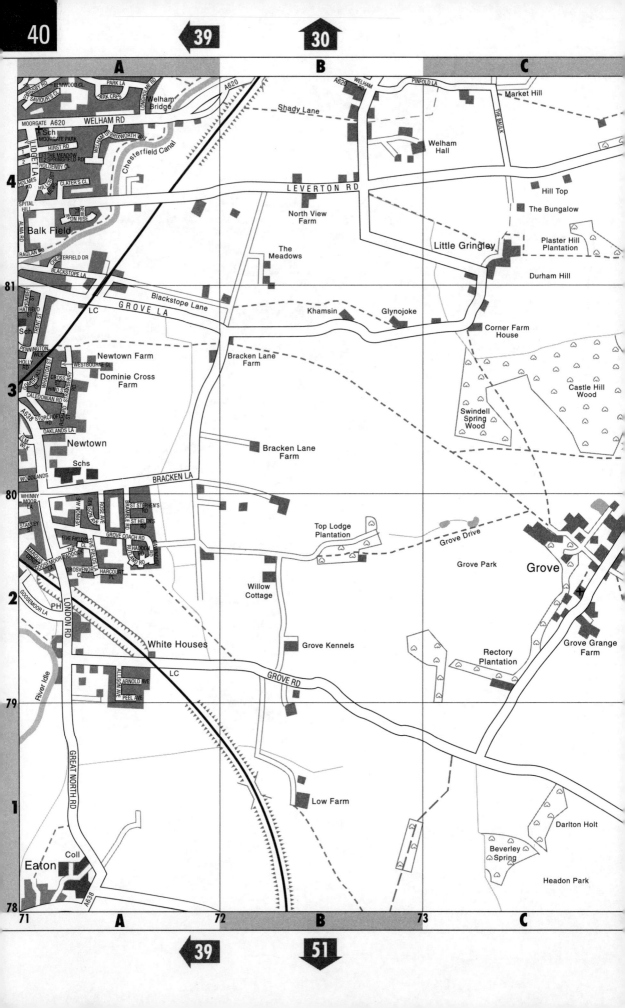

**A** **B** **C**

CRSSBY RD
ELMWOOD CL
PARK LA
PARK CRES
SAVIOURS CT
WELHAM BRIDGE
Shady Lane
PINFOLD LA
Market Hill
MOORGATE A620
WELHAM RD
Welham Hall
THE BALK
A620
WELHAM RD
Sch
Moorgate Park
HIRST RD
LODGE LA
HOLDENBY RD
Chesterfield Canal
BRIXWORTH WAY
WELHAM BY
LEVERTON RD
Hill Top
HOLMES
CLATER'S CL
The Bungalow
SPITAL HILL
NEW ON RISE
ALMA RD
RAGLAN RD
CHESTERFIELD DR
North View Farm
Little Gringley
Plaster Hill Plantation

**4**

Balk Field

The Meadows

Durham Hill

**81**
BLACKSTOPE LA
HUMBER ST
HATFIELD ST
TRENT ST
Blackstope Lane
GROVE LA
Khamsin
Glynojoke
Corner Farm House
LC
Sch
PENNINGTON WLK
HOLLY RD
Newtown Farm
WESTBOURNE CL
Bracken Lane Farm
CROSS HILL
WHARTON ST
HIND ST
STRAWBERRY
Dominie Cross Farm
Castle Hill Wood

**3**
A638
CALEDONIAN RD
STORCROFT RD
OAKLANDS LA
Newtown
Swindell Spring Wood
ELM WK
Schs
Bracken Lane Farm

WOODLANDS
BRACKEN LA

**80**
WHINNY MOOR LA
VERNON AVE
BENISON CL
ROSE AVE
BRAMBLE
ST STEPHEN'S RD
ST HELEN'S RD
Top Lodge Plantation
Grove Drive
Grove
STANLEY ST
FIVE FIELDS CL
GROVE COACH RD
THE FIELDS
HADDON
RUTLAND RD
CAVENDISH
Grove Park
GROSVENOR CL
HARCOURT PL
Grove Grange Farm

**2**
GOOSEMOOR LA
PH
LONDON RD
Willow Cottage
White Houses
Grove Kennels
Rectory Plantation

River Idle
GREAT NORTH RD
LC
ARNOLD AVE
ALLISON AVE
PEEL AVE
GROVE RD

**79**

**1**
Low Farm
Darlton Holt
Beverley Spring
Coll
Eaton
A638
Headon Park

**78**
**71** **A** **72** **B** **73** **C**

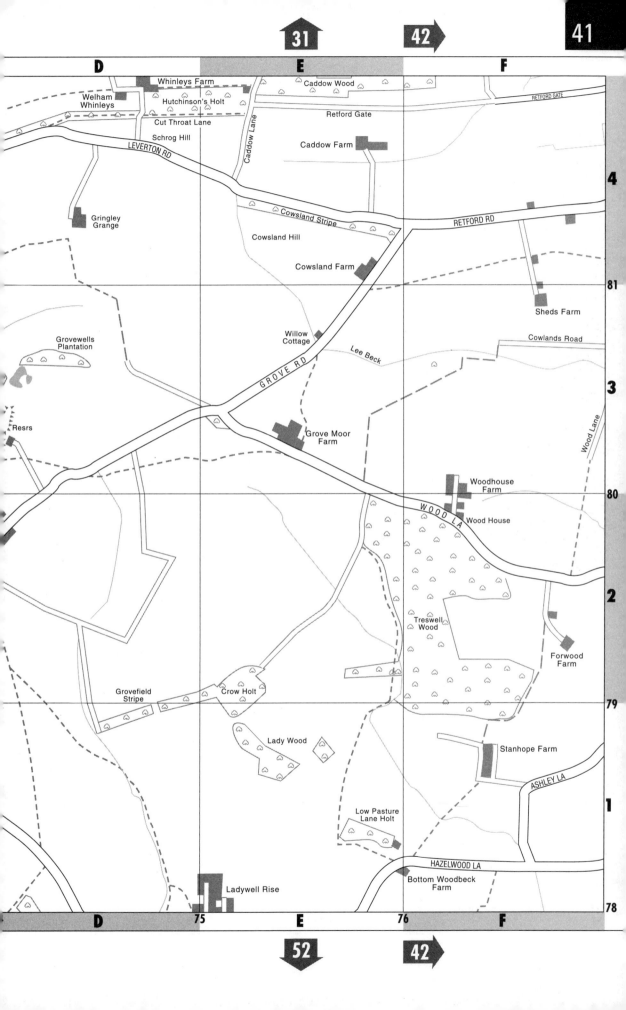

**D** **E** **F**

Welham
Whinleys
Whinleys Farm
Hutchinson's Holt
Cut Throat Lane
Schrog Hill
Caddow Wood
Retford Gate
RETFORD GATE
Caddow Farm
Caddow Lane
LEVERTON RD

**4**

Gringley
Grange
Cowsland Stripe
RETFORD RD
Cowsland Hill
Cowsland Farm

**81**

Sheds Farm

Grovewells
Plantation
Willow
Cottage
Lee Beck
Cowlands Road
GROVE RD

**3**

Resrs
Grove Moor
Farm
Wood Lane

Woodhouse
Farm

**80**

Wood House
WOOD LA

Treswell
Wood

**2**

Forwood
Farm

Grovefield
Stripe
Crow Holt

**79**

Lady Wood
Stanhope Farm
ASHLEY LA

**1**

Low Pasture
Lane Holt

Ladywell Rise
HAZELWOOD LA
Bottom Woodbeck
Farm

**78**

**D** 75 **E** 76 **F**

A B C

Caddow Wood Farm

RETFORD GATE MILL LA Windmill

ST MARTINS RD
SOUTHFIELDS RISE
SOUTHGORE LA
TOWNERS CFT

1 VICARAGE WLK
2 VICARAGE CL
3 ORCHARD CL

ORCHARD AVE

INFIELD

STREET LANE RD

**North Leverton with Habblesthorpe**

Street Lane

RETFORD RD

Railway Inn (PH)

LC

Catchwater Drain

NEWINGS LA

**4** Westholme

STATION RD

Southbank Lane

Priory Farm

MILL LA

RAMPTON LA

COTTAM RD

LC

RETFORD RD

CHURCH ST

The Plough (PH)

Hollowgate Road

MILLFIELD RD

TOWN ST

BROAD LA

**81**

Meadow Dike Lane

Cowsland Road

MEETINGHOUSE LA

GREEN LA

HIGH ST

Brickings Lane

GLOVER CL

Bacon's Farm

Humber Meadow Lane

Wood Lane

Millfield Road

**South Leverton**

**3**

TRESWELL RD

Onslow House

RAMPTON LA

**80**

Rampton Lane

Beckingham Lane

OUTGANG LA

Lee Beck

FOREWOOD LA

NORTHFIELD LA

**Treswell**

Turn-a-beck

Childrens Theme Park

**2**

NEW RD

RECTORY RD

TOWNSIDE CL

GREEN LA

RAMPTON RD

Manor House

ASHLEY LA

TOWN ST

PH

Southfield Road

**79**

Bus Stocks

Lane

COCKING LA

Northfield Road

TRESWELL RD

RAMPTON BREN LA

Northfield Farm

**1**

Greenside Farm

**Rampton**

GREENSIDE AVE

Woodbeck Cottage

SIMON

REES ROW

FEEMING DR

GALEN AVE

DARWIN DR

KELLER CL

Mill House

RETFORD RD

Sch

Moorhades Lane

**78**

77 A 78 B 79 C

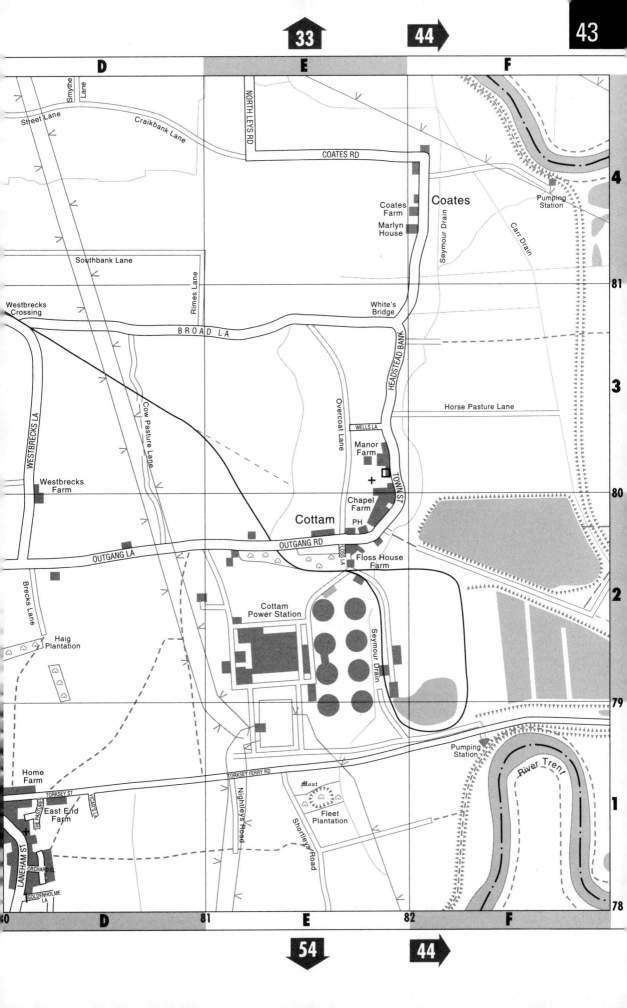

D     E     F

Smythe Lane

Street Lane

Craikbank Lane

NORTH LEYS RD

COATES RD

4

Coates Farm

Coates

Marlyn House

Pumping Station

Seymour Drain

Carr Drain

Southbank Lane

Rimes Lane

81

Westbrecks Crossing

White's Bridge

B R O A D   L A

HEADSTEAD BANK

3

Horse Pasture Lane

WESTBRECKS LA

Cow Pasture Lane

Overcoat Lane

WELLS LA

Manor Farm

TOWN ST

Westbrecks Farm

Cottam

Chapel Farm

PH

80

OUTGANG RD

OUTGANG LA

FLOSS LA

Floss House Farm

Brecks Lane

Cottam Power Station

Seymour Drain

2

Haig Plantation

79

Pumping Station

River Trent

Home Farm

TORKSEY FERRY RD

TORKSEY ST

THE PASTURES

VICARS LA

East End Farm

Nightleys Road

Moat

Fleet Plantation

Shortleys Road

LANEHAM ST

ORCHARD CL

GOLDENHOLME LA

1

80    D     81     E     82     F

78

**A**      **B**      **C**

MOUNT PLEASANT CL

Marton PH

School

TRENT RD

ROMAN ROAD

STOW PARK RD

Marton Grange

Cemy

WAPPING LA

A156

A1500

Windmill

Marlon Rack

TRENT PORT RD

ADAMS WAY

SPAFFORD CL

A1500

LC

TILL BRIDGE LA

**4**

Trent Port
NTL

HIGH ST

Poplar Farm

Ppg Sta

Sewage Works

**81**

Brampton Grange

Marton Moor Farm

LC

Bunker's Hill Warren

**3**

The Lodge

**80**

Manor Farm

Treswell Marsh
Road

River Trent

Torksey Terminal

Golf Course

**Brampton**

West Lawn

**2**

Torksey Viaduct

CH

Ash Holt

Castle Inn (PH)

STATION RD

Vicarage

The Grange Farm

**79**

Caravan Site

MAIN ST

PH

Torksey Common

Dismantled Railway

Castle (rems of)

**Torksey**

Firs Cottage

Cemy

SAND LA

**1**

Firs Farm

Torksey Lock

A156

Caravan Parks

Fossdyke Navigation

Ppg Sta

**78**

**83**    **A**    **84**    **B**    **85**    **C**

Arrow Farm
Firbeck Lane
A619
Half Moon Inn (PH)
Red Hill
DALE LA
A619
Burnt Leys Cottages
Burnt Leys
Steetley Corner
Darfoulds Dike
Ratcliffe Grange
Ratcliffe Cottages
MANSFIELD RD
A60
4
77
Birks Farms
Birks Cottages
New Farm
Whitwell
Hodthorpe
Sewage Works
WELBECK ST
BROAD LA
QUEENS RD
School
Hall Leys Farm
Walling Brook
Ox Pastures Farm
Wallingbrook Wood
3
76
GREEN LA
Tip (disused)
New Cottages
Penny Green
Belph Grange
Millwood Brook
Bismark Plantation
SOUTHFIELD LA
MILLASH LA
Penny Green Cottages
Belph
Springfield Farm
Millwood Lodge
LC
Chy
Tip (disused)
Works
Mill Wood
B6042
HENNYMOOR LA
Ganabrig Wood
West Park
2
75
Ladycroft Wood
Henneymoor Farm
Fishpond Lodge
Burial Ground Plantation
Information Centre
Oaksetts Lodge
1
Caves Cresswell Crags
Pin Hole
Works
Cowclose Wood
Craggs Cottages
CRAGS RD
B6042
Craggs Pond
Church Hole
74

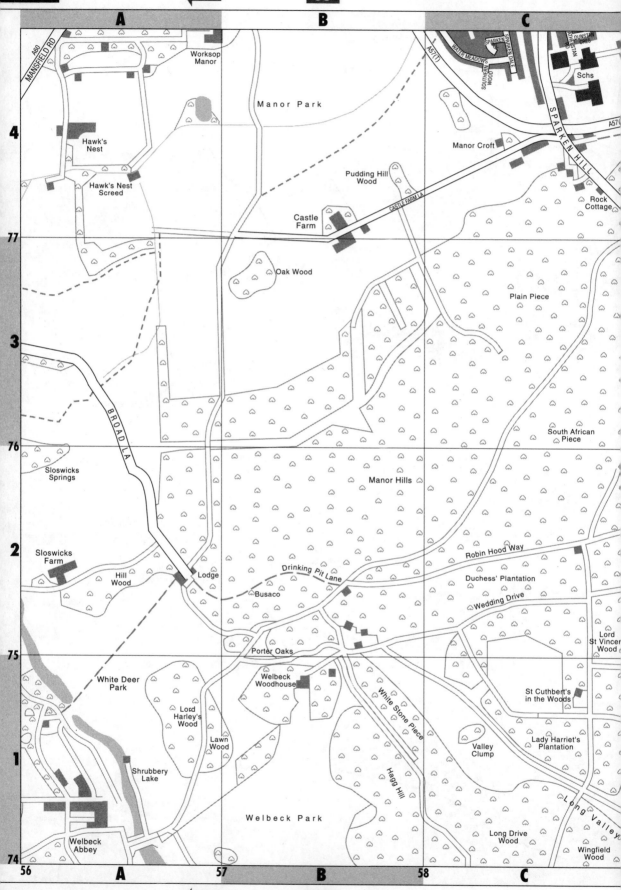

A
B
C

Mansfield Rd
A60

Worksop Manor

Manor Park

Water Meadows
Sparken Stores
Sparken Dale
Southern Down
Athelstan
Dunstan Stores
Schs
Sparken Hill
A57(T)
A57

Manor Croft

4

Hawk's Nest

Pudding Hill Wood

Castle Farm La

Rock Cottage

Hawk's Nest Screed

Castle Farm

77

Oak Wood

Plain Piece

3

Broad La

South African Piece

76

Sloswicks Springs

Manor Hills

2

Sloswicks Farm

Hill Wood

Lodge

Busaco

Drinking Pit Lane

Robin Hood Way

Duchess' Plantation

Wedding Drive

Lord St Vincent Wood

75

Porter Oaks

Welbeck Woodhouse

White Stone Piece

St Cuthbert's in the Woods

White Deer Park

Lord Harley's Wood

Lawn Wood

Valley Clump

Lady Harriet's Plantation

1

Shrubbery Lake

Hagg Hill

Long Valley

Welbeck Park

Long Drive Wood

Wingfield Wood

Welbeck Abbey

74

56
A
57
B
58
C

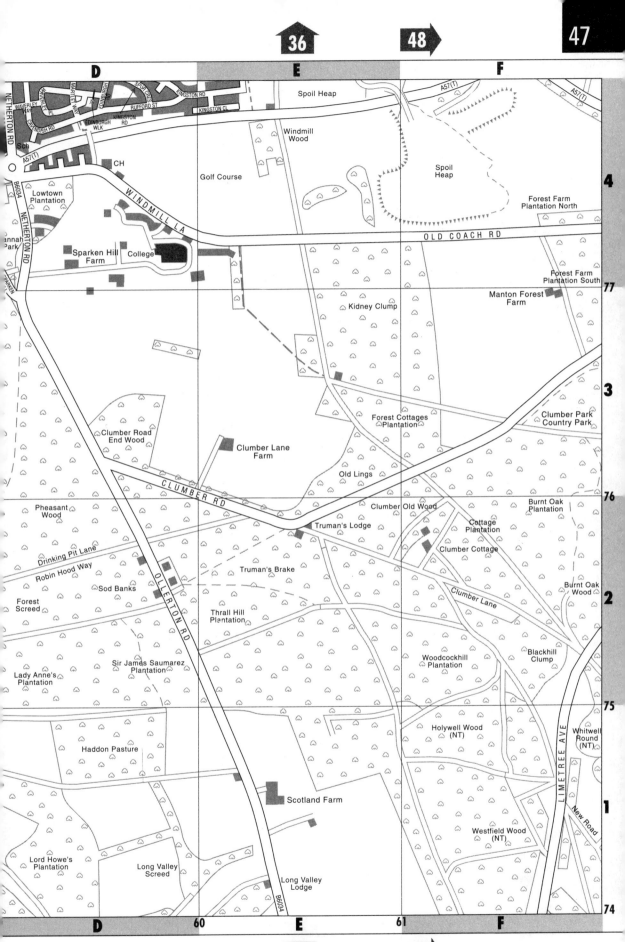

D
E
F

Spoil Heap

Windmill
Wood

NETHERTON RD
KINGSTON RD
RUFFORD ST
WAVERLEY
MARTEN WAY
EDINBURGH
CAVENDISH RD
SPAW CRES
KINGSTON CL
KINGSTON RD
EDINBURGH WLK

A57(T)
A57(T)

Sch

CH

Golf Course

Spoil
Heap

4

B6034

Lowtown
Plantation

NETHERTON RD

WINDMILL LA

Forest Farm
Plantation North

OLD COACH RD

Sparken Hill
Farm

College

annah
Park

Forest Farm
Plantation South

77

Kidney Clump

Manton Forest
Farm

3

Clumber Road
End Wood

Clumber Lane
Farm

Forest Cottages
Plantation

Old Lings

Clumber Park
Country Park

CLUMBER RD

76

Pheasant
Wood

Clumber Old Wood

Burnt Oak
Plantation

Drinking Pit Lane

Truman's Lodge

Cottage
Plantation

Robin Hood Way

Sod Banks

Truman's Brake

Clumber Cottage

OLLERTON RD

Clumber Lane

Burnt Oak
Wood

2

Forest
Screed

Thrall Hill
Plantation

Lady Anne's
Plantation

Sir James Saumarez
Plantation

Woodcockhill
Plantation

Blackhill
Clump

75

Haddon Pasture

Holywell Wood
(NT)

LIMETREE AVE

Whitwell
Round
(NT)

Scotland Farm

New Road

1

Lord Howe's
Plantation

Long Valley
Screed

B6034

Long Valley
Lodge

Westfield Wood
(NT)

74

D
60
E
61
F

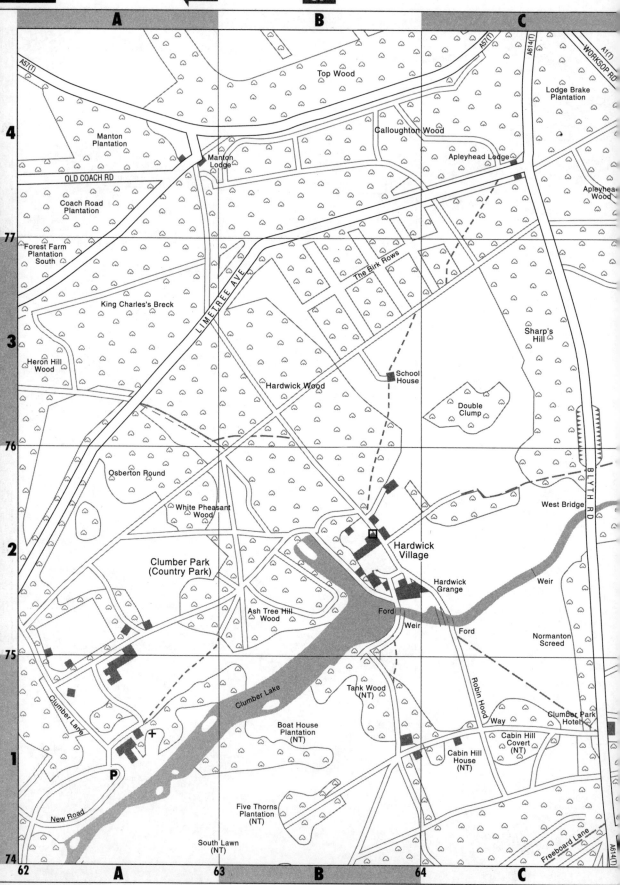

A      B      C

A57(T)

WORKSOP RD

A1(T)

Top Wood

Lodge Brake
Plantation

4

Manton
Plantation

Calloughton Wood

Apleyhead Lodge

Apleyhead
Wood

Manton
Lodge

OLD COACH RD

Coach Road
Plantation

77

Forest Farm
Plantation
South

The Birk Rows

Sharp's
Hill

King Charles's Breck

LIMETREE AVE.

3

Heron Hill
Wood

Hardwick Wood

School
House

Double
Clump

76

Osberton Round

West Bridge

BLYTH RD

White Pheasant
Wood

2

Clumber Park
(Country Park)

Hardwick
Village

Hardwick
Grange

Weir

Ash Tree Hill
Wood

Ford

Weir

Ford

Normanton
Screed

75

Clumber Lane

Clumber Lake

Tank Wood
(NT)

Robin Hood

Way

Clumber Park
Hotel

Boat House
Plantation
(NT)

Cabin Hill
Covert
(NT)

+

1

Cabin Hill
House
(NT)

P

New Road

Five Thorns
Plantation
(NT)

Freeboard Lane

A614(T)

74

South Lawn
(NT)

D    E    F

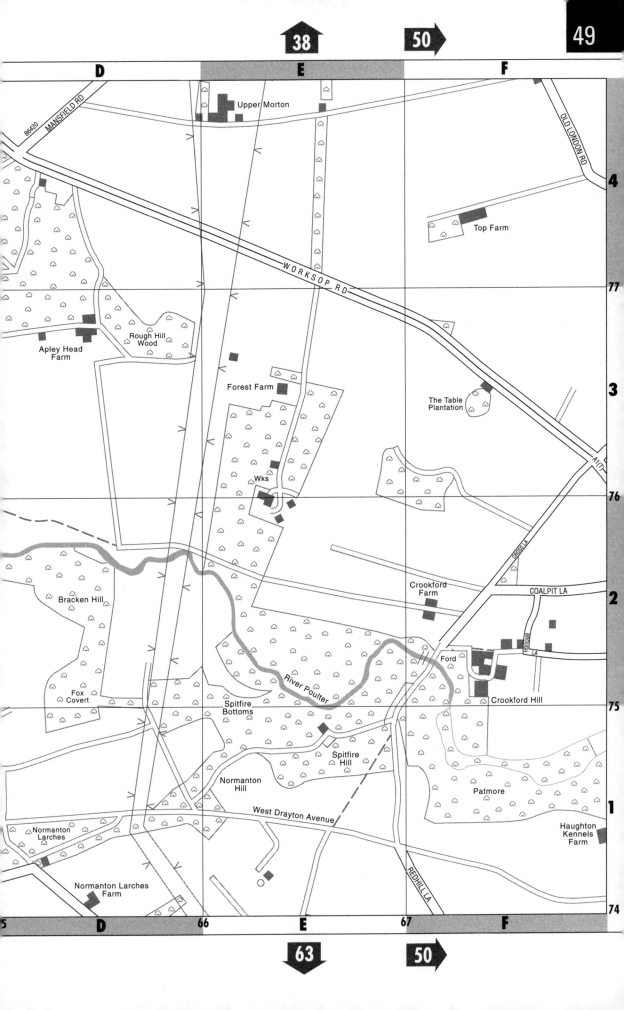

B6420

MANSFIELD RD

Upper Morton

OLD LONDON RD

Top Farm

**4**

WORKSOP RD

**77**

Apley Head
Farm

Rough Hill
Wood

Forest Farm

The Table
Plantation

A1(T)

**3**

**76**

Wks

Crookford
Farm

CROSS LA

COALPIT LA

**2**

Bracken Hill

River Poulter

Ford

BROUGH LA

Crookford Hill

Fox
Covert

Spitfire
Bottoms

**75**

Spitfire
Hill

Normanton
Hill

Patmore

West Drayton Avenue

**1**

Normanton
Larches

Haughton
Kennels
Farm

Normanton Larches
Farm

REDHILL LA

**74**

5    D    66    E    67    F

49
39

A
B
C

4

77

3

76

2

1

Morton Grange

Eaton Breck
Farm

Cleveland House
Farm

Eaton
Bogs

Apple Pie
Plantation

OLD LONDON RD

BRICK YARD RD

Gamston Covert

River Idle

Jockey
House

JOCKEY LA

Saw Mill

Gamston Airport

MUTTONSHIRE HILL

OLLERTON RD

RECTORY LA

B6387

Sch

Church Farm

CHURCH LA

A1(T)

Church Lane

Dover
Holt

WORKSOP RD

COALPIT LA

HOLLY BUSH CL
ELM TREE PL
YEW TREE RD
CEDAR TREE RD
LIME TREE WALK
BEECH RD
MAPLE DR

HIGH ST

TWYFORD LA

Bunker's Hill

DOVER BOTTOM

SANDY LA

HEADLAND AVE

PARK LA

TWYFORD LA

Twyford
Bridge

Pepperley
Hill

Sch

Elkesley

TAWNYWOOD LA
ELM COPPICE WAY

BATTERY LANE

BROUGH LA

River Poulter

Park View
Farm

River Maun

Dobbykes
Lane

Elkesley Wood

Haughton Park
Farm

School
Farm

Little Birch
Holt

OLD LONDON RD

75

Broom Hill

Haughton Kennels
Farm

ROBIN HOOD WAY

Beggar's Rest

West Drayton Avenue

River Meden

Great Birch
Holt

CHURCH LA

GRAVEL PIT LA

Cocked Hat
Plantations

Colliery

Fox
Covert
Holt

GRAVEL PIT LANE

B6387

74

68
A
69
B
70
C

49
64

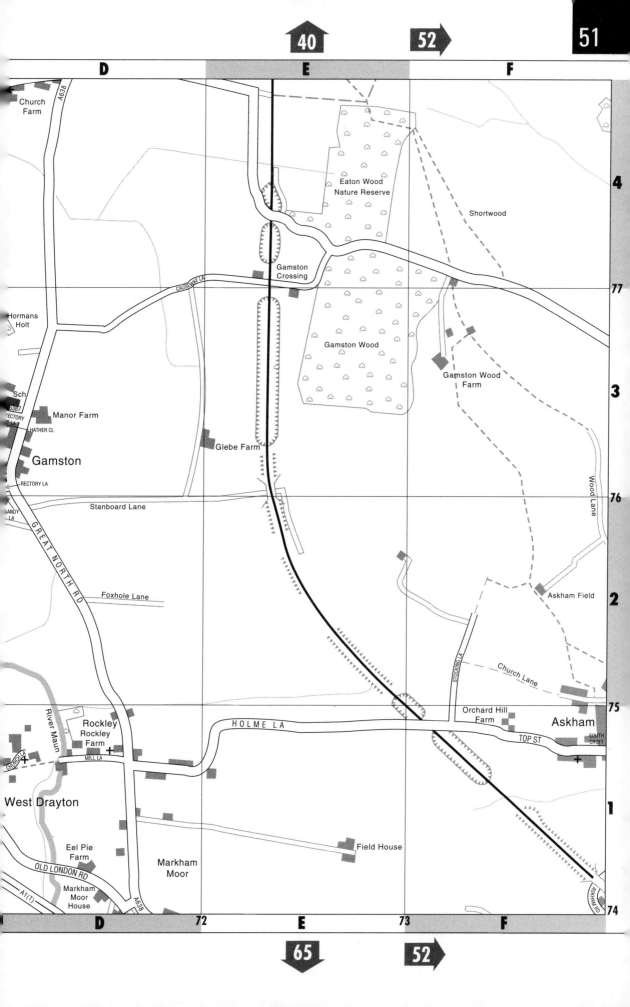

D    E    F

4

Church
Farm

A638

Eaton Wood
Nature Reserve

Shortwood

77

CAUSEWAY LA

Gamston
Crossing

Hormans
Holt

Gamston Wood

3

Sch

RECTORY LA

Manor Farm

HATHER CL

Gamston Wood
Farm

Gamston

RECTORY LA

Glebe Farm

ANDY LA

Stanboard Lane

76

Wood Lane

GREAT NORTH RD

Foxhole Lane

Askham Field

2

STOCKING LA

Church Lane

75

Orchard Hill
Farm

Askham

Rockley
Rockley
Farm

River Maun

HOLME LA

TOP ST

SOUTH
CROFT

CHURCH LA

MILL LA

West Drayton

1

Eel Pie
Farm

Markham
Moor

Field House

OLD LONDON RD

A638

Markham
Moor
House

A1(T)

ASKHAM RD

74

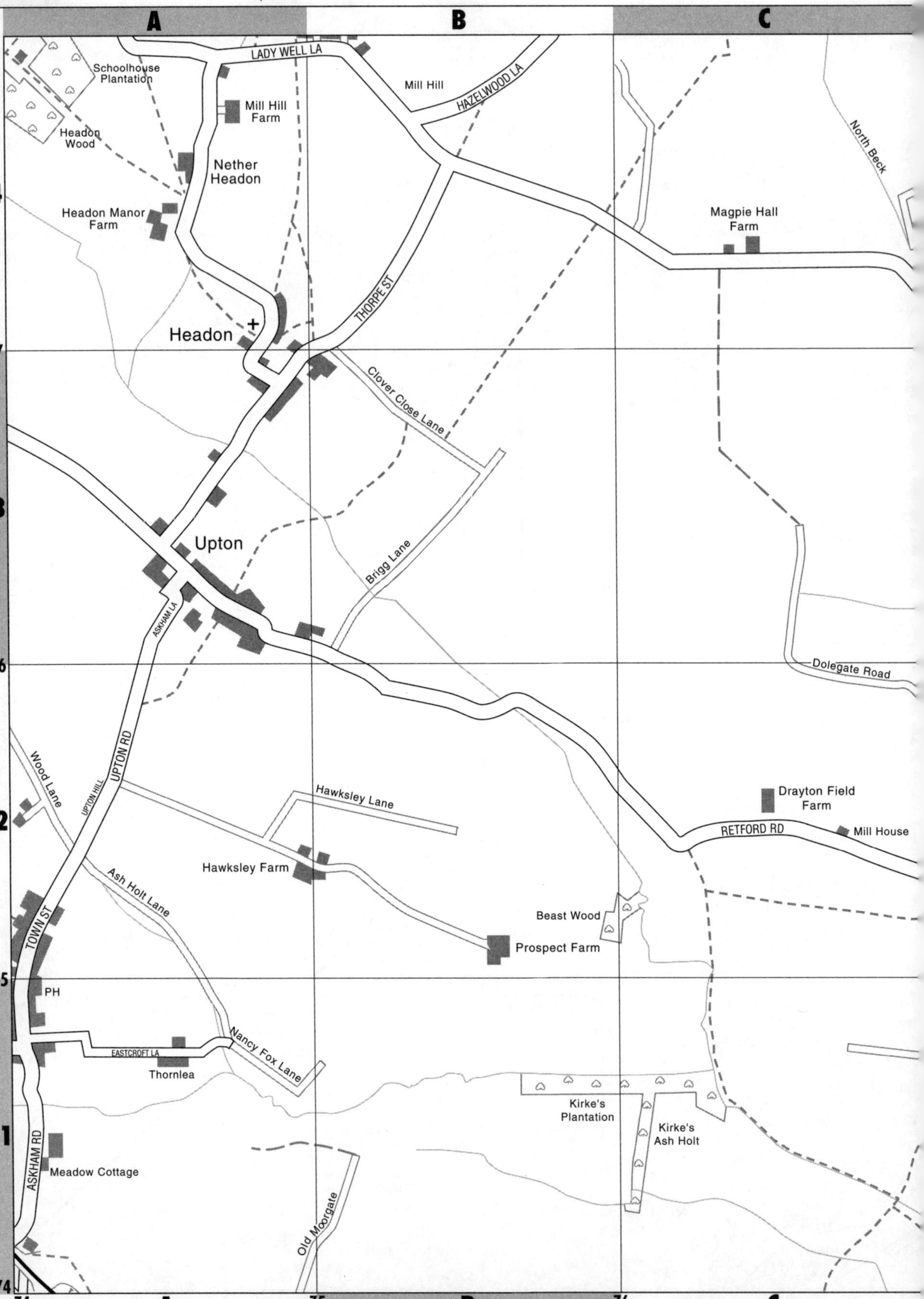

A

B

C

LADY WELL LA

Mill Hill

HAZELWOOD LA

Schoolhouse Plantation

Mill Hill Farm

Headon Wood

Nether Headon

North Beck

Magpie Hall Farm

**4**

Headon Manor Farm

THORPE ST

Headon

**77**

Clover Close Lane

**3**

Upton

Brigg Lane

ASKHAM LA

**76**

Dolegate Road

Wood Lane

UPTON RD

UPTON HILL

Hawksley Lane

Drayton Field Farm

RETFORD RD

Mill House

**2**

Ash Holt Lane

Hawksley Farm

Beast Wood

TOWN ST

Prospect Farm

**75**

PH

EASTCROFT LA

Nancy Fox Lane

Thornlea

Kirke's Plantation

Kirke's Ash Holt

**1**

ASKHAM RD

Meadow Cottage

Old Moorgate

**74**

74

A

75

B

76

C

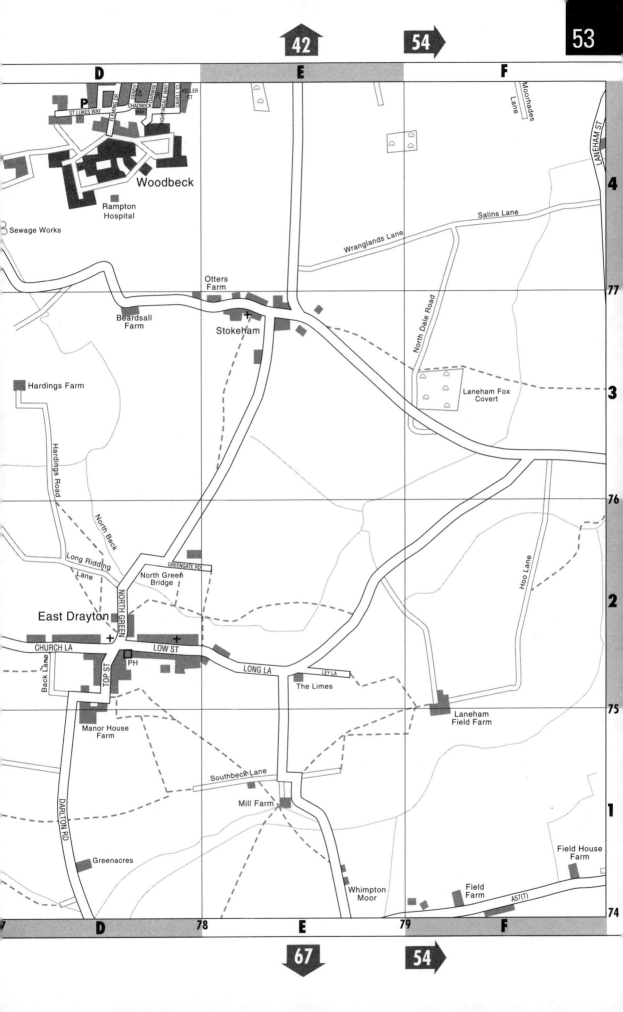

D   E   F

St Lukes Way
FLEMING DR
CANDY DR
DARWIN DR
CHADWICK WAY
NIGHTINGALE WAY
CAVELL CL
KELLER CT
P

Woodbeck

Rampton Hospital

Sewage Works

Moorhades Lane

LANEHAM ST

4

Salins Lane

Wranglands Lane

77

North Dale Road

Otters Farm

Beardsall Farm

Stokeham

Laneham Fox Covert

3

Hardings Farm

Hardings Road

76

Hoo Lane

North Beck

Long Riddling Lane

GREENGATE RD

North Green Bridge

NORTH GREEN

East Drayton

2

CHURCH LA
LOW ST
PH
TOP ST
Back Lane

The Limes

LONG LA

LEY LA

Laneham Field Farm

75

Manor House Farm

DARLTON RD

Southbeck Lane

Mill Farm

Field House Farm

1

Greenacres

Field Farm

A57(T)

Whimpton Moor

74

D   E   F

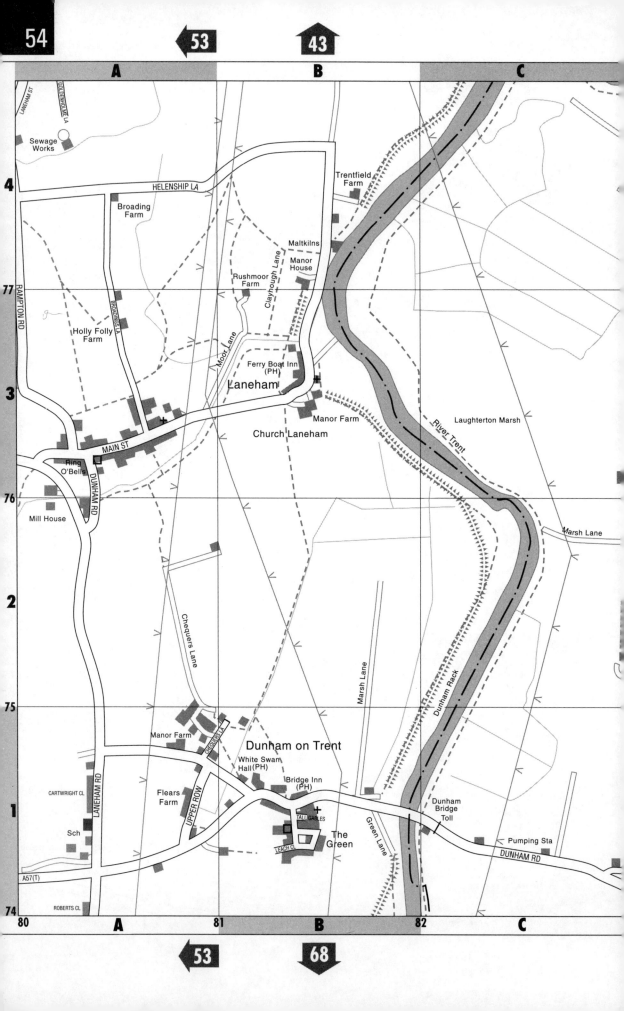

53

43

A

B

C

4

Sewage Works

HELENSHIP LA

LANEHAM ST

GOLDENHOLME LA

Broading Farm

Trentfield Farm

Maltkilns

77

Rushmoor Farm

Clayhough Lane

Manor House

RAMPTON RD

BROADINGS LA

Holly Folly Farm

Moor Lane

Ferry Boat Inn (PH)

Laneham

3

Manor Farm

Church Laneham

Laughterton Marsh

River Trent

Main St

Ring O'Bells

DUNHAM RD

76

Mill House

Marsh Lane

2

Chequers Lane

Marsh Lane

Dunham Rack

75

Manor Farm

CHEQUERS LA

Dunham on Trent

LANEHAM RD

White Swan Hall (PH)

Bridge Inn (PH)

CARTWRIGHT CL

Flears Farm

UPPER ROW

1

Dunham Bridge Toll

Sch

TALL GABLES

The Green

Green Lane

LEACH CL

Pumping Sta

DUNHAM RD

A57(T)

ROBERTS CL

74

80

A

81

B

82

C

53

68

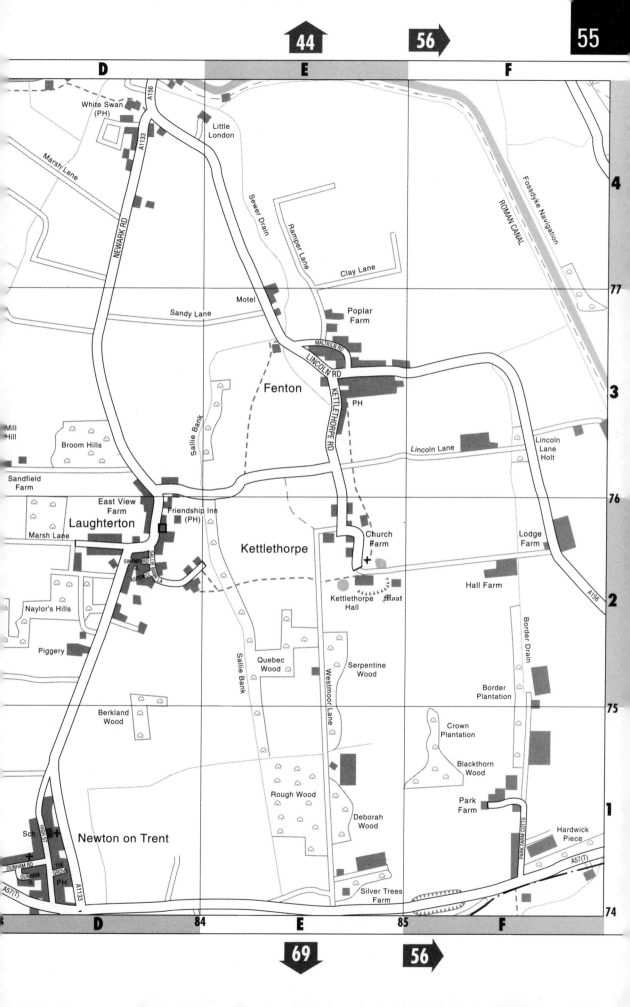

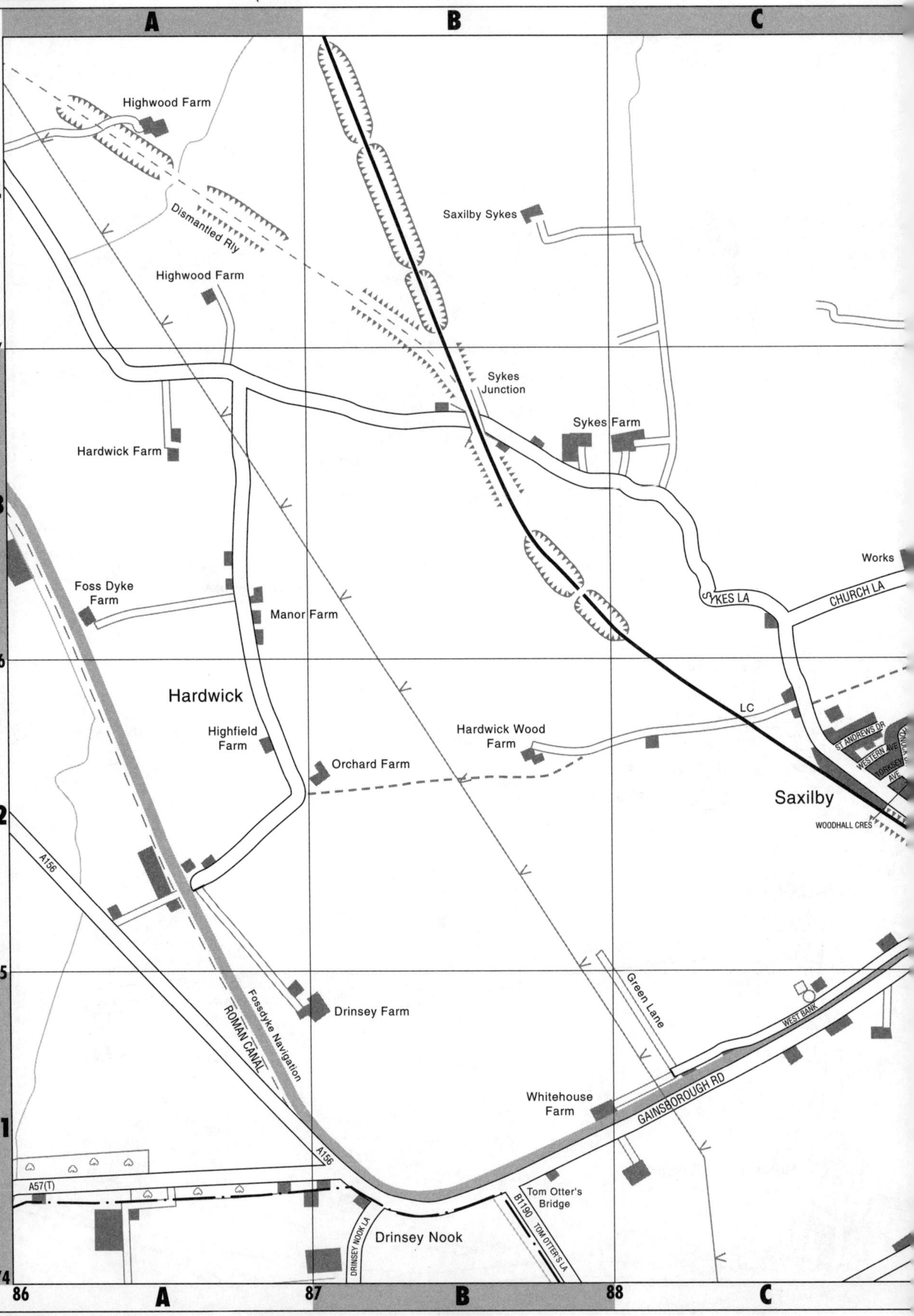

A      B      C

Highwood Farm

4

Dismantled Rly

Saxilby Sykes

Highwood Farm

77

Sykes Junction

Sykes Farm

Hardwick Farm

Works

3

Foss Dyke Farm

Manor Farm

SYKES LA

CHURCH LA

76

Hardwick

LC

Highfield Farm

Hardwick Wood Farm

ST ANDREWS DR

WESTERN AVE

Orchard Farm

Saxilby

2

A156

WOODHALL CRES

75

Drinsey Farm

Green Lane

WEST BANK

ROMAN CANAL

Fossdyke Navigation

GAINSBOROUGH RD

1

Whitehouse Farm

A156

A57(T)

Tom Otter's Bridge

Drinsey Nook

DRINSEY NOOK LA

B1190

TOM OTTER'S LA

74

86      A      87      B      88      C

D E F

4

Ingleby
Hall

Ingleby
Hall
Farm

Manor Farm

CARLTON LA

Moat

STURTON RD

Ingleby Grange

Cornhills Farm

77

Broxholme

BROXHOLME LA

3

Wheelgate
Farm

CHURCH LA

ST OSWALD'S CL

River Till

BROXHOLME LA

76

CHURCH RD

WESTCROFT DR

MEADOW RISE

ROSSDALE

MANOR RD

ALMOND CL

MILL LA

NURSERY CL

MILLFIELD AVE

ELM CL

Eastfield House
Farm

2

SOUTH PARADE

OTTER AVE

ORCHARD

HIGHFIELD RD

Sch

MAYS LA

KELSEY AVE

HIGH ST

+

WILLOW CL

FOSSDYKE

Odder Farm

SKIRBECK DR

OAK CL

FOSSE GR

SYKES LA

THE SIDINGS

WILLIAM ST

BRIDGE PL

QUEENSWAY

B1241

Odda
Farm

Odder

75

Kexilby
Sta

Fire Sta

LC

BRIDGE ST

QUEENSWAY

LINCOLN RD

ROMAN CANAL

WEST BANK

PH

GAINSBOROUGH RD

A57(T)

A57(T)

The Old Mill

Fossdyke Navigation

Moor House
Farm

BROADHOLME RD

Crossing Cottage
LC

River Bank
Farm

1

MANOR CL

Broadholme

Whitehouse
Farm

Bartons Farm

Birchwood Farm

Highland
Farm

Ouseness Farm

74

D 90 E 91 F

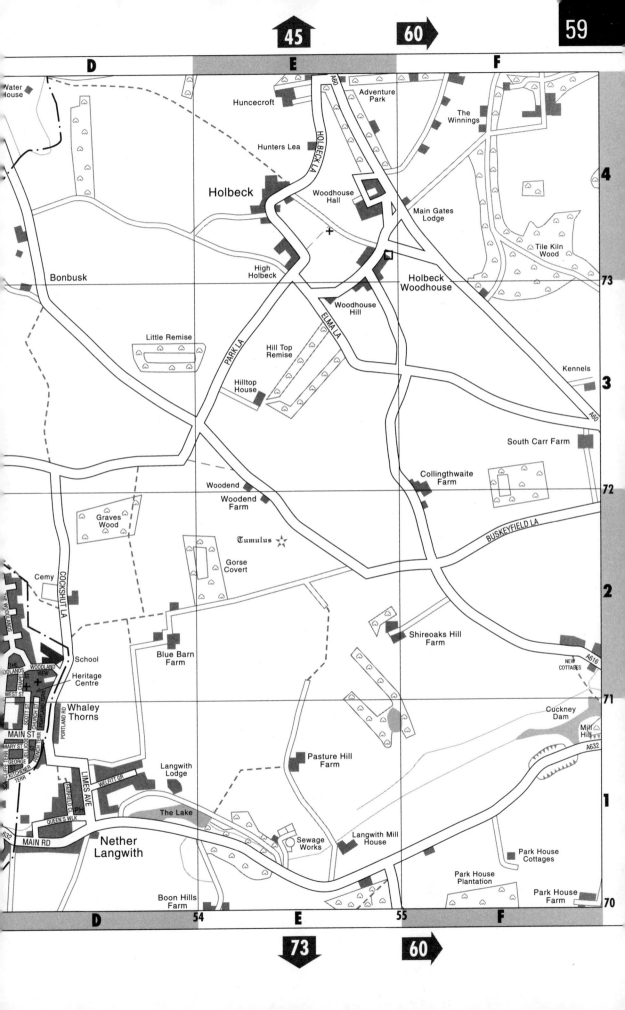

D
E
F

Water House
Huncecroft
Adventure Park
The Winnings

4

Hunters Lea
HOLBECK LA
A60

Holbeck
Woodhouse Hall
Main Gates Lodge
Tile Kiln Wood

Bonbusk
High Holbeck
Holbeck Woodhouse
73

Woodhouse Hill
ELMA LA
Kennels

Little Remise
Hill Top Remise
PARK LA

Hilltop House
South Carr Farm
3
A60

Woodend
Woodend Farm
Collingthwaite Farm
72

Graves Wood
Tumulus
BUSKEYFIELD LA

Cemy
Gorse Covert

THE WOODLANDS
COCKSHUT LA
Shireoaks Hill Farm
2
NEW COTTAGES
A616

School
Blue Barn Farm
WOODLAND VIEW
WEST ST
Heritage Centre

Whaley Thorns
71
Cuckney Dam
Mill Hill
A632

MAIN ST
PORTLAND RD
Pasture Hill Farm

MARY ST
GEORGE
KITCHENER
Langwith Lodge

LIMES AVE
WELFITT GR
The Lake
Langwith Mill House
1

SCHOLIFFE
QUEEN'S WLK
Sewage Works
Park House Plantation
Park House Cottages

MAIN RD
Nether Langwith
Langwith Mill House
Park House Farm

632
Boon Hills Farm
70

D
54
E
55
F

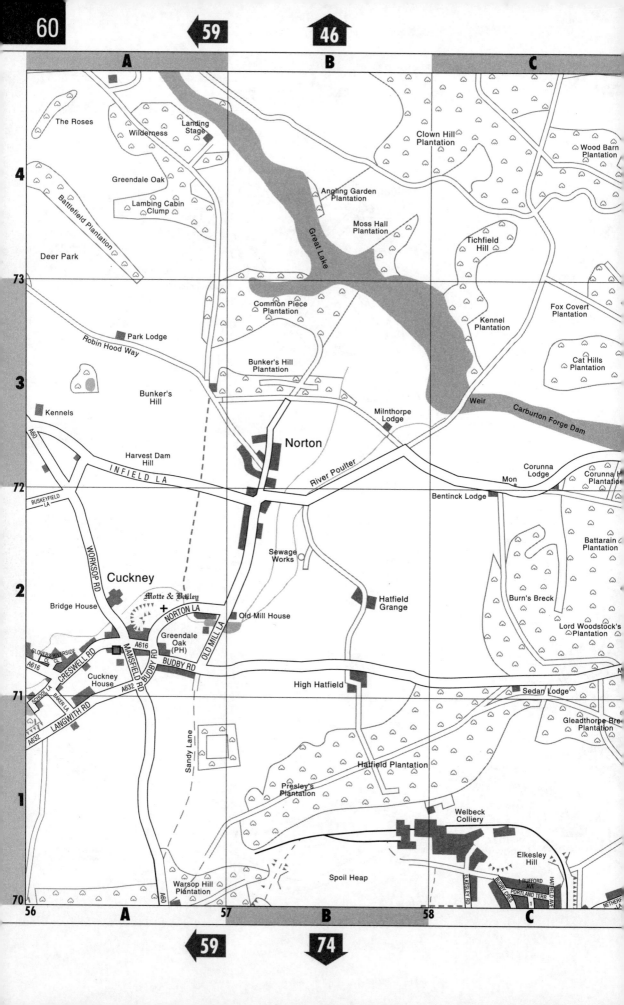

**A   B   C**

4

The Roses

Wilderness

Landing Stage

Clown Hill Plantation

Wood Barn Plantation

Greendale Oak

Lambing Cabin Clump

Battlefield Plantation

Angling Garden Plantation

Moss Hall Plantation

Tichfield Hill

73

Deer Park

Common Piece Plantation

Great Lake

Kennel Plantation

Fox Covert Plantation

3

Park Lodge

Robin Hood Way

Bunker's Hill Plantation

Cat Hills Plantation

Bunker's Hill

Kennels

Milnthorpe Lodge

Weir

Carburton Forge Dam

Harvest Dam Hill

Norton

Corunna Lodge

Corunna H Plantation

INFIELD LA

River Poulter

Mon

72

BUSKEYFIELD LA

Bentinck Lodge

WORKSOP RD

Sewage Works

Battarain Plantation

2

Cuckney

Burn's Breck

Bridge House

Motte & Bailey

+

NORTON LA

Old Mill House

Hatfield Grange

Lord Woodstock's Plantation

Greendale Oak (PH)

OLD MILL LA

GLOVERS RIVERSIDE CL CL

A616

A616

Creswell RD

MANSFIELD RD

BUDBY RD

BUDBY RD

High Hatfield

Sedan Lodge

71

SCHOOL LA

BAKER LA

Cuckney House

A632

Gleadthorpe Bre Plantation

A632

LANGWITH RD

Sandy Lane

Hatfield Plantation

1

Presley's Plantation

Welbeck Colliery

A60

Elkesley Hill

Warsop Hill Plantation

Spoil Heap

ELKESLEY RD

RUFFORD AVE

PORTLAND TERR

BUDBY CRES

HATFIELD AVE

NETHERF

70

56   **A**   57   **B**   58   **C**

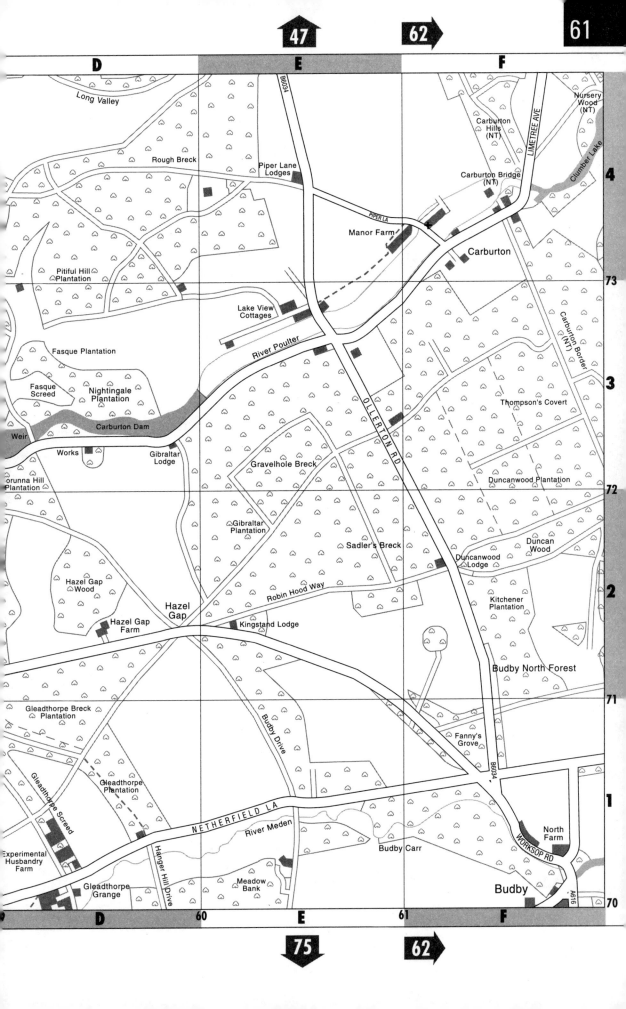

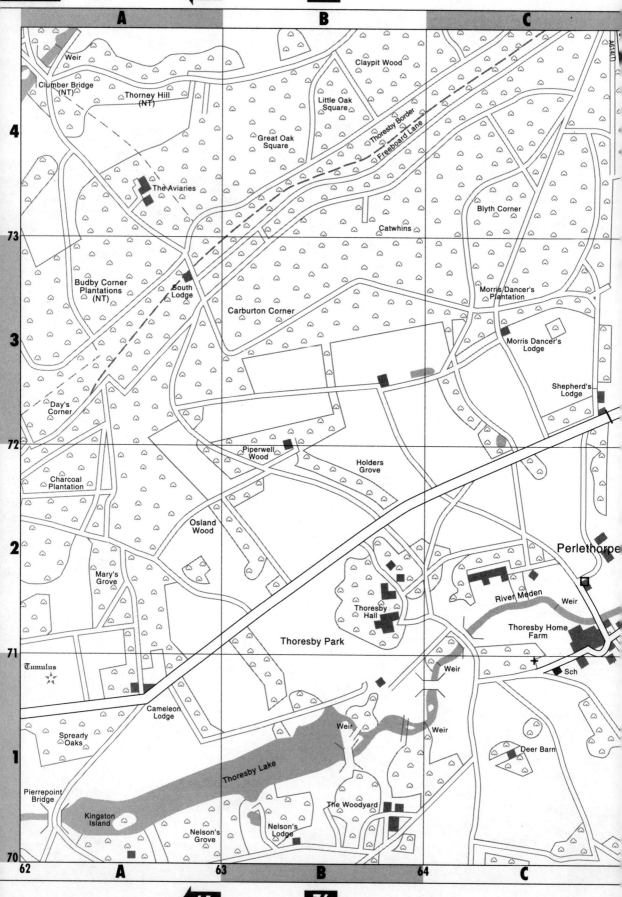

A    B    C

4

73

3

72

2

71

1

70

Weir
Clumber Bridge (NT)
Thorney Hill (NT)
The Aviaries
Budby Corner Plantations (NT)
South Lodge
Day's Corner
Charcoal Plantation
Osland Wood
Mary's Grove
Tumulus
Cameleon Lodge
Spready Oaks
Pierrepoint Bridge
Kingston Island
Nelson's Grove

Claypit Wood
Little Oak Square
Great Oak Square
Thoresby Border
Freeboard Lane
Catwhins
Carburton Corner
Piperwell Wood
Holders Grove
Thoresby Park
Thoresby Hall
Thoresby Lake
Weir
Nelson's Lodge
The Woodyard
Weir

Blyth Corner
Morris Dancer's Plantation
Morris Dancer's Lodge
Shepherd's Lodge
Perlethorpe
River Meden
Weir
Thoresby Home Farm
Sch
Weir
Deer Barn

A6(14T)

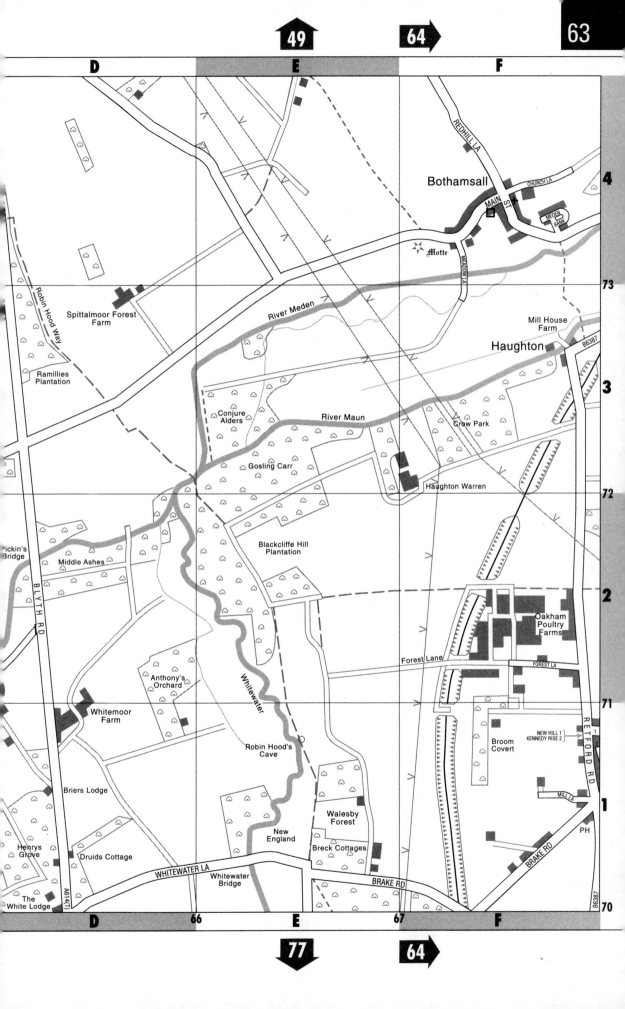

D
E
F

4

Bothamsall

REDHILL LA

CHURCH LA

MAIN ST

MEDEN BANK

Motte

MEADOW LA

73

Spittalmoor Forest Farm

Robin Hood Way

River Meden

Mill House Farm

Haughton

B6387

Ramillies Plantation

3

Conjure Alders

River Maun

Crow Park

Gosling Carr

Haughton Warren

72

Pickin's Bridge

Middle Ashes

Blackcliffe Hill Plantation

2

Oakham Poultry Farms

BLYTH RD

Whitewater

Forest Lane

FOREST LA

Anthony's Orchard

71

Whitemoor Farm

Broom Covert

NEW HILL 1
KENNEDY RISE 2

RETFORD RD

Robin Hood's Cave

MILL LA

Briers Lodge

1

Walesby Forest

New England

Breck Cottages

Henrys Grove

Druids Cottage

PH

WHITEWATER LA

Whitewater Bridge

BRAKE RD

BRAKE RD

The White Lodge

A614(T)

B6387

70

**A**    **B**    **C**

B6387

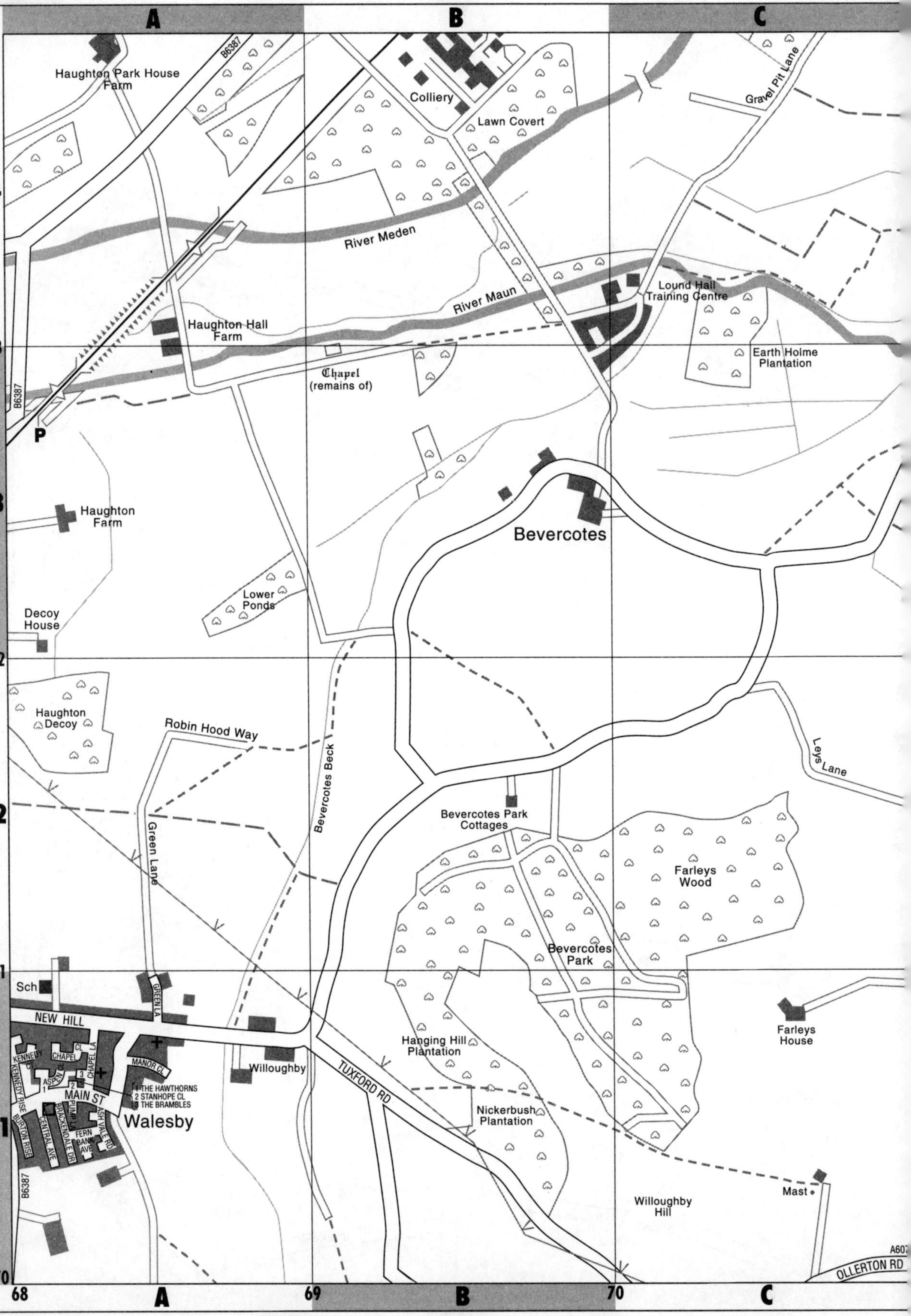

Haughton Park House
Farm

Colliery

Lawn Covert

Gravel Pit Lane

**4**

River Meden

Lound Hall
Training Centre

River Maun

**73**

Haughton Hall
Farm

Earth Holme
Plantation

B6387

Chapel
(remains of)

P

**3**

Haughton
Farm

Bevercotes

Lower
Ponds

Decoy
House

**72**

Haughton
Decoy

Robin Hood Way

Leys Lane

Bevercotes Beck

**2**

Green Lane

Bevercotes Park
Cottages

Farleys
Wood

Bevercotes
Park

**71**

Sch

GREEN LA

NEW HILL

Farleys
House

Willoughby

TUXFORD RD

Hanging Hill
Plantation

KENNEDY RISE
CHAPEL CL
CHAPEL LA
MANOR CL
+
+
+
1 THE HAWTHORNS
2 STANHOPE CL
3 THE BRAMBLES

MAIN ST

Nickerbush
Plantation

**1**

Walesby

Mast

B6387

BRACKENDALE DR
CENTRAL AVE
FERN BANK
BLIDWORTH RISE

Willoughby
Hill

A607

**70**

68    A    69    B    70    C

OLLERTON RD

ASKHAM RD

Old Moorgate

High Brecks Plantation

High Brecks Farm

Brecks Plantation

Low Brecks Farm

A57(T)

A57

4

BROAD GATE

Earthworks

Kingshaugh Farm

PH

HIGH ST

LINCOLN RD

HALL LA

COLLEGE LA

TON ST

TRINITY CRES

PLANTATION AVE

TRINITY CRES

Back Lane

73

Markham Hall

MARK LA

CHURCH ST

NOOK!

QUAKEFIELD RD

Darlton Fie

3

Highfields Farm

72

Darlton Gaps

Lodge Farm

DARLTON RD

Goodhouses Farm

2

PH

Eastfield House

LINCOLN RD

HILLSIDE

A6075

WELBECK PL

FLEMING AVE

GILBERT AVE

HAYES CL

Sch

FARADAY RD

NICHOLAS

WINDSOR DR

ARKWRIGHT

71

LINDEN AVE

MARK LA

MAY FAIR

CATH PL

Tuxford

MARNHAM RD

Merryfields Farm

B1164

ASHVALE RD

A1(T)

CHESTNUT WAY

ASPEN CL

ASPEN WAY

Park Cottage

1

Dismtd Rly

LODGE LA

Lodge La

Peter Barn

Ashvale

GREAT NORTH RD

Lodge Farm

Ruddingwood

Goosemoor Dyke

A1(T)

B1164

70

**A**   **B**   **C**

Ragnall Hall
+
Roberts Farm
**Ragnall**
Chestnut Farm
Old Trent
Dunham Dubs
**4**

Bubble Dyke
**73**
Amblerod Plantation
**North Clifton**
Trentholme Farm
**Fledborough**
**3**
Fledborough Beck
Sewer Dyke
TRENT LA
Mill Hill House
The Gables
+
SILVER ST
Manor House
Hall Farm
MILL LA
**72**
North Clifton Hall
River Trent
Scotchman's Hole
Fledborough Holme
Moor Lane
Fledborough House
Trent Viaduct
Dismantled Railway
**2**
CHURCH LA
Sch
Church Farm
**71**
High Marnham Power Station
Manor Farm
Clifton Plantation
MOOR LA
**1**
SPARROW LA
Brownlow Arms (PH)
South Clifton
BACK ST
FRONT ST
+
Oaklands Farm
A1133
Old Trent
HOLLOWGATE LA
Marnham Hall
Ferry Holme
TRENT LA
Marshgate Farm
COAL YARD LA
**High Marnham**
**70**
**80**   **A**   **81**   **B**   **82**   **C**

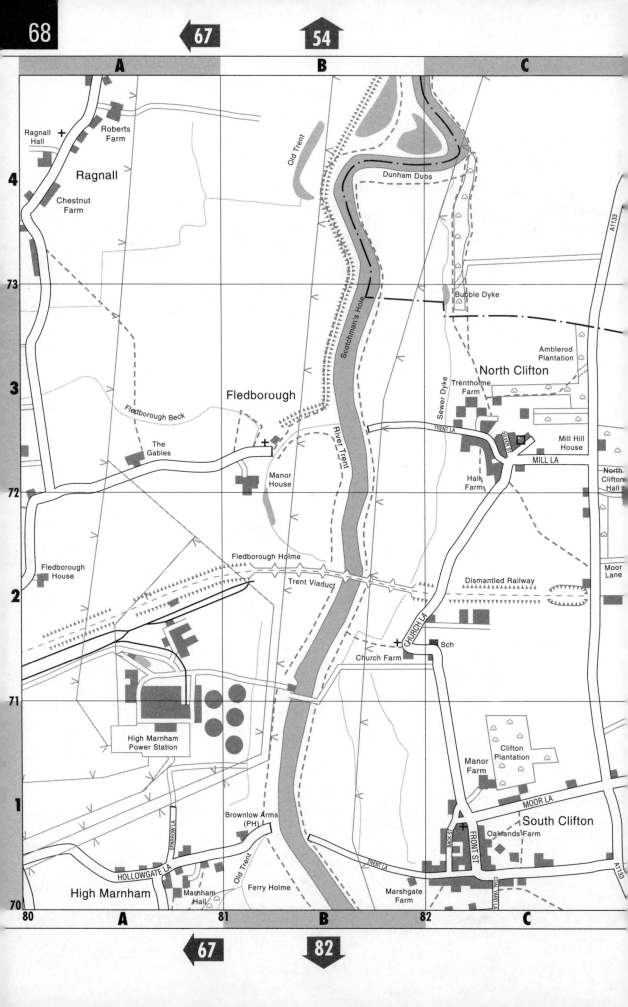

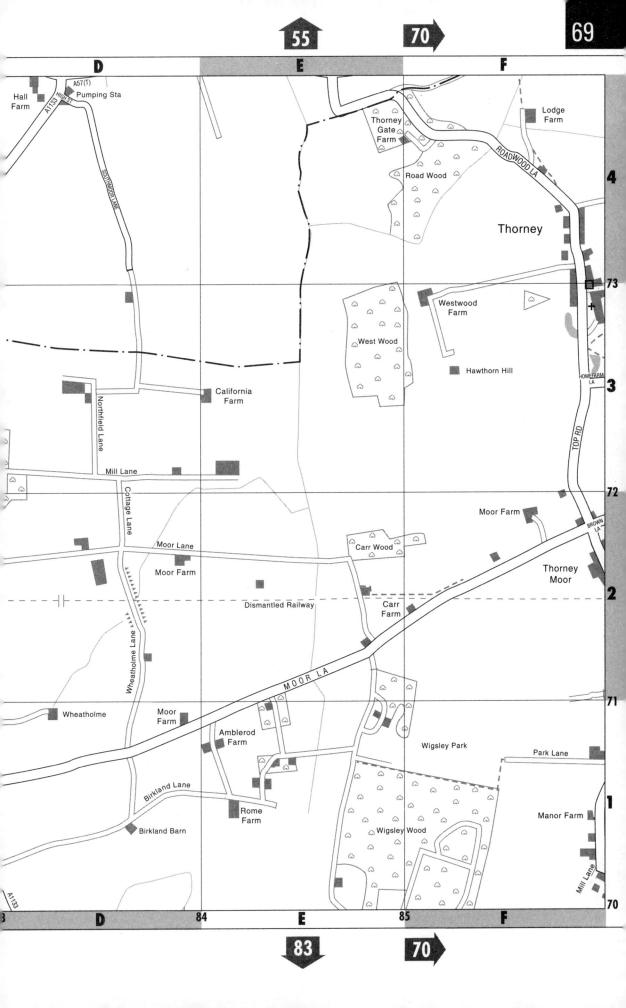

D

E

F

Hall
Farm

A57(T)

Pumping Sta

HIGH ST

A1133

SOUTHMOOR LANE

Lodge
Farm

Thorney
Gate
Farm

ROADWOOD LA

Road Wood

4

Thorney

73

Westwood
Farm

West Wood

Hawthorn Hill

HOMEFARM LA

3

Northfield Lane

California
Farm

Mill Lane

Cottage Lane

TOP RD

72

Moor Farm

BROWN LA

Moor Lane

Moor Farm

Carr Wood

Thorney
Moor

2

Wheatholme Lane

Dismantled Railway

Carr
Farm

MOOR LA

71

Wheatholme

Moor
Farm

Amblerod
Farm

Wigsley Park

Park Lane

Birkland Lane

Rome
Farm

Manor Farm

1

Birkland Barn

Wigsley Wood

Mill Lane

70

D

E

F

84

85

A1133

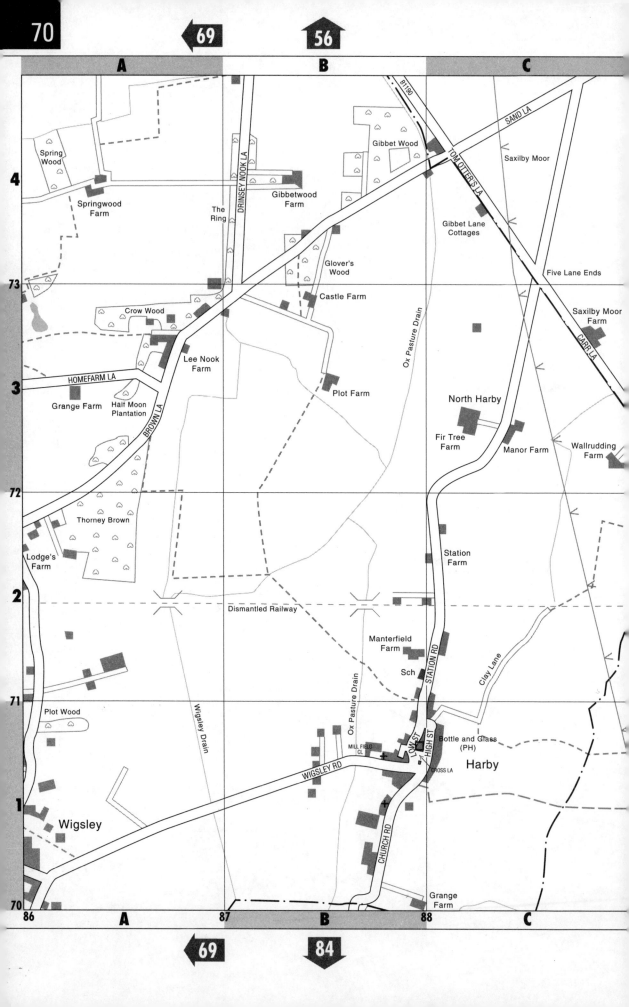

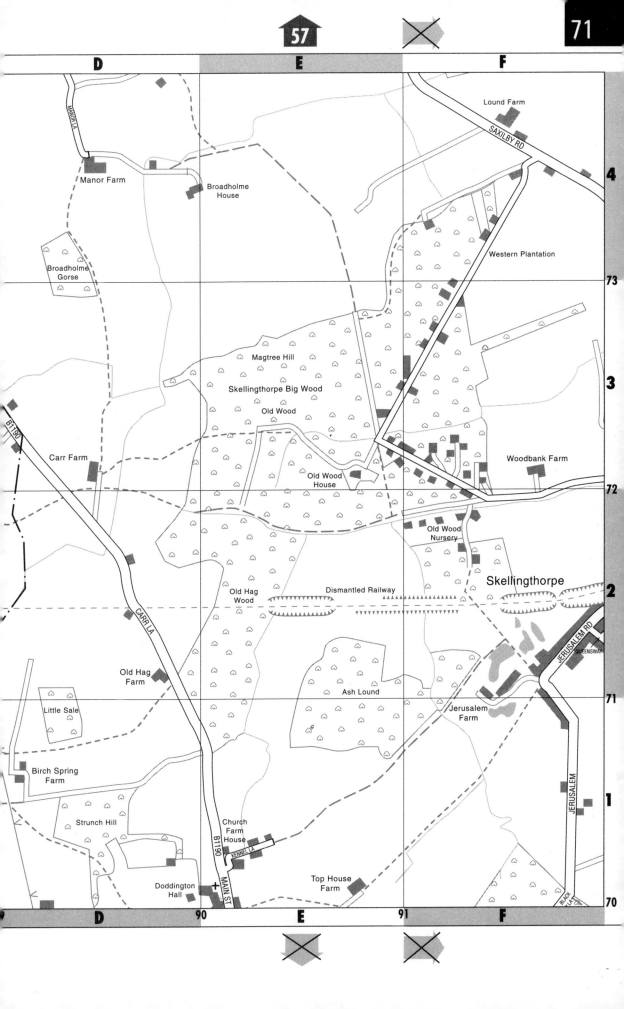

A          B          C

4

A632  MOOR LA

Cross Hills

Upper
Langwith

SCARCLIFFE LA

Scarcliffe
Lanes

River Poulter

Old
Hall

The
Jays

Dismantled Railway

School

Malthouse
Cottages

Langwith

New
Plantatio

Gildwells Farm

PH

69

Scarcliffe

Archaeological Trail

Deans
Plantation

Langwith
Wood

Langwith
Junction

Bradshaw
Wood

School

Schools

Offices

Stubbins Wood

Wks

3

Roseland
Wood

Roseland
Farm

Roseland Lane

SLANT LA

CARTER LA

Carter La by

P P

P

68

COMMON LA

MAIN ST

B6407

Shirebrook

Sch

Sch

CENTRAL DR

FIELD DR

67

Works

Cemy

Dismantled Railway

Hodhill
Farm

WOOD LA

Woodland
Farm

Balkham Lane

Forge La

Archaeological Trail

Green Lane

1

66

B6407

Pleasleypark Farm

50      A      51      B      52      C

73
60

A B C

4

Park House Plantation

Hag's Plantation

Spoil Heap

Dismtld Rly

Meden Vale

BUDBY CRES
FROST AVE
HATFIELD AVE

ELKESLEY RD
JACKSON TERR

EASTLAND TERR
Schs

RUFFORD AVE

P
P

Oakfield Plantation

MARSTON AVE
CARBURTON
MANOR RD
EGMANTON RD

PERLTHORPE AVE
LAXTON DR
EGMANTON RD

KNEESALL CL 1
CAUNTON CL 2
THORESBY CL 3
OSSINGTON CL 4

NETHERFIELD LA

LYNCROFT

P

The Three Lions (PH)

Assarts Farm
LC

LIME CRES

Church Warsop

BIGGIN ST
ELM ST
FOX RD
LAUREL AVE
SYCAMORE ST

Sch

Cemy

Poultry Houses

Assarts Hill Plantation

WOOD LA

CARTER LA

B6031

BISHOP'S WLK

B6031

RECTORY RD
TISSINGTON AVE

ST JOHN'S AVE
ST NIDDOCS
LALLAFAX AVE
SWEETMAN ST
CURZON CTR

GLAMIS RD
MEDEN BANK

MANOR RD

Burns Farm

River Meden

The Bottoms

Broomhill

Lane

Sewage Works

69

EASTLANDS LA
MANOR CT

P

CHURCH RD

3

Sch

1 OLD HALL CL
2 MOORFIELD PL
3 LEEMING CL

OSSINGTON TERR
SOUTHCLIFFE RD
TRENT LA

SHORT LA
GLEBE RD
SOUTHGATE RD

Sod Wall Plantation

Sch
BURNS LA
BIRKLANDS CL

QUEEN ST

RIVER VIEW
HETTS
EASTCLIFFE

SANDY LA
BIRKLAND AVE
MEADOW CROFT

68

CHURCH ST

Sch

APPLETON ST
WOODLAND GR
FITZHERBERT ST
FELL WILSON ST

CUMBERLAND AVE

HAMILTON DR
SAVILLE WAY

EDWARD'S LA
VICTORIA AVE

WORK TERR
KING'S RD

Sch

Liby

PORTLAND TERR
GEORGE AVE
SHORT ST
PRINCESS AVE

MARKET WARSOP

Ling Lane

ALEXANDRA'S DR

STONEBRIDGE LA

STONEBRIDGE CT
GREENDALE CT

CLUMBER ST

HIGH ST

SHERWOOD ST

2

SOOKHOLME LA

MEDEN
WINDSOR CT

SOOKHOLME DR
VALE DR

OLD MILL LA
RIDGEWAY LA

CHERRY GR

LC

MUSGRAVE TERR

NEWARK ST
LONDON TERR
KIRKERS LA

GEORGE AVE

Sch

Blakeley Hill

Norman's Plantation

MANSFIELD RD

ASKEW LA

BENTINCK ST
LITCHFIELD LA
LINGWOOD AVE

Mount Pleasant

67

A60

LANGWITH ROAD
MANSFIELD TERR

WELLINGTON ST

BRACKEN CL
TOP SANDY LA
LING VIEW
MOOR CRES
WINT

Blakeley Lane

Blakeley Hill Plantation

1

OAKFIELD LA

COTTAGE

CAMBER AVE

ROBIN HOOD AVE

JOHN AVE

FRIAR LA

FOREST RISE

Welbeck Colliery Junction

FOREST RD

Bradmer Hill

Windmill (disused)

Windmill Plantation

B6035

A6075

GEORGE

COACH RD

A6075

PEAFIELD LA

B6035

66

56 A 57 B 58 C

73
89

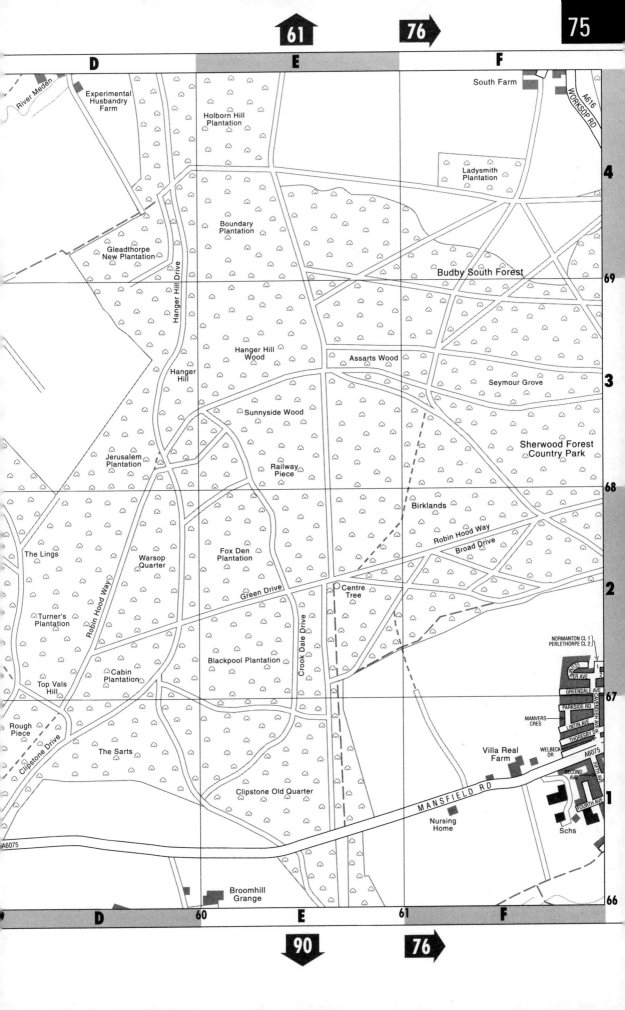

D E F

South Farm

A616 WORKSOP RD

River Meden

Experimental Husbandry Farm

Holborn Hill Plantation

Ladysmith Plantation

**4**

Boundary Plantation

Gleadthorpe New Plantation

Hanger Hill Drive

Budby South Forest

**69**

Hanger Hill Wood

Assarts Wood

Seymour Grove

**3**

Hanger Hill

Sunnyside Wood

Sherwood Forest Country Park

Jerusalem Plantation

Railway Piece

**68**

Birklands

The Lings

Warsop Quarter

Fox Den Plantation

Robin Hood Way

Broad Drive

Robin Hood Way

Green Drive

Centre Tree

**2**

Turner's Plantation

Crook Dale Drive

NORMANTON CL 1
PERLETHORPE CL 2

Blackpool Plantation

GREENDALE AVE

Cabin Plantation

PARKSIDE RD

Top Vals Hill

MANVERS CRES

LINTIN AVE

**67**

Rough Piece

THORESBY DR

WELBECK DR

Villa Real Farm

Clipstone Drive

The Sarts

SECOND AVE

FIFTH AVE

A6075

FOURTH AVE

Clipstone Old Quarter

**1**

Nursing Home

Schs

A6075

Broomhill Grange

Mansfield Rd

**66**

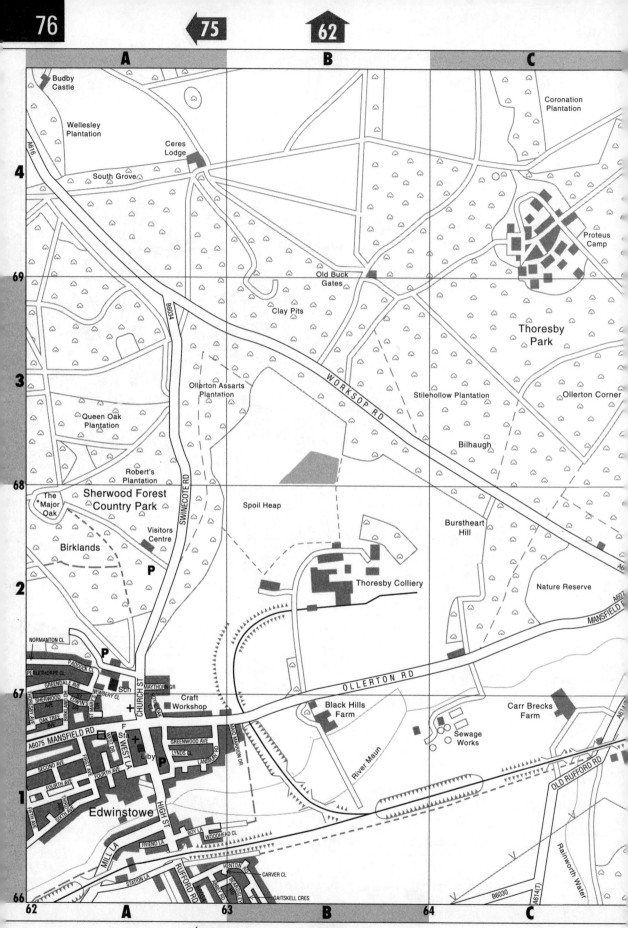

A  B  C

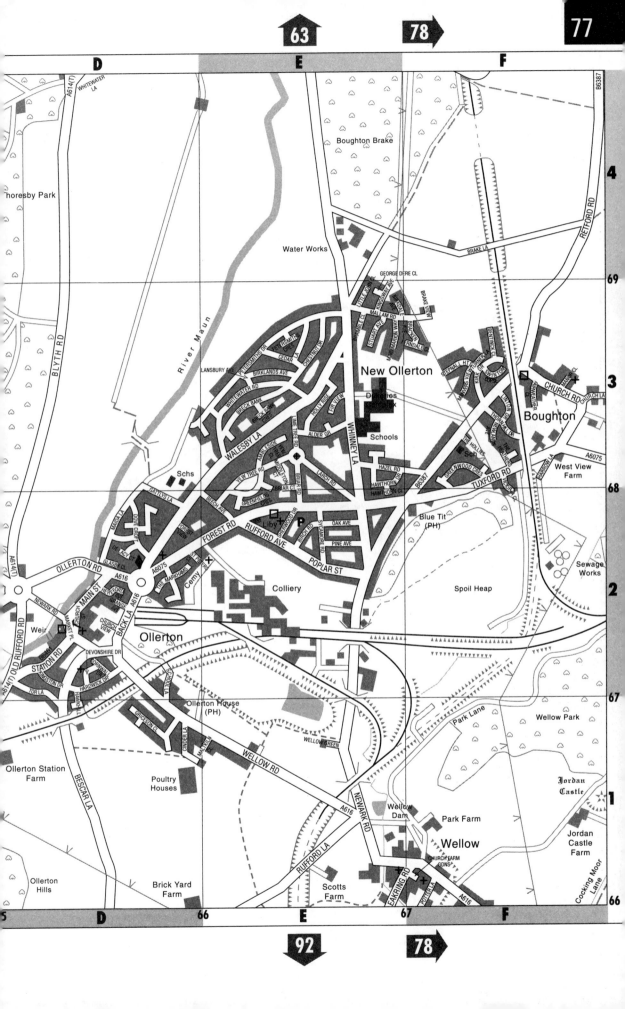

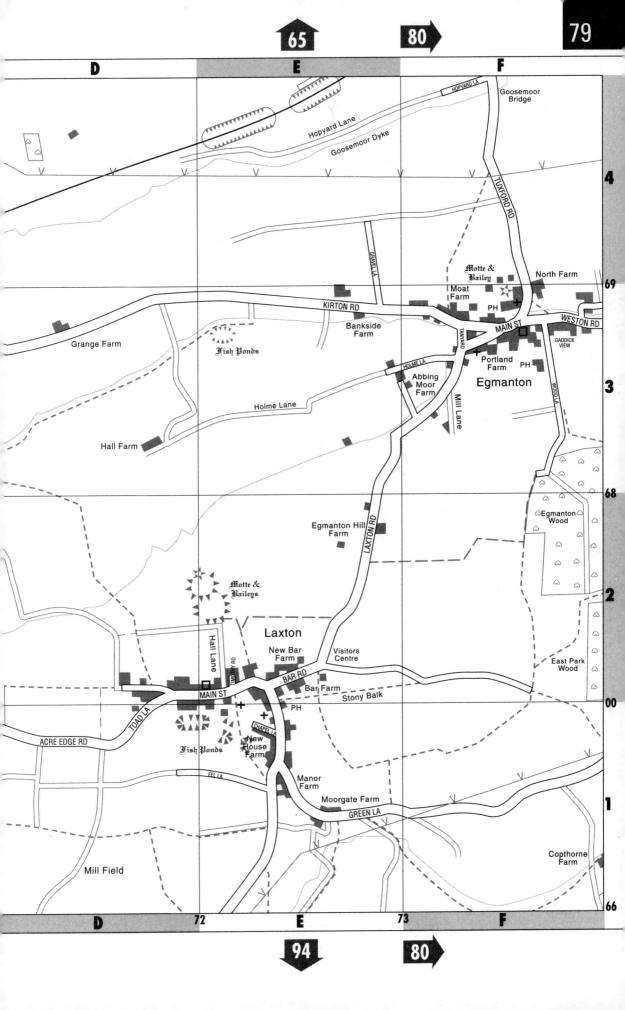

D E F

Hopyard La

Goosemoor
Bridge

Hopyard Lane

Goosemoor Dyke

4

TUXFORD RD

GRAVEL LA

Motte &
Bailey

North Farm

69

Moat
Farm

KIRTON RD

PH

WESTON RD

Grange Farm

Bankside
Farm

Fish Ponds

TANYARD

MAIN ST

GADDICK
VIEW

HOLME LA

Portland
Farm

PH

Egmanton

WOOD LA

3

Abbing
Moor
Farm

Hall Farm

Holme Lane

Mill Lane

68

Egmanton
Wood

Egmanton Hill
Farm

LAXTON RD

2

Motte &
Baileys

East Park
Wood

Laxton

New Bar
Farm

Visitors
Centre

Hall Lane

TIMOTHY RD

BAR RD

Bar Farm

Stony Balk

00

MAIN ST

TOAD LA

PH

ACRE EDGE RD

CHAPEL LA

New
House
Farm

Fish Ponds

EEL LA

Manor
Farm

Moorgate Farm

GREEN LA

1

Mill Field

Copthorne
Farm

66

D E F
72 73

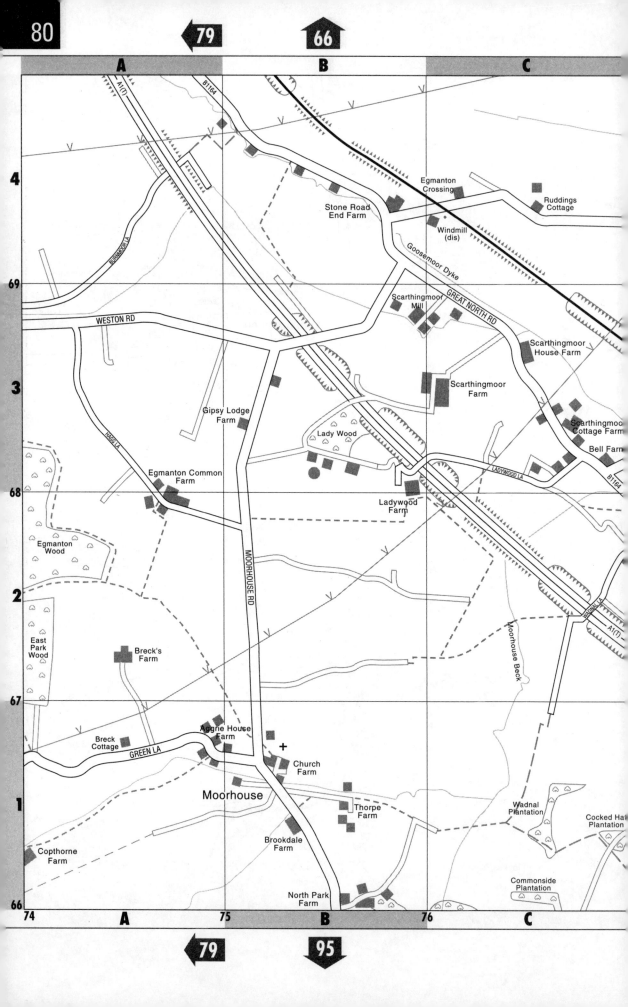

A B C

**Low Marnham**

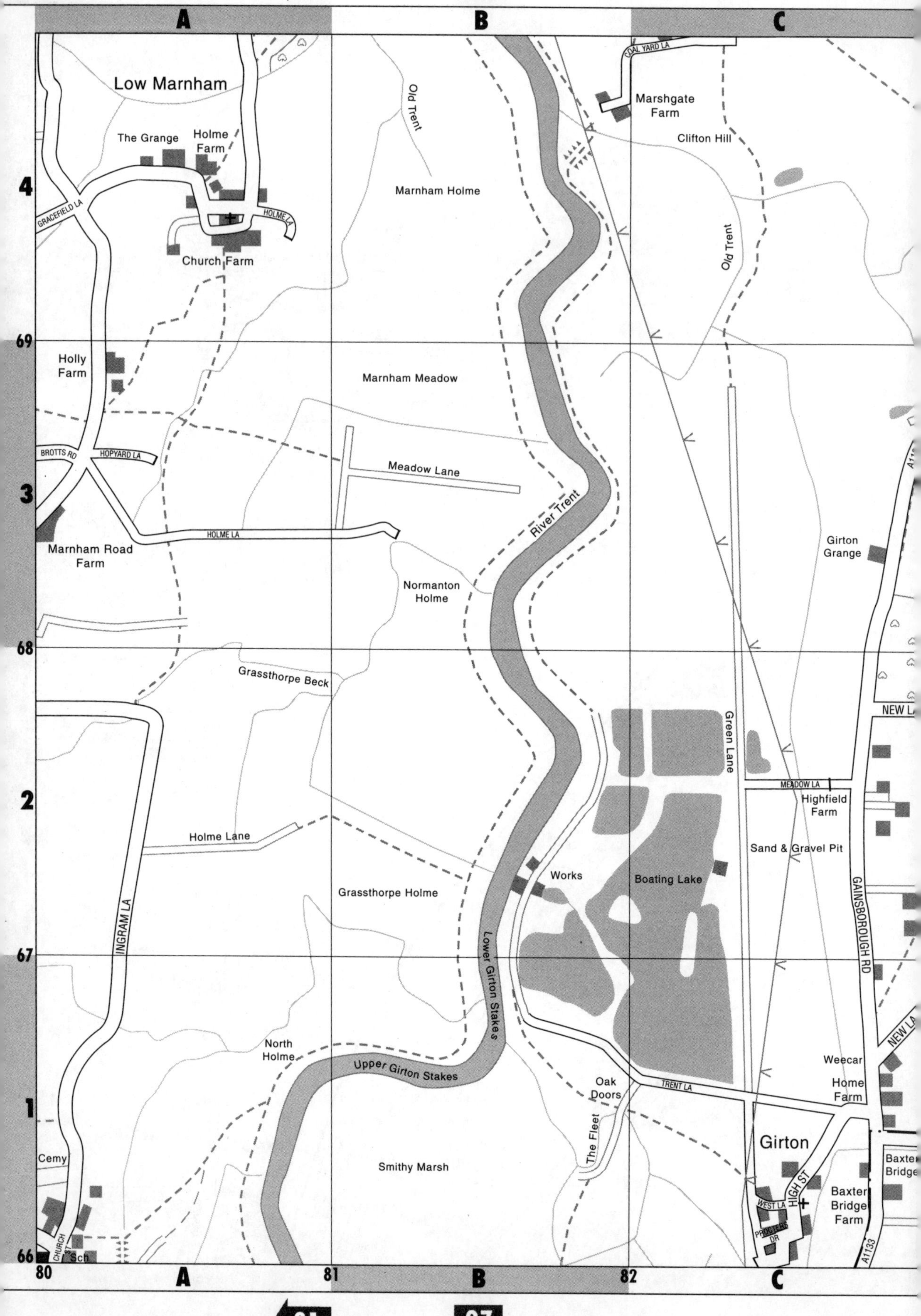

The Grange   Holme Farm

Old Trent

Marshgate Farm

Coal Yard La

Clifton Hill

4

Gracefield La

Holme La

Church Farm

Marnham Holme

Old Trent

69

Holly Farm

Marnham Meadow

Brotts Rd   Hopyard La

Meadow Lane

River Trent

3

Holme La

Marnham Road Farm

Normanton Holme

Girton Grange

68

Grassthorpe Beck

New La

Green Lane

Meadow La

Highfield Farm

Ingram La

Holme Lane

Sand & Gravel Pit

2

Gainsborough Rd

Grassthorpe Holme

Lower Girton Stakes

Works

Boating Lake

67

North Holme

Upper Girton Stakes

Oak Doors

Trent La

New La

Weecar Home Farm

1

The Fleet

Girton

Cemy

Smithy Marsh

West La   High St

Baxter Bridge

Proctors Dr

Baxter Bridge Farm

A1133

Church La   Sch

66

80

A 81 B 82 C

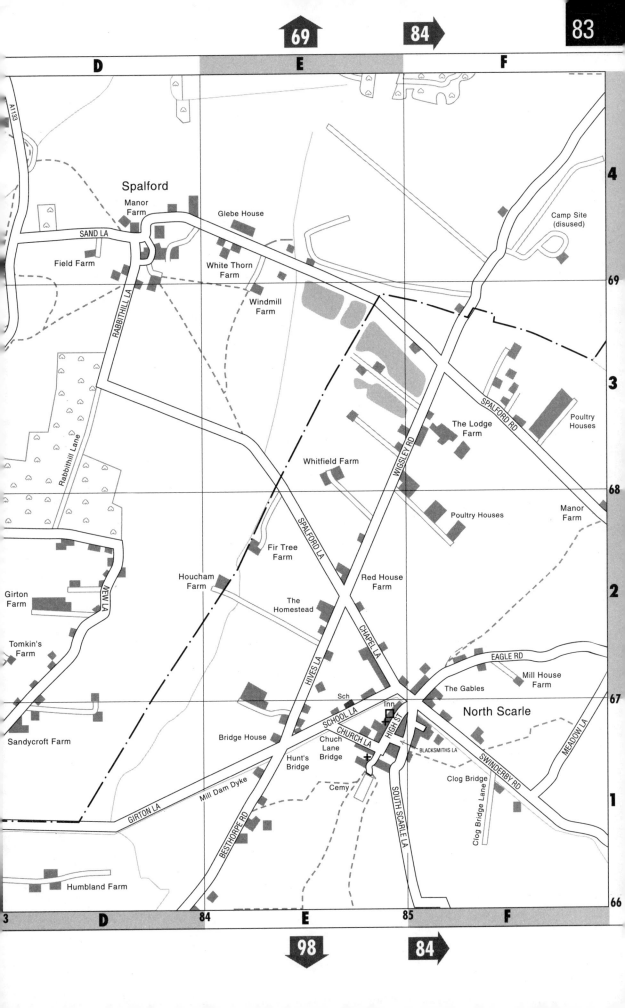

D
E
F

4

Spalford

Manor
Farm

Glebe House

Camp Site
(disused)

SAND LA

Field Farm

White Thorn
Farm

69

RABBITHILL LA

Windmill
Farm

SPALFORD RD

3

Poultry
Houses

Rabbithill Lane

The Lodge
Farm

WIGSLEY RD

Whitfield Farm

68

Poultry Houses

Manor
Farm

NEW LA

Fir Tree
Farm

SPALFORD LA

Girton
Farm

Houcham
Farm

Red House
Farm

2

Tomkin's
Farm

The
Homestead

HIVES LA

CHAPEL LA

EAGLE RD

Mill House
Farm

The Gables

67

Sandycroft Farm

Sch

SCHOOL LA

Bridge House

Inn

North Scarle

CHURCH LA

HIGH ST

BLACKSMITHS LA

Chuch
Lane
Bridge

MEADOW LA

Hunt's
Bridge

SWINDERBY RD

Clog Bridge

Cemy

SOUTH SCARLE LA

GIRTON LA

Mill Dam Dyke

Clog Bridge Lane

1

BESTHORPE RD

Humbland Farm

66

3
D
84
E
85
F

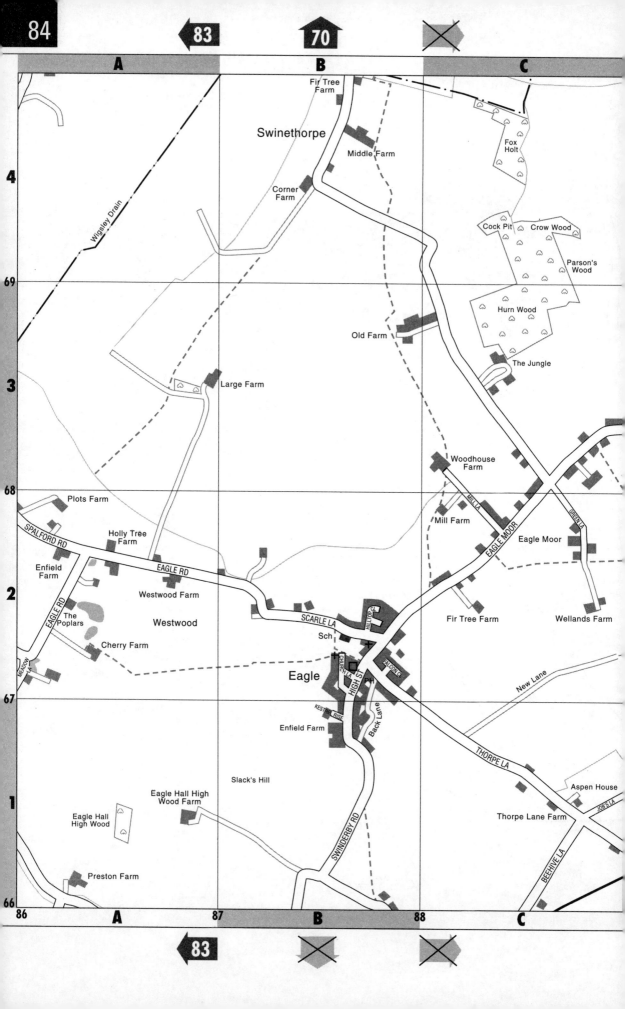

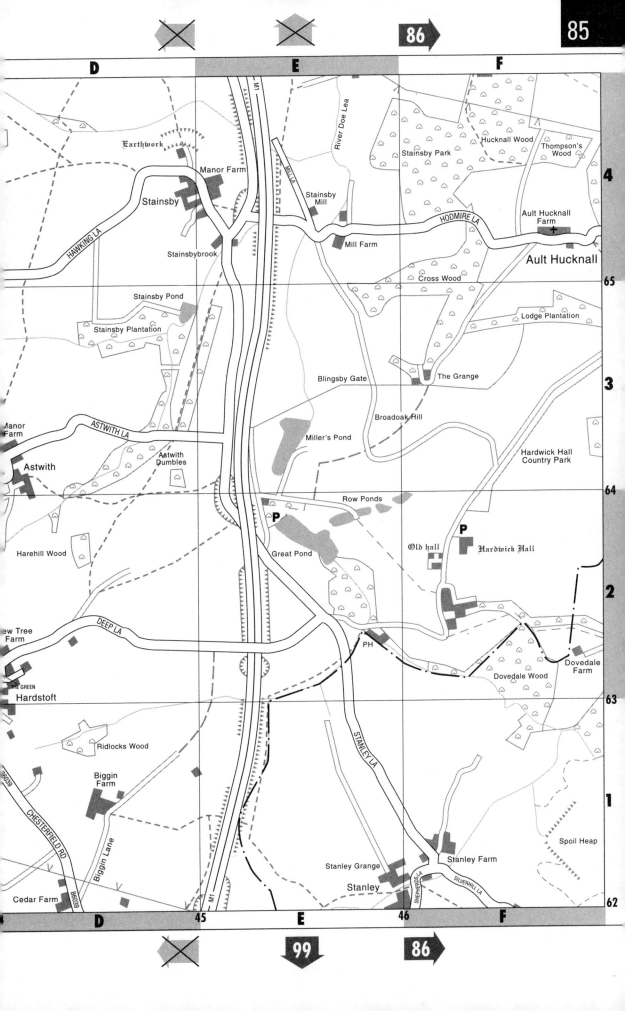

Earthwork

Manor Farm

Stainsby

Stainsbybrook

Stainsby Pond

Stainsby Plantation

HAWKING LA

Stainsby Mill

Mill Farm

River Doe Lea

Stainsby Park

Hucknall Wood

Thompson's Wood

HODMIRE LA

Ault Hucknall Farm

Ault Hucknall

Cross Wood

**4**

**65**

Lodge Plantation

Blingsby Gate

The Grange

**3**

ASTWITH LA

Manor Farm

Astwith

Astwith Dumbles

Broadoak Hill

Miller's Pond

Hardwick Hall Country Park

**64**

Row Ponds

P

Harehill Wood

Great Pond

Old hall

P

Hardwick Hall

**2**

ew Tree Farm

DEEP LA

THE GREEN

Hardstoft

PH

Dovedale Wood

Dovedale Farm

**63**

Ridlocks Wood

STANLEY LA

Biggin Farm

CHESTERFIELD RD

Biggin Lane

B6039

**1**

Spoil Heap

Cedar Farm

Stanley Grange

Stanley

Stanley Farm

SHEPHERDS LA

SILVERHILL LA

M1

**62**

A    B    C

4

Spoil Heap

Hind Car
Wood

River Meden

Nettleworth
Manor

West Croft
Plantation

Littlewood

Hind Car

The Shrubbery

The
Bottoms

LEEMING LA

Northfield
Plantation

Garden
Plantation

Home
Farm

Park Hall

Quarry
Plantation

65

Quarry

Quarry

Park Hall
Farm

Golf Course

CH

Crimea
Farm

Sunnydale

THE FAIRWAYS

Sunnydale
Farm

Schs

GUILDFORD AVE
FARM CROFT RD

BRECHIN CT
SCOTSWOOD RD
DUNDEE DR

BERESFORD RD
CHILTON CRES
MELBOURNE CL

BRISBANE DR
HEREFORD AVE

WORCESTER
MEWS

Playing
Fields

Works

WESTLEIGH
MEADOW BANK

MURIELFIELD WAY

1 THE MYND
2 THE PADDOCKS

SANDRINGHAM CL
KENSINGTON CL
BALMORAL CL

BUCKINGHAM CL

3

BEECH TREE AVE

CHESTNUT GR
LARCH AVE

SYCAMORE RD

BROOKSIDE
AVE

CANTERBURY CL

Schs

NORWICH

LEEMING LA

LEADALE CRES

LOUWIL AVE

WHEATLEY CL

64

COMMON LA

MAPLECROFT AVE
COX'S LA

THE GREEN
BERNARD AVE

WILCOX AVE

HENRY ST
ALFRED CT
AUDREY CRES
MIDDLETON

TEWKESBURY
AVE

KINGSLEY

WELWYN AVE

PEAFIELD LA

Gre
Lane

BROWN AVE

ELM TREE AVE
OAK TR

LABURNUM GR

PARK HALL RD

Allot Gdns

ROLLINE CL

SANDGATE RD

A6075

INWOOD CT
LUDBOROUGH
WLK

Whinney Hill

Sch

1 TRENT WLK
2 BURNASTON CT
3 BLAKENEY CT
4 BRASSINGTON CT
5 TATTERSHALL CT
6 BRIMINGTON CT
7 TRUSLEY WLK
8 REPTON CT
9 THURLBY CT
10 TEALBY CT
11 TORKSEY WLK
12 DRESWELL CT
13 TETFORD WLK
14 CHARLESWORTH
15 CHISWORTH CT
16 CARSINGTON CT
17 OAKTHORPE CT
18 CROXTON CT
19 STOW CT

2

Works

MANVERS ST
OXCLOSE LA

VALE RD

SILVERDALE
MANOR RD

THE
CIRCLE

LIMESTONE
TERR

ALBERT ST

WOODLAND

LEYLA

SALISBURY CL

WARSOP RD A6075

Outgang Lane

River
Maun

NEW MILL LA

STANTON LA

Sch

STATION ST
SPRING HILL
STATION HILL

HIGH ST
MARKET
PL

ALBERT ST

PORTLAND

Liby

WELBECK RD

Cemy

MANSFIELD
WOODHOUSE

63

DEBDALE LA
A6075

SHERWOOD ST
MANSFIELD RD

PRIORY RD
PRIORY
SQ

CHURCH HILL

B6032

BUTT LA
LEEMING LA ST

CHURCH HILL LA

EDGEHILL GR

KING ST

CHESS
BURROW

Maun Valley
Park

Rushpool
Farm

Sch

YORKE ST

Schs

CROW HILL

TENNYSON AVE
BYRON AVE

Works

GLASTONBURY
GLADSTONE

RICHARD

1 ASPEN CT
2 HOLLY CT
3 BULLACE CT
4 CORNEL CT

KINGSTHORPE
CL

OLD MILL LA

1

BEECH HILL
CRES

Sch

MUSKHAM CT 1
NORWELL CT 2
MISTERTON CT 3
MATTERSEY CT 4
THE WOODLANDS 5

YORKE ST
B6032

HALLAM WAY
HALLAM WAY
MILLWAY

ALMOND

WENSLEYDALE

Sewage
Works

ALBANY DR

1 ALBANY PL
2 DOROTHY AVE

OXFORD ST

1 CHARLES
ST

CHESTERFIELD
A617

PLEASANT HILL
DENNISON ST

Sch

Sch

62

53    A    54    B    55    C

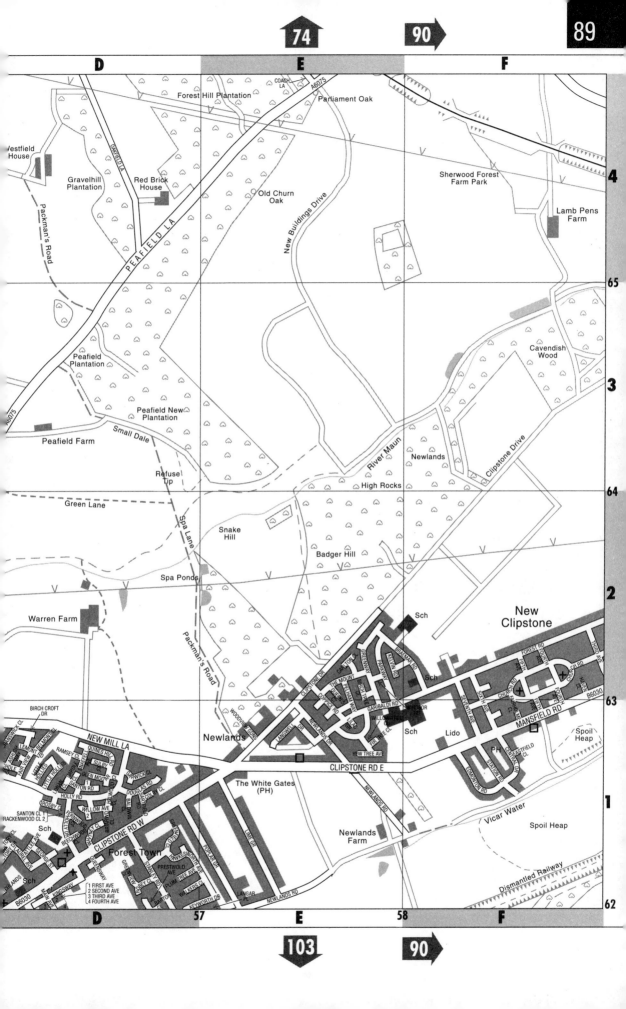

D
E
F

Forest Hill Plantation
COACH LA
A6075
Parliament Oak

Westfield House

Gravelhill Plantation
Red Brick House

CAMBER LA

Sherwood Forest Farm Park

Lamb Pens Farm

4

Packman's Road

PEAFIELD LA

Old Churn Oak

New Buildings Drive

65

Cavendish Wood

Peafield Plantation

3

A6075

Peafield New Plantation

Small Dale

River Maun

Newlands

Clipstone Drive

Peafield Farm

Refuse Tip

High Rocks

64

Green Lane

Spa Lane

Snake Hill

Badger Hill

Warren Farm

Spa Ponds

Packman's Road

2

New Clipstone

Sch

Sch

BROADMAR RD

FOREST RD

THIRD AVE

BIRCH CROFT DR

WOODVILLE GDNS

THE MOUNT
COPPICE RD

CARLTON LA
GREENWAY
PARKWAY

BIRCH TREE RD
BRECKNEN WAY

KENYA RD

SIXTH AVE
FIFTH AVE
FOURTH AVE

WATER RD
B6030

63

NEW MILL LA

Newlands

LANGWITH DR

NEWLANDS RD

GARIBALDI RD
WINDSOR RD

YEW TREE AVE

Sch
Lido

Spoil Heap

RAMSEY CL
QUINES HILL
SILBY RD
BERWICK CL

GEN MOOR CL
DOUGLAS RD
SANTON RD
BALDWIN CL

CLIPSTONE RD W

The White Gates (PH)

CLIPSTONE RD E

PH

CLAYGATE CL

MANSFIELD RD

SANTON CL
RACKENWOOD CL 2

HOLLY RD
CROSBY CL
MALLOW AVE

LIME GR

POPLAR GR

NEWLANDS RD

Newlands Farm

EDMONTON RD

Vicar Water

Spoil Heap

1

Sch

Sch

KINGSWAY

B6030

Forest Town

GEORGE ST

GREENWAY

PRESTWOLD AVE

PLUM TREE AVE
BARTON
WALTERS CL

LANGAR PL

KEYWORTH DR

NEWLANDS RD

Dismantled Railway

62

1 FIRST AVE
2 SECOND AVE
3 THIRD AVE
4 FOURTH AVE

D
57
E
58
F

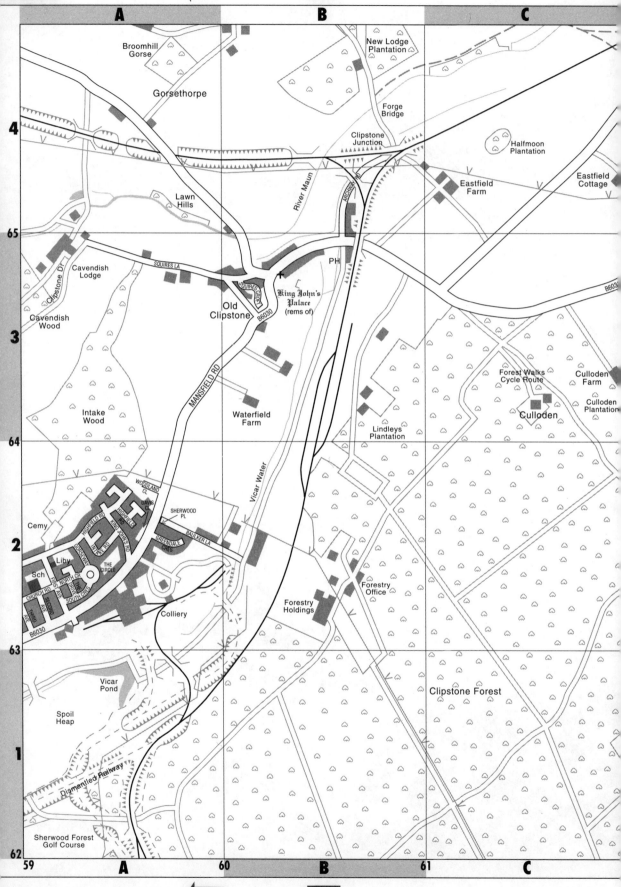

A B C

4

Broomhill
Gorse

Gorsethorpe

New Lodge
Plantation

Forge
Bridge

Clipstone
Junction

Halfmoon
Plantation

Eastfield
Farm

Eastfield
Cottage

River Maun

ARCHWAY RD

Lawn
Hills

65

SQUIRES LA

Cavendish
Lodge

Clipstone Dr

SQUIRES CROFT

B6030

Old
Clipstone

King John's
Palace
(rems of)

PH

B6030

Cavendish
Wood

3

Intake
Wood

MANSFIELD RD

Waterfield
Farm

Forest Walks
Cycle Route

Culloden
Farm

Culloden

Culloden
Plantation

64

Lindleys
Plantation

Vicar Water

WOODLAND
CL

DAVIS
CL

SHERWOOD
PL

HIGHFIELD RD

HIGHFIELD RD

KING JOHN'S RD

BAULKER LA

Cemy

GREENDALE
CRES

2

Liby

THE CROSSWAY

THE CIRCLE

Sch

THE NORTH CR

THE DOWNS CRES

THE SOUTH CRES

Forestry
Office

CHURCH RD

FIRST AVE

SECOND AVE

THIRD AVE

B6030

Colliery

Forestry
Holdings

63

Vicar
Pond

Clipstone Forest

Spoil
Heap

1

Dismantled Railway

Sherwood Forest
Golf Course

62

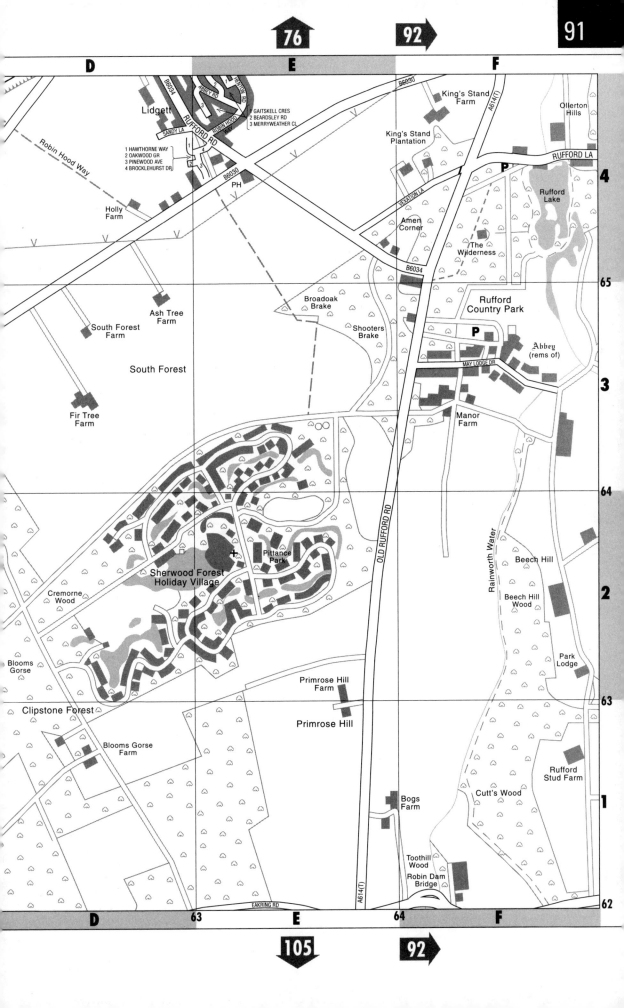

D E F

Lidgett

1 GAITSKELL CRES
2 BEARDSLEY RD
3 MERRYWEATHER CL

1 HAWTHORNE WAY
2 OAKWOOD GR
3 PINEWOOD AVE
4 BROCKLEHURST DR

Robin Hood Way

Holly Farm

King's Stand Farm

King's Stand Plantation

Ollerton Hills

RUFFORD LA

P

Rufford Lake

4

Amen Corner

The Wilderness

Ash Tree Farm

South Forest Farm

Broadoak Brake

Shooters Brake

65

Rufford Country Park

South Forest

P

Abbey (rems of)

Fir Tree Farm

MAY LODGE DR

3

Manor Farm

Sherwood Forest Holiday Village

Pittance Park

64

Rainworth Water

Beech Hill

Cremorne Wood

OLD RUFFORD RD

Beech Hill Wood

2

Blooms Gorse

Park Lodge

Primrose Hill Farm

Clipstone Forest

63

Primrose Hill

Blooms Gorse Farm

Rufford Stud Farm

Bogs Farm

Cutt's Wood

1

Toothill Wood

Robin Dam Bridge

A614(T)

EAKRING RD

62

D 63 E 64 F

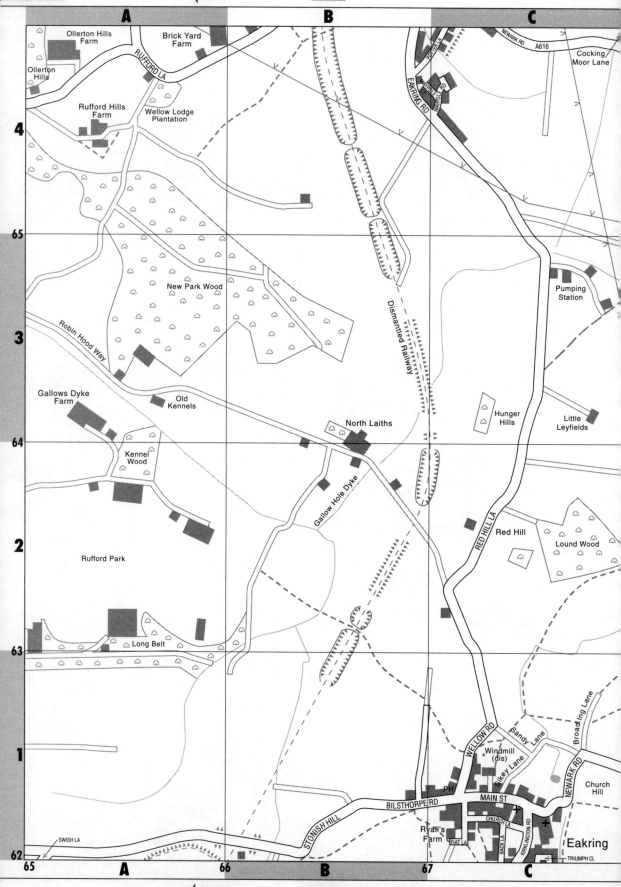

A    B    C

Ollerton Hills Farm
Ollerton Hills
Brick Yard Farm
RUFFORD LA
Rufford Hills Farm
Wellow Lodge Plantation

**4**

NEWARK RD    A616
Cocking Moor Lane

POTTER LA
EAKRING RD

**65**

New Park Wood

Pumping Station

Dismantled Railway

Robin Hood Way

**3**

Gallows Dyke Farm
Old Kennels
North Laiths
Hunger Hills
Little Leyfields

**64**

Kennel Wood
Gallow Hole Dyke

Red Hill
RED HILL LA
Lound Wood

**2**

Rufford Park

Long Belt

**63**

**1**

WELLOW RD
Sandy Lane
Windmill (dis)
Sikey Lane
NEWARK RD
Broading Lane
Church Hill

STONISH HILL
BILSTHORPE RD
PH
MAIN ST
CHURCH LA
Ryall's Farm
BACK LA
FLAT LA
KIRKLINGTON RD
Eakring
TRIUMPH CL

SWISH LA

**62**

65    A    66    B    67    C

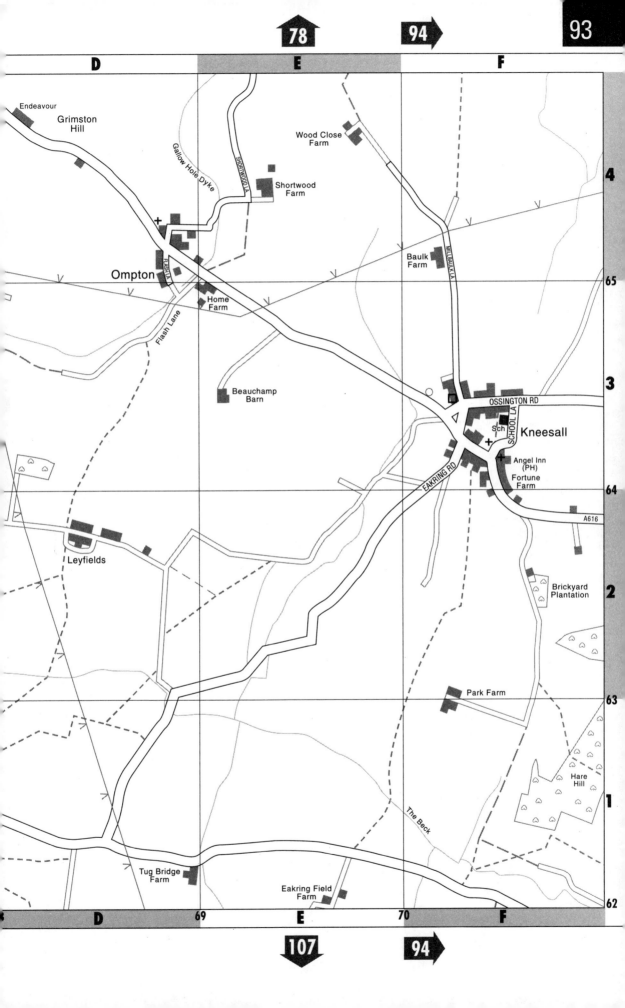

D

E

F

Endeavour

Grimston
Hill

Gallow Hole Dyke

SHORTWOOD LA

Wood Close
Farm

4

Shortwood
Farm

MILL BAULK LA

Baulk
Farm

65

FLASH LA

Ompton

Home
Farm

Flash Lane

Beauchamp
Barn

OSSINGTON RD

3

Sch

SCHOOL LA

Kneesall

Angel Inn
(PH)

Fortune
Farm

EAKRING RD

64

A616

Leyfields

Brickyard
Plantation

2

Park Farm

63

Hare
Hill

1

The Beck

Tug Bridge
Farm

Eakring Field
Farm

62

D 69 E 70 F

A

B

C

South Field

4

Knapeney
Farm

Brockilow
Farm

65

Saywood

Kneesall
Wood

Laxton
Wood

Laxton Middle
Wood

3

Kneesall Green
Farm

Victoria
Plantation

Mainwood
Farm

Hartshorn
Farm

64

A616

High
Wood

Laxton
Lodge

2

Buckshaw
Farm

63

Kneesall
Lodge

Kersall
Lodge

Woodhouse
Gorse

Woodhouse Common
Farm

1

Mill Lane

Kersall

Cocked Hat
Plantation

A616

Manor
Farm

62

71

A

72

B

73

C

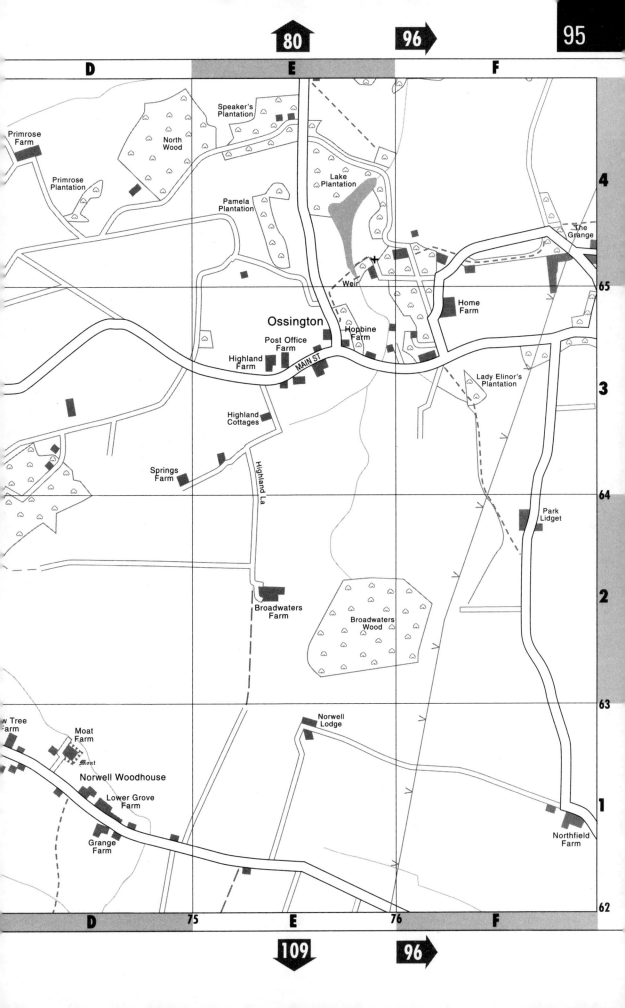

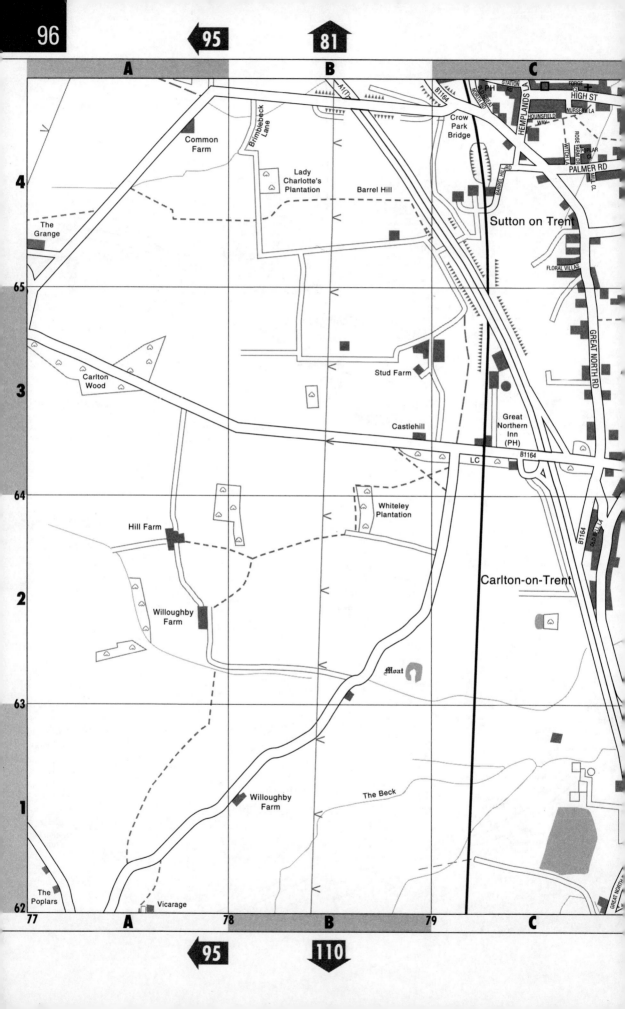

A   B   C

The Grange

Common Farm

Brimblebeck Lane

Lady Charlotte's Plantation

Barrel Hill

Crow Park Bridge

STATION RD

PH

HEMPLANDS LA

HIGH ST

NURSERY LA

HOUNSFIELD WAY

ROSE FARM DR

WITCH LA

POPLAR CL

MILL CL

PALMER RD

Sutton on Trent

FLORAL VILLAS

BARREL HILL RD

GREAT NORTH RD

4

65

Carlton Wood

Stud Farm

Castlehill

Great Northern Inn (PH)

LC   B1164

3

64

Hill Farm

Whiteley Plantation

B1164

OLD BT LA

Carlton-on-Trent

Willoughby Farm

Moat

2

63

Willoughby Farm

The Beck

GREAT NORTH

1

The Poplars

Vicarage

62

77   A   78   B   79   C

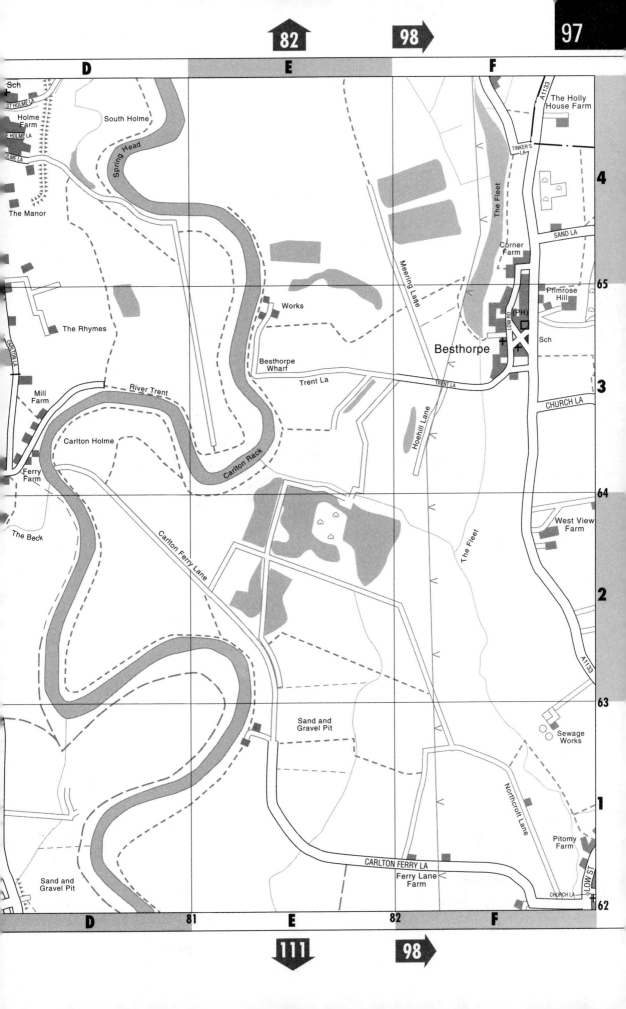

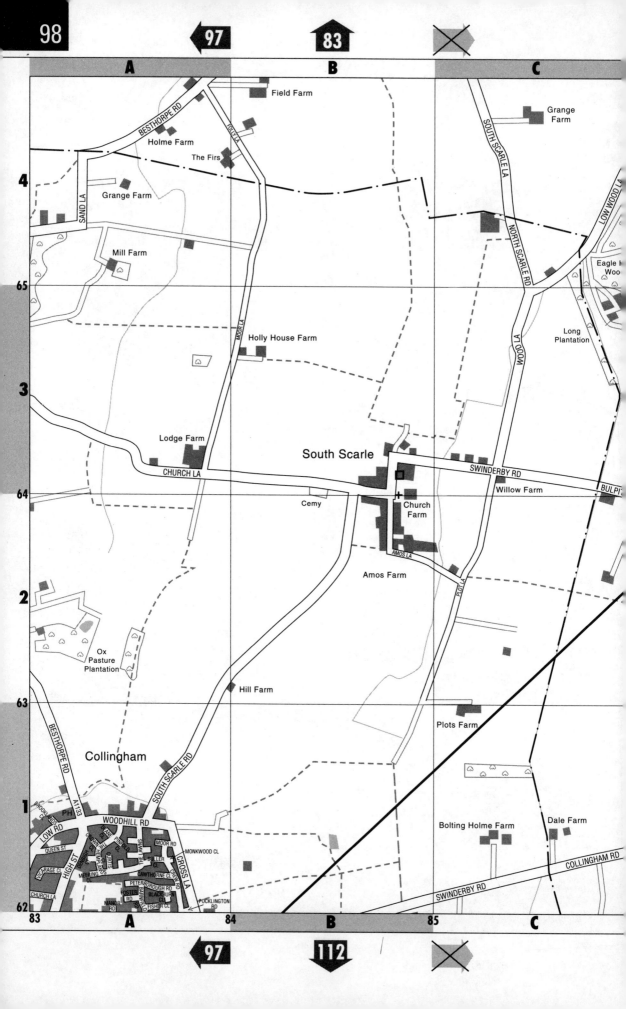

A B C

BESTHORPE RD

Field Farm

Holme Farm

FOLLY LA

SAND LA

The Firs

Grange Farm

SOUTH SCARLE LA

Grange Farm

LOW WOOD LA

NORTH SCARLE RD

4

Mill Farm

Eagle Wood

65

MOOR LA

Holly House Farm

WOOD LA

Long Plantation

3

Lodge Farm

South Scarle

SWINDERBY RD

CHURCH LA

Cemy

Willow Farm

BULPI

64

Church Farm

AMOS LA

Amos Farm

PLOT LA

2

Ox Pasture Plantation

Hill Farm

63

Plots Farm

Collingham

BESTHORPE RD

SOUTH SCARLE RD

Bolting Holme Farm

Dale Farm

1

PH

A1133

WOODHILL RD

BROOK

LOW RD

Queen St

HIGH ST

MOOR RD

MONKWOOD CL

CROSS LA

COLLINGHAM RD

THE LAWN

BULLER CL

SHAW

PINFOLD

DENBY

CURTIS

CAWTHORNE CL

NEW RD

MEERING CL

PETERBOROUGH RD

BLACKBURN CL

SWINDERBY RD

CHURCH LA

MANOR RD

FOSTER RD

BARFIELD CL

FISHER CL

POCKLINGTON RD

62

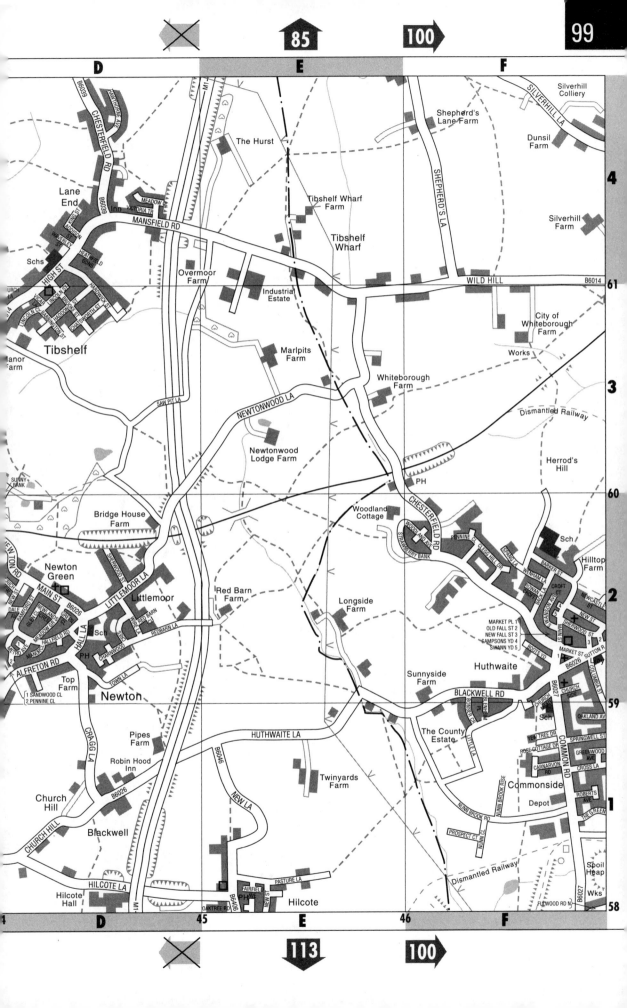

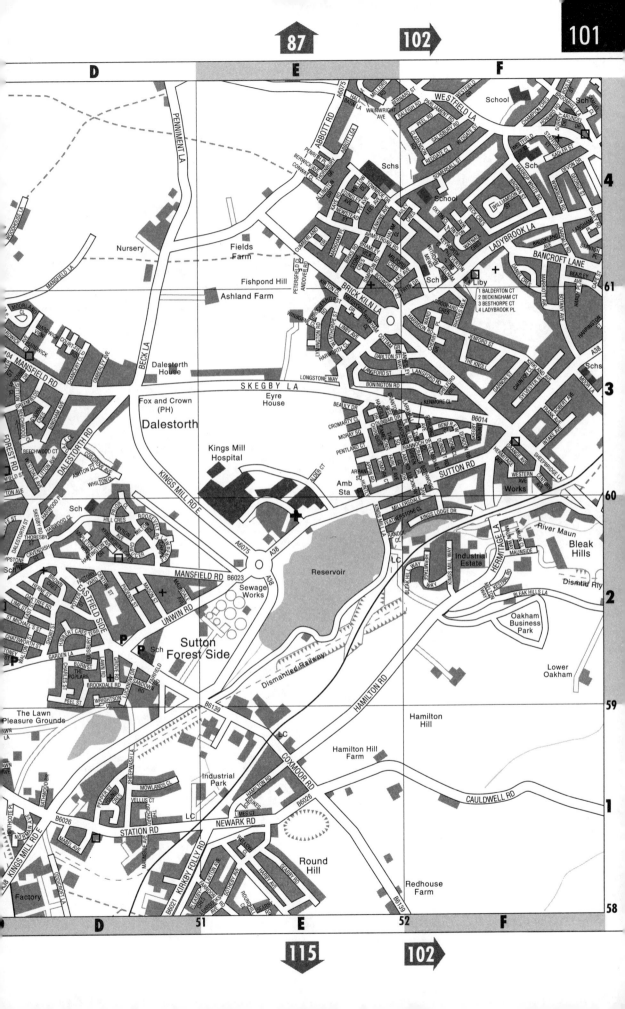

A B C

# MANSFIELD

Ravensdale

Civic Centre
F Sta

The Park
Sewage Works
Sch

Mill
Offices

1 BROWNING ST
2 KIPLING ST
3 BEARDALL ST
Schs

1 WOODHALL CL
2 SHERWOOD HALL GDNS
3 SHERWOOD GRANGE

RAVENSDALE RD
SHERWOOD HALL RD
CLIPSTONE RD W
B6033

Coll

WEST BANK AVE
HADDON RD
WOODHOUSE RD

PECKS HILL

1 WEST HILL

CHESTERFIELD RD S

CLUMBER ST
LEEMING ST
BATH LA
SANDY LA
EAKRING RD

Liby
Mus

4

61

NEWGATE LA

ST JOHN ST
Off
BANCROFT LA
STOCKWELL GATE
ST PETER'S WAY
RATCLIFFE GATE

QUAKER WAY

ROSEMARY ST

Hospl
A38

CARTER LA

3

ROCK HILL
MOUNT MILNER
B6030

Field Mill

River Maun

Recn Gd

Hospl

SOUTHWELL RD W

PORTLAND ST

TA Centre

1 ST MARGARET ST
2 ST CATHERINE ST

WINDSOR GDNS

Berry Hill Quarry

60

SHEEPBRIDGE LA

FOREST RD
BERRY HILL RD

King's Stand

Berry Hill

Dismtld Rly

B6030

WAVERLEY RD

Works

BERRY HILL LA

Berry Hill Hall
Schs

Playing Field

LINDHURST LA

2

High Oakham House

Sch

NOTTINGHAM RD

Robin Down's Hill

Offices

Black Scotch Plantation

NORTH PARK

THE AVENUE

BLACK SCOTCH LA

59

Brook

Cauldwell

Cemy

LICHFIELD LA

CHATSWORTH DR

Cauldwell Wood
Crem
Shining Cliff Plantation

Robin Down La

Coll

Fir's Farm

Black Scotch Lane

1

CAULDWELL RD
DERBY RD
A611

Stonehills Plantation

Rushley Farm
A60

58

53 A 54 B 55 C

**D** **E** **F**

EAKRING RD

SWISH LA

Clipstone Forest

Deerdale Farm

Robin Hood Farm

Letterbox Farm

Birch Belt

Sewage Works

**4**

Machin's Gorse

EAKRING RD

METCALF LA

LANSBURY RD

THE GREEN

NORTH DR

LANSBURY RD

OAK RISE

VALLEY RD

SOUTH DR

VALLEY APP

MICKLEDALE CL

**61**

MICKLEDALE LA

Featherstone House Farm

NEW RD

OLD RD

ALANDALE

THE CRESCENT

CROSS S

CUL-DE-SAC

SCARBOROUGH RD

CHURCH ST

CROMPTON RD

SAVILE RD

Bilsthorpe

Sch

Inkersall Manor

Inkersall Farm

**3**

Rainworth Water

Red Bridge

Hage's Wood

Damside Covert

**60**

HIGHFIELD DR

OLD RUFFORD RD

Crifton Lodge

**2**

Rook Wood

FARNSFIELD RD

Forest Lane

Lockwell House Farm

Dismantled Railway

**59**

Lockwell Hill Wood

A617

Cottage Farm

KIRKLINGTON RD

**1**

Cockett Plantation

A617

Lockwell Hill Farm

COCKETT LA

Cockett Barn Farm

A614(T)

**58**

A B C

4

Bilsthorpe
Colliery

Spoil Heap

Dismantled Railway

Mill Hill

Flat Lane

Mill Lane

SIDE LA

BACK LA

TRIUMPH RD

TRIUMPH CL

KIRKLINGTON RD

Robin Hood Way

Brail Lane

Depot

Spoil Heap

61

Eakring Brail Wood

CHURCH ST

EAKRING RD

BRAIL WOOD RD

BRAIL WOOD CL

Long Springs Wood

Coultas
Farm

3

FERN LA

FOREST VW

BUNGALOW LA

Manor Farm

CHURCH HILL

HORSLEY GATE

CLUMBER WAY

ARCHERS DR

BENET DR

CHEYNE DR

CHAPPEL GDNS

ST MARGARET'S CL

Fox
Holes

WHITESUB LA

Pudding
Poke
Wood

60

MAID MARION
AVE

HUFFORD RD

HIGHFIELDS DR

OAKTREE FORK

WYCAR RD

Fox Holes

Whip Ridding

Redgate
Wood

2

FARNSFIELD RD

Wycar Leys

Belle Eau
Park

Middle Plantation
Farm

Whip Ridding
Farm

Summer House
Plantation

Bilsthorpe Moor

BRACKNER LA

KIRKLINGTON RD

Egg Hatchery

59

A617

Willows
Farm

Swiss
Cottage

1

Upper Hexgreave

Hexgreave
Park

Archway
House

A617

Camp Hill

58

65 A 66 B 67 C

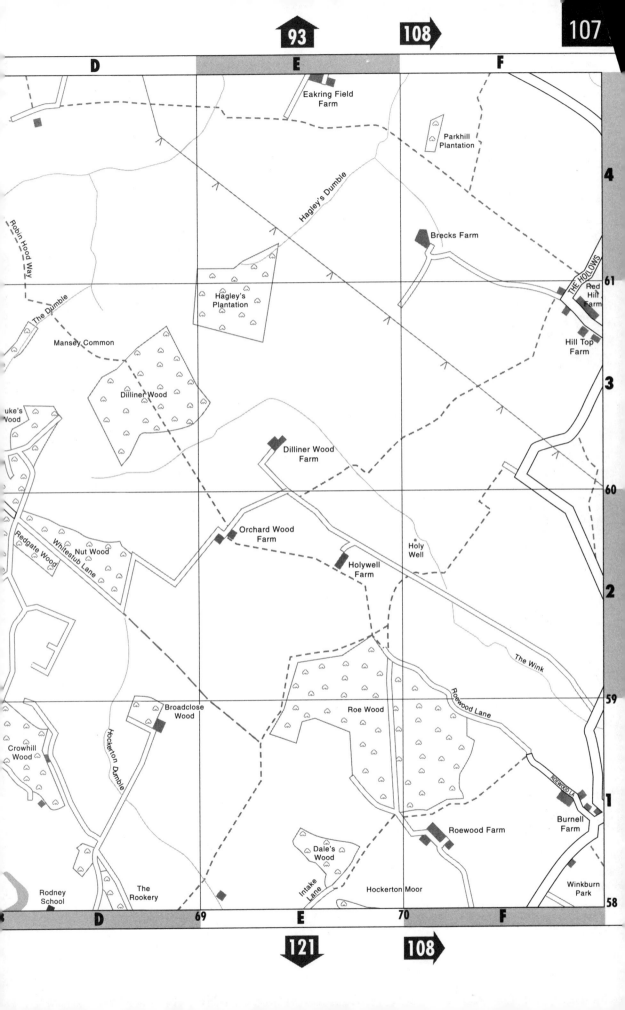

D     E     F

Eakring Field
Farm

Parkhill
Plantation

Robin Hood Way

Hagley's Dumble

Brecks Farm

THE HOLLOWS

Red
Hill
Farm

61

The Dumble

Hagley's
Plantation

Hill Top
Farm

Mansey Common

4

Dilliner Wood

3

uke's
Wood

Dilliner Wood
Farm

60

Redgate Wood

Whitestub Lane

Nut Wood

Orchard Wood
Farm

Holy
Well

Holywell
Farm

The Wink

2

Roewood Lane

59

Broadclose
Wood

Roe Wood

Hockerton Dumble

Crowhill
Wood

ROEWOOD LA

1

Burnell
Farm

Roewood Farm

Dale's
Wood

Rodney
School

The Rookery

Intake
Lane

Hockerton Moor

Winkburn
Park

58

D     69     E     70     F

A B C

Kersall

The Elms
Farm

WOOD LA

THE HOLLOWS

A616

Caunton Common
Farm

Caunton
Lodge Farm

4

Lodge
Cottages

Lodge Farm

61

Maplebeck

Maplebeck
Farm
Low
Farm

CHURCH LA

Holme
Farm

Beesthorpe
Farm

Beesthorpe
Lodge

MILL LA

3

The Beck

Beesthorpe
Hall Farm

Beesthorpe
Hall

MAPLEBECK RD

The
Farmstead

60

Readyfield
Farm

Duke's
Wood

Readyfield
Wood

Earlshaw
Farm

Moat

2

North Lodge
Farm

Mather
Wood

Lady
Wood

Coppice
Wood

59

Lady
Wood

1

Home
Farm

The Wink

Hall
Farm

Winkburn

Winkburn
Hall

Park Spring
Wood

Park Spring
Farm

58

71 A 72 B 73 C

D E F

4

Highfield House

Brunk Wood

Park Wood

School House Farm PH

Southfield Farm

Mount Pleasant

Glebe Farm

Watermill Farm

Mill Bridge

61

Moor La

Flags Farm

Hill House Farm

3

MILL LA

Windmill (dis)

PH

CHAPEL LA

The Woovers

Bathleyford Bridge

Bathleyhill Farm

Bathleyhill Cottages

NORWELL RD

DEAN'S CL

FORD LA

MANOR RD

MAIN ST

AMEN CNR

SCHOOL LA

Sch

PH

The Beck

Home Farm

Holme Farm

Winterset La

CAUNTON RD

60

Caunton

A616

NEWARK RD

Hunger Barn

Newbottles Plantation

Red Lodge

Worner Wood

2

59

Middlethorpe Grange

Dean Hall Farm

Knapthorpe

Knapthorpe Manor

Doncaster's Plantation

1

OLLERTON RD

A616

Cold Harbour Plantation

58

4 D 75 E 76 F

◄ 109

▲ 96

◄ 109

▼ 124

D E F

WHITE HART LA
TEMPERANCE LA
BAPTIST
LOW ST
Horse Pool
WESTFIELD LA
Manor Farm
BELL LA
Westfield Farm
LUNN LA
HIGH ST
4
Westfield Farm
THE GREEN
CHURCH ST
SOUTH END
DYKES END
Cromwell Lock
Weir
A1133
61
The Ness
The Oven
COTTAGE LA
WEST BROOK LA
Sand & Gravel Pit
Willow Farm
Mill Close Farm
River Trent
3
Coney Green
Cottage Lane Crossing
WHITEMOOR LA
60
Slough Dyke
Whitemoor Farm
Lodge Farm
Grange Farm
LC
Trow Bridge
2
South View Farm
Lowfield Farm
Holme
The Hall
LANGFORD LA
LC
HOLME LA
Gothic House Farm
59
The ld Hall
Manor House
Langford
1
Elmtree Farm
A1133
Langford Home Farm
58

D 81 E 82 F

**A** **B** **C**

MANOR RD

SWINDERBY RD

1 TEMPERANCE LA
2 BAPTIST LA

1 CREW RD
2 BARNFIELD RD

Collingham & Swinderby Crossing

High Park Farm

Valley Farm

WINDSOR CL

Sch

HEALEY
CL
LINLEY

REGENTS CL

BREAMER RD

SNOWDON RD

HIGH ST

Liby

THORNTON RD

Breamar Farm

STATION RD

LC

CROSS LA

LC

Collingham Station

GREEN LA

Fishpond Plantation

Potter Hill

North Potter Hill Farm

OAKLANDS

STATION CL

THE PADDOCK

DYKES END

South Collingham Hall

**61**

**4**

LC

WEST BROOK LA

Potter Hill Spinney

A46(T)

ROMAN ROAD

North Scaffold Lane

Potter Hill Plantation

South Potter Hill Farm

**3**

HEWSON'S LA

South Scaffold Lane

The Woodhey

FOLLY LA

SHORT WHEATLEY LA

Wheatley Hill

Wheatley Farm

Villa Farm

**60**

WHITEMOOR LA

WHEATLEY LA

The Havelings

Brickyard Cottage

Brills Hill

**2**

NEWARK RD

Brills Farm

Foss Way
ROMAN ROAD

BROUGH LA

Field House Farm Cottage

Field House Farm

**59**

Corner Farm

Norton Bottoms

Turfmoor

STAPLEFORD LA

The Glebe Farm

Holly Farm

Turf Moor Farm

**1**

Brough

Church Farm

Norwell Lane

Danethorpe

BROUGH RD

Little Danethorpe Farm

A46(T)

**58**

**83** **A** **84** **B** **85** **C**

◄ **113**   **100** ▲

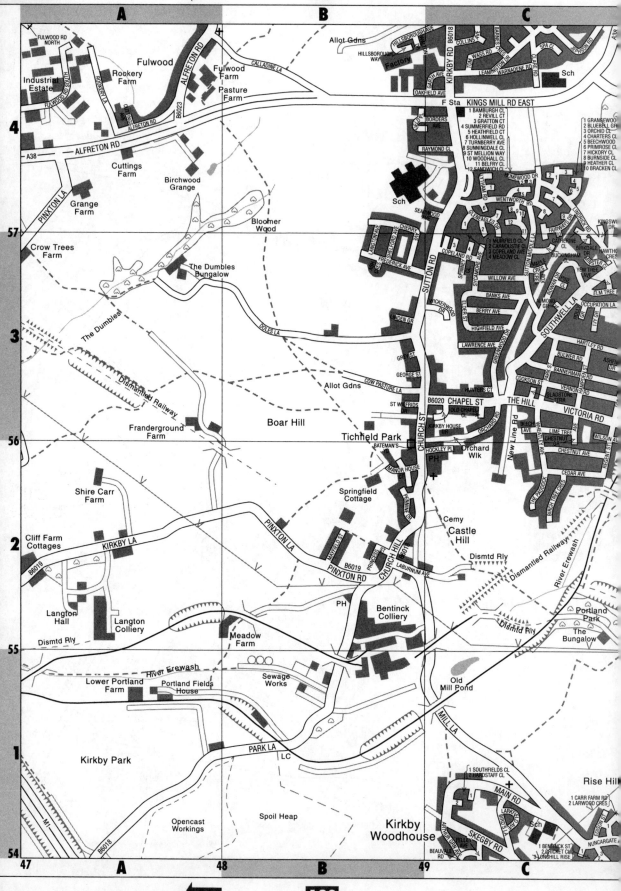

◄ **113**   **129** ▼

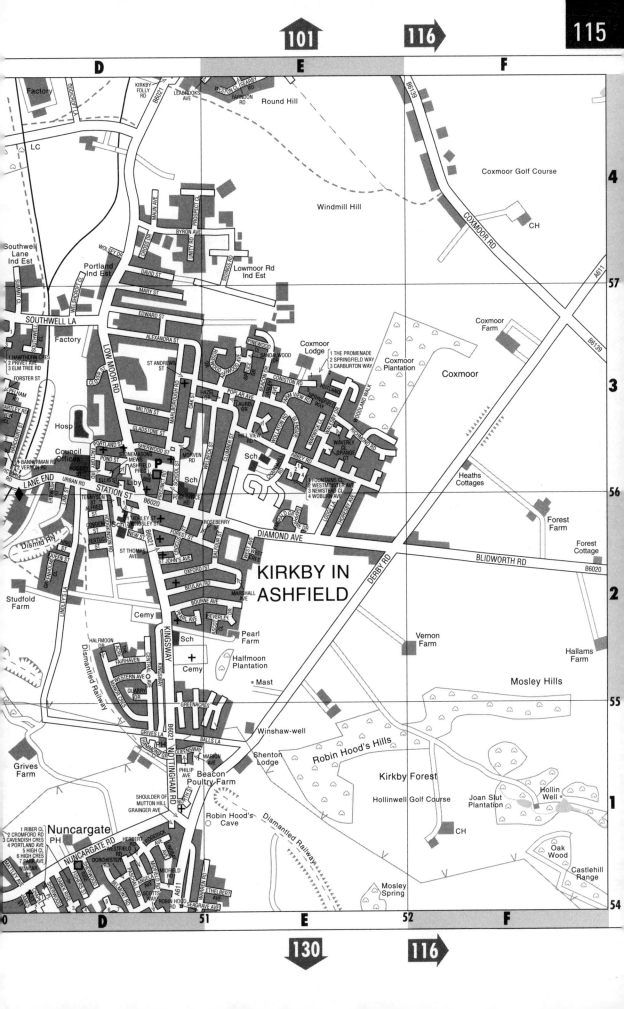

Lindhurst La
Lindhurst Farm
Rainworth
Sch
Rainworth Lodge
The Archer (PH)
BLIDWORTH LA
WARSOP LA
B6020
Cottage Farm
New Farm
Providence Farm
High Park
57
Moat
Fountain Dale
Greenfields
Copt Hill Farm
CROSS LA
Norwood Hill Close
Robin Hood Way
Brick Kiln Hill
MANSFIELD RD
NEW LA
B6020
3
Ling Farm
RICKET LA
Redgate Farm
Norwood Hill Farm
56
MARRIOTS LA
GROVE PARK
BUTLERS DR
B6020
PH
Rock Farm
MAIN ST
PH
Silverland Farm
ROBIN HOOD TERR
PH
SANDY LA
MAIN RD
Fishpool Farm
Tel Ex
FISHPOOL RD
FIELD LA
2
WOODSIDE
THE ARCHES
LOVERIDGE
ASHOVER
BRACKEN
LITTON
CROMFORD
HADDON RD
HEREFORD RD
BRETTON RD
CAROLINE
ASHFORD DR
WEBSTER AVE
1 CHERNSIDE
2 STANLEY CL
3 CASTLETON
Schs
SWINTON RISE
WALTHAM RD
DOWNHAM
55
SOUTHVIEW GDNS
DENBURY RD
BONINGTON
CHERITON DR
Cottage Farm
PH
Bottom Farm
Robin Hood Way
CHURCH DR
CHAPEL LA
WOODLAND RISE
HIGHFIELD CL
RIDGEWOOD GR
MILTON CRES
MILTON DR
WOOD END DR
LEA RD
Jackson's Hill
Sch
MAVIS AVE
BIRCH
CHERNSIDE CL
Ravenshead
HEAVYTREES AVE
VERNON CRES
SILVERWOOD AVE
RIGG LA
1
GORSE HILL
LONGDALE AVE
BARBERS WOOD
ROBIN GR
OAKWOOD DR
ROWAN AVE
PRIORY RD
BIRCHWOOD CL
CHESTNUT AVE
QUARRY RD
LONGDALE
REGINA CRES
Blidworth Dale
54

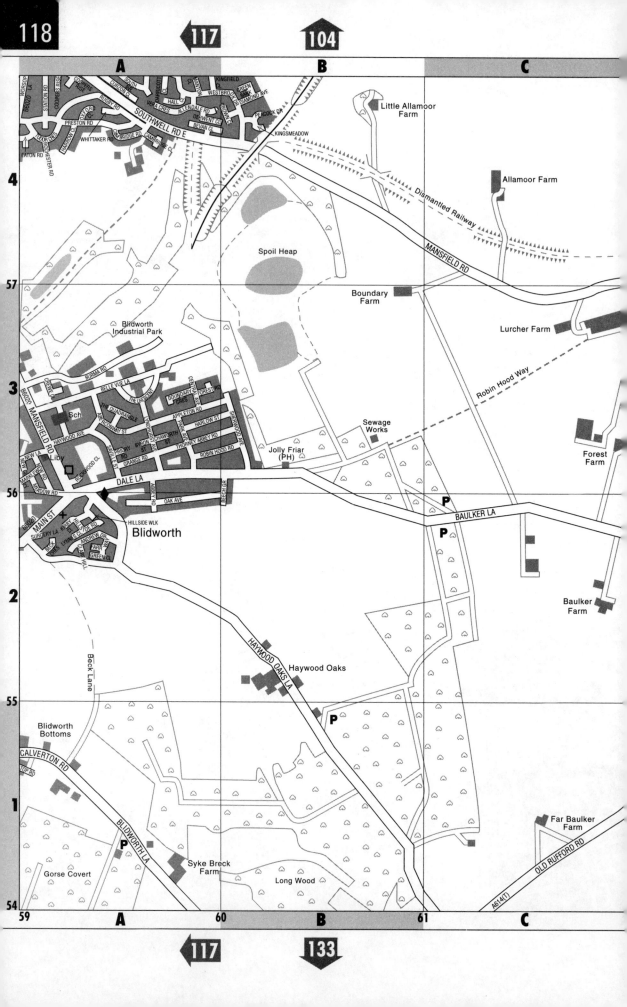

4

57

3

56

2

55

1

54

**Little Allamoor Farm**

**Allamoor Farm**

*Dismantled Railway*

MANSFIELD RD

**Spoil Heap**

**Boundary Farm**

**Lurcher Farm**

**Blidworth Industrial Park**

*Robin Hood Way*

Sch

**Sewage Works**

**Forest Farm**

Liby

DALE LA

**Jolly Friar (PH)**

P

BAULKER LA

P

**Blidworth**

**Baulker Farm**

**Beck Lane**

HAYWOOD OAKS LA

**Haywood Oaks**

P

**Blidworth Bottoms**

CALVERTON RD

**Far Baulker Farm**

BLIDWORTH LA

P

**Syke Breck Farm**

**Long Wood**

**Gorse Covert**

OLD RUFFORD RD

A614(T)

SOUTHWELL RD E

KINGSMEADOW

MANSFIELD RD

ABBEY GR

BEECH GR

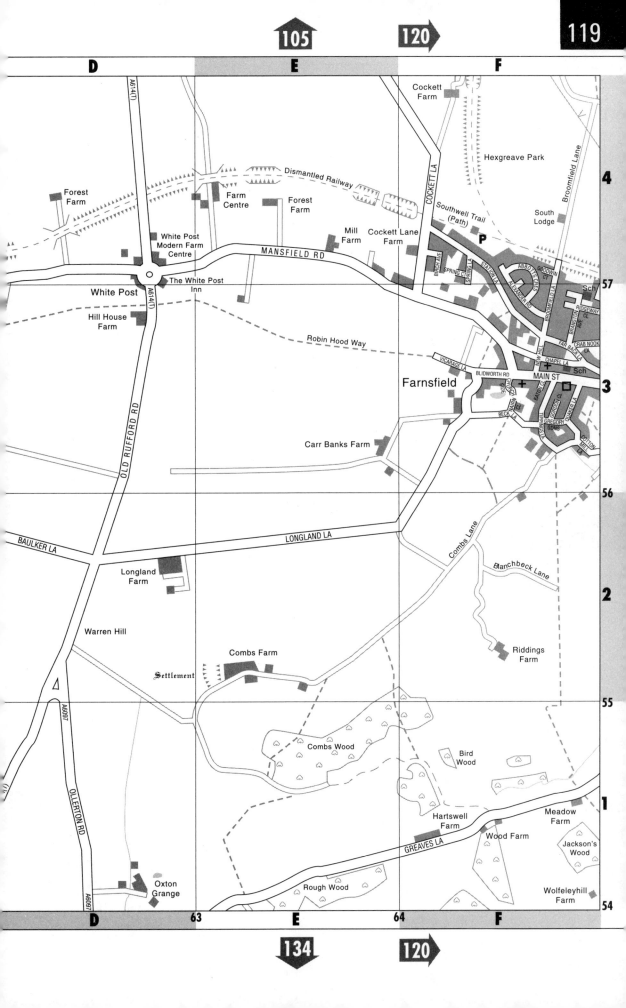

119
106

**A**      **B**      **C**

Lower Hexgreave Farm

Kirklington

KIRKLINGTON RD
A617

Home Farm

NEWARK R.

Hexgreave Park

SOUTHWELL RD

Sch

THE GREEN

Park Plantation

Mill Farm

River Greet

Moor Farm

**4**

RIDGEWAY CL
D'AYNCOURT WK

Osmanthorpe Manor

**57**

MEADOW CL

LONG MEADOW

Robin Hood Way

Spring's Farm

THE RIDGEWAY

WOODLAND
GREENHILL
GREENWOOD CL

Pumping Station

Southwell Trail

MILLDALE RD
WOOD SIDE

GREENWOOD CL

Collyeat House

BRICKYARD LA

Cotton Mill Dyke

Edingley Beck

STATION RD

**3**

MAIN ST

NETHER CL

Sewage Works

Edingley Mill

Valley Farm

Moat

Harlow Fields

CHAPEL LA

SOUTHWELL RD

PH
Sch

STATION RD

CRAB NOOK LANE

COTTON MILL LA

MANSFIELD RD

MAIN ST

**56**

Cotton Mill Farm

ALLESFORD LA

Manor House Farm

Edingley

EDINGLEY HILL

HOLME LA

Diamond Cottage Farm

**2**

LITTLE LA

New Manor Farm

GREAVES LA

Woodendale

Grange Farm

Halam Mill

Old Hall Farm

Littledale

**55**

New Hall Farm

ST HELEN'S LA

Ford

Sch

CARVER'S HOLLOW

Resr

NEWHALL LA

Little Turn Croft Farm

Middlebeck Farm

GRAY LA

JACK LA

PH

HALAM

SCHOOL

**1**

Brockley Farm

Halam

Halam Beck

Wolfeleyhill La

Machin's Farm

ST MICHAEL'S CL

Turncroft Farm

Manor Farm

CHURCH LA

Dovecote
Halam House Farm

Cutlersforth

RADLEY RD

**54**

65     **A**     66     **B**     67     **C**

119
135

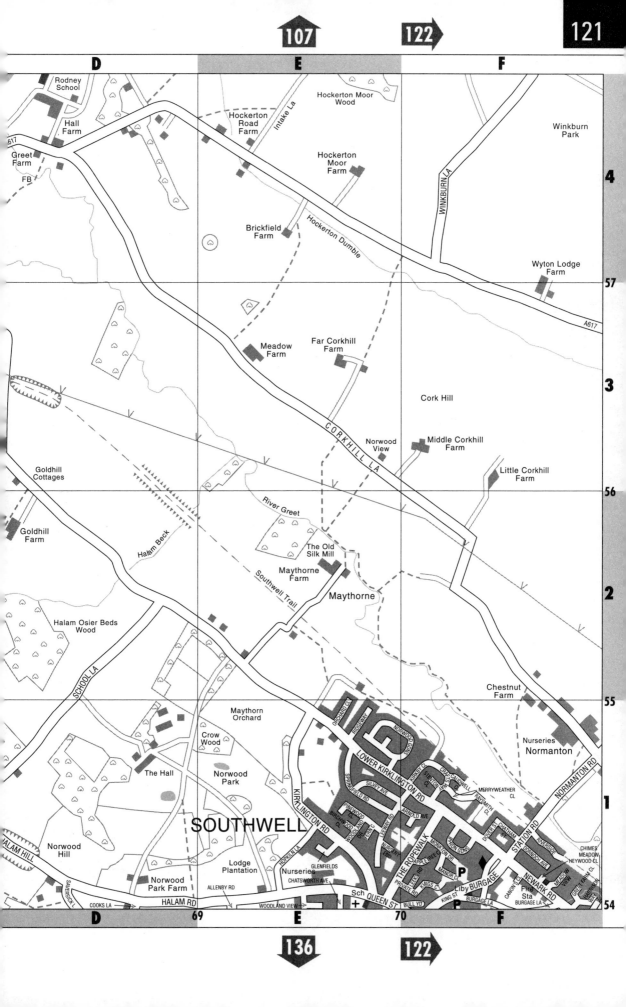

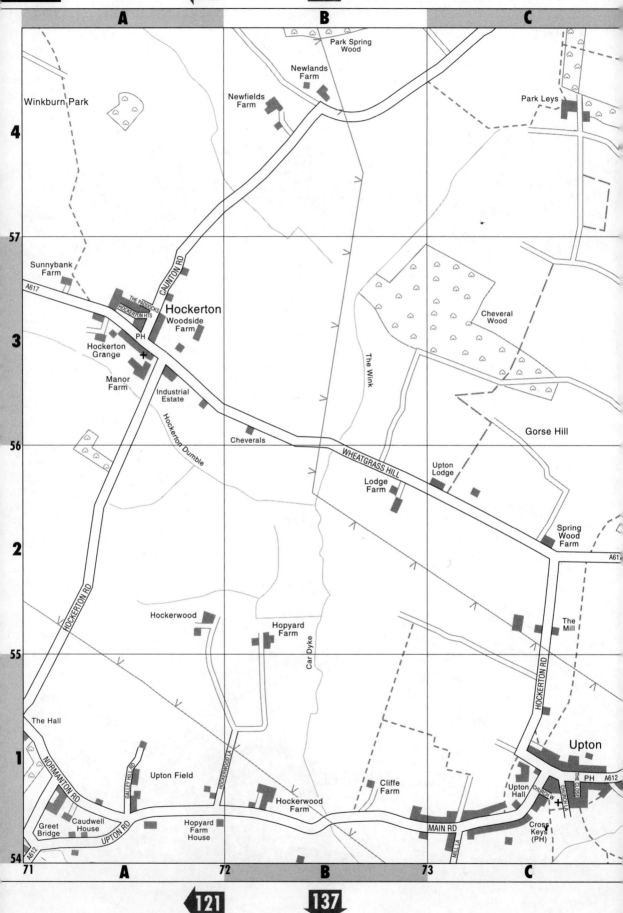

D E F

4

57

3

56

2

55

1

54

Winthorpe Lake

Winthorpe Crossing

High Leys

Hall Farm

Langford Hall

Lodge

A1133

A46(T)

HOLME LA

WOODLANDS

THOROUGHFARE LA

Sch

BRANSTON CL

PICKLINGTON CRES

GAINSBOROUGH RD

CHAPEL LA

THE DRIVE

The Hall

PH

HARGON LA

SPRING LA

Winthorpe

THE SPINNEY

A1133

DROVE LA

Winthorpe Bridge

River Trent

Winthorpe Rack

Crankley Point

Bridge House

Foss Way
ROMAN ROAD

A46(T)

Newark and Nottingham Agricultural Society's Showground

Airfield (disused)

Sewage Works

LC

WINTHORPE RD

A17(T)

South Airfield Farm

North Airfield Farm

Newark Crossing

STEPHEN RD

Sch

ALEXANDER AVE

FLEMING DR

WORKSOP RD

DEERING AVE

NORMAN AVE

HOLLIES AVE

PARK AVE

CHESTNUT AVE

GAINSBOROUGH DR

WINTHORPE RD

LINCOLN RD

CLIFTON CRES

STANHOPE RD

TERRY AVE

MIDDLETON RD

B6166

PEMBROKE CRES

Depot

The Bungalow

South Airfield Farm

TILFORD DR

BRUNEL DR

Newark Branch

Works

DUBELL'S LA

HATCHET'S LA

HATCHET'S LA

LINCOLN ROAD BRIDGE

MAPLE AVE

WINTHORPE RD

HILL'S

YORKE DR

FENTON DR

FIR'S WOOD CL

STRAWBERRY HALL LA

BESTWOOD WLK

WHITTLE CL

HIGGEAR

Beaconfield Farm

The Nook

LINCOLN ST

NORTH GATE

TRENT LA

MALKIN

MADIN GN

BRUNEL DR

WELLAND CL

JESSOP WAY

Newark Northgate Station

ABBOTT'S WAY

NORTHERN RD

STANLEY ST

WITHAM

CROMWELL WAY

TRENCHARD AVE

MATCHE RD

HARVEY AVE

Cotswold

VALIANT RD

CRANBERRY RD

PENSWICK RD

THE PADDOCKS

PARK LANDS CL

HALL GDNS

SYCAMORE DR

NEWARK RD

Depot

THE MOUNT
MOUNT LA

CURRIE RD

NURSERY

WARBURTON

GEORGE ST

APPLETON GATE

QUEEN'S RD

Amb

Stn

LAWRENCE PL

CLIFT NOOK LA

VICTORIA ST

WEST BECK RD

SLEAFORD RD

FRIARY

MAGNUS

WELLINGTON RD

Works

Greenways

BEACON HILL RD

A17(T)

ALLIANCE ST 1
RIMMER'S RD 2
WINHAM RD 3
BEYRICK RD 4

chs

D 81 E 82 F

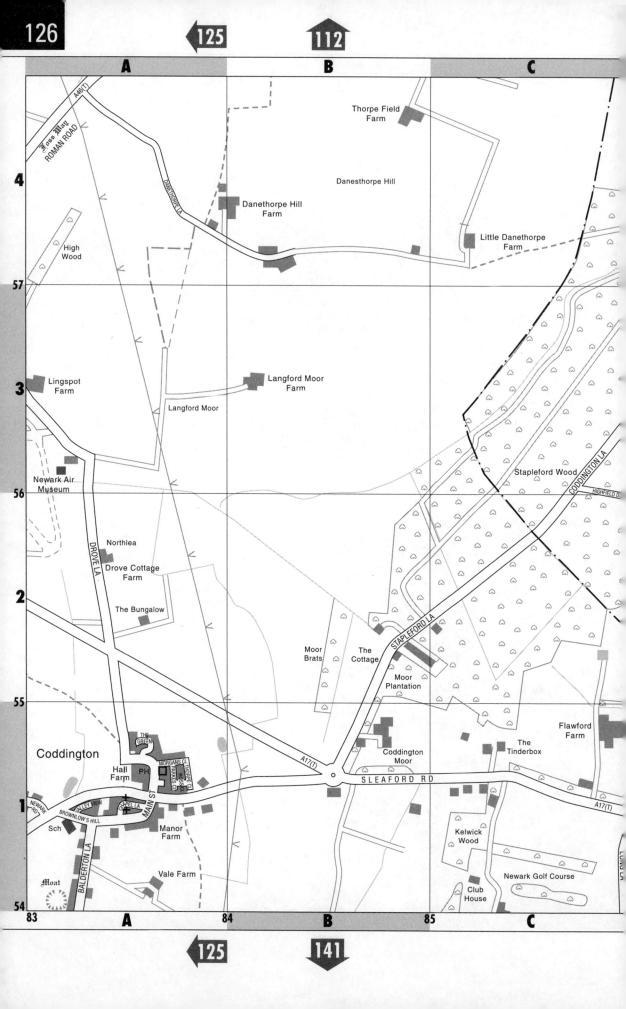

A   B   C

4

57

3

56

2

55

1

54

83   A   84   B   85   C

Thorpe Field Farm

Danesthorpe Hill

Danethorpe Hill Farm

Little Danethorpe Farm

High Wood

Fosse Way
ROMAN ROAD
A46(T)

DANETHORPE LA

Lingspot Farm

Langford Moor Farm

Langford Moor

Newark Air Museum

Stapleford Wood

CODDINGTON LA

HIGHFIELD D

Northlea

Drove Cottage Farm

DROVE LA

The Bungalow

Moor Brats

The Cottage

Moor Plantation

STAPLEFORD LA

Flawford Farm

The Tinderbox

Coddington

THE GREEN
MORGANS CL
THORPE CL
RUSS CL
PARKES CL
CHAPEL LA

Hall Farm

PH

Coddington Moor

SLEAFORD RD

A17(T)

A17(T)

MAIN ST

NEWARK RD
VALLEY VIEW
BROWNLOW'S HILL

Sch

Manor Farm

Vale Farm

BALDERTON LA

Moat

Kelwick Wood

Newark Golf Course

Club House

LONG LA

Stapleford Moor
BROUGH RD
Moor Farm
ing's Ride
CODDINGTON LA
Lodge Drive
Stapleford Wood
Grange Drive
HIGHFIELD DR
Four Acres
Stapleford Moor
SLEAFORD RD
Barnby Manor
A17(T)
College Plantation
SLEAFORD RD

NEWARK RD
Woodland View
Moor Lane
Stapleford House
Clay Lane
Stapleford Grange
Highfield House
DANGER AREA
DANGER AREA
DANGER AREA
Rifle Range
Youle Dike

BRECKS LA
THE PADDOCKS
NORTON RD
The Hall
Church Lane Sch
Stapleford
Poplar Tree Farm
BROUGHTON RD
The Laurels
Broughton Clays
The Elms
River Witham
Top Covert Farm
Top Covert
Hanley Farm
Whitegate House
WOODGATE LA
Beckingham Training Camp
Sewage Works

4
57
3
56
2
55
1
54

D    E    F
87    88

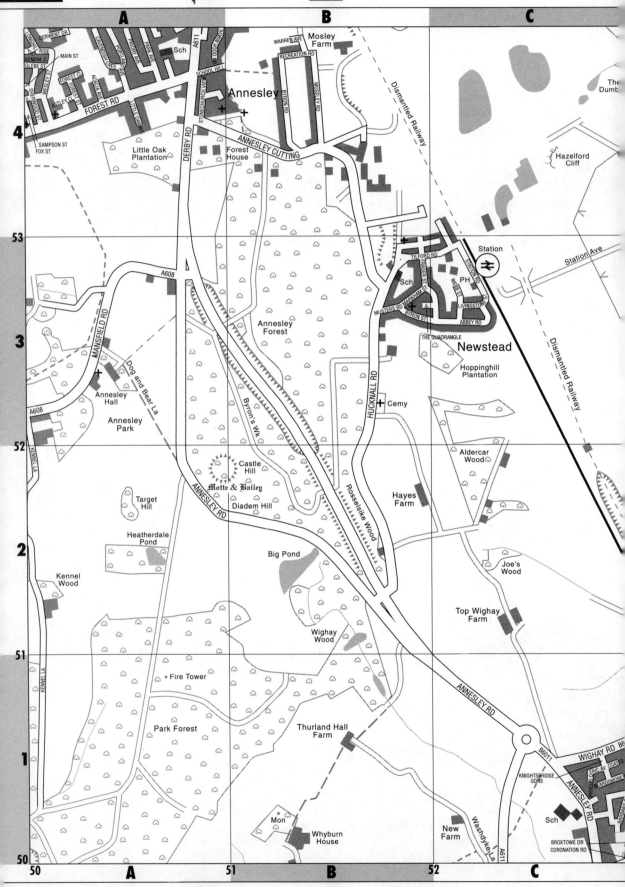

**A**     **B**     **C**

SANDFIELD AVE

REGINA CRES

QUARRY RD

QUARRY CL

QUARRY RD

CHAPEL LA

Blidworth Dale

Appleton Dale

P

Trumper's Park

**4**

A60

KIGHILL LA

Kighill Farm

RIGG LA

P

Blidworth Lodge

**53**

LONGDALE LA

Sand Holes

Wildman's Wood

Sand Pit

Longdale Farm

**3**

Longdale Plantation

Robin Hood Way

Reservoir

Pumping Station

**52**

Barracks Farm

MANSFIELD RD

Forest Farm

**2**

New Plantation

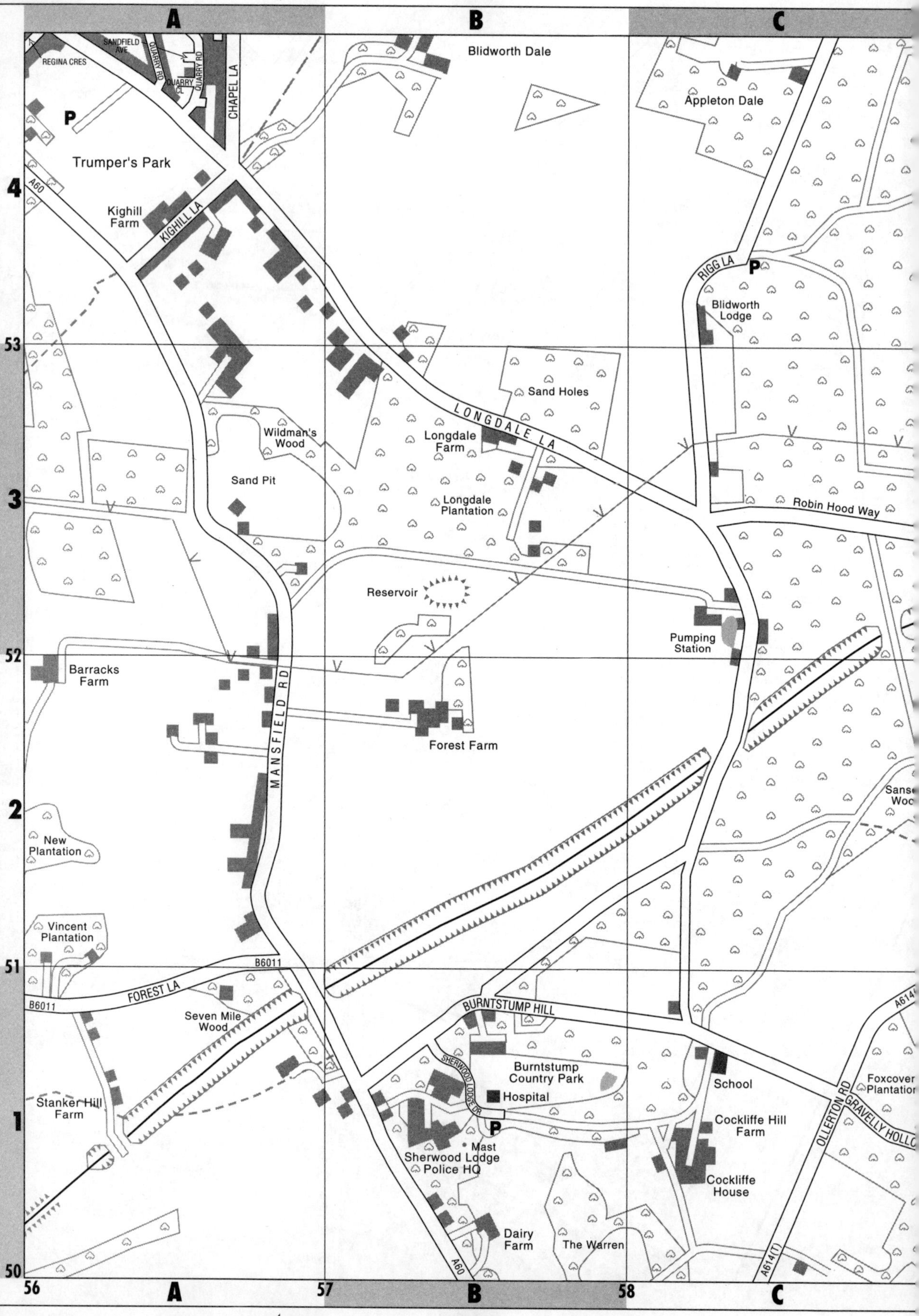

Sanse Woo

Vincent Plantation

**51**

B6011

B6011

FOREST LA

Seven Mile Wood

BURNTSTUMP HILL

A614

A614(T)

Burntstump Country Park

School

Foxcover Plantation

Stanker Hill Farm

SHERWOOD LODGE DR

Hospital

Cockliffe Hill Farm

OLLERTON RD

GRAVELLY HOLLO

**1**

P

Mast

Sherwood Lodge Police HQ

Cockliffe House

Dairy Farm

The Warren

A60

A614(T)

**50**

56    **A**    57    **B**    58    **C**

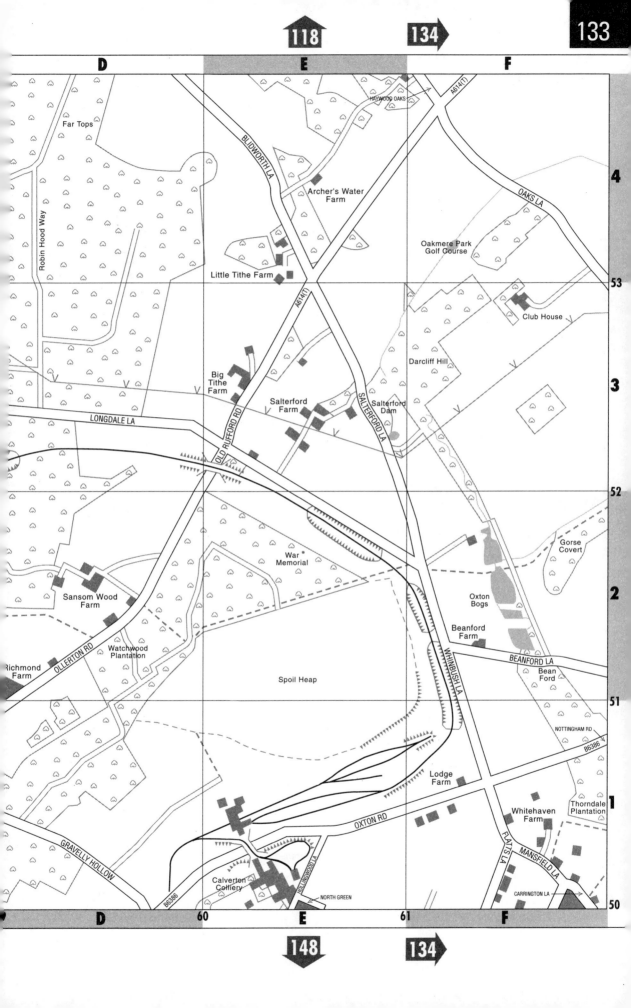

D   E   F

4

3

2

53

52

51

1

50

Far Tops

Robin Hood Way

BLIDWORTH LA

HAYWOOD OAKS

A614(T)

OAKS LA

Archer's Water
Farm

Oakmere Park
Golf Course

Little Tithe Farm

Club House

A614(T)

Darcliff Hill

Big
Tithe
Farm

OLD RUFFORD RD

LONGDALE LA

Salterford
Farm

SALTERFORD LA

Salterford
Dam

Gorse
Covert

War
Memorial

Oxton
Bogs

Sansom Wood
Farm

Beanford
Farm

BEANFORD LA

Bean
Ford

Richmond
Farm

OLLERTON RD

Watchwood
Plantation

WHINBUSH LA

Spoil Heap

Lodge
Farm

NOTTINGHAM RD

B6386

Thorndale
Plantation

Whitehaven
Farm

FLATS LA

MANSFIELD LA

OXTON RD

GRAVELLY HOLLOW

B6386

HOLLINGWOOD LA

Calverton
Colliery

NORTH GREEN

CARRINGTON LA

D   60   E   61   F

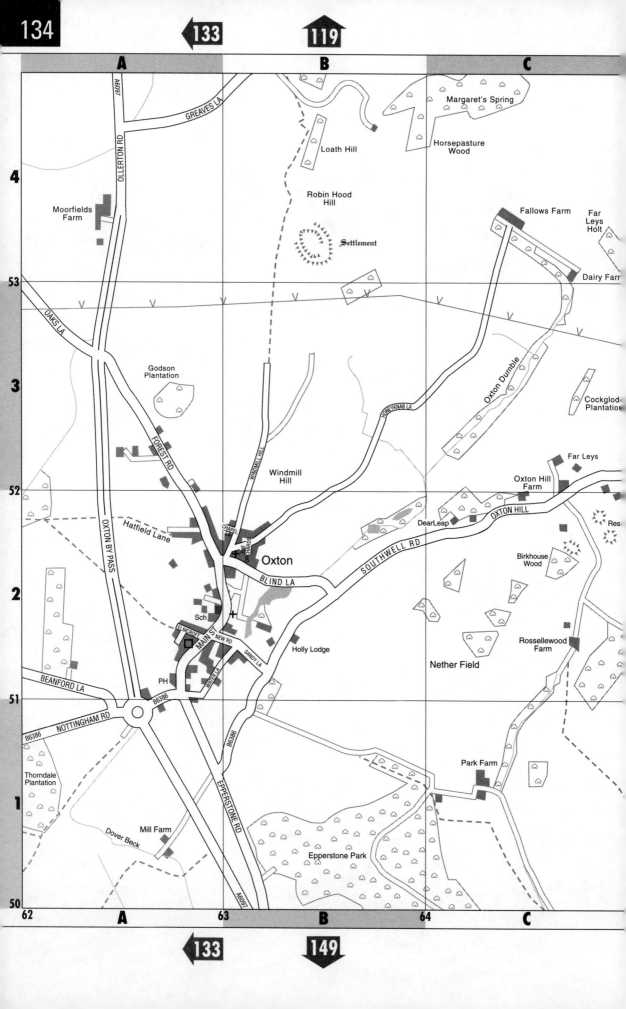

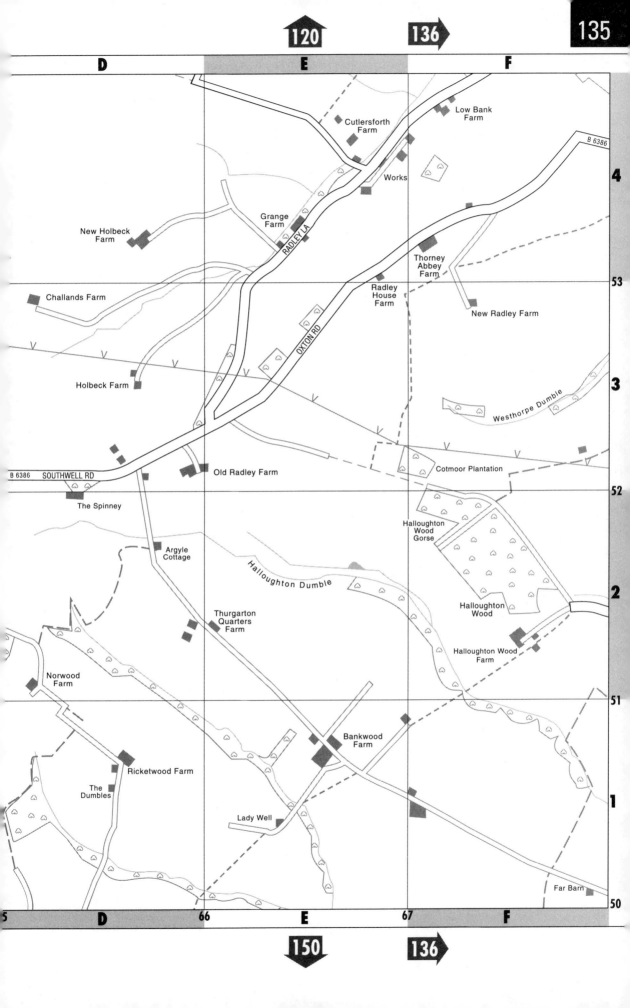

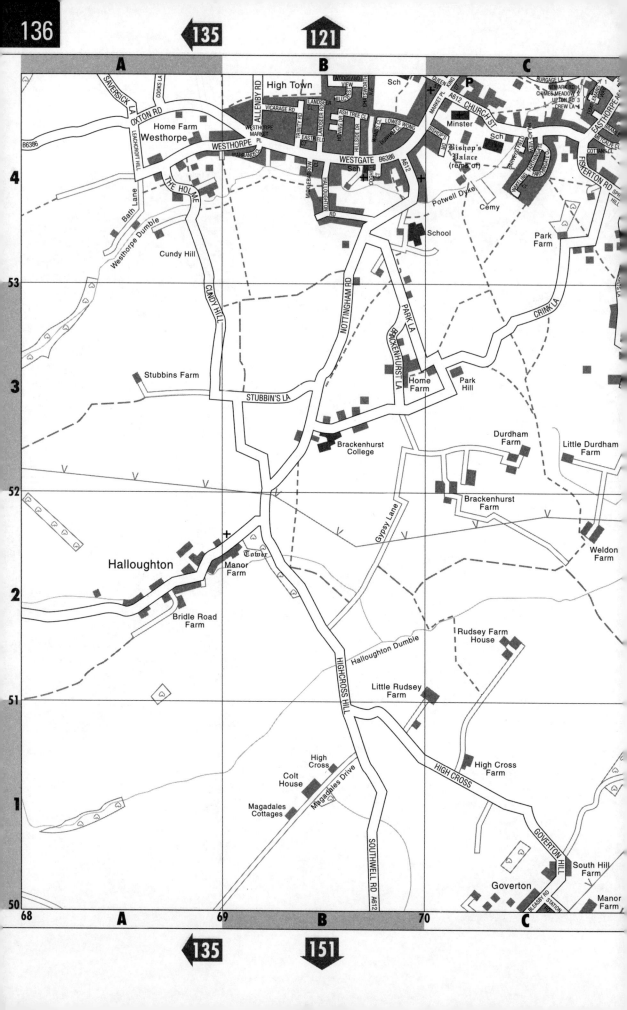

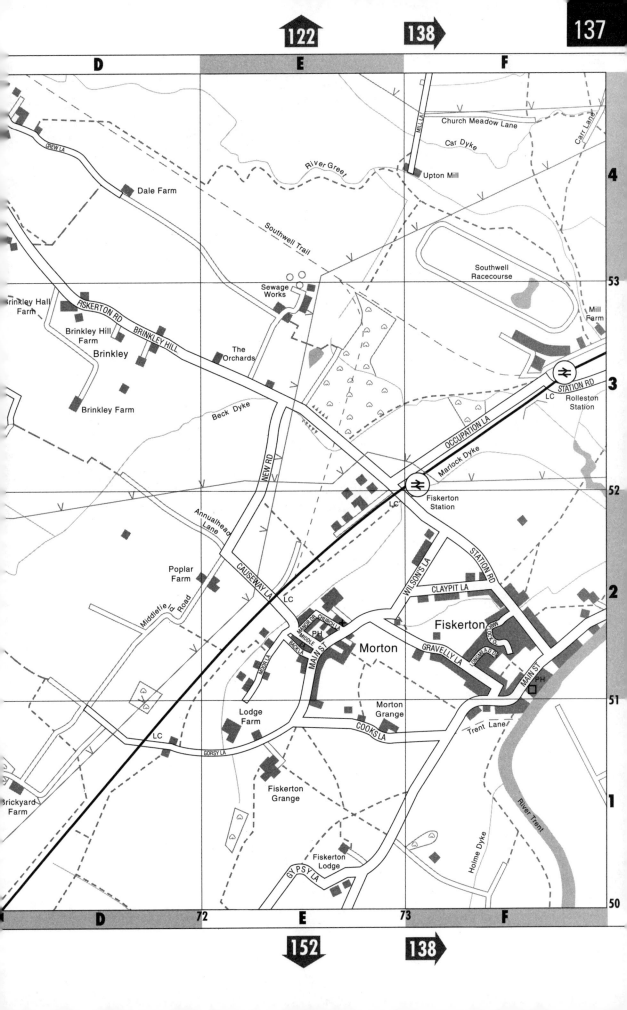

**A**  **B**  **C**

Staythorpe

PINGLEY CL  PINGLEY LA

BETHY GDNS

LC

4

Staythorpe
Power Station

Baggarley Rack

STAYTHORPE RD

LC

53

Greenaway

Rolleston
Gorse

Rundell Dyke

The
Crown Inn

LC

STATION RD

Ferry
(foot)

The Lazy Otter
(PH)

NORTHEN GR
WYKE LA
CHAPEL LA
MARSH S
MAIN S

3

Rolleston

Rolleston Field

CHURCH ST
WYKE LA
GREBE END
WEST END
CROSS SCHOOL LA
ST PETERS LA

Norwood
Farm

FISKERTON RD

Swillow Lane

OLD HALL CL

River Green

52

River Trent

Fiskerton
Mill

2

MAIN ST

Gawburn Nip

51

FOSSE RD
FOSSE RD
ROMAN ROAD

A46 (T)

Gawburn Holt

1

P

Wharf
Farm

Stoke
Hall

A46 (T)

Thorpe

CHURCH LA

The Park

50

74          75          76

**A**  **B**  **C**

# NEWARK-ON-TRENT

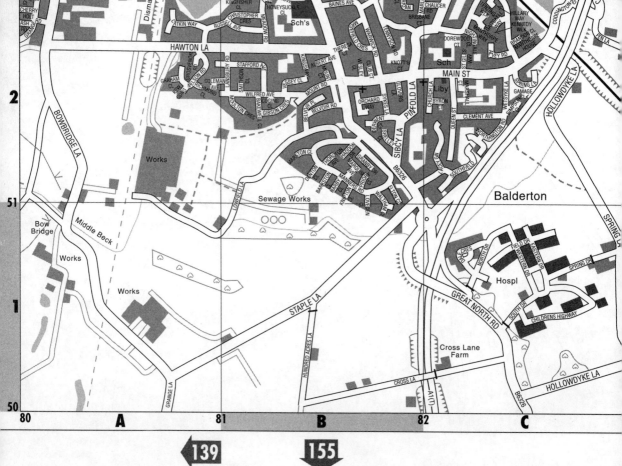

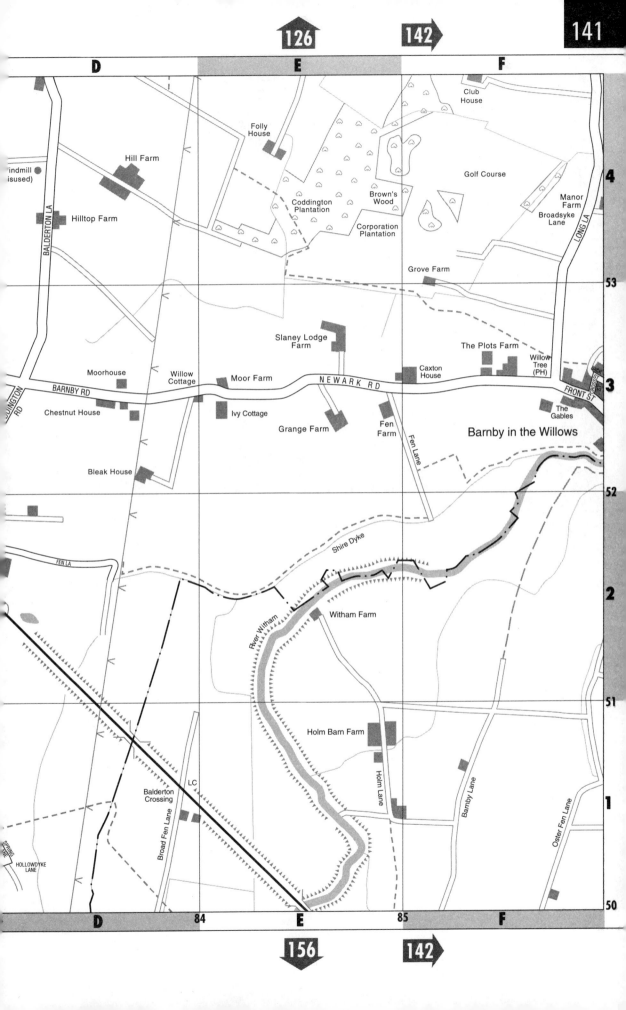

D
E
F

Club House

Folly House

Hill Farm

Golf Course

(Windmill (disused)

4

Coddington Plantation

Brown's Wood

Manor Farm

Hilltop Farm

Broadsyke Lane

BALDERTON LA

Corporation Plantation

LONG LA

Grove Farm

53

Slaney Lodge Farm

The Plots Farm

Willow Tree (PH)

FRONT ST

Moorhouse

Willow Cottage

Moor Farm

NEWARK RD

Caxton House

BARNBY RD

3

ODDINGTON RD

The Gables

Chestnut House

Ivy Cottage

Grange Farm

Fen Farm

Barnby in the Willows

Fen Lane

Bleak House

52

FEN LA

Shire Dyke

River Witham

Witham Farm

2

51

Holm Barn Farm

Holm Lane

Bamby Lane

Oster Fen Lane

LC

Balderton Crossing

Broad Fen Lane

1

SPRING LANE

HOLLOWDYKE LANE

50

D
84
E
85
F

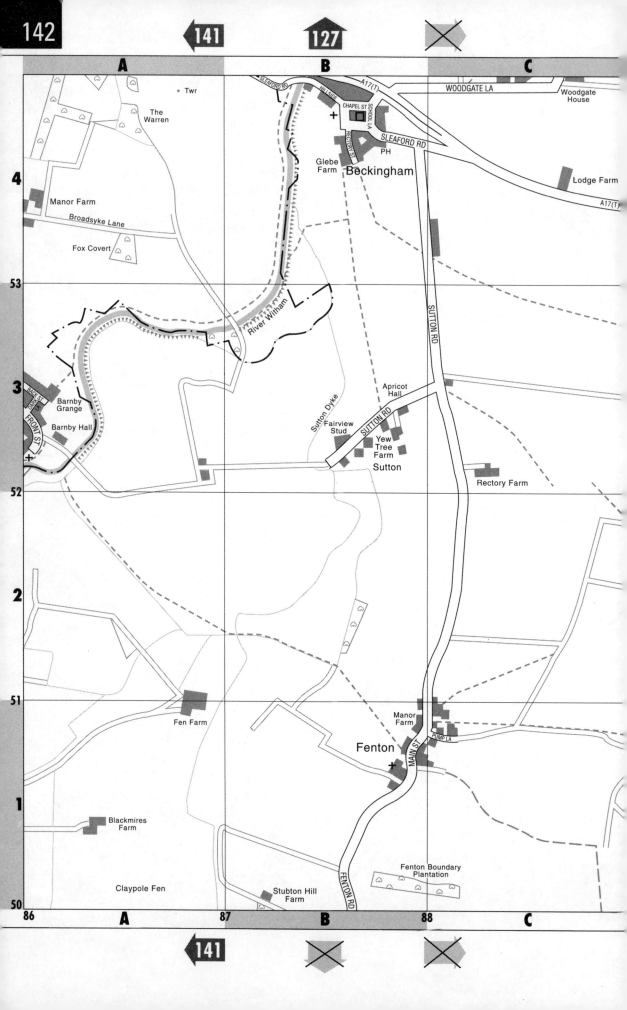

A   B   C

Twr

The Warren

**4**

Manor Farm

Broadsyke Lane

Fox Covert

SLEAFORD RD

HILLSIDE

A17(T)

WOODGATE LA

Woodgate House

CHAPEL ST

SCHOOL LA

RECTORY ST

Glebe Farm

SLEAFORD RD

PH

**Beckingham**

Lodge Farm

A17(T)

**53**

River Witham

SUTTON RD

**3**

BACK ST

DARK LA

Barnby Grange

FRONT ST

Barnby Hall

Sutton Dyke

Fairview Stud

Apricot Hall

SUTTON RD

Yew Tree Farm

**Sutton**

Rectory Farm

**52**

**2**

**51**

Fen Farm

Manor Farm

PUMP LA

**Fenton**

MAIN ST

**1**

Blackmires Farm

**50**

Claypole Fen

Stubton Hill Farm

FENTON RD

Fenton Boundary Plantation

D E F

Lower
Stoneyford
Farm

Gin
Farm

Dismtd
Rly

Hobsic

BROAD LA

CORDY LA

4

BOAT LA

Inn

Brinsley Gin

Stoneyford

The Moor

Gladstone
Dr

CHURCH LA

Crowfields
Farm

Hall Farm

HALL LA

Brinsley

49

rk Farm

River Erewash

New Farm

STONEY LA

PH

Coneygrey
Plantation

Brinsley
Brook

3

Crow Wood

ALDERCAR LA

MANSFIELD RD

Dismtd Rly.

48

Aldercar

CROMFORD RD

Hall
Farm

COCKERHOUSE RD

Sch

UPPER DUNSTEAD RD

HALL RD

Eastwood Hall

GREENHILLS RD

2

Langley
Mill

LOWER DUNSTEAD RD

Langley
Park

ARGYLE ST

Nether Green Brook

EASTWOOD

Sch

GRANGE VIEW

Sch

P

DERBY RD

P
P

NOTTINGHAM RD

47

P

Heanor

ALDRED'S LA

STATION RD

Langley Mill
Station

WESLEY ST

NEW DERBY RD

A608

DERBY RD

Bailey
Grove

Sch

CHURCH ST

MILNHAY RD

MIDLAND RD

1

Langley

LACEY FIELDS RD

LEE LA

Sewage
Works

Erewash Canal

Works

Cemy

A610

CHEWTON ST

HAND'S RD

BREACH RD

Sch

Lacey Fields
Farm

TINSLEY RD

143
129

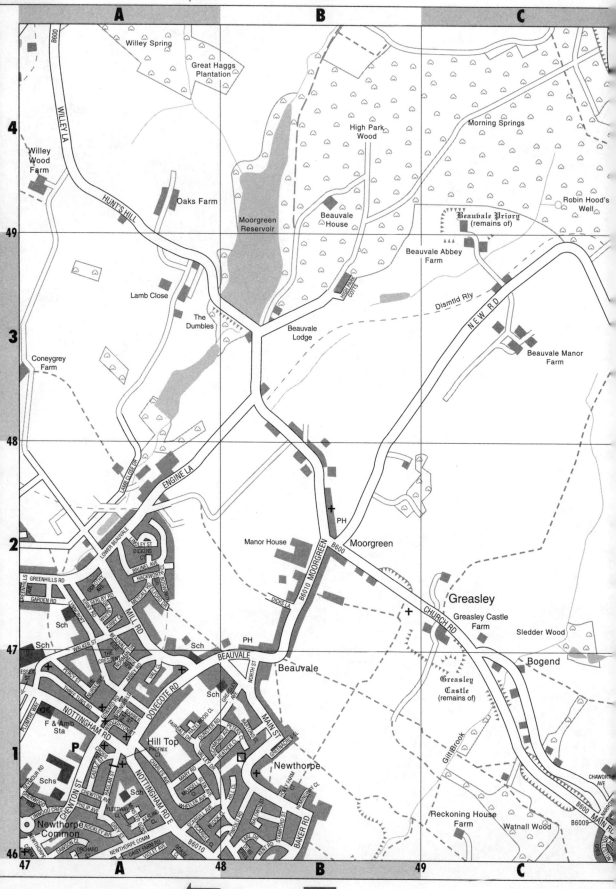

143
158

A    B    C

1 BROXTOWE DR
2 BENTINCK ST
3 NEWSTEAD TERR
4 VICTORIA ST

ST ANDREW'S CL
ST MARY'S WAY
GEORGE ST
ST JAMES'S CT
ST GEORGE'S
PEVERIL
MONTAGUE ST
ANNESLEY RD
SPRING ST EAST
OGLE ST
CARLINGFORD AVE
MAGDALE WAY
BAKER ST
TITCHFIELD ST
PERLETHORPE AV
THORESBY DALE

Leisure Centre
1 KERSALL GDNS
2 KNEESALL GR

LINBY RD
LINBY CL
LINBY AV

HOLBECK
MINSTER WAY
BISHOPS WAY
WINDSOR CL
BALMORAL CL
LEEN VIEW CT
MILLS
PAPPLEWICK LA

PEARTREE
CLEARBROOK
COPELAND AVE
HUDSON ST
LEEN AVE
EDM DNS
OAKENHALL AVE
CAVENDISH AVE

Sch

Hucknall Station

STATION RD
Govt Off

P

River Leen

The Duck Ponds

B683

Sports Ground

GOOSEDALE LA

WOOD LA
BEECH AVE
LDYCRFT AV
WEST TERR
WEST ST
WILLIAM RD
DERBYSHIRE LA
CENTRAL AVE
WATNALL RD
MOSLEY
MKT PL
Liby
SOUTH ST
HIGH ST
CHAPEL ST
VINE TERR
Offices
MANSON CRES
KING EDWARD
TENNYSON
BYRON ST
LITCHFIELD ST
DUKE ST
BEARDALL ST
PORTLAND RD
WOODSTOCK
LINGFORD
BATHS
PRIESTER
WIGWAM LA
WIDMAN

Sch
Coll

49

Butler's Hill
1 RUFFORD CL
2 CAVENDISH CL
3 BUTLERS CL

MOOR RD

Cobbler's Hill

SANDY LA
WINDMILL AVE
CHTSWRTH
STORTH AVE
ORCHARD ST
CROFT ST
ALLWOOD GDNS
LABURNUM GR
CHERRY AV
HOLLY CL
LILAC CL
BUS AVE
HENRY ST
WINIFRED ST
WHYBURN ST
BROOKSIDE
SHERWOOD ST
MARTIN CL
BUCKYARD DR
LAKELAND
John's ST
LEIGH
WINFRED ST
BESTWOOD RD
BRICKYARD

Bestwood FP
LC

Westhouse Farm

LONG HILL RISE
BRIDGE ST
ACEY AV
ASHDALE AVE
HAZEL GR
Park
Cemy

Hazelgrove

Broomhill

THE SPINNEY
CORONATION RD
HILL RD
Schs
THE MOUNT
KEEPERS CL
BROAD VALLEY
BESTON CL

Bestwood Village

48

GLENDON DR
ARLINGTON CL
SHORTWOOD AVE
A611
HAZEL MEADOWS
ELDER GR
LIME TREE RD
BROOMHILL RD
FISHERS
MIMOSA CL

Allot Gdns

Broomhill Farm

The Lodge (PH)

NOTTINGHAM RD

Allot Gdns

Leen Valley Country Park

SCHOOL WLK
MAYES RISE
LAMCASTER
THE WLK
PARK RD
ST ALBANS RD

Broadvalley Farm

P

Shaft (dis)

Farley's Lane

SHERTON AVE

River Leen

Bestwood Country Park

2

Airfield

Home Wood

City Golf Course

Barker's Wood

Bulwell Hall Park

47

Dismild Riv

HOWDEN RD

LONGFORD CRES

WOODLEA
MANOR CRES
ASTON DR
FENTON
CALDON GREEN
LAWTON DR

HUCKNALL LA
A6002 MOOR BRIDGE
B683
WOODBRIDGE GDNS

BESTWOOD RD

Mills
OLD MILL RD

HEXHAM GDNS 1
TITHE GDNS 2
MOIRFIELD RD 3
LYTHAM GDNS 4
MEREGILL CL 5
ECTON CL 6
TERTON RD 7
HELMSDALE GDNS 8
THOR GDNS 9
CARLSWARK GDNS 10

1 COLINWOOD AVE
2 JENNESS AVE
3 CROWTHORNE GDNS
4 HOUSTON CL

BROWNLOW DR
HILLFIELD
BARDFIELD GDNS
HAVERHILL CRES

GLIST GDNS
LARS CL
RUSHY CL
DUNDON CL
ROSENEATH AVE
WANSTEAD WAY
BRAMHALL CL
DUNLIN CT
DUNGANNON
CULLEN CL

Dismild Riv
HUCKNALL RD

REVELSTOKE WAY
REVELSTOKE AVE
ABBOTSBURY CL
CROWTHORNE AVE
BARRHEAD CL
BLANTYRE AVE

EARLSFIELD DR
ELMSHAM AVE
BESTWOOD PARK DR W
RISE PARK
LANGBANK AVE
RISE PARK RD
STANSTEAD AVE

Rise Park

Schs
OLD FARM
Liby RD
PINE HILL CL
SHALDON CL
TOP VALLEY DR

1

NORWICH GDNS
ACLE GDNS
A6002
FRISERBROUGH WLK
SOUTHGLADE
RISEBOROUGH WLK
CAMBERLEY
SANDHURST RD
WINGBOURNE CT
NAOMI CT

CH
Sch

46

53    A    54    B    55    C

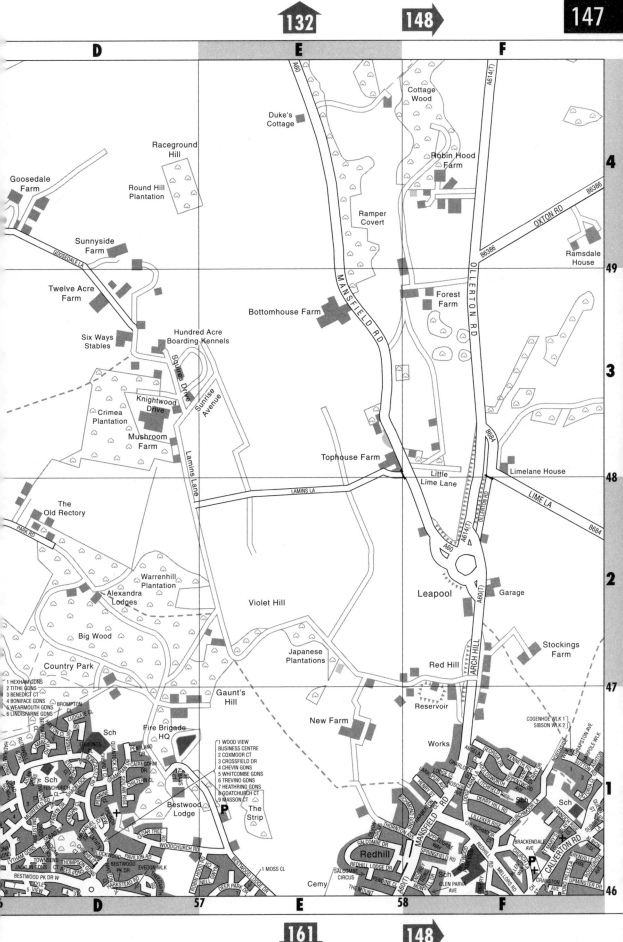

132  148

D   E   F

4

49

3

48

2

47

1

46

Goosedale Farm
Sunnyside Farm
GOOSEDALE LA
Twelve Acre Farm
Six Ways Stables
Hundred Acre Boarding Kennels
SQUIRES DRIVE
Crimea Plantation
Knightwood Drive
SUNRISE AVENUE
Mushroom Farm
LAMINS LANE
The Old Rectory
PARK RD
Warrenhill Plantation
Alexandra Lodges
Big Wood
Country Park
Raceground Hill
Round Hill Plantation

Duke's Cottage
Cottage Wood
A60
Robin Hood Farm
Ramper Covert
MANSFIELD RD
Bottomhouse Farm
Forest Farm
OLLERTON RD
B6386
OXTON RD
B6386
Ramsdale House
Limelane House
B684
Tophouse Farm
Little Lime Lane
LAMINS LA
LIME LA
B684
A60
A614(T)
OLLERTON RD
Leapool
Garage
ARCH HILL
Red Hill
Stockings Farm
Reservoir
Violet Hill
Japanese Plantations
Gaunt's Hill
New Farm
Works
1 HEXHAM GDNS
2 TITHE GDNS
3 BENEDICT CT
4 BONIFACE GDNS
5 WEARMOUTH GDNS
6 LINDISFARNE GDNS
BROMPTON CL
LUDGATE CL
Sch
Fire Brigade HQ
EDMONDS
QUANTOCK CL
PENTLAND DR
CAIRNGORM DR
GRAMPIAN DR
CHILTERN CL
ALBANS CT
Sch
FENCHURCH CL
PENNINE CL
CEDAR TREE
LOCKWOOD
PAVILION RD
WOODCHURCH RD
Bestwood Lodge
P
The Strip
1 WOOD VIEW BUSINESS CENTRE
2 COXMOOR CT
3 CROSSFIELD DR
4 CHEVIN GDNS
5 WHITCOMBE GDNS
6 TREVINO GDNS
7 HEATHRING GDNS
8 GOATCHURCH CT
9 MASSON CT
1 MOSS CL
Cemy
Redhill
Redhill Lodge Dr
SALCOMBE CIRCUS
GLEN PARVA AVE
THE MOUNT
A60(T)
MANSFIELD RD
THORNTON AVE
SALCOMBE RD
SPRINGFIELD RD
RICHMOND GDNS
GARDEN
HENRY RD
LILLEKER RISE
DERBY HILL RD
CHURCHMOOR
Sch
REDHILL
MELLORS RD
CALVERTON RD
BRACKENDALE AVE
P
CRANSTON AVE
UPMINSTER DR
Sch
COGENHOE WLK 1
SIBSON WLK 2
THRAPSTON AVE
SUTTON RD
NORTHOLT
SUTTON RD
GRENVILLE RISE
ROSEDALE
JACKLIN GDNS
TOWNSEND
BESTWOOD PK DR W
KYLE VIEW
BESTWOOD PK DR
HARKSTEAD RD
EVEDON WLK
NELL CLOSE
DEER PARK DR
ROBIN HOOD DR
BESTWOOD LODGE DR

D   E   F

161  148

57   58

D  E  F

arrington
Farm
ROADFIELDS
RICHMOND AVE

OXTON BY PASS
EPPERSTONE RD

A6097

CARRINGTON LA
THE HOLLIES
PARK RD E

GRIMESMOOR RD
THE BAINBRIDGE

CROOKDOLE L
DUNELM DR

Calverton

DOVER BECK CL
SPRINGWOOD CL

Crookdole La

ROES LA  PADDOCK CL

MOOR RD

THE GROVE

Works

BONNER LA

Calverton
Lido

Dover Beck

MOOR LA

Caravan
Park

Grimesmoor Dyke

Grimesmoor

Criftin
Farm

Epperstone
Park

Kennels

MAIN ST

4

49

3

Foxwood
House

FOXWOOD LA

Wynhill

Cemy

PRIVATE RD  ASH GROVE
RISE HILL

SUNNINGDALE DR

DOVER BECK DR

WHITES CROFT

THE MEADOWS

BROAD CL

FIELD LA

ALDENE WAY
OLDACRES

HAWTHORNE CL

BURNHAM AV

SHELT HILL

Shelt
Hill
Farm

Fox
Covert

Epperstone
Manor

Sports
Gd

EPPERSTONE BY PASS

48

A6097

Nursery

WESTFIELDS LA

PARK AVE

MAIN ST

Sch
FOLD CL

FOLD CRES

BUCKLAND
DR

HOLME CL

SMALL'S CROFT

PH

OLD MANOR CL

CHARNWOOD WAY

Manor
Farm

LOWDHAM LA

2

BANK HILL

The
Bank

Stanley
Wood

Bank Hill
Farm

Woodborough

LINGWOOD LA

Wood Barn
Farm

Hungerhill La

Well
Cottage

GREEN LA

Hunger Hill

Jericho
Farm

Ploughman
Wood

Lowdham
Grange

LONG MEADOW
HILL

THE GREEN

Hunters Hill
Farm

47

1

46

D  63  E  64  F

A    B    C

4

Hill Farm

Cottage Farm

Green Acres

Brockwood Farm

Starling Hall

Thurgarton Beck

ROMAN BUILDING (remains of)

Foxhole Wood

Thistly Coppice

Souther Wood

Southerwood Barn

49

Eastwood Farm

Hagg Farm

Hagg Lane

Hagg Cottage

CHAPEL LA

Order Beck

NEELS CROFT

CHURCH LA

Epperstone

Bentley Wood

3

Main St

PH

BLAND LA

LEDT LA

PARR LA

Netherfield Farm

Order Beck

LOWDHAM RD

Playing Field

Netherfield Farm House

48

A6097

Wash Bridge

Leland's Dumble

LOWDHAM LA

Nursery

Epperstone By-Pass

Old Epperstone Rd

Car Holt Farm

GONALSTON LA

Dover Beck

2

Lowdham Mill

Eliment Hill Farm

Nurseries

Vicarage

Carr Beck Barn

Epperstone Rd

The Hut

The Hermitage

Cliff Mill

47

Cliff Mill Farm

Long Meadow Hill

HILL SYKE

ROCKLEYS VIEW

Grove Farm

The Old Hall

THE LEYS

MOUNT CRESENT

NURSERY GDNS

Sch

RID TRENCON IN RD

OGE HILL

Barker Hill

Barker Hill

Norrisdene

SOUTHWELL RD

THE PRIORS

Liby

ST MARY'S CL

Blackthorne Dr

STONE BANK

TON LA

TON LA

Main St

CRANLEIGH DR

1

Cocker Beck

LAMBLEY RD

RED LA

PLOUGH LA

MANOR HOUSE CL

MARL DA LA

1 Nottingham Rd
2 Victoria Ave
3 Worcester Cl

WILLOW HOLT

BEAGHSIDE

THE COPPICE

SOMERVALE CL

NEWTON IN RD

LIME TREE GDNS

BLENHEIM AVE

LANGDALE CRES

BLENHEIM AVE

ROSES

RUSSEY CL

PH

46

Lowdham

A6097

A612

STATION RD

CAYTHORPE RD

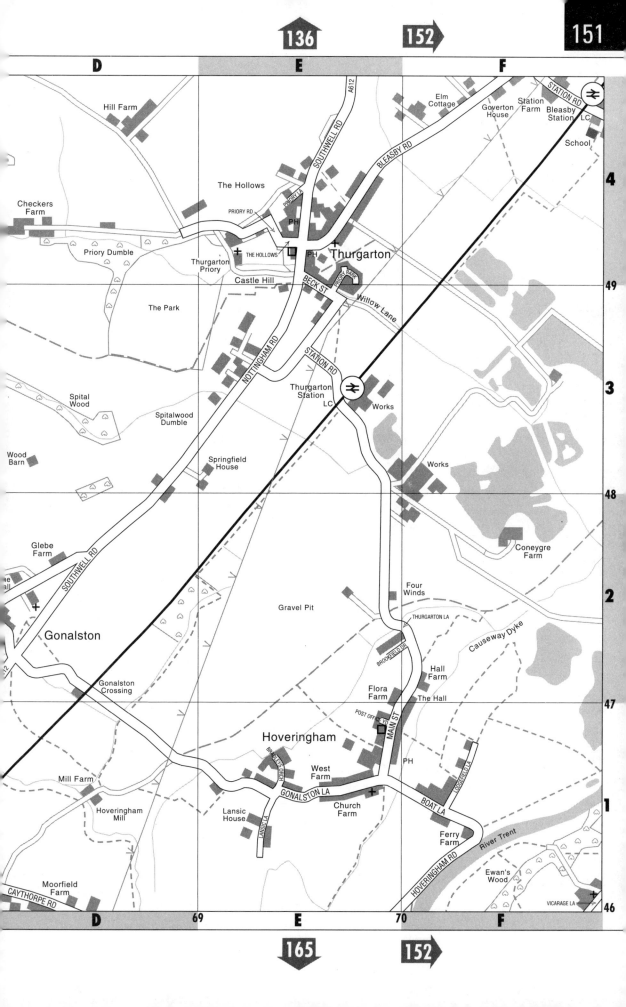

136
152

**D**    **E**    **F**

Hill Farm

Elm Cottage

Station Farm

Goverton House

Bleasby Station

STATION RD

LC

School

Checkers Farm

The Hollows

PRIORY RD

PRIORY LA

SOUTHWELL RD

BLEASBY RD

A612

Priory Dumble

Thurgarton Priory

THE HOLLOWS

PH

PH

**Thurgarton**

Castle Hill

BECK ST

PRIORY PARK

Willow Lane

**4**

**49**

The Park

NOTTINGHAM RD

STATION RD

Thurgarton Station

LC

Works

**3**

Spital Wood

Spitalwood Dumble

Wood Barn

Springfield House

Works

**48**

Glebe Farm

SOUTHWELL RD

Gravel Pit

Four Winds

THURGARTON LA

Causeway Dyke

Coneygre Farm

**2**

**Gonalston**

Gonalston Crossing

BROOKFIELD DR

Hall Farm

The Hall

Flora Farm

POST OFFICE YD

MAIN ST

PH

**47**

Mill Farm

BRADLEY'S BROOK

Hoveringham Mill

Lansic House

LANSIC LA

GONALSTON LA

West Farm

Church Farm

**Hoveringham**

BOAT LA

RODGEFIELD LA

Ferry Farm

HOVERINGHAM RD

River Trent

Ewan's Wood

VICARAGE LA

**1**

Moorfield Farm

CAYTHORPE RD

**46**

**D**    **E**    **F**

69      70

165
152

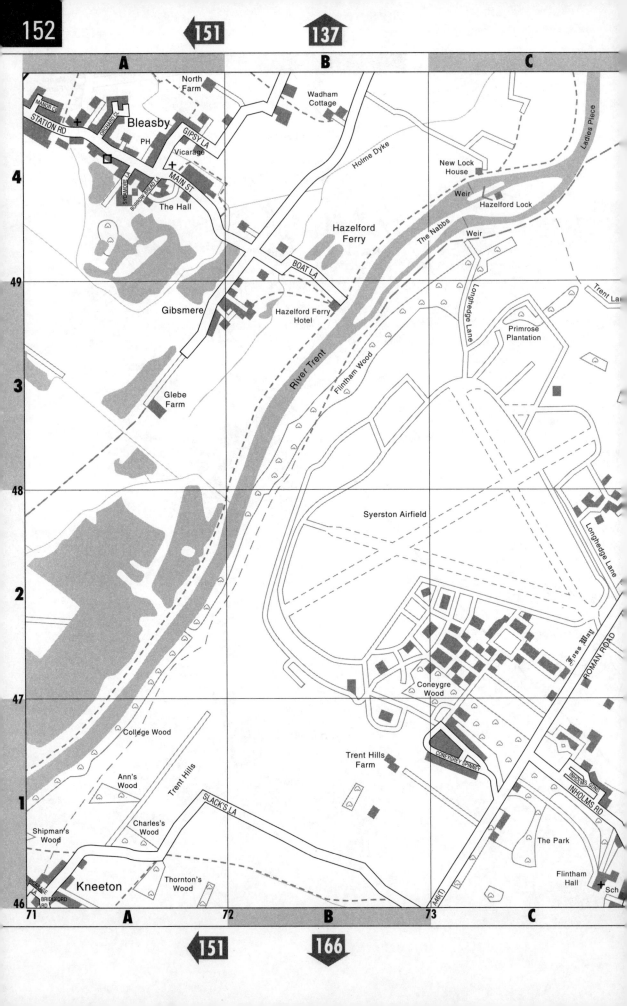

D
E
F

Stoke Wood

SCHOOL LA

Hall Farm

Sch

PH

East Stoke

HUMBER LA

BROWNLOW CL

A46(T)

The Old Vicarage

MOOR LA

Battle of Stoke Field 1487

4

49

Fosse Way

Trent Lane

ROMAN ROAD

ELSTON LA

Mill Hill House

Cedar Cottage

Elston Lodge Farm

Stoke Fields Farm

3

Elston Towers

Lady Pit Farm

LODGE LA

LOW ST

PINFOLD LA

SPINNEY

Elston Chapel

Codders Dyke

Elston

Sch

48

Elston Hall

TOP ST

GREENGATE

Syerston

The Rookery

Croft House

HAWKSWORTH RD

Low Farm

MOOR LA

Gundykes Plantation

The Windmill

MILL RD

PETTAL DRI

WINSTON DRI

DARRACH CL

CARRGATE LA

PH

Sewage Works

Carrgate Lane

PADDOCKS CL 1
THE PADDOCKS 2

BRECKS LA

2

Hawksworth Road

DOGHILL LA

Ash Holt

47

Longhedge Lane

Lineham Plantation

LINEHAM LA

Sewage Works

Hill Farm

DEADWONG LA

Brecks Plantation

1

Flintham

Sch

MAIN ST

WOOD'S LA

46

D
75
E
76
F

A  B  C

4

49

Thorpe
Lodge

Honies Farm

Car Dyke

The Grange

3

MOOR LA

River Devon

48

Fox Covert

Manor
Farm

2

Carrgate Lane

CROSS LA

Meadow Farm

The Old
Hall Farm

Cotham

Devon Farm

LANE

47

Dismantled Railway

Back Dyke

1

Grange Farm

BRECKS LA

Elston
Grange

Station
House

46

77  A  78  B  79  C

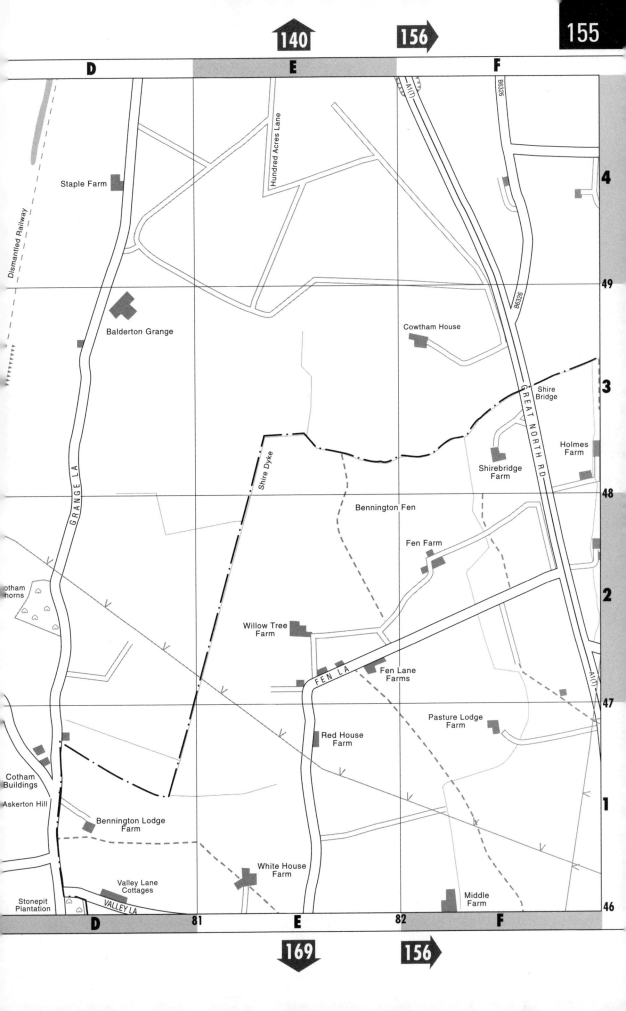

D E F

Dismantled Railway

Staple Farm

Hundred Acres Lane

A1(T)
B6326

4

49

Balderton Grange

Cowtham House

3

Shire Bridge

GREAT NORTH RD
B6326

Shire Dyke

Shirebridge Farm

Holmes Farm

48

Bennington Fen

Fen Farm

...tham ...horns

2

Willow Tree Farm

FEN LA
Fen Lane Farms

A1(T)

47

Red House Farm

Pasture Lodge Farm

Cotham Buildings

Askerton Hill

1

Bennington Lodge Farm

White House Farm

Valley Lane Cottages

Middle Farm

Stonepit Plantation

VALLEY LA

46

D 81 E 82 F

GRANGE LA

155
141

**A**      **B**      **C**

Balderfields

Balderfield

Broad Fen Lane

Well Fen Lane

Barnby Lane

Cross Lane

Oster Fen Lane

Liberty Gates Crossing

**Claypole**

FB

Brunts Farm

LC

SHIRE LA

Piggery

Witham View

WELL FEN LA

BARNBY LA

CHAPEL LA

SCHOOL LA

RECTORY LA

TOWN ST

Sch

PH

CHAPEL CL

REDTHORN WAY

TINSLEY CL

STUBTON RD

LC

Claypole Bridge

Mill Road

Hough Lane

DODDINGTON LA

Sandhills

Mill Farm

Weir

River Witham

Holmes Lane

The Willows

Doddington Bridge

DODDINGTON LA

Coach Road

Bridge Farm

Syke Lane

GREAT NORTH RD

A1(T)

Manor Farm

MANOR HOUSE LA

CLAYPOLE LA

Long Lane

GREEN LA

CLENSEY LA

MAIN ST

Red House Farm

HOUGHAM RD

The Wheatsheaf (PH)

**Dry Doddington**

Hill Farm

**A**      **B**      **C**

83      84      85

155

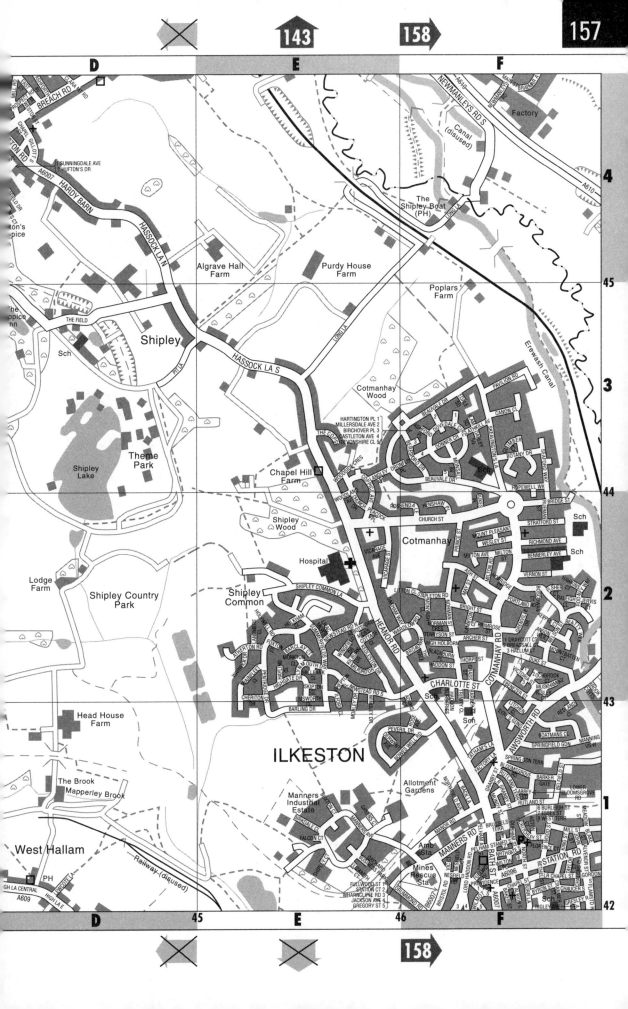

A     B     C

NEWTHORPE COMM
MYVERN CL
COMMONS CL
HALLS LA
LODGE RD
DAISY FARM RD
PRIMROSE
FOXGLOVE RD
RD
CLOSE
NOTTINGHAM RD
B6010
HAMPDEN ST
VERNON PL
BAKER RD
SOUTH ST

Newthorpe
Common

THE HEATH HIGH MEADOW
JUNIPER CT
ACORN AVE
ROBIN RD
AZALEA CT
AZALEA CL
VELVET CL
GILTBROOK
SILVERBIRCH
CRES

BASON CL
BRANDRETH
LLOYD DR
GOODMAN LA
BRADWELL CL
BRACKENFIELD DR
SMITHURST RD
BRANTHAM
BENWAY
LEECH CT

Giltbrook

RESERVOIR
ROLLESTON
CRES

Reservoir

MILLFIELD RD
HIGH SPANIA
OXGBURY RD

4

HALLS LA
CONIFER
TURBERRY
BRASSINGTON CL
WEIGHTMAN
BEWLAY

A610

Depot

GILT HILL
Gilt Hill
Farm
Sch
ARTIC WAY
GILT HILL
B6010
A6096

STOCKS RD
GRASSBANK CL
STONEBANK CL
HIGH SPANIA

HARDY ST
Sch
PARKHAM
NORMAN ST
TEWKESBURY DR
EASTWOOD RD
MAWS LA
BEVERLEY
STRATHGLEN CL
ASCOT AVE
WETHERBY CL

Kimberley

CHURCH HILL
Coll
MAIN ST
HIGH ST

45

Sewage Works

DIGBY ST
BROXTOWE AVE
AINSWORTH DR
WENTWORTH CL
VALLEY RD
HALEY CL
GOODWIN DR

GIN CLOSE WAY
A6096
Hogs Head
(PH)
AWSWORTH LA

Dismantled Railway

SPRING HILL

3

MEADOW RD
ATTEWELL
RD
STATION RD
MAIN ST
DOUGLAS AVE
CROFT
CRES
Grasscroft
Farm
Swingate

Viaduct
PARK HILL
SHAKESPEARE RD
MANOR DR
Sch
Manor Farm
Sch
Babbington
Hall
BABBINGTON LA

44

BARLOW DR (N)
HAWTHORNE
RISE
TULIP
MYNO
BARLOW DR (S)
CHESTERMAN
CL
Sch
BONNER'S RD
THE LANE
Awsworth
Babbington
Swingate Farm

2

Stenson's
Lock
NEWTON'S LA
ST MORRIS RD
MIDDLETON ST
ABBOT RD
THE GLEBE
AWSWORTH LA
PH
Cossall
Common
WESTBY LA
Babbington
House Farm
Swingate Farm

AWSWORTH RD

Common
Farm
Strelley Park
Farm

43

River Erewash
Erewash Canal
CORONATION RD
STOCKMAN RD
Cossall
Marsh
Spring Wood

WENTWORTH ST
STATION RD
Nottingham Canal (disused)
Turkey Fields
Farm

1

MILL ST
CANAL ST
A6096
STATION RD
WILLOUGHBY ST
LOWER MIDDLETON ST
TEMAN ST
Works
Almshouses
P
Cossall
Grange
Farm
Oldmoor
Farmhouse

THE ROPEWALK
GORDON ST
RUPERT
FAIRFIELD
RD
THE ROPEWORK
SEEDBED CENTRE
CHURCH LA
MILL LA
DEAD LA
Manor
Farm
ROBINETTES LA

42

47    A    48    B    49    C

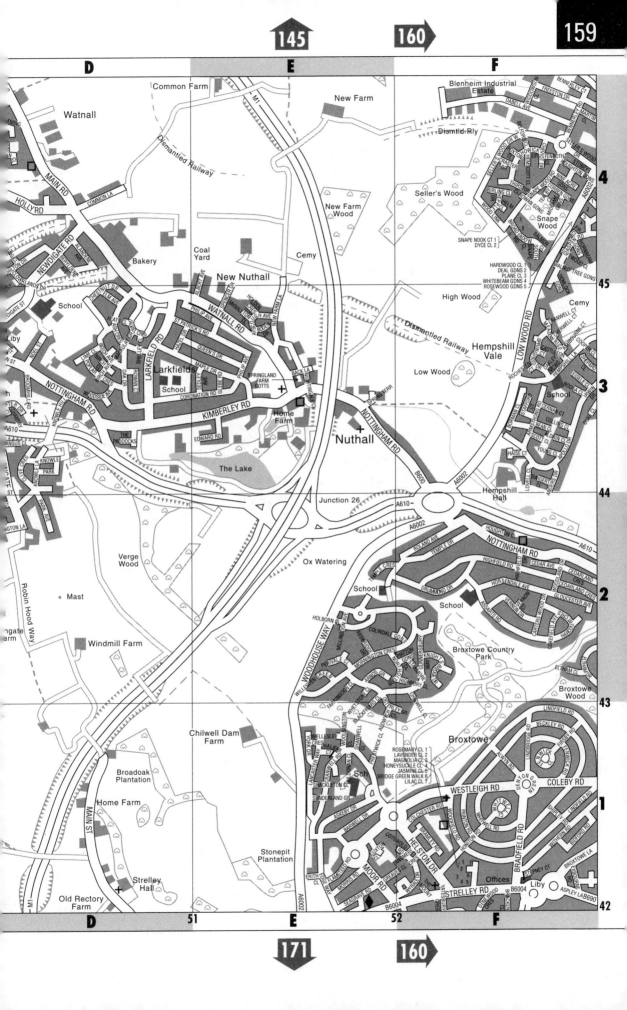

D   E   F

4

45

3

44

2

43

1

42

149
164
175
164

D E F

4 45 3 44 2 43 1 42

63 64

Lambley

Burton Joyce

Bateman House
Nursery
Harlow Wood Farm
Cocker Beck
PARK LA
Works
Broughton Park
Bulcote Wood

GREEN LA
THE DUMBLES
CATFOOT LA
CHURCH ST
ORCHARD RISE
STEELES WAY
MILL LA
CHAPEL LA
TRINITY CRES
WILLOW CRES
MAIN ST
MOSS LA
GRANGE CT
Cemy
Cornwall's Hill
Stockhill Farm
Sch
PH
Lambley Dumble
FLAMSTEAD AVE
CROMWELL CRES

Bulcote Lodge Farm

Stockhill Farm
Earthwork
Lodge Farm

SPRING LA
Wicketwood Hill
The Mount
BLACKACRE
GREENACRE
HILLCREST
FOXHILL RD
PADLEYS LA
CLOSE CL
WILLOW CL
OLIVER DR
ORCHARD CL
HILL SIDE DR
LAMBLEY
CROMWELL RD
GLEN RD
BRIDLE RD
COVERT CL
GROVE CL
LAMBLEY LA
Rose Cotts
Brooklyn Ave
Sch
A612
MEADOW LA

Wood Farm

LAMBLEY LA

Crock Dumble

Gedling Wood
Barron's Plantation

MAIN ST
LENTON AVE
CHURCH RD
ST HELEN'S
PARK AVE
VICARAGE WK
ASH CL
Glebe Farm
GLEBE DR
FRENCH ST
CROW PARK DR
MASSE
CRAGMOOR RD
HARRIS DR
MILL FIELD RD
STATION RD
LC
Burton Joyce Station

Gedling Wood
Gedling Wood Farm
White Gates
Gedling House

BULCOTE RD
WOODSIDE RD
NEW Plantation
NOTTINGHAM RD
WADSWORTH DR

River Trent
STOKE LA

SAGE VIEW RD
OAK TREE CL
ALMOND WLK
ACORN DR
MAPLE DR
YALDALE
YEW TREE LA
WOOD LA
SAFELY CL
WATERHOUSE LA
Sch
Sch
Sch
CONISBROUGH AVE
BURTON RD
LINDEN GR
A612
BEAUMARIS DR
RAGLAN DR
HARTINGTON CL
STOKE LA
THE CHESTNUTS
CORRINGHAM WK
WILLOW CRES
MAIN RD
THE ORCHARDS
WAVERLEY AVE
TENNYSON AVE
VERNON
FLORENCE
SHEARING
SMILLANDS

Sewage Works

Ferry Boat Inn (PH)
STOKE FERRY LA

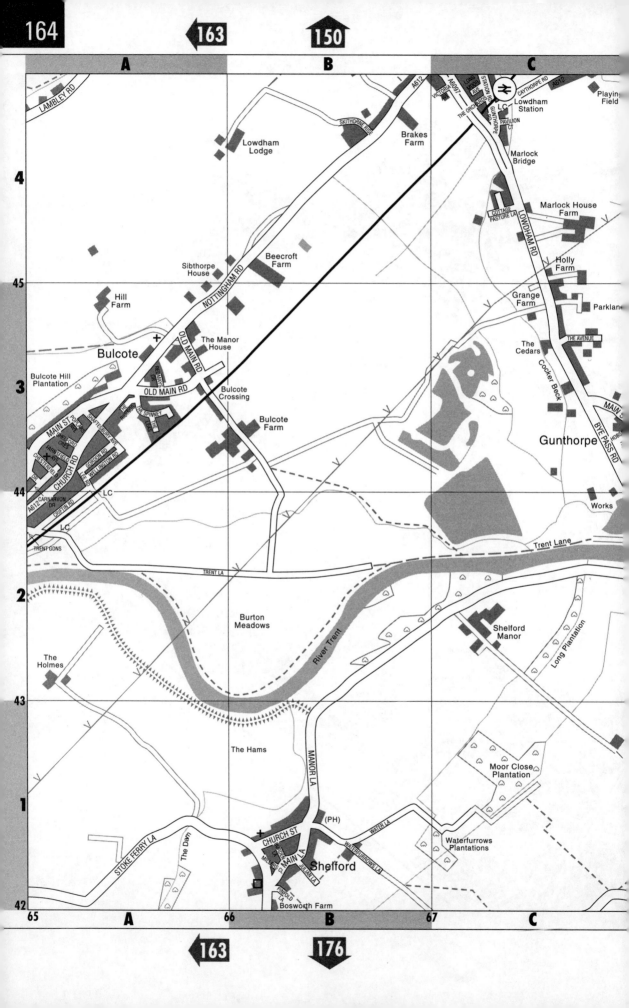

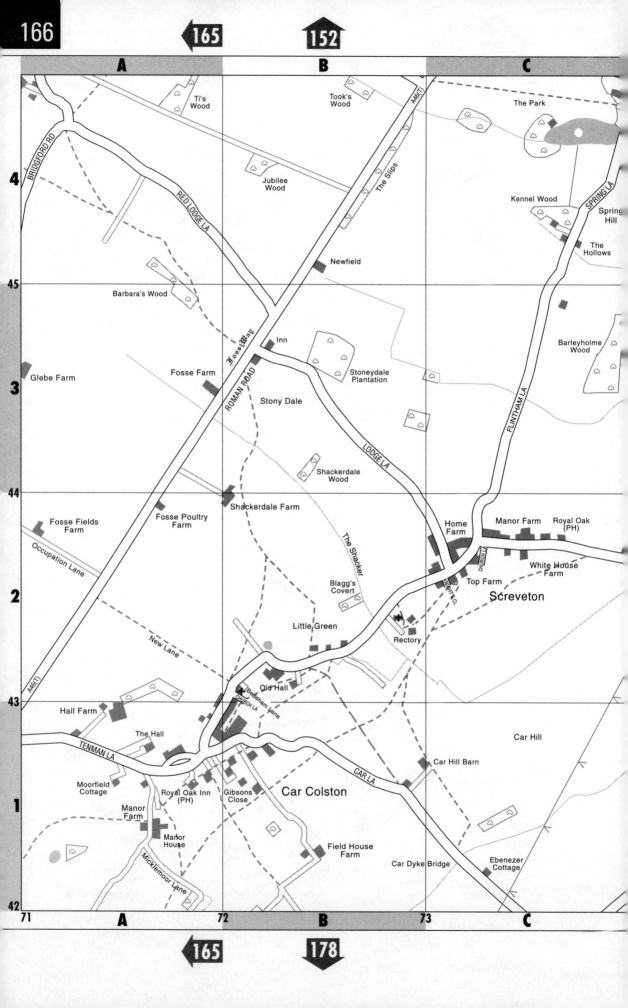

**A**      **B**      **C**

Ti's Wood

Took's Wood

The Park

4

BRIDGFORD RD

RED LODGE LA

Jubilee Wood

The Slips

A46(T)

Kennel Wood

Spring Hill

SPRING LA

The Hollows

Newfield

45

Barbara's Wood

Inn

Barleyholme Wood

3

Glebe Farm

Fosse Farm

Fosse La

ROMAN ROAD

Stony Dale

Stoneydale Plantation

FLINTHAM LA

Shackerdale Wood

LODGE LA

44

Fosse Fields Farm

Fosse Poultry Farm

Shackerdale Farm

Home Farm

Manor Farm

Royal Oak (PH)

Occupation Lane

The Shacker

White House Farm

2

Blagg's Covert

CHURCH LA

KNIGHT CL

Top Farm

Screveton

New Lane

Little Green

Rectory

A46(T)

Old Hall

Bodeham Lane

CHURCH LA

43

Hall Farm

The Hall

Car Hill

Car Hill Barn

TENMAN LA

CAR LA

Moorfield Cottage

Royal Oak Inn (PH)

Gibsons Close

Car Colston

1

Manor Farm

Manor House

Field House Farm

Car Dyke Bridge

Ebenezer Cottage

Micklemoor Lane

42

**71**    **A**     **72**    **B**     **73**    **C**

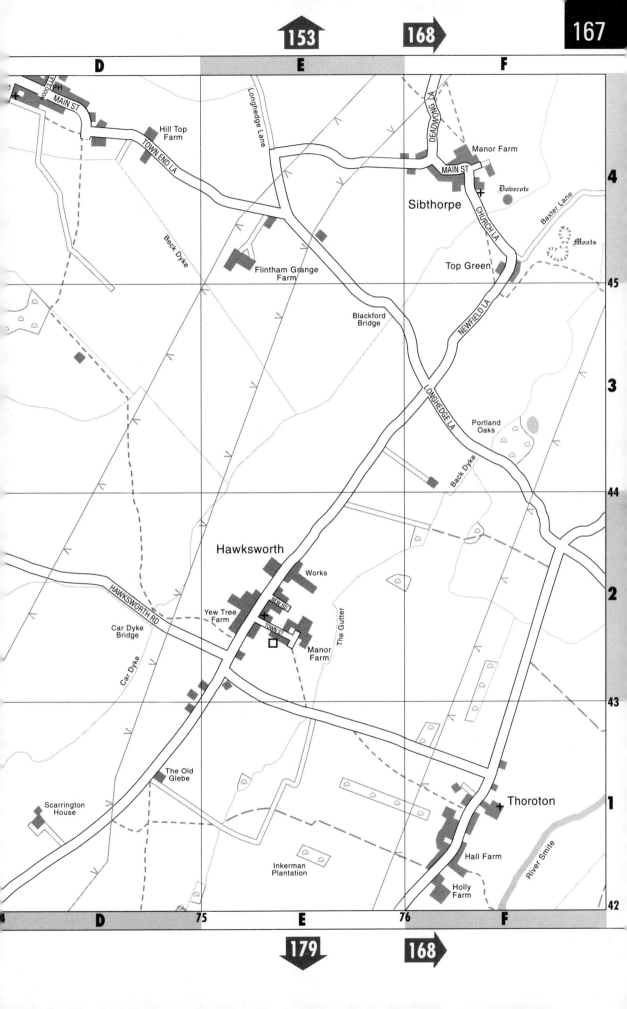

**D**  **E**  **F**

4

Sibthorpe

45

3

44

2

43

1

42

Hill Top Farm

MAIN ST

TOWN END LA

Longhedge Lane

Beck Dyke

Flintham Grange Farm

DEADWONG LA

Manor Farm

MAIN ST

Dovecote

CHURCH LA

Top Green

Baxter Lane

Moats

Blackford Bridge

NEWFIELD LA

LONGHEDGE LA

Portland Oaks

Back Dyke

Hawksworth

Works

HAWKSWORTH RD

Car Dyke Bridge

Yew Tree Farm

NEW RD

TOWN ST

Manor Farm

The Gutter

Car Dyke

The Old Glebe

Scarrington House

Thoroton

Hall Farm

River Smite

Inkerman Plantation

Holly Farm

**D**  75  **E**  76  **F**

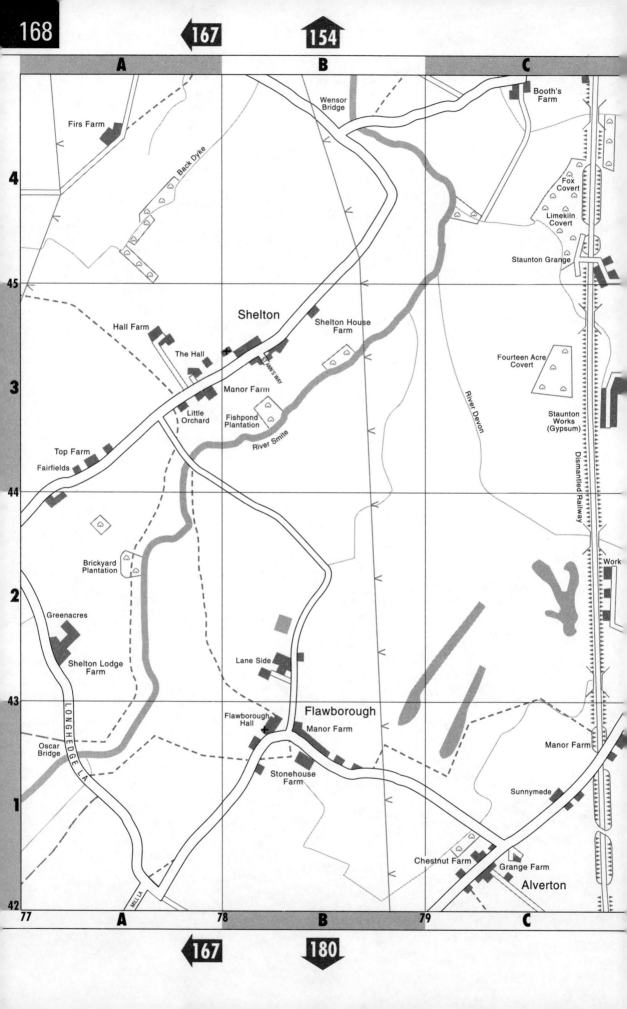

A | B | C

Firs Farm

Back Dyke

**4**

Wensor Bridge

Booth's Farm

Fox Covert

Limekiln Covert

Staunton Grange

**45**

Shelton

Shelton House Farm

Hall Farm

The Hall

ST ANN'S WAY

Manor Farm

Little Orchard

Fishpond Plantation

River Smite

Fourteen Acre Covert

River Devon

**3**

Staunton Works (Gypsum)

Top Farm

Fairfields

**44**

Brickyard Plantation

Dismantled Railway

Work

**2**

Greenacres

Shelton Lodge Farm

Lane Side

**43**

Flawborough

Flawborough Hall

Manor Farm

Manor Farm

LONGHEDGE LA

Oscar Bridge

Stonehouse Farm

Sunnymede

**1**

Chestnut Farm

Grange Farm

Alverton

MILL LA

**42**

77 | 78 | 79

A | B | C

Back Dyke

Big Sykes Covert

Moor Drain

Moor Lane

FEN LA

VALLEY LA

MOOR LA

Costa Hill

A1(T)

Authorpe Farm

Charlton Farm

HIGH ST

Chapelside Farm

Staunton Arms (PH)

Riverside Cottages

Staunton in the Vale

Staunton Park

Jubilee Plantation

Staunton Hall

The Rookery

Folly Hill

Follyhill Cottage

NEW RD

Mar Plantation

The Old Rectory

Kilvington

Waterloo Plantation

Three Shire Oak

Normanton Thorns

Three Shires Farm

Winter Beck

River Devon

Willow Farm

Normanton Lodge

Rowe Farm

Rowe Farm

Airfield (disused)

A     B     C

Oldmoor Wood

FARFIELD RD

Cemy

PARK CRES

CHICHESTER CT

POTTERS WAY

WORTLEY CL

CAVENDISH CT

FARM CT

TRESSALL CL

Lock

**Larklands**

HEATHFIELD AVE

DORIS RD

MILLFIELD CL

Sch

HOLMFIELD CRES

CHAMBERS AVE

LEE CRES

4

SUDBURY AVE

WADE AVE

OUNDLE DR

ANDREW AVE

ARKLANDS AVE

GREEN LA

PARK RD

KENSINGTON GDNS

BIRCH

WALNUT

HORNBEAM CL

Lock

River Erewash

Shortwood
Farm

ALBANY ST

SMEDLEY AVE

EREWASH DR

Meadow
Farm

Field House

41

ASHDALE RD

CAROLINE CT

POWTRELL PL

A609

Sch

CAVENDISH RD

SHAW ST W

WESTWICK ST

SHAW ST E

**Gallows Inn**

CHARLES CL

CHARLES RD

JULIAN CL

BROOKSBY LA

STOREY LA

FURNACE RD

BUTTERTON CL

GLEBE CRES

ST JAMES AVE

KENSINGTON GDNS

BROOMFIELD LA

MANNERS RD

INGLEFIELD

NOTTINGHAM RD

Lock

Grange
Wood

Trowell
Service
Area

Trowell Moor

WATERLOO LA

Robin Hood Way

COOK DR

TRIANGLE

THE MALL

SHIPSTONE ST

GALLOWS
INN CL

Uplands
Farm

ELLESMERE DR

COSSALL RD

Shortwood
House

Moor
Cottages

3

KIMBERLEY

1 NEWDIGATE ST
2 STANHOPE ST
3 LITTLE HALLAM LA

Nottingham Canal
(disused)

**Trowell**

LITTLE HALLAM LA

HADLEY ST

ST DEVON ST

CORPORATION RD

MIDDLETON RD

CROMWELL AVE

WINDSOR CR

THE FORGE

Trowell
Junction

ILKESTON RD

HARDYS

NOTTINGHAM RD

Trowell Hall

DORRITERRACE

CRANMER AVE

HALL PER CRES

TROWELL AVE

HILL RISE

HILL RISE

Sch

Potter's
Plantation

QUEENS AVE

FREDERICK AVE

LONGFIELD

MITCHELL TERR

HALLAM FIELDS RD

A6007

DERBYSHIRE AVE

40

Factories

Hallam Fields
Lock

STANTLEY CRES

CHURCH CL

KINGSTON AVE

CROMPTON RD

**Hallam Fields**

Erewash Canal

Sewage
Works

Swancar
Farm

WEXHAM AVE

Crompton Road
Industrial Estate

Works

Field Farm

2

Dismtd Rly

STAPLEFORD RD

NORTHERN DR

WORK LA

TROWELL GR

Stapleford
Hill

Works

Stanton Works

SPRING
DALE GDNS

TROWELL RD

A6007

39

LC

Junction
Lock

BUTTERMEAD AVE

FIONA DR

NORWOOD AVE

ROTHBURY AVE

CAVENDISH CRES

DEVONSHIRE DR

Field Farm

LC

LC

LC

Works

BRAMBRIDGE

PASTURE RD

ILKESTON RD

MAYBERRY

P

LOW'S LA

PH

HARTWOOD DR

COVENTRY LA

P

1

**Stanton-
by-Dale**

SEVEN OAKS RD

HARTWOOD DR

MOORBRIDGE LA

NEWDALE

B6003

THE CRESCENT

FARADAY CT

1 SHERIDAN CT
2 ADELAIDE CL
3 CANBERRA CL
4 DRYDEN CT

WASHINGTON DR

B6004

HICKINGS LA

EWE LAMB CL

QUARRY HILL

Golf
Course

GOLF CLUB RD

CH

M1

STANTON GATE

Stanton
Gate

PASTURE RD

B6003

Sch

RYECROFT
ST

SPRINGFIELD
CT

HILLFIELD RD

SHERWIN RD

TRENTON
CL

STANLEY
DR

38

47     A     48     B     49     C

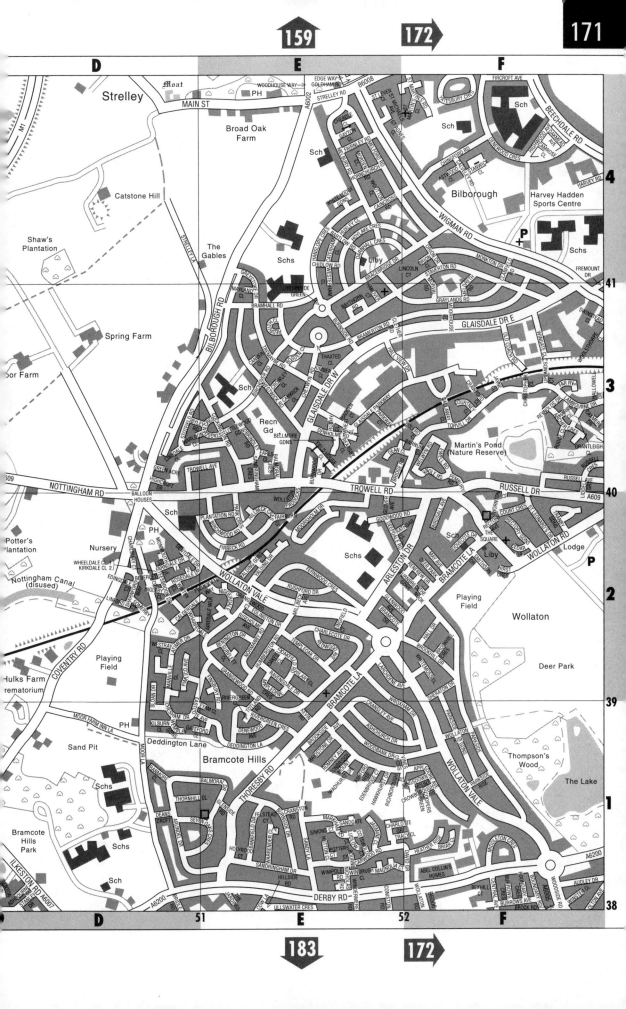

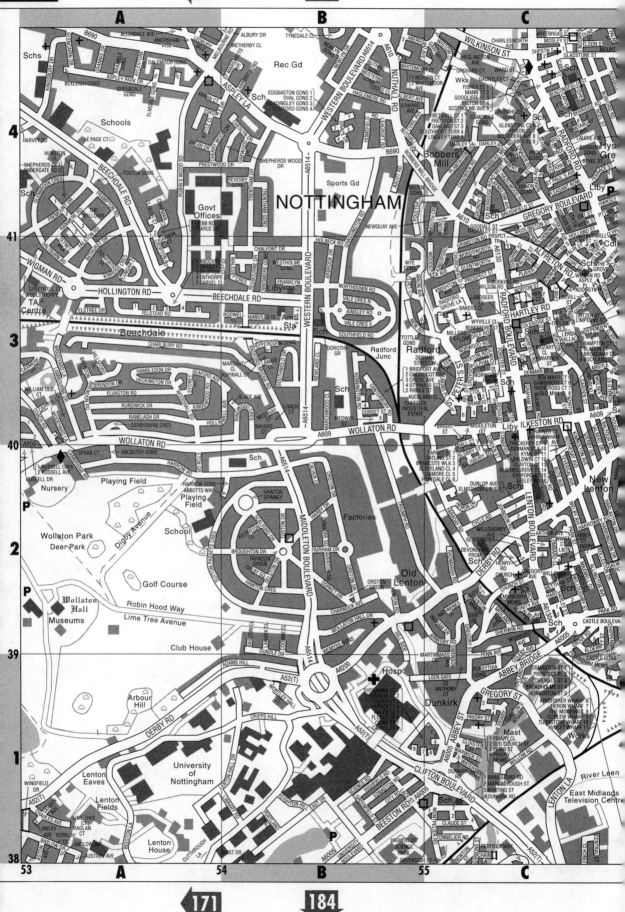

NOTTINGHAM

Wollaton Park
Deer Park

Golf Course

Wollaton
Hall

Museums

Robin Hood Way

Lime Tree Avenue

Club House

Arbour
Hill

University
of
Nottingham

Lenton
Eaves

Lenton
Fields

Lenton House

Beechdale

Radford

Old
Lenton

Dunkirk

East Midlands
Television Centre

New
Lenton

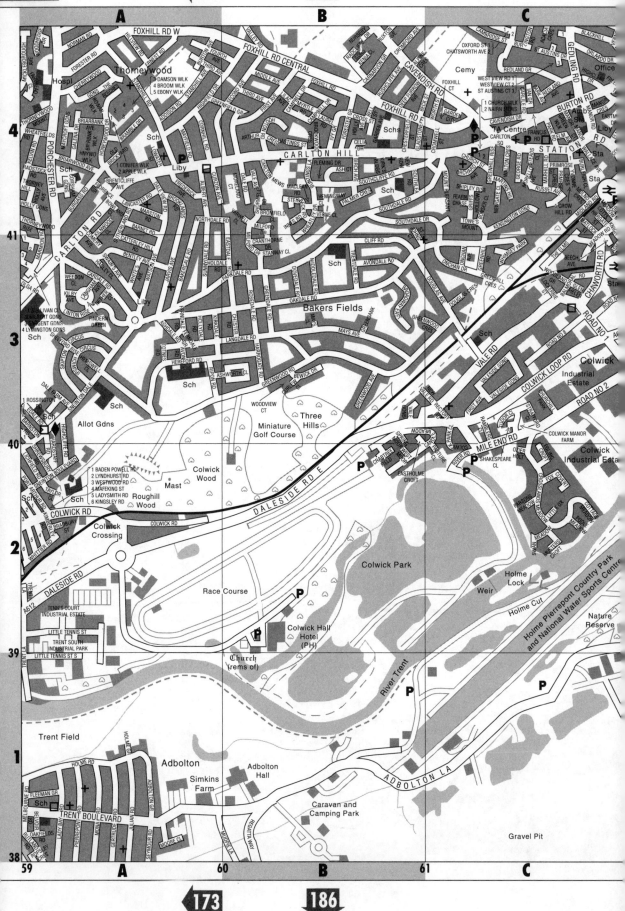

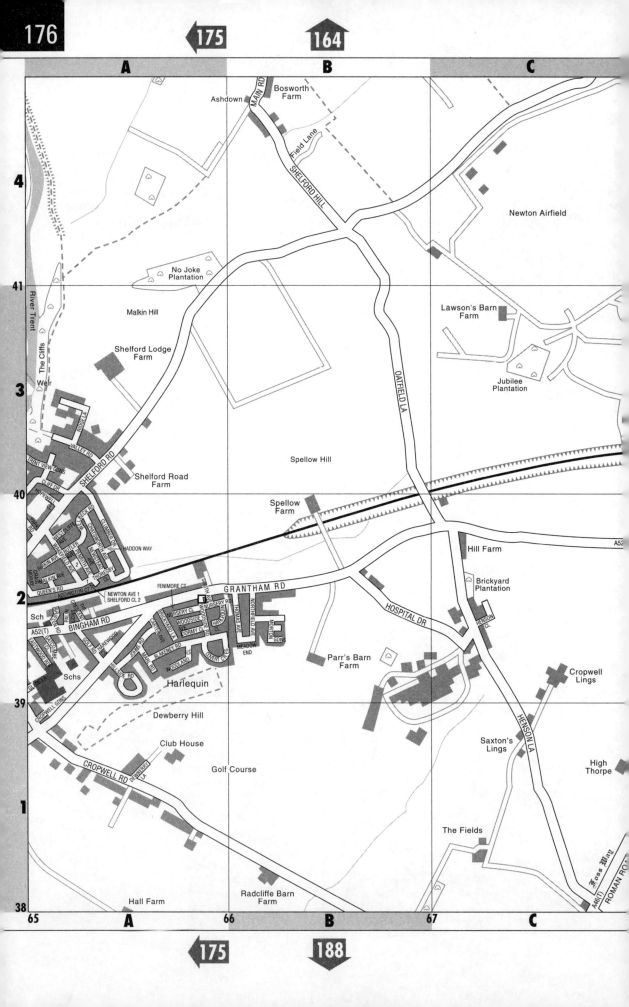

D
E
F

4

41

3

40

39

1

38

Newton House Farm

Newton

FAIRWAY CRES
FRIAR WY
TRENCHARD RD
TRENCHARD CL

Castle Hill

Burrowsmoor Holt

MARGIDVNVM ROMAN TOWN (site of)

High Westing Farm

Dawson's Plantation

NEWTON GDNS

Foss Road Farm

Foss Hill
ROMAN ROAD

CHAPEL LA
Moor Bridge

Parson's Hill

MOORBRIDGE RD
Bingham Industrial Park

Bingham Station

LC
Dismtd Rly

LC
LC

1 STAINMORE GR
2 WINDSOR CT
3 RADNOR GR
4 QUANTOCK GR
5 NEWSTEAD GR
6 RUFFORD GR
7 SHERWOOD GR

CARNARVON

WESTERN AVE
MARGARET
HILL DR
BISHOP'S RD
Sch
SCHOOL LA
CARNARVON PL
WESTFIELD RD
CARNARVON PL
ORCHARD AVE

GILLOTTS CL
NEWGATE ST
MARKET
Liby
P
UNION ST
CHURCH ST
Court

ST MARYS RD
GROVE RD
HOLME RD
MANOR RD

Lodge Farm
Saxondale

A46(T)

BRENDON GR
HARDWICK
THE BECK
FOREST RD
STEEPLE
LONG ACRE
Fire Sta
Jebb's Lane

LONG ACRE E
GRANTHAM RD

GRIZEDALE
BALMORAL
GLENDALE
BOWLAND
ROCKINGHAM GR
CHARNWOOD GR
NOTTINGHAM RD
STANHOPE WAY

THE CROFTS
MELVYN DR
THE PADDOCKS
FISHER LA
THE BANKS

Cemy

Newgate Farm

MEADOWSWEET HILL
CAMPION WAY
MUSTERS RD
PORCHESTER RD
CLAWORTH RD
RUPERT RD
SPINNEY
LARGAR

WIVERTON RD
School

BINGHAM

Foss Farm

Toot Hill

Mill Hill

Linear Park

A52(T)

Lings Farm

A46(T)

A52(T)

Top Brackendale Farm

TITHBY RD

Spring Farm

Cropwell Grove Farm

New Banks Farm

Whitefield Farm

**A**    **B**    **C**

**4**

Thoroughfare Holt

Bottom Plantation

**41**

Holme Farm

The Old Vicarage
Hall
LONGMOO...
HAWKSWORTH RD

Scarrington

MAIN ST
THE SAUCERS
Manor Farm

MILL LA

**3**

Sewage Works

NEW LA

MOOR LA

ABBEY LA

WALNUT C...
S...

Abbey Farm

FIELDS DR

ABBEY CL

**40**

ST MARYS RD
GROVE RD   LC
BROWNES RD

PRIORS CL
ABBEY RD
VICTORIA R
NURSERY RD
CARR ... RD
DOUGLAS RD
BANES RD

BUTT RD
HOLME RD
COGLEY LA

Sch

ASH CL GDNS

LC

Aslockton Hall

THE CAPES
BEVERLEY AVE
GREEN WLK
SMITE CL
COTTAGE A...

Brocker Farm

LONG ACRE E
DARK LA
RAYM DND DR
ROWAN CL
LARCH CL
POPLAR CL
OAK AVE
HOLLY C
WILLOW RD
HAZEL CL
BLACKTHORD C
JUNIPER CNS

Nursery

HM Young Offender Institution

ASH CL
CEDAR CL
MAPLE CL
BEECH AVE
ELM A
DERRY LA

Sewage Works

**2**

SYCAMORE CL

**GRANTHAM RD**

BELVOIR CL
CROMWELL RD
CRANMER A

A52(T)

**GRANTHAM RD**

Aslockton Grange

**39**

River Smite

GRANBY LA

CONERY LA

**1**

Starnhill Farm

Thorough Bridge

Dismantled Railway

Starnhill Plantation

Vicars Croft

**38**

71    **A**    72    **B**    73    **C**

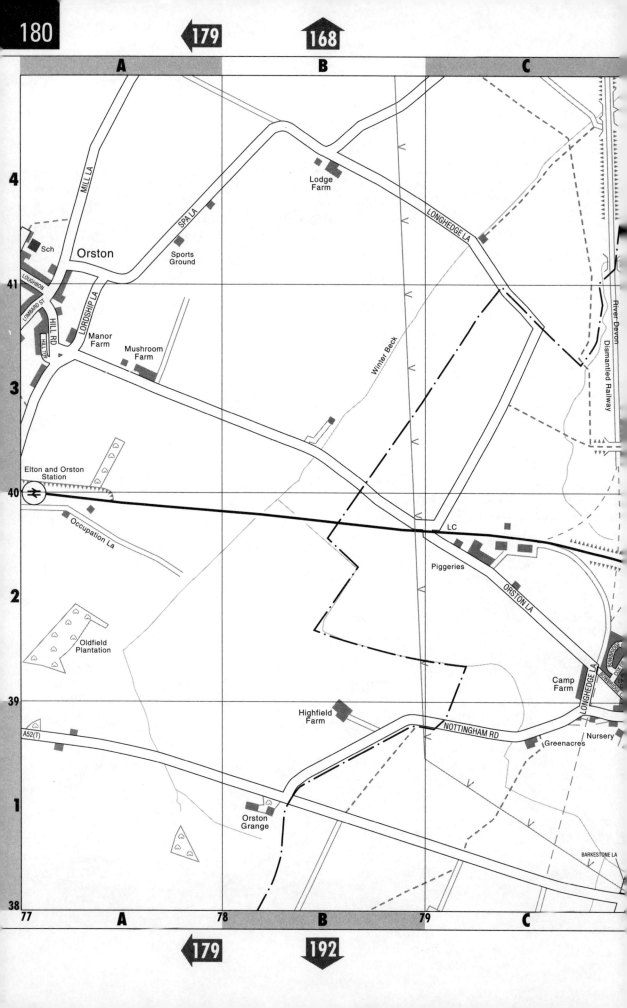

D | E | F

4

41

3

40

2

39

1

38

**River Devon**

Piggery

Airfield
(disused)

Ease
Drain

Normanton
Hall

Normanton
House

Peacock
Farm

Normanton

Little Covert
Farm

Elm Farm

Home Farm

NORMANTON LA

Sewage
Works

Beacon Hill

The
Nook
COX RD

Rectory
Farm

Beckingthorpe

LC

STROUD CT

LC STATION RD

Station

Bottesford

WIMBISH CLOSE

PINFOLD CL

THE PIT

KINGSTONE AVE

FABIS CLOSE

FARRIER'S WAY

CHURCH VIEW

DEVON LA

THE SQUARE

RECTORY LA

CHURCH ST

QUEEN ST

MARKET ST

CHAPEL ST

Ford

Walford Cl

ST MARY'S LA

WYGGESTON
AVE

CHAPEL HILL

EASTHORPE RD

DARRELL CT

RUTLAND L

FLEMING AVE

VAUGHAN AVE

HIGH ST

WEST END CL
NOTTINGHAM RD
BOWBRIDGE LA

PH

St Mary's La

HAND'S WLK

THE PADDOCKS

GRANTBY DR

NORTH CREST

SILVERWOOD RD

BELVOIR RD

BELVOIR AVE

BARKESTONE LA

WALNUT
RD

SOUTH KEEP

Schs

The
Elms

Manor
Farm

MANOR RD

GREEN LA

Easthorpe

EASTHORPE VIEW

South
View

River Devon

GRANTHAM RD

SKERRY LA

Castleview
Farm

CASTLE VIEW RD

MUSTON LA

Winterbeck
Bridge

A52(T)

A52(T)

CASTLE VIEW RD

EASTHORPE LA

Corner
Farm

SKERRY LA

A52(T)

Hospital
Farm

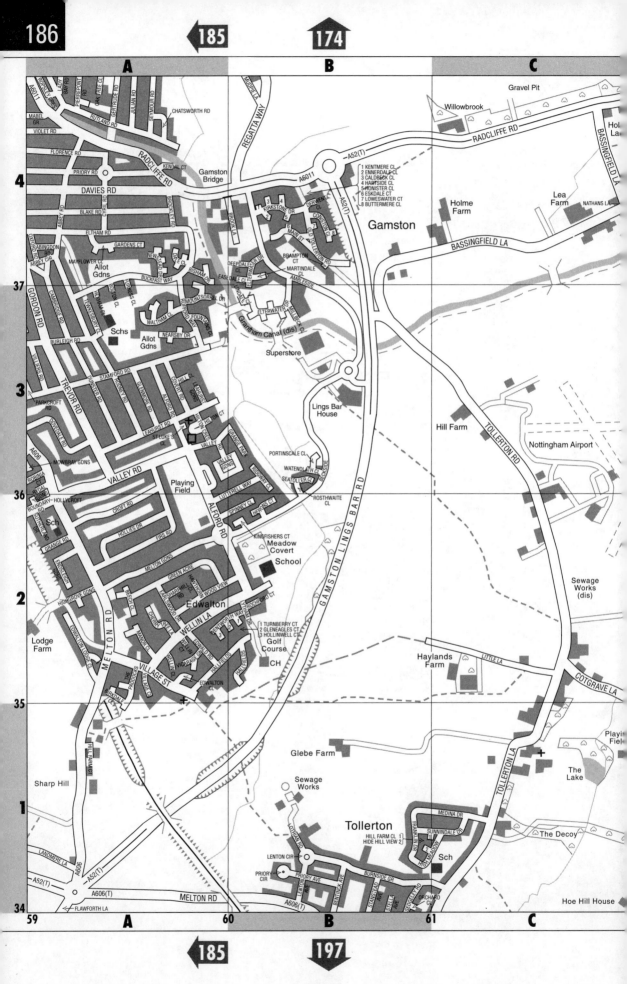

A    B    C

4

37

3

36

2

35

1

34

59    A    60    B    61    C

Gravel Pit

Willowbrook

RADCLIFFE RD

Hol La

BASSINGFIELD LA

A52(T)

A6011

1 KENTMERE CL
2 ENNERDALE CL
3 CALDBECK CL
4 HARTSIDE CL
5 HONISTER CL
6 ESKDALE CL
7 LOWESWATER CT
8 BUTTERMERE CL

Holme Farm

Lea Farm

NATHANS LA

Gamston

BASSINGFIELD LA

ROUSLEY RD
LADY BAY RD
HEREFORD RD
OAK TREE CL
JULIAN RD
SEYMOUR RD

CHATSWORTH RD

MABEL GR
VIOLET RD

RUTLAND RD

FLORENCE RD

RADCLIFFE RD

KENDAL CT

Gamston Bridge

PRIORY RD

DAVIES RD

ABBEY RD

BLAKE RD

BROCKLEY RD

ELTHAM RD

GARDENS CT

ABINGDON RD

ABBEY CIR

Mayflower CL

Allot Gdns

NEWSTEAD CL

CLARE CL

BISHAM DR

KIRKSTONE DR

DERWENT CL

OLD TOLLERTON RD

CONISTON CL

MAIN ST

BRAMPTON CT

MARTINDALE CL

AMBLESIDE

BROOK LA

DEEPDALE CL
EASEDALE CL
ELTERWATER

GORDON RD

CAMBRIDGE RD
HENKSBURY RD

BURGESS CL
BOLTON CL
MOUNT SORREL DR

WALTHAM CL

FOUNTAINS CL

NEARSBY DR

Schs

Allot Gdns

BURLEIGH RD

VILLIERS RD

STAMFORD RD

DUNSTER RD

ROONEY RD

GLENMORE RD

ALFORD RD

LEAHURST GDNS

COVERT RD

HILTON CT

Gramham Canal (dis)

Superstore

ELTERWATER

MILLBECK CL

Lings Bar House

PARKCROFT RD

TREVOR RD

MOWBRAY GDNS

DOVEDALE RD

ROBINIA CT
RYDAL
SYDNEY

ST LUKE'S CL

LEAHURST GDNS

GRANBY PARK

VALLEY GDNS

BUCKWATER

Portinscale CL
WATENDLATH CL
SEATOLLER CL

BECKSIDE

Hill Farm

TOLLERTON RD

Nottingham Airport

VALLEY RD

Playing Field

ALFORD RD

LUTTRELL WAY

SPINNEY CL

HOPKINS CT

Rosthwaite CL

Sch

Boundary-Hollycroft

SUTHERLAND RD
GRANGE RD

CROFT RD

HOLLIES DR

FIRS RD

KINGFISHERS CT

Meadow Covert

School

Sewage Works (dis)

EDINBORO

HIGHGROVE GDNS

MELTON GDNS

GREEN ACRE

HAYWARD CL

WOODVIEW

GAMSTON LINGS BAR RD

MELTON RD

WELLIN LA

Edwalton

HAWTHORN RD

BISHARP CL

WENTWORTH WAY

BROCHERD CT

1 TURNBERRY CT
2 GLENEAGLES CT
3 HOLLINWELL CT

Golf Course

Haylands Farm

LITTLE LA

Lodge Farm

EDWALTON LODGE CL

GREGORY CL

MANOR CL

WELLIN CT

EDWALTON CL

HALLFIELDS

HALL FIELDS

CH

COTGRAVE LA

The PADDOCKS

VILLAGE ST

VILLAGE ST

VICARAGE GREEN

Edwalton CL

HILL FARM RD

Glebe Farm

TOLLERTON LA

Playi Fiel

The Lake

Sharp Hill

Sewage Works

Tollerton

MEDINA DR

FRANKLIN DR

SUNNINDALE DR

HIGH MEADOW

Sch

The Decoy

LANDMERE LA

A52(T)

A606

A606(T)

MELTON RD

LOTHAM LA

LENTON CIR

PRIORY CIR

PRIORY AVE

BURNSIDE GR

HILL FARM CL
HIDE HILL VIEW

BENTINCK AVE

STANSTEAD AVE

STELLA AVE

ORCHARD

SELBY RD

Hoe Hill House

FLAWFORTH LA

A606(T)

D E F

4

37

3

36

2

35

1

34

RADCLIFFE RD
A52(T)

Polser Brook

Bassingfield

Caravan Site

Sewage Works

Thornton's Holt Farm

Shepherd's (PH)

North Farm

Nursery

Cotgrave Place

Slag Heap

Cotgrave Bridge

Cotgrave Colliery

Grantham Canal (dis)

Slag Heap

Thurlbeck Dyke

Peashill Farm

Windmill Hill

Sewage Works

MAIN RD

MILL
Chichester Dr
Morkinshire Cres
MORKINSHIRE LA
THURGON
Bingham Rd
THE PARK
PINFOLD CL
HOLLYGATE LA
EAST ACRES
CHURCH LA
THE CROSS
Sch
BINGHAM RD
COLSTON RD
HOMESTEAD
SCOTLAND BANK
THE PRECINCT
AVONDALE
MILLER HIVES CL
CANDLEBY CT
CANDLEBY LA
RISEGATE
WOODGATE LA
RECTORY LA
WOODGATE CL
BAKER'S HOLLOW
PLUMTREE RD
SCRIMSHIRE LA
HAZEL GR
FERRY
MENSING AV
GREEN PLAT
DRING CT
FOREST
1 LAMMLANDS
Sch
1
Schs
GREENFIELDS DR
ASH LEA CL
ASHOLME
CARTERSHOLT
RING LEAS
WHITE FURROWS
FERN LEA
DAISY
MANNS LEYS
NEWTHORN
NEWBOUND
SPINNEY
CORN
TOFT CL
DALESIDE
FOXHILL
THE DALE
WESTWAY
BARNWOOD
OTHORPE RD
RUMCIE
GRIPPS COMM
SAXON WAY
WARWICK GDNS
KINGSTON CT
THE WARREN
MILLERS BRIDGE 1
INGLEBY CL 2
BONNY MEAD

COTGRAVE LA

COTGRAVE RD

Collerton Wood
Hoehill Farm

GILLNER LA
CHURCH GATE
Manor Farm
Blackberry Farm
Wolds Lane
Clipston

Mill Lane

Brickyard Plantation

Scotton's Hill

A B C

4

Stragglethorpe

Cropwell
Court

New Barn
Farm

The
Grov

The
Limes

Barnsfie
Farm

37

Brown's
Cottages

Foss
Bridge

Berry
Hill

Sports
Gnd

Spoil
Heap

Hollygate
Farm

3

Cotgrave
Colliery

HOLLYGATE LA

Mann's
Bridge

Foss Way

ROMAN RD

36

Spoil
Heap

Hollygate
Bridge

NOTTINGHAM RD

Hollygate
Industrial
Park

Works

2

TROUTBECK

COLSTON GATE

Cropwell
Bridge

RIVERMEAD
AVONDALE
DEANSCOURT
LINGFORD
SPRING
MEADOW
WILLOWDENE
GRASSMERE
BRIAR DALE
HENDRE
CLOSE

Gypsum
Quarry

Hazeldean
Cottage

HAZELWOOD

Foss
House

CHENNEL NOOK
LITTLE
MEADOW
BRAMBLEWAY
THORNTON CT
RING LEAS
CROSSE

35

Cotgrave

Reservoir

WOODVIEW
WHITELANDS
BURHILL
CLOVERDALE
EASTWOLD
LAKENDALE
OAKENWOOD

Smith's
Round
Hill

Cotgrave
Gorse

Long
Plantation

Wolds
Farm

Groundwells
Farm

1

THURLBECK
SAXON WAY
W FENTONS
H SKINNING
BRIAR GATE
FOSS TILE

Cropwell
Wolds

Limekiln Inn
(PH)

SWAB'S LA

COLSTO

EDDINGTON CL
E MOOR

Stone Pit
Plantation

Limekiln
Farm

34

OWTHORPE RD

A46(T)

The Old
Farm House

65

A

66

B

67

C

D    E    F

Newlands

HARDIGATE RD

RADCLIFFE RD

Cropwell Butler

MAIN ST

BACK LA

THE POSTS

PH

CARPENTERS CL
CARPENTERS CL

HO LA

BUTLERS

Cemy

CROPWELL BISHOP RD

Lower
Brackendale
Farm

TITHBY RD

Manor
Farm

Tithby

Holly
Tree
Farm

TITHBY RD

BINGHAM RD

Wiverton
Hall
Farm

37

New
Plantation

Meadow Lane

3

36

Cropwell Bishop

HUEY NOOK RD
PARKIN CL
COOPER CL
NEVIN LA
NEWBERY CL
BROWNHILL CL
MARSHALL
FIELD LA
HEY NOOK RD
BARRATT CL
RICHARDS CL
CLARKE CL
OLD LENTON CL

THIRLBY RD
HARDYS CL
HALL DR
KENDAL CL
THE MALTINGS
ST GILES WAY
ST MARTIN CL
STOCKWELL LA
DOBEN CL
CHURCH ST
SPRINGFIELD CL
ETHELDENE
CROPWELL BUTLER RD

PH
Sch

NOTTINGHAM RD

Home
Farm

Spring
Hill

Fern
Hill

Fern
Hill

Fern
Hill

FERN RD

Mill Hill

Pasture Lane

Fern Hill
Farm

Ash Holt

Langar
Lane
Covert

Langar
Lane
Bridge

2

35

River Smite

NEW RD

Edmondthorpe
Lodge

Winifred
Wood

1

Old
Brickyard
Plantation

Blue
Hill

COLSTON RD

Colston
Bridge

Home
Farm

Blanches
Gorse

WASH PIT LA

34

D    69    E    70    F

189
178

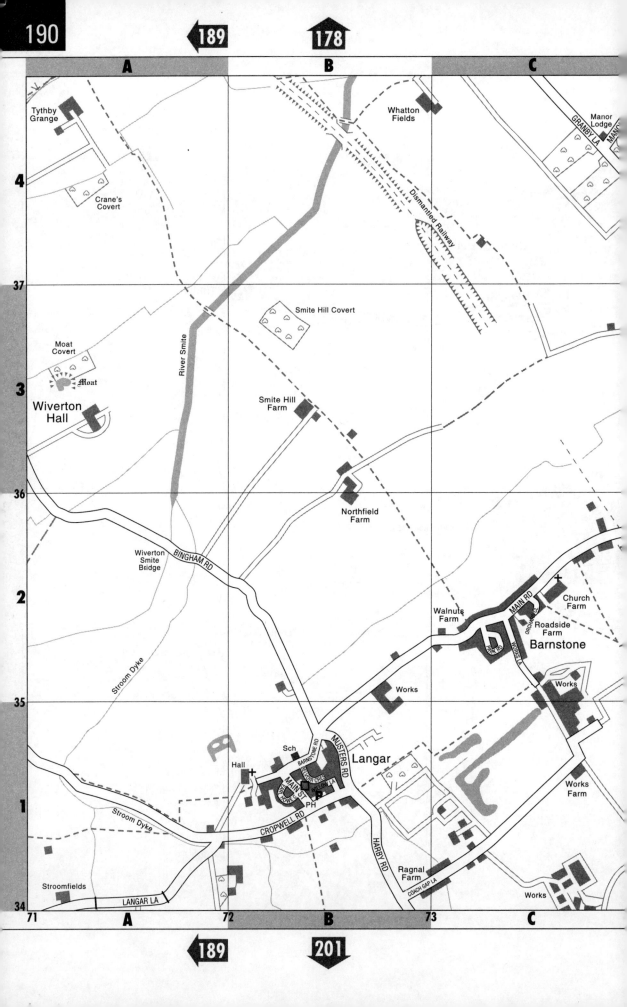

189
201

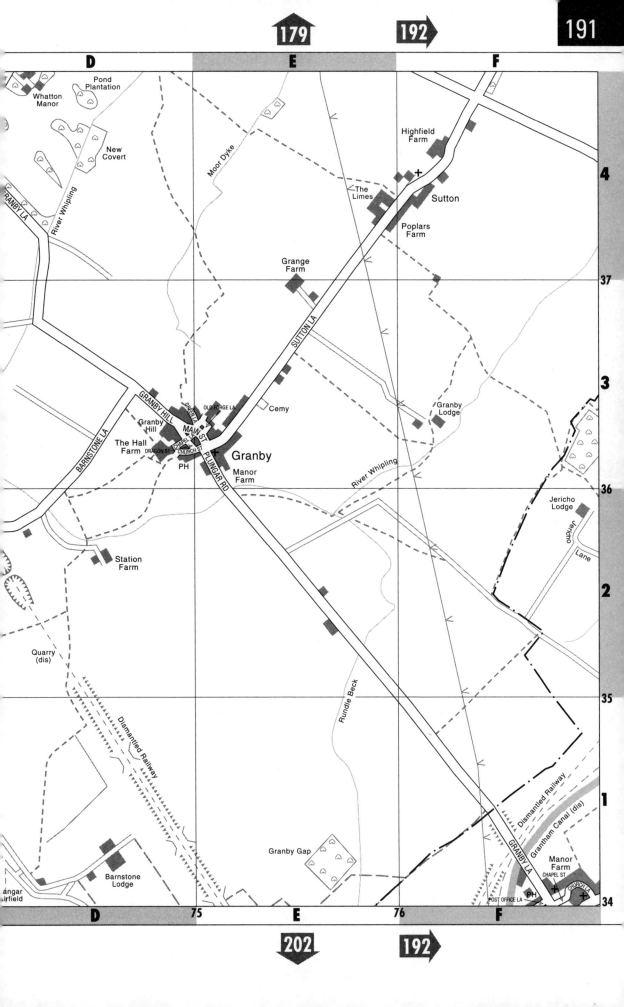

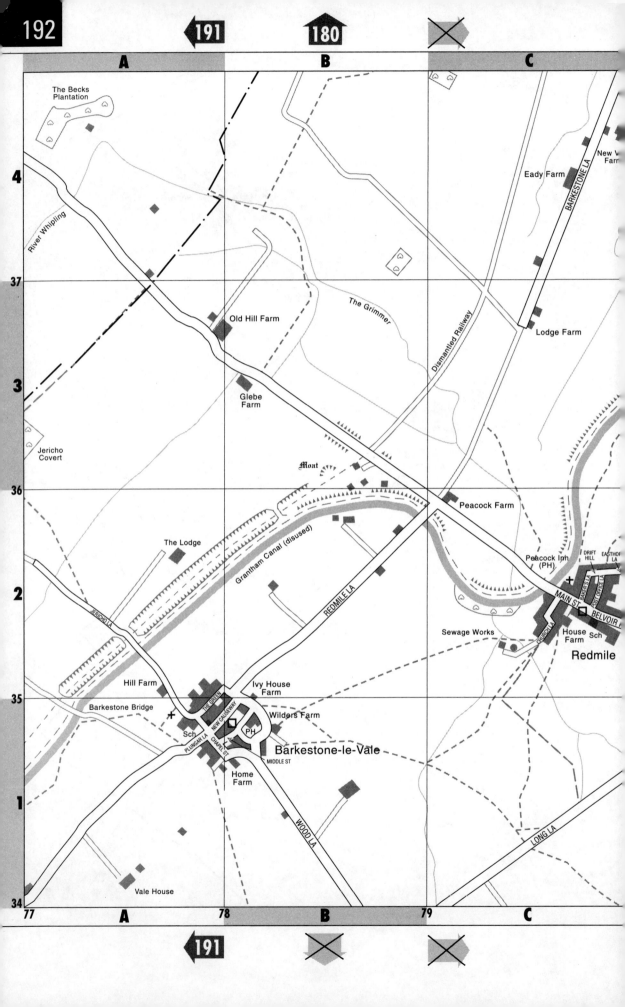

A
B
C

The Becks
Plantation

River Whipling

4

Eady Farm

BARKESTONE LA

New V
Farm

37

The Grimmer

Old Hill Farm

Dismantled Railway

Lodge Farm

3

Glebe
Farm

Jericho
Covert

Moat

Peacock Farm

36

The Lodge

Grantham Canal (disused)

REDMILE LA

Peacock Inn
(PH)

DRIFT
HILL

EASTHOF
LA

BAKERS LA

POST OFFICE LA

2

JERICHO LA

MAIN ST

BELVOIR

Sewage Works

CHURCH LA

House
Farm

Sch

Redmile

Hill Farm

Ivy House
Farm

35

Barkestone Bridge

THE GREEN

NEW CAUSEWAY

Wilders Farm

Sch

PLUNGAR LA

CHAPEL ST

PH

Barkestone-le-Vale

MIDDLE ST

Home
Farm

1

WOOD LA

LONG LA

Vale House

34
77
A
78
B
79
C

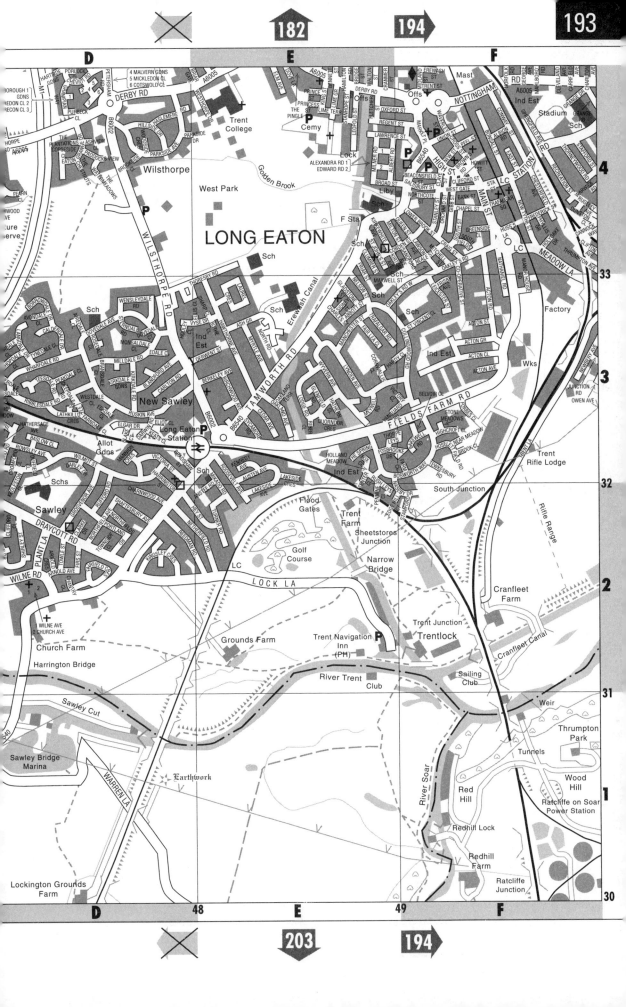

A　　　　　　B　　　　　　C

**4**

Nottingham Rd
Station Rd
HARLAXTON DR
SOMERSET CL
Sewage Works
The Warren
Attenborough Nature Reserve
Barton Island
Golden Brook
Long Eaton Sailing Club
River Erewash
Attenborough Junction
River Trent
FB
1 WARWICK RD
2 LITCHFIELD CL
3 RUGELEY AVE
CLIFTON AVE
LC
Grange Farm
Brands Wood

**33**

LC
1 THRUMPTON AVE
2 CHATSWORTH AVE
MEADOW LA
Trent Meadows (Picnic area)
Old Farm
CHESTNUT LA
BROWN LA
CHURCH
NEW RD
Brands Wood
PASTURE LA
Home Farm
JUNCTION RD
RIVER LA
LITTLE LA
Manor Farm
**Barton in Fabis**
MANOR RD

**3**

GREEN ST

**32**

Cranfleet Lock
Cranfleet Canal
Glebe Farm
Fields Farm

**2**

Ferry Farm
**Thrumpton**
Thrumpton Park
Thrumpton Hall
CHURCH LA
Manor Farm
Crowhole Wood

**31**

Church Farm
Wood Farm
Gotham Hill
Old Wood
Twenty Lands Plantation
Hillside Cottage
Gotham Hill Wood
Wright's Hill
Wright's Hill Plantation
Cottagers Hill

**1**

Cottagers Hill Spinney
Old Wood
Morley's Barn Farm
Power Station
A453(T)
Stonepit Wood

**30**

50　　　　　A　　　51　　　B　　　52　　　C

D
E
F

4

33

Plumtree

3

32

2

31

1

30

FLAWFORTH LA

...hire ...arm

Flawford House

Barn Farm

Blackcliffe Hill

BRADMORE LA

BENTINCK AVE

A606(T)

STANSTEAD AV

STELLA

A AVE

BERKELEY

MOOR AVE

TOLLERTON LA

MELTON RD

MAIN RD

CHURCH LA

ST LONGS

BEARLE BLVD

PH

OLD MELTON RD

Hall Farm

CLIPSTON LA

THE LEYS

COTGRAVE RD

A606(T)

The Poplars

Chestnut Farm

STATION RD

Plumtree Park

PARK RD

PARK TER

PARK AVE

GREEN CL

POPLARS CL

PARK SIDE

PLATT LA

Sch

BROOKDALE

BRIAR CL

ROSE GR

NICKER HILL

HILLCREST RD

BELVEDERE

BROADWOOD

VILLA RD

NORMANTON LA

NOWLANDS DR

COVERT CL

HIGHBURY RD

ABBOT CL

FRANKLYN GDNS

ADAMS HILL

CLIFFORD CL

LYNCOMBE GDNS

RANCLIFFE AVE

DEVILLE AVE

BISHOPS CL

SIDMOUTH CL

WYNDBECK DR

WOLDS RISE

2

DEBDALE LA

SPINNEY RD

HAYES RD

GORSE RD

PLANTATION RD

THE DALE

DALE RD

THELDA AVE

ASHLEY CRES

ASHLEY RD

GRANTOCK

CHERRY AVE

PARK LANE VIEW

FAIRWAY

INTAKE RD

FAIRHAM RD

CROFT RD

HIGHFIELD

ROSE HILL

NOTTINGHAM RD

RANNOCK GDNS

CHURCH DR

Sch

Liby

BEECH AVE

31

PARK AVE W

PARK AVE E

WEST CL

EAST CL

CHARNWOOD

Sch

ELM AVE

ELM CL

WINDMILL CT

LAUREL AVE

ASH GR

Cotton's Plantation

Greenhays Farm

Woodfields

BUNNY LA

HAWTHORN CL

PH

THE SQUARE

SELBY LA

Keyworth

Rancliffe Wood

Wheatcroft Farm

Hillside Farm

WRIGHTS ORCHARD

FAB PASTURE CL

HOLME CL

COMMERCIAL RD

MAIN ST

CEDAR DR

Holly Farm

PENDOCK LA

KEYWORTH LA

WYSALL RD

Sewage Works

BARROW SLADE

LINGS LA

PH

Long Plantation

Bunny Park

New Holme Farm

Lings Lane Farm

197
187

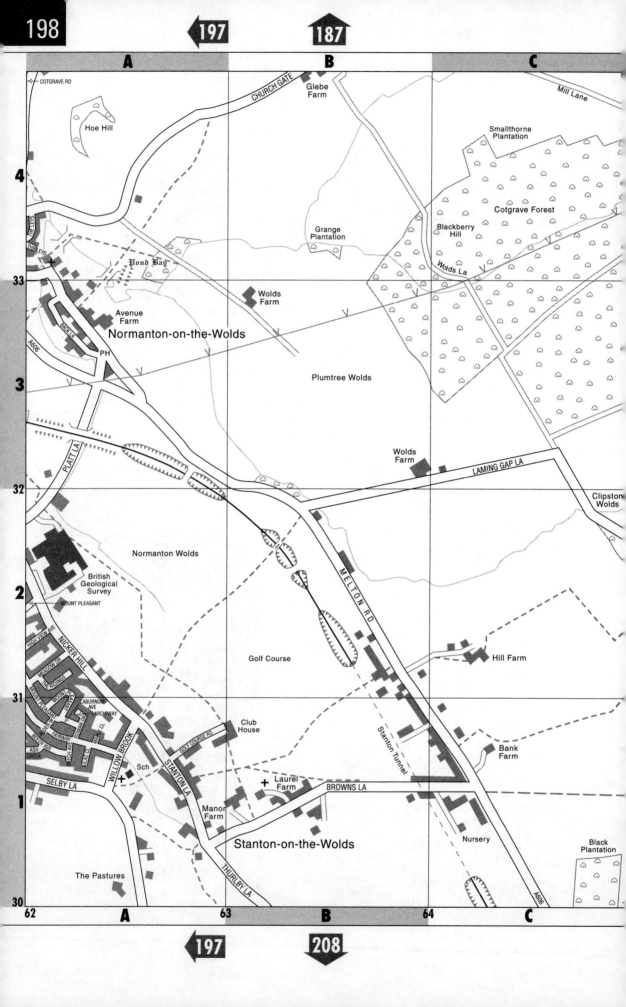

A      B      C

← COTGRAVE RD

Hoe Hill

CHURCH GATE

Glebe Farm

Mill Lane

Smallthorne Plantation

**4**

Cotgrave Forest

Grange Plantation

Blackberry Hill

THE LEYS

THE LEYS

Pond Bay

Wolds La

**33**

Wolds Farm

BACK LA

Avenue Farm

**Normanton-on-the-Wolds**

A606

PH

Plumtree Wolds

**3**

PLATT LA

Wolds Farm

LAMING GAP LA

**32**

Clipston Wolds

Normanton Wolds

MELTON RD

British Geological Survey

MOUNT PLEASANT

**2**

Golf Course

Hill Farm

HIGH VIEW AVE

NICKER HILL

MEADOW DR

THE RIDINGS

MAIN RD

MAIN RD

**31**

LABURNUM AVE

LARCHWAY

Club House

Stanton Tunnel

Bank Farm

MAPLE CL

RIVIAN DR

FAIRWAY

GOLF COURSE RD

WILLOW BROOK

BEECH AVE

LILAC CL

ASH GROVE

STANTON LA

Sch

Laurel Farm

BROWNS LA

SELBY LA

Manor Farm

Nursery

**1**

Black Plantation

**Stanton-on-the-Wolds**

The Pastures

THURLBY LA

A606

**30**

62      A      63      B      64      C

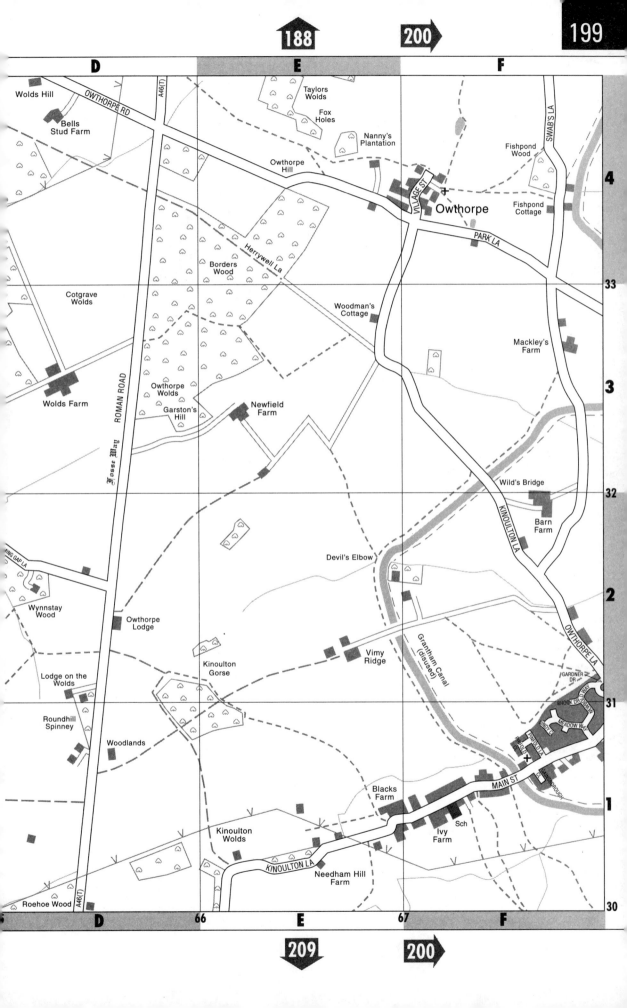

D
E
F

4

33

3

32

2

31

1

30

Wolds Hill
OWTHORPE RD
A46(T)
Taylors
Wolds
Fox
Holes
Nanny's
Plantation
SWAB'S LA

Bells
Stud Farm
Owthorpe
Hill
Fishpond
Wood

Borders
Wood
Herrywell La
VILLAGE ST
Owthorpe
Fishpond
Cottage

Cotgrave
Wolds
PARK LA

Woodman's
Cottage
Mackley's
Farm

ROMAN ROAD

Owthorpe
Wolds

Wolds Farm
Garston's
Hill
Newfield
Farm

Fosse Way

Wild's Bridge

KINOULTON LA

Barn
Farm

RAMING GAP LA

Devil's Elbow

Wynnstay
Wood
Owthorpe
Lodge

Grantham Canal
(disused)
OWTHORPE LA

Lodge on the
Wolds
Kinoulton
Gorse
Vimy
Ridge
GARDNER
DR

Roundhill
Spinney

BROOK DR
MEADOW WAY

Woodlands

Blacks
Farm
MAIN ST

Kinoulton
Wolds
Ivy
Farm
Sch

A46(T)

Roehoe Wood
Needham Hill
Farm
KINOULTON LA

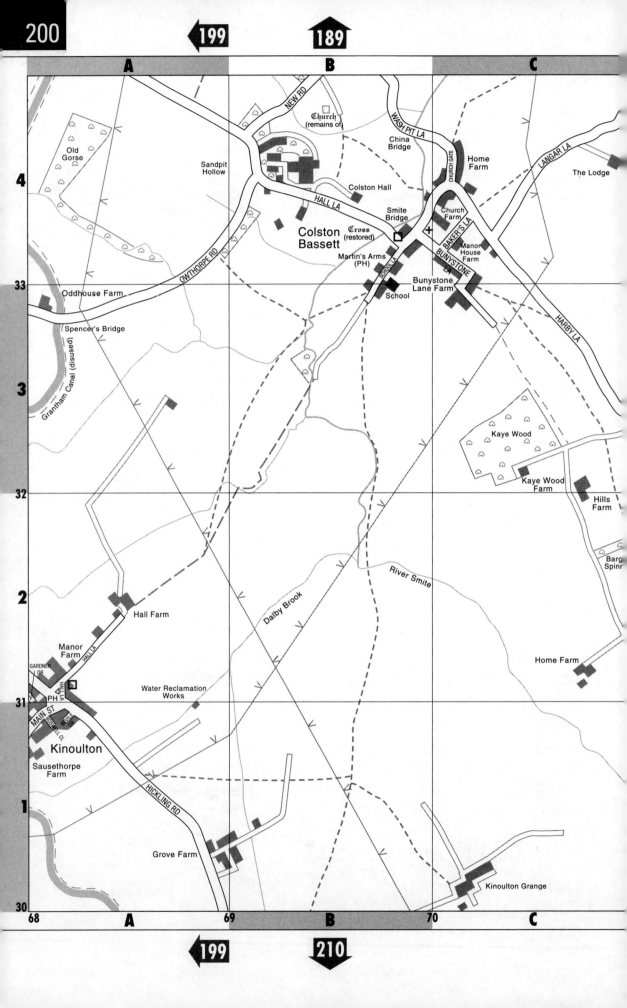

**A**    **B**    **C**

NEW RD

Church
(remains of)

WASH PIT LA

China
Bridge

Old
Gorse

Sandpit
Hollow

HALL LA

Colston Hall

LANGAR LA

Home
Farm

The Lodge

**4**

Smite
Bridge

CHURCH GATE

Church
Farm

OWTHORPE RD

Colston
Bassett

Cross
(restored)

Martin's Arms
(PH)

BAKER'S LA

Manor
House
Farm

BUNYSTONE LA

SCHOOL LA

Bunystone
Lane Farm

Oddhouse Farm

**33**

School

HARBY LA

Spencer's Bridge

Grantham Canal (disused)

Kaye Wood

**3**

Kaye Wood
Farm

Hills
Farm

**32**

Barg
Spinn

River Smite

**2**

Hall Farm

Dalby Brook

Home Farm

Manor
Farm

HALL LA

GARDNER DR

SMITH DR

Water Reclamation
Works

**31**

PH

MAIN ST

RUSSELL CL

NEVILE CR

Kinoulton

Sausethorpe
Farm

HICKLING RD

**1**

Grove Farm

Kinoulton Grange

**30**

68    **A**    69    **B**    70    **C**

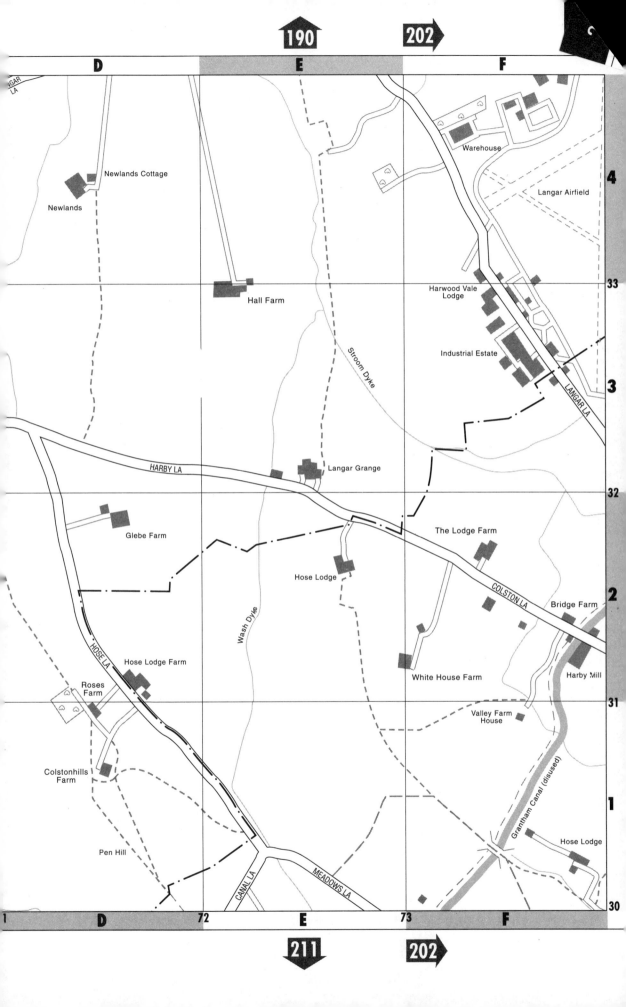

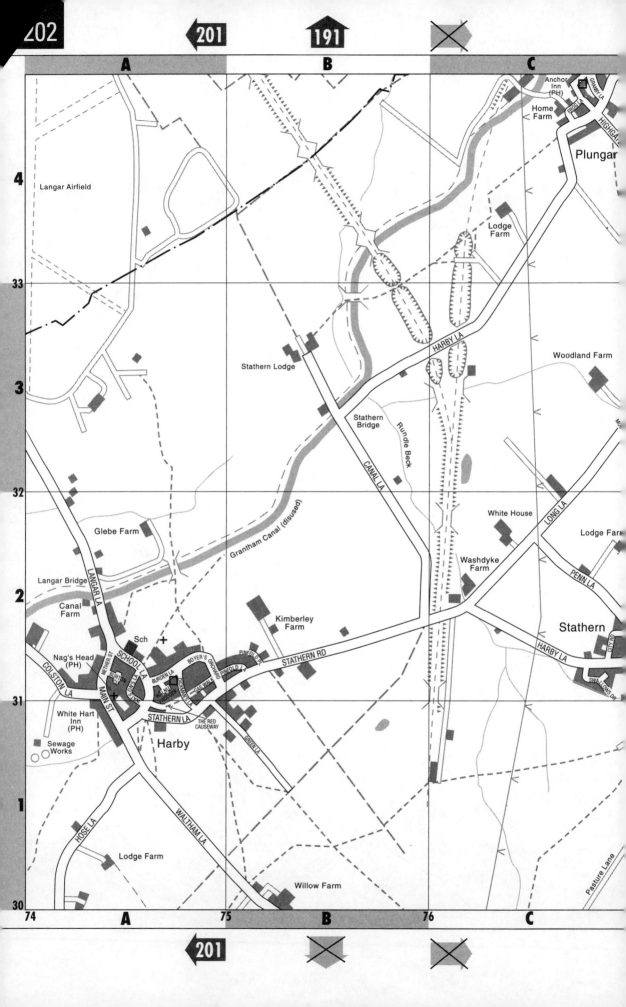

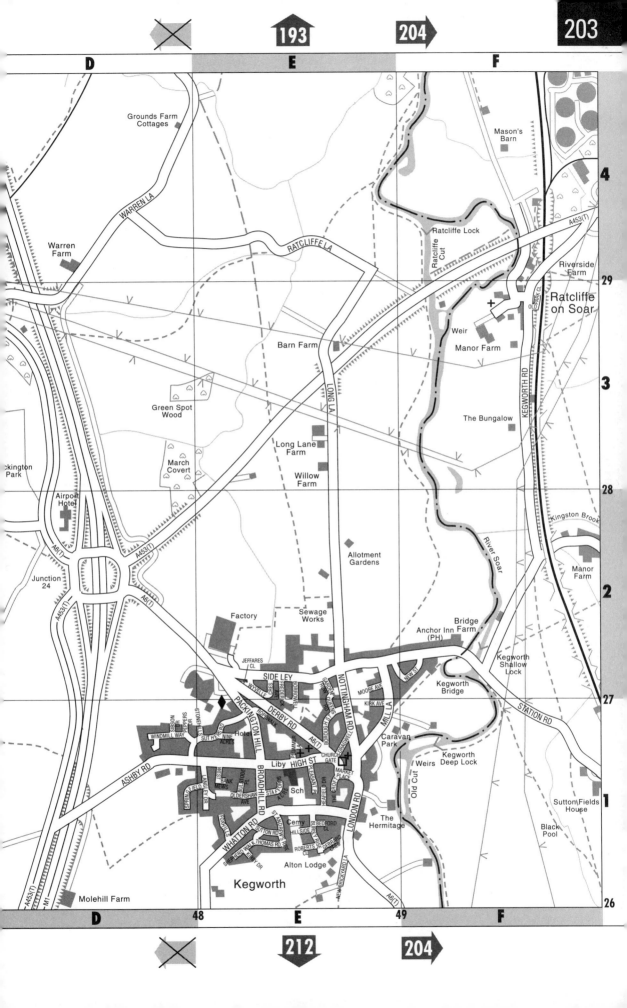

D E F

4

Grounds Farm
Cottages

Mason's
Barn

WARREN LA

RATCLIFFE LA

Ratcliffe Lock

Riverside
Farm

Warren
Farm

29

Ratcliffe
Cut

Ratcliffe
on Soar

Weir

Barn Farm

Manor Farm

LONG LA

KEGWORTH RD

3

Green Spot
Wood

The Bungalow

Long Lane
Farm

March
Covert

Willow
Farm

28

ckington
Park

Airport
Hotel

Kingston Brook

River Soar

Manor
Farm

A6(T)

A453(T)

A6(T)

Junction
24

Allotment
Gardens

2

A453(T)

Factory

Sewage
Works

Bridge
Anchor Inn Farm
(PH)

Kegworth
Shallow
Lock

JEFFARES
CL

SIDE LEY

NEW ST

Kegworth
Bridge

27

A453(T)

M1

DERBY RD

NOTTINGHAM RD

MOORE AVE

KIRK AVE

MILL LA

Kegworth
Deep Lock

STATION RD

PACKINGTON HILL

A6(T)

Caravan
Park

SIBSON
DR

WINDMILL WAY

Hotel

Weirs

Liby

HIGH ST

CHURCH
GATE

MARKET
PLACE

Sutton Fields
House

1

ASHBY RD

BROADHILL RD

Sch

LONDON RD

The Hermitage

Black
Pool

WHATTON RD

Cemy

HILLSIDE

Alton Lodge

Kegworth

26

Molehill Farm

A453(T)

A6(T)

D 48 E 49 F

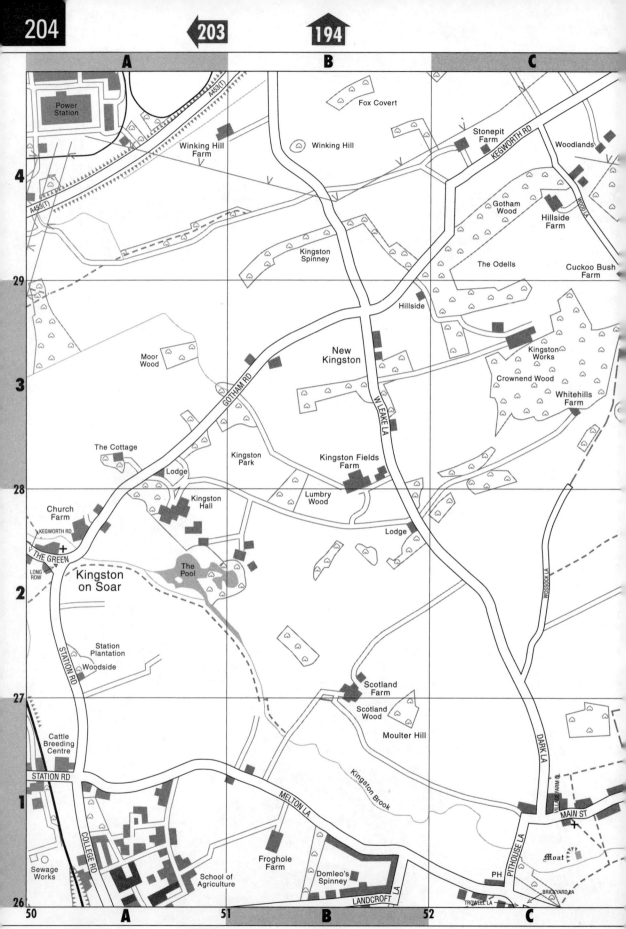

Power
Station

A453(T)

A453(T)

Winking Hill
Farm

Fox Covert

Winking Hill

Stonepit
Farm

KEGWORTH RD

Woodlands

Gotham
Wood

Hillside
Farm

Kingston
Spinney

The Odells

Cuckoo Bush
Farm

Hillside

Moor
Wood

New
Kingston

Kingston
Works

Crownend Wood

Whitehills
Farm

GOTHAM RD

W LEAKE LA

The Cottage

Kingston
Park

Kingston Fields
Farm

Lodge

Church
Farm

Kingston
Hall

Lumbry
Wood

KEGWORTH RD.

Lodge

+

THE GREEN

LONG
ROW

The Pool

Kingston
on Soar

KOSSOCK LA

Station
Plantation

STATION RD

Woodside

Scotland
Farm

Scotland
Wood

Moulter Hill

27

Cattle
Breeding
Centre

DARK LA

Kingston Brook

VILLAGE FARM DL

STATION RD

MELTON LA

MAIN ST

1

COLLEGE RD

Sewage
Works

School of
Agriculture

Froghole
Farm

Domleo's
Spinney

PH

PITHOUSE LA

Moat

X

LANDCROFT LA

TROWELL LA

BRICKYARD LA

26

50

A

51

B

52

C

D
E
F

MOOR LA

Fairholme
Farm

Gotham Moor
Farm

FYRES LA

HILL RD

Dismantled Railway

Paradise

4

Works

Cuckoo
Bush

29

Cuckoo
Bush Farm

Tumulus

LEAKE RD

Ridgeway
Plantation

Kismet

Hotchley Hill
Farm

Court Hill
Shiddock's
Spinney

BUNNY LA

Hotchley
Bungalows

3

Golf Course

Highthorn
Farm

Hotchley
Hill

Leake New
Wood

West Leake
Hills

Moat

Gypsum
Works

28

Crow Wood
Hill

Railway (disused)

Stone
House

CH

Sports
Ground

Mine

Sharpley
Hill

2

Grange
Farm

The
Cottage

Crow
Wood

STOCKING LA

Rushcliffe
Lodge

RUSHCLIFFE GR

STONE CRES

ANGRAVE RD

SHARPLEY DR

Ash
Spinney

Fir Dale
Plantation

WEAVERS CL

ST MARY'S CRES

ELM AVE

R HOLME RD

MANOR RD

GOTHAM RD

The
Heavens

SWEET LEYS DR

HOLME AVE

27

Fox
Hill

Fox Hill
Farm

LANTERN LA

Foxhill Wood

Schs

BROCKHILL RD

FISHERS

CARLTON CRES

MONKS MEADOW

TAFT LEYS RD

STONEBRIDGE DR

Kingston Brook

West Leake

East Leake

BATEMAN RD

SOUTHWELL CL

MANOR FARM
MEADOW

DE FERRERS CL

F Sta
P
Liby

1

MAIN ST

THE KEEP

Masts

BIRCH LEA

ROPE WALK

YORK CL

EXETER RD

TRURO CL

WINCHESTER CL

CHURCH

COSTOCK RD

Sewage
Works

Allot
Gdns

W LEAKE RD

STATION RD

FIELD END CL

ROSE AVE

SYCAMORE

TWENTYL...

OAK CRES

BROOKSIDE
AVE

OLD RECTORY CL
BROOKSIDE
Sch

SCHOOL G

BURTON WK

School G

THE NOOK

POTTERS

CROMWELL DR

HAWLEY CL

BISHOP AVE

OLD HOPYS

OLDERSHAW RD

MEETING HOUSE CL

CASTLE HILL

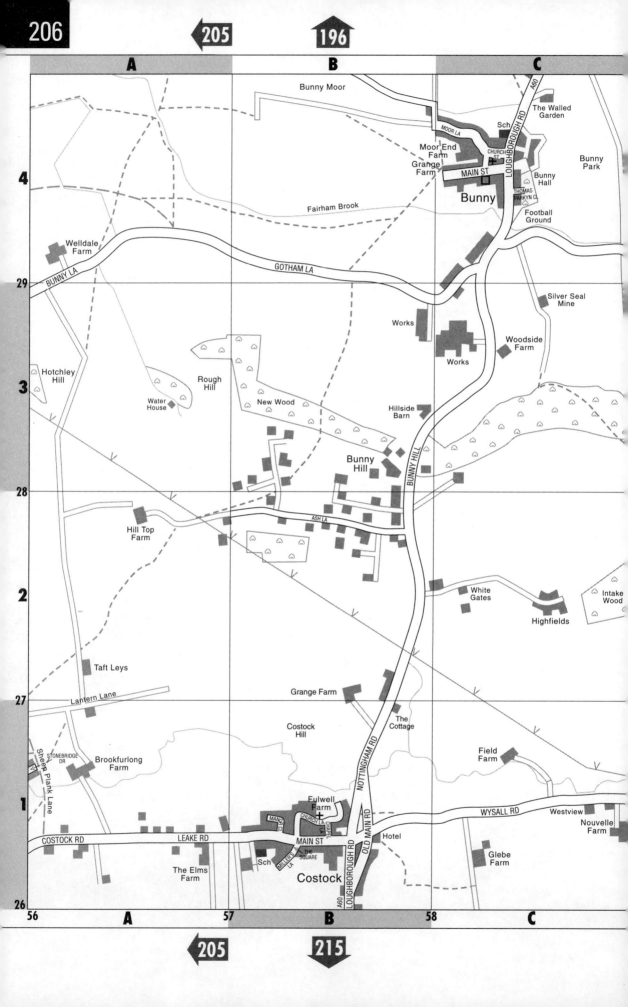

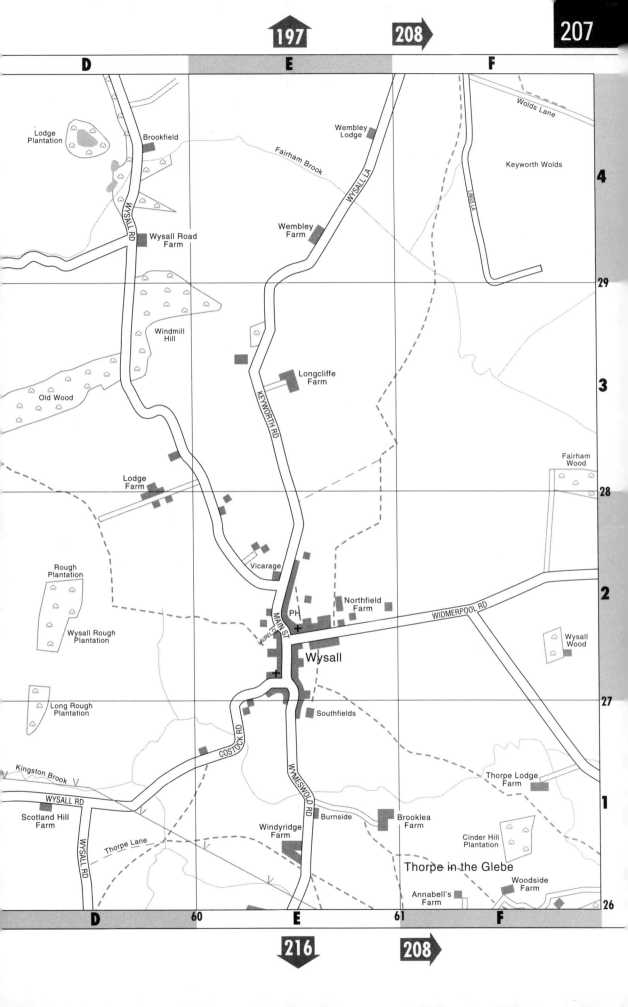

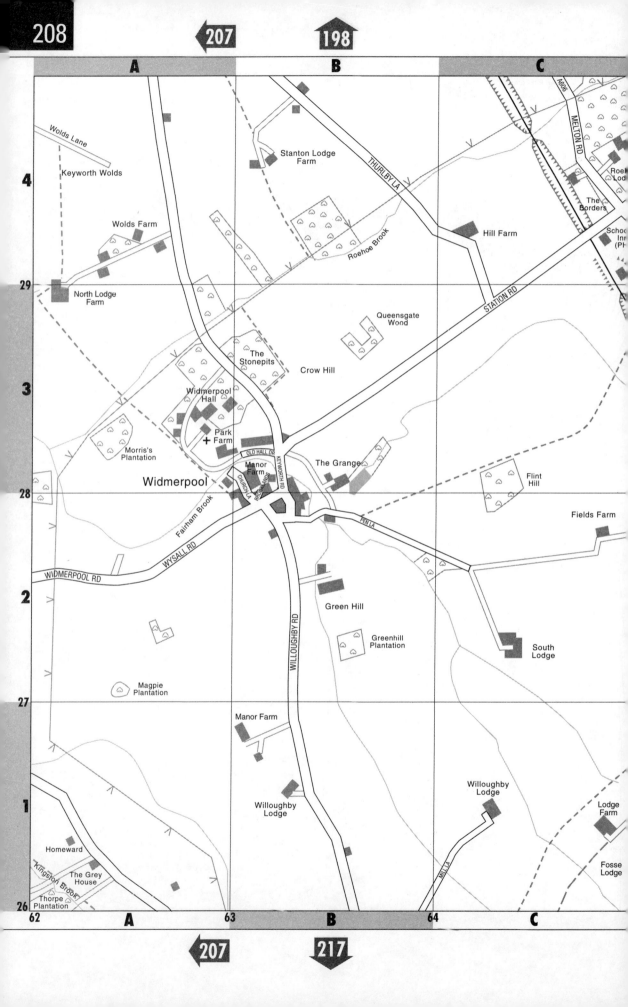

**A**     **B**     **C**

Wolds Lane

Keyworth Wolds

Stanton Lodge
Farm

THURLBY LA

4

Wolds Farm

Roehoe Brook

Hill Farm

STATION RD

29

North Lodge
Farm

Queensgate
Wood

The
Stonepits

Crow Hill

3

Widmerpool
Hall

Morris's
Plantation

Park
Farm

OLD HALL DR

The Grange

Flint
Hill

Manor
Farm

KEYWORTH RD

28

Widmerpool

CHURCH LA

BROOKSIDE

Fairham Brook

PEN LA

Fields Farm

WYSALL RD

WIDMERPOOL RD

WILLOUGHBY RD

Green Hill

Greenhill
Plantation

South
Lodge

2

Magpie
Plantation

27

Manor Farm

1

Willoughby
Lodge

Willoughby
Lodge

Lodge
Farm

MILL LA

Homeward

Kingston Brook

The Grey
House

Fosse
Lodge

26

Thorpe
Plantation

62     **A**     63     **B**     64     **C**

A606

MELTON RD

Roe
Lod

The
Borders

Scho
Inn
(PH

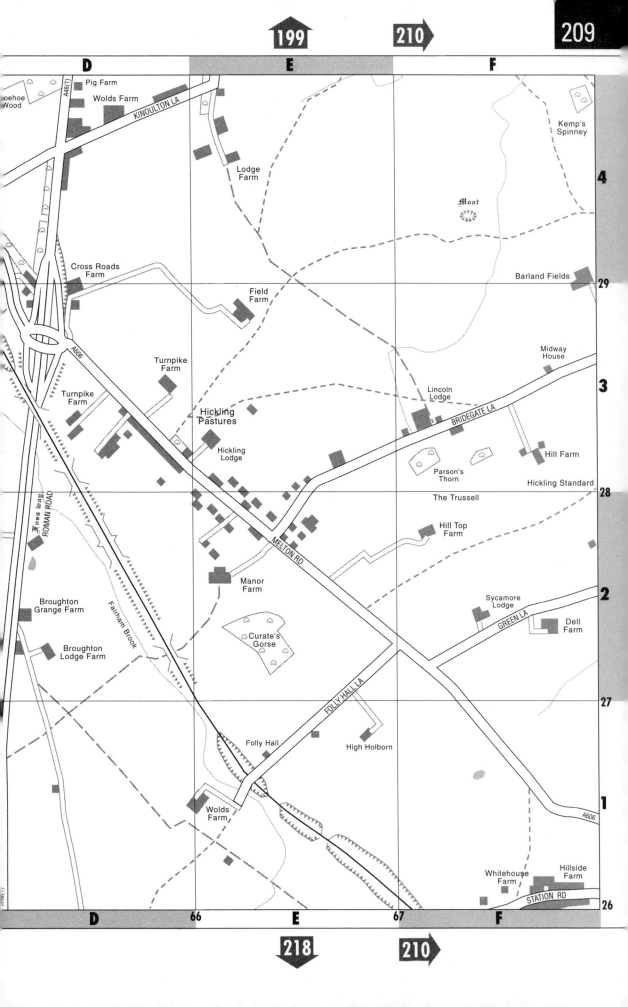

D
E
F

Pig Farm
Wolds Farm
KINOULTON LA
Kemp's Spinney
oehoe Wood

Lodge Farm

**Moat**

4

Cross Roads Farm

Barland Fields

29

Field Farm

Midway House

A606

Turnpike Farm

Lincoln Lodge

BRIDEGATE LA

3

Turnpike Farm

Hickling Pastures

Hill Farm

Hickling Lodge

Parson's Thorn

Hickling Standard

28

The Trussell

ROMAN ROAD
Foss way

Hill Top Farm

MELTON RD

Manor Farm

Broughton Grange Farm

Sycamore Lodge

2

Fairham Brook

Curate's Gorse

GREEN LA

Dell Farm

Broughton Lodge Farm

27

FOLLY HALL LA

Folly Hall

High Holborn

1

A606

Wolds Farm

Whitehouse Farm

Hillside Farm

STATION RD

26

209
200

A                    B                    C

4

Clarke's
Bridge

Bridge
Farm

Bridge
Farm                Hickling RD

Grantham Canal (disused)          Canal
Farm

The Plough Inn
(PH)

Church
Farm            Waterlane
Farm

Elms Farm

Hickling

29

Cricket
Ground          MARSH'S
PADDOCK     Burial
Ground          CLAWSON LA

BRIDEGATE LA          Manor
House                          Canal
Farm

Hickling RD

MAIN ST          The Green

CHARLES ACRES

LONG LA

3                            PUDDING LA

Oak
Farm

Castle
View

28

Hickling Standard

GREEN LA          Dalby Brook          Sherbrooke Fox
Covert

River Smite

2

27

Muxlow
Hill                                                                Bridge
Farm

BROUGHTON LA

1

A606          Sulney
Fields

COLONELS LA

CHURCH LA

Upper
Broughton

CLAWSON LA

The Golden Fleece
(PH)

TOP GREEN          CHAPEL LA

STA
RD          BOTTOM GREEN          MELTON RD

CHURCH END

26          Corner Farm          NOTTINGHAM RD          A606

68                    A          69                    B          70          C

209          219

**D**　　**E**　　**F**

The Grange

Long Clawson Bridge

MEADOWS LA

Bridge House

Grantham Canal (disused)

CANAL LA

Wash Dyke

Hose Thorns

Marriott's Bridge

Works

STROUDS CL

COAL

CHAPEL LA

HARBY LA

**4**

Hose Lodge

**Hose**

PH

MIDDLE

ST

GREEN

HOME

PASTURE

GREEN

DAIRY LA

CHURCH CL

Sch

BOLTON LA

Homeleigh Farm

Black Horse (PH)

**29**

PASTURE LA

CANAL LA

Dam Dyke

HOSE LA

Brook Farm

Glebe Farm

**3**

Highfield Farm

Sewage Works

**28**

Hall Farm

Dovecote Farm

Old Hall Farm

WATER LA

**2**

HICKLING LA

Rushland Farm

EAST END

PH

Bakers Farm

THE SANDS

Manor House

West End Farm

CHURCH LA

SCHOOL LA

Sch

Long Clawson

Hollytree Farm

BACK LA

PH

**27**

BROUGHTON LA

WEST END

RICHARDS PL

CLAXTON RISE

SANDPIT LA

KINGS RD

MILL LA

WALTHAM LA

Hill Farm

Cemy

Brockhill Cottage

CORONATION AVE

Sherbrook Farm

Mill Farm

MELTON RD

Windmill (disused)

**1**

Slyborough Hill

Old Mill House

Sandpit Farm

**26**

**D**　72　**E**　73　**F**

A      B      C

ASHBY RD A453(T)

M1

M42

M1

A42

A42

M1

SOAR LA

A6(T)

Springhouse
Farm

WHATTON RD

4

PH

Slade
Spinney

Devil's
Elbow

25

Slade
Farm

LONDON RD

River So

Windmill
Farm

Lodge

His
Lordships

Intensive Dairy
Unit

Home
Farm

Woodyard
Plantation

3

KEGWORTH LA

Five Acre

Whatton
House

Ash
Spinney

Gallow's
Wood

Gorse
Covert

24

Manor
House
Farm

Marylea
Farm

Lodge

B5401   WEST END

Whatton
Fields
Farm

Long Whatton

MILL LA

Long Whatton
Mill

M1

2

+

MAIN ST

MANOR CL

BARRIE RD

PH

Manor
Farm

Long Whatton Brook

Long Whatton
Mill

Sch

+

Sewage
Works

THE GREEN

PH

PIPER CL

HATHERN RD

23

Rose Hill

SPRING LA

OAKLEY DR

B5401

Hathern
Turn

SMITHY LA

WHATTON RD

DERBY RD

ZOUCH P

A60

B5324

DRY POT LA

Works

WIDE LA

P

1

Piper
Farm

SHEPSHED RD

B588

Mitchell's
Spring
Farm

Oakley Wood

Oakley Grange
Farm

22

B5324

M1

47      A      48      B      49      C

BRICKYARD LA

Coll
LANDCROFT LA

Glebe
Farm

Valley
Farm
Cemy

SOAR LA

MARLE PIT HILL
COLLEGE RD

Coll

California
Farm

4

Sutton
Bonington

Hall Farm

California
Plantation

PH
BOLLARD LA
BUCK ST

The Hall

St Anne's
Manor

HUNGARY LA

TROWELL LA

Cold Harbour
Plantation

MAIN ST

25

PH

+

Cold Harbour
Farm

A6006

ST ANNE'S LA
SWAN LA

PASTURE LA

PH
PADDOCKS
GATE'S LEA

REMPSTONE RD

PH
Sch
Park Lane
Farm

3

The
Cedars

ORCHARD CL
WILLOW POOL LA

CHARNWOOD AVE

SHEPHERD'S CL

Industrial
Estate

PARK LA

SUTTON CL
CHARNWOOD FIELDS

24

BUTT LA

Tebbutt's
Farm

MOOR LA

2

Zouch
Lock

Zouch Cut

PH

FAR LA

PH

Zouch
Farm

MAIN ST

Normanton on Soar

Zouch

P

River Soar

Sch

Butt
Lane
Bridge

ZOUCH RD

Zouch
Bridge

MAIN ST

SOAR ST
PH

23

The
Stints

Village Rd

PASTURE LA

STANFORD RD

Ferry

Bowley's
Barn
Farm

Cemy

Bowley's
Bridge

1

ROWAN AVE
HAWTHORNE AV
GREEN HILL RISE

LibY
THE GREEN
GREEN HILL

WIDE LA

PENFOLD LA

LABURNUM CL
Sch
WESLEY CL
CROSS ST
ST PETER'S AVE

NARROW LA
THE FARTHINGS
GLADSTONE ST
OLD FORGE CL

Hathern

River
Soar

HIGH MEADOW
LOVEDAY ST
LOUGHBOROUGH RD
SWAN INN YD
OLD WAY

22

RD A6(T)
LANGHAM CL
TANNER'S LA
ANCHOR LA

0    D    51    E    52    F

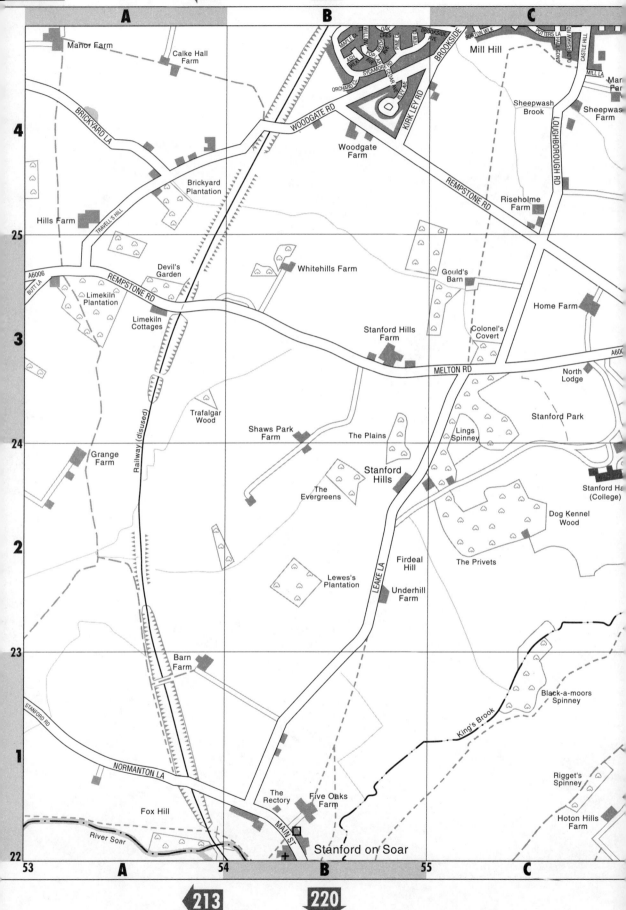

213
205

A                B                C

Manor Farm

Calke Hall
Farm

Mill Hill

BROOKSIDE

BRICKYARD LA

WOODGATE RD

KIRK LEY RD

Sheepwash
Brook

Sheepwash
Farm

Mar
Par

LOUGHBOROUGH RD

CASTLE HILL

MILL LA

Woodgate
Farm

REMPSTONE RD

Riseholme
Farm

Brickyard
Plantation

4

Hills Farm

TRAVELL'S HILL

25

A6006

BUTT LA

Devil's
Garden

Whitehills Farm

Gould's
Barn

Home Farm

REMPSTONE RD

Limekiln
Plantation

Limekiln
Cottages

Stanford Hills
Farm

Colonel's
Covert

A600

MELTON RD

North
Lodge

3

Railway (disused)

Trafalgar
Wood

Shaws Park
Farm

The Plains

Lings
Spinney

Stanford Park

24

Grange
Farm

The
Evergreens

Stanford
Hills

Stanford Ha
(College)

Dog Kennel
Wood

STANFORD RD

LEAKE LA

Firdeal
Hill

The Privets

2

Lewes's
Plantation

Underhill
Farm

Barn
Farm

23

King's Brook

Black-a-moors
Spinney

NORMANTON LA

1

Rigget's
Spinney

Fox Hill

The
Rectory

Five Oaks
Farm

MAIN ST

Hoton Hills
Farm

River Soar

Stanford on Soar

22

53         A       54        B      55        C

D      E      F

Canaan Farm

Hill Farm

Oaklands Farm

The Lings Farm

Sheepwash Brook

**4**

WYSALL RD

**25**

A60

LOUGHBOROUGH RD

MELTON RD

Lings Farm

Rempstone Hall (Convent)

Rempstone Hall Farm

SCHOOL LA

PH

MAIN ST

Dales Farm

WYMESWOLD RD

THE OLD ENGINE YARD

A6006

**3**

Damhead Plantation

Sutcliffe Plantation

**Rempstone**

Cherry Hill

Sutcliffe Hill

**24**

Stanford Park

Floodgate Plantation

**2**

King's Bridge

King's Brook

New Covert

REMPSTONE RD

**23**

Gorse Farm

Sewage Works

New Covert Farm

HOLLYTREE CL

Harts Farm

PH

WYMESWOLD RD

**1**

**Hoton**

THE THREE TERRACE LA

Peartree Farm

Wymeswold Airfield (disused)

LOUGHBOROUGH RD

B675 PRESTWOLD LA B675

OLD PARSONAGE LA

A60

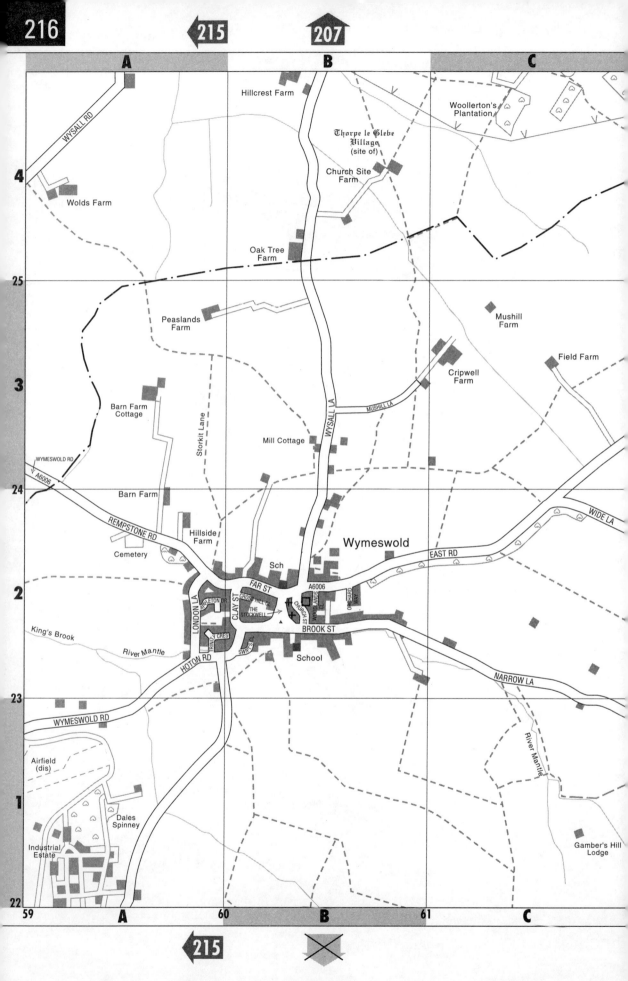

A B C

WYSALL RD

Hillcrest Farm

Woollerton's
Plantation

Thorpe le Glebe
Village
(site of)

Church Site
Farm

4

Wolds Farm

Oak Tree
Farm

25

Mushill
Farm

Peaslands
Farm

Field Farm

Cripwell
Farm

3

Barn Farm
Cottage

Storkit Lane

WYSALL LA

MUSHILL LA

Mill Cottage

WYMESWOLD RD

A6006

24

Barn Farm

WIDE LA

REMPSTONE RD

Hillside
Farm

Wymeswold

EAST RD

Cemetery

Sch

King's Brook

FAR ST

A6006

2

LONDON LA

CLAY ST

CROS HILL CL
THE
STOCKWELL

MANOR
LANDS CL

ORCHARD
WAY

River Mantle

SWAN ST

TRINITY CRES

CHURCH ST

BROOK ST

HOTON RD

School

NARROW LA

River Mantle

23

WYMESWOLD RD

Airfield
(dis)

1

Dales
Spinney

Gamber's Hill
Lodge

Industrial
Estate

22

59 A 60 B 61 C

D
E
F

Triangle
Plantation

Eelpool
Field

**Willoughby-on
-the-Wolds**

Field Farm

Bryans Lane

MILL LA

WIDMERPOOL LA

A46(T)

4

Willoughby
Gorse

Old Hall
Farm

CHURCH LA

Sch

MAIN ST

Green Lane

LONDON LA

MOB LA

CHAPEL LA

PH

Broughton
Lodge

WEST THORPE

BACK LA

25

Barrack
Cottages

HADES LA

OCCUPATION LA

3

Turnpost
Farm

Kingston Brook

24

Dungehill
Farm

HADES LA

A46(T)

6006

Eller's
Gorse

2

Hill Farm

WIDE LA

Ella's
Farm

Pasture
Lodge

23

Highthorn
Farm

NARROW LA

Common
Farm

Wymeswold
Lodge

Kingston Brook

Willoughby Fields
Farm

PADDY'S LA  A6006

1

River Mantle

Wolds Farm

The Lodge

A46(T)

22

A

B

C

Manor Barn Farm

A46(T)

Manor Farm

STATION RD

Brookside Cottage

4

The Willoughby Hotel

Top Cottage

Fairham Brook

Longcliff Hill

25

Dalby Brook

Wad House

Spruce Haven

3

A46(T)

NOTTINGHAM LA

Dalby Lodges

North Lodge

Beazley's Farm

North Lodge Farm

Sch

24

LONGCLIFF HILL

STATION LA

DEBDALE HILL   HAWTHORN RD

CROSS LA   CHAPEL LA

Old Dalby

PH

Wood's Hill

Vale View Farm

MAIN RD

CHURCH LA   PARADISE LA

2

Hall Plantation

Fishpond Plantation

Woodhill Farm

WOOD HILL

Thorney Hollow

Hill Top Farm

23

Old Dalby Wood

Upper Grange Farm

Yard Farm

LAWN LA

Grange Cottages

Wavendon Grange

Old Dalby Wood House

Dalby Wolds

GIBSON'S LA

Old Dalby Grange

Home Lodge Farm

1

A6006

Lower Grange Farm

Bridgets Covert

SIX HILLS LA

PADDY'S LA

Lodge Farm

22

65

A

66

B

67

C

D     E     F

CHURCH END

HECADECK LA

Moat
Farm

CHAPEL LA

MIDDLE LA

KING ST

BLACKSMITHS CK

A606

Nether
Broughton

Manor
Farm

River Smite

**4**

PH

The
Grange

NOTTINGHAM RD

Sewage
Works

Thompson
Walk

**25**

GREAVES
AVE

QUEENSWAY

Hatton
Lodge

OLD DALBY LA

Broughton
Lodges

THE CRESCENT

PRINCES DR

EARLS RD

Playing Field

MARQUIS RD

DUKES RD

Lodge Farm

**3**

A606

Broughton
Lodge

ATION LA

STATION LA

Old Dalby
Depot

Greenhill
Farm

**24**

Crompton's
Plantation

Stonepit
Spinney

Stonepits
Farm

Marriott's
Spinney

Green Hill

**2**

Air Shafts

Grimston Tunnel

Saxelby Lodge
Farm

Friars Well
Farm

Wartnaby

Tunnel
Farm

Marriott's
Wood

**23**

Old Dalby Wood

SIX HILLS LA

Tunnel
Farm

Barnes Hill
Plantation

Friars
Well

Resr

Tunnel
Plantation

Ten Acres
Plantation

Ppg
Sta

ROMAN ROAD

**1**

PERKIN'S LA

Barn
Farm

Grimston
Gorse

Saxelby
Pastures

Grimston

**22**

| | A | B | C |
|---|---|---|---|

**4**

Loughborough Meadows

Summerpool Brook

Moat Hill Spinney

Moat Hill

Fishpond Spinney

STANFORD LA

Sewage Works

Allot Gdns

Engineering Works

Park Farm

Hermitage Brook

**21**

Works

1 STANFORD HILL
2 CHURCH LANDS
3 FOX COVERT
4 CABIN LEAS

Works

Loughborough Station

LOUGHBOROUGH RD

Cotes

MEADOW LA

MEADOW LA IND ESTATE

NOTTINGHAM RD

A60  B676 BARROW RD

LOUGHBOROUGH RD

**3**

BELTON RD

A6004

RATCLIFFE RD  A6004

Cotes Mill (PH)

Cotes Bridge

River Soar

Bandalls Farm

PH EDWARD ST

Works  B589

Allsopp's Lane

Weirs

Dismtd Rly

LC

**20**

DERBY RD

BROOMHEAD ST

**LOUGHBOROUGH**

QUEEN'S RD

Wolsey Way

Little Moorlane Bridge

Moor Farm

BAXTER GATE

Mus

EMPRESS RD

Little Moor La

Hosp

PINFOLD GATE

Thomas St

**2**

GRANBY ST

WHARNCLIFFE RD

Moor Farm

Moor Lane

ASHBY RD

WOOD GATE

SOUTHFIELD RD

Moors Farm

BROWNS LA

Offs

GREAT CENTRAL RD

Moor Lane Farm

Loughborough Moors

**19**

FOREST RD

BEECHES RD

Grand Union Canal
Leicester Navigation

Towing Path

Woodthorp Bridge

BEACON RD

PARK RD

LEICESTER RD

TA Centre

Miller's Bridge

**1**

EPINAL WAY

SHELTHORPE RD

A6004

Great Central Railway

Quorn Fields Farm

BEACON RD

PH HOLT DR

Coll & Sch

Cemy

Charnwood Water

**18**

PARKLANDS DR

Shelthorpe

Crem

A6(T)  LOUGHBOROUGH RD

USER'S NOTES

# EXPLANATION OF THE STREET INDEX REFERENCE SYSTEM

Street names are listed alphabetically and show the locality, the page number and a reference to the square in which the name falls on the map page.

Example:          Southlands Dr. Mort.....................................................15   D2

Southlands Dr      This is the full street name, which may have been abbreviated on the map.

Mort      This is the abbreviation for the town, village or locality in which the street falls.

15      This is the page number of the map on which the street name appears.

D2      The letter and figure indicate the square on the map in which the centre of the street falls. The square can be found at the junction of the vertical column carrying the appropriate letter and the horizontal row carrying the appropriate figure.

### ABBREVIATIONS USED IN THE INDEX
Road Names

| | | | |
|---|---|---|---|
| Approach | App | Lane | La |
| Avenue | Ave | North | N |
| Boulevard | Bvd | Orchard | Orch |
| Broadway | Bwy | Parade | Par |
| By-Pass | By-Ps | Passage | Pas |
| Causeway | Cswy | Place | Pl |
| Common | Comm | Pleasant | Plea |
| Corner | Cnr | Precinct | Prec |
| Cottages | Cotts | Promenade | Prom |
| Court | Ct | Road | Rd |
| Crescent | Cres | South | S |
| Drive | Dri | Square | Sq |
| Drove | Dro | Street,Saint | St |
| East | E | Terrace | Terr |
| Gardens | Gdns | Walk | Wlk |
| Grove | Gr | West | W |
| Heights | Hts | Yard | Yd |

**Key to abbreviations of Town, Village and Rural locality names used in the index of street names.**

| Place | Abbr. | Ref. |
|---|---|---|
| Aldercar | Ald | 143 D2 |
| Allt Hucknall | Al Hu | 85 F4 |
| Alverton | Alv | 168 C1 |
| Annesley Woodhouse | Ann Wo | 129 F4 |
| Arnold | Arn | 162 A4 |
| Askham | Askh | 51 F1 |
| Aslockton | Aslo | 179 D3 |
| Austerfield | Aust | 3 E1 |
| Averham | Aver | 123 F1 |
| Awsworth | Awsw | 158 B2 |
| Babworth | Babw | 39 D1 |
| Balderton | Bald | 140 C2 |
| Barkestone-le-Vale | B-le-V | 192 B1 |
| Barnby in the Willows | B in W | 141 F3 |
| Barnby Moor | Ba Mo | 28 B3 |
| Barnstone | Barns | 190 C2 |
| Barton in Fabis | B in F | 194 C3 |
| Bathley | Bath | 110 A2 |
| Bawtry | Baw | 10 A4 |
| Beckingham | Beck | 14 A1 |
| Beckingham | Beckin | 142 B4 |
| Beeston | Bees | 183 E4 |
| Besthorpe | Best | 97 F3 |
| Bestwood Village | Bes Vil | 146 C2 |
| Bevercotes | Bev | 64 B3 |
| Bilsthorpe | Bils | 105 F3 |
| Bingham | Bing | 177 F2 |
| Bircotes | Bir | 9 E2 |
| Blaxton | Blax | 1 A1 |
| Bleasby | Bleas | 152 A4 |
| Blidworth | Blid | 118 A2 |
| Blyth | Blyth | 18 A2 |
| Blyton | Blyt | 15 F4 |
| Bole | Bole | 23 F1 |
| Bothamsall | Both | 63 F4 |
| Bottesford | Bott | 181 E2 |
| Boughton | Boug | 77 F3 |
| Bradmore | Brad | 196 C2 |
| Brampton | Bram | 44 B2 |
| Brinsley | Brin | 143 F3 |
| Broadholme | Broad | 57 D1 |
| Broxholme | Brox | 57 F3 |
| Budby | Budby | 61 F1 |
| Bulcote | Bulc | 164 A3 |
| Bunny | Bunny | 206 C4 |
| Burton Joyce | Bu Jo | 163 F2 |
| Calverton | Calv | 149 D4 |
| Car Colston | Car Co | 166 B1 |
| Carlton | Carl | 162 B1 |
| Carlton in Lindrick | C in L | 25 F3 |
| Carlton on Trent | C on T | 96 C2 |
| Caunton | Caun | 109 D2 |
| Caythorpe | Cayt | 165 D4 |
| Clarborough | Clar | 30 C2 |
| Claypole | Clayp | 156 B4 |
| Clayworth | Clay | 21 E3 |
| Clipston | Clip | 187 E1 |
| Coddington | Codd | 126 A1 |
| Collingham | Coll | 98 A1 |
| Colston Bassett | Co Ba | 200 B4 |
| Cossall | Coss | 158 B1 |
| Costock | Cost | 206 B1 |
| Cotes | Cotes | 220 C3 |
| Cotgrave | Cotg | 188 A1 |
| Cotham | Coth | 154 C2 |
| Cottam | Cott | 43 E3 |
| Cromwell | Crom | 110 C4 |
| Cropwell Bishop | Cr Bi | 189 D2 |
| Cropwell Butler | Cr Bu | 189 D4 |
| Cuckney | Cuck | 60 A2 |
| Darlton | Darl | 67 D4 |
| Dry Doddington | Dry Do | 156 C1 |
| Dunham on Trent | D on T | 54 B1 |
| Eagle | Eagle | 84 B2 |
| Eakring | Eakr | 92 C1 |
| East Bridgford | E Brid | 165 F2 |
| East Drayton | E Dray | 53 D2 |
| East Leake | E Lea | 205 F1 |
| East Markham | E Mark | 65 F3 |
| East Stockwith | E Stock | 7 F1 |
| East Stoke | E Sto | 153 E4 |
| Eastwood | East | 143 F2 |
| Eaton | Eaton | 40 A1 |
| Edingley | Edin | 120 B2 |
| Edwinstowe | Edwin | 76 A1 |
| Egmanton | Egma | 79 F3 |
| Elkersley | Elk | 50 A2 |
| Elmton | Elmt | 58 A4 |
| Elston | Elst | 153 F3 |
| Elton | Elton | 179 F1 |
| Epperstone | Epp | 150 A3 |
| Everton | Ever | 11 D2 |
| Farndon | Farn | 139 D2 |
| Farnsfield | Farns | 119 F3 |
| Fenton | Fent | 55 E3 |
| Fenton | Fenton | 141 B1 |
| Finningley | Finn | 1 A2 |
| Firbeck | Fir | 16 A3 |
| Fiskerton | Fisk | 137 F2 |
| Flawborough | Flaw | 168 B1 |
| Fledborough | Fled | 68 B3 |
| Flintham | Flint | 153 D1 |
| Gainsborough | Gain | 24 C3 |
| Gamston | Gam | 186 B4 |
| Gamston | Gams | 51 D3 |
| Girton | Girt | 82 C1 |
| Glapwell | Glap | 86 B4 |
| Gonalston | Gona | 151 D2 |
| Gotham | Goth | 195 D1 |
| Granby | Gran | 191 E3 |
| Grassthorpe | Grass | 81 F2 |
| Greasley | Greas | 144 C2 |
| Grimston | Grim | 219 D1 |
| Gringley on the Hill | G on H | 12 B1 |
| Grove | Grove | 40 C2 |
| Gunthorpe | Gunt | 164 C3 |
| Halam | Halam | 120 C1 |
| Halloughton | Hall | 136 A2 |
| Harby | Harby | 202 A1 |
| Harby | Harby | 70 C1 |
| Hardwick | Hardw | 56 A3 |
| Harworth | Har | 8 C3 |
| Hathern | Hath | 213 D1 |
| Haughton | Haug | 63 F3 |
| Hawksworth | Hawk | 167 E2 |
| Hawton | Hawt | 139 F2 |
| Haxey | Haxey | 6 B4 |
| Hayton | Hayt | 30 B3 |
| Headon | Head | 52 A4 |
| Heanor | Hean | 143 D1 |
| Hickling | Hick | 210 A4 |
| High Marnham | H Marn | 68 A1 |
| Hockerton | Hock | 122 A3 |
| Hodsock | Hod | 26 C4 |
| Holbeck | Holb | 59 E4 |
| Holme | Holme | 111 D2 |
| Holme Pierrepont | Ho Pi | 175 D2 |
| Hose | Hose | 211 F4 |
| Hoton | Hoton | 215 E1 |
| Hoveringham | Hover | 151 E1 |
| Hucknall | Huck | 145 F3 |
| Ilkeston | Ilk | 157 E1 |
| Kegworth | Kegw | 203 E1 |
| Kelham | Kelh | 124 A2 |
| Kersall | Kers | 94 A1 |
| Kettlethorpe | Kettl | 55 E2 |
| Keyworth | Keyw | 197 F1 |
| Kilvington | Kilv | 169 D1 |
| Kimberley | Kim | 158 C3 |
| Kingston on Soar | K on S | 204 A2 |
| Kinoulton | Kinou | 200 A1 |
| Kirkby-in-Ashfield | K-in-A | 115 E2 |
| Kirklington | Kirk | 120 C4 |
| Kirton | Kirt | 78 B3 |
| Kneesall | Knee | 93 F3 |
| Kneeton | Kneet | 152 A1 |
| Lambley | Lamb | 163 E4 |
| Laneham | Lane | 54 B3 |
| Langar | Lang | 190 B1 |
| Langford | Langf | 111 F1 |
| Langley Mill | La Mi | 143 D2 |
| Langold | Lan | 16 C2 |
| Laxton | Lax | 79 E2 |
| Lea | Lea | 24 C1 |
| Letwell | Let | 16 A2 |
| Linby | Linby | 131 D2 |
| Long Clawson | Lo Cl | 211 E2 |
| Long Eaton | Lo Ea | 193 E4 |
| Long Whatton | Lo Wh | 212 B2 |
| Loughborough | Lough | 220 B2 |
| Lound | Lound | 29 E4 |
| Low Marnham | L Marn | 82 A4 |
| Lowdham | Lowd | 150 B1 |
| Maltby | Malt | 16 A4 |
| Mansfield | Mans | 102 B4 |
| Maplebeck | Mapl | 108 A3 |
| Market Warsop | Mar War | 74 B2 |
| Marton | Mart | 44 A4 |
| Mattersey | Matt | 20 B4 |
| Misson | Miss | 4 A1 |
| Misterton | Mist | 6 C1 |
| Morton | Mort | 15 D2 |
| Morton | Morton | 137 E2 |
| Nether Broughton | Ne Br | 219 E4 |
| Nether Langwith | Ne La | 59 D1 |
| New Clipstone | N Clip | 89 F4 |
| Newark-on-Trent | N-on-T | 140 B4 |
| Newstead | News | 130 C3 |
| Newton | New | 177 D4 |
| Newton | Newt | 99 D2 |
| Newton on Trent | Ne on T | 55 D1 |
| Normanton on Soar | N on S | 213 F2 |
| Normanton on Trent | Nor on T | 81 E3 |
| Normanton-on-the-Wolds | N-on-W | 198 A3 |
| North Clifton | N Clift | 68 C3 |
| North Leverton with Habblesthorpe | N Le Ha | 42 B4 |
| North Muskham | N Musk | 110 C1 |
| North Scarle | N Sca | 83 F1 |
| North Wheatley | N Whea | 31 E4 |
| Norton | Nort | 60 B3 |
| Norwell | Norw | 110 A4 |
| Nottingham | Nott | 172 C4 |
| Nuthall | Nuth | 159 E3 |
| Old Dalby | Ol Da | 218 C2 |
| Oldcotes | Old | 17 D3 |
| Ollerton | Oll | 77 D2 |
| Ompton | Omp | 93 D4 |
| Orston | Orst | 180 A4 |
| Ossington | Oss | 95 E3 |
| Owthorpe | Owth | 199 F4 |
| Oxton | Oxt | 134 B2 |
| Papplewick | Papp | 131 F2 |
| Perlethorpe | Perl | 62 C2 |
| Pinxton | Pinx | 113 E1 |
| Pleasley | Plea | 87 D3 |
| Plumtree | Plum | 197 F3 |
| Plungar | Plun | 202 C4 |
| Radcliffe on Trent | R on T | 175 F2 |
| Ragnall | Ragn | 68 A4 |
| Rainworth | Rain | 117 F4 |
| Rampton | Ramp | 42 C1 |
| Ranskill | Ran | 19 D2 |
| Ratcliffe on Soar | R on S | 203 F3 |
| Ravenshead | Raven | 117 D1 |
| Redmile | Redm | 192 C2 |
| Rempstone | Remp | 215 E3 |
| Retford | Ret | 39 F4 |
| Rhodesia | Rhod | 35 D3 |
| Rolleston | Roll | 138 A3 |
| Ruddington | Rudd | 196 C3 |
| Rufford | Ruff | 104 C4 |
| Sandiacre | Sand | 182 A3 |
| Saundby | Saun | 23 E3 |
| Saxilby | Sax | 56 C2 |
| Scaftworth | Scaf | 10 B2 |
| Scarcliffe | Scarc | 72 A3 |
| Scarrington | Scarr | 178 C4 |
| Screveton | Screv | 166 C2 |
| Scrooby | Scro | 9 F1 |
| Selston | Sels | 128 C4 |
| Shelford | Shel | 164 B1 |
| Shelton | Shelt | 168 B3 |
| Shipley | Ship | 157 D3 |
| Shirebrook | Shireb | 72 B2 |
| Shireoaks | Shire | 34 C3 |
| Sibthorpe | Sibt | 167 F4 |
| Skellingthorpe | Skel | 71 F2 |
| South Clifton | S Clift | 68 C1 |
| South Leverton | S Lev | 42 B3 |
| South Muskham | S Musk | 124 B4 |
| South Normanton | S Norm | 113 D4 |
| South Scarle | S Sca | 98 B3 |
| South Wheatley | S Whea | 31 F4 |
| Southwell | South | 121 E1 |
| Spalford | Spal | 83 D4 |
| Stanford on Soar | S on S | 214 B1 |
| Stanton-by-Dale | S-by-D | 170 A1 |
| Stanton-on-the-Wolds | S-on-W | 198 B1 |
| Stapleford | Stap | 182 C4 |
| Stapleford | Staple | 127 E4 |
| Stathern | Stat | 202 C2 |
| Staunton in the Vale | S in V | 169 D2 |
| Staythorpe | Stay | 138 B4 |
| Stoke Bardolph | St Ba | 175 F4 |
| Strelley | Stre | 171 D4 |
| Sturton Le Steeple | S Le S | 32 B3 |
| Styrrup | Styr | 8 B1 |
| Sutton Bonington | Su Bo | 213 D4 |
| Sutton in Ashfield | S in A | 100 B1 |
| Sutton on Trent | S on T | 96 C4 |
| Sutton-cum-Lound | Sutt | 28 C3 |
| Swinethorpe | Swine | 84 B4 |
| Syerston | Syer | 153 E2 |
| Thonock | Thon | 15 F2 |
| Thorney | Thor | 69 F4 |
| Thoroton | Thoro | 167 F1 |
| Thorpe | Thorpe | 138 C1 |
| Thorpe in the Glebe | T in G | 207 F1 |
| Thorpe Salvin | Th Sa | 34 A3 |
| Thrumpton | Thrum | 194 B2 |
| Thurgarton | Thur | 151 E4 |
| Tibshelf | Tibs | 99 D3 |
| Tickhill | Tick | 8 A4 |
| Tithby | Tith | 189 F3 |
| Tollerton | Toll | 186 B1 |
| Torksey | Tork | 44 A1 |
| Torworth | Torw | 19 D1 |
| Treswell | Tres | 42 B2 |
| Trowell | Trow | 170 B3 |
| Tuxford | Tux | 66 A1 |
| Upper Broughton | Up Br | 210 A1 |
| Upton | Upt | 52 A3 |
| Upton | Upton | 122 C1 |
| Walesby | Wale | 64 A1 |
| Walkeringham | Walker | 13 F3 |
| Walkerith | Walk | 14 B3 |
| Wallingwells | Wall | 25 E3 |
| Wellow | Wellow | 92 C4 |
| West Bridgford | W Brid | 185 E3 |
| West Burton | W Burt | 32 B4 |
| West Drayton | W Dray | 51 D1 |
| West Hallam | We Ha | 157 D1 |
| West Leake | W Lea | 205 D1 |
| West Markham | W Mark | 65 D3 |
| West Stockwith | W Sto | 7 E1 |
| Weston | West | 81 D2 |
| Whatton | What | 179 D2 |
| Whitwell | Whit | 45 D3 |
| Widmerpool | Widm | 208 A3 |
| Wigsley | Wig | 70 A1 |
| Willoughby-on-the-Wold | W-on-W | 217 E4 |
| Winkburn | Wink | 108 A1 |
| Winthorpe | Wint | 125 E3 |
| Wiseton | Wise | 21 D4 |
| Wiverton Hall | Wi Ha | 190 A3 |
| Woodbeck | Wood | 53 D4 |
| Woodborough | Woodb | 149 E2 |
| Woodsetts | Woods | 25 D1 |
| Worksop | Work | 36 A2 |
| Wroot | Wroot | 2 A4 |
| Wymeswold | Wyme | 216 B2 |
| Wysall | Wys | 207 E2 |

| Name | Pg | Grid |
|------|----|------|
| 1st Ave. Nott | 173 | D4 |
| 2nd Ave. Nott | 173 | D4 |
| 3rd Ave. Nott | 173 | D4 |
| 4th Ave. Nott | 173 | D4 |
| A'court St. Nott | 172 | C3 |
| Aaron Cl. Nott | 185 | D4 |
| Abba Cl. Kim | 158 | C4 |
| Abbey Bridge. Nott | 172 | C1 |
| Abbey Cir. W Brid | 186 | A4 |
| Abbey Cl. Aslo | 178 | C3 |
| Abbey Ct. Huck | 145 | F4 |
| Abbey Ct. Bees | 183 | F4 |
| Abbey Ct. Mans | 102 | C4 |
| Abbey Ct. Nott | 172 | C2 |
| Abbey Dr. Bees | 183 | F4 |
| Abbey Gr. Nott | 173 | F4 |
| Abbey La. Aslo | 178 | C3 |
| Abbey Rd. Bing | 178 | A2 |
| Abbey Rd. Blid | 118 | A3 |
| Abbey Rd. East | 144 | A1 |
| Abbey Rd. Edwin | 91 | E4 |
| Abbey Rd. K-in-A | 115 | E3 |
| Abbey Rd. Mans | 102 | C4 |
| Abbey Rd. Matt | 20 | B4 |
| Abbey Rd. News | 130 | C3 |
| Abbey Rd. W Brid | 186 | A4 |
| Abbey St. Ilk | 157 | F1 |
| Abbey St. Nott | 172 | C1 |
| Abbey St. Work | 35 | F1 |
| Abbeydale Dr. Mans | 102 | B2 |
| Abbeyfield Rd. Nott | 184 | C4 |
| Abbot Cl. Keyw | 197 | F2 |
| Abbot St. Awsw | 158 | B2 |
| Abbots Cl. Arn | 161 | E3 |
| Abbots Dr. Huck | 145 | F3 |
| Abbots Rd. Huck | 145 | F3 |
| Abbots Wlk. Huck | 145 | F3 |
| Abbotsbury Cl. Nott | 146 | C1 |
| Abbotsford Dr. Nott | 173 | E3 |
| Abbotsford Mews. Ilk | 157 | E2 |
| Abbott Lea. Mans | 101 | E4 |
| Abbott Rd. Mans | 101 | E4 |
| Abbott St. Lo Ea | 193 | E3 |
| Abbott's Way. N-on-T | 125 | D1 |
| Abbotts Cres. Farns | 119 | F4 |
| Abbotts Croft. Mans | 87 | F1 |
| Abbotts Way. Nott | 172 | B2 |
| Abel Collin's Homes. Bees | 171 | F1 |
| Abercarn Cl. Nott | 160 | A4 |
| Aberconway St. Blid | 118 | A3 |
| Aberdeen St. Nott | 173 | F3 |
| Aberford Ave. Nott | 172 | B4 |
| Abingdon Dr. Rudd | 196 | B4 |
| Abingdon Gdns. Arn | 162 | A3 |
| Abingdon Gdns. Bees | 183 | E2 |
| Abingdon Rd. W Brid | 186 | A4 |
| Abingdon Sq. Nott | 160 | A1 |
| Abington Ave. S in A | 100 | C3 |
| Acacia Ave. Ann Wo | 130 | A4 |
| Acacia Ave. Gain | 15 | E1 |
| Acacia Cl. Huck | 146 | A3 |
| Acacia Cres. Carl | 162 | C1 |
| Acacia Ct. Mans | 88 | C1 |
| Acacia Rd. Bald | 140 | B3 |
| Acacia Wlk. Bees | 183 | F3 |
| Academy Cl. Nott | 160 | C2 |
| Acaster Cl. Bees | 184 | A2 |
| Acer Cl. Pinx | 113 | E2 |
| Ackford Dr. Work | 35 | E2 |
| Acland St. Gain | 15 | E1 |
| Acle Gdns. Nott | 146 | A1 |
| Acle Gdns. Nott | 160 | A4 |
| Acorn Ave. Greas | 158 | B4 |
| Acorn Bank. W Brid | 185 | D2 |
| Acorn Bsns Park. Mans | 102 | A3 |
| Acorn Cl. Bald | 140 | B3 |
| Acorn Dr. Carl | 163 | D1 |
| Acorn Park. Nott | 184 | C4 |
| Acorn Ridge. Shireb | 72 | B3 |
| Acre Edge Rd. Lax | 78 | C1 |
| Acre The. K-in-A | 115 | D2 |
| Acreage La. Shireb | 72 | C1 |
| Acton Ave. Lo Ea | 193 | F3 |
| Acton Ave. Nott | 160 | B2 |
| Acton Cl. Lo Ea | 193 | F3 |
| Acton Gr. Lo Ea | 193 | F3 |
| Acton Rd. Arn | 161 | F4 |
| Acton Rd. Lo Ea | 193 | F3 |
| Acton St. Lo Ea | 193 | F3 |
| Adam St. Ilk | 170 | A3 |
| Adams Ct. Ilk | 157 | F2 |
| Adams Hill. Keyw | 197 | F2 |
| Adams Hill. Nott | 172 | B1 |
| Adams Way. Mart | 44 | B4 |
| Adamsway. Mans | 103 | D2 |
| Adbolton Ave. Carl | 162 | C1 |
| Adbolton Gr. W Brid | 174 | A1 |
| Adbolton La. Ho Pi | 174 | C1 |
| Adderley Cl. Nott | 161 | D3 |
| Addington Ct. R on T | 176 | A2 |
| Addington Rd. Nott | 172 | C3 |
| Addison Dr. Huck | 145 | F4 |
| Addison Rd. Carl | 174 | A4 |
| Addison St. Nott | 173 | D3 |
| Addison St. Tibs | 99 | D4 |
| Addison Villas. East | 143 | F1 |
| Adel Dr. Carl | 162 | C1 |
| Adelaide Cl. Gain | 24 | C3 |
| Adelaide Cl. Staple | 170 | C1 |
| Adelaide Gr. Nott | 160 | C4 |
| Adenburgh Dr. Bees | 183 | E1 |
| Adrian Cl. Bees | 182 | C1 |
| Adrians Cl. Mans | 102 | C3 |
| Aegir Cl. Gain | 24 | C3 |
| Aeneas Ct. Nott | 173 | D4 |
| Agnes Villas. Nott | 161 | F1 |
| Aidan Gdns. Bes Vil | 147 | D1 |
| Ainsdale Cres. Nott | 160 | A2 |
| Ainsdale Green. Ret | 39 | E2 |
| Ainsley Rd. Nott | 172 | B3 |
| Ainsworth Dr. Nott | 173 | D1 |
| Aintree Cl. Nott | 158 | C4 |
| Airedale Ave. Tick | 8 | A4 |
| Airedale Cl. Lo Ea | 193 | D3 |
| Airedale Ct. Bees | 183 | D2 |
| Airedale Wlk. Nott | 171 | E2 |
| Airedale. Work | 36 | A4 |
| Aisby Wlk. Gain | 24 | C4 |
| Aitchison Ave. Huck | 145 | F4 |
| Alandale Ave. Shireb | 72 | C3 |
| Alandale. Bils | 105 | F3 |
| Alandene Rd. Kim | 159 | D4 |
| Albany Cl. Arn | 161 | F4 |
| Albany Cl. Mans | 88 | B1 |
| Albany Ct. Staple | 170 | C1 |
| Albany Dr. Mans | 88 | B1 |
| Albany Pl. Mans | 88 | B1 |
| Albany Rd. Nott | 173 | D4 |
| Albany Sq. Nott | 173 | D2 |
| Albany St. Gain | 15 | E1 |
| Albany St. Ilk | 170 | A3 |
| Albemarle Rd. Arn | 161 | E2 |
| Albert Ave. Bald | 140 | B2 |
| Albert Ave. Carl | 174 | A4 |
| Albert Ave. Nott | 172 | B4 |
| Albert Ave. Nuth | 159 | E3 |
| Albert Ave. Sels | 128 | A2 |
| Albert Ave. Staple | 182 | B4 |
| Albert Ball Cl. Nott | 160 | C4 |
| Albert Dr. Nott | 172 | C3 |
| Albert Pl. Lough | 220 | A2 |
| Albert Prom. Lough | 220 | B2 |
| Albert Rd. Bees | 184 | A4 |
| Albert Rd. Bunn | 196 | C1 |
| Albert Rd. Hello | 173 | A2 |
| Albert Rd. Lo Ea | 193 | E4 |
| Albert Rd. Nott | 172 | C2 |
| Albert Rd. Ret | 39 | F3 |
| Albert Rd. Sand | 182 | A3 |
| Albert Rd. W Brid | 185 | F4 |
| Albert Sq. S in A | 100 | C1 |
| Albert St. Bott | 181 | D2 |
| Albert St. Carl | 162 | C1 |
| Albert St. East | 143 | F2 |
| Albert St. Huck | 146 | A4 |
| Albert St. Lough | 220 | A2 |
| Albert St. Mans | 88 | B2 |
| Albert St. Mans | 102 | A3 |
| Albert St. Mar War | 74 | A3 |
| Albert St. N-on-T | 139 | F4 |
| Albert St. Nott | 173 | E2 |
| Albert St. R on T | 175 | F2 |
| Albert St. S in A | 100 | B3 |
| Albert St. S Norm | 113 | D3 |
| Albert St. Staple | 182 | B4 |
| Albert St. Work | 35 | F2 |
| Alberta Ave. Sels | 129 | D4 |
| Alberta Terr. Nott | 173 | D4 |
| Albine Rd. Shireb | 72 | C3 |
| Albion Centre The. Ilk | 157 | F1 |
| Albion Cl. Work | 35 | F2 |
| Albion Rd. Lo Ea | 193 | F4 |
| Albion Rd. S in A | 100 | C1 |
| Albion Rise. Nott | 147 | F1 |
| Albion St. Bees | 183 | F4 |
| Albion St. Mans | 87 | F1 |
| Albion St. N-on-T | 139 | F4 |
| Albion St. Nott | 173 | E2 |
| Albion Terr. Mist | 7 | D1 |
| Albury Dr. Nott | 160 | A1 |
| Alcester St. Nott | 184 | C4 |
| Alcock Ave. Mans | 102 | C4 |
| Aldene Ct. Bees | 183 | E3 |
| Aldene Way. Woodb | 149 | E2 |
| Alder Cl. Bald | 140 | B3 |
| Alder Cl. Mans | 88 | C1 |
| Alder Cl. Shireb | 72 | B3 |
| Alder Cl. Work | 35 | F1 |
| Alder Ct. Mans | 101 | E3 |
| Alder Gdns. Nott | 160 | A4 |
| Alder Gr. Mans | 88 | A3 |
| Alder Gr. Oll | 77 | E3 |
| Alder Way. Keyw | 198 | A1 |
| Alder Way. S in A | 100 | B2 |
| Alder Way. Shireb | 72 | B2 |
| Aldercar La. Ald | 143 | D3 |
| Aldermens Cl. Nott | 173 | E1 |
| Alderney St. Nott | 172 | C2 |
| Alderson Cl. Tick | 8 | A4 |
| Alderson Dr. Tick | 8 | A4 |
| Alderson Rd. Work | 35 | F1 |
| Alderton Rd. Nott | 161 | E3 |
| Aldgate Cl. Nott | 160 | A4 |
| Aldred St E. Work | 36 | A1 |
| Aldred St W. Work | 36 | A1 |
| Aldred St. Work | 36 | A1 |
| Aldred's La. Hean | 143 | D1 |
| Aldridge Cl. Bees | 182 | C1 |
| Aldrin Cl. Nott | 159 | F3 |
| Aldworth Cl. Nott | 161 | E3 |
| Aldwych Cl. Bes Vil | 147 | D1 |
| Aldwych Cl. Nott | 159 | E1 |
| Alec Rose Gr. Gain | 24 | C4 |
| Alexander Ave. N-on-T | 125 | D2 |
| Alexander Ave. Sels | 128 | B4 |
| Alexander Cl. Huck | 131 | D1 |
| Alexander Rd. Farns | 119 | F3 |
| Alexander St. East | 143 | F1 |
| Alexander Terr. Pinx | 113 | E1 |
| Alexandra Ave. Mans | 88 | A3 |
| Alexandra Ave. Mans | 102 | A2 |
| Alexandra Cres. Bees | 184 | A3 |
| Alexandra Rd. Har | 9 | D2 |
| Alexandra Rd. Lo Ea | 193 | E4 |
| Alexandra St. K-in-A | 115 | D3 |
| Alexandra St. Mar War | 74 | A3 |
| Alexandra St. Nott | 173 | D3 |
| Alexandra St. Staple | 182 | B3 |
| Alexandra Terr. S in A | 100 | B3 |
| Alford Cl. Bees | 184 | A3 |
| Alford Rd. W Brid | 186 | A3 |
| Alfred Ave. Carl | 162 | A1 |
| Alfred Cl. Nott | 173 | E3 |
| Alfred Ct. Mans | 102 | A4 |
| Alfred St Central. Nott | 173 | E3 |
| Alfred St N. Nott | 173 | E3 |
| Alfred St S. Nott | 173 | F3 |
| Alfred St. Gain | 15 | E1 |
| Alfred St. K-in-A | 115 | D2 |
| Alfred St. Lough | 220 | A3 |
| Alfred St. Pinx | 113 | E2 |
| Alfred St. S in A | 100 | C2 |
| Alfreton Rd. Newt | 99 | D2 |
| Alfreton Rd. Nott | 172 | C3 |
| Alfreton Rd. Pinx | 113 | E2 |
| Alfreton Rd. S in A | 100 | B1 |
| Alfreton Rd. S Norm | 113 | D3 |
| Alfreton Rd. Sels | 128 | B4 |
| Alfreton Rd. Sels | 129 | D2 |
| Alison Ave. Huck | 131 | E1 |
| Alison Wlk. Nott | 173 | E3 |
| Allandale Ave. Bees | 183 | E1 |
| Allandale Ave. Nott | 160 | A1 |
| Allandale Rd. Rain | 118 | A4 |
| Allandale Way. Mans | 88 | C1 |
| Allesford La. Edin | 120 | A2 |
| Alliance St. N-on-T | 125 | D1 |
| Allington Ave. Nott | 172 | C2 |
| Allington Dr. Mans | 101 | E4 |
| Allison Ave. Ret | 40 | A2 |
| Allison Gdns. Bees | 183 | E2 |
| Allsopp Dr. Work | 35 | F3 |
| Allwood Gdns. Huck | 146 | A3 |
| Alma Cl. Carl | 163 | D1 |
| Alma Cl. Nott | 173 | E3 |
| Alma Hill. Kim | 158 | C4 |
| Alma Rd. Nott | 173 | E3 |
| Alma Rd. Ret | 40 | A4 |
| Alma Rd. Sels | 128 | C3 |
| Alma Rd. Sels | 129 | D3 |
| Alma St. Nott | 173 | D4 |
| Almond Ave. Shireb | 72 | C3 |
| Almond Cl. Huck | 145 | A3 |
| Almond Cl. Kim | 158 | C4 |
| Almond Cl. Sax | 57 | D2 |
| Almond Gr. K-in-A | 114 | C3 |
| Almond Gr. Work | 35 | F1 |
| Almond Rise. Mans | 88 | C1 |
| Almond Wlk. Carl | 163 | D2 |
| Alnwick Cl. Nott | 160 | B3 |
| Alpha Terr. Nott | 173 | D3 |
| Alpine Cres. Carl | 174 | B4 |
| Alpine St. Nott | 160 | C1 |
| Alport Pl. Mans | 103 | D4 |
| Althea Ct. Nott | 161 | D1 |
| Althorpe St. Nott | 173 | D3 |
| Alton Ave. Nott | 185 | D2 |
| Alton Cl. W Brid | 185 | E2 |
| Alum Ct. Nott | 160 | C4 |
| Alvenor St. Ilk | 157 | F1 |
| Alverstone Rd. Nott | 161 | E1 |
| Alvey Rd. Bald | 140 | C2 |
| Alwood Gr. Nott | 184 | B1 |
| Alwyn Rd. Nott | 159 | F1 |
| Amanda Ave. C in L | 25 | F3 |
| Amanda Rd. Har | 8 | C2 |
| Amber Dr. Hean | 143 | D1 |
| Amber Hill. Nott | 161 | D4 |
| Ambergate Rd. Nott | 172 | A4 |
| Amberley St. Nott | 173 | D2 |
| Ambleside Dr. East | 143 | E2 |
| Ambleside Grange. Work | 35 | F4 |
| Ambleside Rd. Nott | 160 | A1 |
| Ambleside Way. Carl | 175 | D4 |
| Ambleside. Gam | 186 | B4 |
| Ambleside. Oll | 77 | E3 |
| Amcott Ave. Mist | 14 | A4 |
| Amcott Way. Ret | 39 | F4 |
| Amen Cnr. Caun | 109 | D3 |
| Amersham Rise. Nott | 160 | A1 |
| Amesbury Circ. Nott | 160 | A2 |
| Amos La. S Sca | 98 | B2 |
| Ampthill Rise. Nott | 161 | D2 |
| Anastasia Cl. Gain | 15 | E2 |
| Ancaster Gdns. Nott | 172 | A2 |
| Anchor La. Hath | 213 | D1 |
| Anchor Rd. East | 143 | E1 |
| Anders Dr. Nott | 159 | F3 |
| Anderson Cres. Bees | 183 | F4 |
| Anderson Ct. Nott | 161 | D4 |
| Andover Cl. Nott | 172 | A3 |
| Andover Rd. Mans | 101 | E4 |
| Andover Rd. Nott | 160 | C3 |
| Andrew Ave. Carl | 162 | A1 |
| Andrew Ave. Ilk | 170 | A4 |
| Andrew Dr. Blid | 118 | A2 |
| Andrews Dr. La Mi | 143 | D2 |
| Anfield Cl. Bees | 183 | D1 |
| Anford Cl. Nott | 160 | A3 |
| Angel Alley. Nott | 173 | E2 |
| Angel Row. Nott | 173 | E2 |
| Angela Ave. Ann Wo | 115 | D1 |
| Angela Cl. Nott | 147 | F1 |
| Angell Green. Nott | 195 | E4 |
| Anglia Way. Mans | 103 | D2 |
| Angrave Cl. Nott | 173 | F4 |
| Angus Cl. Arn | 148 | A1 |
| Angus Cl. Kim | 159 | D3 |
| Anmer Cl. Nott | 173 | D1 |
| Annan Ct. Nott | 172 | A4 |
| Anne's Cl. Carl | 162 | A1 |
| Annesley Cutting. Ann Wo | 130 | B4 |
| Annesley Gr. Nott | 173 | E3 |
| Annesley La. Sels | 129 | D3 |
| Annesley Rd. Ann Wo | 130 | A2 |
| Annesley Rd. Huck | 130 | C1 |
| Annesley Rd. Huck | 145 | F4 |
| Annesley Rd. Linby | 130 | C1 |
| Annesley Rd. W Brid | 185 | F4 |
| Annesley Way. Mans | 101 | E3 |
| Anslow Ave. Nott | 184 | A4 |
| Anslow Ave. S in A | 100 | C3 |
| Anson Wlk. Ilk | 157 | F2 |
| Anstee Rd. Lo Ea | 193 | E3 |
| Anstey Rise. Nott | 173 | F3 |
| Anston Ave. Work | 35 | F3 |
| Antill St. Staple | 182 | B3 |
| Apley Cl. Gain | 24 | C4 |
| Apollo Dr. Nott | 159 | F3 |
| Apple Tree La. Carl | 162 | C1 |
| Apple Wlk. Carl | 174 | A4 |
| Appleby Cl. N-on-T | 140 | B4 |
| Appleby Rd. Plea | 86 | C3 |
| Appledore Ave. Bees | 171 | F1 |
| Appledore Ave. Nott | 171 | F1 |
| Appledorne Way. Nott | 147 | F1 |
| Appleton Dr. Wyme | 216 | B3 |
| Appleton Gate. N-on-T | 125 | D1 |
| Appleton Rd. Bees | 184 | A2 |
| Appleton Rd. Blid | 118 | A3 |
| Appleton St. Mar War | 74 | A2 |
| Appletree Cl. South | 121 | F1 |
| Applewood Gr. Nott | 161 | E2 |
| Arboretum St. Nott | 173 | D3 |
| Arbrook Dr. Nott | 172 | B3 |
| Arbutus Cl. Nott | 184 | B1 |
| Arcade The. N-on-T | 139 | F4 |
| Arcadia Ave. Shireb | 72 | C3 |
| Arch Hill. Bes Vil | 147 | F2 |
| Archdale Rd. Nott | 161 | E3 |
| Archer Cres. Nott | 171 | F3 |
| Archer Rd. Staple | 182 | C3 |
| Archer St. Ilk | 157 | F2 |
| Archers Dr. Bils | 106 | A3 |
| Archway Rd. N Clip | 90 | B4 |
| Arden Cl. Huck | 146 | B3 |
| Arden St. Nott | 184 | A4 |
| Arden Gr. Bing | 177 | E3 |
| Ardleigh Cl. Nott | 146 | B1 |
| Ardsley Cl. Hean | 143 | D1 |
| Argosy Cl. Baw | 9 | F4 |
| Argyle St. Mar War | 73 | F2 |
| Argyle St. La Mi | 143 | E2 |
| Argyle St. Mans | 102 | B3 |
| Argyle St. Nott | 172 | C3 |
| Ariel Cl. Nott | 160 | C3 |
| Arkers Cl. Nott | 160 | B2 |
| Arklow Cl. Nott | 160 | A1 |
| Arkwright St N. Nott | 173 | E1 |
| Arkwright St S. Nott | 173 | E1 |
| Arkwright Wlk. Nott | 173 | E1 |
| Arleston Dr. Nott | 171 | E2 |
| Arlington Ave. Mans | 88 | |
| Arlington Cl. Huck | 146 | |
| Arlington Dr. Nott | 161 | |
| Arlington Way. Ret | 39 | |
| Armadale Cl. Arn | 162 | |
| Armfield Rd. Arn | 162 | |
| Armitage Dr. Lo Ea | 194 | |
| Armstrong Rd. Mans | 101 | |
| Armstrong Rd. Mans | 101 | |
| Armstrong Rd. Nott | 159 | |
| Armstrong Rd. Ret | 39 | |
| Arndale Rd. Nott | 161 | |
| Arne Ct. Nott | 173 | |
| Arnesby Rd. Nott | 172 | |
| Arno Ave. Nott | 173 | |
| Arno Vale Gdns. Arn | 161 | |
| Arno Vale Rd. Arn | 161 | |
| Arnold Ave. Lo Ea | 193 | |
| Arnold Ave. South | 121 | |
| Arnold Cres. Lo Ea | 193 | |
| Arnold La. Carl | 162 | |
| Arnold Rd. Nott | 161 | |
| Arnos Gr. Nuth | 159 | |
| Arnot Hill Rd. Arn | 161 | |
| Arnside Cl. Nott | 161 | |
| Arnside Rd. Nott | 161 | |
| Arnside. Staple | 182 | |
| Arran Cl. Staple | 170 | |
| Arran Sq. Mans | 101 | |
| Arthur Ave. Nott | 172 | |
| Arthur Ave. Staple | 182 | |
| Arthur Cres. Carl | 174 | |
| Arthur Green Ave. Ann Wo | 114 | |
| Arthur Mee Rd. Staple | 182 | |
| Arthur Rd. Gain | 15 | |
| Arthur Short Cl. Whit | 45 | |
| Arthur St. Carl | 175 | |
| Arthur St. Mans | 102 | |
| Arthur St. Nott | 173 | |
| Arthur St. Pinx | 113 | |
| Artic Way. Kim | 158 | |
| Arum Croft. Ret | 39 | |
| Arun Dale. Mans | 88 | |
| Arundel Cl. Gain | 15 | |
| Arundel Cl. Sand | 182 | |
| Arundel Dr. Bees | 171 | |
| Arundel Dr. C in L | 25 | |
| Arundel Dr. Mans | 101 | |
| Arundel Dr. Ran | 19 | |
| Arundel Dr. Nott | 173 | |
| Arundel Way. Ret | 39 | |
| Arundel Wlk. Har | 9 | |
| Ascot Ave. Kim | 158 | |
| Ascot Cl. K-in-A | 115 | |
| Ascot Dr. Arn | 161 | |
| Ascot Dr. Huck | 145 | |
| Ascot Dr. Mans | 102 | |
| Ascot Park Est. Sand | 182 | |
| Ascot Rd. Nott | 172 | |
| Ascott Gdns. W Brid | 185 | |
| Ash Cl. Bing | 178 | |
| Ash Cl. Bu Jo | 163 | |
| Ash Cl. Huck | 145 | |
| Ash Cl. Pinx | 113 | |
| Ash Cl. Work | 35 | |
| Ash Cres. K-in-A | 114 | |
| Ash Cres. Kim | 159 | |
| Ash Ct. Carl | 174 | |
| Ash Gr. Brin | 143 | |
| Ash Gr. Gain | 15 | |
| Ash Gr. Hath | 213 | |
| Ash Gr. Keyw | 198 | |
| Ash Gr. Lo Ea | 193 | |
| Ash Gr. S in A | 100 | |
| Ash Gr. Sand | 182 | |
| Ash Gr. Sels | 128 | |
| Ash Gr. Shireb | 72 | |
| Ash Gr. Staple | 182 | |
| Ash Grove. Woodb | 149 | |
| Ash La. Cost | 206 | |
| Ash Lea Cl. Cotg | 187 | |
| Ash Mount Rd. La Mi | 143 | |
| Ash Rd. N-on-T | 139 | |
| Ash St. Ilk | 157 | |
| Ash Tree Ave. Baw | 9 | |
| Ash Tree Cl. South | 136 | |
| Ash Tree Cres. Mans | 88 | |
| Ash Tree Sq. Bees | 183 | |
| Ash Vale Rd. Wale | 64 | |
| Ash Villas. Nott | 161 | |
| Ash Wlk. E Lea | 214 | |
| Ashbourne Cl. Bees | 171 | |
| Ashbourne Ct. Nott | 159 | |
| Ashbourne Rd. Sels | 129 | |
| Ashbourne St. Nott | 173 | |
| Ashbourne St. Scarc | 72 | |
| Ashburnham Ave. Nott | 172 | |
| Ashburnham Ave. Nott | 172 | |
| Ashby Ave. Mans | 88 | |
| Ashby Rd. Kegw | 203 | |
| Ashby Rd. Kegw | 212 | |
| Ashby Rd. Lo Wh | 212 | |
| Ashby Rd. Lough | 220 | |
| Ashby Sq. Lough | 220 | |
| Ashchurch Dr. Nott | 171 | |
| Ashcroft Rd. Gain | 24 | |
| Ashcroft. Ret | 39 | |

...hdale Ave. Huck ............ 146 A3
...hdale Rd. Arn .............. 162 A4
...hdale Rd. Ilk .............. 170 A3
...hdale Rd. Nott ............. 174 A3
...hdown Cl. Nott ............. 185 D3
...hdown Gr. Bing ............. 177 E2
...hdown Way. Mist ............... 6 C1
...he Cl. Arn ................. 162 A4
...her La. Rudd ............... 196 B3
...hfield Ave. Bees ........... 184 A3
...hfield Ave. Mans ........... 102 A4
...hfield Dr. K-in-A .......... 114 C3
...hfield Prec. K-in-A ........ 115 D3
...hfield Rd. Nott ............ 173 F2
...hfield Rd. S in A .......... 100 A2
...hfield St. S in A .......... 101 D3
...hford Dr. Raven ............ 117 D2
...hford Pl. Ilk .............. 157 F3
...hford Rise. Nott ........... 171 E1
...hford Rise. S in A ......... 100 B2
...hforth Ave. Hean ........... 143 D1
...hforth St. Nott ............ 173 E3
...hgate. S in A .............. 100 B2
...hington Dr. Arn ............ 148 A1
...hland Rd (W). S in A ....... 100 A2
...hland Rd. S in A ........... 100 B2
...hlands Cl. S in A .......... 100 A2
...hlea. Mist ................... 6 C1
...hleigh Way. Mans ............ 89 D1
...hley Cl. Bees .............. 183 E3
...hley Cres. Keyw ............ 197 F2
...hley Ct. Work ............... 35 F3
...hley Gr. Huck .............. 145 F4
...hley La. Tres ............... 41 F1
...hley La. Wood ............... 41 F1
...hley Rd. Keyw .............. 197 F2
...hley Rd. Work ............... 35 F3
...hley St. Nott .............. 173 F3
...hley Terr. Work ............. 35 F2
...hling St. Nott ............. 173 E1
...hmore Ave. S in A .......... 100 B1
...hover Cl. Nott ............. 173 F4
...hover Cl. Raven ............ 117 D2
...hton Ct. S in A ............ 101 D3
...hvale Rd. Tux ............... 66 A1
...hview Cl. Lo Ea ............ 193 D4
...hville Cl. Nott ............ 173 D1
...hwater Dr. Carl ............ 162 B3
...hwell Ave. Mans ............. 88 C3
...hwell Gdns. Nott ........... 172 C4
...hwick Cl. Nott ............. 185 D3
...hwood Ave. K-in-A .......... 115 E3
...hwood Cl. Mans .............. 88 C3
...hworth Ave. Rudd ........... 196 B4
...hworth Cl. N-on-T .......... 140 B4
...hworth Cl. Nott ............ 174 B3
...hworth Cres. Carl .......... 162 A1
...hworth Cres. N Le Ha ........ 32 B1
...skeby Dr. Nott ............. 159 E1
...skew La. Mar War ............ 74 A2
...skham Rd. Ashkh ............. 51 F1
...skham Rd. E Mark ............ 51 F1
...slockton Dr. Nott .......... 160 B1
...spen Cl. Bing .............. 178 A2
...spen Cl. Kettl .............. 55 D2
...spen Cl. Tux ................ 66 A1
...spen Cl. Wale ............... 64 A1
...spen Ct. Mans ............... 88 C1
...spen Cl. Tux ................ 66 A1
...spen Rd. Nott .............. 159 F4
...sper St. Carl .............. 175 D4
...spinall Ct. Nott ........... 172 B3
...spley La. Nott ............. 172 B4
...spley Park Dr. Nott ........ 172 A4
...spley Rd. Nott ............. 172 C3
...spley Rd. S in A ........... 100 B2
...squith Mews. Mans .......... 102 C3
...squith St. Gain ............. 15 D1
...squith St. Mans ............ 102 C3
...ssarts Rd. Nuth ............ 159 F2
...stcote Cl. Hean ............ 143 D1
...ster Rd. Nott .............. 173 F4
...stle Ct. Arn ............... 162 B3
...stley Cl. Ann Wo ........... 130 A4
...stley Dr. Nott ............. 161 F1
...ston Ave. Nott ............. 172 A1
...ston Ct. Ilk ............... 157 F1
...ston Dr. Nott .............. 146 B1
...ston Green. Bees ........... 182 C2
...stral Dr. Nott ............. 145 E2
...strid Gdns. Nott ........... 160 C3
...stwith La. Al Hu ............ 85 D3
...stwood Cl. Nott ............ 171 F4
...thelstan Rd. Work ........... 35 F1
...therfield Gdns. East ....... 143 F2
...therton Rd. Ilk ............ 157 E2
...therton Rd. Ship ........... 157 E2
...therton Rise. Nott ......... 160 A2
...thorpe Gr. Nott ............ 160 C2
...tkin La. Mans .............. 102 A2
...ttenborough La. Bees ....... 183 E1
...ttenborough La. Bees ....... 183 E1
...ttercliffe Terr. Nott ...... 173 E1
...ttewell Rd. Awsw ........... 158 A3
...ttlee Ave. Mans ............. 89 D1

Aubrey Rd. Nott ................ 161 D1
Auckland Cl. Nott ............. 172 C3
Auckland Rd. Huck ............. 145 E3
Auckland Rd. Ret .............. 39 E4
Audley Dr. Nott ............... 171 F1
Audon Ave. Bees ............... 183 F3
Audrey Cres. Mans ............. 88 B3
Augustine Gdns. Bes Vil ...... 147 D1
Ault Hucknall La. Al Hu ....... 86 A4
Aumberry Gap. Lough .......... 220 A2
Aurillac Way. Ret ............. 29 E1
Austen Ave. Lo Ea ............ 193 E3
Austen Ave. Nott ............. 173 D4
Austin Cl. Mans .............. 102 C4
Austin St. Nott .............. 160 B4
Austin St. Shireb ............. 73 D2
Austins Dr. Sand ............. 182 A2
Austrey Ave. Nott ............ 184 A4
Avalon Cl. Nott .............. 160 C3
Ave A. Nott .................. 173 E2
Ave B. Nott .................. 173 E2
Ave C. Nott .................. 173 E2
Ave D. Nott .................. 173 E2
Ave E. Nott .................. 173 F3
Avebury Cl. Nott ............. 195 E4
Avenue Cl. Nott .............. 160 C4
Avenue Rd. Ret ................ 39 F3
Avenue The. Calv ............. 148 C4
Avenue The. Gain .............. 15 F1
Avenue The. Gunt ............. 164 C3
Avenue The. Mans ............. 102 C2
Avenue The. N-on-T ........... 140 A4
Avenue The. S in A ........... 100 C1
Averham Cl. Mans ............. 101 E3
Averton Sq. Nott ............. 172 B2
Aviemore Cl. Arn ............. 162 A4
Avocet Wharf. Nott ........... 172 C1
Avon Ave. Huck ............... 145 F2
Avon Cl. Ann Wo .............. 129 F4
Avon Gdns. W Brid ............ 185 F4
Avon Pl. Bees ................ 184 A4
Avon Rd. Carl ................ 162 C1
Avon Rd. Nott ................ 174 A3
Avon Rise. Ret ................ 40 A4
Avon Vale Rd. Lough .......... 220 B1
Avon Way. Mans ............... 103 D3
Avon Way. Work ................ 35 F4
Avonbridge Cl. Arn ........... 148 B1
Avondale Cl. Lo Ea ........... 193 D3
Avondale Rd. Carl ............ 174 B3
Avondale. Cotg ............... 188 A2
Avondale. Mans ............... 102 C4
Avonlea Cl. Ilk .............. 170 A3
Awsworth La. Awsw ............ 158 B2
Awsworth La. Awsw ............ 158 B3
Awsworth La. Kim ............. 158 B3
Awsworth Rd. Ilk ............. 157 F1
Axford Cl. Carl .............. 162 C1
Aylesham Ave. Arn ............ 161 F3
Aylestone Dr. Nott ........... 172 A4
Ayr St. Nott ................. 173 D3
Ayscough Ave. Nuth ........... 159 E3
Ayton Cl. Nott ............... 173 D1
Azalea Ct. Greas ............. 158 B4
Azimghur Rd. What ............ 179 D2

Babbacombe Way. Huck ... 145 E3
Babbington Cres. Carl ........ 162 C1
Babbington La. Kim ........... 158 C2
Babbington St. Tibs ........... 99 D3
Babington Ct. Bees ........... 183 E3
Babworth Cres. Ret ............ 39 E3
Babworth Ct. Mans ............ 102 B4
Babworth Rd. Babw ............. 39 E3
Babworth Rd. Ret .............. 39 E3
Back La. Clayp ............... 156 B3
Back La. Cotes ............... 220 C3
Back La. Cr Bu ............... 189 D3
Back La. E Mark ............... 66 A4
Back La. Eakr ................ 106 C4
Back La. Halam ............... 120 C1
Back La. Ilk ................. 157 F1
Back La. Lo Cl ............... 211 E2
Back La. Miss .................. 4 A1
Back La. Morton .............. 137 E2
Back La. N-on-W .............. 198 A3
Back La. Nuth ................ 159 E3
Back La. Oll .................. 77 D2
Back La. Ran .................. 19 D2
Back La. S in A ............... 99 F2
Back La. S in A .............. 100 C3
Back La. Th Sa ................ 34 A3
Back La. W-on-W .............. 217 D3
Back St. B in W .............. 142 A3
Back St. E Stock .............. 7 F1
Back St. S Clift .............. 68 C1
Back Terr. Ret ................ 39 F4
Bacon Cl. Greas .............. 158 A4
Bacon St. Gain ................ 24 B3
Bacton Ave. Nott ............. 160 A4
Bacton Gdns. Nott ............ 160 A4
Baden Powell Rd. Nott ........ 174 A2
Bader Rise. Matt .............. 20 A4
Bader. Nott .................. 185 D4
Badger Cl. Huck .............. 145 E3
Baggaley Cres. Mans ........... 88 A1
Bagnall Ave. Arn ............. 161 E4
Bagnall Rd. Nott ............. 160 B2

Bagshaw St. Mans .............. 87 D2
Baildon Cl. Nott ............. 172 B2
Bailey Brook Cres. La Mi ... 143 D2
Bailey Brook Ind Est. Hean .. 143 D1
Bailey Cl. Arn ............... 161 E4
Bailey Cres. Mans ............ 101 F4
Bailey Ct. R on T ............ 175 F1
Bailey Grove Rd. East ........ 143 E1
Bailey La. R on T ............ 175 F1
Bailey Rd. N-on-T ............ 139 F3
Bailey St. Carl .............. 175 D4
Bailey St. Nott .............. 160 C1
Bailey St. Staple ............ 182 B3
Bainbridge Rd. Lough ........ 220 B1
Bainbridge Rd. Mar War ....... 74 A2
Bainbridge Terr. S in A ...... 100 B3
Bainbridge The. Calv ......... 149 D4
Baines Ave. Bald ............. 140 B2
Baines Rd. Gain ............... 24 C4
Bainton Gr. Nott ............. 184 C1
Baker Ave. Arn ............... 148 A1
Baker La. Greas .............. 144 B1
Baker Rd. Mans ................ 88 B3
Baker St. Huck ............... 146 A4
Baker St. Ilk ................ 157 F1
Baker St. Nott ............... 173 D4
Baker's Hollow. Cotg ......... 187 F2
Baker's La. Co Ba ............ 200 C4
Baker's La. Bees ............. 183 F2
Bakerdale Rd. Nott ........... 174 A3
Bakers Cl. Nott .............. 172 C3
Bakewell Ave. Carl ........... 162 C1
Bakewell Cl. Bald ............ 140 B2
Bakewell Dr. Nott ............ 160 C4
Bakewell Rd. Lo Ea ........... 193 F3
Bala Dr. Nott ................ 161 D4
Balderton Cl. Mans ........... 101 F4
Balderton Gate. N-on-T ....... 140 A4
Balderton La. Codd ........... 141 D4
Baldwin Cl. Mans .............. 89 D1
Baldwin Ct. Nott ............. 172 C3
Baldwin St. Greas ............ 144 B1
Balfour Rd. Nott ............. 172 C3
Balfour Rd. Staple ........... 182 B3
Balfour St. Gain .............. 15 E1
Balfour St. K-in-A ........... 115 E2
Balfron Gdns. Nott ........... 173 D1
Ball Hill. S Norm ............ 113 E3
Ball St. Nott ................ 173 F4
Ballantrae Cl. Arn ........... 162 A4
Ballerat Cres. Nott .......... 160 C4
Balloon Houses. Nott ......... 171 D2
Balls La. K-in-A ............. 115 E1
Balmoral Ave. W Brid ......... 185 F4
Balmoral Cl. C in L ........... 25 F3
Balmoral Cl. Mans ............. 88 C3
Balmoral Cl. Sand ............ 182 A2
Balmoral Cres. Nott .......... 171 E3
Balmoral Ct. Har .............. 9 D3
Balmoral Dr. Bees ............ 171 E1
Balmoral Dr. Har .............. 9 D3
Balmoral Dr. Mans ............. 87 F1
Balmoral Dr. Huck ............ 146 A4
Balmoral Rd. Bing ............ 177 E2
Balmoral Rd. Carl ............ 174 C3
Balmoral Rd. Nott ............ 173 D3
Bamburgh Cl. K-in-A .......... 114 C4
Bamford Dr. Mans ............. 103 D3
Bamford St. Newt .............. 99 D2
Bampton Cl. Nott ............. 172 C3
Bampton St. Lough ............ 220 A2
Banbury Ave. Bees ............ 182 C2
Bancroft La. Mans ............ 101 F4
Bancroft Rd. N-on-T .......... 140 A3
Bancroft St. Nott ............ 160 B4
Banes Rd. Bing ............... 178 A2
Bangor Wlk. Nott ............. 173 E4
Bank Ave. S in A ............. 100 C1
Bank End Rd. Fin ............... 1 B2
Bank End Rd. Mis ............... 1 B2
Bank Hill. Lamb .............. 149 D2
Bank Hill. Woodb ............. 149 D2
Bank Pl. Nott ................ 173 E2
Bank Side. Ret ................ 39 F2
Bank St. La Mi ............... 143 E2
Bank St. Lo Ea ............... 193 F4
Bankfield Dr. Bees ........... 171 E1
Banks Ave. K-in-A ............ 114 C3
Banks Cl. Arn ................ 162 A3
Banks Cres. Bing ............. 177 F2
Banks Paddock. Bing .......... 177 F2
Banks Rd. Bees ............... 182 C1
Banks The. Bing .............. 177 F2
Bankwood Cl. Nott ............ 160 A1
Bannerman Rd. K-in-A ......... 114 C3
Bannerman Rd. Nott ........... 160 B3
Baptist La. Coll ............. 111 F4
Bar Gate. N-on-T ............. 124 C1
Bar La. Nott ................. 160 B1
Bar Lane Ind Park. Nott ...... 160 B1
Bar Rd N. Beck ............... 23 E4
Bar Rd S. Beck ............... 23 E4
Bar Rd. Beck ................. 23 E4
Bar Rd. Lax ................... 79 E2
Barbara Sq. Huck ............. 130 C1

Barber Cl. Ilk ............... 157 F2
Barber St. East .............. 144 A1
Barbers Wood Cl. Raven ... 117 D1
Barbury Dr. Nott ............. 195 E4
Barclay Ct. Ship ............. 157 E2
Barden Rd. Arn ............... 162 A2
Bardfield Gdns. Nott ......... 146 B1
Bardney Dr. Nott ............. 160 A4
Bardsey Gdns. Nott ........... 161 D4
Barent Cl. Nott .............. 160 C3
Barent Wlk. Nott ............. 160 C3
Barker Ave E. Sand ........... 182 A3
Barker Ave N. Sand ........... 182 A3
Barker Ave. S in A ........... 100 B4
Barker Ave. Sels ............. 128 A2
Barker Gate. Huck ............ 145 F4
Barker Gate. Ilk ............. 157 F1
Barker Gate. Nott ............ 173 E2
Barker Hades Rd. Let .......... 16 A2
Barker Hill. Lowd ............ 150 C1
Barker St. S in A ............. 99 F2
Barker's La. Bees ............ 183 F2
Barkestone La. Bott .......... 181 D1
Barkestone La. Bott .......... 192 C4
Barkla Cl. Nott .............. 195 E4
Barkston Cl. Bald ............ 140 B2
Barley Brook Dr. La Mi ...... 143 D2
Barley Brook Wlk. La Mi ..... 143 D2
Barley Cft. S Norm ........... 113 D2
Barley Croft. W Brid ......... 185 E2
Barley Dale Dr. Staple ....... 170 B1
Barleylands. Rudd ............ 196 B3
Barling Dr. Ship ............. 157 E1
Barlock Rd. Nott ............. 160 C2
Barlow Dr (N). Awsw .......... 158 A2
Barlow Dr (S). Awsw .......... 158 A2
Barn Cl. Cotg ................ 187 F1
Barn Cl. Mans ................ 102 C3
Barn Cl. Work ................. 36 A4
Barn Croft. Bees ............. 183 D3
Barnards Pl. Lo Cl ........... 211 E2
Barnby Gate. N-on-T .......... 140 A4
Barnby La. Clayp ............. 156 B4
Barnby Rd. Bald .............. 140 B3
Barnby Rd. N-on-T ............ 140 B3
Barnby Wlk. Nott ............. 161 D2
Barndale Cl. Nott ............ 185 E2
Barnes Cres. S in A .......... 114 C4
Barnes Ct. Ret ................ 29 E1
Barnes Rd. Nott .............. 160 C4
Barnet Rd. Nott .............. 174 A4
Barnfield Cl. Lo Wh .......... 212 A4
Barnfield Rd. Coll ............ 98 A1
Barnfield. Nott .............. 185 D2
Barnsley Terr. Nott .......... 173 E1
Barnston Rd. Nott ............ 174 A3
Barnum Cl. Nott .............. 171 F3
Barons Cl. Carl .............. 162 C1
Barra Mews. Nott ............. 173 D1
Barrack La. Nott ............. 172 C2
Barrack Row. Lough ........... 220 A3
Barratt Cl. Bees ............. 183 E1
Barratt Cl. Cr Bi ............ 189 D2
Barratt Cres. Bees ........... 183 E1
Barratt La. Bees ............. 183 E1
Barrel Hill Rd. S on T ........ 96 C4
Barrhead Cl. Nott ............ 146 C1
Barringer Rd. Mans ........... 102 C4
Barrington Cl. R on T ........ 175 F1
Barrow Rd. Cotes ............. 220 C3
Barrow Slade. Keyw ........... 197 F1
Barrow St. Lough ............. 220 A2
Barrowhill Wlk. Mans ......... 103 D3
Barrows Hill La. Sels ........ 128 B3
Barry St. Nott ............... 160 A4
Barrydale Ave. Bees .......... 183 F3
Bartlow Rd. Nott ............. 171 E4
Bartlow Rd. Nott ............. 171 E4
Barton Cl. Mans ............... 89 D1
Barton Cl. Rudd .............. 196 A3
Barton La. B in F ............ 195 D3
Barton La. Bees .............. 183 E1
Barton La. Nott .............. 184 B1
Barton Rd. Lo Ea ............. 194 A3
Barton St. Bees .............. 184 A3
Bartons Cl. Greas ............ 144 B1
Barwell Dr. Nott ............. 159 E1
Basa Cres. Nott .............. 160 C4
Basford Rd. Nott ............. 160 B3
Baskin La. Bees .............. 183 E2
Baslow Ave. Carl ............. 162 C1
Baslow Cl. Lo Ea ............. 193 D3
Baslow Dr. Nott .............. 172 A1
Baslow Way. Mans ............. 103 D3
Bassett Cl. Kim .............. 158 C3
Bassett Rd. Kim .............. 158 C4
Bassett The. Shireb .......... 72 B3
Bassingfield La. Gam ......... 186 C4
Bassingfield La. Ho Pi ....... 186 C4
Baston Cl. Nott .............. 172 C3
Bateman Gdns. Nott ........... 172 C4
Bateman Rd. E Lea ............ 205 F1
Bateman's Yd. K-in-A ......... 114 B2
Bath La. Mans ................ 102 B4
Bath La. Mar War .............. 73 D3
Bath St. Ilk ................. 157 F1
Bath St. Mans ................ 102 A3

Bath St. Nott ................ 173 E3
Bath St. S in A .............. 100 C2
Bathley La. S Musk ........... 110 A1
Bathley La. S Musk ........... 124 A4
Bathley St. Nott ............. 173 E1
Baths La. Huck ............... 146 A4
Bathurst Dr. Nott ............ 172 A3
Bathurst Terr. Scarc ......... 58 C1
Bathwood Dr. Mans ............ 101 F3
Bathwood Dr. S in A .......... 101 D1
Batley La. Al Hu .............. 86 C2
Baulk La. Bees ............... 182 C3
Baulk La. Bees ............... 182 C4
Baulk La. Har .................. 8 C3
Baulk La. Torw ................ 19 D1
Baulk La. Work ................ 35 F3
Baulk The. Clar ............... 40 C4
Baulk The. Work ............... 35 F3
Baulker La. Blid ............. 118 C2
Baulker La. Farns ............ 119 D3
Baulker La. N Clip ............ 90 A2
Baum's La. Mans .............. 102 B3
Bawtry Cl. Har ................. 8 C2
Bawtry Rd. Aust ............... 10 B4
Bawtry Rd. Blyth .............. 18 A3
Bawtry Rd. Ever ............... 11 D2
Bawtry Rd. Har ................. 9 D3
Bawtry Rd. Miss ................ 4 A2
Bawtry Rd. Tick ................ 8 B4
Bawtry Wlk. Nott ............. 173 F3
Baxter Hill. Mans ............. 86 C2
Baxter St. Lough ............. 220 A2
Bayard Ct. Nott .............. 172 B3
Bayard St. Gain ............... 15 E1
Bayliss Rd. Carl ............. 162 B2
Bayswater Rd. Kim ............ 158 C4
Baythorn Rd. Nott ............ 171 E3
Beacon Dr. K-in-A ............ 115 E3
Beacon Dr. Lough ............. 220 A1
Beacon Hill Dr. Huck ......... 145 E3
Beacon Hill Rd. G on H ........ 13 D1
Beacon Hill Rd. N-on-T ....... 140 B4
Beacon Hill Rise. Nott ....... 173 F3
Beacon Hts. N-on-T ........... 140 B4
Beacon Rd. Bees .............. 184 A3
Beacon Rd. Lough ............. 220 A1
Beacon Way. N-on-T ........... 140 B4
Beaconsfield St. Lo Ea ....... 193 F4
Beaconsfield St. Nott ........ 172 C4
Bean Ave. Work ................ 36 A2
Beanford La. Calv ............ 133 F2
Beanford La. Oxt ............. 134 A2
Beardall St. Huck ............ 146 A3
Beardall St. Mans ............ 102 A4
Beardsall's Row. Ret .......... 39 F4
Beardsley Gdns. Nott ......... 173 D1
Beardsley Rd. Edwin ........... 76 B1
Beardsmore Gr. Huck .......... 130 C1
Beast Market Hill. N-on-T .... 124 C1
Beast Market Hill. Nott ...... 173 E2
Beatty Wlk. Ilk .............. 157 F2
Beauclerk Dr. Nott ........... 160 C4
Beaufit La. Pinx ............. 113 F1
Beaufort Ct. W Brid .......... 185 E2
Beaufort Dr. Bees ............ 183 E3
Beaufort St. Gain ............. 15 E2
Beaulieu Gdns. W Brid ........ 185 E3
Beauly Dr. Mans .............. 101 E3
Beaumaris Dr. Bees ........... 183 D2
Beaumaris Dr. Carl ........... 163 D1
Beaumond Cross. N-on-T ... 139 F4
Beaumont Ave. Mans ........... 102 C3
Beaumont Cl. Keyw ............ 197 F2
Beaumont Cl. Staple .......... 170 C1
Beaumont Gdns. W Brid ........ 185 E2
Beaumont Rd. Lough ........... 220 A1
Beaumont Rise. Work ........... 35 E2
Beaumont St. Gain ............. 24 B4
Beaumont St. Nott ............ 173 F2
Beaumont Wlk. N-on-T ......... 125 D1
Beauvale Cres. Huck .......... 145 E3
Beauvale Dr. Ilk ............. 157 F3
Beauvale Rd. Ann Wo .......... 114 C1
Beauvale Rd. Huck ............ 145 F3
Beauvale Rd. Nott ............ 173 E1
Beauvale Rise. East .......... 144 A2
Beauvale. East ............... 144 B1
Beaver Pl. Work ............... 35 F2
Beazley Ave. Mans ............ 101 F4
Beck Ave. Calv ............... 148 C4
Beck Cres. Blid .............. 118 A2
Beck Cres. Mans .............. 101 F4
Beck La. Clay ................. 21 F2
Beck La. Farns ............... 119 F3
Beck La. Mans ................ 101 D3
Beck St. Carl ................ 174 C4
Beck St. Nott ................ 173 E3
Beck St. Thur ................ 151 E4
Beckenham Rd. Nott ........... 172 C3
Beckett Ave. C in L ........... 25 E4
Beckett Ave. Gain ............. 15 F1
Beckett Ave. Mans ............. 87 F1
Beckett Ct. Carl ............. 162 B2
Beckford Rd. Nott ............ 173 F2
Beckhampton Rd. Nott ....... 161 D4
Beckingham Ct. Mans ......... 101 F4
Beckingham Rd. Walker ...... 14 A2

## Beckingthorpe Dr. Bott

Beckingthorpe Dr. Bott ....... 181 D2
Beckland Hill. E Mark ......... 65 F3
Beckley Rd. Nott ............... 159 F1
Beckside. W Brid ............... 186 B3
Bed Hill La. Ruff ............... 92 C2
Bedale Ct. Bees ............... 183 D2
Bedale Rd. Nott ............... 161 E3
Bedale. Work ................... 36 A4
Bede House La. N-on-T ...... 140 A4
Bede Ling. W Brid ............. 185 E3
Bedford Ave. Mans ........... 102 C4
Bedford Cl. Kegw ............. 203 E1
Bedford Ct. Baw ................. 9 F4
Bedford Ct. Staple ............ 170 C1
Bedford Gr. Nott ............... 160 B3
Bedford Row. Nott ............ 173 E3
Bedford Sq. Lough ............ 220 A2
Bedford St. Lough ............. 220 A2
Bedlington Gdns. Nott ....... 161 F1
Bee Hive La. Lough ........... 220 A2
Beech Ave. Arn ................ 162 A2
Beech Ave. Bees .............. 184 A3
Beech Ave. Bing ............... 178 A2
Beech Ave. Carl ............... 174 C3
Beech Ave. E Lea ............. 214 B4
Beech Ave. Gain ............... 15 F1
Beech Ave. Huck .............. 146 A4
Beech Ave. K-in-A ............ 114 C3
Beech Ave. Keyw ............. 198 A1
Beech Ave. Kim ................ 159 D3
Beech Ave. Lo Ea ............. 182 C1
Beech Ave. Mans ............. 102 A3
Beech Ave. Nott ............... 173 D4
Beech Ave. Oll ................... 77 E2
Beech Ave. Pinx ............... 113 F2
Beech Ave. Raven ............ 116 C2
Beech Ave. S in A ............ 100 A2
Beech Ave. Sand .............. 182 A4
Beech Ave. Tick ................... 8 A4
Beech Ave. Work ............... 35 F3
Beech Cl. G on H ............... 12 C1
Beech Cl. Nott ................. 160 B2
Beech Cl. R on T ............. 175 F1
Beech Cl. W Brid ............. 186 A2
Beech Cres. Glap .............. 86 A4
Beech Ct. Arn .................. 162 A2
Beech Ct. Sels ................ 129 D2
Beech Gr. Bild ................. 118 B3
Beech Gr. C in L ................ 25 F4
Beech Gr. S Norm ............ 113 D3
Beech Hill Ave. Mans .......... 87 F1
Beech Hill Cres. Mans ........ 87 F1
Beech Hill Dr. Mans ........... 87 F1
Beech Rd. Har ................... 9 D3
Beech Rd. Sels ................ 129 D2
Beech St. S in A .............. 100 B4
Beech Tree Ave. Mans ........ 88 A3
Beech Wlk. Elk .................. 50 A2
Beecham Ave. Nott ........... 173 F3
Beechcroft. Work ............... 36 A3
Beechdale Ave. S in A ....... 100 C2
Beechdale Cres. S in A ...... 100 C2
Beechdale Rd. Mans ........... 89 D1
Beechdale Rd. Nott ........... 172 A4
Beecher La. Beck ............... 14 A1
Beeches Rd. Lough ........... 220 B1
Beeches The. Carl ............ 174 A4
Beeches The. S in A .......... 100 B4
Beeches The. Tux .............. 65 F1
Beechways. Ret ................. 39 E2
Beechwood Cl. Mans .......... 89 D1
Beechwood Cl. S in A ........ 101 D3
Beechwood Cres. Babw ....... 37 F3
Beechwood Ct. S in A ........ 101 D3
Beechwood Dr. Babw ......... 38 B3
Beechwood Rd. Arn ........... 162 A4
Beechwood Rd. K-in-A ....... 114 C4
Beehive La. Eagle .............. 84 C1
Beehive St. Ret ................. 39 F3
Beeley Ave. S in A ........... 100 C1
Beeley Cl. Mans ............... 103 D3
Beeston Cl. Bes Vil ........... 146 C2
Beeston Ct. Nott .............. 160 B3
Beeston Fields Dr. Bees ..... 183 E4
Beeston La. Nott .............. 184 A4
Beeston Rd. N-on-T .......... 140 A3
Beeston Rd. Nott .............. 172 B1
Behay Gdns. Stay ............. 138 B4
Beighton Ct. Mans ............ 103 D3
Beighton St. S in A ........... 100 C2
Belconnen Rd. Nott ........... 161 D3
Belfmoor Cl. Whit .............. 45 D3
Belford Cl. Nott ............... 159 F4
Belfry Cl. K-in-A .............. 114 C4
Bell La. Coll ................... 111 F4
Bell La. Nott ................... 185 D4
Bell La. West ................... 81 D3
Bell St. Carl ................... 174 B4
Bellamy Rd. Mans ............ 103 D1
Bellar Gate. Nott ............. 173 E2
Belle Vue La. Blid ............ 118 A3
Belle-isle Rd. Huck .......... 146 A4
Belleville Dr. Nott ............ 161 D4
Bellevue Ct. Nott ............. 173 F3
Bellmore Gdns. Nott ......... 171 E3
Bells La. Nott .................. 160 A2
Bellsfield Cl. Whit ............. 45 D3
Belmond Cl. N-on-T .......... 139 F3

Belmont Ave. Nott ............ 160 B4
Belmont Cl. Bees ............. 183 D2
Belmont Cl. Huck ............. 146 A2
Belmont Cl. Mans .............. 89 D1
Belmont Rd. Ann Wo ........ 115 D1
Belper Ave. Carl .............. 162 B1
Belper Cres. Carl ............. 162 B1
Belper Rd. Nott ............... 172 C4
Belper St. Mans ............... 102 B4
Belper Way. Mans ............ 102 B4
Belsay Rd. Nott ............... 161 D4
Belsford Ct. Greas ........... 159 D4
Belt Rd The. Gain .............. 15 F2
Belton Cl. Sand ............... 182 A2
Belton Dr. W Brid ............ 185 D2
Belton Rd W Ext. Lough .... 220 A3
Belton Rd. Lough ............. 220 A3
Belton St. Nott ................ 172 C4
Belvedere Ave. Nott ......... 172 C4
Belvedere St. Mans .......... 102 A3
Belvoir Ave. Bott ............. 181 D1
Belvoir Cl. Aslo ............... 178 C2
Belvoir Cl. Lo Ea ............. 193 F3
Belvoir Cres. N-on-T ........ 140 A3
Belvoir Hill. Nott .............. 173 F2
Belvoir Pl. Bald ............... 140 B2
Belvoir Rd. Bald .............. 140 B2
Belvoir Rd. Bott ............... 181 D1
Belvoir Rd. Carl ............... 175 D4
Belvoir Rd. Redm ............. 192 C2
Belvoir St. Huck .............. 145 F4
Belvoir St. Nott ............... 161 F1
Belvoir Terr. Mort .............. 15 D2
Belward St. Nott .............. 173 E2
Belwood Cl. Nott ............. 184 C1
Bembridge Ct. Bees .......... 183 D4
Bembridge Dr. Nott ......... 161 D3
Bembridge. Work .............. 36 A3
Ben Mayo Ct. Nott ........... 172 C3
Ben St. Nott ................... 172 C3
Benedict Ct. Bes Vil ......... 147 D1
Benet Dr. Bils ................. 106 A3
Benington Dr. Nott ........... 171 E2
Benner Ave. Ilk ............... 170 A3
Bennerley Ave. Ilk ........... 157 F2
Bennerley Rd. Nott .......... 159 F4
Bennett Ave. Mans ........... 102 C3
Bennett Rd. Carl .............. 162 A2
Bennett St. Lo Ea ............ 182 B1
Bennett St. Nott .............. 161 F1
Bennett St. Sand ............. 182 A3
Benneworth Cl. Huck ........ 145 F3
Bennington Wlk. Mans ........ 88 C2
Bentick St. Mans ............. 102 B4
Bentinck Ave. Toll ........... 186 B1
Bentinck Cl. Boug .............. 77 F3
Bentinck Cl. Nott ............. 173 F2
Bentinck Rd. Carl ............. 162 B1
Bentinck Rd. N-on-T ......... 139 F3
Bentinck St. Ann Wo ........ 114 C1
Bentinck St. Ann Wo ........ 129 F4
Bentinck St. Huck ............ 145 F4
Bentinck St. S in A ........... 100 C2
Bentinck Terr. Mar War ....... 74 A2
Bentley Ave. Nott ............ 174 A3
Bentwell Ave. Arn ............ 162 A4
Beresford Dr. Ilk ............. 157 F3
Beresford Rd. Lo Ea ......... 193 D3
Beresford Rd. Mans ........... 88 B3
Beresford St. Mans .......... 102 B3
Beresford St. Nott ........... 172 C3
Berkeley Ave. Lo Ea ......... 193 E3
Berkeley Ave. Nott ........... 173 E4
Bernard Ave. Huck ........... 131 D1
Bernard Ave. Mans ............ 88 A3
Bernard St. Mans ............. 101 F4
Bernard St. Nott .............. 161 D1
Bernisdale Cl. Nott .......... 146 C1
Berridge Rd. Nott ............ 172 C4
Berridge Rd. Nott ............ 173 D4
Berridge Road West. Nott .. 172 C4
Berriedale Cl. Arn ............ 162 B4
Berristow La. S Norm ....... 113 E4
Berry Ave. K-in-A ............ 114 C3
Berry Hill Gdns. Mans ...... 102 C2
Berry Hill Gr. Carl ........... 162 C1
Berry Hill La. Mans .......... 102 B2
Berry Hill Rd. Mans .......... 102 B2
Berry Park Lea. Mans ....... 102 B2
Berwick Ave. Mans ........... 101 E4
Berwick Cl. Nott .............. 161 E3
Berwin Cl. Lo Ea .............. 182 A1
Beryldene Ave. Kim .......... 159 D4
Bescar La. Oll ................... 77 D1
Bescoby St. Ret ................ 39 F4
Besecar Ave. Carl ............ 162 C1
Besecar Cl. Carl .............. 162 C1
Bessell La. Bees .............. 182 B3
Bessell La. Staple ............ 182 B3
Bessingham Dr. W Brid ..... 185 E2
Besthorpe Cl. Mans .......... 101 F4
Besthorpe Rd. Coll ............ 98 A1
Besthorpe Rd. N Sca .......... 83 E1
Bestwick Ave. Hean .......... 143 D1
Bestwood Ave. Arn ........... 161 F4
Bestwood Cl. Arn ............. 161 F4

Bestwood Lodge Dr. Bes Vil 161 E4
Bestwood Lodge Dr. Nott .. 161 E4
Bestwood Park Dr W. Nott . 146 C1
Bestwood Park Dr. Nott ..... 161 D4
Bestwood Park View. Nott .. 147 F1
Bestwood Rd. Huck .......... 146 B3
Bestwood Rd. Nott ........... 146 B1
Bestwood Rd. Pinx ........... 113 F1
Bestwood Terr. Nott ......... 160 B4
Bethel Gdns. Huck ........... 145 E3
Bethel St. Ilk .................. 157 F1
Bethel Terr. Shire .............. 34 C3
Bethnal Wlk. Nott ............ 160 A4
Betula Cl. Nott ................ 184 B1
Beulah Rd. K-in-A ............ 115 D2
Bevan Cl. Rain ................ 118 A4
Bevel St. Nott ................. 172 C4
Bevercotes Rd. Tux ........... 65 E2
Beverley Cl. Nott ............. 171 D2
Beverley Cl. Rain ............. 104 B1
Beverley Dr. Codd ............ 125 F1
Beverley Dr. K-in-A .......... 115 E2
Beverley Dr. Kim ............. 158 C4
Beverley Dr. Mans ........... 102 B1
Beverley Gdns. Carl ......... 162 C1
Beverley Rd. Har ............... 9 D2
Beverley Sq. Nott ............ 173 F3
Beverley Wlk. C in L .......... 25 F4
Beverleys Ave. Aslo ......... 178 C2
Bewcastle Rd. Bes Vil ...... 147 D1
Bewcastle Rd. Nott .......... 147 D1
Bewick Dr. Nott ............... 174 B3
Bexhill Ct. Bees ............... 171 F1
Bexwell Cl. Nott .............. 195 F4
Biant Cl. Nott .................. 160 A2
Bidford Rd. Nott .............. 159 F1
Bidwell Cres. Goth ........... 195 D1
Big Barn La. Mans ............ 102 C3
Big La. Clar ..................... 30 B2
Biggin St. Lough .............. 220 A2
Bigsby Rd. Ret .................. 30 A1
Biko Sq. Nott .................. 172 C4
Bilberry Wlk. Nott ........... 173 F4
Bilbie Wlk. Nott ............... 173 E3
Billborough Rd. Nott ........ 171 E3
Billesdon Dr. Nott ............ 171 E3
Billingsley Ave. Pinx ........ 113 E2
Bilsthorpe Rd. Eakr ........... 92 B1
Bingham Ave. S in A ......... 101 D3
Bingham Rd. Cotg ............ 187 F2
Bingham Rd. Mans ........... 103 D2
Bingham Rd. Nott ............ 161 E1
Bingham Rd. R on T .......... 176 A2
Bingham Rd. Wi Ha .......... 189 F3
Birch Ave. Bees ............... 184 A2
Birch Ave. Carl ................ 174 B4
Birch Ave. Farns .............. 119 F4
Birch Ave. Ilk .................. 170 A4
Birch Ave. Kim ................ 159 D3
Birch Ave. Rain ............... 104 B1
Birch Cl. Kim .................. 159 D3
Birch Cl. Ramp .................. 42 C1
Birch Cl. Raven ............... 117 D1
Birch Croft Dr. Mans .......... 89 D1
Birch Cl. Tux .................... 65 F1
Birch Gr. Gain .................. 15 E1
Birch Gr. Mans ................ 103 D2
Birch Gr. Shireb ................ 72 B3
Birch Lea. Arn ................. 161 E4
Birch Lea. E Lea .............. 205 E1
Birch Pas. Nott ............... 173 D3
Birch Rd. Bald ................. 140 B3
Birch Rd. Oll ..................... 77 E2
Birch Rd. Whit .................. 45 E3
Birch St. Mar War .............. 73 F3
Birch Tree Cl. Mans ........... 89 E2
Birch Tree Cres. K-in-A ..... 114 C2
Birchdale Ave. Huck ......... 146 A3
Birchen Holme. S Norm ..... 113 D2
Birchenhall Ct. Farn ......... 139 D2
Birches The. Raven .......... 117 D2
Birchfield Rd. Arn ............ 148 A1
Birchlands. Mans .............. 88 C1
Birchover Pl. Ilk .............. 157 F3
Birchover Rd. Nott ........... 171 E3
Birchwood Ave. Lo Ea ...... 193 D4
Birchwood Ave. Lo Ea ...... 193 E3
Birchwood Cl. Raven ........ 117 D1
Birchwood Cl. S in A ........ 100 C3
Birchwood Cl. S Norm ...... 113 D2
Birchwood Cl. South ......... 121 E1
Birchwood Dr. Raven ........ 117 D1
Birchwood Dr. S in A ........ 100 B4
Birchwood Rd. Nott .......... 171 E2
Bird's La. Ann Wo ............ 114 C1
Birdcroft La. Walker ........... 14 A3
Birding St. Mans ............... 88 A1
Birdsall Ave. Nott ............ 171 F2
Birkdale Ave. Boug ............ 77 E3
Birkdale Cl. Ilk ................. 157 E1
Birkdale Cl. W Brid .......... 186 A2
Birkdale Gr. K-in-A ........... 114 C3
Birkdale Gr. Ret ................ 39 E2
Birkdale Way. Nott ........... 160 A4
Birkdale. Work .................. 36 A3
Birkin Ave. Bees .............. 183 D1

Birkin Ave. Nott ............... 172 C4
Birkin Ave. R on T ........... 176 A2
Birkin Ave. Rudd ............. 196 B4
Birkland Ave. Arn ............ 162 A2
Birkland Ave. Mans ........... 88 B2
Birkland Ave. Mar War ....... 74 A2
Birkland Ave. Nott ........... 173 E3
Birkland Dr. Edwin ............ 76 A1
Birkland St. Mans ............ 102 B4
Birklands Ave. Oll .............. 77 E3
Birklands Ave. Work ........... 36 B1
Birklands Cl. Mar War ........ 74 A3
Birks Cl. Whit ................... 45 E3
Birks Rd. Mans ................ 101 E4
Birley St. Staple .............. 182 B3
Birling Cl. Nott ................ 159 F4
Birrel St. Gain .................. 15 D1
Birrell Rd. Nott ............... 173 D4
Bisham Dr. W Brid ........... 186 A4
Bishop Alexandra Ct. N-on-T 139 F4
Bishop St. East ............... 143 F1
Bishop St. Lough ............. 220 B2
Bishop St. Mans .............. 102 A3
Bishop St. S in A ............. 100 C2
Bishop's Dr. South ........... 136 C4
Bishop's Wlk. Mar War ....... 74 A3
Bishopdale Cl. Lo Ea ........ 193 D3
Bishopdale. Work .............. 36 A4
Bishopfield La. Ran ............ 19 D3
Bishops Cl. Keyw ............. 197 F2
Bishops Hill. Mans ........... 103 F1
Bishops Rd. Bing ............. 177 E3
Bishops Way. Huck .......... 146 A4
Bispham Dr. Bees ............ 182 C1
Black La. Swine ................. 71 F1
Black Scotch La. Mans ...... 102 C2
Blackacre. Lamb .............. 163 F3
Blackburn Cl. Coll ............. 98 A1
Blackburn Pl. Ilk ............. 157 F2
Blackcliff Field Cl. Whit ...... 45 D3
Blacketts Wlk. Nott .......... 195 E4
Blackfriars Cl. Nuth .......... 159 E2
Blackham Rd. Lough ......... 220 A1
Blackhill Dr. Carl ............. 174 C4
Blackrod Cl. Bees ............ 183 D1
Blacksmith La. Kelh .......... 124 A2
Blacksmith La. Torw ........... 19 D1
Blacksmiths Cl. Ne Br ....... 219 E4
Blacksmiths La. N Sca ........ 83 E1
Blackstone Wlk. Nott ........ 173 E1
Blackstope La. Ret ............. 40 A4
Blackthorn Cl. Bing .......... 178 A2
Blackthorne Cl. Bald ........ 140 A3
Blackthorne Dr. East ........ 143 E1
Blackthorne Dr. Lowd ....... 150 B1
Blackwell Rd. S in A ........... 99 F3
Bladon Cl. Nott ............... 161 F1
Bladon Cl. Nott ............... 172 C3
Bladon Rd. Rudd ............. 196 A4
Blair Ct. Nott .................. 173 E1
Blair Gr. Sand ................. 182 A2
Blaise Cl. Nott ................ 195 F4
Blake Cl. Arn ................... 162 A4
Blake Cres. Mans ............ 102 C4
Blake Ct. Lo Ea ............... 193 D3
Blake Rd. Staple .............. 182 C3
Blake Rd. W Brid ............. 186 A4
Blake St. Ilk ................... 157 F1
Blake St. Mans ................. 88 A1
Blakeney Ct. Mans ............ 88 C2
Blakeney Dr. Mans ........... 102 B2
Blakeney Rd. R on T ......... 176 A2
Blakeney Wlk. Arn ........... 161 F3
Bland La. Epp ................. 150 A3
Blandford Ave. Lo Ea ....... 193 D3
Blandford Gdns. W Brid .... 185 E3
Blandford Rd. Bees .......... 183 E3
Blankney Cl. Sax .............. 57 D2
Blankney St. Nott ............ 160 C2
Blantyre Ave. Nott ........... 146 C1
Blatherwick Rd. N-on-T ..... 140 B4
Blatherwick's Yd. Arn ....... 161 F4
Bleachers Yd. Nott .......... 160 C1
Bleak Hill Way. Mans ....... 101 F2
Bleak Hills La. Mans ........ 101 F2
Bleasby Cres. S in A ........ 101 D1
Bleasby Rd. Bleas ........... 151 E4
Bleasby Rd. Thur ............. 151 E4
Bleasby St. Nott .............. 173 F2
Bleasdale Cl. Carl ............ 163 D1
Blenheim Ave. Carl .......... 162 B1
Blenheim Ave. Lowd ......... 150 C1
Blenheim Cl. Mans ............ 88 B1
Blenheim Cl. Rudd ........... 196 A4
Blenheim Dr. Bees ........... 183 E3
Blenheim Gdns. E Brid ...... 165 E1
Blenheim La. Huck ........... 145 F1
Blenheim La. Stre ............ 145 F1
Blenheim Pl. S in A ............ 99 F2
Blenhiem Ct. Sand ........... 182 A2
Bley Ave. E Lea ............... 214 B4
Blidworth La. Blid ............ 133 E4
Blidworth La. Mans .......... 103 E1
Blidworth La. Rain ........... 117 F4
Blidworth Rd. Farns .......... 119 F3
Blidworth Rd. K-in-A ........ 115 F2
Blidworth Waye. Papp ....... 131 E2

Blidworth Waye. Raven ..... 131 F...
Blind La. Oxt ................... 134 B...
Bloomgrove Rd. Ilk .......... 157 F...
Bloomsgrove St. Nott ....... 172 C...
Blue Bell Hill Rd. Nott ...... 173 E...
Blue Bell Yd. Tux .............. 65 F...
Bluebell Cl. Huck ............. 145 E...
Bluebell Cl. S in A ........... 100 C...
Bluebell Cl. Sels .............. 128 C...
Bluebell Gr. K-in-A .......... 114 C...
Bluecoat Cl. Nott ............ 173 E...
Bluecoat St. Nott ............ 173 E...
Blundell Cl. Nott ............. 173 F...
Blyth Cl. Mans .................. 87 E...
Blyth Gdns. Nott ............. 161 F...
Blyth Gr. Work .................. 36 A...
Blyth Rd. Babw ................. 48 C...
Blyth Rd. Bir ..................... 8 C...
Blyth Rd. Elk .................... 48 C...
Blyth Rd. Hod ................... 27 F...
Blyth Rd. Old .................... 16 C...
Blyth Rd. Oll ..................... 77 C...
Blyth Rd. Perl ................... 63 D...
Blyth Rd. Ran .................... 19 D...
Blyth Rd. Styr ..................... 8 C...
Blyth Rd. Styr ................... 18 A...
Blyth Rd. Tick .................... 8 C...
Blyth Rd. Work .................. 36 A...
Blyth St. Nott .................. 161 F...
Blyton Rd. Thon ................ 15 E...
Blyton Wlk. Nott .............. 161 D...
Boar La. N-on-T ............... 139 F...
Boat La. Ald .................... 143 D...
Boat La. E Sto ................ 152 B...
Boat La. Hover ................. 151 F...
Boatmans Cl. Ilk .............. 157 F...
Bobbers Mill Bridge. Nott .. 172 B...
Bobbers Mill Rd. Nott ....... 172 C...
Boden Dr. Nuth ................ 159 E...
Boden St. Nott ................ 172 C...
Bodmin Ave. Huck ........... 145 E...
Bodmin Ct. Mans ............. 103 D...
Bodmin Dr. Nott .............. 160 B...
Bohem Rd. Lo Ea ............ 182 B...
Bold Cl. Nott ................... 160 A...
Bolero Cl. Nott ................ 171 F...
Bolham La. Ret .................. 29 F...
Bolingey Way. Huck ......... 145 E...
Bollard's La. Su Bo ........... 213 D...
Bolsover St. Huck ............ 146 A...
Bolsover St. Mans ........... 102 B...
Bolton Ave. Bees ............. 183 E...
Bolton Cl. W Brid ............ 186 A...
Bolton La. Hose .............. 211 F...
Bolton Terr. R on T .......... 175 F...
Bond St. Arn ................... 161 F...
Bond St. Nott .................. 173 F...
Bonemill La. Clar .............. 30 B...
Bonemill La. Work ............. 35 F...
Bonetti Cl. Arn ................ 162 B...
Boniface Gdns. Bes Vil ..... 147 D...
Bonington Dr. Arn ........... 161 F...
Bonington Rd. Arn ........... 162 A...
Bonington Rd. Mans ......... 101 F...
Bonner Hill. Calv ............. 148 C...
Bonner La. Calv ............... 149 D...
Bonner's Rd. Awsw .......... 158 B...
Bonnington Cl. Nott ......... 160 A...
Bonnington Cres. Nott ...... 161 E...
Bonny Mead. Cotg ........... 187 F...
Bonsal Ct. Mans .............. 103 D...
Bonsall St. Lo Ea ............ 193 F...
Bonser Cl. Carl ............... 174 C...
Bonser Cres. S in A ........... 99 F...
Bonser Gdns. S in A ........ 100 B...
Booth Ave. Plea ................ 87 D...
Booth Cl. Nott ................ 173 E...
Booth Cres. Mans ............. 87 E...
Booth St. Mans ................. 88 A...
Boots Yd. S in A ................ 99 F...
Borders Ave. K-in-A ......... 114 C...
Borlace Cres. Staple ........ 182 C...
Borman Cl. Nott .............. 159 F...
Borough St. Kegw ............ 203 E...
Borrow Bread La. Bleas ..... 152 A...
Borrowdale Dr. Lo Ea ....... 193 D...
Borrowell. Kegw .............. 203 E...
Boscowan Ct. Ilk ............. 157 F...
Bosden Cl. Nott ............... 171 E...
Bosley Sq. Nott ............... 184 A...
Bostock's La. Sand ........... 182 A...
Boston St. Nott ............... 173 E...
Boswell Cl. Kinou ............ 200 A...
Boswell Cl. Mans ............. 102 B...
Bosworth Dr. Greas .......... 144 A...
Bosworth St. Mans ........... 101 E...
Bosworth Way. Lo Ea ....... 193 F...
Bosworth Wlk. Nott .......... 173 C...
Botany Ave. Mans ............ 101 F...
Botany Ave. Nott ............. 173 F...
Botany Cl. W Brid ............ 185 E...
Botany Dr. Ilk .................. 157 F...
Bothe Cl. Lo Ea .............. 193 E...
Bottle La. Nott ................ 173 E...
Bottleacre La. Lough ........ 220 A...
Bottom Green. Up Br ........ 210 A...
Bottom Row. N-on-T ......... 140 A...
Boughton Cl. S in A .......... 100 C...

227

oughton Ind Est. Kirton

Bull Yd. South

oughton Ind Est. Kirton 78 A3
ughton Rd. Rhod 35 D3
uld St. Mans 87 F1
undary Cl. Shireb 72 C3
undary Cres. Bees 171 F1
undary Cres. Blid 118 A3
undary Ct. N-on-T 139 F4
undary La. East 143 E2
oundary Rd. Bees 183 F4
oundary Rd. N-on-T 139 F4
oundary Rd. W Brid 185 F2
oundary Row. Work 35 F1
oundary Wlk. Scarc 58 C1
ourne Ave. K-in-A 115 D2
ourne Ave. Sels 129 D4
ourne Cl. Bees 171 E1
ourne Dr. Raven 117 D1
ourne Mews. Carl 175 D3
ourne St. Carl 175 D3
ournmoor Ave. Nott 184 C1
ovill St. Nott 172 C3
ovington Ct. Ret 29 F1
ow St. Mans 88 C2
Bowbridge Gdns. Bott 181 D2
Bowbridge La. Bald 140 A2
Bowbridge La. Bott 180 C2
Bowbridge Rd. N-on-T 140 A3
Bowden Dr. Bees 184 A3
Bowers Ave. Nott 173 E4
Bowes Well Rd. Ilk 157 F1
Bowland Cl. Nott 174 A4
Bowland Rd. Bing 177 E2
Bowler Ct. Lough 220 B2
Bowling Green Rd. Gain 15 D1
Bowling St. Mans 102 B3
Bowlwell Ave. Nott 160 C4
Bowne St. S in A 100 C2
Bowness Ave. Nott 160 B1
Box Cres. K-in-A 114 C3
Boxley Dr. W Brid 185 E2
Boy La. Edwin 76 A1
Boyce Gdns. Nott 161 F1
Boycroft Ave. Nott 173 F4
Boyd Cl. Arn 148 A1
Boyer St. Lough 220 B2
Boyer's Orchard. Harb 202 A2
Boynton Dr. Nott 161 F1
Bracadale Rd. Nott 146 C1
Bracebridge Ave. Work 36 A2
Bracebridge Ct. Work 36 A1
Bracebridge Dr. Nott 171 E4
Bracebridge. Work 36 A2
Bracey Rise. W Brid 185 F2
Bracken Ave. Boug 77 F3
Bracken Cl. Carl 162 B1
Bracken Cl. Gain 15 D2
Bracken Cl. K-in-A 114 C4
Bracken Cl. Lo Ea 182 A1
Bracken Cl. Mar War 74 B2
Bracken Cl. Nott 159 F1
Bracken Hill La. Miss 4 A3
Bracken Hill. Mans 103 D3
Bracken La. Ret 40 A3
Bracken Rd. Lo Ea 182 A1
Brackendale Ave. Arn 161 F4
Brackendale Dr. Wale 64 A1
Brackenfield Ave. Mans 88 C2
Brackenfield Dr. Greas 158 A4
Brackenfield Rise. Raven 117 D2
Brackenhurst La. South 136 B3
Brackenwood Cl. Mans 89 D1
Brackhills Cl. Mans 88 C1
Bracknell Cres. Nott 160 B1
Brackner La. Kirk 106 A2
Bracton Dr. Nott 173 F3
Bradbourne Ave. Nott 185 D3
Bradbury St. Nott 174 A2
Bradden Ave. Staple 170 C1
Bradder La. Mans 102 A3
Bradfield Rd. Nott 159 F1
Bradforth Ave. Mans 103 D4
Bradgate Cl. Sand 182 A2
Bradgate Rd. Nott 173 D4
Bradley St. Sand 182 B3
Bradley Wlk. Nott 195 F4
Bradley. Nott 195 F4
Bradleys Orch. Hover 151 E1
Bradman Gdns. Arn 162 A3
Bradmore Ave. Rudd 196 B4
Bradmore Ct. Mans 103 D2
Bradmore La. Plum 197 E3
Bradmore Rise. Nott 161 E2
Bradshaw St. Lo Ea 193 D3
Bradwell Cl. Greas 158 B4
Bradwell Dr. Nott 161 D4
Braemar Ave. East 143 F1
Braemar Dr. Carl 163 D1
Braemar Rd. Mans 89 F2
Braemar Rd. Nott 160 B4
Brail Wood Cl. Bils 106 A3
Brail Wood Rd. Bils 106 A3
Brailsford Ct. Mans 103 D3
Brailsford Rd. Nott 172 C1
Brake La. Boug 77 F4
Brake Rd. Wale 63 F1
Brake View. Boug 77 F3
Bramber Gr. Nott 195 F4
Bramble Cl. Bees 183 E1
Bramble Cl. Boug 77 E3
Bramble Cl. Lo Ea 182 A1
Bramble Cl. Nott 160 B2
Bramble Cl. Shireb 72 C3
Bramble Ct. Carl 162 C1
Bramble Dr. Carl 174 A4
Bramble Gdns. Nott 172 A4
Bramble La. Mans 103 D3
Bramble Rd. Ret 40 A2
Bramble Way. Har 8 C2
Brambles The. Wale 64 A1
Brambleway. Cotg 188 A1
Brambling Cl. Mans 102 C4
Bramcote Ave. Bees 183 E3
Bramcote Ct. Mans 103 D2
Bramcote Dr W. Bees 183 E4
Bramcote Dr. Bees 183 F4
Bramcote Dr. Nott 171 E2
Bramcote Dr. Ret 39 E3
Bramcote La. Bees 183 E3
Bramcote La. Nott 171 E2
Bramcote Rd. Bees 183 F4
Bramcote Wlk. Nott 172 C3
Bramerton Rd. Nott 171 E3
Bramhall Rd. Nott 171 E3
Bramley Cl. South 136 C4
Bramley Ct. Kim 158 C3
Bramley Ct. S in A 100 C2
Bramley Rd. Nott 159 F1
Bramley Wlk. Mans 101 E4
Bramoote St. Nott 172 C3
Brampton Ave. Hean 143 D1
Brampton Ct. Gam 186 B4
Brampton Dr. Staple 182 C3
Brancaster Cl. Nott 160 A2
Brancliffe La. Shire 34 C4
Brand La. S in A 100 B3
Brand St. Nott 173 F1
Brandish Cres. Nott 184 B1
Brandon Cl. Bald 140 C2
Brandreth Ave. Nott 173 F4
Brandreth Ave. S in A 100 B2
Brandreth Dr. Greas 158 A4
Branklene Cl. Kim 158 C4
Branksome Wlk. Nott 173 E1
Bransdale Cl. Lo Ea 193 D3
Bransdale Rd. Nott 184 B1
Bransdale. Work 36 A4
Branston Ave. Farns 119 F3
Branston Cl. Wint 125 E3
Branston Gdns. W Brid 185 E2
Branston Wlk. Nott 161 E2
Brantford Ave. Nott 184 C1
Brassington Cl. Greas 158 A4
Brassington Ct. Mans 88 C2
Braunton Cl. Huck 145 E3
Brayton Cres. Nott 160 B3
Breach Rd. Hean 157 D4
Breadsall Ct. Ilk 157 F2
Breamer Rd. Coll 112 A4
Brechin Cl. Arn 148 A1
Brechin Ct. Mans 88 A3
Brechin. Work 36 A3
Breck Bank Cres. Oll 77 E3
Breck Bank. Oll 77 E3
Breck Hill Rd. Arn 161 F2
Breck La. Matt 20 A4
Breckbank. Mans 88 C1
Brecks La. Elst 154 A1
Brecks La. Stap 127 F4
Brecks Rd. Ret 39 E2
Breckswood Dr. Nott 195 F4
Brecon Cl. Lo Ea 193 D4
Brecon Cl. Nott 160 A2
Brecon Cl. Rain 104 B1
Bredon Cl. Lo Ea 193 D4
Breedon St. Lo Ea 182 B1
Brendon Ct. Bees 183 D4
Brendon Dr. Kim 158 C4
Brendon Dr. Nott 172 A3
Brendon Gdns. Nott 172 A3
Brendon Gr. Bing 177 E3
Brendon Rd. Nott 172 A3
Brendon Way. Lo Ea 182 A1
Brentcliffe Ave. Nott 174 A4
Bretby Ct. Mans 103 D3
Brett Cl. Huck 145 F3
Bretton Rd. Raven 117 D2
Brewery La. Ever 11 E2
Brewery La. Ret 39 F3
Brewery St. Kim 158 C3
Brewster Rd. Nott 173 F4
Brewsters Cl. Bing 177 F2
Brewsters Way. Ret 29 E1
Briar Ave. Sand 182 A2
Briar Cl. Bees 171 F1
Briar Cl. Huck 145 F3
Briar Cl. Keyw 197 F2
Briar Cl. Rain 104 A1
Briar Cl. S in A 100 B3
Briar Cl. Work 35 E1
Briar Ct. Har 8 C2
Briar Ct. Nott 173 D1
Briar Ct. Oll 77 E3
Briar Gate. Cotg 188 A1
Briar Gate. Lo Ea 182 A1
Briar La. Mans 103 D2
Briar Lea. Ret 39 E2
Briar Lea. Work 35 E1
Briar Rd. Greas 158 B4
Briar Rd. Oll 77 E3
Briarbank Ave. Carl 174 A4
Briarbank Wlk. Carl 174 A4
Briars The. Miss 4 B2
Briarwood Ave. Nott 174 A4
Briarwood Cl. Mans 89 D1
Briarwood Ct. Nott 161 F2
Briber Hill. Blyth 18 A1
Briber Rd. Blyth 18 A1
Brick Kiln La. Mans 101 E4
Brick Yard Rd. Gams 50 B3
Brickcliffe Rd. E Lea 205 F1
Brickenell Rd. Calv 148 C3
Brickenhole La. Walker 13 F3
Brickings Way. S Le S 32 B3
Brickley Cres. E Lea 205 F1
Brickyard Dr. Huck 146 B3
Brickyard La. E Brid 165 E1
Brickyard La. Farns 120 A3
Brickyard La. Miss 4 B2
Brickyard La. R on T 176 A2
Brickyard La. S Norm 113 D3
Brickyard La. Su Bo 213 F4
Brickyard La. W Lea 214 A4
Brickyard La. Walker 13 E3
Brickyard. Huck 146 B3
Bride Church La. Tick 8 A4
Bridegate La. Hick 209 F3
Bridge Ave. Bees 183 F3
Bridge Cl. Whit 45 D3
Bridge Ct. Huck 146 A3
Bridge End Ave. Sels 128 C4
Bridge End Ave. Sels 129 D4
Bridge Farm La. Nott 184 C1
Bridge Gr. W Brid 185 F4
Bridge Green Walk. Nott 159 F1
Bridge Pl. Sax 57 D2
Bridge Pl. Work 35 F2
Bridge Rd. Gain 24 B4
Bridge Rd. Nott 171 E3
Bridge St. Gain 24 B4
Bridge St. Ilk 157 F2
Bridge St. La Mi 143 E2
Bridge St. Lo Ea 182 B1
Bridge St. Lough 220 A2
Bridge St. Mans 102 B4
Bridge St. N-on-T 139 F4
Bridge St. Sand 182 B3
Bridge St. Sax 57 D2
Bridge St. Work 35 F1
Bridgegate. Ret 39 F4
Bridgend Cl. Staple 182 B3
Bridgeway Centre. Nott 173 E1
Bridgeway Ct. Nott 173 E1
Bridgford Rd. Kneet 166 A4
Bridgford Rd. W Brid 185 F4
Bridgford St. Mans 102 C3
Bridgnorth Dr. Nott 184 C1
Bridgnorth Way. Bees 182 C2
Bridle Cl. S in A 100 A3
Bridle Rd. Bees 183 D4
Bridle Rd. Bu Jo 163 F3
Bridle Ways. E Brid 165 E1
Bridlesmith Gate. Nott 173 E2
Bridleway The. Mans 88 C1
Bridlington St. Nott 172 C4
Bridport Ave. Nott 172 B3
Brielen Rd. R on T 176 A2
Brierfield Ave. Nott 185 D2
Brierley Green. Carl 175 D4
Brierly Cotts. S in A 100 C2
Brierly Rd. S in A 100 B2
Bright Sq. Mans 87 E1
Bright St. Gain 24 B4
Bright St. Ilk 157 F2
Bright St. Nott 172 C3
Bright St. S Norm 113 D3
Brightmoor St. Nott 173 E3
Brimington Ct. Mans 88 C2
Brindley Rd. Nott 171 E3
Brinkhill Cres. Nott 184 C2
Brinkley Hill. South 137 D3
Brinsley Cl. Nott 160 A1
Brinsley Hill. Brin 128 B1
Brisbane Cl. Mans 88 B3
Brisbane Ct. Bald 140 B2
Brisbane Dr. Nott 160 C4
Brisbane Dr. Staple 170 C1
Bristol Rd. Ilk 157 F1
Britannia Ave. Nott 160 C3
Britannia Rd. Lo Ea 182 B1
Britannia Terr. Gain 24 B4
British Fields. Tux 65 E2
Brittania Ct. N-on-T 139 F4
Britten Gdns. Nott 173 F3
Brixham Rd. Huck 145 E3
Brixton Rd. Nott 172 C3
Brixworth Way. Ret 40 A4
Broad Cl. Woodb 149 E2
Broad Eadow Rd. Nott 159 F4
Broad Gate. Darl 66 C4
Broad Gate. E Mark 66 C4
Broad Gores. Clar 30 B2
Broad La. Brin 143 F4
Broad La. Cott 43 D3
Broad La. S Lev 43 D3
Broad La. Whit 45 E3
Broad La. Work 45 E3
Broad Meer. Cotg 187 F2
Broad Oak Cl. Nott 173 F4
Broad Oak Dr. Brin 143 F4
Broad Oak Dr. Staple 182 B3
Broad Pl. Whit 45 E3
Broad St. Lo Ea 193 E4
Broad St. Lough 220 A2
Broad St. Nott 173 E3
Broad Valley Dr. Bes Vil 146 C2
Broad Wlk. Nott 160 B2
Broadfields. Calv 148 C4
Broadgate Ave. Bees 184 A4
Broadgate La. Bees 184 A4
Broadgate La. Kelh 123 F3
Broadgate. Bees 184 A4
Broadhill Rd. Kegw 203 E1
Broadholme Rd. Sax 57 D1
Broadholme St. Nott 172 C2
Broadhurst Ave. Nott 160 B1
Broadings La. Lane 54 A3
Broadlands. S Norm 113 D2
Broadlands. Sand 182 A2
Broadleigh Cl. W Brid 185 E2
Broadmead. Bu Jo 163 F3
Broadstairs Rd. Bees 182 C1
Broadstone Cl. W Brid 185 E3
Broadway Ct. Nott 172 C3
Broadway East. Carl 174 B3
Broadway The. Mans 102 B3
Broadway. Ilk 157 F2
Broadway. Nott 173 E2
Broadwood Ct. Bees 184 A4
Broadwood Rd. Nott 161 D4
Brockdale Gdns. Keyw 197 F2
Brockenhurst Rd. Mans 101 E3
Brockhall Rise. Hean 143 D1
Brockhurst Gdns. Nott 173 F3
Brocklehurst Dr. Edwin 91 E4
Brocklesby Cl. Gain 24 C4
Brockley Rd. W Brid 186 A4
Brockton Ave. Farn 139 D3
Brockwell The. S Norm 113 D2
Brockwood Cres. Keyw 197 F2
Bromfield Cl. Nott 174 B4
Bromley Ave. N-on-T 140 A3
Bromley Cl. Nott 160 A3
Bromley Pl. Nott 173 D2
Bromley Rd. W Brid 185 F3
Brompton Cl. Bes Vil 147 D1
Brompton Way. W Brid 185 E2
Bronte Ct. Nott 173 D3
Brook Ave. Arn 162 A4
Brook Cl. Greas 144 B1
Brook Cl. Lo Ea 193 F3
Brook Cl. Nott 160 A3
Brook Cotts. Ilk 157 F2
Brook Ct. Hean 143 D1
Brook Dr. Kinou 199 F1
Brook Gdns. Arn 162 A4
Brook La. Gam 186 B4
Brook Rd. Bees 183 F4
Brook Side. Lough 220 A2
Brook St. Huck 146 A4
Brook St. Nott 173 E3
Brook St. S in A 100 C1
Brook St. Tibs 99 D3
Brook Terr. Work 35 F1
Brook Vale Rd. La Mi 143 E1
Brook View Ct. Keyw 197 F1
Brook View Dr. Keyw 197 F1
Brookdale Ct. Nott 161 E3
Brookdale Rd. S in A 101 D2
Brooke Cl. Bald 140 B3
Brooke Cl. Work 36 B2
Brooke St. Ilk 170 A3
Brooke St. Sand 182 A3
Brookfield Ave. Huck 146 A3
Brookfield Ave. S in A 100 B2
Brookfield Cres. Shireb 72 C3
Brookfield Ct. Nott 173 E1
Brookfield Dr. Hover 151 E2
Brookfield Gdns. Arn 162 A4
Brookfield Rd. Arn 161 F4
Brookfield Rd. Arn 162 A4
Brookhill Ave. Pinx 113 E2
Brookhill Cres. Nott 171 F2
Brookhill Dr. Nott 171 F2
Brookhill La. Pinx 113 F3
Brookhill Leys Rd. East 143 F1
Brookhill Rd. Pinx 113 E1
Brookhill St. Staple 182 B3
Brookland Ave. Mans 101 F4
Brookland Cl. Gunt 165 D3
Brookland Dr. Bees 183 E3
Brooklands Cl. Coll 98 A1
Brooklands Cres. Carl 163 D1
Brooklands Dr. Carl 163 D1
Brooklands Rd. Nott 174 A4
Brooklands. Widm 208 B2
Brooklyn Ave. Bu Jo 163 F3
Brooklyn Cl. Nott 160 B3
Brooklyn Rd. Nott 160 B3
Brooksby La. Nott 184 C2
Brookside Ave. E Lea 205 E1
Brookside Ave. Mans 88 B3
Brookside Ave. Nott 171 E1
Brookside Cl. Lo Ea 193 D4
Brookside Gdns. Rudd 196 A4
Brookside Rd. Rudd 196 A4
Brookside Wlk. Har 9 D2
Brookside. E Lea 214 C4
Brookside. Greas 143 F2
Brookside. Huck 146 A3
Brookside. Lowd 150 B1
Brookthorpe Way. Nott 185 D2
Brookvale Cl. Mans 103 D3
Brookwood Cres. Carl 174 B4
Broom Cl. Calv 148 C4
Broom Cl. Tick 8 A4
Broom Rd. Calv 148 C4
Broom Wlk. Carl 174 A4
Broome Cl. Bald 140 A3
Broomfield Cl. Sand 182 A3
Broomfield La. Farns 119 F3
Broomfield La. Matt 19 F4
Broomhead St. Lough 220 B2
Broomhill Ave. Ilk 170 A3
Broomhill La. Mans 101 F4
Broomhill Rd. Huck 146 A3
Broomhill Rd. Kim 159 D3
Broomhill Rd. Nott 160 B3
Broomston La. Haxey 2 C1
Brora Rd. Nott 160 B4
Brotts La. Nor on T 81 F3
Brotts Rd. Nor on T 81 F3
Brough La. Coll 112 A2
Brough La. Elk 50 A2
Brough Rd. Stap 127 D4
Brough Rd. Staple 112 C1
Brougham Ave. Mans 87 E1
Broughton Dr. Notts 172 B2
Broughton La. Lo Cl 211 D1
Broughton Rd. Stap 127 F4
Broughton St. Bees 183 F4
Brown Ave. Mans 88 A2
Brown Cres. S in A 101 D2
Brown La. B in F 194 C3
Brown La. Thor 70 A3
Brown St. Mans 101 F4
Brown St. Notts 172 C4
Brown's Flats. Kim 158 C3
Brown's La. E Brid 165 E2
Brown's Rd. Lo Ea 193 F4
Brownes Rd. Bing 178 A3
Brownhill Cl. Cr Bi 189 D2
Browning Cl. Arn 161 E4
Browning Cl. Work 36 A3
Browning Rd. Bald 140 C3
Browning St. Mans 102 A4
Brownlow Cl. E Sto 153 E4
Brownlow Dr. Nott 146 C1
Brownlow Rd. Mans 87 F1
Brownlow's Hill. Codd 126 A1
Browns Croft. Nott 160 B2
Browns La. Lough 220 A2
Browns La. S-on-W 198 B1
Broxholme La. Brox 57 F3
Broxholme La. Sax 57 E3
Broxton Rise. Nott 160 A2
Broxtowe Ave. Kim 158 B3
Broxtowe Ave. Nott 160 B1
Broxtowe Dr. Huck 131 D1
Broxtowe Dr. Mans 102 B3
Broxtowe Hall Cl. Nott 160 A1
Broxtowe La. Nott 160 A1
Broxtowe St. Nott 161 E1
Bruce Cl. Nott 173 E1
Bruce Dr. W Brid 185 E4
Brunel Ave. Greas 144 A2
Brunel Cl. Styr 8 C1
Brunel Dr. N-on-T 125 E1
Brunnen The. S Norm 113 D2
Brunner Ave. Shireb 72 C2
Brunswick Dr. Staple 182 C3
Brunt St. Mans 102 B3
Brunt's La. E Brid 165 E1
Brushfield St. Nott 172 C4
Brussels Terr. Ilk 157 F1
Brusty Pl. Bu Jo 163 F3
Bryans Close La. Miss 3 F2
Brynsmoor Rd. Brin 143 F4
Buck's La. Su Bo 213 D4
Buckfast Way. W Brid 186 A4
Buckingham Ave. Huck 146 A4
Buckingham Cl. K-in-A 114 C3
Buckingham Cl. Mans 88 C3
Buckingham Ct. Sand 182 A2
Buckingham Rd. Arn 161 F3
Buckingham Rd. Sand 182 A2
Buckingham Rise. Work 35 F4
Buckland Ct. Nott 172 C3
Buckland Dr. Woodb 149 E2
Bucklee Dr. Calv 148 C4
Bucklow Cl. Nott 160 B1
Budby Ave. Mans 102 C3
Budby Cres. Mar War 74 C4
Budby Rd. Cuck 60 A2
Budby Rise. Huck 146 A4
Bulcote Dr. Bu Jo 163 E2
Bulcote Rd. Nott 184 C2
Bulgrave Mews. W Brid 185 E2
Bulham La. S on T 81 F1
Bull Close Rd. Nott 184 C4
Bull Yd. South 121 F1

Bull Yd. Work .......... 35 F1
Bullace Ct. Mans .......... 88 C1
Bullace Rd. Nott .......... 173 F4
Buller Cl. Coll .......... 98 A1
Buller St. Ilk .......... 170 A3
Buller Terr. Nott .......... 161 E2
Bullivant Ave. Elmt .......... 58 B4
Bullivant St. Nott .......... 173 E3
Bullock Cl. Mans .......... 88 A3
Bullpit Rd. Bald .......... 140 C3
Bulpit La. Eagle .......... 98 C3
Bulstode Pl. Kegw .......... 203 E1
Bulwell High Rd. Nott .......... 160 A4
Bulwell La. Nott .......... 160 B2
Bulwer Rd. K-in-A .......... 114 C3
Bulwer Rd. Nott .......... 172 C3
Bunbury St. Nott .......... 173 E1
Bungalow La. Bils .......... 106 A3
Bunny Hill. Bunn .......... 206 B3
Bunny Hill. Cost .......... 206 B3
Bunny La. E Lea .......... 205 F3
Bunny La. Keyw .......... 197 F1
Bunting St. Nott .......... 172 C1
Buntings La. Carl .......... 174 B4
Bunyan Green Rd. Sels .......... 128 B4
Bunystone La. Co Ba .......... 200 C4
Burbage Ct. Mans .......... 103 D3
Burden La. Harb .......... 202 A2
Burden La. Shel .......... 164 B1
Burder St. Lough .......... 220 B3
Burfield Ave. Lough .......... 220 A2
Burford Rd. Nott .......... 172 C4
Burford St. Arn .......... 161 F4
Burgage La. South .......... 121 F1
Burgage. South .......... 121 F1
Burgass Rd. Nott .......... 174 A4
Burge Cl. Nott .......... 173 E1
Burgh Hall Cl. Bees .......... 183 E1
Burhill. Cotg .......... 188 A1
Burke St. Nott .......... 173 D3
Burleigh Cl. Carl .......... 174 C4
Burleigh Rd. Lough .......... 220 A2
Burleigh Rd. W Brid .......... 186 A3
Burleigh Sq. Bees .......... 183 E2
Burleigh St. Ilk .......... 157 F1
Burley Rise. Kegw .......... 203 E1
Burlington Ave. Nott .......... 161 D2
Burlington Ave. Shireb .......... 72 C3
Burlington Dr. Mans .......... 87 F1
Burlington Rd. Carl .......... 174 C4
Burlington Rd. Nott .......... 161 E2
Burma Rd. Blid .......... 118 A3
Burmaston Rd. Mans .......... 103 D3
Burn St. S in A .......... 101 D2
Burnaby St. Nott .......... 160 B2
Burnaston Ct. Mans .......... 88 C2
Burnbreck Gdns. Nott .......... 171 F2
Burndale Wlk. Nott .......... 160 C4
Burneham Cl. E Brid .......... 165 E1
Burnham Ave. Bees .......... 183 F2
Burnham Ct. Mans .......... 102 B2
Burnham St. Nott .......... 161 E1
Burnham Way. Nott .......... 173 E2
Burnmoor La. Egma .......... 80 A4
Burnor Pool. Calv .......... 148 C4
Burns Ave. Mans .......... 88 B1
Burns Ave. Nott .......... 173 D3
Burns La. Mar War .......... 74 A3
Burns Rd. Work .......... 36 A2
Burns St. Mans .......... 102 A4
Burns St. Nott .......... 173 D3
Burns The. Mar War .......... 74 B3
Burnside Cl. K-in-A .......... 114 C4
Burnside Dr. Bees .......... 171 E1
Burnside Gr. Toll .......... 186 B1
Burnside Green. Nott .......... 171 E3
Burnside Rd. Nott .......... 171 E3
Burnside Rd. W Brid .......... 185 F3
Burnt Oaks Cl. Mans .......... 88 B2
Burntleys Rd. Hayt .......... 30 B4
Burntstump Hill. Arn .......... 132 B1
Burnwood Ave. Mans .......... 103 D4
Burnwood Dr. Nott .......... 171 E3
Burr La. Ilk .......... 157 F1
Burrows Ave. Bees .......... 171 F1
Burrows Cres. Bees .......... 171 F1
Burrows Ct. Nott .......... 173 E1
Burtness Rd. Nott .......... 184 C1
Burton Ave. Carl .......... 174 A4
Burton Cl. Carl .......... 175 D4
Burton Cl. Harb .......... 202 A2
Burton Dr. Bees .......... 183 E2
Burton La. What .......... 179 D2
Burton Mandeville Ct. Nott . 173 E1
Burton Rd. Carl .......... 175 D4
Burton Rd. S in A .......... 100 B2
Burton Rise. Wale .......... 64 A1
Burton St. Gain .......... 24 B4
Burton St. Lough .......... 220 A1
Burton St. Nott .......... 173 E3
Burton Wlk. E Lea .......... 214 C4
Burton Wlks. Lough .......... 220 A1
Burwell Ct. Mans .......... 88 C2
Burwell St. Nott .......... 172 C3
Bush Cl. Nott .......... 160 C4
Bushmead Mews. Work .......... 35 F1
Buskeyfield La. Nort .......... 59 F2

Bute Ave. Nott .......... 172 C2
Butler Ave. R on T .......... 176 A2
Butler Cl. Cr Bu .......... 189 D3
Butler Cres. Mans .......... 87 E1
Butler Dr. Blid .......... 117 F2
Butlers Cl. Huck .......... 146 B3
Butt Hill. Whit .......... 45 D3
Butt La. E Brid .......... 165 F1
Butt La. Mans .......... 88 B1
Butt La. N on S .......... 213 F2
Butt Rd. Bing .......... 178 A2
Butt St. Sand .......... 182 A3
Buttercup Cl. Bald .......... 140 B3
Butterhall Cl. Whit .......... 45 D3
Buttermead Cl. Staple .......... 170 B1
Buttermere Cl. Gam .......... 186 B4
Buttermere Ct. Nott .......... 161 E1
Buttermere Dr. Bees .......... 183 E4
Butterton Cl. Ilk .......... 170 A4
Buttery La. S in A .......... 100 C4
Buxton Ave. Carl .......... 162 C1
Buxton Ct. Ilk .......... 157 E1
Buxton Rd. Mans .......... 87 E1
Byard La. Nott .......... 173 E2
Bycroft Rd. Mort .......... 15 E2
Bye Pass Rd. Gunt .......... 164 C3
Bye Path Rd. Ret .......... 39 F4
Bye-pass Rd. Bees .......... 183 E2
Byfield Cl. Nott .......... 172 C3
Byford Cl. Nott .......... 161 F1
Byley Rd. Nott .......... 171 D3
Byrne Ct. Arn .......... 162 A3
Byron Ave. K-in-A .......... 115 D4
Byron Ave. Lo Ea .......... 182 A2
Byron Ave. Mans .......... 88 B1
Byron Ave. S in A .......... 101 D2
Byron Cl. Darl .......... 67 D4
Byron Cl. N-on-T .......... 140 A3
Byron Cres. Awsw .......... 158 B2
Byron Cres. Raven .......... 116 C2
Byron Ct. Bald .......... 140 C2
Byron Ct. Nott .......... 173 F2
Byron Ct. Staple .......... 170 C1
Byron Gdns. South .......... 121 F1
Byron Gr. Nott .......... 161 E2
Byron Rd. Ann Wo .......... 130 B4
Byron Rd. W Brid .......... 185 F4
Byron St. Arn .......... 161 E3
Byron St. Blid .......... 118 A3
Byron St. Huck .......... 146 A3
Byron St. Ilk .......... 157 F1
Byron St. Mans .......... 102 A4
Byron St. News .......... 130 A3
Byron St. Shireb .......... 72 C2
Byron Way. Work .......... 36 A2

Cabin Leas. Lough .......... 220 A3
Cad La. Nor on T .......... 81 F4
Caddaw Ave. Huck .......... 146 A3
Cadlan Cl. Nott .......... 161 D4
Cadlan Ct. Nott .......... 161 D4
Caenby Cl. Gain .......... 24 C4
Caernarvon Pl. Bees .......... 183 D2
Caincross Rd. Nott .......... 171 E4
Cairngorm Dr. Bes Vil .......... 147 D1
Cairns Cl. Nott .......... 161 D3
Cairns St. Nott .......... 161 D3
Cairnsmore Cl. Lo Ea .......... 182 A1
Cairo St. Nott .......... 160 C1
Caister Rd. Nott .......... 195 F4
Caithness Ct. Nott .......... 161 D1
Calcroft Cl. Nott .......... 160 B1
Caldbeck Cl. Gam .......... 186 B4
Caldbeck Ct. Bees .......... 183 D2
Caldbeck Wlk. Nott .......... 161 D4
Calder Wlk. Nott .......... 160 A4
Calderdale Dr. Lo Ea .......... 193 D3
Calderdale. Nott .......... 171 D2
Calderhall Gdns. Nott .......... 161 E4
Caldwell St. Lough .......... 220 A2
Caledon Rd. Nott .......... 161 D2
Caledonian Rd. Ret .......... 40 A2
Calf Croft. Whit .......... 45 D3
California Rd. Farn .......... 139 D2
Calladine La. S in A .......... 114 B4
Callaway Cl. Nott .......... 171 F1
Calstock Rd. Arn .......... 161 F3
Calveley Rd. Nott .......... 171 F4
Calver Cl. Nott .......... 172 B2
Calver St. Mans .......... 88 C2
Calverton Ave. Carl .......... 162 A1
Calverton Cl. Bees .......... 183 D1
Calverton Ct. Mans .......... 103 D2
Calverton Rd. Arn .......... 148 A1
Calverton Rd. Blid .......... 118 A1
Camb's La. N Whea .......... 31 F4
Cambell Gdns. Arn .......... 148 B1
Camberley Rd. Nott .......... 160 A4
Camborne Cres. Ret .......... 29 F1
Camborne Dr. Nott .......... 160 B1
Cambourne Gdns. Raven .. 116 C1
Cambrai Terr. Work .......... 35 F2
Cambria Mews. Nott .......... 173 E4
Cambria Rd. Mans .......... 87 E2
Cambridge Cl. Rain .......... 118 A4
Cambridge Cres. Staple .......... 170 B1
Cambridge Gdns. Arn .......... 162 A3

Cambridge Rd. Har .......... 8 C2
Cambridge Rd. Nott .......... 172 A2
Cambridge Rd. Rain .......... 118 A4
Cambridge Rd. W Brid .......... 186 A3
Cambridge St. Carl .......... 174 C4
Cambridge St. Lough .......... 220 A3
Cambridge St. Mans .......... 102 A3
Camdale Cl. Bees .......... 183 D3
Camden Cl. Nott .......... 173 F2
Camelia Ave. Nott .......... 184 B1
Camelot Ave. Nott .......... 161 D1
Camelot Cres. Rudd .......... 196 A4
Camelot St. Rudd .......... 196 A4
Cameron St. Nott .......... 161 E1
Camerons The. Mans .......... 101 E3
Camomile Cl. Nott .......... 160 C4
Camomile Gdns. Nott .......... 172 C4
Campbell Cl. Work .......... 35 F4
Campbell Dr. Carl .......... 174 B4
Campbell Gr. Nott .......... 173 E3
Campbell St. Gain .......... 15 D1
Campbell St. La Mi .......... 143 E2
Campbell St. Nott .......... 173 E3
Campden Green. Nott .......... 184 C1
Campion St. Arn .......... 161 F4
Campion Way. Bing .......... 177 E2
Camrose Cl. Nott .......... 171 F4
Canal La. Hose .......... 211 F4
Canal La. Lo Cl .......... 211 E3
Canal La. Stat .......... 202 B3
Canal La. W Sto .......... 7 E1
Canal Rd. Work .......... 35 F2
Canal Side. Bees .......... 184 A2
Canal St. Ilk .......... 158 A1
Canal St. Lo Ea .......... 182 B1
Canal St. Nott .......... 173 E2
Canal St. Ret .......... 39 F3
Canal St. Sand .......... 182 B3
Canal Terr. Work .......... 36 A2
Canberra Cl. Staple .......... 170 C1
Canberra Cres. W Brid .......... 185 E2
Canberra Gdns. W Brid .......... 185 E2
Canberra Rd. Codd .......... 125 F1
Candle Meadow. Nott .......... 174 B3
Candleby Cl. Cotg .......... 187 F2
Candleby Ct. Cotg .......... 187 F2
Candleby La. Cotg .......... 187 F2
Candlemass Ct. Mans .......... 88 B1
Canning Circus. Nott .......... 173 D3
Cannock Way. Lo Ea .......... 194 A4
Cannon Sq. Ret .......... 39 F4
Cannon St. Nott .......... 161 E2
Canon Cl. Ilk .......... 157 F3
Canon's Cl. South .......... 121 F1
Canonbie Cl. Arn .......... 148 A1
Cantabury Ave. Nott .......... 172 C4
Cantelope Rd. Ilk .......... 170 A4
Canterbury Cl. Mans .......... 88 B3
Canterbury Ct. Nott .......... 173 D3
Canterbury Rd. Nott .......... 172 B3
Canterbury Wlk. C in L .......... 25 F2
Cantley Ave. Carl .......... 162 C1
Cantrell Rd. Nott .......... 160 B4
Canver Cl. Nott .......... 171 E3
Canwick Cl. Nott .......... 171 E3
Cape St. Mans .......... 101 F4
Capenwray Gdns. Nott .......... 161 E4
Capes The. What .......... 178 C2
Capitol Ct. Nott .......... 172 A3
Caporn Cl. Nott .......... 160 B3
Capps Pl. Tux .......... 66 A1
Car La. Car Co .......... 166 B1
Carburton Ave. Mar War .... 74 B4
Carburton Way. K-in-A .......... 115 E3
Cardale Rd. Mans .......... 87 E2
Cardale Rd. Nott .......... 174 A3
Cardiff St. Nott .......... 173 F3
Cardinal Cl. Nott .......... 173 F3
Cardinal Hinsley Cl. N-on-T 139 E2
Cardington Cl. Nott .......... 146 C1
Cardle Cl. Mans .......... 89 D1
Cardwell St. Nott .......... 172 C4
Carew Rd. Nott .......... 184 C1
Carey Rd. Nott .......... 160 B4
Carisbrook Ave. Mans .......... 103 D4
Carisbrooke Ave. Bees ...... 184 A4
Carisbrooke Ave. Carl .......... 163 D1
Carisbrooke Ave. Nott .......... 161 E1
Carisbrooke Dr. Nott .......... 161 E1
Carlile Rd. Carl .......... 174 C4
Carlin St. Nott .......... 160 A4
Carling Ave. Work .......... 35 E2
Carlingford Rd. Huck .......... 146 A4
Carlisle Ave. Nott .......... 160 B4
Carlisle St. Gain .......... 15 E1
Carlswark Gdns. Nott .......... 146 C1
Carlton Ave. Work .......... 35 F3
Carlton Cl. Hean .......... 143 D2
Carlton Cl. Mans .......... 89 E2
Carlton Cl. N-on-T .......... 139 F3
Carlton Cl. Work .......... 35 F4
Carlton Cres. E Lea .......... 205 F1
Carlton Ferry La. Coll .......... 97 E1
Carlton Fold. Nott .......... 173 F2
Carlton Hall La. C in L .......... 25 F2
Carlton Hill. Carl .......... 174 B4
Carlton La. Brox .......... 57 F4

Carlton La. S on T .......... 97 D3
Carlton Mews. Carl .......... 174 B4
Carlton Rd. Lo Ea .......... 193 D3
Carlton Rd. N-on-T .......... 140 A3
Carlton Rd. Nott .......... 173 F3
Carlton Rd. Work .......... 35 F3
Carlton Sq. Carl .......... 174 C4
Carlton St. Mans .......... 88 B1
Carlton St. Nott .......... 173 E2
Carlyle Rd. W Brid .......... 185 F4
Carman Cl. Greas .......... 159 D4
Carmel Gdns. Arn .......... 161 F3
Carnarvon Cl. Bing .......... 177 F3
Carnarvon Dr. Bu Jo .......... 164 A3
Carnarvon Gr. Carl .......... 162 C1
Carnarvon Gr. Carl .......... 174 B4
Carnarvon Gr. S in A .......... 100 C3
Carnarvon Pl. Bing .......... 177 E2
Carnarvon Rd. S in A .......... 99 F1
Carnarvon Rd. W Brid .......... 185 F3
Carnarvon St. Carl .......... 175 D3
Carnarvon St. S in A .......... 100 A4
Carnforth Cl. Staple .......... 182 B3
Carnforth Ct. Nott .......... 161 E4
Carnoustie Cl. K-in-A .......... 114 C4
Carnoustie. Work .......... 36 A3
Carnwood Rd. Nott .......... 161 D3
Carolgate. Ret .......... 39 F3
Caroline Cl. Raven .......... 117 D2
Caroline Ct. Ilk .......... 170 A3
Caroline Wlk. Nott .......... 173 E4
Carpenter Ave. Mans .......... 87 E1
Carpenters Cl. Cr Bu .......... 189 D3
Carr Cl. S Norm .......... 113 E4
Carr Farm Rd. Ann Wo ...... 114 C1
Carr Hill Way. Ret .......... 29 F1
Carr La. Blyt .......... 15 E4
Carr La. E Stock .......... 7 F1
Carr La. Gain .......... 24 B3
Carr La. Harb .......... 71 D2
Carr La. Mar War .......... 74 A2
Carr La. Mist .......... 6 C1
Carr La. S Norm .......... 113 D4
Carr La. Swine .......... 71 D2
Carr Rd. Bing .......... 178 A3
Carr Rd. G on H .......... 12 B3
Carr Rd. Ret .......... 39 F3
Carr View. Ever .......... 11 E2
Carradale Cl. Arn .......... 162 B4
Carrfield Ave. Bees .......... 182 C1
Carrfield Ave. Lo Ea .......... 182 C1
Carrgate La. Elst .......... 153 F3
Carrington La. Calv .......... 149 D4
Carrington St. Nott .......... 173 E2
Carroll Gdns. Nott .......... 173 E1
Carsic La. S in A .......... 100 C2
Carsic Rd. S in A .......... 100 B2
Carside Ave. S in A .......... 100 B1
Carsington Ct. Mans .......... 88 C2
Carson Rd. Gain .......... 15 E1
Carswell Cl. N-on-T .......... 139 F3
Cartbridge. Cotg .......... 187 F1
Carter Ave. R on T .......... 176 A2
Carter Ave. Rudd .......... 196 B3
Carter Gate. N-on-T .......... 139 F4
Carter La E. S Norm .......... 113 E3
Carter La W. S Norm .......... 113 E3
Carter La W. Shireb .......... 72 B2
Carter La. Mans .......... 102 C3
Carter La. Mar War .......... 73 E2
Carter La. Shireb .......... 72 C2
Carter Rd. Bees .......... 183 D1
Carter Rd. Bees .......... 183 D2
Carters Wood Dr. Nuth ...... 159 F2
Cartwright Cl. D on T .......... 54 A1
Cartwright St. Lough .......... 220 B3
Cartwright St. Shire .......... 34 C4
Carver Cl. Edwin .......... 76 A1
Carver St. Nott .......... 172 C4
Carver's Hollow. Edin .......... 120 A1
Carwood Rd. Bees .......... 171 E1
Caskgate St. Gain .......... 24 B4
Casper Ct. Nott .......... 161 D4
Castellan Rise. Nott .......... 161 E4
Casterton Rd. Nott .......... 161 D4
Castle Brewery Ct. N-on-T . 139 F4
Castle Bridge Rd. Nott .......... 173 D1
Castle Bvd. Nott .......... 173 D2
Castle Cl. Bott .......... 181 E1
Castle Cl. Calv .......... 148 C4
Castle Farm La. Work .......... 46 B3
Castle Gate. N-on-T .......... 139 F4
Castle Gate. Nott .......... 173 E2
Castle Gate. Tick .......... 8 A4
Castle Gdns. Nott .......... 172 C2
Castle Gr. Nott .......... 173 D2
Castle Hill. E Lea .......... 205 F1
Castle Marina Rd. Nott .......... 173 D1
Castle Meadow Rd. Nott .......... 173 D1
Castle Meadow Ret Pk Nott 173 D2
Castle Park. Nott .......... 173 D1
Castle Pl. Nott .......... 173 E2
Castle Quay. Nott .......... 173 D1
Castle Rd. Nott .......... 173 E2
Castle Rising. N-on-T .......... 139 F4
Castle St. East .......... 144 A1
Castle St. Mans .......... 88 A2

Castle St. Mans .......... 102 A
Castle St. Nott .......... 173 F
Castle St. Work .......... 35 F
Castle View Rd. Bott .......... 181 E
Castle View. Ald .......... 143 D
Castle View. W Brid .......... 185 F
Castledine St Ext. Lough ... 220 A
Castledine St. Lough .......... 220 E
Castlefields. Nott .......... 173 E
Castleton Ave. Arn .......... 161 F
Castleton Ave. Carl .......... 162 C
Castleton Ave. Ilk .......... 157 F
Castleton Cl. Huck .......... 145 E
Castleton Cl. Mans .......... 88 B
Castleton Cl. Nott .......... 173 C
Castleton Cl. Raven .......... 117 D
Castleton Ct. Nott .......... 159 F
Caterham Cl. Nott .......... 171 E
Catfoot La. Lamb .......... 162 C
Catherine Ave. Mans .......... 88 B
Catherine Cl. K-in-A .......... 114 C
Catherine Cl. Nott .......... 160 A
Catkin Dr. Greas .......... 158 B
Catkin Way. Bald .......... 140 A
Catlow Wlk. Nott .......... 161 E
Caton Cl. S in A .......... 100 B
Cator Cl. Carl .......... 162 B
Cator La N. Bees .......... 183 E
Cator La. Bees .......... 183 E
Cator Rd. Mans .......... 87 E
Catriona Cres. Arn .......... 148 A
Catterley Hill Rd. Nott .......... 174 A
Cattle Market Rd. Nott .......... 173 E
Cattle Rd. Mist .......... 6 B
Catton Rd. Arn .......... 162 A
Caudwell Cl. South .......... 121 F
Caudwell Dr. Mans .......... 102 B
Cauldwell Rd. S in A .......... 101 F
Caulton St. Nott .......... 172 C
Caunt's Cres. S in A .......... 100 B
Caunton Ave. Nott .......... 161 F
Caunton Cl. Mans .......... 101 F
Caunton Cl. Mar War .......... 74 B
Caunton Rd. Bath .......... 109 F
Caunton Rd. Hock .......... 122 A
Causeway La. Gams .......... 51 D
Causeway La. Morton .......... 137 E
Causeway Mews. Nott .......... 173 D
Causeway. Lea .......... 24 C
Cavan Ct. Nott .......... 173 E
Cave's La. Walker .......... 13 E
Cavell Cl. Nott .......... 184 B
Cavell Cl. Wood .......... 53 D
Cavell Ct. Nott .......... 172 B
Cavendish Ave. Carl .......... 162 B
Cavendish Ave. Edwin .......... 75 F
Cavendish Ave. N-on-T .......... 140 A
Cavendish Ave. Nott .......... 161 E
Cavendish Ave. S in A .......... 100 C
Cavendish Cl. Huck .......... 146 B
Cavendish Cres N. Nott .......... 173 D
Cavendish Cres S. Nott .......... 173 D
Cavendish Cres. Ann Wo ... 130 A
Cavendish Cres. Carl .......... 162 B
Cavendish Cres. Staple .......... 170 C
Cavendish Ct. Nott .......... 173 D
Cavendish Dr. Carl .......... 174 C
Cavendish Dr. Lea .......... 24 C
Cavendish Pl. Bees .......... 183 F
Cavendish Rd E. Nott .......... 173 D
Cavendish Rd W. Nott .......... 173 D
Cavendish Rd. Carl .......... 162 B
Cavendish Rd. Ilk .......... 170 A
Cavendish Rd. Lo Ea .......... 182 B
Cavendish Rd. Ret .......... 40 A
Cavendish Rd. Work .......... 47 D
Cavendish St. Arn .......... 161 F
Cavendish St. Mans .......... 88 A
Cavendish St. Nott .......... 184 C
Cavendish St. S in A .......... 101 D
Cavendish St. Scarc .......... 72 C
Cavendish Vale. Nott .......... 161 E
Cawdron Wlk. Nott .......... 184 C
Cawston Gdns. Nott .......... 160 A
Cawthorn Cl. Coll .......... 98 A
Cawthorne Way. Mans .......... 102 C
Caxmere Dr. Nott .......... 171 F
Caythorpe Cres. Nott .......... 161 E
Caythorpe Ct. Mans .......... 88 C
Caythorpe Rd. Cayt .......... 151 D
Caythorpe Rd. Gunt .......... 150 C
Caythorpe Rise. Nott .......... 161 E
Cecil St. Gain .......... 15 E
Cecil St. Nott .......... 172 C
Cedar Ave. Bees .......... 184 A
Cedar Ave. E Lea .......... 214 B
Cedar Ave. K-in-A .......... 114 C
Cedar Ave. Lo Ea .......... 193 E
Cedar Ave. Mans .......... 88 B
Cedar Ave. N-on-T .......... 125 D
Cedar Ave. Nuth .......... 159 F
Cedar Cl. Gain .......... 15 D
Cedar Cl. S in A .......... 100 B
Cedar Cl. Sand .......... 182 A
Cedar Dr. Bees .......... 184 A
Cedar Dr. Keyw .......... 197 F
Cedar Dr. Sels .......... 128 C

Cedar Gr. Arn ... 162 A4
Cedar Gr. Huck ... 146 A3
Cedar Gr. Nott ... 171 F2
Cedar Gr. S Norm ... 113 D2
Cedar La. Oll ... 77 E3
Cedar Rd. Bees ... 183 F3
Cedar Rd. Lough ... 220 B1
Cedar Rd. Nott ... 173 D4
Cedar St. Mans ... 102 B3
Cedar Tree Rd. Bes Vil ... 147 D1
Cedar Tree Rd. Elk ... 50 A2
Cedarland Cres. Nuth ... 159 F2
Cedars The. Nott ... 161 E2
Celia Dr. Carl ... 174 B4
Cemetery Rd. Staple ... 182 C4
Cemetery Rd. Work ... 36 A1
Central Ave S. Arn ... 161 F4
Central Ave. Arn ... 161 F4
Central Ave. Arn ... 162 A2
Central Ave. Bees ... 183 E4
Central Ave. Bees ... 183 F4
Central Ave. Blid ... 118 A3
Central Ave. Elmt ... 58 B4
Central Ave. Huck ... 146 A3
Central Ave. K-in-A ... 115 D2
Central Ave. Mans ... 102 B3
Central Ave. Nott ... 161 D1
Central Ave. S Norm ... 113 D3
Central Ave. Sand ... 182 A3
Central Ave. Staple ... 182 C4
Central Ave. W Brid ... 185 F4
Central Ave. Wale ... 64 A1
Central Ave. Work ... 35 F2
Central Cl. Shireb ... 72 C2
Central Ct. Nott ... 172 C1
Central Dr. Baw ... 10 A4
Central Dr. Elst ... 153 F2
Central Dr. N Clip ... 89 F1
Central Dr. Shireb ... 72 C2
Central St. Nott ... 173 F3
Central St. R on T ... 101 D2
Central Wlk. Huck ... 146 A4
Centre Way. R on T ... 175 F2
Century Ave. Mans ... 101 F3
Century Rd. Ret ... 39 F3
Cernan Ct. Nott ... 159 F3
Cerne Cl. Nott ... 184 C1
Chaceley Way. Nott ... 185 D2
Chad Gdns. Bes Vil ... 147 D1
Chadborn Ave. Goth ... 195 D1
Chadburn Rd. Mans ... 102 C4
Chaddesden The. Nott ... 173 E4
Chadwick Rd. Nott ... 172 C4
Chadwick Way. Wood ... 53 D4
Chaffinch Cl. Mans ... 102 C4
Chain Bridge Rd. Lound ... 29 E4
Chain La. N-on-T ... 139 F4
Chain La. Nott ... 172 C1
Chainbridge La. Lound ... 29 E4
Chalfield Cl. Nott ... 184 B1
Chalfont Dr. Nott ... 172 B3
Chalons Cl. Ilk ... 157 F1
Chamberlain Cl. Nott ... 184 B1
Chambers Ave. Ilk ... 170 A4
Champion Cres. Mans ... 101 F4
Chancery Cl. S in A ... 101 D3
Chancery La. Ret ... 39 F4
Chancery The. Bees ... 183 E4
Chandos Ave. Carl ... 175 D4
Chandos Ct. Tux ... 65 F2
Chandos St. Carl ... 175 D4
Chandos St. Nott ... 173 F4
Chantrey Cl. Bees ... 183 E2
Chantrey Rd. W Brid ... 185 F4
Chantry Cl. Kim ... 159 D3
Chantry Cl. Lo Ea ... 193 D2
Chantry Cl. N-on-T ... 139 F3
Chantry Wlk. Tux ... 65 F2
Chapel Bar. Nott ... 173 D2
Chapel Cl. Mist ... 6 C1
Chapel Cl. Wale ... 64 A1
Chapel Garth. Orst ... 179 F3
Chapel Gate. C in L ... 26 A3
Chapel La. Arn ... 161 F4
Chapel La. Aslo ... 179 D3
Chapel La. Bath ... 110 A2
Chapel La. Bing ... 177 F3
Chapel La. Caun ... 109 D3
Chapel La. Clayp ... 156 B4
Chapel La. Codd ... 126 A1
Chapel La. Cost ... 206 B1
Chapel La. Cotg ... 187 F2
Chapel La. Epp ... 150 A3
Chapel La. Ever ... 11 E2
Chapel La. Farn ... 138 C2
Chapel La. Farns ... 119 F3
Chapel La. Gran ... 191 D3
Chapel La. Hose ... 211 F4
Chapel La. Lamb ... 163 D4
Chapel La. Lax ... 79 E1
Chapel La. Mort ... 15 D2
Chapel La. N Sca ... 83 E2
Chapel La. Ne Br ... 219 E4
Chapel La. Ol Da ... 218 C2
Chapel La. Oxt ... 134 B2
Chapel La. Raven ... 117 D1
Chapel La. Up Br ... 210 A1

Chapel La. W-on-W ... 217 E4
Chapel La. Wale ... 64 A1
Chapel La. Wint ... 125 E3
Chapel Mews Ct. Bees ... 183 D4
Chapel Pl. Kim ... 158 C3
Chapel Rd. Sels ... 128 C3
Chapel St. Ann Wo ... 115 D1
Chapel St. B-le-V ... 192 A1
Chapel St. Beckin ... 142 B4
Chapel St. Bees ... 183 D4
Chapel St. Bott ... 181 D2
Chapel St. East ... 143 F1
Chapel St. Hean ... 157 D4
Chapel St. Huck ... 146 A4
Chapel St. Ilk ... 157 F1
Chapel St. K-in-A ... 114 C3
Chapel St. Kim ... 158 C3
Chapel St. Lo Ea ... 193 F4
Chapel St. Orst ... 179 F4
Chapel St. Plun ... 191 F1
Chapel St. Rudd ... 196 B3
Chapel St. Scarc ... 59 D2
Chapel St. Sels ... 129 D4
Chapel Staith. Gain ... 24 B4
Chapel Wlk. Work ... 35 F1
Chapelgate. Ret ... 39 F4
Chapman Ct. Nott ... 172 A4
Chapman St. Lough ... 220 B2
Chappel Gdns. Bils ... 106 A2
Chapter Dr. Kim ... 159 D3
Chard St. Nott ... 160 C1
Charlbury Ct. Bees ... 171 D2
Charlbury Rd. Nott ... 172 A3
Charlecote Dr. Nott ... 171 E2
Charlecote Park Dr. W Brid ... 185 E2
Charles Ave. Bees ... 183 E2
Charles Ave. East ... 144 A1
Charles Ave. Nott ... 172 A1
Charles Ave. Sand ... 182 A3
Charles Ave. Staple ... 182 C4
Charles Cl. Carl ... 162 C1
Charles Cl. Ilk ... 170 A3
Charles St. Arn ... 161 F4
Charles St. Gain ... 15 E1
Charles St. Huck ... 146 A4
Charles St. Lo Ea ... 193 E4
Charles St. Lough ... 220 A3
Charles St. Mans ... 88 A1
Charles St. Mans ... 88 B2
Charles St. N-on-T ... 140 A4
Charles St. Rudd ... 196 B4
Charles St. S in A ... 101 D2
Charlesworth Ave. Nott ... 172 C4
Charlesworth Ct. Mans ... 88 C2
Charlotte Cl. Kirton ... 78 A3
Charlotte Cl. N-on-T ... 140 A4
Charlotte Cl. Nott ... 147 F1
Charlotte Gr. Bees ... 171 E1
Charlton Ave. Lo Ea ... 182 C1
Charlton Gr. Bees ... 183 F3
Charlton Rd. C in L ... 26 A1
Charnock Ave. Nott ... 172 B2
Charnwood Ave. Bees ... 183 F3
Charnwood Ave. Keyw ... 197 F1
Charnwood Ave. Lo Ea ... 193 D2
Charnwood Ave. Sand ... 182 A2
Charnwood Ave. Su Bo ... 213 D3
Charnwood Cres. Newt ... 99 D2
Charnwood Fields. Su Bo ... 213 D3
Charnwood Gr. Bing ... 177 E2
Charnwood Gr. Huck ... 145 F4
Charnwood Gr. Mans ... 88 A3
Charnwood Gr. Mans ... 103 D4
Charnwood Gr. W Brid ... 185 F4
Charnwood La. Arn ... 162 A3
Charnwood Prec. Lough ... 220 A2
Charnwood Rd. Lough ... 220 A1
Charnwood St. S in A ... 100 B1
Charnwood Way. Woodb ... 149 E2
Charter Pl. Tux ... 66 A2
Charters Cl. K-in-A ... 114 C4
Chartwell Ave. Rudd ... 196 A4
Chartwell Gr. Carl ... 162 B3
Chartwell Rd. K-in-A ... 115 E3
Chatham Ct. N-on-T ... 139 F4
Chatham St. Nott ... 173 E3
Chatsworth Ave. Bees ... 183 E1
Chatsworth Ave. Carl ... 162 C1
Chatsworth Ave. Lo Ea ... 194 A3
Chatsworth Ave. Nott ... 160 C1
Chatsworth Ave. R on T ... 176 A2
Chatsworth Ave. Sels ... 129 D4
Chatsworth Ave. Shireb ... 72 C3
Chatsworth Ave. South ... 121 E1
Chatsworth Cl. Mans ... 102 C1
Chatsworth Cl. S in A ... 100 C3
Chatsworth Cl. Sand ... 182 A2
Chatsworth Ct. Har ... 9 D3
Chatsworth Ct. Huck ... 146 A3
Chatsworth Dr. Huck ... 146 A3
Chatsworth Rd. N-on-T ... 140 A3
Chatsworth Rd. W Brid ... 186 A4
Chatsworth Rd. Work ... 35 F4
Chatsworth St. S in A ... 101 D2
Chatsworth St. Tibs ... 99 D3
Chaucer Cres. S in A ... 101 D2

Chaucer Rd. Bald ... 140 C2
Chaucer St. Ilk ... 157 F1
Chaucer St. Mans ... 102 A4
Chaucer St. Nott ... 173 D3
Chaworth Ave. Greas ... 145 D1
Chaworth Rd. Bing ... 177 E2
Chaworth Rd. Carl ... 174 C3
Chaworth Rd. W Brid ... 185 F3
Chaworth St. Blid ... 118 A3
Cheadle Cl. Carl ... 162 A1
Cheadle Cl. Nott ... 171 E4
Cheapside. Nott ... 173 E2
Cheapside. Work ... 36 A1
Cheddar Cl. Rain ... 104 B1
Cheddar Rd. Nott ... 195 F4
Chedington Ave. Carl ... 162 B3
Chediston Vale. Nott ... 161 D4
Chedworth Cl. Nott ... 173 F3
Chelmorton Cl. Mans ... 88 C2
Chelmsford Rd. Nott ... 160 C1
Chelmsford Terr. Nott ... 160 C1
Chelsea St. Nott ... 160 C1
Cheltenham Cl. Bees ... 182 C1
Cheltenham Ct. Mans ... 102 C4
Cheltenham St. Nott ... 160 C2
Chennel Nook. Cotg ... 188 A1
Chepstow Rd. Nott ... 195 F4
Chepstow Wlk. Mans ... 102 C4
Chequers La. D on T ... 54 A1
Cherhill Cl. Nott ... 195 E4
Cheriton Cl. Mans ... 87 F1
Cheriton Dr. Raven ... 117 D1
Cheriton Dr. Ship ... 157 E2
Chermside Cl. Raven ... 117 D1
Chernside. Raven ... 117 D2
Cherry Ave. Huck ... 146 A3
Cherry Ave. K-in-A ... 114 B4
Cherry Cl. Arn ... 161 F4
Cherry Cl. S Norm ... 113 D4
Cherry Cl. Shireb ... 72 C3
Cherry Gr. Mans ... 101 F3
Cherry Gr. Mar War ... 74 B2
Cherry Hill. Keyw ... 197 F2
Cherry Holt. N-on-T ... 139 F3
Cherry Holt. Ret ... 29 E1
Cherry La. Mans ... 102 A2
Cherry Orch. Cotg ... 187 F2
Cherry Orchard Mnt. Nott ... 161 D4
Cherry St. Bing ... 177 F2
Cherry Tree Ave. Shire ... 34 C4
Cherry Tree Cl. Brin ... 143 F4
Cherry Tree Cl. Mans ... 88 A2
Cherry Tree Cl. R on T ... 175 F1
Cherry Tree La. W Brid ... 186 A2
Cherry Tree Rd. Gain ... 15 F1
Cherry Tree Wlk. Ran ... 19 E3
Cherry Wood Dr. Nott ... 172 A4
Cherryholt Cl. E Brid ... 165 E2
Cherryholt La. E Brid ... 165 E2
Cherrywood Gdns. Carl ... 174 A4
Chertsey Cl. Nott ... 161 F1
Cherwell Cl. Nott ... 159 F3
Chesham Dr. Bees ... 171 D1
Chesham Dr. Nott ... 161 D1
Cheshire Way. Sels ... 128 B2
Chesil Ave. Nott ... 172 B3
Chesil Cotts. Nott ... 172 B3
Cheslyn Dr. Nott ... 172 B4
Chess Burrow. Mans ... 88 B1
Chester Cl. Lough ... 220 A2
Chester Green. Bees ... 182 C1
Chester Rd. Nott ... 174 B3
Chester St. Mans ... 87 F1
Chesterfield Ave. Bing ... 177 F3
Chesterfield Ave. Carl ... 162 B1
Chesterfield Ave. Lo Ea ... 193 F4
Chesterfield Ct. Carl ... 162 B2
Chesterfield Dr. Bu Jo ... 164 A3
Chesterfield Dr. Ret ... 40 A4
Chesterfield Rd N. Mans ... 87 E2
Chesterfield Rd S. Mans ... 102 A4
Chesterfield Rd. Plea ... 86 C4
Chesterfield Rd. S in A ... 99 F2
Chesterfield Rd. Tibs ... 85 D1
Chesterfield St. Carl ... 174 B4
Chesterman Cl. Awsw ... 158 A2
Chesterton Dr. Work ... 36 A3
Chestnut Ave. Bees ... 183 F3
Chestnut Ave. Bing ... 177 F2
Chestnut Ave. Carl ... 162 A1
Chestnut Ave. Gain ... 15 E1
Chestnut Ave. K-in-A ... 114 A2
Chestnut Ave. N-on-T ... 125 D2
Chestnut Ave. Raven ... 117 D1
Chestnut Ave. Ret ... 39 F2
Chestnut Cl. Bott ... 181 E2
Chestnut Cl. Work ... 35 F1
Chestnut Dr. Baw ... 9 F4
Chestnut Dr. Kim ... 159 D3
Chestnut Dr. Mans ... 102 C1
Chestnut Dr. Oll ... 77 E3
Chestnut Dr. S Norm ... 113 D2
Chestnut Dr. Sels ... 128 C4
Chestnut Dr. Shireb ... 72 B2
Chestnut Gr. Arn ... 162 A4
Chestnut Gr. Bu Jo ... 163 F2
Chestnut Gr. Carl ... 162 C1
Chestnut Gr. Farn ... 139 D2

Chestnut Gr. Huck ... 146 A2
Chestnut Gr. K-in-A ... 114 C3
Chestnut Gr. Mans ... 88 A3
Chestnut Gr. Nott ... 173 E4
Chestnut Gr. R on T ... 175 F2
Chestnut Gr. Sand ... 182 A4
Chestnut Gr. W Brid ... 185 E4
Chestnut Hill. Mans ... 102 C1
Chestnut Hill. Newt ... 99 D1
Chestnut La. B in F ... 194 C3
Chestnut Mews. Mans ... 102 C1
Chestnut Rd. La Mi ... 143 D2
Chestnut Rd. Lan ... 16 C2
Chestnut St. Lough ... 220 A2
Chestnut Way. Tux ... 66 A1
Chestnuts The. Carl ... 163 D1
Chestnuts The. Lo Ea ... 193 D4
Chestnuts The. Nott ... 161 F1
Chestnuts The. R on T ... 175 F2
Chettles Ind Est. Nott ... 172 B3
Chetwyn Rd. Nott ... 171 E3
Chetwynd Rd. Bees ... 183 E3
Chetwynd Rd. Bees ... 183 E2
Cheverton Ct. Nott ... 173 E4
Chevin Gdns. Nott ... 147 D1
Cheviot Cl. Bes Vil ... 147 D1
Cheviot Ct. C in L ... 25 F4
Cheviot Dr. Nott ... 159 F4
Cheviot Rd. Lo Ea ... 182 A1
Chewton Ave. East ... 144 A1
Chewton St. East ... 144 A1
Cheyne Dr. Bils ... 106 A2
Cheyne Wlk. Baw ... 9 F4
Cheyne Wlk. Ret ... 39 E2
Cheyny Cl. Nott ... 173 E1
Chichester Cl. Ilk ... 170 A4
Chichester Cl. Nott ... 160 C4
Chichester Dr. Cotg ... 187 F2
Chichester Wlk. C in L ... 25 F4
Chidlow Rd. Nott ... 171 E4
Chigwell Cl. Nuth ... 159 F2
Chillon Way. Huck ... 145 E3
Chiltern Cl. Bes Vil ... 147 D1
Chiltern Gdns. Lo Ea ... 182 A1
Chiltern Way. C in L ... 25 F4
Chiltern Way. Nott ... 161 D4
Chilton Cres. Mans ... 88 B3
Chilton Dr. Kim ... 159 D4
Chilvers Cl. Nott ... 161 D4
Chilwell Ct. Nott ... 160 B4
Chilwell La. Bees ... 183 E3
Chilwell Rd. Bees ... 183 F3
Chilwell Retail Park. Bees ... 183 D1
Chilwell St. Nott ... 172 C2
Chimes Meadow. South ... 136 C4
Chine Gdns. W Brid ... 185 E3
Chine The. S Norm ... 113 D2
Chingford Rd. Nott ... 171 F4
Chippendale St. Not ... 172 C2
Chippenham Rd. Nott ... 161 E4
Chirnside. Mans ... 101 E3
Chisbury Green. Nott ... 195 E4
Chisholm Way. Nott ... 161 D3
Chisworth Ct. Mans ... 88 C2
Christchurch Rd. Huck ... 145 E2
Christina Ave. Nott ... 160 B2
Christina Cres. Nott ... 160 B2
Christine Cl. Huck ... 131 E1
Christopher Cl. Nott ... 171 F3
Christopher Cres. Bald ... 140 B2
Chrysalis Way. East ... 143 E2
Church Ave. Arn ... 161 F4
Church Ave. Lo Ea ... 193 D2
Church Ave. Nott ... 172 C2
Church Ave. S in A ... 100 B1
Church Cl. Arn ... 161 F4
Church Cl. Bing ... 177 F3
Church Cl. E Lea ... 205 F1
Church Cl. Hose ... 211 F4
Church Cl. Mar War ... 74 A3
Church Cl. N Whea ... 31 F4
Church Cl. Nott ... 173 E3
Church Cl. Trow ... 170 B2
Church Cres. Bees ... 183 D2
Church Croft. W Brid ... 185 F4
Church Ct. R on T ... 175 F2
Church Dr E. Arn ... 161 F4
Church Dr. Arn ... 161 F4
Church Dr. Huck ... 146 A4
Church Dr. Ilk ... 157 F2
Church Dr. Keyw ... 197 F2
Church Dr. Mist ... 6 C1
Church Dr. Nott ... 161 D1
Church Dr. Nott ... 161 D1
Church Dr. Raven ... 117 D1
Church Dr. Sand ... 182 A4
Church Dr. Shireb ... 72 C2
Church Dr. W Brid ... 185 F4
Church End. Ne Br ... 210 B1
Church Farm Gdns. Wellow ... 77 F1
Church Field Cl. C in L ... 26 A3
Church Gate. Clip ... 187 E1
Church Gate. Clip ... 198 B4
Church Gate. Co Ba ... 200 C4
Church Gate. Kegw ... 203 E1
Church Gate. Lough ... 220 A2
Church Gdns. S in A ... 100 B1

Church Gr. Nott ... 172 C2
Church Hill Ave. Mans ... 88 B2
Church Hill. Bils ... 106 A3
Church Hill. K-in-A ... 114 B2
Church Hill. Kim ... 158 C3
Church Hill. Mans ... 88 B2
Church Hill. N Whea ... 31 F4
Church Hill. Newt ... 99 D1
Church La. S in A ... 100 C1
Church La. Aver ... 123 F1
Church La. B in F ... 194 C3
Church La. Bald ... 140 C2
Church La. Bees ... 183 E1
Church La. Best ... 98 A3
Church La. Bing ... 177 F3
Church La. Both ... 63 F4
Church La. Boug ... 77 F3
Church La. Boug ... 78 A3
Church La. Brin ... 143 F4
Church La. C in L ... 25 F2
Church La. Car Co ... 166 B2
Church La. Clar ... 30 C2
Church La. Clay ... 21 E3
Church La. Coll ... 98 A1
Church La. Coss ... 158 B3
Church La. Cost ... 206 B1
Church La. Cotg ... 187 F2
Church La. Crom ... 110 C4
Church La. E Dray ... 53 D2
Church La. E Sto ... 138 A1
Church La. Eagle ... 84 B2
Church La. Eakr ... 92 C1
Church La. Epp ... 150 A3
Church La. Gams ... 50 C2
Church La. Halam ... 120 C1
Church La. Har ... 8 C2
Church La. Hayt ... 30 B3
Church La. Huck ... 131 D1
Church La. Let ... 16 A1
Church La. Linby ... 131 D1
Church La. Lo Cl ... 211 E2
Church La. Mans ... 102 B3
Church La. Mapl ... 108 A3
Church La. Mist ... 6 C1
Church La. Morton ... 137 E2
Church La. N Clift ... 68 B2
Church La. N Sca ... 83 E1
Church La. Nott ... 147 F1
Church La. Nott ... 160 B4
Church La. Ol Da ... 218 C2
Church La. Plea ... 87 D3
Church La. Plum ... 197 F4
Church La. Plun ... 191 F1
Church La. Red ... 192 C2
Church La. Ret ... 39 F2
Church La. S Clift ... 68 B2
Church La. S in A ... 100 C1
Church La. S Musk ... 124 C1
Church La. S Sca ... 98 A3
Church La. Sax ... 56 C3
Church La. Screv ... 166 C2
Church La. Sels ... 128 B4
Church La. Sels ... 129 D2
Church La. Sibt ... 167 F4
Church La. Staple ... 182 B4
Church La. Thrum ... 194 B2
Church La. Tibs ... 99 D3
Church La. Tick ... 8 A1
Church La. Up Br ... 210 A1
Church La. Upton ... 122 C1
Church La. W Dray ... 50 C1
Church La. W-on-W ... 217 E4
Church La. Widm ... 208 A3
Church Lands. Lough ... 220 A3
Church Mead. S in A ... 99 F2
Church Meadow. Calv ... 148 C4
Church Mews. Nott ... 173 E1
Church Rd. Bes Vil ... 146 C2
Church Rd. Bir ... 9 E2
Church Rd. Bu Jo ... 163 F2
Church Rd. Greas ... 144 C2
Church Rd. Harby ... 70 B1
Church Rd. Mar War ... 74 A3
Church Rd. N Clip ... 89 F2
Church Rd. Nott ... 173 E3
Church Rd. Sax ... 57 D2
Church Side. Farns ... 119 F3
Church Side. Mans ... 102 B3
Church Side. S in A ... 99 F2
Church Sq. Nott ... 172 C2
Church St E. Pinx ... 113 E2
Church St W. Pinx ... 113 E2
Church St. Arn ... 161 F4
Church St. Baw ... 10 A3
Church St. Beck ... 14 A1
Church St. Bees ... 183 D1
Church St. Bees ... 183 F3
Church St. Bing ... 177 F3
Church St. Bils ... 105 F3
Church St. Bott ... 181 D1
Church St. Bunn ... 206 C4
Church St. Carl ... 174 C4
Church St. Coll ... 111 F4
Church St. Cr Bi ... 189 D2
Church St. E Mark ... 66 A3
Church St. East ... 143 F1
Church St. Edwin ... 76 A1
Church St. Ever ... 11 E2

230

Church St. Farn Coronation Rd. Nu

Church St. Farn 138 C2
Church St. Gain 15 E1
Church St. Goth 195 D1
Church St. Gran 191 D3
Church St. Hath 213 D1
Church St. Ilk 157 F2
Church St. K-in-A 114 B3
Church St. Lamb 163 E4
Church St. Lan 16 C1
Church St. Mans 87 D2
Church St. Mans 88 B2
Church St. Mans 102 A4
Church St. Mar War 74 A3
Church St. Mist 6 C1
Church St. N Whea 31 F4
Church St. N-on-T 139 F4
Church St. Nott 160 C1
Church St. Nott 172 C3
Church St. Oll 77 D2
Church St. Orst 179 F4
Church St. Rudd 196 B4
Church St. S in A 100 B1
Church St. S in A 100 C1
Church St. S Le S 32 B2
Church St. S Lev 42 B4
Church St. S Norm 113 D3
Church St. S on T 97 D4
Church St. Sand 182 A4
Church St. Scarc 59 D1
Church St. Shel 164 B1
Church St. South 136 C4
Church St. Staple 182 B4
Church St. What 179 D2
Church St. Wyme 216 B2
Church View Cl. Bes Vil 147 D1
Church View. Beck 14 A1
Church View. Bott 181 D2
Church View. Carl 162 C1
Church View. Glap 86 A4
Church View. Oll 77 D2
Church View. Plea 86 C4
Church View. S in A 100 B3
Church View. Scro 10 A1
Church Way. Sutt 29 D3
Church Wlk. Baw 10 A4
Church Wlk. Brin 143 F4
Church Wlk. Carl 174 C4
Church Wlk. East 143 F1
Church Wlk. Har 8 C2
Church Wlk. Staple 182 C4
Church Wlk. Upton 122 C1
Church Wlk. West 81 D3
Church Wlk. What 179 D2
Church Wlk. Work 35 F2
Churchdale Ave. Staple 170 C1
Churchfield Ct. Nott 147 D1
Churchfield Dr. Rain 103 F1
Churchfield La. Nott 172 C3
Churchfield Terr. Nott 160 C1
Churchgate. Ret 39 F4
Churchill Cl. Arn 161 F4
Churchill Dr. N-on-T 139 F3
Churchill Dr. Rudd 196 A4
Churchill Dr. Staple 182 C4
Churchill Gdns. Mans 88 B2
Churchill Park. Carl 174 C3
Churchill Way. Lea 24 C2
Churchmoor Ct. Nott 147 F1
Churchmoor La. Nott 147 F1
Churchside Gdns. Nott 172 C4
Churnet Cl. Nott 184 C2
Cinder La. Oll 77 D1
Cinderhill Gr. Carl 162 C1
Cinderhill Rd. Nott 160 A3
Cinderhill Wlk. Nott 160 A3
Circle The. Mans 88 A2
Citadel St. Nott 172 C3
City Rd. Bees 184 A3
City Rd. Nott 172 B1
City Rd. Stat 202 C2
City The. Bees 184 A3
City The. Bees 184 A4
Clandon Dr. Nott 161 D1
Clanfield Rd. Nott 171 F4
Clapham St. Nott 172 C3
Clapton La. Nott 184 C1
Clara Mount Rd. Hean 143 D1
Clarborough Dr. Arn 162 A3
Clarborough Hill. Clar 30 C2
Clare Cl. Nott 160 C2
Clare Hill. Blid 118 A2
Clare Rd. S in A 114 C4
Clare St. Nott 173 E3
Clare Valley. Nott 173 D2
Clarehaven. Staple 182 C3
Claremont Ave. Bees 183 E4
Claremont Ave. Huck 146 A3
Claremont Dr. W Brid 185 E2
Claremont Rd. Gain 24 C3
Claremont Rd. Nott 161 D1
Clarence Rd. Work 35 F2
Clarence Rd. Bees 183 E2
Clarence St. Lough 220 B3
Clarence St. Mans 87 E2
Clarence St. Mans 102 A3
Clarence St. Nott 173 F3
Clarendon Ct. Nott 173 D4
Clarendon Dr. Work 35 E3
Clarendon Rd. Mans 101 F4
Clarendon St. Nott 173 D3
Clarewood Gr. Nott 195 F4
Clarges St. Nott 160 B3
Clark La. Tux 65 F1
Clarke Ave. Arn 161 F4
Clarke Ave. N-on-T 139 F3
Clarke Cl. Cr Bi 189 D2
Clarke Dr. Lo Ea 193 D2
Clarke Rd. Nott 173 F1
Clarke's La. Bees 183 F2
Clarkson Dr. Bees 184 A3
Clater's Cl. Ret 40 A4
Claude St. Nott 172 C1
Clawson La. Hick 210 B3
Clawson La. Ne Br 210 C1
Claxton Rise. Lo Cl 211 E1
Clay Ave. Carl 162 A2
Clay St. Wyme 216 B2
Claye St. Lo Ea 193 F4
Clayfield Cl. Nott 160 A3
Claylands Ave. Work 35 E3
Claylands Cl. Work 35 E3
Claylands La. Work 35 E3
Claypit La. Fisk 137 F2
Claypole La. Dry Do 156 C1
Claypole Rd. Nott 172 C4
Claythorn Dr. Gain 24 C4
Clayton Cl. N-on-T 140 A3
Clayton Ct. Nott 172 C3
Clayton's Wharf. Nott 172 C1
Clayworth Comm. Clay 21 F2
Clayworth Ct. Mans 103 D2
Clayworth Rd. G on H 12 C1
Clegg Hill Dr. S in A 99 F2
Clement Ave. Bald 140 C2
Clensey La. Dry Do 156 C1
Clerkson St. Mans 102 A3
Clerkson's Alley. Mans 102 A4
Clether Rd. Nott 171 E3
Cleve Ave. Bees 182 C2
Cleveland Ave. Lo Ea 182 C1
Cleveland Cl. C in L 25 F4
Cleveland Cl. Nott 172 C3
Cleveland Sq. N-on-T 139 F3
Cleveland St. Gain 24 B4
Cleveleys Rd. Bees 182 C2
Clevely Way. Nott 184 C2
Cliff Bvd. Kim 158 C4
Cliff Cres. R on T 175 F2
Cliff Dr. R on T 176 A3
Cliff Gate. E Mark 65 E4
Cliff La. K in A 113 F2
Cliff Nook La. N-on-T 125 D1
Cliff Rd. Carl 174 B3
Cliff Rd. Nott 173 E2
Cliff Rd. R on T 175 F2
Cliff St. Mans 102 B4
Cliff The. Nott 160 A2
Cliff Way. R on T 175 F2
Cliffe Hill Ave. Staple 182 B4
Cliffgrove Ave. Bees 183 E3
Cliffhill La. Aslo 179 E3
Cliffhill La. Thoro 179 E3
Cliffmere Wlk. Nott 184 B1
Clifford Ave. Bees 183 F4
Clifford Cl. Keyw 197 F2
Clifford Cl. Lo Ea 193 D2
Clifford St. Lo Ea 193 F4
Clifford St. Mans 102 A2
Clifford St. Nott 172 C3
Clifton Ave. Lo Ea 194 A4
Clifton Ave. Rudd 196 B4
Clifton Bvd. Nott 184 C4
Clifton Cres. Bees 183 F2
Clifton Cres. N-on-T 125 E2
Clifton Gr. Carl 162 C1
Clifton Gr. Mans 102 C2
Clifton La. Nott 184 C2
Clifton La. Rudd 196 A4
Clifton Pl. Mans 102 A4
Clifton Rd. Rudd 196 A4
Clifton St. Bees 184 A3
Clifton Terr. Nott 173 D2
Clifton Way. Ret 39 E4
Clinthill La. Whit 45 D4
Clinton Ave. Brin 143 E3
Clinton Ave. Nott 173 D4
Clinton Ct. Nott 173 E3
Clinton Gdn La. Tux 65 F1
Clinton St E. Nott 173 E3
Clinton St W. Nott 173 E3
Clinton St. Arn 161 F4
Clinton St. Bees 183 F4
Clinton St. N-on-T 139 F4
Clinton St. Work 36 A1
Clinton Terr. Gain 24 B4
Clipston La. N-on-W 197 F4
Clipstone Ave. Arn 162 A2
Clipstone Ave. Mans 102 B4
Clipstone Ave. Nott 173 E3
Clipstone Ave. S in A 101 D2
Clipstone Dr. Mans 89 E2
Clipstone Rd E. Mans 89 E1
Clipstone Rd W. Mans 89 D1
Clive Cres. Kim 159 D3
Cliveden Green. Nott 184 B1
Cloister St. Nott 172 C1
Cloisters The. Bees 184 A4
Close Quarters. Bees 183 E4
Close The. Aver 123 F1
Close The. Bees 183 E2
Close The. Mans 103 F1
Close The. N-on-T 140 A4
Close The. Nott 161 E2
Close The. Shireb 72 C3
Close The. Upton 122 C1
Closes Side La. E Brid 165 F2
Cloud Ave. Staple 182 C4
Clouds Hill. Nott 195 F4
Cloudside Ct. Sand 182 A4
Cloudside Rd. Sand 182 A4
Clough Ct. Nott 172 A4
Clover Cl. Work 36 A4
Clover Green. Nott 160 B2
Clover Rise. Greas 158 B4
Clover St. K-in-A 115 D3
Cloverdale. Cotg 188 A1
Cloverlands Dr. Kim 159 D4
Cloverlands. W Brid 185 E2
Club Ct. Bald 140 B2
Clumber Ave. Arn 162 A2
Clumber Ave. Bees 183 E3
Clumber Ave. Brin 128 C1
Clumber Ave. Carl 175 D4
Clumber Ave. Edwin 75 F2
Clumber Ave. N-on-T 140 A3
Clumber Ave. Nott 173 D4
Clumber Ave. Rain 103 F1
Clumber Cres N. Nott 173 D2
Clumber Cres S. Nott 173 D2
Clumber Cres. S in A 100 B3
Clumber Ct. Ilk 157 F3
Clumber Ct. Mans 87 F1
Clumber Ct. Mar War 74 A2
Clumber Ct. Nott 173 D2
Clumber Dr. Mans 87 F1
Clumber Dr. R on T 176 A2
Clumber Pl. Work 35 F2
Clumber Rd E. Nott 173 D2
Clumber Rd W. Nott 173 D2
Clumber Rd. W Brid 185 F4
Clumber Rd. Work 47 D3
Clumber St. Huck 146 B3
Clumber St. K-in-A 115 E3
Clumber St. Lo Ea 193 E4
Clumber St. Mans 102 A4
Clumber St. Mar War 74 A2
Clumber St. Nott 173 E3
Clumber St. Ret 39 F3
Clumber St. S in A 100 B1
Clumber Way. Bils 106 A3
Clun Ct. Mans 88 B1
Co-operative Ave. Huck 146 A4
Co-operative St. Lo Ea 193 F3
Co-operative St. S in A 100 B3
Coach Dr. Greas 143 F2
Coach Rd. Mar War 74 B1
Coach Rd. Nott 172 A3
Coal La. Hose 211 F4
Coal Yard La. S Clift 82 C4
Coalpit La. Elk 49 F2
Coates Ave. Huck 130 C1
Coates Rd. N Le Ha 43 E4
Coatsby Rd. Kim 158 C4
Cobden Pl. Mans 87 F1
Cobden St. Gain 24 B4
Cobden St. K-in-A 115 D2
Cobden St. Lo Ea 193 F4
Cobden St. Lough 220 B2
Cobden St. Nott 172 C3
Coburn St. S in A 100 C1
Cobwell Rd. Ret 39 F3
Cochrane Terr. S in A 100 B3
Cock Hill La. Baw 10 A3
Cockayne Cl. Sand 182 A2
Cocker Beck. Lamb 163 E4
Cockerhouse Rd. East 143 F1
Cockett La. Farns 119 F4
Cockhill Cl. Baw 10 A3
Cocking Hill. Wellow 78 B2
Cocking La. Tres 42 B1
Cockington Rd. Nott 171 E3
Cockshut La. Holb 59 D2
Cockshut La. Ne La 59 D2
Coddington La. Stap 127 D3
Coddington Rd. Bald 140 C3
Codrington Gdns. Nott 161 E4
Cogenhoe Wlk. Nott 147 F1
Coggin's La. Mar War 74 B3
Coghill Ct. South 136 B4
Coging Cl. Bald 140 B2
Cogley La. Bing 178 A2
Cohen Cl. Arn 162 A3
Cokefield Ave. Nuth 159 F2
Colbeck St. Work 35 F2
Colborn St. Nott 173 F4
Colby Cl. Mans 89 D1
Coleby Ave. Nott 172 C2
Coleby Rd. Nott 159 F1
Coleby Rd. Nott 160 A1
Coleman Ave. Bald 140 A2
Coleridge Cres. Arn 161 E4
Coleridge Rd. Bald 140 C3
Coleridge Rd. Work 36 A3
Coleridge St. Nott 172 C3
Colesbourne Rd. Nott 184 C1
Colgrove Rd. Lough 220 A1
Colin Broughton Ct. Nott 160 B4
Colindale Gdns. Nuth 159 F2
Colinwood Ave. Nott 146 C1
College Dr. Nott 184 B1
College Dr. Nott 184 C2
College La. E Mark 66 A4
College La. Work 36 A1
College Rd. Bees 183 F3
College Rd. Su Bo 204 A1
College St. E Brid 165 E2
College St. Lo Ea 182 B1
College St. Nott 173 D2
Colley La. West 81 D2
Colleymoor Leys La. Nott 184 C1
Collier Ave. Mans 88 A3
Colliery Cl. Nott 173 D1
Colliery Rd. Bir 9 D2
Collin Ave. Sand 182 A2
Collin Gn. Nott 161 E2
Collin St. Bees 183 F3
Collin St. Nott 173 E2
Collingham Rd. Eagle 98 C1
Collingham Rd. Mans 87 E1
Collington St. Bees 183 F3
Collington Way. W Brid 185 E3
Collingwood Cl. Nott 184 C2
Collingwood Rd. Lo Ea 193 F3
Collins Ave. S in A 114 C4
Collins Ave. S Norm 113 D4
Collins Cl. Nott 159 F3
Collins Wlk. Ret 39 F4
Collis Cl. N-on-T 140 B4
Collison St. Nott 172 C3
Colly Gate. Kim 159 D3
Collyer Rd. Calv 148 B4
Collygate Rd. Nott 173 E1
Colmon Cl. Nott 161 D4
Colmon Wlk. Nott 161 D4
Colne Ct. Mans 88 B1
Colonel's La. Up Br 210 A1
Colonsay Cl. Staple 170 B2
Colsterdale. Work 36 A4
Colston La. Harb 202 A2
Colston Cres. W Brid 185 E2
Colston Gate. Cotg 188 A2
Colston La. Hose 201 F2
Colston Rd. Cr Bi 189 D1
Colston Rd. Mans 103 D2
Colston Rd. Nott 160 B4
Colton St. Mist 6 C1
Columbia Ave. Mans 102 C3
Columbia Ave. S in A 100 B1
Columbia Cl. Sels 129 D4
Columbia St. S in A 99 F2
Columbia St. S in A 100 A1
Colville St. Nott 173 D4
Colville Terr. Gain 24 B4
Colville Terr. Nott 173 D4
Colville Villas. Nott 173 D4
Colwick Cl. Mans 87 F1
Colwick Loop Rd. Carl 175 D4
Colwick Manor Farm. Carl 174 C3
Colwick Park Cl. Carl 174 C3
Colwick Rd. Nott 174 A2
Colwick Rd. W Brid 173 F1
Comery Ave. Nott 174 A3
Comfrey Cl. Nott 160 C4
Commerce Sq. Nott 173 E2
Commercial Ave. Bees 183 F3
Commercial Gate. Mans 102 A3
Commercial Rd. Keyw 197 F1
Commercial Rd. Nott 160 A4
Commercial St. Mans 102 A3
Commodore Gdns. Nott 160 B1
Common La. Bees 183 D3
Common La. Blyth 18 A2
Common La. Huck 145 E3
Common La. Kim 159 D4
Common La. Mans 88 A2
Common La. Plea 72 B2
Common La. Ran 19 E2
Common La. S Le S 32 B2
Common La. Scarc 72 B2
Common La. Shireb 72 B2
Common La. Tick 8 A4
Common Rd. Ret 39 F4
Common Rd. S in A 99 F1
Common Rd. S in A 113 F4
Common Rd. Th Sa 34 A3
Common Side. Sels 128 C4
Common The. Huck 145 E3
Common The. S Norm 113 D3
Commons Cl. Greas 158 A4
Compton Acres. W Brid 185 D3
Compton Rd. Nott 161 D2
Compton St. Scarc 72 C4
Comyn Gdns. Nott 173 E3
Conduit Cl. Nott 173 E1
Conery Gdns. What 179 D2
Conery La. What 178 C1
Coneygrey Spinney. Flint 152 C1
Conifer Cres. Nott 195 F4
Conifer Wlk. Carl 174 A4
Coningsby Cl. Gain 24 C4
Coningsby Gdns E. Arn 161 F2
Coningsby Rd. Arn 161 F3
Coningswath Rd. Carl 162
Conisborough Terr. Nott 173
Conisbrough Ave. Carl 163
Coniston Ave. Nott 160
Coniston Cl. Gam 186
Coniston Rd. Bees 183
Coniston Rd. Huck 145
Coniston Rd. K-in-A 115
Coniston Rd. Lo Ea 182
Coniston Rd. Work 35
Connaught Rd. Gain 15
Connelly Cl. Arn 162
Connery Mews. Bees 183
Connery The. Huck 146
Conrad Cl. Work 36
Constance St. Nott 161
Convent St. Nott 173
Conway Ave. Carl 175
Conway Cl. Mans 101
Conway Cl. Nott 173
Conway Cres. Carl 175
Conway Dr. C in L 25
Conway Gdns. Arn 161
Conway Gdns. Ret 39
Conway Rd. Carl 175
Conway Rd. Huck 145
Conway St. Lo Ea 193
Conway Wlk. Nott 173
Cook Dr. Ilk 170
Cooks La. Morton 137
Cooks La. South 136
Cookson Ave. Carl 162
Cookson St. K-in-A 114
Coombe Cl. Nott 172
Cooper Cl. Arn 162
Cooper Cl. Cr Bi 189
Cooper Cl. Nott 159
Cooper Ct. Lough 220
Cooper St. Carl 175
Coopers Green. Bees 171
Coopers Rise. Rain 104
Cope St. Nott 172
Copeland Ave. K-in-A 114
Copeland Ave. Staple 182
Copeland Gr. Bing 177
Copeland Rd. Huck 146
Copeland Rd. K-in-A 114
Copenhagen Ct. Nott 161
Copper Hill. Grass 81
Coppice Ave. Ilk 157
Coppice Cl. Huck 145
Coppice Dr. East 143
Coppice Gr. Nott 161
Coppice Rd. Arn 162
Coppice Rd. Mans 89
Coppice Rd. Work 35
Coppice The. Ba Mo 28
Coppice The. Shireb 72
Coppice View. S Norm 113
Copplestone Dr. Carl 162
Copse Cl. Bu Jo 163
Copse The. Bees 183
Copse The. Farn 139
Copse The. Huck 146
Copse The. Ilk 157
Copse The. S in A 100
Copseside Cl. Lo Ea 193
Copsewood. S Norm 113
Corben Gdns. Nott 159 F4
Corby Rd. Nott 161 F1
Cordy La. Brin 143 F4
Cordy La. Sels 143 F4
Corene Ave. S in A 100 C1
Coriander Dr. Nott 160 B2
Corinth Rd. Nott 184 C1
Corkhill La. Kirk 121 E3
Corkhill La. South 121 E3
Corn Cl. Cotg 187 F1
Corn Cl. S Norm 113 D3
Cornel Ct. Mans 88 C1
Cornell Dr. Arn 162 B4
Corner The. Lowd 150 B1
Corneries The. Lough 220 A2
Cornfield Ave. S Norm 113 D2
Cornfield Rd. Kim 158 C4
Cornhill Rd. Carl 174 A4
Cornley Rd. Mist 6 B2
Cornwall Ave. Bees 184 B2
Cornwall Ave. Mans 102 C3
Cornwall Cl. Sels 128 B2
Cornwall Dr. Oll 77 D2
Cornwall Rd. Arn 161 E4
Cornwall Rd. Ret 30 A1
Cornwall Rd. Shire 34 C4
Cornwallis Cl. Lo Ea 193 E3
Coronation Ave. Lo Cl 211 D1
Coronation Ave. Miss 4 A2
Coronation Ave. Nott 185 D4
Coronation Ave. Plea 86 C4
Coronation Ave. Sand 182 A4
Coronation Dr. Mans 103 D4
Coronation Dr. S Norm 113 D3
Coronation Dr. Shireb 72 C1
Coronation Rd. Arn 161 F2
Coronation Rd. Bes Vil 146 C2
Coronation Rd. Coss 158 A1
Coronation Rd. Huck 145 F4
Coronation Rd. Nuth 159 E3

| | | |
|---|---|---|
| ronation St. Bald | 140 | B3 |
| ronation St. Mans | 102 | B3 |
| ronation St. Ret | 39 | F3 |
| ronation St. S in A | 100 | C1 |
| ronation St. Whit | 45 | D3 |
| rporation Oaks. Nott | 173 | E4 |
| rporation Rd. Ilk | 170 | A3 |
| rporation St. Mans | 102 | A4 |
| rringham Rd. Gain | 15 | F1 |
| sby Rd. Nott | 173 | F2 |
| sgrove Ave. S in A | 101 | D3 |
| ssall Rd. Cross | 170 | B3 |
| ssall Rd. Trow | 170 | B3 |
| sthorpe Ind Est. C in L | 16 | C1 |
| sthorpe Villas. C in L | 16 | C1 |
| stock Ave. Nott | 161 | D2 |
| stock Rd. E Le | 206 | A1 |
| stock Rd. T in G | 207 | E1 |
| stock Rd. Wys | 207 | E1 |
| tes Rd. Lough | 220 | C3 |
| tgrave Ave. Carl | 162 | C1 |
| tgrave La. Toll | 187 | D1 |
| tgrave Rd. Mans | 87 | F1 |
| tgrave Rd. N-on-W | 187 | D1 |
| tmanhay Rd. Ilk | 157 | F2 |
| oton Cl. Mans | 88 | C2 |
| oton Cl. Nott | 185 | D2 |
| tswold Cl. Lo Ea | 193 | D4 |
| tswold Ct. Bees | 171 | E1 |
| tswold Ct. C in L | 25 | F4 |
| tswold Gr. Mans | 103 | D3 |
| tswold Rd. Nott | 159 | F1 |
| ttage Ave. Aslo | 178 | C2 |
| ttage Cl. Ilk | 157 | E2 |
| ttage La. Coll | 111 | F3 |
| ttage La. Mar War | 74 | B1 |
| ttage Meadow. Carl | 174 | C2 |
| ttage Pasture La. Gunt | 164 | C4 |
| ttage Terr. Nott | 173 | D3 |
| ttam Dr. Nott | 161 | D4 |
| ttam Gdns. Nott | 161 | D4 |
| ttam Gr. Mans | 101 | E3 |
| ttam Rd. S Lev | 42 | C4 |
| ttam Cl. South | 136 | C4 |
| ttesmore Rd. Nott | 172 | C2 |
| otton Mill La. Farns | 120 | A3 |
| oulby Cl. Clayp | 156 | C3 |
| oulton's Ave. S in A | 100 | B2 |
| oulton's Cl. S in A | 100 | B2 |
| ounty Bsns Park. Nott | 173 | F1 |
| ounty Rd. Carl | 162 | B2 |
| ounty Rd. Nott | 173 | F1 |
| ourt Cres. Nott | 171 | F2 |
| ourt Gdns. W Brid | 185 | D2 |
| ourt St. Nott | 172 | C4 |
| ourt Yd. Bees | 183 | D4 |
| ourt-Field Rd. S in A | 101 | D3 |
| ourtenay Gdns. Nott | 173 | E4 |
| ourtlett Way. Nott | 160 | A3 |
| ourtney Cl. Nott | 171 | F3 |
| ove Rd. Haxey | 2 | C3 |
| ovedale Rd. Nott | 161 | E3 |
| oventry Dr. Work | 36 | A3 |
| oventry Rd. Bees | 171 | D2 |
| oventry Rd. Bees | 184 | A4 |
| oventry Rd. Nott | 160 | A3 |
| overate. Work | 36 | A4 |
| overt Cl. Bu Jo | 163 | F3 |
| overt Cl. Huck | 146 | B3 |
| overt Cl. Keyw | 197 | F2 |
| overt Rd. W Brid | 186 | A3 |
| ow La. Bees | 183 | E4 |
| ow La. N-on-T | 124 | C1 |
| ow Pasture La. K-in-A | 114 | B3 |
| owan St. Nott | 173 | E3 |
| owdray Cl. Lough | 220 | A1 |
| owdrey Gdns. Arn | 162 | A3 |
| owlairs. Nott | 160 | C4 |
| owley St. Nott | 160 | C2 |
| owpasture La. S in A | 100 | C1 |
| owper Cl. Work | 36 | A3 |
| owper Rd. Arn | 161 | F2 |
| owper Rd. Greas | 158 | A4 |
| owpes Cl. S in A | 100 | C2 |
| ox Dr. Bott | 180 | C2 |
| ox's Hill. Gain | 15 | E1 |
| ox's La. Mans | 88 | A3 |
| oxmoor Ct. Nott | 147 | D3 |
| oxmoor Rd. K in A | 116 | A3 |
| oxmoor Rd. S in A | 101 | E1 |
| rab La. N Musk | 110 | C1 |
| rab Nook La. Farns | 119 | F3 |
| rabtree Field. Nott | 174 | B2 |
| rabtree La. Beck | 23 | D4 |
| rabtree La. H Marn | 67 | E1 |
| rabtree Rd. Nott | 160 | A3 |
| raddock St. Lough | 220 | A2 |
| rafts Way. South | 121 | F1 |
| ragdale Rd. Nott | 161 | E3 |
| ragg La. Newt | 99 | D1 |
| ragmoor Rd. Bu Jo | 163 | F2 |
| rags Rd. Elmt | 45 | D1 |
| rags Rd. Whit | 45 | D1 |
| raig Moray. R on T | 176 | A2 |
| raig St. Lo Ea | 193 | F4 |
| Craigs Green. Mans | 101 | F3 |
| Craigston Rd. C in L | 25 | F3 |
| Crammond Cl. Nott | 173 | D1 |
| Crampton Ave. Mans | 102 | C4 |
| Crampton Cl. S in A | 100 | A2 |
| Crampton Ct. Nott | 161 | D4 |
| Cranworth Gr. Nott | 161 | E2 |
| Cranberry Cl. W Brid | 185 | D3 |
| Cranbourne Cl. Staple | 170 | B1 |
| Cranbourne Gr. Huck | 145 | F4 |
| Cranbrook St. Nott | 173 | E2 |
| Cranford Gdns. W Brid | 185 | E2 |
| Cranleigh Dr. Lowd | 150 | B1 |
| Cranmer Ave. Aslo | 178 | C2 |
| Cranmer Gr. Mans | 87 | E2 |
| Cranmer Rd. Nott | 173 | E4 |
| Cranmer Rd. N-on-T | 139 | F3 |
| Cranmer St. Ilk | 157 | F1 |
| Cranmer St. Lo Ea | 182 | B1 |
| Cranmer St. Nott | 173 | E4 |
| Cranmore Cl. Arn | 148 | A1 |
| Cransley Ave. Nott | 171 | E1 |
| Cranston Ave. Nott | 147 | F1 |
| Cranston Rd. Bees | 171 | E1 |
| Cranswick Cl. Mans | 89 | D1 |
| Cranthorpe Dr. Nott | 174 | B3 |
| Crantock Gdns. Keyw | 197 | F2 |
| Cranwell Cl. Nott | 159 | F3 |
| Cranwell Rd. Nott | 159 | F1 |
| Craster Dr. Nott | 159 | F4 |
| Craster St. S in A | 100 | C1 |
| Crathie Rd. C in L | 25 | F3 |
| Craven Rd. Nott | 172 | C4 |
| Crawford Ave. Staple | 182 | B4 |
| Crawford Cl. Nott | 171 | F3 |
| Crawford Rise. Arn | 162 | B4 |
| Crees La. Farn | 139 | D3 |
| Crescent Ave. Carl | 162 | C1 |
| Crescent Rd. Sels | 128 | B3 |
| Crescent The. Arn | 161 | F2 |
| Crescent The. Beck | 14 | A1 |
| Crescent The. Bees | 183 | D1 |
| Crescent The. Bees | 183 | E2 |
| Crescent The. Bir | 9 | E2 |
| Crescent The. Blid | 118 | A3 |
| Crescent The. Bils | 105 | F3 |
| Crescent The. E Lea | 205 | F1 |
| Crescent The. East | 144 | A1 |
| Crescent The. Lea | 24 | C1 |
| Crescent The. Mans | 102 | B2 |
| Crescent The. Ne Br | 219 | D3 |
| Crescent The. Nott | 173 | A2 |
| Crescent The. R on T | 176 | A2 |
| Crescent The. Ret | 39 | E3 |
| Crescent The. S in A | 100 | B4 |
| Crescent The. Shireb | 72 | C3 |
| Crescent The. Staple | 170 | C1 |
| Cresswell Rd. Bees | 183 | D3 |
| Cresswell Rd. Work | 35 | F2 |
| Cresswell St. Work | 35 | F2 |
| Cresta Gdns. Nott | 161 | E1 |
| Creswell Ct. Mans | 88 | C2 |
| Creswell Rd. Cuck | 60 | A2 |
| Crew La. South | 137 | D4 |
| Crew Rd. Coll | 98 | A1 |
| Crewe Cl. Blid | 118 | A3 |
| Crewe Cl. Nott | 172 | C3 |
| Crewe Rd. Bir | 9 | D2 |
| Cribb Cl. Nott | 185 | D4 |
| Crich View. Newt | 99 | D2 |
| Crich View. Nott | 161 | E1 |
| Cricket Cl. Ann Wo | 129 | F4 |
| Cricket Field La. Ret | 39 | F4 |
| Cricketers Ct. W Brid | 173 | F1 |
| Criftin Rd. Bu Jo | 164 | A2 |
| Crink La. South | 136 | C3 |
| Cripps Hill. Nott | 172 | B1 |
| Critch's Flats. Kim | 158 | C3 |
| Critchley St. Ilk | 157 | F1 |
| Crocus St. K-in-A | 115 | D2 |
| Crocus St. Nott | 173 | E1 |
| Croft Ave. Huck | 146 | A3 |
| Croft Ave. Mans | 102 | B1 |
| Croft Cl. Pinx | 113 | E2 |
| Croft Cres. Awsw | 158 | B3 |
| Croft Ct. S in A | 99 | F2 |
| Croft Dr. Tick | 8 | A4 |
| Croft Farm Close. Ever | 11 | D2 |
| Croft Gdns. Ol Da | 218 | C2 |
| Croft Rd. Arn | 161 | F4 |
| Croft Rd. Fin | 1 | A1 |
| Croft Rd. Keyw | 197 | F2 |
| Croft Rd. W Brid | 186 | A2 |
| Croft Rise. E Brid | 165 | E2 |
| Croft The. Beck | 23 | E4 |
| Croft The. Kegw | 203 | E1 |
| Croft The. N-on-T | 140 | A4 |
| Croft The. Ret | 39 | F4 |
| Croft The. S in A | 100 | B3 |
| Croft The. S Norm | 113 | D3 |
| Croft Way. Ever | 11 | E2 |
| Croft Wlk. Whit | 45 | D3 |
| Crofton Cl. Bees | 183 | E2 |
| Crofton Cl. Nott | 172 | A3 |
| Crofton Rd. Bees | 183 | E1 |
| Crofts The. Bing | 177 | F2 |
| Cromarty Cl. Mans | 101 | E3 |
| Cromarty Ct. Nott | 173 | D1 |
| Cromdale Cl. Arn | 148 | B1 |
| Cromer Rd. Nott | 173 | F4 |
| Cromford Ave. Carl | 174 | B4 |
| Cromford Ave. Mans | 102 | A2 |
| Cromford Cl. Ald | 143 | D2 |
| Cromford Cl. Lo Ea | 193 | D3 |
| Cromford Rd. Ald | 143 | D2 |
| Cromford Rd. Ann Wo | 115 | D1 |
| Cromford Rd. W Brid | 185 | F3 |
| Cromford St. Gain | 15 | E1 |
| Crompton Rd. Mans | 87 | E2 |
| Crompton Rd. Bils | 105 | F3 |
| Crompton Rd. Ilk | 170 | A2 |
| Crompton St. Plea | 86 | C4 |
| Crompton St. S in A | 100 | A4 |
| Cromwell Ave. Ilk | 170 | A3 |
| Cromwell Cres. Lamb | 163 | D4 |
| Cromwell Dr. E Lea | 205 | F1 |
| Cromwell Rd. Aslo | 178 | C2 |
| Cromwell Rd. Bees | 183 | F3 |
| Cromwell Rd. N-on-T | 140 | A4 |
| Cromwell St. Carl | 174 | C4 |
| Cromwell St. Gain | 24 | B3 |
| Cromwell St. Greas | 158 | B4 |
| Cromwell St. Mans | 102 | B3 |
| Cromwell St. Nott | 173 | D3 |
| Cromwell Way. Lea | 24 | C2 |
| Crook's Ave. Mans | 88 | B2 |
| Crookdale La. Calv | 148 | C4 |
| Crooked Billet St. Mort | 15 | D2 |
| Crookes Ave. Plea | 87 | D3 |
| Croome Cl. Lough | 220 | B1 |
| Cropston Cl. W Brid | 185 | F2 |
| Cropton Gr. Bing | 177 | E2 |
| Cropton Rd. Nott | 172 | A3 |
| Cropwell Bishop Rd. Cr Bu | 189 | D3 |
| Cropwell Butler Rd. Cr Bi | 189 | D2 |
| Cropwell Ct. Mans | 102 | B4 |
| Cropwell Gdns. R on T | 176 | A1 |
| Cropwell Green. Nott | 173 | F3 |
| Cropwell Rd. R on T | 176 | A1 |
| Crosby Cl. Mans | 89 | D1 |
| Crosby Rd. W Brid | 185 | F4 |
| Cross Dr. K-in-A | 115 | D4 |
| Cross Dr. Rain | 104 | A1 |
| Cross Hill Cl. Wyme | 216 | B2 |
| Cross Hill. G on H | 12 | C1 |
| Cross La. Aust | 3 | E3 |
| Cross La. Bald | 140 | B1 |
| Cross La. Blid | 117 | E3 |
| Cross La. Coll | 112 | B4 |
| Cross La. E Brid | 165 | E2 |
| Cross La. E Sto | 154 | A2 |
| Cross La. Elk | 49 | F2 |
| Cross La. Elst | 154 | A2 |
| Cross La. Farn | 138 | C2 |
| Cross La. G on H | 5 | D1 |
| Cross La. Harby | 71 | B1 |
| Cross La. S in A | 100 | A1 |
| Cross La. S in A | 101 | B3 |
| Cross St. Arn | 161 | F4 |
| Cross St. B in W | 141 | F3 |
| Cross St. Bees | 183 | F4 |
| Cross St. Bils | 105 | F3 |
| Cross St. Carl | 174 | B4 |
| Cross St. Carl | 175 | D4 |
| Cross St. East | 144 | A1 |
| Cross St. Gain | 24 | B4 |
| Cross St. Hath | 213 | D1 |
| Cross St. Lan | 16 | C2 |
| Cross St. Lo Ea | 193 | D4 |
| Cross St. Lough | 220 | B3 |
| Cross St. Mans | 88 | A1 |
| Cross St. Mort | 15 | D2 |
| Cross St. N-on-T | 140 | A4 |
| Cross St. Ret | 40 | A3 |
| Cross St. S Le S | 32 | B3 |
| Cross St. Sand | 182 | B3 |
| Cross The. C in L | 26 | A3 |
| Cross The. Cotg | 187 | F2 |
| Crossdale Dr. Keyw | 197 | F2 |
| Crossdale Wlk. Nott | 160 | C4 |
| Crossfield Dr. Nott | 161 | D4 |
| Crossgate Dr. Nott | 173 | D1 |
| Crosshill. Cotg | 188 | A2 |
| Crosslands Meadow. Carl | 174 | C2 |
| Crossley Ave. S in A | 100 | A2 |
| Crossley Hill La. C in L | 26 | B2 |
| Crossley St. Nott | 161 | D1 |
| Crossman St. Nott | 161 | E1 |
| Crossways Dr. E Brid | 165 | E2 |
| Crossways. E Mark | 66 | A4 |
| Crossways. Ret | 39 | F4 |
| Crow Hill Cl. Mans | 102 | A4 |
| Crow Hill Dr. Mans | 102 | A4 |
| Crow Hill La. Mans | 88 | A1 |
| Crow Hill Rd. Carl | 174 | C4 |
| Crow Hill. Mans | 87 | D3 |
| Crow La. S Musk | 124 | B4 |
| Crow Park Ave. S on T | 81 | F1 |
| Crow Park Dr. Bu Jo | 163 | F2 |
| Crowborough Ave. Bees | 171 | F1 |
| Crowley Cl. Nott | 171 | E3 |
| Crown Ave. Mans | 103 | D4 |
| Crown Cl. Coll | 98 | A1 |
| Crown Cl. Rain | 118 | B4 |
| Crown Ct. S Le S | 32 | B3 |
| Crown Farm Way. Mans | 103 | D4 |
| Crown St. Mans | 102 | C3 |
| Crown St. N-on-T | 139 | F4 |
| Crown St. Work | 35 | F2 |
| Crowthorne Cl. Nott | 146 | C1 |
| Crowthorne Gdns. Nott | 146 | C1 |
| Croxall Cl. Nott | 184 | C2 |
| Croxton Ct. Mans | 88 | C2 |
| Croydon Rd. Nott | 172 | C3 |
| Crummock Cl. Bees | 183 | E4 |
| Cuckney Hill. Mar War | 74 | A4 |
| Cuillin Cl. Lo Ea | 182 | A1 |
| Cul-de-sac. Bils | 105 | F3 |
| Culdrose Wlk. Nott | 161 | F1 |
| Cullen's Ct. Nott | 161 | E1 |
| Cullin Cl. Nott | 146 | C1 |
| Cumberland Ave. Bees | 183 | E3 |
| Cumberland Ave. Mar War | 74 | A3 |
| Cumberland Cl. Bir | 9 | E2 |
| Cumberland Cl. C in L | 25 | F4 |
| Cumberland Cl. Sels | 128 | B2 |
| Cumberland Dr. Mans | 101 | E2 |
| Cumberland Pl. Nott | 173 | D2 |
| Cumbria Rd. Work | 36 | A3 |
| Cundy Hill. South | 136 | A3 |
| Cunningham Cl. Matt | 19 | F4 |
| Cunningham Cl. Matt | 20 | A4 |
| Cupar St. Mar War | 74 | C3 |
| Curie Ct. Nott | 172 | C1 |
| Curlew Cl. Nott | 174 | B3 |
| Curlew Wharf. Nott | 172 | C1 |
| Currie Rd. N-on-T | 125 | D1 |
| Curtis Cl. Coll | 98 | A1 |
| Curtis St. Huck | 146 | A3 |
| Curzon Ave. Carl | 174 | B4 |
| Curzon Cl. Rain | 118 | A4 |
| Curzon Ct. Nott | 173 | E3 |
| Curzon Dr. Work | 35 | E4 |
| Curzon Gdns. Nott | 173 | E3 |
| Curzon Pl. Nott | 173 | E3 |
| Curzon St. Carl | 175 | D4 |
| Curzon St. Gain | 15 | E1 |
| Curzon St. Goth | 195 | D1 |
| Curzon St. Lo Ea | 182 | A1 |
| Curzon St. Lough | 220 | A2 |
| Cusworth Way. Work | 35 | E2 |
| Cuttings Ave. S in A | 114 | A4 |
| Cuxton Cl. Nott | 159 | E1 |
| Cycle Rd. Nott | 172 | C2 |
| Cypress Cl. Huck | 145 | E3 |
| Cyprus Ave. Bees | 183 | F4 |
| Cyprus Rd. Nott | 161 | E1 |
| Cyril Ave. Bees | 183 | F4 |
| Cyril Ave. Nott | 172 | B4 |
| Cyril Ave. Staple | 182 | B4 |
| Cyril Rd. W Brid | 186 | A4 |
| D'Ayncourt Wk. Farns | 120 | A3 |
| Dabek Rise. Ann Wo | 115 | D1 |
| Dabell Ave. Nott | 159 | F4 |
| Dadley Rd. C in L | 25 | F4 |
| Dadsley Rd. Tick | 8 | A4 |
| Dagmar Gr. Bees | 184 | A3 |
| Dagmar Gr. Nott | 161 | E1 |
| Dairy La. Hose | 211 | F4 |
| Daisy Cl. Cotg | 187 | F1 |
| Daisy Farm Rd. Greas | 158 | B4 |
| Daisy Rd. Carl | 162 | A1 |
| Dakeyne St. Nott | 173 | F3 |
| Dalbeattie Cl. Arn | 162 | A4 |
| Dalby Sq. Nott | 172 | B2 |
| Dale Ave. Carl | 162 | A1 |
| Dale Ave. Carl | 174 | B4 |
| Dale Ave. Lo Ea | 182 | B1 |
| Dale Ave. Newt | 99 | D2 |
| Dale Cl. Huck | 145 | E3 |
| Dale Cl. Ret | 39 | F2 |
| Dale Cl. S in A | 101 | D3 |
| Dale Cl. Scarc | 58 | C1 |
| Dale Cl. Scarc | 72 | C4 |
| Dale Cl. W Brid | 186 | A4 |
| Dale Cres. Bald | 140 | C1 |
| Dale Farm Ave. Nott | 173 | F3 |
| Dale Gr. Nott | 173 | F2 |
| Dale La. Al Hu | 86 | B4 |
| Dale La. Bees | 183 | D3 |
| Dale La. Blid | 118 | A3 |
| Dale Rd. Carl | 174 | B4 |
| Dale Rd. Keyw | 197 | F2 |
| Dale Rd. Kim | 158 | C3 |
| Dale Rd. Mar War | 74 | B3 |
| Dale St. Mans | 88 | A1 |
| Dale St. Nott | 173 | F3 |
| Dale View Rd. Nott | 174 | A4 |
| Dalebrook Cres. Huck | 145 | E3 |
| Dalemoor Gdns. Nott | 172 | A4 |
| Dales Ave. S in A | 100 | C3 |
| Dales La. Miss | 4 | C2 |
| Daleside E. Nott | 174 | B2 |
| Daleside Rd. Nott | 174 | A2 |
| Daleside. Cotg | 187 | F1 |
| Dalestorth Ave. Mans | 87 | E1 |
| Dalestorth Cl. S in A | 101 | D1 |
| Dalestorth Rd. S in A | 101 | D2 |
| Dalestorth S. in A | 101 | D2 |
| Daleswood Cres. S Norm | 113 | D2 |
| Dalkeith Terr. Nott | 172 | C4 |
| Dallas St. Mans | 102 | A3 |
| Dallas York Rd. Bees | 184 | A3 |
| Dalley Cl. Staple | 182 | C4 |
| Dalton Cl. Staple | 182 | C3 |
| Daltons Cl. Ald | 143 | D2 |
| Dam Rd. Tick | 8 | A3 |
| Dame Flogan St. Mans | 102 | A3 |
| Dame La. Miss | 4 | A1 |
| Damson Wlk. Carl | 174 | A4 |
| Danbury Mount. Nott | 161 | E1 |
| Dane Cl. Nott | 173 | E3 |
| Dane Ct. Nott | 173 | E3 |
| Danes Cl. Arn | 161 | E4 |
| Danes Rd. Gain | 15 | F1 |
| Danesfield Rd. Work | 35 | F1 |
| Daneshill Rd. Lound | 20 | A1 |
| Daneshill Rd. Sutt | 19 | E1 |
| Daneshill Rd. Torw | 19 | E1 |
| Danethorpe La. Coll | 126 | A4 |
| Danethorpe Vale. Nott | 161 | E2 |
| Daniel Cres. Mans | 101 | F4 |
| Daniels Way. Huck | 145 | F2 |
| Danners Hill. Papp | 131 | F3 |
| Darfield Cl. Tick | 8 | A4 |
| Darfield Dr. Hean | 143 | D1 |
| Dark La. B in W | 142 | A3 |
| Dark La. Bing | 178 | A2 |
| Dark La. W Lea | 204 | C1 |
| Dark La. What | 179 | D2 |
| Darkey La. Staple | 182 | C3 |
| Darley Ave. Bees | 182 | C2 |
| Darley Ave. Carl | 162 | C1 |
| Darley Ave. K-in-A | 115 | E3 |
| Darley Ave. Nott | 172 | C4 |
| Darley Dale La. Mans | 102 | B2 |
| Darley Dr. Lo Ea | 193 | D3 |
| Darley Rd. Nott | 172 | C4 |
| Darley Sq. Ilk | 157 | F3 |
| Darlton Dr. Arn | 162 | A4 |
| Darlton Rd. E Dray | 53 | D1 |
| Darlton Rd. Tux | 66 | B2 |
| Darlton St. Mans | 101 | E3 |
| Darnal Cl. Nott | 160 | C4 |
| Darnhall Cres. Nott | 171 | E4 |
| Daron Gdns. Nott | 161 | D4 |
| Darrel Rd. Ret | 39 | F3 |
| Darricott Cl. Rain | 118 | A4 |
| Darvel Cl. Nott | 172 | A3 |
| Darwin Cl. Elst | 153 | F2 |
| Darwin Cl. Mans | 102 | B2 |
| Darwin Cl. Nott | 160 | C4 |
| Darwin Dr. Wood | 42 | A1 |
| Darwin Rd. Lo Ea | 193 | D3 |
| Darwin St. Gain | 24 | B3 |
| Davey Rd. Mans | 102 | A4 |
| David Gr. Bees | 171 | E1 |
| David La. Nott | 160 | B2 |
| David St. K-in-A | 115 | D4 |
| Davids La. Gunt | 165 | D3 |
| Davidson Cl. Arn | 162 | B4 |
| Davidson St. Nott | 173 | F2 |
| Davies Ave. S in A | 100 | C2 |
| Davies Cl. S in A | 100 | C2 |
| Davies Rd. W Brid | 186 | A4 |
| Davis Cl. N Clip | 90 | A2 |
| Dawber St. Work | 35 | E4 |
| Dawlish Cl. Huck | 145 | E3 |
| Dawlish Ct. East | 143 | D4 |
| Dawlish Dr. Nott | 161 | D3 |
| Dawn Cl. Huck | 131 | E1 |
| Dawn View. Staple | 170 | B1 |
| Dawn's La. Aslo | 179 | D3 |
| Dawson Cl. East | 144 | A1 |
| Dawver Rd. Kim | 158 | C3 |
| Day St. Mar War | 74 | A2 |
| Daybell Cl. Bott | 181 | D2 |
| Daybrook Ave. Nott | 161 | E2 |
| Daybrook St. Nott | 161 | E2 |
| De Ferrers Cl. E Lea | 205 | F1 |
| De Lacy Ct. Oll | 77 | D2 |
| De Morgan Cl. Sels | 129 | D1 |
| De Vere Gdns. Arn | 162 | A3 |
| Deabill St. Carl | 175 | D3 |
| Dead La. Cross | 170 | B4 |
| Deadwong La. Sibt | 153 | F1 |
| Deakins Pl. Nott | 172 | C3 |
| Deal Gdns. Nott | 159 | F4 |
| Dean Ave. Carl | 162 | A2 |
| Dean Cl. Mans | 102 | B2 |
| Dean Rd. Arn | 161 | F3 |
| Dean St. La Mi | 143 | E2 |
| Dean St. Nott | 173 | E2 |
| Dean's Cl. Caun | 109 | D3 |
| Deane Cl. Coll | 98 | A1 |
| Deans Cl. Mist | 6 | C1 |
| Deans Croft. Bees | 171 | D1 |
| Deanscourt. Cotg | 188 | A2 |
| Deansgate. Plea | 87 | D3 |
| Death La. Clay | 5 | F1 |
| Debdale Gate. Mans | 88 | A1 |
| Debdale Hill. Ol Da | 218 | C2 |
| Debdale La. Keyw | 197 | F2 |
| Debdale La. Mans | 88 | A1 |
| Debdhill Rd. Mist | 6 | A1 |
| Deddington La. Bees | 171 | E1 |
| Deep Furrow Ave. Carl | 174 | B4 |
| Deep La. Al Hu | 85 | D2 |

Deepdale Ave. Staple ...... 182 B3
Deepdale Cl. Gam ...... 186 B4
Deepdale Gdns. S in A ...... 100 C2
Deepdale Pk. S in A ...... 100 C2
Deepdale Rd. Lo Ea ...... 193 D3
Deepdale Rd. Mans ...... 88 C1
Deepdale Rd. Nott ...... 171 E2
Deepdale St. S in A ...... 100 C2
Deepdene Cl. Nott ...... 160 A1
Deepdene Way. Nott ...... 160 A1
Deeps La. Miss ...... 4 A4
Deer Park Dr. Bes Vil ...... 147 E1
Deer Park Dr. Bes Vil ...... 161 E4
Deer Park Dr. Nott ...... 147 E1
Deer Park Dr. Nott ...... 161 E4
Deer Park. Nott ...... 171 F2
Deerleap Dr. Arn ...... 161 E4
Deers Acre. Lough ...... 220 A3
Deetleton Cl. Sels ...... 129 D4
Delamere Cl. Mans ...... 102 B2
Delamere Dr. Mans ...... 102 B2
Delia Ave. Huck ...... 131 E1
Dell Lea. Mans ...... 103 D2
Dell The. Ann Wo ...... 129 F4
Dell Way. Nott ...... 184 C1
Dellwood Cl. Carl ...... 162 B1
Delta St. Nott ...... 160 C1
Delville Ave. Keyw ...... 197 F2
Denacre Ave. Lo Ea ...... 182 C1
Denay Cl. Rain ...... 104 B1
Denbigh Ct. Coll ...... 98 A1
Denbury Rd. Raven ...... 117 D1
Denby Dr. Mans ...... 102 B1
Dendy Dr. Wood ...... 53 D4
Dene Cl. Matt ...... 20 A4
Dene The. Work ...... 35 E1
Denehurst Ave. Nott ...... 160 B1
Denewood Ave. Bees ...... 171 E1
Denewood Cres. Nott ...... 171 F4
Denholme Rd. Nott ...... 171 E3
Denison Ave. Ret ...... 40 A2
Denison St. Bees ...... 183 F4
Denison St. Nott ...... 172 C3
Denman Cl. Ret ...... 39 E4
Denman Street C. Nott ...... 172 C3
Denman Street E. Nott ...... 172 C3
Denman Street W. Nott ...... 172 C3
Denmark Gr. Hello ...... 173 A2
Dennett Cl. Nott ...... 173 F3
Dennis Ave. Bees ...... 183 F4
Dennis St. Carl ...... 175 D4
Dennis St. Work ...... 35 F1
Dennor Dr. Mans ...... 88 C3
Denstone Rd. Nott ...... 173 F3
Dentdale Dr. Nott ...... 171 D2
Denton Ave. Sand ...... 182 A3
Denton Cl. Bald ...... 140 B2
Denton Cl. Mans ...... 88 C1
Denton Dr. W Brid ...... 185 E2
Denton Green. Nott ...... 159 F1
Denver Ct. Staple ...... 170 C1
Deptford Cres. Nott ...... 160 B3
Derby Gr. Nott ...... 172 C3
Derby Rd. Ann Wo ...... 130 A4
Derby Rd. Bees ...... 171 E1
Derby Rd. East ...... 143 E1
Derby Rd. East ...... 143 E2
Derby Rd. Hath ...... 212 C1
Derby Rd. K-in A ...... 116 A4
Derby Rd. K-in A ...... 115 E2
Derby Rd. Kegw ...... 203 E1
Derby Rd. Lo Ea ...... 193 D4
Derby Rd. Lough ...... 220 A3
Derby Rd. Mans ...... 102 A1
Derby Rd. Nott ...... 172 C2
Derby Rd. S in A ...... 102 A1
Derby Rd. Sand ...... 182 A3
Derby Rd. Staple ...... 182 B3
Derby Sq. Lough ...... 220 A2
Derby St. Arn ...... 161 F4
Derby St. Bees ...... 183 F4
Derby St. Mans ...... 102 B3
Derby St. Nott ...... 173 D3
Derbyshire Ave. Trow ...... 170 B2
Derbyshire Cres. Nott ...... 172 A3
Derbyshire Dr. Sels ...... 128 B2
Derbyshire La. Huck ...... 146 A4
Dereham Dr. Arn ...... 162 A3
Derry Dr. Nott ...... 147 F1
Derry Hill Rd. Nott ...... 147 F1
Derry La. Bing ...... 178 A2
Derwent Ave. Ilk ...... 157 E1
Derwent Ave. Mans ...... 103 D3
Derwent Cl. Bees ...... 183 F2
Derwent Cl. Gam ...... 186 B4
Derwent Cl. Mans ...... 103 D3
Derwent Cl. Mar War ...... 74 B3
Derwent Cl. Rain ...... 118 A4
Derwent Cl. Work ...... 35 F3
Derwent Cres. Arn ...... 162 A3
Derwent Ct. Bald ...... 140 B2
Derwent Ct. Nott ...... 173 D3
Derwent Dr. Ann Wo ...... 130 A4
Derwent Dr. Huck ...... 146 A2
Derwent Dr. Sels ...... 129 D4
Derwent St. Lo Ea ...... 193 E3
Derwent Terr. Nott ...... 161 E1
Derwent Way. N-on-T ...... 125 D1

Desborough Rd. Sels ...... 128 B4
Desford Cl. Nott ...... 161 D2
Devitt Dr. Huck ...... 131 E1
Devon Circus. Nott ...... 147 E1
Devon Cl. Sand ...... 182 A3
Devon Dr. Mans ...... 101 F4
Devon Dr. Nott ...... 161 E1
Devon Dr. Rudd ...... 196 B4
Devon La. Bott ...... 181 D2
Devon Rd. N-on-T ...... 139 F3
Devon St. Ilk ...... 170 A3
Devon St. Nott ...... 173 F3
Devonshire Av. Lo Ea ...... 194 A4
Devonshire Ave. Bees ...... 183 F3
Devonshire Cl. Ilk ...... 157 F3
Devonshire Cl. S in A ...... 100 A1
Devonshire Cres. Nott ...... 161 E1
Devonshire Dr. East ...... 143 F1
Devonshire Dr. Oll ...... 77 D2
Devonshire Dr. Scarc ...... 58 C1
Devonshire Dr. Scarc ...... 72 C4
Devonshire Dr. Staple ...... 170 B1
Devonshire Prom. Nott ...... 172 C2
Devonshire Rd. Har ...... 8 C2
Devonshire Rd. Nott ...... 161 D1
Devonshire Rd. Ret ...... 39 E3
Devonshire Rd. W Brid ...... 185 F3
Devonshire Sq. Lough ...... 220 A2
Devonshire St. Plea ...... 87 D4
Devonshire St. Work ...... 35 F1
Dewberry La. R on T ...... 176 A1
Dial The. Cotg ...... 187 F1
Diamond Ave. K-in-A ...... 115 E2
Diamond Ave. Rain ...... 118 B4
Dickens Ct. Greas ...... 144 A2
Dickens Rd. Work ...... 36 A2
Dickenson Terr. Gain ...... 24 B4
Dickman's La. Harb ...... 202 A2
Dicks La. Greas ...... 144 B2
Dickson Dr. Rudd ...... 196 B3
Didcot Dr. Nott ...... 160 B1
Digby Ave. Carl ...... 162 B2
Digby Cl. Nott ...... 172 C2
Digby Hall Dr. Carl ...... 162 B2
Digby St. Coss ...... 158 A1
Digby St. Kim ...... 158 B4
Dingley Cl. Mans ...... 88 C3
Dingley Cl. Nott ...... 172 A3
Dirca Cl. Nott ...... 195 E4
Diseworth Gr. Nott ...... 173 E1
Distillery St. Rudd ...... 196 B3
Division Rd. Shireb ...... 72 C2
Dixie St. Sels ...... 128 A2
Dobbin Cl. Cr Bi ...... 189 D2
Dock Rd. Work ...... 35 F2
Dockholm Rd. Lo Ea ...... 182 B1
Doddington La. Clayp ...... 156 C3
Doddington La. Dry Do ...... 156 A1
Dog and Duck La. Mort ...... 15 D2
Doghill La. Syer ...... 153 D1
Dogwood Ave. Nott ...... 160 A4
Doles La. K-in-A ...... 114 B3
Doles La. Whit ...... 45 D4
Dolphin Ct. Nott ...... 161 D4
Dominie Cross Rd. Ret ...... 39 F3
Donbas Cl. Nott ...... 160 A2
Doncaster Ave. Sand ...... 182 A3
Doncaster Gr. Lo Ea ...... 182 C1
Doncaster Rd. Baw ...... 10 A4
Doncaster Rd. C in L ...... 25 F4
Doncaster Rd. Haxey ...... 2 C2
Doncaster Rd. Lan ...... 16 C2
Doncaster Rd. Tick ...... 8 A4
Doncaster Terr. Nott ...... 173 E1
Donington Rd. Nott ...... 184 C1
Donkey La. Brad ...... 196 C2
Donner Cres. Ilk ...... 157 F3
Dooland Dr. Nott ...... 161 F1
Dorchester Dr. Mans ...... 102 B1
Dorchester Gdns. W Brid ...... 185 F2
Dorchester Rd. Ann Wo ...... 115 D1
Dorchester Rd. Har ...... 9 D3
Dorchester Rd. Kim ...... 158 C4
Doreen Dr. S in A ...... 100 B1
Dorewood Ct. Bald ...... 140 C2
Doris Rd. Ilk ...... 170 A4
Dorket Cl. Arn ...... 148 A1
Dorket Dr. Nott ...... 172 B2
Dorking Rd. Nott ...... 172 C3
Dormy Cl. Bees ...... 183 E4
Dormy Cl. Mans ...... 88 C3
Dormy Cl. R on T ...... 176 A2
Dormy Ct. Nott ...... 160 B4
Dorner Ave. N-on-T ...... 139 E4
Dornoch Ave. Nott ...... 161 E1
Dornoch Ave. South ...... 121 F1
Dorothy Ave. East ...... 144 A2
Dorothy Ave. Huck ...... 131 D1
Dorothy Ave. Mans ...... 88 B1
Dorothy Ave. Sand ...... 182 A3
Dorothy Dr. Mans ...... 88 C1
Dorothy Gr. Nott ...... 172 B3
Dorset Dr. Ilk ...... 8 C2
Dorset Gdns. W Brid ...... 185 E3
Dorset St. Nott ...... 172 B3
Dorset Way. Mans ...... 103 D2
Dorterry Cres. Ilk ...... 170 A3

Dorton Ave. Gain ...... 24 C4
Douglas Ave. Awsw ...... 158 B3
Douglas Ave. Carl ...... 174 C3
Douglas Cl. R on T ...... 175 F1
Douglas Cres. Carl ...... 174 C3
Douglas Ct. Bees ...... 183 D1
Douglas Rd. Bing ...... 178 A2
Douglas Rd. Lo Ea ...... 182 A1
Douglas Rd. Mans ...... 89 D1
Douglas Rd. Nott ...... 172 C3
Douglas Rd. S in A ...... 100 B1
Douro Dr. Arn ...... 148 A1
Dove Cl. Work ...... 35 F4
Dove Croft. Oll ...... 77 D2
Dove St. Bees ...... 129 D4
Dove La. Lo Ea ...... 193 E4
Dove St. Nott ...... 160 A4
Dovecoat St. Hath ...... 213 D1
Dovecote Cl. E Brid ...... 165 E2
Dovecote Dr. Nott ...... 171 F2
Dovecote La. Bees ...... 184 A3
Dovecote Rd. East ...... 144 A1
Dovedale Ave. Lo Ea ...... 193 D3
Dovedale Ave. S in A ...... 100 B1
Dovedale Circ. Ilk ...... 157 F3
Dovedale Cl. Mans ...... 102 B2
Dovedale Ct. Lo Ea ...... 193 D3
Dovedale Rd. Nott ...... 174 B3
Dovedale Rd. W Brid ...... 186 A3
Dovenby Rd. Nott ...... 184 C1
Dover Beck Cl. Calv ...... 149 D4
Dover Beck Cl. Raven ...... 116 C1
Dover Beck Dr. Woodb ...... 149 E2
Dover Bottom. Elk ...... 50 B2
Dover St. South ...... 121 F1
Doveridge Ave. Carl ...... 175 D4
Doveridge Ct. Raven ...... 117 D2
Doveridge Rd. Carl ...... 175 D4
Downes Cl. Nott ...... 160 A4
Downham Cl. Arn ...... 162 A3
Downham Gdns. Raven ...... 117 D1
Downing Cl. Nott ...... 160 A4
Downing Gdns. Nott ...... 160 A4
Downing St. Nott ...... 160 A4
Downing St. S in A ...... 100 C2
Downing St. S Norm ...... 113 D3
Downs The. Nott ...... 185 D2
Dowson St. Nott ...... 173 F3
Doyne Ct. Nott ...... 173 E1
Dragon St. Gran ...... 191 D3
Dragwell. Kegw ...... 203 E1
Drake St. Gain ...... 24 B3
Draycott Cl. Ilk ...... 157 F2
Draycott Rd. Lo Ea ...... 193 D2
Drayton Ave. Mans ...... 87 E1
Drayton St. Nott ...... 161 E1
Drift Hill. Redm ...... 192 C2
Drift The. Nott ...... 184 C2
Drinsey Nook La. Thor ...... 70 B4
Drive The. Park La. Ret ...... 30 A1
Drive The. Bees ...... 183 F2
Drive The. Gain ...... 24 C4
Drive The. N Clip ...... 90 A2
Drive The. Wint ...... 125 E3
Dronfield Pl. Ilk ...... 157 F3
Drove La. Codd ...... 126 A2
Drove La. Langf ...... 125 F3
Drove La. Langf ...... 125 F2
Drovers Ct. Gain ...... 24 C3
Droversdale Rd. Bir ...... 9 E2
Drummond Ave. Carl ...... 175 D4
Drummond Dr. Nuth ...... 159 F2
Drummond Rd. Ilk ...... 157 F1
Drury La. Tick ...... 8 A4
Dry Pot La. Lo Wh ...... 212 A1
Dryden Ave. Bald ...... 140 C3
Dryden Ct. Staple ...... 170 C1
Dryden Dale. Work ...... 36 A2
Dryden St. Nott ...... 173 D3
Drysdale Cl. Nott ...... 160 A3
Duchess Gdns. Nott ...... 160 A4
Duchess St. Elmt ...... 58 C4
Duchess St. Nott ...... 160 A4
Duchess St. Whit ...... 45 D4
Ducie La. Bole ...... 23 F2
Dudley Ct. Bees ...... 183 D4
Duesbury The. S Norm ...... 113 D2
Duffield Cl. Lo Ea ...... 193 D3
Duffield Ct. Nott ...... 160 C4
Duke Cl. Nott ...... 160 A3
Duke Cres. Greas ...... 144 B1
Duke Pl. Work ...... 35 F2
Duke St. Arn ...... 161 F4
Duke St. Huck ...... 146 A4
Duke St. Ilk ...... 157 F2
Duke St. Lough ...... 220 A3
Duke St. Nott ...... 160 A4
Duke St. Nott ...... 160 C1
Duke St. Ret ...... 39 F3
Duke St. S in A ...... 100 A2
Duke St. S in A ...... 100 C1
Duke St. S Norm ...... 113 D3
Duke St. Whit ...... 45 D4
Duke William Mount. Nott ...... 173 D2
Duke's Dr. Al Hu ...... 86 A4
Duke's Pl. Nott ...... 173 E2
Duke's Terr. Baw ...... 10 A4
Dukeries Cl. Work ...... 35 E3

Dukeries Cres. Work ...... 36 B1
Dukeries Way. Work ...... 35 E3
Dukes Cl. S in A ...... 101 E1
Dukes Pl. Ilk ...... 157 F2
Dukes Rd. Ne Br ...... 219 D3
Dulverton Vale. Nott ...... 160 A2
Dulwich Rd. Nott ...... 172 C3
Dumb Hall La. Shire ...... 34 A2
Dumb Hall La. Th Sa ...... 34 A2
Dumbles The. Lamb ...... 163 D4
Dunbar Cl. Jacks ...... 15 F1
Dunbar Dr. Mans ...... 101 E3
Dunblane Rd. Brad ...... 196 B3
Duncan Ave. Raven ...... 117 D1
Duncombe Cl. Nott ...... 173 F4
Duncroft Ave. Carl ...... 162 C1
Dundas Cl. Nott ...... 173 E3
Dundee Dr. Mans ...... 88 A3
Dunelm Cl. S in A ...... 100 B2
Dunelm Dr. Calv ...... 149 D4
Dungannon Rd. Nott ...... 195 F4
Dunham Cl. Ne on T ...... 55 D1
Dunham Cl. South ...... 136 B4
Dunham Rd. Lane ...... 54 A3
Dunham Rd. Ne on T ...... 54 C1
Dunholme Ave. N-on-T ...... 139 F4
Dunholme Cl. Gain ...... 24 C4
Dunholme Cl. Nott ...... 160 A4
Dunholme Rd. Gain ...... 24 C4
Dunkery Rd. Nott ...... 195 F4
Dunkirk Rd. Nott ...... 172 C1
Dunlop Ave. Nott ...... 172 C2
Dunn Brigg. Mans ...... 88 B1
Dunnett Rd. Mans ...... 101 F3
Dunoon Cl. Nott ...... 146 C1
Dunoon Rd. Mans ...... 101 F3
Dunsby Cl. Nott ...... 184 C1
Dunsford Dr. Carl ...... 162 B3
Dunsil Dr. Nott ...... 185 D4
Dunsil Rd. Pinx ...... 113 E1
Dunsmore Cl. Bees ...... 184 A2
Dunstall Wlk. Gain ...... 24 C4
Dunstan Cres. Work ...... 35 F1
Dunstan St. Carl ...... 175 D4
Dunster Rd. East ...... 144 A1
Dunster Rd. Gain ...... 15 F1
Dunster Rd. W Brid ...... 186 A3
Dunston Cl. Lo Ea ...... 193 F4
Dunvegan Dr. Nott ...... 146 C1
Dunwoody Cl. Mans ...... 102 C4
Durham Ave. Nott ...... 173 F2
Durham Cl. Mans ...... 88 B2
Durham Cl. Nott ...... 173 F2
Durham Cl. Work ...... 36 A4
Durham Cres. Nott ...... 160 B3
Durham Gr. Ret ...... 30 A1
Durham St. Ilk ...... 157 F1
Durlston Cl. W Brid ...... 185 D3
Durnford St. Nott ...... 160 C1
Dursley Cl. Nott ...... 160 A3
Dyce Cl. Nott ...... 159 F4
Dykes End. Coll ...... 112 A4
Dylan Thomas Rd. Nott ...... 161 E4
Dyscarr Cl. Lan ...... 16 C2

E Moor. Cotg ...... 188 A1
Eagle Cl. Arn ...... 162 A4
Eagle Cl. Bees ...... 183 E4
Eagle Ct. Nott ...... 160 B4
Eagle Moor. Eagle ...... 84 C2
Eagle Pl. Ret ...... 39 F4
Eagle Rd. N Sca ...... 83 F2
Eagle Rd. N Sca ...... 84 A2
Eakring Cl. Mans ...... 102 C4
Eakring Rd. Bils ...... 105 F4
Eakring Rd. Knee ...... 93 F3
Eakring Rd. Mans ...... 103 E4
Eakring Rd. Rain ...... 104 B4
Eakring Rd. Ruff ...... 104 B4
Eakring Rd. Wellow ...... 92 B4
Ealing Ave. Nott ...... 160 B2
Eardley Rd. Nott ...... 160 C3
Earl Cres. Carl ...... 162 C2
Earl Dr. Greas ...... 144 B1
Earles Ct. Nott ...... 29 E1
Earls Cl. Nott ...... 171 E3
Earls Rd. Ne Br ...... 219 D3
Earlswood Dr. W Brid ...... 186 A2
Earp Ave. N-on-T ...... 140 A4
Easedale Cl. Gam ...... 186 B4
Easegill Ct. Nott ...... 160 C4
East Acres. Cotg ...... 187 F2
East Circus St. Nott ...... 173 D2
East Cl. Keyw ...... 197 F1
East Cres. Bees ...... 184 A3
East End. Lo Cl ...... 211 E2
East Gr. Bing ...... 177 F2
East Gr. Nott ...... 173 D4
East St. Bing ...... 177 F2
East St. Goth ...... 195 D1
East St. Har ...... 9 D4
East St. Hean ...... 157 D4
East St. Lo Ea ...... 193 F4
East St. Nott ...... 173 E3
East St. Ret ...... 39 F3

East St. S in A ...... 101
East St. Saundby ...... 23
East View. Baw ...... 10
East View. E Mark ...... 65
East View. Shireb ...... 72
East View. W Brid ...... 185
East Wlk. Ret ...... 39
Eastcliffe Ave. Carl ...... 162
Eastcote Ave. Bees ...... 171
Eastcroft La. Askh ...... 52
Eastdale Rd. Nott ...... 174
Eastern Ave. Gain ...... 15
Eastern Ct. N-on-T ...... 140
Eastern Dr. Bald ...... 140
Eastern Terrace La. N-on-T ...... 140
Eastfield Cl. N Clip ...... 89
Eastfield Ct. South ...... 136
Eastfield Dr. S Norm ...... 113
Eastfield Side. S in A ...... 101
Eastfield. N Musk ...... 110
Eastfield. N Whea ...... 31
Eastgate. Nor on T ...... 81
Eastgate. Work ...... 35
Eastglade Rd. Nott ...... 161
Eastham Cl. Nott ...... 173
Eastham Rd. Arn ...... 162
Eastholme Croft. Nott ...... 174
Easthorpe La. Redm ...... 192
Easthorpe Rd. Bott ...... 181
Easthorpe St. Rudd ...... 196
Easthorpe View. Bott ...... 181
Easthorpe. South ...... 136
Eastland Terr. Mar War ...... 74
Eastlands La. Mar War ...... 74
Eastleigh Dr. Mans ...... 88
Eastmoor Dr. Carl ...... 174
Eastwell St. Huck ...... 146
Eastwold. Cotg ...... 188
Eastwood Ave. Mar War ...... 74
Eastwood Cl. Huck ...... 145
Eastwood La. Miss ...... 4
Eastwood Rd. Kim ...... 158
Eastwood Rd. R on T ...... 175
Eastwood St. Nott ...... 160
Easy Par. Whit ...... 45
Eather Ave. Mans ...... 88
Eaton Ave. Arn ...... 162
Eaton Cl. Bees ...... 184
Eaton Cl. Farns ...... 119
Eaton Cl. Mans ...... 103
Eaton Cl. Sutt ...... 28
Eaton Grange Dr. Lo Ea ...... 193
Eaton Rd. Rain ...... 118
Eaton St. Nott ...... 161
Eatons Rd. Staple ...... 182
Ebenezer St. Ilk ...... 157
Ebenezer St. La Mi ...... 143
Ebers Gr. Nott ...... 173
Ebers Rd. Nott ...... 173
Ebony Wlk. Carl ...... 174
Ebury Rd. Nott ...... 161
Eckington Terr. Nott ...... 173
Eckington Wlk. Mans ...... 103
Eclipse Yd. Mans ...... 102
Ecton Cl. Nott ...... 146
Ecton Cl. Nott ...... 160
Edale Cl. Huck ...... 145
Edale Cl. Lo Ea ...... 193
Edale Cl. Mans ...... 103
Edale Ct. S in A ...... 100
Edale Rd. Mans ...... 103
Edale Rd. Nott ...... 174
Edale Rise. Bees ...... 182
Edale Sq. Ilk ...... 157
Eddington Cl. Cotg ...... 188
Eddison Cl. Work ...... 36
Eddleston Dr. Nott ...... 184
Edelin Rd. Lough ...... 220
Eden Cl. Arn ...... 162
Eden Low. Mans ...... 88
Edenbridge Ct. Nott ...... 171
Edenhall Gdns. Nott ...... 184
Edgar Ave. Mans ...... 102
Edgbaston Gdns. Nott ...... 172
Edgcote Way. Nott ...... 161
Edge Hill Ct. Lo Ea ...... 193
Edge Way. Nott ...... 159
Edgehill Gr. Mans ...... 88
Edgewood Dr. Huck ...... 145
Edgewood Rd. Kim ...... 158
Edginton St. Nott ...... 173
Edgware Rd. Nott ...... 160
Edinbane Cl. Nott ...... 146
Edinburgh Dr. Bing ...... 177
Edinburgh Rd. Work ...... 47
Edinburgh Wlk. Work ...... 47
Edingale Ct. Bees ...... 171
Edingley Ave. Mans ...... 101
Edingley Ave. Nott ...... 161
Edingley Hill. Edin ...... 120
Edingley Sq. Nott ...... 161
Edison St. Ann Wo ...... 114
Edlington Dr. Nott ...... 171
Edmond Gr. Huck ...... 146
Edmonds Cl. Bes Vil ...... 147

| | | |
|---|---|---|
| monton Rd. Mans | 89 | F1 |
| haston Rd. Nott | 172 | B1 |
| wald Rd. W Brid | 186 | A2 |
| waltam Ave. W Brid | 185 | F4 |
| walton Cl. W Brid | 186 | A2 |
| walton Ct. Mans | 103 | D2 |
| walton Ct. Nott | 160 | C3 |
| walton Lodge Cl. W Brid | 186 | A2 |
| ward Ave. N-on-T | 139 | F4 |
| ward Ave. Nott | 172 | B4 |
| ward Ave. S in A | 100 | C2 |
| ward Ave. Sels | 128 | A2 |
| ward Cl. Huck | 145 | E2 |
| ward Rd. East | 144 | A1 |
| ward Rd. Gain | 15 | E1 |
| ward Rd. Lo Ea | 193 | E4 |
| ward Rd. Nuth | 159 | E3 |
| ward Rd. W Brid | 185 | F4 |
| ward St. Ald | 143 | D2 |
| ward St. K-in-A | 115 | D3 |
| ward St. Lough | 220 | A3 |
| ward St. Mar War | 74 | A3 |
| ward St. Staple | 182 | B4 |
| ward St. Work | 35 | F2 |
| wards Ct. Work | 35 | E2 |
| wards La. Nott | 161 | D3 |
| wards La. Nott | 161 | E2 |
| wards La. Nott | 161 | E3 |
| win St. Arn | 161 | E3 |
| win St. S in A | 100 | C2 |
| winstowe Dr. Nott | 161 | E2 |
| winstowe Dr. Sels | 129 | D4 |
| l La. Lax | 79 | E1 |
| l Pool Rd. Ever | 11 | F1 |
| l Pool Rd. Wise | 11 | F1 |
| lwood Rd. Huck | 145 | D2 |
| an Cl. Rain | 104 | B1 |
| erton Cl. Mans | 103 | D4 |
| erton Dr. Staple | 170 | B1 |
| erton Rd. Arn | 161 | E2 |
| erton St. Nott | 173 | E4 |
| erton Wlk. Nott | 173 | E4 |
| gling Croft. Carl | 174 | C2 |
| gmanton Rd. Mans | 103 | D2 |
| gmanton Rd. Mar War | 74 | B4 |
| gmanton Rd. Tux | 65 | F1 |
| gmont Ct. Nott | 173 | E1 |
| gypt Rd. Nott | 160 | C1 |
| der Cl. Shireb | 72 | B2 |
| ghth Ave. Mans | 103 | D4 |
| sele Cl. Nott | 159 | F3 |
| kowe St. Nott | 160 | C1 |
| and St. Shireb | 72 | C3 |
| and St. Nott | 160 | C1 |
| der Cl. Arn | 148 | A1 |
| der Gdns. Nott | 161 | D4 |
| der Gr. Huck | 146 | A2 |
| der St. K-in-A | 114 | C3 |
| der St. S in A | 100 | C4 |
| don Rd. Bees | 183 | E1 |
| don St. N-on-T | 139 | F4 |
| don St. Tux | 65 | F2 |
| eanor Ave. Ilk | 170 | A3 |
| eanor Cres. Staple | 182 | C4 |
| ford Rise. Nott | 173 | F3 |
| gar Dr. Lo Ea | 193 | D3 |
| gar Rd. Nott | 173 | F4 |
| liot Cl. Lo Ea | 193 | D3 |
| liot Wlk. Nott | 195 | E4 |
| lizabeth Cl. Huck | 145 | F3 |
| lizabeth Cl. Ilk | 157 | E1 |
| lizabeth Gr. Carl | 162 | C1 |
| lizabeth Rd. N-on-T | 139 | F3 |
| llastone Ave. Nott | 161 | E4 |
| llerby Ave. Nott | 184 | C1 |
| llerslie Cl. N-on-T | 125 | D1 |
| llerslie Gr. Sand | 182 | A3 |
| llesmere Cl. Arn | 162 | A4 |
| llesmere Dr. Trow | 170 | B3 |
| llesmere Rd. Mans | 102 | C4 |
| llesmere Rd. W Brid | 185 | F2 |
| llington Rd. Arn | 148 | A1 |
| lliott St. Nott | 173 | D3 |
| llis Ave. Huck | 146 | A3 |
| llis Cl. Lo Ea | 193 | E3 |
| llis Ct. Nott | 173 | E3 |
| llis Gr. Bees | 183 | F3 |
| llis St. K-in-A | 115 | D3 |
| llsworth Rise. Nott | 160 | C3 |
| lm Ave. Bees | 183 | E1 |
| lm Ave. Bees | 183 | F3 |
| lm Ave. Bing | 178 | A2 |
| lm Ave. Carl | 174 | C4 |
| lm Ave. E Lea | 205 | F2 |
| lm Ave. Huck | 145 | F3 |
| lm Ave. Keyw | 197 | D2 |
| lm Ave. Kim | 159 | D3 |
| lm Ave. Lo Ea | 193 | E4 |
| lm Ave. N-on-T | 140 | A3 |
| lm Ave. Sand | 182 | A4 |
| lm Bank Dr. Nott | 173 | E4 |
| lm Bank. Nott | 173 | E4 |
| lm Cl. Keyw | 197 | D2 |
| lm Cl. N-on-T | 140 | A2 |
| lm Cl. Nott | 173 | E4 |
| Elm Cl. Pinx | 113 | E2 |
| Elm Cl. Sax | 57 | D2 |
| Elm Dr. Carl | 174 | C4 |
| Elm Gr. Arn | 148 | A1 |
| Elm Gr. Mar War | 74 | A3 |
| Elm Tree Ave. Mans | 88 | A2 |
| Elm Tree Ave. Shireb | 72 | B2 |
| Elm Tree Ave. W Brid | 185 | E4 |
| Elm Tree Ct. Work | 35 | F1 |
| Elm Tree Dr. Baw | 9 | F4 |
| Elm Tree Pl. Elk | 50 | A2 |
| Elm Tree Rd. K-in-A | 114 | C3 |
| Elm Tree St. Mans | 102 | B4 |
| Elm Wlk. Ret | 40 | A3 |
| Elma La. Holb | 59 | E3 |
| Elmbridge. Nott | 161 | D4 |
| Elmcroft. Oxt | 134 | A2 |
| Elmdale Gdns. Nott | 172 | A4 |
| Elmhurst Ave. Carl | 162 | B1 |
| Elmhurst Ave. S Norm | 113 | D2 |
| Elmhurst Cl. S Norm | 113 | D2 |
| Elmhurst Rd. Mans | 88 | C1 |
| Elmore Ct. Nott | 173 | D3 |
| Elms Cl. Remp | 215 | E3 |
| Elms Cl. Rudd | 196 | B3 |
| Elms Gdns. Brad | 196 | B3 |
| Elms Gr. Lough | 220 | B2 |
| Elms Park. Rudd | 196 | B3 |
| Elms Rd. Work | 35 | F2 |
| Elms The. Carl | 174 | C3 |
| Elms The. Kim | 158 | C4 |
| Elmsfield Ave. Hean | 143 | D1 |
| Elmsham Ave. Nott | 146 | C1 |
| Elmsmere Dr. Old | 17 | D3 |
| Elmswood Gdns. Nott | 161 | E2 |
| Elmton Cl. Mans | 58 | B4 |
| Elmton Rd. Elmt | 58 | B4 |
| Elmtree Ave. Sels | 128 | C4 |
| Elmtree Cl. Shire | 34 | C4 |
| Elmtree Rd. Calv | 148 | B4 |
| Elmwood Cl. Ret | 30 | A1 |
| Elnor St. La Mi | 143 | E2 |
| Elsham Wlk. Gain | 24 | C4 |
| Elson St. Nott | 172 | C4 |
| Elston Cl. Mans | 87 | E1 |
| Elston Gdns. Nott | 184 | C2 |
| Elston Hall. Elst | 153 | E3 |
| Elston La. Elst | 153 | E3 |
| Elswick Cl. Nott | 161 | D4 |
| Elswick Dr. Bees | 184 | B2 |
| Elterwater Dr. Gam | 186 | B3 |
| Eltham Cl. Nott | 159 | F2 |
| Eltham Dr. Nott | 160 | A1 |
| Eltham Rd. W Brid | 186 | A4 |
| Elton Cl. Bald | 140 | B2 |
| Elton Cl. Mans | 103 | D3 |
| Elton Cl. Staple | 182 | B4 |
| Elton Rd N. Nott | 161 | D1 |
| Elton Rd. Mans | 102 | C3 |
| Elton Rd. Nott | 161 | D1 |
| Elvaston Ct. Mans | 103 | D3 |
| Elvaston Dr. Lo Ea | 193 | D2 |
| Elvaston Rd. Nott | 172 | A3 |
| Ely Cl. Mans | 88 | B2 |
| Emerald Cl. Mans | 87 | F1 |
| Emerald Gr. K-in-A | 115 | E2 |
| Emerys Rd. Carl | 175 | D4 |
| Emmanuel Ave. Bes Vil | 147 | D1 |
| Emmanuel Ave. Carl | 162 | A1 |
| Emneth Cl. Nott | 173 | F4 |
| Empingham Cl. Bees | 183 | D1 |
| Empire St. Mans | 102 | B3 |
| Empress Rd. Lough | 220 | B2 |
| Emsworth Ave. Ret | 29 | F1 |
| Emsworth Cl. Ship | 157 | E2 |
| Ena Ave. Nott | 173 | F3 |
| Enderby Cres. Gain | 24 | C4 |
| Enderby Cres. Mans | 102 | C3 |
| Enderby Gdns. Nott | 147 | F1 |
| Enderby Sq. Nott | 183 | F4 |
| Endsleigh Gdns. Bees | 183 | F4 |
| Endsleigh Gdns. W Brid | 186 | A2 |
| Enfield St. Bees | 183 | F4 |
| Engine La. Greas | 144 | A2 |
| England Cres. Hean | 143 | D1 |
| Ennerdale Cl. Gam | 186 | B4 |
| Ennerdale Rd. Lo Ea | 182 | A1 |
| Ennerdale Rd. Nott | 161 | E3 |
| Ennismore Mews. W Brid | 185 | E1 |
| Enright Cl. N-on-T | 139 | F3 |
| Enthorpe St. Nott | 172 | A3 |
| Epinal Way. Lough | 220 | A1 |
| Epperstone By-Ps. Lowd | 150 | A2 |
| Epperstone By-Ps. Woodb | 150 | A2 |
| Epperstone Cl. Mans | 103 | D1 |
| Epperstone Rd. Lowd | 150 | B1 |
| Epperstone Rd. Oxt | 134 | A1 |
| Epperstone Rd. W Brid | 185 | F4 |
| Epsom Rd. Bees | 182 | C2 |
| Epsom St. Mans | 102 | C3 |
| Erdington Way. Bees | 182 | C2 |
| Erewash Dr. Ilk | 170 | A3 |
| Erewash Gdns. Nott | 161 | D4 |
| Erewash Gr. Bees | 182 | C1 |
| Erewash Rd. Pinx | 113 | F1 |
| Erewash Sq. Ilk | 170 | A3 |
| Erewash St. Ald | 128 | A3 |
| Erewash St. K-in-A | 115 | D3 |
| Erewash St. Lo Ea | 193 | F4 |
| Eric Ave. Huck | 130 | C1 |
| Erica Dr. S Norm | 113 | D4 |
| Erith Cl. Nott | 159 | E1 |
| Ernest Rd. Carl | 162 | A1 |
| Erskine Rd. Nott | 161 | D1 |
| Esher Gr. Nott | 161 | E1 |
| Eskdale Cl. Lo Ea | 193 | D3 |
| Eskdale Cl. Gam | 186 | B4 |
| Eskdale Dr. Bees | 183 | D3 |
| Eskdale Dr. Nott | 172 | A4 |
| Eskdale Dr. Work | 35 | F4 |
| Essex Dr. Bir | 9 | E2 |
| Essex Rd. Bir | 9 | E2 |
| Essex St. East | 143 | F1 |
| Essex St. Ilk | 157 | F1 |
| Estefeld Cl. Tick | 8 | A4 |
| Estwic Ave. East | 143 | F2 |
| Ethel Ave. Carl | 162 | A1 |
| Ethel Ave. Huck | 131 | E1 |
| Ethel Rd. W Brid | 185 | F4 |
| Ethelbert Ave. Ann Wo | 115 | E1 |
| Etheldene. Cr Bi | 189 | D2 |
| Etherington St. Gain | 24 | B4 |
| Eton Cl. N-on-T | 139 | F3 |
| Eton Gr. Nott | 172 | A2 |
| Eton Rd. W Brid | 185 | F3 |
| Eucalyptus Ave. Nott | 184 | B1 |
| Eugene Gdns. Nott | 173 | E1 |
| Eugene St. Nott | 173 | E2 |
| Evans Ave. S in A | 100 | B2 |
| Evans Rd. Nott | 160 | B2 |
| Evedon Wlk. Nott | 147 | D1 |
| Evelyn St. Bees | 184 | A4 |
| Evelyn St. Nott | 173 | F2 |
| Eversley Wlk. Nott | 161 | D4 |
| Everton Sluice La. Ever | 11 | E2 |
| Everton St. Mans | 87 | F1 |
| Evesham Mews. Work | 35 | F1 |
| Ewart Rd. Nott | 173 | D4 |
| Ewe Lamb Cl. Bees | 170 | C1 |
| Ewe Lamb La. Staple | 170 | C1 |
| Ewell Rd. Nott | 171 | F3 |
| Exbourne Rd. Nott | 159 | F1 |
| Exbury Gdns. W Brid | 185 | D2 |
| Exchange Rd. W Brid | 185 | F4 |
| Exchange St. Ret | 39 | F4 |
| Exchange Wlk. Nott | 173 | E2 |
| Exeter Cl. Carl | 162 | C1 |
| Exeter Cl. E Lea | 205 | E1 |
| Exeter Rd. Nott | 173 | D4 |
| Exeter Rd. W Brid | 185 | F3 |
| Export Dr. S in A | 113 | F4 |
| Exton Rd. Nott | 161 | D2 |
| Eyam Cl. Bees | 171 | E1 |
| Eyam Cl. Mans | 103 | D3 |
| Eyre St. Nott | 173 | F2 |
| Eyre's Gdns. Ilk | 157 | F1 |
| Eyres La. Goth | 205 | D4 |
| Fabis Dr. Nott | 184 | C2 |
| Fackley Rd. S in A | 100 | A4 |
| Fackley Rd. S in A | 100 | B3 |
| Fackley Way. S in A | 100 | B3 |
| Factory La. Bees | 183 | F3 |
| Factory La. Ilk | 157 | F1 |
| Factory Rd. K-in-A | 115 | D3 |
| Factory St. Lough | 220 | B2 |
| Factory Yard. S in A | 101 | D2 |
| Failsworth Cl. Nott | 184 | C2 |
| Fair Lea Cl. Lo Ea | 193 | E3 |
| Fair Vale. Norw | 110 | A4 |
| Fair View. Mans | 89 | D1 |
| Fairbank Cres. Nott | 161 | E1 |
| Fairburn Cl. Nott | 171 | E2 |
| Faircroft Ave. Sand | 182 | A3 |
| Fairdale Dr. East | 144 | A1 |
| Fairfax Cl. Gain | 24 | C3 |
| Fairfax Cl. Nott | 160 | C1 |
| Fairfield Ave. Bald | 140 | B3 |
| Fairfield Ave. Farn | 139 | D3 |
| Fairfield Ave. Newt | 99 | E1 |
| Fairfield Cl. Ne La | 59 | D1 |
| Fairfield Cl. Nott | 185 | D3 |
| Fairfield Cres. Lo Ea | 193 | D2 |
| Fairfield Dr. Mans | 103 | D4 |
| Fairfield Rd. S in A | 101 | D3 |
| Fairfield St. Bing | 177 | F2 |
| Fairfield. Ret | 39 | F2 |
| Fairham Ave. Goth | 195 | D1 |
| Fairham Cl. Rudd | 196 | A4 |
| Fairham Dr. Nott | 172 | B2 |
| Fairham Rd. Keyw | 197 | E2 |
| Fairhaven. K-in-A | 115 | D2 |
| Fairholme Cl. N Clip | 89 | F1 |
| Fairholme Dr. Mans | 87 | F1 |
| Fairisle Cl. Nott | 185 | D1 |
| Fairland Cres. W Brid | 185 | F2 |
| Fairlawn Pl. Nott | 161 | E1 |
| Fairlawns. Mans | 103 | D4 |
| Fairlie Ave. Mans | 101 | E3 |
| Fairlight Way. Nott | 161 | D4 |
| Fairmaid Gr. Nott | 184 | C1 |
| Fairmead Cl. Nott | 174 | A4 |
| Fairnley Rd. Nott | 171 | E4 |
| Fairview Ave. Sels | 128 | C4 |
| Fairview Ct. W Brid | 185 | E1 |
| Fairview Rd. Arn | 161 | F2 |
| Fairway Ave. Gain | 15 | D2 |
| Fairway Cres. New | 177 | D4 |
| Fairway Dr. Bees | 183 | E3 |
| Fairway Dr. Nott | 160 | B4 |
| Fairway. Keyw | 198 | A1 |
| Fairway. N-on-T | 139 | E3 |
| Fairway. Ret | 39 | E2 |
| Fairways Dr. K-in-A | 114 | C4 |
| Fairways The. Mans | 88 | B3 |
| Fairweather Cl. Boug | 77 | F3 |
| Fal Paddock. Mans | 88 | B1 |
| Falcon Cl. Eagle | 84 | B2 |
| Falcon Cl. Ilk | 157 | E1 |
| Falcon Gr. Nott | 161 | D1 |
| Falcon St. Lough | 220 | B3 |
| Falcon St. Nott | 161 | D1 |
| Falconers Wlk. Arn | 161 | E4 |
| Falconwood Gdns. Nott | 184 | B1 |
| Fallow Cl. Nott | 184 | C1 |
| Fallow Cl. Ret | 29 | F1 |
| Fallow Cl. Work | 36 | A4 |
| Falston Rd. Nott | 172 | A4 |
| Falstone Ave. N-on-T | 140 | A3 |
| Far Back La. Farns | 119 | F3 |
| Far Croft Ave. S in A | 100 | B2 |
| Far Holme La. S on T | 97 | D4 |
| Far La. N on S | 213 | E2 |
| Far New Cl. Sand | 182 | A3 |
| Far Pasture Cl. Keyw | 197 | F1 |
| Far Rd. Fled | 67 | E2 |
| Far Rye. Nott | 171 | F3 |
| Far St. Brad | 196 | C2 |
| Far St. Wyme | 216 | B2 |
| Faraday Ave. Tux | 66 | A2 |
| Faraday Ct. Staple | 170 | C1 |
| Faraday Rd. Mans | 102 | C3 |
| Faraday Rd. Nott | 172 | C2 |
| Farfield Ave. Bees | 183 | F4 |
| Farfield Gr. Bees | 183 | F4 |
| Farfield Rd. Ilk | 170 | A4 |
| Farley St. Nott | 160 | A4 |
| Farleys La. Huck | 146 | A3 |
| Farm Ave. Huck | 145 | E2 |
| Farm Cl. E Brid | 165 | E2 |
| Farm Cl. Ilk | 170 | A4 |
| Farm Cl. Lo Ea | 193 | F3 |
| Farm Cl. Nott | 184 | C1 |
| Farm Croft Rd. Mans | 88 | B3 |
| Farm Gr. Work | 36 | A4 |
| Farm La. E Mark | 65 | F4 |
| Farm Rd. Arn | 162 | A4 |
| Farm Rd. Bees | 183 | E3 |
| Farm View Rd. K-in-A | 115 | E3 |
| Farm View. Ret | 39 | F2 |
| Farmer St. Brad | 196 | C2 |
| Farmhouse Cl. Bott | 181 | D2 |
| Farmilo Cres. Mans | 87 | F1 |
| Farmway. Mans | 88 | B1 |
| Farnborough Rd. Nott | 185 | D1 |
| Farndale Cl. Lo Ea | 193 | D3 |
| Farndale Cl. S in A | 100 | C3 |
| Farndale Dr. Nott | 171 | D2 |
| Farndale Rd. S in A | 100 | C3 |
| Farndale. Work | 36 | A4 |
| Farndon Dr. Bees | 182 | C2 |
| Farndon Gr. Work | 35 | E4 |
| Farndon Green. Nott | 172 | B2 |
| Farndon Rd. N-on-T | 139 | E3 |
| Farndon Rd. S in A | 101 | E1 |
| Farndon Way. Mans | 101 | F4 |
| Farnes Ct. Work | 36 | A3 |
| Farnham Rd. Lough | 220 | A1 |
| Farnsfield Ave. Bu Jo | 164 | A3 |
| Farnsfield Cl. Mans | 103 | D2 |
| Farnsfield Rd. Bils | 105 | F2 |
| Farnsworth Ave. Mans | 103 | F1 |
| Farnsworth Cl. Greas | 145 | D1 |
| Farr Way. Blid | 118 | A2 |
| Farrar Cl. N-on-T | 125 | D1 |
| Farrendale Cl. Mans | 88 | B1 |
| Farringdon Cl. Nott | 159 | E2 |
| Farthingate Cl. South | 136 | C4 |
| Farthingate. South | 136 | C4 |
| Farthings The. Hath | 213 | D1 |
| Farwells Cl. Nott | 160 | B2 |
| Faulconbridge Cl. Nott | 160 | A3 |
| Fawcett St. Gain | 15 | E1 |
| Fearn Chase. Carl | 174 | C4 |
| Fearn Cl. Lo Ea | 193 | D4 |
| Fearnleigh Dr. Nott | 160 | B1 |
| Fearnley St. Nott | 160 | A4 |
| Featherston Ave. Work | 36 | A1 |
| Featherstone Cl. Mans | 101 | E2 |
| Featherstone Cres. Carl | 162 | B2 |
| Felen Cl. Nott | 161 | D4 |
| Fell Croft. Farn | 139 | D3 |
| Fell Side. Arn | 162 | A3 |
| Fell Wilson St. Mar War | 74 | B2 |
| Felley Ave. Ann Wo | 114 | C1 |
| Felley Mill La N. Sels | 129 | E1 |
| Fellows Rd. Bees | 183 | F4 |
| Fellows Yd. Plum | 197 | F4 |
| Felly Cl. Huck | 145 | F3 |
| Felly Mill La S. Sels | 129 | D1 |
| Felstead Ct. Bees | 171 | E1 |
| Felton Cl. Bees | 183 | D3 |
| Felton Rd. Nott | 173 | E1 |
| Fen La. Bald | 141 | D2 |
| Fen La. Dry Do | 155 | E2 |
| Fenchurch Cl. Bes Vil | 147 | D1 |
| Fenimore Ct. R on T | 176 | A2 |
| Fennel St. Lough | 220 | A2 |
| Fenroth Cl. Nott | 159 | F4 |
| Fenton Cl. N-on-T | 125 | D1 |
| Fenton Dr. Nott | 146 | B1 |
| Fenton Rd. Clayp | 142 | B1 |
| Fenton Rd. Nott | 160 | C2 |
| Fenwick Cl. Nott | 159 | F1 |
| Fenwick Rd. Nott | 159 | F1 |
| Fenwick St. Mar War | 74 | A2 |
| Ferguson Ave. Mans | 88 | A2 |
| Fern Ave. Nott | 161 | F1 |
| Fern Bank Ave. Wale | 64 | A1 |
| Fern Cl. Bils | 106 | A3 |
| Fern Cl. Raven | 117 | D1 |
| Fern Cl. Shireb | 72 | C3 |
| Fern Cl. South | 121 | E1 |
| Fern Cres. East | 143 | E2 |
| Fern Lea Ave. Cotg | 187 | F1 |
| Fern Rd. Cr Bi | 189 | D2 |
| Fern St. S in A | 100 | B2 |
| Ferndale Cl. Bees | 183 | F1 |
| Ferndale Cl. Boug | 77 | F3 |
| Ferndale Gr. Nott | 174 | A3 |
| Ferndale Rd. Nott | 174 | A3 |
| Ferngill Cl. Nott | 173 | D1 |
| Fernleigh Ave. Carl | 162 | A1 |
| Fernleigh Rise. Mans | 88 | B1 |
| Fernwood Cl. Mans | 89 | D1 |
| Fernwood Cres. Nott | 171 | E2 |
| Fernwood Dr. R on T | 175 | F2 |
| Ferny Hollow Cl. Nott | 160 | C4 |
| Ferous Cl. Nott | 195 | F4 |
| Ferrers Wlk. Nott | 173 | F3 |
| Ferriby Terr. Nott | 173 | E1 |
| Ferry La. Ever | 11 | E2 |
| Ferry La. N Musk | 110 | C1 |
| Festival Ave. Har | 9 | D2 |
| Festival Dr. Lough | 220 | A3 |
| Festus Cl. Nott | 173 | E3 |
| Festus St. Carl | 175 | D4 |
| Festus St. K-in-A | 115 | D2 |
| Fiat La. Eakr | 92 | C1 |
| Field Ave. Huck | 145 | E2 |
| Field Cl. Bees | 183 | D2 |
| Field Cl. Carl | 162 | C1 |
| Field Cl. Mans | 88 | B3 |
| Field Cl. Work | 36 | A4 |
| Field Dr. Bald | 140 | C1 |
| Field Dr. Shireb | 72 | C1 |
| Field End Cl. E Lea | 205 | E1 |
| Field House Cl. Nott | 171 | E3 |
| Field La. Al Hu | 86 | B3 |
| Field La. Bees | 183 | D2 |
| Field La. Blid | 117 | F2 |
| Field La. Cr Bi | 189 | D2 |
| Field La. Mort | 15 | D2 |
| Field La. Woodb | 149 | E2 |
| Field Pl. S in A | 114 | B4 |
| Field The. Ship | 157 | D3 |
| Fielden Ave. Mans | 87 | E1 |
| Fields Ave. Rudd | 196 | B3 |
| Fields Dr. Aslo | 178 | C3 |
| Fields Farm Rd. Lo Ea | 193 | F3 |
| Fieldway. Nott | 185 | D2 |
| Fiennes Cres. Nott | 173 | D2 |
| Fifth Ave. Edwin | 75 | F1 |
| Fifth Ave. Mans | 103 | D4 |
| Fifth Ave. N Clip | 89 | F2 |
| Fiftyeights Rd. Fin | 1 | B2 |
| Filey St. Nott | 160 | B4 |
| Finch Cl. Nott | 184 | C4 |
| Finchley Cl. Nott | 184 | B1 |
| Findern Cl. Mans | 103 | D3 |
| Findern Green. Nott | 174 | A3 |
| Fingal Cl. Nott | 184 | C1 |
| Fingle St. N Le Ha | 32 | B1 |
| Fingleton. Work | 36 | A3 |
| Finkell St. G on H | 12 | C2 |
| Finningley Rd. Mans | 103 | D2 |
| Finsbury Ave. Lough | 220 | B2 |
| Finsbury Ave. Nott | 173 | F2 |
| Finsbury Rd. Bees | 171 | E2 |
| Finsbury Rd. Bes Vil | 147 | D1 |
| Fir Cl. Nott | 159 | F4 |
| Fir Cl. Shireb | 72 | B3 |
| Fir Dale. Cotg | 188 | A2 |
| Fir Tree Cl. Mans | 89 | E1 |
| Fir View. Oll | 77 | E1 |
| Firbank Ct. Bees | 183 | D3 |
| Firbeck Ave. Mans | 102 | C3 |
| Firbeck Cres. Lan | 16 | C2 |
| Firbeck Rd. Arn | 162 | A4 |
| Firbeck Rd. Nott | 171 | E1 |
| Fircroft Ave. Nott | 171 | E4 |
| Fircroft Dr. Huck | 145 | E3 |
| Firemen's Row. S in A | 100 | C1 |
| Firs Ave. Bees | 183 | F4 |
| Firs Rd. W Brid | 186 | A2 |
| Firs St. Lo Ea | 193 | D2 |
| Firs The. Nott | 161 | E2 |
| Firsby Rd. Nott | 159 | F1 |
| First Ave. Carl | 162 | C1 |
| First Ave. Carl | 174 | B4 |
| First Ave. Carl | 174 | C3 |

234

First Ave. Edwin Glen St. S in

First Ave. Edwin 76 A1
First Ave. Mans 89 D1
First Ave. Mans 103 F1
First Ave. N Clip 90 A2
First Holme La. S on T 97 D4
Firth Cl. Arn 148 B1
Firth Rd. Ret 39 E4
Fish Pond Dr. Nott 173 D2
Fisher Ave. Arn 161 F3
Fisher Cl. Coll 98 A1
Fisher Cl. E Lea 205 F1
Fisher Ct. Ilk 157 F2
Fisher Gate. Nott 173 E2
Fisher La. Bing 177 F2
Fisher La. Mans 102 B3
Fisher St. Nott 172 C4
Fishers St. Ann Wo 115 D1
Fishpool Rd. Blid 117 E2
Fiskerton Ct. Mans 103 D2
Fiskerton Rd. Roll 138 A3
Fiskerton Rd. South 137 D3
Fitzherbert St. Mar War 74 B2
Five Acres. Nott 185 D2
Five Fields Cl. Ret 40 A2
Five Fields La. Ret 40 A2
Flagholme. Cotg 187 F1
Flamingo Ct. Nott 173 D1
Flamstead Ave. Lamb 163 D4
Flamstead Rd. Ilk 157 F1
Flamsteed Rd. Nott 159 E1
Flash La. Omp 93 D4
Flat La. Fir 16 A3
Flatts La. Calv 133 F1
Flatts La. Calv 148 C4
Flatts La. Sels 128 B2
Flatts The. Bees 183 D3
Flawforth Ave. Rudd 196 B3
Flawforth La. Rudd 196 C4
Flaxendale. Cotg 188 A1
Flaxton Way. Nott 160 C4
Fleam Rd. Nott 184 C2
Fleeman Gr. W Brid 174 A1
Fleet Cl. Nott 172 B3
Fleetway Cl. East 144 A1
Fleetway. Work 35 F4
Fleming Ave. Bott 181 E2
Fleming Ave. Tux 66 A2
Fleming Cl. Greas 159 D4
Fleming Dr. Carl 174 B4
Fleming Dr. N-on-T 125 D2
Fleming Dr. Wood 53 D4
Fleming Gdns. Nott 184 B1
Fletcher Gate. Nott 173 E2
Fletcher Rd. Bees 184 A4
Fletcher St. Lo Ea 193 E4
Flewitt Gdns. Nott 173 F3
Flint Ave. Mans 88 C1
Flintham Dr. Nott 161 E2
Flintham La. Screv 166 C3
Flixton Rd. Kim 158 C4
Flood Rd The. Beck 24 A4
Floral Villas. S on T 96 C4
Florence Ave. Lo Ea 182 C1
Florence Boot Cl. Nott 184 A4
Florence Cres. Carl 175 D4
Florence Ct. Ilk 157 F1
Florence Gr. Nott 174 A4
Florence Rd. Carl 175 D4
Florence Rd. W Brid 186 A4
Florence St. Huck 146 A3
Florence Terr. Gain 24 B4
Florey Ct. Nott 172 C1
Florey Wlk. Nott 195 E4
Floss La. Cott 43 E2
Flowers Cl. Arn 162 A3
Flying Horse Wlk. Nott 173 E2
Foljambe Terr. Nott 173 E3
Folkton Gdns. Nott 161 F1
Folly Hall La. Hick 209 E2
Folly La. No Sc 98 A4
Folly La. Staple 112 C3
Folly Nook La. Ran 19 D3
Forbes Cl. Lo Ea 193 F3
Ford La. Caun 109 D3
Ford St N. Nott 161 D1
Ford St. Nott 161 D1
Fordbridge La. S Norm 113 D4
Fordham Green. Nott 195 F4
Foredrift Cl. Goth 195 D1
Forest Ave. Mans 102 B3
Forest Cl. Ann Wo 130 A4
Forest Cl. Cotg 187 F2
Forest Cl. Rain 104 B1
Forest Cl. Sels 129 D4
Forest Ct. Nott 173 D3
Forest Gr. Nott 173 D3
Forest Gr. Nott 173 D4
Forest Hill Rd. Work 36 A4
Forest Hill. Mans 102 B1
Forest La. Papp 131 F2
Forest La. Wale 63 F2
Forest La. Work 36 B1
Forest Link. Bils 106 A3
Forest Rd E. Nott 173 D4
Forest Rd W. Nott 173 D3
Forest Rd. Ann Wo 130 A4
Forest Rd. Bing 177 E2
Forest Rd. Blid 118 A3
Forest Rd. Calv 148 B4
Forest Rd. Lough 220 A2
Forest Rd. Mans 102 B3
Forest Rd. Mar War 74 B1
Forest Rd. N Clip 89 F2
Forest Rd. Oll 77 E2
Forest Rd. Oxt 134 A3
Forest Rd. S in A 101 D3
Forest Rise. Mar War 74 B1
Forest St. Ann Wo 130 A4
Forest St. K-in-A 115 D2
Forest St. S in A 100 C1
Forest View Dr. Huck 145 F4
Forest View. Oll 77 D2
Forest View. Ret 39 E2
Forester Cl. Bees 183 E2
Forester Gr. Carl 174 B4
Forester Rd. Carl 174 A4
Forester St. Carl 175 D4
Forewood La. Tres 42 A2
Forge Ave. Calv 148 C4
Forge Cl. S Musk 124 B4
Forge Cl. S on T 96 C4
Forge Hill. Bees 183 E2
Forge The. Trow 170 A3
Forman St. Nott 173 E3
Forrests Yd. Work 35 F1
Forster Ave. N-on-T 139 F3
Forster St. Gain 15 E1
Forster St. K-in-A 114 C3
Forster St. Nott 172 C3
Forsythia Gdns. Nott 172 C1
Fosbrooke Dr. Lo Ea 193 E3
Fossdyke Gdns. Sax 57 D2
Fosse Gr. Sax 57 D2
Fosse Rd. Farn 139 D2
Fosse Wlk. Cotg 188 A1
Fossett's Ave. Sels 128 C4
Foster Ave. Bees 183 F3
Foster Rd. Coll 98 A1
Foster St. Mans 102 B3
Fosters La. Bing 177 F2
Foston Cl. Mans 103 D3
Fothergill Ct. Nott 173 E4
Fountain Dale Ct. Nott 173 E4
Fountain Hill Rd. Walker 13 E4
Fountain Hill. Walker 13 E4
Fountains Cl. K-in-A 115 E3
Fountains Cl. W Brid 186 A3
Fourth Ave. Carl 174 B4
Fourth Ave. Edwin 75 F1
Fourth Ave. Edwin 76 A1
Fourth Ave. Mans 103 D4
Fourth Ave. Mans 103 F1
Fourth Ave. N Clip 89 F2
Fowler St. Hello 173 A2
Fox Cl. Lo Ea 193 E3
Fox Covert La. Mist 14 A4
Fox Covert La. Nott 184 B1
Fox Covert. Carl 174 C2
Fox Covert. Lough 220 A3
Fox Gr. Nott 160 C4
Fox Grove Ct. Nott 160 C2
Fox Hill. Cotg 187 F1
Fox Meadow. Huck 145 F3
Fox Rd. W Brid 173 F1
Fox Rd. Whit 45 D3
Fox St. Ann Wo 130 A4
Fox St. S in A 100 C2
Foxby Hill. Gain 24 C3
Foxby La. Gain 24 C3
Foxearth Ave. Nott 185 D1
Foxes Cl. Nott 173 D2
Foxglove Cl. Bald 140 B2
Foxglove Cl. Work 36 A1
Foxglove Rd. Greas 158 B4
Foxhall Rd. Nott 173 D4
Foxhill Cl. S in A 100 A2
Foxhill Ct. Carl 174 C4
Foxhill Rd Central. Carl 174 B4
Foxhill Rd E. Carl 174 B4
Foxhill Rd W. Carl 174 A4
Foxhill Rd. Bu Jo 163 F3
Foxhill Rd. Carl 174 B4
Foxhills. Kegw 203 E1
Foxhollies Gr. Nott 161 D2
Foxton Cl. Nott 159 F4
Foxwood Gr. Calv 148 C4
Foxwood La. Woodb 149 D3
Fradley Cl. Nott 146 B1
Frampton Rd. Nott 172 A4
Frances Gr. Huck 131 D1
Frances St. Sels 128 B1
Francis Chichester Wlk. Gain 24 C4
Francis Gr. Nott 160 C2
Francis Rd. Carl 174 C4
Francis St. Mans 102 C4
Francis St. Nott 173 D3
Francklin Rd. Lowd 150 B1
Frank Ave. Mans 101 F3
Franklin Cl. Nott 161 E4
Franklin Dr. Toll 186 B1
Franklin Rd. Sels 128 A2
Franklyn Gdns. Keyw 197 F2
Franklyn Gdns. Nott 172 B3
Fraser Cres. Carl 162 A1
Fraser Rd. Carl 162 A1
Fraser Rd. Nott 173 E1
Fraser Sq. Carl 162 A1
Fraser St. News 130 B3
Freckingham St. Nott 173 E2
Freda Ave. Carl 162 B1
Freda Cl. Carl 162 B2
Frederick Ave. Carl 174 A4
Frederick Ave. Ilk 170 A3
Frederick Ave. K-in-A 114 B3
Frederick Ave. Kegw 203 E2
Frederick Rd. Staple 182 B4
Frederick St. Lo Ea 193 F4
Frederick St. Lough 220 A2
Frederick St. Mans 102 B3
Frederick St. Ret 39 F3
Frederick St. S in A 100 B1
Frederick St. Work 35 F2
Freeby Ave. Mans 88 B3
Freehold St. Lough 220 B2
Freeland Cl. Bees 182 C2
Freeman's La. S Le S 32 B3
Freemans Rd. Carl 175 D4
Freemans Terr. Carl 175 D4
Freemantle Wlk. Nott 160 C4
Freeston Dr. Nott 159 F4
Freeth St. Nott 173 F1
Freiston St. Nott 172 C4
Fremount Dr. Nott 172 A4
French St. Ilk 170 A3
French Terr. Scarc 59 D1
Fretwell St. Nott 172 C4
Fria'rs Cres. N-on-T 139 F3
Friar La. Mar War 74 B1
Friar La. Nott 173 D2
Friar St. Lo Ea 193 E4
Friar St. Nott 172 C1
Friar Wlk. New 177 E4
Friars Cl. Sels 129 D4
Friars Ct. Nott 173 D2
Friary Cl. Nott 172 C1
Friary Rd. N-on-T 140 A4
Friary The. Nott 172 C1
Friday La. Carl 162 C1
Friend La. Edwin 76 A1
Friesland Dr. Sand 182 A3
Frinton Rd. Nott 159 F1
Frisby Ave. Lo Ea 193 F3
Fritchley Ct. Mans 103 D3
Frith Gr. Mans 101 F4
Frithwood La. Elmt 58 B4
Frobisher Gdns. Nott 161 E3
Frog La. Plun 202 C4
Frogmore St. Nott 173 E3
Front St. B in W 141 F3
Front St. E Stock 7 E1
Front St. Mort 15 D2
Front St. S Clift 68 C1
Frost Ave. La Mi 143 D2
Fryar Rd. Greas 143 F2
Fulford Ave. Ret 39 E4
Fulforth St. Nott 173 E3
Fuller St. Rudd 196 B3
Fullwood Ave. Ilk 157 F1
Fullwood Cl. Bees 183 E2
Fullwood St. Ilk 157 F1
Fulwood Cres. Nott 160 A1
Fulwood Rd N. S in A 114 A4
Fulwood Rd S. S in A 114 A4
Furlong Ave. Arn 161 F4
Furlong Cl. Staple 182 B4
Furlong St. Arn 161 F4
Furnace Rd. Ilk 170 A3
Furness Cl. W Brid 186 A4
Furness Rd. Nott 160 B2
Furnival St N. Work 36 A1
Furnival St. Work 36 A1
Furze Gdns. Nott 173 E4
Fylde Cl. Bees 182 C1
Fylingdale Way. Nott 171 E2

Gable's Lea. Su Bo 213 D3
Gabor Cl. Nott 195 E4
Gabrielle Cl. Nott 160 B2
Gadd St. Nott 172 C3
Gaddick View. Egma 79 F3
Gainas Ave. Gain 15 E1
Gainsborough Cl. Kinou 199 F1
Gainsborough Cl. Staple 182 C3
Gainsborough Dr. N-on-T 125 D2
Gainsborough Rd. Baw 10 A3
Gainsborough Rd. Ever 11 E1
Gainsborough Rd. Girt 82 C2
Gainsborough Rd. Lea 24 C1
Gainsborough Rd. N Whea 22 C1
Gainsborough Rd. S Le S 32 B3
Gainsborough Rd. Saundby 23 E3
Gainsborough Rd. Sax 56 C1
Gainsborough Rd. Sax 57 D2
Gainsborough Rd. Wint 125 E3
Gainsborough Rd. Wise 12 B1
Gainsford Cl. Nott 160 C3
Gainsford Cres. Nott 160 C3
Gaitskell Cres. Edwin 76 B1
Gaitskell Way. Bald 140 C2
Gale Cl. Bees 184 A3
Galen Ave. Wood 42 A1
Galen Ct. Nott 172 C1
Galena Dr. Carl 174 A4
Galley Hill Rd. Upton 122 A1
Gallows Inn Cl. Ilk 170 A3
Galway Ave. Bir 9 E3
Galway Cres. Ret 39 E4
Galway Dr. Bir 9 E3
Galway Rd. Arn 161 F4
Galway Rd. Bir 9 E3
Galway Rd. Nott 172 C2
Gamage Cl. Bald 140 C2
Gamble St. Nott 173 D3
Gamston Cres. Nott 161 E2
Gamston Lings Bar Rd. W Brid 186 B2
Gamston Rd. Mans 103 D2
Gant Ct. Tick 8 A4
Ganton Cl. Nott 161 F1
Garden Ave. Carl 174 B4
Garden Ave. Plea 86 C4
Garden Ave. Rain 104 A1
Garden Ave. Shireb 72 C2
Garden City. Carl 174 C4
Garden La. S in A 101 D2
Garden Rd. Bing 177 E2
Garden Rd. East 144 A2
Garden Rd. Huck 145 F4
Garden Rd. Mans 102 A3
Garden Row. Kegw 203 E2
Garden St. Nott 172 C3
Gardendale Ave. Nott 184 B1
Gardendale Ave. Nott 195 E4
Gardenia Cres. Carl 162 A1
Gardenia Gr. Carl 162 A1
Gardens Ct. W Brid 186 A4
Gardiner Terr. S in A 100 B3
Gardinia Cl. Bees 183 D1
Gardner Dr. Kinou 199 F2
Garfield Cl. Staple 170 C1
Garfield Rd. Nott 172 C3
Garfield St. Gain 15 E1
Garforth Cl. Nott 172 C4
Garibaldi Rd. Mans 89 E1
Garnet Ct. Nott 173 F3
Garnet St. Carl 174 C4
Garnon St. Mans 101 F3
Garratt Ave. Mans 102 B4
Garrett Gr. Nott 184 B1
Garsdale Dr. Nott 185 D2
Garside St. Work 36 A2
Garth Ave. S in A 114 C4
Garth Rd. Mans 102 A2
Garton Cl. Bees 183 D3
Garton Cl. Nott 160 A3
Garton Rd. Lough 220 A2
Garwick Cl. Mans 89 D1
Gas St. Sand 182 B3
Gas Walk. Harb 202 A2
Gatcombe Cl. R on T 176 A2
Gatcombe Gr. Sand 182 A2
Gateford Ave. Work 35 E3
Gateford Cl. Bees 171 E1
Gateford Cl. Work 35 E4
Gateford Gdns. Work 35 E3
Gateford Glade. Work 35 E3
Gateford Rd. Work 35 E3
Gateford Rise. Work 35 E4
Gateside Rd. Nott 173 D1
Gatling St. Nott 172 C3
Gattlys La. Oll 77 D2
Gaul St. Nott 160 A4
Gauntley Ct. Nott 172 C4
Gauntley St. Nott 172 C4
Gautries Cl. Nott 161 D4
Gawthorne St. Nott 161 D1
Gayhurst Green. Nott 160 C3
Gayhurst Rd. Nott 160 C3
Gaynor Ct. Nott 172 A3
Gayrigg Ct. Bees 183 D2
Gayton Cl. Nott 171 E4
Gaywood Cl. Nott 195 F4
Gedling Gr. Nott 173 D3
Gedling Rd. Arn 162 A3
Gedling Rd. Carl 174 C4
Gedling St. Mans 102 A3
Gedling St. Nott 173 E2
Gedney Ave. Nott 173 F4
Gelding Gr. Arn 161 F4
Gell Rd. Bees 183 D2
George Ave. Bees 183 F3
George Ave. Lo Ea 182 C1
George Dere Cl. Boug 77 E3
George Rd. Carl 174 C4
George Rd. W Brid 185 F4
George St. Gain 15 D1
George St. Huck 146 A4
George St. La Mi 143 D2
George St. Mans 88 B2
George St. Mans 89 D1
George St. Mans 101 F4
George St. Mar War 73 F1
George St. Mar War 74 A2
George St. N-on-T 125 D1
George St. Nott 161 F3
George St. Nott 173 E3
George St. Pinx 113 E2
George St. Ret 39 F3
George St. S in A 100 A2
George St. Scarc 59 D1
George St. Work 35 F2
George Yd. Lough 220 A2
George's La. Calv 148
Georgia Dr. Nott 147
Georgina Rd. Bees 183
Gerrard Cl. Bes Vil 147
Gerrard Cres. Kegw 203
Gertrude Rd. W Brid 174
Gervase Gdns. Nott 184
Ghest Villas. C in L 16
Ghost House La. Bees 183
Ghost House La. Bees 183
Gibb St. Lo Ea 193
Gibbet Hill La. Scro 9
Gibbons Ave. Staple 182
Gibbons St. Nott 172
Gibdyke. Miss 4
Gibson Cres. Bald 140
Gibson Rd. Nott 173
Gibson's La. Ol Da 218
Gifford Gdns. Nott 173
Gilbert Ave. Goth 195
Gilbert Ave. Tux 66
Gilbert Gdns. Nott 174
Gilbert Rd. Bir 9
Gilcroft St. Mans 102
Gilcroft St. S in A 100
Gilead St. Nott 160
Giles Ave. W Brid 185
Gill Green Wlk. Clar 30
Gill St. Nott 173
Gill St. S in A 100
Gill St. Sels 129
Gillies The. Mans 101
Gillot St. Hean 157
Gillotts Cl. Bing 177
Gilpet Ave. Nott 173
Gilstrap Cl. N-on-T 140
Gilt Hill. Kim 158
Giltbrook Cres. Greas 158
Giltway. Greas 158
Gin Close Way. Awsw 158
Gin Close Way. Kim 158
Gipsy La. Bleas 152
Girton La. N Sca 83
Girton Rd. Nott 161
Gisburn Cl. Nott 185
Glade Ave. Nott 172
Glade The. Nott 195 F
Gladehill Rd. Arn 161
Gladstone Ave. Goth 195
Gladstone Ave. Lough 220
Gladstone Dr. Brin 143 F
Gladstone Rd. N-on-T 139 F
Gladstone St. Bees 183 F
Gladstone St. Carl 174 E
Gladstone St. Gain 15 E
Gladstone St. Hath 213 D
Gladstone St. K-in-A 115 D
Gladstone St. La Mi 143 E
Gladstone St. Lo Ea 193 E
Gladstone St. Lough 220 A
Gladstone St. Mans 88 E
Gladstone St. Mans 102 E
Gladstone St. Nott 172 C
Gladstone St. Nott 173
Gladstone St. S Norm 113 E
Gladstone St. Work 35 F
Gladstone Terr. K-in-A 114 C
Gladstone Terr. Mans 88 E
Gladys St. Nott 161 D
Glaisdale Dr E. Nott 171 F
Glaisdale Dr W. Nott 171 E
Glaisdale Parkway. Nott 171 E
Glaisdale. Work 36 A
Glamis Rd. C in L 25 F
Glamis Rd. Nott 161 D
Glannis Sq. Mar War 74 B
Glapton Rd. Nott 173 E
Glaramara Cl. Nott 173 D
Glasby Cl. Oll 77 D
Glasshouse St. Nott 173 E
Glastonbury Cl. Mans 88 B
Glaven Cl. Mans 88 B
Glebe Ave. Mar War 74 B
Glebe Ave. Pinx 113 E
Glebe Cl. N Whea 31 F
Glebe Cl. Work 35 E
Glebe Cres. Ilk 170 A
Glebe Dr. Bu Jo 163 E
Glebe Farm Cl. W Brid 185 E
Glebe Farm View. Carl 162 C
Glebe Rd. Carl 162 B
Glebe Rd. Nuth 159 E
Glebe Rd. W Brid 185 F
Glebe St. Ann Wo 129 F
Glebe St. Bees 183 F
Glebe St. Huck 146 A
Glebe St. Lough 220 B
Glebe The. Awsw 158 A
Glebe The. Ret 39 E
Glebe View. Mans 102 C
Glen Ave. East 144 A
Glen Cl. Newt 99 D
Glen Eagles Way. Ret 39 E
Glen Helen. Carl 174 C
Glen Mooar Cl. Mans 89 D
Glen Parva Ave. Nott 147 F
Glen Rd. Bu Jo 163 F
Glen St. S in A 100 C

...n The. Nott .... 184 C1
...nbrook Cres. Nott .... 172 A4
...nbrook. Cotg .... 188 A2
...ncairn Rd. Nott .... 172 A4
...ncoe Rd. Nott .... 184 C1
...ncoe Rd. Nott .... 185 D1
...ncoyne Rd. Nott .... 195 F4
...ndale Cl. Carl .... 162 B1
...ndale Ct. Bees .... 183 F2
...ndale Gdns. Arn .... 161 F4
...ndoe Gr. Bing .... 177 E2
...ndon Dr. Huck .... 146 A3
...ndon Dr. Nott .... 161 D2
...neagles Ct. W Brid .... 186 B2
...neagles Dr. Arn .... 148 A1
...neagles Dr. K-in-A .... 114 C4
...nfield Ave. Kim .... 158 B4
...nfield Rd. Lo Ea .... 193 E3
...nlivet Gdns. Nott .... 184 C1
...nloch Dr. Nott .... 195 F4
...nmore Rd. W Brid .... 186 A3
...norchy Cres. Nott .... 160 C4
...nsford Gdns. Nott .... 146 C1
...nside Rd. Bees .... 171 E1
...nside. Arn .... 162 A3
...nside. K-in-A .... 115 E3
...nstone Ct. Nott .... 172 C4
...nthorn Cl. Shire .... 34 C4
...ntworth Rd. Nott .... 172 C3
...nwood Ave. Nott .... 171 E2
...nis Rd. Nott .... 160 C4
...ossop Rd. Mans .... 103 D3
...oucester Ave. Bees .... 183 F3
...oucester Ave. Nott .... 172 C2
...oucester Ave. Nuth .... 159 F2
...oucester Ave. Sand .... 182 A2
...oucester Rd. Work .... 36 A4
...over Ave. Nott .... 171 E2
...over Cl. S Lev .... 42 B3
...overs Cl. Cuck .... 60 A2
...overs La. Bald .... 140 B2
...oatchurch Ct. Nott .... 147 D1
...oatland Cl. Nott .... 161 D4
...odber Rd. Huck .... 145 F3
...odfrey St. Carl .... 175 D3
...odfrey's Ct. Work .... 35 F2
...odkin Dr. Ald .... 143 D2
...oldenholme La. Ramp .... 43 D1
...oldfinch Cl. Mans .... 102 C4
...oldham Rd. Nott .... 171 E4
...oldsmith Rd. Bald .... 140 B3
...oldsmith Rd. Work .... 36 A3
...oldsmith St. Mans .... 102 A4
...oldsmith St. Nott .... 173 D3
...oldswong Terr. Nott .... 173 E4
...oldthorpe Ave. Lan .... 16 C2
...oldthorpe Cl. Lan .... 16 C2
...olf Club Rd. S-by-D .... 170 A1
...olf Course Rd. S-on-W .... 198 A1
...olf Rd. R on T .... 176 A2
...omersall Ct. Ret .... 40 A3
...onalston La. Epp .... 150 B2
...onalston La. Gona .... 150 B2
...onalston La. Hover .... 151 E1
...oodacre St. Mans .... 102 B4
...oodall Cres. Huck .... 146 B3
...oodall St. Nott .... 172 C4
...oodhand Cres. Mans .... 101 F3
...oodliffe St. Nott .... 172 C4
...oodman Cl. Greas .... 158 B4
...oodwin Cl. N-on-T .... 140 B4
...oodwin St. Farns .... 119 F4
...oodwin Dr. Kim .... 158 C3
...oodwin St. Nott .... 173 D3
...oodwood Ave. Arn .... 161 F4
...oodwood Dr. Bees .... 182 C1
...oodwood Rd. Nott .... 171 E2
...oodwood Way. Mans .... 102 C4
...oose Gate. Nott .... 173 E2
...oosedale La. Bes Vil .... 147 D4
...oosemoor La. Ret .... 39 F2
...opher Rd. N-on-T .... 139 F3
...ordon Ave. Mans .... 102 C3
...ordon Cl. Bees .... 183 E1
...ordon Cl. Farns .... 119 F3
...ordon Cl. Work .... 36 A2
...ordon Cres. S Norm .... 113 D2
...ordon Rd. Bu Jo .... 164 A3
...ordon Rd. Lough .... 220 A3
...ordon Rd. Nott .... 173 F3
...ordon Rd. W Brid .... 185 F4
...ordon Rise. Nott .... 161 F1
...ordon Sq. W Brid .... 185 F4
...ordon St. Gain .... 24 B3
...ordon St. Ilk .... 158 A1
...ordon St. Nott .... 160 B2
...ordonbrae. Mans .... 102 B2
...ordondale Rd. Mans .... 88 A1
...orman Ct. Arn .... 162 A4
...orse Ave. Mans .... 103 D3
...orse Cl. Calv .... 148 B4
...orse Cl. Greas .... 158 B4
...orse Cl. Nott .... 160 C3
...orse Hill. Raven .... 117 D1
...orse Rd. Keyw .... 197 E2
...orse Rd. N-on-T .... 139 F3
...orselands Ave. Work .... 36 B1
...orseway. N Clip .... 90 A2

Gorsey Rd. Hello .... 173 A2
Gorsy La. Morton .... 137 E1
Gosforth Ct. Nott .... 173 E1
Gotham La. Bunn .... 206 B4
Gotham Rd. E Lea .... 205 F2
Gotham Rd. K on S .... 204 B3
Gothic Cl. Nott .... 160 C2
Goverton Hill. Bleas .... 136 C1
Goverton Sq. Nott .... 160 B3
Goyden Cl. Nott .... 161 D4
Grace Ave. Bees .... 184 A3
Grace Dr. Nott .... 172 B4
Gracefield La. L Marn .... 81 F4
Grafton Ave. Arn .... 161 F3
Grafton Ct. K-in-A .... 114 C4
Grafton Ct. Nott .... 173 D3
Grafton St. Work .... 35 F2
Graham Cl. Bald .... 140 A2
Graham St. Nott .... 172 C3
Grainger Ave. Ann Wo .... 115 D1
Grainger Ave. W Brid .... 185 F2
Grainger St. Nott .... 173 F1
Graingers Terr. Huck .... 146 A3
Grampian Dr. Bes Vil .... 147 D1
Grampian Way. Lo Ea .... 193 D4
Granby Ave. Mans .... 102 A4
Granby Ave. N-on-T .... 140 A3
Granby Ct. Bing .... 177 E2
Granby Dr. Bald .... 140 B2
Granby Dr. Bott .... 181 D1
Granby Hill. Gran .... 191 D3
Granby La. Aslo .... 178 B1
Granby La. Plun .... 191 F1
Granby La. What .... 178 B1
Granby St. Ilk .... 157 F1
Granby St. Lough .... 220 A2
Grandfield Ave. R on T .... 175 F2
Grandfield Cres. R on T .... 175 F2
Grange Ave. Baw .... 9 F4
Grange Ave. Bees .... 183 F3
Grange Ave. Mans .... 101 F3
Grange Ave. Mist .... 14 A4
Grange Ave. N-on-T .... 139 F2
Grange Ave. Oll .... 77 D2
Grange Ave. Rudd .... 196 B4
Grange Cl. C in L .... 26 A3
Grange Cl. Lamb .... 163 E4
Grange Cl. Mist .... 14 A4
Grange Cl. Nott .... 185 D4
Grange Cres. Carl .... 162 C2
Grange Ct. K-in-A .... 115 E3
Grange Dr. Har .... 9 D3
Grange Dr. Lo Ea .... 193 F4
Grange Dr. Mist .... 14 A4
Grange La. Bald .... 155 D2
Grange La. Coth .... 155 D2
Grange Park. W Brid .... 186 B3
Grange Rd. Arn .... 161 F2
Grange Rd. Blid .... 118 A3
Grange Rd. Lo Ea .... 193 F4
Grange Rd. Nott .... 160 B2
Grange Rd. Ret .... 39 F2
Grange Rd. W Brid .... 186 A2
Grange St. Lough .... 220 A3
Grange The. N Musk .... 110 C2
Grange The. Ret .... 39 F2
Grange The. S Norm .... 113 D2
Grange View Rd. Carl .... 163 D1
Grange View. East .... 143 F2
Grange View. Har .... 9 D3
Grange Wlk. Mist .... 7 D1
Grangelea Gdns. Bees .... 183 E4
Granger Ct. Lough .... 220 A2
Grangewood Ct. Nott .... 171 E2
Grangewood Rd. K-in-A .... 114 C4
Grangewood Rd. Nott .... 171 E2
Grannis Dr. Nott .... 172 A4
Grant St. Nott .... 172 C3
Grantham Cl. Greas .... 158 B4
Grantham Rd. Bing .... 178 B3
Grantham Rd. Bott .... 181 E1
Grantham Rd. R on T .... 175 F1
Grantham Rd. R on T .... 176 B2
Grantleigh Cl. Nott .... 171 F3
Granton Ave. Nott .... 195 F4
Granton Rise. Mans .... 101 E3
Granville Ave. Lo Ea .... 182 B1
Granville Cres. R on T .... 175 F1
Granville Ct. Nott .... 173 F3
Granville Gr. Nott .... 173 F3
Granville St. Lough .... 220 A2
Grasmere Cl. Gain .... 15 F1
Grasmere Cl. Huck .... 145 F4
Grasmere Rd. Bees .... 183 E4
Grasmere Rd. Lo Ea .... 182 A1
Grasmere Rd. Work .... 35 F4
Grasmere St. Sand .... 182 A3
Grass St. Ilk .... 157 F2
Grassingdale Cl. Carl .... 162 B1
Grassington Rd. Nott .... 172 B4
Grassmere. Cotg .... 188 A2
Grassthorpe Rd. S on T .... 81 F1
Gravel La. Egma .... 79 E4
Gravel Pit La. W Dray .... 50 C1
Gravelholes La. Mist .... 6 C1
Gravelly Hollow. Calv .... 133 D1
Gravelly La. Fisk .... 137 F2
Gravelly La. Morton .... 137 F2

Graveney Gdns. Arn .... 162 B3
Graves Moor La. Blyth .... 18 C1
Graves Moor La. Torw .... 18 C1
Gray La. Halam .... 120 C1
Gray St. Lough .... 220 A1
Graylands Rd. Nott .... 171 F3
Grazingfield. Nott .... 185 D2
Greasley Ave. East .... 144 B1
Greasley Ct. Mans .... 103 D2
Greasley St. Nott .... 160 A4
Great Central Rd. Lough .... 220 B2
Great Central Rd. Mans .... 102 B3
Great Freeman St. Nott .... 173 E3
Great Hoggett Dr. Bees .... 183 D3
Great La. E Mark .... 65 F4
Great North Rd. Ba Mo .... 28 B3
Great North Rd. Bald .... 155 F3
Great North Rd. C on T .... 96 C3
Great North Rd. Crom .... 110 C3
Great North Rd. Dry Do .... 155 F3
Great North Rd. E Mark .... 65 E3
Great North Rd. Eaton .... 40 A1
Great North Rd. Gams .... 51 D2
Great North Rd. Kelh .... 124 B3
Great North Rd. N Musk .... 110 C3
Great North Rd. N-on-T .... 124 B3
Great North Rd. Ran .... 19 D2
Great North Rd. S Musk .... 124 B3
Great North Rd. S on T .... 96 C3
Great North Rd. Scro .... 10 A1
Great North Rd. Sutt .... 28 B3
Great North Rd. Torw .... 19 D2
Great North Rd. Tux .... 65 E3
Great North Rd. W Dray .... 51 D2
Great North Rd. West .... 81 E2
Great Northern Cl The. Nott .... 173 E1
Great Northern Rd. East .... 143 E1
Great Northern Way. Carl .... 175 D4
Greaves Cl. Ne Br .... 219 E3
Greaves Cl. Arn .... 162 A3
Greaves Cl. N-on-T .... 140 B4
Greaves Cl. Nott .... 159 E1
Greaves La. Edin .... 120 A2
Greaves La. Oxt .... 119 F1
Grebe Cl. Bald .... 140 B3
Greek St. Nott .... 173 D3
Green Acre. Nott .... 171 D3
Green Acre. W Brid .... 186 A2
Green Ave. Carl .... 175 D4
Green Bank. Rain .... 118 B4
Green Cl. Blid .... 118 A2
Green Cl. Huck .... 146 B3
Green Cl. Keyw .... 197 F2
Green Cl. Newt .... 99 D2
Green Cres. Sels .... 128 C3
Green Farm Rd. Sels .... 128 B3
Green Hill Rise. Hath .... 213 D1
Green Hill. Hath .... 213 D1
Green La. Babw .... 38 C3
Green La. Bath .... 110 A1
Green La. Bott .... 181 E1
Green La. Coll .... 112 A4
Green La. Darl .... 67 E2
Green La. Dry Do .... 156 C2
Green La. Eagle .... 84 C2
Green La. Gran .... 191 D3
Green La. Harb .... 202 B1
Green La. Hick .... 210 A2
Green La. Ilk .... 170 A4
Green La. Lamb .... 149 D1
Green La. Lax .... 79 E1
Green La. Lax .... 80 A1
Green La. Lea .... 24 C2
Green La. Mans .... 87 D1
Green La. Mans .... 102 B2
Green La. Nott .... 184 C1
Green La. Plea .... 86 B4
Green La. S Lev .... 42 B3
Green La. Scro .... 18 C4
Green La. Tres .... 42 B2
Green La. Wale .... 64 A1
Green La. Whit .... 45 E3
Green Leys. W Brid .... 185 E2
Green Mile La. Babw .... 28 A1
Green Mile La. Babw .... 38 C4
Green Platt. Cotg .... 187 F2
Green Rd. G on H .... 13 D1
Green St. B in F .... 195 D4
Green St. Nott .... 173 E1
Green The. Al Hu .... 85 D2
Green The. B-le-V .... 192 A1
Green The. Bees .... 183 F2
Green The. Bils .... 105 F4
Green The. C in L .... 26 A3
Green The. Codd .... 126 A1
Green The. Coll .... 111 F4
Green The. E Lea .... 205 F1
Green The. Elst .... 153 E2
Green The. Gain .... 24 C4
Green The. Glap .... 86 A4
Green The. Har .... 8 C2
Green The. Hath .... 213 D1
Green The. Hose .... 211 F4
Green The. K on S .... 204 A2
Green The. Kirk .... 120 C4
Green The. Lo Wh .... 212 B2
Green The. Lowd .... 149 F1
Green The. Mans .... 88 A3

Green The. Orst .... 179 F4
Green The. R on T .... 175 F2
Green The. S in A .... 99 F1
Green Wlk. Nott .... 178 C2
Green's Farm La. Carl .... 163 D1
Greenacre Ave. Hean .... 143 D2
Greenacre Rd. Work .... 36 A3
Greenacre. Lamb .... 163 F3
Greenacre. Mans .... 102 C3
Greenacre. S in A .... 100 B3
Greenacres Cl. Greas .... 144 B1
Greenacres Dr. S Norm .... 113 D3
Greenacres. K-in-A .... 115 D1
Greenbank. Carl .... 174 B3
Greenclose La. Lough .... 220 A2
Greencroft. Nott .... 184 C2
Greendale Ave. Edwin .... 76 A2
Greendale Cl. Mar War .... 74 A2
Greendale Cres. N Clip .... 90 A2
Greendale Gdns. Nott .... 172 A4
Greendale Rd. Arn .... 161 F3
Greendale Rd. Nott .... 174 B3
Greenfield Ave. Whit .... 45 E3
Greenfield Cl. Mans .... 89 D1
Greenfield Gr. Carl .... 174 B4
Greenfield St. Nott .... 172 B1
Greenfields Cres. Oll .... 77 E2
Greenfields Dr. Cotg .... 187 F1
Greenfields. Ald .... 143 D2
Greenfields. S in A .... 101 D3
Greengate Rd. E Dray .... 53 D2
Greengate. Syer .... 153 D2
Greengates Ave. Arn .... 161 F2
Greenhill Cres. Carl .... 174 C3
Greenhill La. Ann Wo .... 129 F4
Greenhill Rd. Carl .... 174 C3
Greenhill Rise. Carl .... 174 C3
Greenhills Rd. East .... 143 F2
Greenhills Ave. East .... 144 A2
Greenhills Rd. East .... 144 A2
Greenholme Cl. K-in-A .... 115 D2
Greenland Cres. Bees .... 183 E2
Greenland Rd. S in A .... 100 C4
Greens Ct. Ilk .... 157 E1
Greens La. Nott .... 159 D3
Greenside Ave. Ramp .... 42 C1
Greenside Cl. Lo Ea .... 193 F4
Greensquare Rd. K in A .... 113 F1
Greenvale. Farns .... 120 A3
Greenview Cl. Mans .... 89 D1
Greenway Cl. R on T .... 175 F2
Greenway The. Sand .... 182 A3
Greenway. C in L .... 26 A3
Greenway. Mans .... 89 E2
Greenway. N-on-T .... 139 F3
Greenway. Ret .... 39 E2
Greenwich Ave. Nott .... 160 B2
Greenwood Ave. Edwin .... 76 A1
Greenwood Ave. Har .... 8 C3
Greenwood Ave. Huck .... 145 F4
Greenwood Ave. Ilk .... 170 A4
Greenwood Ave. Mans .... 88 A2
Greenwood Ave. Nott .... 174 B3
Greenwood Ave. S in A .... 99 F1
Greenwood Cl. Farns .... 120 A3
Greenwood Cotts. Mans .... 102 C4
Greenwood Cres. Boug .... 77 F3
Greenwood Cres. Carl .... 174 C3
Greenwood Dr. K-in-A .... 114 C3
Greenwood Gdns. Rudd .... 196 B3
Greenwood Rd. Carl .... 174 B3
Greenwood Rd. Nott .... 174 B3
Greenwood Vale. Huck .... 145 F4
Greet Farm Cl. South .... 121 F1
Greetwell Cl. Nott .... 172 A3
Gregory Bvd. Nott .... 173 D4
Gregory Ave. Ald .... 143 D2
Gregory Ave. Carl .... 162 A1
Gregory Ave. La Mi .... 143 D2
Gregory Ave. Nott .... 172 C2
Gregory Cl. Staple .... 182 C4
Gregory Cres. Har .... 8 C2
Gregory Ct. Bees .... 183 D2
Gregory Ct. Nott .... 172 C2
Gregory Gdns. Farns .... 119 F3
Gregory St. Ilk .... 157 F1
Gregory St. Lough .... 220 A2
Gregory St. Nott .... 172 C2
Grenville Dr. Ilk .... 157 F2
Grenville Dr. Staple .... 182 C4
Grenville Rd. Bees .... 184 A2
Grenville Rise. Nott .... 147 F1
Gresham Cl. N-on-T .... 140 C4
Gresham Cl. W Brid .... 185 E4
Gresham Gdns. Arn .... 162 A3
Gresham Gdns. W Brid .... 185 E4
Gresley Ave. Baw .... 10 A4
Gresley Rd. Ilk .... 157 F1
Gresley Rd. Ret .... 39 E3
Gressy Rd. Nott .... 184 C1
Gretton Cl. Clayp .... 156 B3
Gretton Rd. Carl .... 162 A2
Grey St. East .... 144 A1
Grey St. Gain .... 15 D1
Grey St. K-in-A .... 114 B3
Greyfriar Gate. Nott .... 173 E2
Greys Rd. Arn .... 161 F2

Greystoke Dr. Nott .... 171 E4
Greystones Rd. Gain .... 15 D2
Greythorn Dr. W Brid .... 185 E2
Griceson Cl. Oll .... 77 D1
Grierson Ave. Nott .... 161 D4
Griffs Hollow. Carl .... 174 C4
Grimesmoor Rd. Calv .... 149 D4
Grimsby Terr. Nott .... 173 E3
Grimston Rd. Nott .... 172 C4
Grindon Cres. Nott .... 146 B1
Gringley Rd. Clay .... 21 F3
Gringley Rd. G on H .... 21 F3
Gringley Rd. Mist .... 6 C1
Gringley Rd. Walker .... 13 F2
Gripps Comm. Cotg .... 187 F1
Grisedale Ct. Bees .... 183 D2
Gritley Mews. Nott .... 173 D1
Grives La. K-in-A .... 115 D1
Grizedale Gr. Bing .... 177 D2
Grosvenor Ave. Lo Ea .... 193 D2
Grosvenor Ave. Nott .... 161 E1
Grosvenor Ave. S in A .... 100 B1
Grosvenor Rd. Bald .... 140 A2
Grosvenor Rd. East .... 143 F1
Grosvenor Rd. Har .... 9 D2
Grouville Dr. Arn .... 162 A3
Grove Ave. Bees .... 183 F3
Grove Ave. Nott .... 173 D3
Grove Cl. Bu Jo .... 163 F3
Grove Coach Rd. Ret .... 40 A2
Grove La. Ret .... 40 A3
Grove Mews. East .... 143 F1
Grove Park. Mist .... 6 C1
Grove Rd. Grove .... 41 E3
Grove Rd. Mar War .... 74 A3
Grove Rd. Nott .... 172 C2
Grove Rd. Ret .... 40 B2
Grove Rd. S in A .... 101 D2
Grove Rd. S Lev .... 41 E3
Grove St. Bald .... 140 B3
Grove St. Bees .... 184 A3
Grove St. Mans .... 88 A2
Grove St. Mans .... 102 A3
Grove St. Ret .... 39 F4
Grove The. Beck .... 14 A1
Grove The. Calv .... 149 D4
Grove The. Ne on T .... 55 D1
Grove The. Nott .... 161 D1
Grove The. Nott .... 172 C3
Grove Way. Mans .... 88 A2
Grove Wood Rd. Mist .... 6 C1
Grove Wood Terr. Mist .... 6 C1
Grover Ave. Carl .... 162 A2
Groveside Cres. Bees .... 184 B2
Groveview Rd. Bald .... 140 B3
Grundy Ave. Sels .... 128 B4
Grundy Nook. Whit .... 45 D3
Grundy St. Nott .... 172 C4
Guildford Ave. Mans .... 88 B3
Guildhall St. N-on-T .... 140 A4
Gunn Cl. Nott .... 160 A4
Gunnersbury Way. Nuth .... 159 F2
Gunthorpe Cl. Nott .... 161 D2
Gunthorpe Dr. Nott .... 161 E2
Gunthorpe Rd. Carl .... 162 B2
Gunthorpe Rd. Gunt .... 164 C4
Gunthorpe Rd. Haxey .... 7 F4
Gutersloh Ct. Staple .... 182 C4
Gwenbrook Ave. Bees .... 183 F3
Gwenbrook Rd. Bees .... 183 F3
Gwndy Gdns. Nott .... 161 D4

Habblesthorpe Cl. N Le Ha .... 32 C1
Habblesthorpe Rd. N Le Ha .... 32 C1
Hackers Cl. E Brid .... 165 E4
Hackworth Cl. Greas .... 144 A2
Hadbury Rd. Nott .... 160 C2
Hadden Cl. Nott .... 171 E3
Haddon Cl. Carl .... 162 B1
Haddon Cl. Huck .... 146 A3
Haddon Cl. Sels .... 129 D4
Haddon Cres. Bees .... 183 E1
Haddon Dr. Bald .... 140 B2
Haddon Nurseries. Ilk .... 157 F2
Haddon Pl. Shireb .... 72 B3
Haddon Rd. Mans .... 102 A4
Haddon Rd. Raven .... 117 D2
Haddon Rd. Ret .... 40 A2
Haddon Rd. W Brid .... 185 F3
Haddon St. Ilk .... 157 F1
Haddon St. Nott .... 161 D1
Haddon S in A .... 100 C2
Haddon S. Tibs .... 99 D3
Haddon Way. R on T .... 176 A2
Hades La. W-on-W .... 217 E3
Hades La. Wyme .... 217 E3
Hadfield Wlk. Mans .... 103 D3
Hadleigh Cl. Bees .... 182 C1
Hadley St. Ilk .... 170 A3
Hadrian Gdns. Bes Vil .... 147 D1
Hadstock Cl. Sand .... 182 A2
Hagg La. Egma .... 80 A3
Hagg La. Miss .... 10 C1
Hagley Cl. Nott .... 174 A3
Haileybury Cres. W Brid .... 185 F3
Haileybury Rd. W Brid .... 185 F3
Hainton Cl. Gain .... 24 C4
Haise Ct. Nott .... 159 F3

## Halam Cl. Mans — Heyward St. Mar

| Name | Page | Grid |
|---|---|---|
| Halam Cl. Mans | 101 | E4 |
| Halam Hill. Halam | 121 | D1 |
| Halberton Dr. W Brid | 185 | E2 |
| Haldane St. Gain | 15 | D1 |
| Hales Cl. Cotg | 187 | F2 |
| Haley Cl. Kim | 158 | B3 |
| Halfmoon Dr. K-in-A | 115 | D2 |
| Halifax Ct. Nott | 159 | E1 |
| Halifax Pl. Nott | 173 | E2 |
| Hall Barn La. Mans | 101 | E4 |
| Hall Cl The. E Mark | 66 | A4 |
| Hall Cl. R on T | 175 | F2 |
| Hall Cl. Rain | 118 | A4 |
| Hall Croft. Bees | 183 | F3 |
| Hall Dr. Clay | 21 | E3 |
| Hall Dr. Cr Bi | 189 | D2 |
| Hall Dr. Goth | 195 | D1 |
| Hall Dr. Nott | 171 | F2 |
| Hall Dr. Sand | 182 | A3 |
| Hall Gdns. Bees | 183 | D4 |
| Hall Gdns. E Lea | 214 | C4 |
| Hall La. Brin | 143 | E3 |
| Hall La. Co Ba | 200 | B4 |
| Hall La. E Mark | 66 | A4 |
| Hall La. Kinou | 200 | A2 |
| Hall La. Newt | 99 | D2 |
| Hall Rd. Ald | 143 | E2 |
| Hall St. Mans | 102 | C3 |
| Hall St. Nott | 161 | E2 |
| Hall St. S in A | 100 | C3 |
| Hall View Dr. Nott | 171 | E3 |
| Hall View. Matt | 20 | A4 |
| Hall's Rd. G on H | 13 | D2 |
| Hallam Fields Rd. Ilk | 170 | A2 |
| Hallam Rd. Bees | 183 | F3 |
| Hallam Rd. Carl | 162 | A4 |
| Hallam's La. Arn | 161 | F4 |
| Hallams La. Bees | 183 | E3 |
| Hallamway. Mans | 88 | B1 |
| Hallcroft Ave. Ret | 39 | F4 |
| Hallcroft Rd. Ret | 29 | E1 |
| Hallfield Rd. Newt | 99 | D2 |
| Hallfields. W Brid | 186 | A2 |
| Hallifax Ave. Mar War | 74 | A4 |
| Halloughton Rd. South | 136 | B4 |
| Hallowell Dr. Nott | 171 | F2 |
| Halls La. Greas | 158 | A4 |
| Halls Rd. Staple | 182 | B3 |
| Hallum Ct. Ilk | 157 | F2 |
| Halstead Cl. Bees | 183 | E2 |
| Halstead Cl. Nott | 160 | A2 |
| Haltham Green. Gain | 24 | C4 |
| Haltham Wlk. Nott | 195 | E4 |
| Hambledon Dr. Nott | 172 | A3 |
| Hambleton Cl. Lo Ea | 182 | A1 |
| Hambleton Ct. C in L | 25 | F4 |
| Hambling Cl. Nott | 160 | A4 |
| Hamilton Cl. Arn | 148 | B1 |
| Hamilton Cl. Bees | 182 | C1 |
| Hamilton Dr. Mar War | 74 | A2 |
| Hamilton Dr. Nott | 173 | D2 |
| Hamilton Dr. R on T | 175 | F2 |
| Hamilton Gdns. Nott | 161 | D1 |
| Hamilton Rd. Lo Ea | 182 | B1 |
| Hamilton Rd. Nott | 173 | D4 |
| Hamilton Rd. S in A | 101 | E1 |
| Hamilton St. Mans | 102 | C3 |
| Hamilton St. Work | 35 | F3 |
| Hamlet La. S Norm | 113 | D3 |
| Hamlet The. S Norm | 113 | D3 |
| Hammerwater Dr. Mar War | 74 | A2 |
| Hammond Gr. K-in-A | 115 | D1 |
| Hampden St. Nott | 173 | D3 |
| Hampden Gr. Bees | 183 | F3 |
| Hampden St. Greas | 158 | B4 |
| Hampden St. K-in-A | 114 | C3 |
| Hampshire Ct. Sels | 128 | A2 |
| Hampshire Dr. Sand | 182 | A3 |
| Hampstead Rd. Nott | 161 | F1 |
| Hampton Cl. Bees | 182 | C2 |
| Hampton Rd. W Brid | 185 | F3 |
| Hanbury Ct. Mans | 103 | D3 |
| Hand's Rd. Hean | 143 | D1 |
| Hand's Wlk. Bott | 181 | D1 |
| Handel St. Nott | 173 | F3 |
| Handley Ct. N-on-T | 124 | C1 |
| Hanford Way. Lough | 220 | A3 |
| Hangar Hill. Whit | 45 | D3 |
| Hankin St. Huck | 146 | B3 |
| Hanley Ave. Bees | 183 | D4 |
| Hanley St. Nott | 173 | D3 |
| Hannah Cres. Nott | 185 | D4 |
| Hanover Ct. Nott | 171 | E3 |
| Hanslope Cres. Nott | 171 | E4 |
| Hanson Ave. Huck | 146 | A4 |
| Hanstubbin Rd. Sels | 128 | C3 |
| Hanton Ave. Sels | 129 | D1 |
| Hanworth Gdns. Arn | 161 | E4 |
| Harberton Cl. Nott | 147 | F1 |
| Harby Ave. Mans | 88 | B3 |
| Harby Ave. S in A | 101 | E1 |
| Harby Cl. Bald | 140 | B2 |
| Harby Dr. Nott | 172 | B2 |
| Harby La. Co Ba | 200 | C3 |
| Harby La. Hose | 211 | F4 |
| Harby La. Lang | 201 | D3 |
| Harby La. Plun | 202 | C3 |
| Harby La. Stat | 202 | C2 |
| Harby La. Stat | 202 | C3 |
| Harcourt Cres. Nuth | 159 | F2 |
| Harcourt Pl. Ret | 40 | A2 |
| Harcourt Rd. Nott | 173 | D4 |
| Harcourt St. Bees | 183 | F3 |
| Harcourt St. K-in-A | 115 | D3 |
| Harcourt St. Mans | 102 | B3 |
| Harcourt St. N-on-T | 140 | A4 |
| Harcourt Terr. Nott | 173 | E3 |
| Harden Ct. Nott | 195 | E4 |
| Hardie Ave. S Norm | 113 | D3 |
| Hardigate Rd. Cr Bu | 189 | D4 |
| Hardstaff Cl. Ann Wo | 114 | C1 |
| Hardstaff Cl. Ret | 29 | E1 |
| Hardstaff Rd. Nott | 174 | A2 |
| Hardwick Ave. N-on-T | 139 | F4 |
| Hardwick Ave. Rain | 103 | F1 |
| Hardwick Ave. S in A | 101 | D3 |
| Hardwick Ave. Shireb | 72 | C2 |
| Hardwick Cl. S in A | 101 | D3 |
| Hardwick Cres. Work | 36 | A1 |
| Hardwick Ct. Har | 9 | D3 |
| Hardwick Dr. Oll | 77 | D2 |
| Hardwick Dr. Sels | 129 | D4 |
| Hardwick Gr. Nott | 172 | C2 |
| Hardwick Gr. W Brid | 173 | F1 |
| Hardwick La. S in A | 100 | C1 |
| Hardwick Rd E. Work | 36 | A1 |
| Hardwick Rd W. Work | 36 | A1 |
| Hardwick Rd. Nott | 161 | E2 |
| Hardwick St. Nott | 173 | D2 |
| Hardwick St. Mans | 102 | B4 |
| Hardwick St. S in A | 100 | C1 |
| Hardwick St. Scarc | 72 | C4 |
| Hardwick St. Shireb | 73 | D2 |
| Hardwick St. Tibs | 99 | D4 |
| Hardwick View. S in A | 101 | D3 |
| Hardwicke Rd. Bees | 183 | E2 |
| Hardwood Cl. Nott | 159 | F4 |
| Hardy Barn. Ship | 157 | D4 |
| Hardy Cl. Lo Ea | 193 | E3 |
| Hardy Pl. Mans | 101 | F4 |
| Hardy St. Kim | 158 | C4 |
| Hardy St. Nott | 173 | D3 |
| Hardy St. Work | 35 | F1 |
| Hardy's Dr. Carl | 162 | C1 |
| Hardys Cl. Cr Bi | 189 | D2 |
| Hareholme St. Mans | 102 | A4 |
| Harewood Ave. N-on-T | 139 | F4 |
| Harewood Ave. Nott | 160 | B3 |
| Harewood Ave. Ret | 39 | E3 |
| Harewood Cl. R on T | 176 | A2 |
| Harewood Ct. Har | 9 | D3 |
| Harewood Ct. Sand | 182 | A2 |
| Harewood Rd. Work | 35 | F4 |
| Hargon La. Wint | 125 | E3 |
| Harkstead Rd. Nott | 147 | D1 |
| Harlaxton Dr. Lo Ea | 194 | A4 |
| Harlaxton Dr. Nott | 172 | C2 |
| Harlaxton Wlk. Nott | 173 | E3 |
| Harlech Rise. Bees | 183 | D2 |
| Harlequin Ct. East | 143 | E2 |
| Harles Acres. Hick | 210 | B3 |
| Harley St. Nott | 172 | C2 |
| Harlow Ave. Mans | 102 | B2 |
| Harlow Cl. Mans | 88 | B3 |
| Harlow Cl. S in A | 100 | C3 |
| Harlow Gr. Carl | 162 | C1 |
| Harlow St. Blid | 118 | A3 |
| Harmston Rise. Nott | 160 | C2 |
| Harold Ave. Ald | 143 | D2 |
| Harold St. Nott | 173 | F2 |
| Harpenden Sq. Nott | 160 | A2 |
| Harpole Wlk. Nott | 147 | F1 |
| Harriett St. Staple | 182 | B4 |
| Harrimans La. Nott | 184 | C3 |
| Harrington Dr. Nott | 172 | C2 |
| Harrington St. Lo Ea | 193 | D3 |
| Harrington St. Mans | 102 | A3 |
| Harrington St. Work | 35 | E1 |
| Harris Cl. Nott | 171 | F3 |
| Harris Rd. Bees | 183 | E3 |
| Harrison Ct. Bing | 177 | E2 |
| Harrison Dr. Lan | 16 | C2 |
| Harrison Rd. Mans | 101 | F3 |
| Harrison Rd. Staple | 182 | B4 |
| Harrison Way. South | 121 | F1 |
| Harrogate Rd. Nott | 174 | B3 |
| Harrogate St. Carl | 174 | C3 |
| Harrop White Rd. Mans | 101 | F4 |
| Harrow Cl. Gain | 15 | F1 |
| Harrow Cl. Rain | 118 | A4 |
| Harrow Gdns. Nott | 172 | B2 |
| Harrow Rd. Boug | 77 | F3 |
| Harrow Rd. Huck | 145 | E3 |
| Harrow Rd. Nott | 172 | A2 |
| Harrow Rd. W Brid | 185 | F3 |
| Harrowby Rd. Nott | 172 | C2 |
| Harstoft Ave. Work | 35 | F3 |
| Hart Ave. Sand | 182 | A3 |
| Hart St. Nott | 172 | C2 |
| Hartcroft Rd. Nott | 161 | D3 |
| Hartford Cl. Nott | 173 | E1 |
| Hartill Dr. Mans | 101 | E3 |
| Hartington Ave. Carl | 162 | B1 |
| Hartington Ave. Huck | 145 | E3 |
| Hartington Cl. Carl | 163 | D1 |
| Hartington Ct. Mans | 103 | D3 |
| Hartington Dr. S in A | 101 | D2 |
| Hartington Dr. Sels | 129 | D4 |
| Hartington Pl. Ilk | 157 | F3 |
| Hartington Rd. Nott | 161 | E2 |
| Hartington St. Scarc | 72 | C4 |
| Hartland Rd. Work | 35 | F1 |
| Hartley Ct. Nott | 172 | C3 |
| Hartley Dr. Bees | 184 | A3 |
| Hartley Rd. K-in-A | 114 | C3 |
| Hartley Rd. Nott | 172 | C3 |
| Hartness Rd. Nott | 184 | B1 |
| Hartside Cl. Gam | 186 | B4 |
| Hartside Gdns. Lo Ea | 193 | D4 |
| Hartwell St. Nott | 173 | E3 |
| Hartwood Dr. Staple | 170 | B1 |
| Harvest Cl. Nott | 160 | C4 |
| Harvest Cl. Work | 36 | A4 |
| Harvey Ave. Codd | 125 | F1 |
| Harvey Cl. Rudd | 196 | B3 |
| Harvey Croft. Trow | 170 | B2 |
| Harvey Ct. Nott | 172 | C1 |
| Harvey Rd. Mans | 102 | C3 |
| Harvey Rd. Nott | 171 | F4 |
| Harvey's Field. South | 136 | C4 |
| Harwell La. Ever | 11 | D2 |
| Harwell Sluice La. Ever | 11 | D3 |
| Harwich Cl. Nott | 160 | A4 |
| Harwill Cres. Nott | 160 | A1 |
| Harwood Cl. Arn | 162 | A4 |
| Harwood Cl. S in A | 101 | D2 |
| Harwood Pl. S in A | 101 | D2 |
| Harworth Ave. Blyth | 18 | A3 |
| Harworth Cl. Mans | 101 | E3 |
| Haslam St. Nott | 173 | D2 |
| Haslemere Gdns. Raven | 116 | C1 |
| Haslemere Rd. Lo Ea | 193 | D4 |
| Haslemere Rd. Nott | 172 | B4 |
| Hassock La N. Ship | 157 | D4 |
| Hassock La S. Ship | 157 | E3 |
| Hassocks La. Bees | 184 | A4 |
| Hassop Wlk. Mans | 103 | D3 |
| Hastings St. Carl | 174 | B4 |
| Hastings St. Lough | 220 | A2 |
| Haswell Rd. Nott | 160 | A3 |
| Hatchet's La. N-on-T | 125 | D2 |
| Hatfield Ave. Mar War | 74 | C4 |
| Hatfield Ave. Sand | 182 | A2 |
| Hatfield Cl. Rain | 104 | A1 |
| Hatfield Dr. W Brid | 185 | E2 |
| Hatfield Rd. Nott | 161 | E1 |
| Hatfield St. Ret | 40 | A3 |
| Hather Cl. Gams | 51 | D3 |
| Hatherleigh Cl. Carl | 162 | B3 |
| Hatton Cl. Lo Ea | 193 | E3 |
| Hathern Green. Nott | 184 | A4 |
| Hathern Rd. Lo Wh | 212 | B1 |
| Hathersage Ave. Lo Ea | 193 | D3 |
| Hathersage Way. S in A | 100 | C2 |
| Hathersage Wlk. Mans | 103 | D3 |
| Hatley Cl. Nott | 173 | D1 |
| Hatton Cl. Bes Vil | 147 | D1 |
| Hatton Ct. Mans | 103 | D3 |
| Hatton Gdns. N-on-T | 140 | A4 |
| Hatton Gdns. Nott | 159 | F2 |
| Haughgate Hill. N Whea | 22 | A1 |
| Haven Cl. N Clip | 89 | F2 |
| Haven Cl. S in A | 100 | B2 |
| Haven Cl. W Brid | 185 | E3 |
| Haven Hill. Fir | 16 | B3 |
| Haven Hill. Malt | 16 | B3 |
| Havenden Gdns. Nott | 172 | C4 |
| Havenwood Rise. Nott | 195 | E4 |
| Haverhill Cres. Nott | 146 | B1 |
| Haversham Cl. Nott | 160 | B1 |
| Hawarden Terr. Nott | 172 | C4 |
| Hawbush Rd. West | 81 | D3 |
| Hawkesworth Ave. Mans | 89 | D1 |
| Hawkhill Cl. Oll | 77 | D2 |
| Hawkhurst Dr. Nott | 171 | E1 |
| Hawking La. Al Hu | 85 | D4 |
| Hawkins Ct. Ilk | 157 | F2 |
| Hawkridge St. Nott | 173 | E3 |
| Hawksley Gdns. Nott | 184 | B1 |
| Hawksley Rd. Nott | 172 | C4 |
| Hawkswood Cl. Bees | 183 | D2 |
| Hawksworth Ave. Nott | 161 | E2 |
| Hawksworth Rd. Scarr | 178 | C4 |
| Hawksworth Rd. Screv | 167 | D2 |
| Hawksworth Rd. Syer | 153 | D2 |
| Hawksworth St. Nott | 173 | F3 |
| Hawksworth Rd. W Brid | 173 | F1 |
| Hawksworth St. Gain | 24 | B4 |
| Hawley Cl. E Lea | 205 | F1 |
| Hawson Way. Work | 35 | E4 |
| Hawthorn Ave. Gain | 15 | E1 |
| Hawthorn Ave. Glap | 86 | A4 |
| Hawthorn Ave. Huck | 145 | F4 |
| Hawthorn Ave. Staple | 182 | B3 |
| Hawthorn Cl. Beck | 23 | D4 |
| Hawthorn Cl. Boug | 77 | E3 |
| Hawthorn Cl. Keyw | 197 | F1 |
| Hawthorn Cl. Ol Da | 218 | C2 |
| Hawthorn Cl. W Brid | 186 | A2 |
| Hawthorn Cres. Arn | 148 | A1 |
| Hawthorn Cres. K-in-A | 115 | D3 |
| Hawthorn Ct. Nott | 173 | D1 |
| Hawthorn Dr. Boug | 77 | E3 |
| Hawthorn Gr. Gain | 15 | E1 |
| Hawthorn Way. C in L | 25 | F4 |
| Hawthorne Ave. Hath | 213 | D1 |
| Hawthorne Ave. Lo Ea | 193 | F3 |
| Hawthorne Ave. Shireb | 72 | B2 |
| Hawthorne Ave. Tibs | 99 | D4 |
| Hawthorne Cl. S in A | 100 | A3 |
| Hawthorne Cl. Woodb | 149 | E2 |
| Hawthorne Cres. Farn | 139 | D2 |
| Hawthorne Gr. Bees | 184 | A3 |
| Hawthorne Rd. Pinx | 113 | C2 |
| Hawthorne Rise. Awsw | 158 | A2 |
| Hawthorne Way. Edwin | 91 | E4 |
| Hawthorns The. Mar War | 74 | A2 |
| Hawthorns The. Wale | 64 | A1 |
| Hawton Cl. Gain | 15 | F1 |
| Hawton Cl. Mans | 87 | F1 |
| Hawton Cres. Nott | 172 | B2 |
| Hawton La. Bald | 140 | A2 |
| Hawton Rd. N-on-T | 139 | F3 |
| Hawton Spinney. Nott | 172 | B2 |
| Haxey Gate Rd. Haxey | 6 | C3 |
| Haxey Gate Rd. Mist | 6 | C3 |
| Haxey Rd. Mist | 6 | C2 |
| Haycroft Cl. Mans | 88 | C3 |
| Haycroft Way. E Brid | 165 | E1 |
| Hayden La. Huck | 131 | D1 |
| Hayden La. Linby | 131 | D1 |
| Haydn Ave. Nott | 173 | D3 |
| Haydn Rd. Nott | 161 | D1 |
| Haydock Cl. Kim | 158 | C4 |
| Hayes Cl. Pinx | 113 | E2 |
| Hayes Rd. Keyw | 197 | F2 |
| Hayland Dr. Nott | 160 | B1 |
| Hayles Cl. Nott | 161 | D3 |
| Hayling Cl. Ship | 157 | E2 |
| Haynes Ave. Trow | 170 | B3 |
| Haynes Cl. Nott | 184 | C2 |
| Haynes Cl. Tux | 66 | A2 |
| Hayward Ave. Lough | 220 | B1 |
| Haywood Ave. Blid | 118 | A3 |
| Haywood Ct. Nott | 173 | F2 |
| Haywood Oaks La. Blid | 118 | B2 |
| Haywood Rd. Carl | 162 | A2 |
| Haywood St. Nott | 173 | F2 |
| Hayworth Rd. Sand | 182 | A3 |
| Hazel Bank. Mans | 102 | C4 |
| Hazel Cl. Boug | 178 | A2 |
| Hazel Cres. Shireb | 72 | B2 |
| Hazel Dr. Nuth | 159 | D3 |
| Hazel Gr. Arn | 162 | A2 |
| Hazel Gr. Bald | 140 | B3 |
| Hazel Gr. Huck | 146 | A3 |
| Hazel Gr. K-in-A | 115 | E3 |
| Hazel Gr. Mans | 88 | A3 |
| Hazel Gr. S Norm | 113 | D3 |
| Hazel Hill Cres. Nott | 161 | D4 |
| Hazel Meadows. Huck | 146 | A3 |
| Hazel St. Nott | 160 | A4 |
| Hazel St. S in A | 100 | B4 |
| Hazelbank Ave. Nott | 161 | F1 |
| Hazelby Rd. Elmt | 58 | C4 |
| Hazelhurst Gdns. Nott | 160 | A4 |
| Hazelwood Cl. East | 144 | A1 |
| Hazelwood Cl. Mans | 89 | D1 |
| Hazelwood Dr. Huck | 145 | E3 |
| Hazelwood La. Head | 41 | F1 |
| Hazelwood Rd. Nott | 172 | C4 |
| Hazelwood. Cotg | 188 | A2 |
| Headingley Gdns. Nott | 172 | B4 |
| Headland Ave. Elk | 50 | A2 |
| Headstead Bank. Cott | 43 | E3 |
| Heafield Dr. Kegw | 203 | E1 |
| Healdswood St. S in A | 100 | B4 |
| Healey Cl. Coll | 112 | A4 |
| Healey Cl. Nott | 173 | E1 |
| Heanor Rd. Ilk | 157 | E2 |
| Heanor Wlk. Mans | 103 | D3 |
| Heapham Cres. Gain | 24 | C4 |
| Heapham Rd. Gain | 24 | C4 |
| Heard Cres. Bees | 183 | F4 |
| Heath Ave. Mans | 103 | D4 |
| Heath Gdns. Lo Ea | 193 | D4 |
| Heath The. Greas | 158 | A4 |
| Heathcoat St. Lough | 220 | A2 |
| Heathcoat St. Nott | 173 | E3 |
| Heathcote Pl. S in A | 101 | D1 |
| Heather Cl. Greas | 144 | B1 |
| Heather Cl. K-in-A | 114 | C3 |
| Heather Cl. Nott | 173 | E4 |
| Heather Cl. S Norm | 113 | D2 |
| Heather Cl. Tick | 8 | A4 |
| Heather Croft. W Brid | 185 | E2 |
| Heather Rd. Carl | 162 | B1 |
| Heather Rise. Bees | 171 | F1 |
| Heather Way. Mans | 103 | D3 |
| Heatherley Dr. Mans | 88 | C1 |
| Heatherley Dr. Nott | 160 | C2 |
| Heathers The. Boug | 77 | F3 |
| Heathervale. W Brid | 185 | D3 |
| Heathfield Ave. Ilk | 170 | A4 |
| Heathfield Cl. K-in-A | 114 | C4 |
| Heathfield Gdns. Ret | 39 | F4 |
| Heathfield Gdns. Tibs | 99 | D4 |
| Heathfield Gr. Bees | 183 | E2 |
| Heathfield Rd. Nott | 160 | |
| Heathing Gdns. Nott | 147 | |
| Heathland Cl. Mans | 103 | |
| Heaton Cl. N-on-T | 140 | |
| Heaton Cl. Nott | 161 | |
| Heaton St. Gain | 24 | |
| Heavytrees Ave. Raven | 117 | |
| Hecadeck La. Ne Br | 219 | |
| Heckdyke La. Haxey | 7 | |
| Heckington Dr. Nott | 172 | |
| Heddington Gdns. Arn | 161 | |
| Heddon Bar. Mans | 88 | |
| Hedley St. Nott | 173 | |
| Hedley Villas. Nott | 161 | |
| Helen Cl. Bees | 183 | |
| Helenship La. Lane | 54 | |
| Hellebore Cl. Nott | 160 | |
| Helm Cl. Nott | 159 | |
| Helmsdale Cl. Arn | 148 | |
| Helmsdale Cl. Mans | 101 | |
| Helmsdale Gdns. Nott | 146 | |
| Helmsley Rd. Mans | 103 | |
| Helston Dr. Nott | 159 | |
| Helvellyn Cl. Nott | 173 | |
| Hemingway Cl. Carl | 174 | |
| Hemingway Cl. Greas | 144 | |
| Hemlock Ave. Lo Ea | 182 | |
| Hemlock Ave. Staple | 182 | |
| Hemlock Gdns. Nott | 159 | |
| Hemmingfield Cl. Work | 35 | |
| Hemmingfield Cres. Work | 35 | |
| Hemmingfield Rd. Work | 36 | |
| Hemmingfield Way. Work | 36 | |
| Hemplands La. S on T | 96 | |
| Hemplands The. Coll | 98 | |
| Hempshill La. Nott | 160 | |
| Hemsby Gdns. Nott | 160 | |
| Hemscott Cl. Nott | 159 | |
| Hemsley Dr. East | 143 | |
| Hemswell Cl. Nott | 174 | |
| Hendon Rise. Nott | 173 | |
| Hendre Gdns. Nott | 161 | |
| Henley Cl. Carl | 175 | |
| Henley Ct. Gain | 15 | |
| Henley Gdns. Staple | 170 | |
| Henley Rise. Nott | 161 | |
| Henning Gdns. Nott | 161 | |
| Henning La. S in A | 100 | |
| Hennymoor Cl. Whit | 45 | |
| Hennymoor La. Whit | 45 | |
| Henrietta St. Nott | 160 | |
| Henry Ave. Mans | 88 | |
| Henry Ct. Nott | 173 | |
| Henry Rd. Bees | 184 | |
| Henry Rd. Nott | 172 | |
| Henry Rd. W Brid | 185 | |
| Henry St. Huck | 146 | |
| Henry St. Nott | 147 | |
| Henry St. Nott | 173 | |
| Henry St. S in A | 100 | |
| Henshaw Pl. Ilk | 157 | |
| Henson Cl. Cr Bu | 176 | |
| Henson La. Cr Bu | 176 | |
| Henson's Sq. Bees | 183 | |
| Henton Rd. Edwin | 76 | |
| Hepple Dr. Nott | 159 | |
| Herald Cl. Bees | 184 | |
| Herbert Rd. Ann Wo | 115 | |
| Herbert Rd. Nott | 161 | |
| Herbert St. Lough | 220 | |
| Herbert St. Mans | 102 | |
| Hereford Ave. Mans | 88 | |
| Hereford Ave. Oll | 77 | |
| Hereford Cl. Work | 36 | |
| Hereford Cl. Arn | 161 | |
| Hereford Rd. Carl | 162 | |
| Hereford Rd. Nott | 174 | |
| Hereford Rd. Raven | 117 | |
| Herewood Cl. Shireb | 72 | |
| Hermes Cl. Baw | 9 | |
| Hermitage Ave. Mans | 101 | |
| Hermitage La. Mans | 101 | |
| Hermitage Sq. Nott | 173 | |
| Hermitage Way. Mans | 101 | |
| Hermitage Wlk. Nott | 173 | |
| Hermon St. Nott | 173 | |
| Herne St. S in A | 101 | |
| Heron Dr. Nott | 172 | |
| Heron Way. Bald | 140 | |
| Heron Wharf. Nott | 172 | |
| Herons Ct. W Brid | 186 | |
| Herrick Rd. Lough | 220 | |
| Herril Ings. Tick | 8 | |
| Hervey Green. Nott | 184 | |
| Heskey Cl. Nott | 173 | |
| Heskey Wlk. Nott | 173 | |
| Heslington Ave. Nott | 172 | |
| Hethbeth Ct. Nott | 173 | |
| Hethersett Gdns. Nott | 160 | |
| Hetley Rd. Bees | 183 | |
| Hett's La. Mar War | 74 | |
| Hewett St. Mar War | 73 | |
| Hewson's La. Coll | 112 | |
| Hexham Ave. Ilk | 170 | |
| Hexham Cl. W Brid | 186 | |
| Hexham Gdns. Bes Vil | 147 | |
| Hey St. Lo Ea | 193 | |
| Heyward St. Mans | 102 | B4 |

# eywood Cl. South

wood Cl. South .......... 121 F1
wood Cl. Mans .......... 102 B4
bert Cres. S in A .......... 101 D2
bert Rd. Mans .......... 102 B4
kings La. Staple .......... 182 C4
kling Ct. Mans .......... 102 B4
kling La. Lo Cl .......... 211 D2
kling Rd. Carl .......... 162 A1
kling Rd. Kinou .......... 200 A1
kling Way. Cotg .......... 188 A1
kman Cres. Mort .......... 15 E2
kman St. Gain .......... 24 C4
kman St. Gain .......... 24 B4
kory Cl. K-in-A .......... 114 C4
e Hill View. Toll .......... 186 B1
h Church St. Nott .......... 161 D1
h Cl. Ann Wo .......... 115 D1
h Common La. Aust .......... 3 D3
h Common La. Tick .......... 9 D4
h Cres. Ann Wo .......... 115 D1
h Cross St. Nott .......... 173 E3
h Cross. Bleas .......... 136 C1
h Field La. Aust .......... 3 D2
gh Hoe Ct. Work .......... 36 A2
gh Hoe Dr. Work .......... 36 A2
gh Hoe Rd. Work .......... 36 A2
gh Holborn. Ilk .......... 157 F2
h Hurst. Calv .......... 148 C4
gh La Central. WeHa .......... 157 D1
gh La E. WeHa .......... 157 D1
gh Leys Rd. Huck .......... 145 F3
gh Meadow. Baw .......... 9 F4
gh Meadow. Hath .......... 213 D1
gh Meadow. Toll .......... 186 B1
gh Oakham Dr. Mans .......... 102 A2
gh Oakham Hill. Mans .......... 102 A2
gh Oakham Rd. Mans .......... 102 A2
gh Park Cotts. Greas .......... 144 B3
gh Pavement. Nott .......... 173 E2
h Pavement. S in A .......... 100 C1
gh Rd. Bees .......... 183 D1
gh Rd. Bees .......... 183 E2
gh Rd. Bees .......... 184 A4
gh Rd. C in L .......... 26 A3
gh Ridge. Mans .......... 88 C1
gh Spania. Kim .......... 158 C4
gh St. Arn .......... 161 F4
gh St. Baw .......... 10 A4
gh St. Beck .......... 23 D4
gh St. Blyth .......... 18 A1
gh St. Bott .......... 181 D1
gh St. Brin .......... 128 B1
gh St. Coll .......... 98 A1
gh St. Coll .......... 112 A4
gh St. E Mark .......... 65 F4
gh St. Eagle .......... 84 B2
gh St. Edwin .......... 76 A1
gh St. Elk .......... 50 A2
gh St. Ever .......... 11 E2
gh St. G on H .......... 12 C1
gh St. Gain .......... 24 B4
gh St. Girt .......... 82 C1
gh St. Harby .......... 70 C1
gh St. Huck .......... 146 A4
gh St. Kegw .......... 203 E1
gh St. Kim .......... 158 C3
gh St. Lo Ea .......... 193 F4
gh St. Lough .......... 220 A2
gh St. Mans .......... 87 D3
gh St. Mans .......... 88 B2
gh St. Mans .......... 102 A3
gh St. Mar War .......... 74 A2
gh St. Mart .......... 44 B4
gh St. Miss .......... 4 B1
gh St. Mist .......... 6 C1
gh St. N Sca .......... 83 E1
gh St. Ne on T .......... 55 D1
gh St. Nott .......... 173 E2
gh St. Orst .......... 179 F4
gh St. Ret .......... 39 F2
gh St. Rudd .......... 196 B4
gh St. S in A .......... 100 A2
gh St. S in A .......... 100 B1
gh St. S in A .......... 100 B3
gh St. S in V .......... 169 D2
gh St. S Lev .......... 42 B3
gh St. S Norm .......... 113 D3
gh St. S on T .......... 96 C4
gh St. Sax .......... 57 D2
gh St. Staple .......... 182 C4
gh St. Tibs .......... 99 D4
gh St. Walker .......... 13 F3
High Street Ave. Arn .......... 161 F4
High Street Pl. Nott .......... 173 E2
High Tor. S in A .......... 100 C4
High View Ave. Keyw .......... 198 A2
High View Rd. S Norm .......... 113 E4
Highbank Dr. Nott .......... 195 F4
Highbury Ave. Nott .......... 160 B3
Highbury Cl. Nuth .......... 159 F2
Highbury Rd. Keyw .......... 197 F2
Highbury Rd. Nott .......... 160 B3
Highbury Wlk. Nott .......... 160 B3
Highclere Dr. Carl .......... 174 C4
Highcliffe Ave. Shireb .......... 72 B2
Highcliffe Rd. Nott .......... 174 A2
Highcroft Cl. Lo Ea .......... 193 F3
Highcroft Dr. Nott .......... 171 D3

Highcroft. Arn .......... 161 F2
Highcross Ct. Nott .......... 172 C3
Highcross Hill. South .......... 136 B2
Highfield Ave. K-in-A .......... 114 C3
Highfield Ave. Mans .......... 88 A1
Highfield Ave. Shireb .......... 72 B3
Highfield Cl. Gain .......... 15 F1
Highfield Cl. Mans .......... 88 A1
Highfield Cl. Raven .......... 117 D1
Highfield Ct. Bees .......... 183 F3
Highfield Dr. Bils .......... 105 F2
Highfield Dr. Carl .......... 174 A4
Highfield Dr. Nuth .......... 159 F2
Highfield Dr. S Norm .......... 113 D3
Highfield Dr. Stap .......... 127 D2
Highfield Gr. W Brid .......... 185 F4
Highfield Grove. C in L .......... 26 A3
Highfield La. Work .......... 36 B1
Highfield Rd. Baw .......... 10 A4
Highfield Rd. Bees .......... 183 D2
Highfield Rd. Keyw .......... 197 F2
Highfield Rd. N Clip .......... 90 A2
Highfield Rd. Nott .......... 172 B1
Highfield Rd. Nuth .......... 159 F2
Highfield Rd. S in A .......... 100 B2
Highfield Rd. Sax .......... 57 D2
Highfield Rd. W Brid .......... 185 F4
Highfield La. Lo Ea .......... 182 B1
Highfield Terr. Mans .......... 102 A3
Highfield Villas. C in L .......... 25 F4
Highfield Way. Mans .......... 102 A3
Highfield. Ret .......... 29 E1
Highfields Science Pk. Nott 172 C1
Highgate Cl. Carl .......... 162 B1
Highgate Dr. Ship .......... 157 E2
Highgate La. Plun .......... 202 C4
Highgrove Ave. Bees .......... 183 E3
Highgrove Gdns. W Brid .......... 186 A2
Highland Cl. Mans .......... 88 B2
Highland Gr. Work .......... 36 A3
Highland Rd. Mans .......... 102 C1
Highurst St. Nott .......... 173 D3
Highwood Ave. Nott .......... 171 F4
Highwray Gr. Nott .......... 184 B1
Hilary Cl. Nott .......... 171 E2
Hilcot Dr. Nott .......... 160 B1
Hilcote La. Newt .......... 99 D1
Hilcote St. S Norm .......... 113 D3
Hill Cl. East .......... 144 B1
Hill Cl. W Brid .......... 186 A3
Hill Cres. Gain .......... 15 F1
Hill Cres. S in A .......... 101 D2
Hill Crest Gr. Nott .......... 161 D2
Hill Crest. Shireb .......... 72 B2
Hill Dr. Bing .......... 177 E3
Hill Farm Cl. Toll .......... 186 B1
Hill Farm Ct. W Brid .......... 186 A1
Hill Fields. S Norm .......... 113 D2
Hill Rd. Bes Vil .......... 146 C2
Hill Rd. Goth .......... 205 D4
Hill Rd. Har .......... 8 C2
Hill Rd. Orst .......... 180 A3
Hill Rise. Trow .......... 170 B2
Hill Side. Nott .......... 172 B2
Hill St. Mans .......... 87 D3
Hill St. Ret .......... 39 F2
Hill St. Work .......... 35 F1
Hill Syke. Lowd .......... 150 A1
Hill The. K-in-A .......... 114 C3
Hill Top Ave. Shireb .......... 72 C2
Hill Top Ct. Har .......... 9 D2
Hill Top. Orst .......... 180 A3
Hill View Rd. Bees .......... 183 D1
Hill View Rd. K-in-A .......... 115 E3
Hill Vue Ave. N-on-T .......... 140 A4
Hill Vue Gdns. N-on-T .......... 140 A4
Hillary Way. Bald .......... 140 C2
Hillbeck Cres. Nott .......... 171 E2
Hillcrest Ave. S Norm .......... 113 D2
Hillcrest Cl. Kim .......... 159 D4
Hillcrest Dr. Huck .......... 145 E3
Hillcrest Gdns. Bu Jo .......... 163 F3
Hillcrest Mews. Ret .......... 40 A4
Hillcrest Rd. Keyw .......... 197 F2
Hillcrest View. Carl .......... 162 A1
Hillcrest. South .......... 136 B4
Hillfield Gdns. Nott .......... 146 C1
Hillfield Rd. Staple .......... 170 C1
Hillgrove Gdns. Nott .......... 161 D4
Hilliers Ct. Nott .......... 160 C4
Hillington Rise. Nott .......... 161 E4
Hillmoor St. Mans .......... 87 E2
Hills Rd. Arn .......... 161 F2
Hillsborough Ave. S in A .......... 114 B4
Hillsborough Way. S in A .......... 114 B4
Hillsford Cl. Nott .......... 172 A3
Hillside Ave. Arn .......... 162 A2
Hillside Ave. Mist .......... 7 D1
Hillside Cres. Bees .......... 183 F4
Hillside Cres. Work .......... 35 F3
Hillside Dr. Bu Jo .......... 163 F3
Hillside Dr. Lo Ea .......... 193 D4
Hillside Dr. South .......... 136 B4
Hillside Gr. Sand .......... 182 A3
Hillside Rd. Bees .......... 183 D2
Hillside Rd. Bees .......... 183 E4
Hillside Rd. Blid .......... 118 A2
Hillside Rd. R on T .......... 176 A2

Hillside Wlk. Blid .......... 118 A2
Hillside. Beckin .......... 142 B4
Hillside. Kegw .......... 203 E1
Hillside. La Mi .......... 143 D2
Hillside. Tux .......... 66 A2
Hillsway Cres. Mans .......... 102 A2
Hillsway. Shireb .......... 72 B2
Hilltop Cl. Eagle .......... 84 B2
Hilltop Rd. Pinx .......... 113 E2
Hillview Ave. Nott .......... 161 E1
Hillview Cres. Clar .......... 30 C2
Hillview Rd. Carl .......... 162 A1
Hillview Rd. Ret .......... 39 F2
Hilton Cres. W Brid .......... 186 A3
Hilton Ct. W Brid .......... 186 A3
Hilton Rd. Carl .......... 162 A2
Hind St. Ret .......... 40 A3
Hindlow Ct. Mans .......... 103 D3
Hine Ave. N-on-T .......... 140 C4
Hinsley Cl. Arn .......... 162 A4
Hirst Cres. Nott .......... 171 F2
Hirst Rd. Ret .......... 40 A4
Hives La. N Sca .......... 83 E2
Hobart Cl. Nott .......... 173 E1
Hobart Dr. Staple .......... 170 C1
Hobhouse Rd. Mans .......... 87 E1
Hobsic Cl. Brin .......... 143 E4
Hobsic La. Sels .......... 128 C4
Hobson's Acre. Gunt .......... 165 D3
Hockerton Rd. South .......... 122 A2
Hockerton Rd. Upton .......... 122 C1
Hockerwood La. Upton .......... 122 B1
Hockerwood. Nott .......... 184 C2
Hockley Pl. K-in-A .......... 114 C2
Hockley. Nott .......... 173 E2
Hodgkin Cl. Nott .......... 184 B1
Hodgkinson Rd. K-in-A .......... 115 D2
Hodgkinson St. Carl .......... 175 D3
Hodmire La. Al Hu .......... 85 F4
Hodsock La. C in L .......... 26 A3
Hoe La. Cr Bu .......... 189 D3
Hoe Nook. Cr Bi .......... 189 D2
Hoe View Rd. Cr Bi .......... 189 D2
Hoefield Cres. Nott .......... 160 A3
Hoewood Rd. Nott .......... 160 A4
Hogan Gdns. Nott .......... 147 D1
Hogarth Cl. Staple .......... 182 C3
Hogarth St. Nott .......... 173 F3
Hogg La. R on T .......... 175 F2
Hoggetts Cl. Bees .......... 183 D3
Holbeck La. Holb .......... 59 E4
Holbeck Rd. Huck .......... 131 D1
Holbeck Rd. Nott .......... 172 B3
Holbeck Way. Rain .......... 104 A1
Holbein Cl. Lough .......... 220 B2
Holborn Ave. Nott .......... 173 F2
Holborn Cl. Nuth .......... 159 E2
Holborn Pl. Nott .......... 160 B4
Holbrook Cl. Plea .......... 87 D3
Holbrook Ct. Mans .......... 103 D3
Holbrook Ct. Nott .......... 195 F4
Holbrook St. Hean .......... 143 D1
Holby Cl. Nott .......... 160 C4
Holcombe Cl. Nott .......... 160 A1
Holdale Rd. Nott .......... 174 A3
Holden Cres. N-on-T .......... 139 F3
Holden Cres. Nuth .......... 159 E3
Holden Rd. Bees .......... 183 F4
Holden St. Mans .......... 102 A3
Holden St. Nott .......... 173 D3
Holdenby Cl. Ret .......... 40 A4
Holderness Cl. Har .......... 9 D2
Holding. Work .......... 36 A3
Holds La. Torw .......... 19 D1
Holgate Rd. Nott .......... 173 E1
Holgate Wlk. Huck .......... 145 F3
Holgate. Nott .......... 184 B1
Holkham Ave. Bees .......... 183 E3
Holkham Cl. Arn .......... 162 A3
Holkham Cl. Ship .......... 157 E2
Holland Cl. Goth .......... 195 D1
Holland Cres. Sels .......... 129 D4
Holland Meadow. Lo Ea .......... 193 E3
Holland St. Nott .......... 172 C4
Holles St. Work .......... 35 F1
Hollies Ave. Codd .......... 125 D2
Hollies Cres. Nott .......... 173 D2
Hollies Dr. W Brid .......... 186 A2
Hollies The. Boug .......... 77 F3
Hollies The. East .......... 143 F1
Hollies The. Rain .......... 104 A1
Hollies The. Sand .......... 182 A3
Hollington Rd. Nott .......... 172 A3
Hollington Way. Mans .......... 103 D4
Hollingwood La. Calv .......... 133 E1
Hollingworth Ave. Sand .......... 182 A2
Hollins The. Calv .......... 149 D4
Hollinwell Ave. Nott .......... 172 B3
Hollinwell Cl. K-in-A .......... 114 C4
Hollinwell Ct. W Brid .......... 186 A2
Hollis St. Nott .......... 161 D1
Hollow Stone. Nott .......... 173 E2
Holloway Cl. E Brid .......... 165 E2
Hollowdyke La. Bald .......... 140 C1
Hollowdyke La. Bald .......... 140 C2

Hollowgate La. H Marn .......... 68 A1
Hollows The. Lo Ea .......... 194 A4
Hollows The. Mapl .......... 108 A4
Hollows The. Nott .......... 185 D2
Hollows The. Thur .......... 151 E4
Holly Ave. Carl .......... 174 B4
Holly Ave. Nott .......... 174 A4
Holly Ave. Nott .......... 185 D4
Holly Bush Cl. Elk .......... 50 A2
Holly Cl. Bing .......... 178 A2
Holly Cl. Huck .......... 146 A3
Holly Ct. Bees .......... 183 E4
Holly Ct. Har .......... 8 C2
Holly Ct. Mans .......... 88 C1
Holly Ct. Ret .......... 39 F3
Holly Dr. Mans .......... 89 D1
Holly Farm Ct. Greas .......... 144 B1
Holly Gdns. Nott .......... 173 F4
Holly Gr. K-in-A .......... 114 C3
Holly Hill Rd. Sels .......... 128 C3
Holly Hill Rd. Sels .......... 129 D3
Holly La. Bees .......... 183 F3
Holly Rd. Kim .......... 159 D4
Holly Rd. Mans .......... 89 D1
Holly Rd. Ret .......... 40 A3
Holly Rise. Oll .......... 77 E3
Hollycroft. W Brid .......... 186 A2
Hollydale Rd. Nott .......... 174 A3
Hollydene Cl. Huck .......... 145 E3
Hollydene Cres. Nott .......... 160 A2
Hollygate La. Cotg .......... 188 A3
Hollyhouse Dr. S Norm .......... 113 D3
Hollythorpe Pl. Huck .......... 145 E3
Hollytree Cl. Hoton .......... 215 E1
Holme Ave. E Lea .......... 205 F2
Holme Cl. Woodb .......... 149 E2
Holme Gr. W Brid .......... 174 A1
Holme La. E Mark .......... 51 E1
Holme La. Edin .......... 120 C2
Holme La. Egma .......... 79 F3
Holme La. Halam .......... 120 C2
Holme La. Ho Pi .......... 175 E2
Holme La. Holm .......... 125 E4
Holme La. L Marn .......... 82 A4
Holme La. Langf .......... 111 F2
Holme La. Nor on T .......... 82 A3
Holme La. R on T .......... 175 E2
Holme La. W Dray .......... 51 E1
Holme La. Wint .......... 125 E4
Holme Rd. Bing .......... 178 A2
Holme Rd. W Brid .......... 174 A1
Holme St. Nott .......... 173 F1
Holme The. South .......... 136 A4
Holmecroft Ave. S in A .......... 100 C3
Holmefield Cres. Ilk .......... 170 A4
Holmefield Rd. Whit .......... 45 D3
Holmefield Wlk. Mans .......... 103 D3
Holmes Cl. La Mi .......... 143 D2
Holmes Rd. Ret .......... 39 F4
Holmewood Cres. Nott .......... 161 D3
Holmewood Dr. Greas .......... 158 A4
Holmfield Cl. Work .......... 36 A3
Holmfield Rd. Bees .......... 183 E2
Holmhurst Cl. Work .......... 35 F3
Holmsfield. Keyw .......... 197 F1
Holmwood Rd. Rain .......... 104 B1
Holroyd Ave. Nott .......... 173 F2
Holt Dr. Lough .......... 220 A1
Holt Gr. Calv .......... 148 C4
Holt The. N-on-T .......... 139 E3
Holwood Ct. Nott .......... 160 A3
Holyoake Rd. Carl .......... 162 B2
Holyrood Ct. Bees .......... 171 E1
Holywell Rd. Ship .......... 157 E2
Home Cl. Arn .......... 161 E4
Home Croft The. Bees .......... 183 D4
Home Farm Cl. Goth .......... 195 D1
Home Fm Ct. Sels .......... 128 B3
Home Meadows. Tick .......... 8 A3
Home Pastures. Hose .......... 211 F4
Homecroft Dr. Sels .......... 128 C4
Homefarm La. Thor .......... 70 A3
Homefield Ave. Arn .......... 148 A1
Homefield Rd. Nott .......... 172 B4
Homelands The. S in A .......... 100 C1
Homestead. Ald .......... 143 D2
Homesteads The. Mar War .. 74 A2
Homewood Dr. K-in-A .......... 114 C4
Honeyknab La. Oxt .......... 134 B3
Honeys La. Bart .......... 139 D1
Honeysuckle Cl. Bald .......... 140 B2
Honeysuckle Cl. Nott .......... 159 F1
Honeywood Dr. Carl .......... 174 A4
Honeywood Wlk. Carl .......... 174 A4
Honing Dr. South .......... 136 B4
Honingham Cl. Arn .......... 161 F4
Honingham Rd. Arn .......... 161 F4
Honister Cl. Gam .......... 186 B4
Honister Cl. Mans .......... 102 B3
Honister Cl. Nott .......... 195 E4
Honister Ct. Mans .......... 102 B3
Honiton Cl. Bees .......... 183 D1
Honiton Rd. Nott .......... 159 F1
Hood St. Nott .......... 161 E1
Hooley Cl. Lo Ea .......... 193 D3
Hooley Pl. Nott .......... 161 E2
Hooley St. Sels .......... 128 C3
Hoopers Wlk. Nott .......... 173 E1

Hooton Rd. Carl .......... 174 B4
Hooton St. Nott .......... 173 F3
Hope Cl. Nott .......... 173 D1
Hope Dr. Nott .......... 173 D2
Hope St. Bees .......... 183 F4
Hope St. Mans .......... 102 B3
Hopedale Cl. Nott .......... 172 C3
Hopewell Cl. R on T .......... 176 A2
Hopewell Wlk. Ilk .......... 157 F3
Hopkiln La. South .......... 121 E1
Hopkins Ct. East .......... 143 F2
Hopyard La. Egma .......... 79 F4
Hopyard La. Nor on T .......... 82 A3
Horace Ave. Staple .......... 182 B3
Hornbeam Cl. Ilk .......... 170 A4
Hornbeam Gdns. Nott .......... 159 F4
Hornbuckle Ct. Nott .......... 172 C3
Hornchurch Rd. Nott .......... 171 E4
Hornsby Wlk. Nott .......... 160 C4
Horridge St. Ilk .......... 157 F2
Horsendale Ave. Nuth .......... 159 F2
Horsewells St. G on H .......... 12 C1
Horsham Dr. Nott .......... 160 C4
Horsley Cres. La Mi .......... 143 D2
Hose La. Hose .......... 201 D2
Hose La. Hose .......... 202 A1
Hose La. Hose .......... 211 F3
Hose La. Lo Cl .......... 211 F3
Hoselett Field Rd. Lo Ea .......... 193 F3
Hosiery St. K-in-A .......... 115 D3
Hospital Dr. R on T .......... 176 B2
Hospital Rd. Ret .......... 39 F4
Hoten Rd. Nott .......... 173 F2
Hoton Rd. Wyme .......... 216 A2
Hotspur Cl. Nott .......... 160 C3
Hotspur Rd. Gain .......... 15 E1
Houfton Rd. Mans .......... 102 C4
Hougham Rd. Dry Do .......... 156 C1
Houghton Cl. Nuth .......... 159 F2
Houldsworth Rise. Nott .......... 147 F1
Hound Rd. W Brid .......... 185 F4
Hounds Gate. Nott .......... 173 D2
Hounsfield Cl. N-on-T .......... 140 C4
Hounsfield Way. S on T .......... 96 C4
Houseman Gdns. Nott .......... 173 E1
Houston Cl. Nott .......... 146 C1
Hove Rd. Nott .......... 160 C3
Hoveringham Rd. Cayt .......... 165 E4
Hoveringham Rd. Hover .......... 165 E4
Howard Cl. Lo Ea .......... 182 C1
Howard Rd. Bir .......... 9
Howard Rd. Mans .......... 101 F4
Howard St. Lough .......... 220 A3
Howard St. Nott .......... 173 E3
Howard St. S in A .......... 100 C2
Howard St. Work .......... 36 A1
Howbeck La. Clar .......... 30 C2
Howbeck Rd. Arn .......... 162 A4
Howden Rd. Nott .......... 146 B1
Howe Rd. Lough .......... 220 A1
Howells Cl. Nott .......... 161 E4
Howes Ct. N-on-T .......... 140 A4
Howick Dr. Nott .......... 159 F4
Howitt St. Hean .......... 143 D1
Howitt St. Lo Ea .......... 193 F4
Hoylake Cres. Nott .......... 171 E4
Hoyland Ave. Nott .......... 172 C1
Hubert St. Nott .......... 172 C3
Hucklow Ct. Mans .......... 103 D3
Hucknall Cres. Carl .......... 162 C1
Hucknall La. Nott .......... 146 B1
Hucknall Rd. Ann Wo .......... 130 B3
Hucknall Rd. News .......... 130 B3
Hucknall Rd. Nott .......... 160 C3
Huddlestones Whrf. N-on-T 139 F4
Hudson Dr. Lough .......... 220 B2
Hudson St. Nott .......... 173 F3
Hufton's Ct. Ship .......... 157 D4
Hufton's Dr. Ship .......... 157 D4
Hugessen Ave. Huck .......... 146 B4
Hugget Gdns. Nott .......... 161 D4
Humber Cl. Nott .......... 173 E1
Humber La. E Sto .......... 153 D4
Humber Rd S. Bees .......... 184 A3
Humber Rd. Bees .......... 184 A4
Humber Rd. Lo Ea .......... 182 B1
Humber St. Ret .......... 40 A4
Humber St. Work .......... 35 F2
Humberston Rd. Nott .......... 171 E2
Hume St. Lough .......... 220 B2
Hundred Acre La. C in L .......... 26 B2
Hundred Acres La. Bald .......... 140 B3
Hundreds La. G on H .......... 5 D2
Hungary La. Su Bo .......... 213 D4
Hungerhill Rd. Nott .......... 173 E4
Hungerton St. Nott .......... 172 C3
Hunston Cl. Nott .......... 172 A4
Hunt's Hill. Greas .......... 144 A4
Hunter Rd. Arn .......... 162 B3
Hunter's Dr. G on H .......... 12 C1
Hunters Cl. Nott .......... 185 D3
Hunters Ct. K-in-A .......... 114 C3
Huntingdon Dr. Nott .......... 173 D2
Huntingdon St. Nott .......... 173 E3
Huntingdon Wlk. Bees .......... 182 C1
Huntingdon Wlk. Sand .......... 182 A3
Huntly Cl. Mans .......... 101 E3
Huntly Cl. Nott .......... 184 C1

Huntsman Pl. Torw ............. 19 D1
Hurcomb St. Nott ............. 173 F4
Hurst Cl. Mans .............. 103 F1
Hurt's Yd. Nott ............... 173 E2
Hurts Croft. Bees ........... 183 E2
Huss's La. Lo Ea ............ 193 F4
Hutchinson Green. Nott ..... 173 E3
Huthwaite La. Newt .......... 99 E1
Huthwaite Rd. S in A ........ 100 B1
Hutton Cl. Bees ............. 171 E1
Hutton St. Nott .............. 173 F2
Huxley Cl. Nott .............. 171 E4
Hyde Cl. Nott ............... 184 C2
Hyson Cl. Nott .............. 172 C4
Hyson St. Nott .............. 172 C4

Ian Gr. Carl ................. 174 C4
Icle View. Ret ................ 29 F1
Idle Bank. Haxey ............. 2 B2
Idle Bank. Miss ............... 5 E4
Idle Bank. Wroot ............. 2 B2
Idlewells Shpg Cntr. S in A 100 C1
Ilam Sq. Ilk ................. 157 F3
Ilford Rd. Ship ............. 157 E2
Ilion St. Mans ............... 87 F1
Ilkeston Rd. Bees ........... 171 D1
Ilkeston Rd. Hean ........... 157 D4
Ilkeston Rd. S-by-D ......... 182 B4
Ilkeston Rd. Sand ........... 182 B4
Ilkeston Rd. Staple ......... 170 C1
Ilkeston Rd. Trow ........... 170 B3
Imperial Ave. Bees .......... 183 F3
Imperial Ave. Carl .......... 162 C1
Imperial Rd. Bees ........... 183 F3
Imperial Rd. Nott ........... 160 B3
Inchwood Cl. Bees ........... 182 C1
Incinerator Rd. Nott ........ 173 F1
Independent St. Nott ........ 172 C3
Infield La. N Le Ha .......... 32 C1
Infield La. Nort ............. 60 A3
Infield La. West ............. 81 D2
Ingham Gr. Nott ............. 172 C2
Ingham Rd. Baw ............... 9 F4
Ingham Rd. Lo Ea ........... 182 B1
Ingleborough Gdns. Lo Ea . 193 D4
Ingleby Cl. Cotg ........... 187 F1
Ingleby Cl. Nott ............ 171 D2
Inglefield Rd. Ilk .......... 170 A3
Inglemere Cl. Work .......... 36 A3
Inglewood Rd. Nott ......... 184 C1
Ingram La. Grass ............ 82 A2
Ingram La. S on T ........... 82 A2
Ingram Rd. Nott ............ 160 B3
Ingram Terr. Nott ........... 160 B3
Ings Rd. G on H ............. 12 C3
Inham Circus. Bees .......... 183 D3
Inham Cl. Bees .............. 183 D3
Inham Fields Cl. Gunt ....... 165 D3
Inham Rd. Bees .............. 183 D3
Inholms Gdns. Flint ......... 152 C1
Inholms Rd. Flint ........... 152 C1
Inkerman Rd. Sels ........... 128 C3
Inkerman St. Sels ........... 128 C3
Innes Rd. Carl .............. 174 B4
Institute St. S in A ........ 100 B3
Instow Rise. Nott ........... 173 E3
Intake Ave. Mans ............ 101 F3
Intake Rd. Keyw ............. 197 E2
Intake Rd. N Clip ........... 90 A2
Iona Cl. Gain ............... 15 F1
Iona Dr. Staple ............. 170 B1
Iona Gdns. Bes Vil .......... 147 D1
Ipswich Circus. Nott ........ 174 A3
Ireland Ave. Bees ........... 184 A3
Ireland Cl. Bees ............ 184 A3
Iremonger Rd. Nott .......... 173 E1
Irene Terr. Nott ............ 160 C1
Ireton Gr. Bees ............. 183 F3
Ireton St. Bees ............. 183 F3
Ireton St. Nott ............. 173 D3
Irwin Dr. Nott .............. 160 A3
Isaac's La. Staple .......... 182 B4
Isabella St. Nott ........... 173 E2
Island St. Nott ............. 173 E2
Islay Cl. Nott .............. 147 F1
Islay Cl. Staple ............ 170 B2
Ivatt Cl. Baw ............... 10 A4
Iveagh Cl. Mar War .......... 74 B3
Ives Cl. W Brid ............. 185 E2
Ivy Cl. Greas ............... 144 C1
Ivy Gr. Carl ................ 174 B4
Ivy Gr. K-in-A .............. 114 C3
Ivy Gr. Nott ................ 173 D4
Ivy La. East ................ 143 F1
Ivy Lodge La. Let ........... 16 A2
Ivy Row. What ............... 179 D2

Jacklin Gdns. Nott .......... 147 D1
Jackson Ave. Ilk ............ 157 F1
Jackson Ave. Sand ........... 182 A3
Jackson Terr. Mar War ....... 74 C4
James St. Ann Wo ............ 115 D1
James St. Arn ............... 161 F4
James St. Kim ............... 158 C3
James St. Work ............... 35 F3
James William Turner Ave. S in A
................................100 C1
James' Yd. Mans ............. 102 B4

Japan Rd. Gain .............. 15 D1
Jardine. Work ............... 36 A3
Jardines The. Bees .......... 171 E1
Jarrow Gdns. Nott ........... 146 C1
Jarvis Ave. Nott ............ 174 A3
Jasmin Cl. Shireb ........... 72 B3
Jasmine Cl. Bees ............ 171 E1
Jasmine Cl. Nott ............ 159 F1
Jasmine Cl. Nott ............ 184 B1
Jasmine Rd. Nott ............ 160 C2
Jasper Cl. R on T ........... 175 F1
Jayne Cl. Carl .............. 163 D1
Jayne Cl. Nott .............. 171 F3
Jedburgh Cl. Nott ........... 173 E3
Jedburgh Wlk. Nott .......... 173 E3
Jeffares Cl. Kegw ........... 203 E2
Jellicoe St. Scarc .......... 59 D1
Jenford St. Mans ............ 101 F3
Jenkins Ave. Mans ........... 101 E4
Jenned Rd. Arn .............. 148 A1
Jenner St. Nott ............. 161 D1
Jenness Ave. Nott ........... 146 C1
Jennison St. Mans ........... 88 A1
Jenny Beckett's La. Mans .. 102 C2
Jephson Rd. S in A .......... 114 C4
Jericho La. B-le-V .......... 192 A2
Jermyn Dr. Bes Vil .......... 147 D1
Jersey Gdns. Nott ........... 173 F3
Jersey St. N-on-T ........... 139 F3
Jerusalem Rd. Skel .......... 71 F2
Jerusalem. Skel ............. 71 F1
Jervis Ct. Ilk .............. 157 F2
Jesmond Rd. Nott ............ 160 B3
Jessop Cl. N-on-T ........... 125 E1
Jessop Way. N-on-T .......... 125 E1
Jessop's La. Carl ........... 162 C1
Job La. Matt ................ 20 A4
Job's La. Eagle ............. 84 C1
Jockey La. Elk .............. 50 A3
John Carroll Ct. Nott ....... 173 F3
John St. Ilk ................ 157 F1
John St. Nott ............... 160 C1
John St. S in A ............. 100 C2
John St. Work ............... 35 F2
Johns Rd. R on T ............ 176 A2
Johnson Ave. Huck ........... 146 A3
Johnson Dr. Mans ............ 102 B2
Joyce Ave. Bees ............. 182 C2
Joyce Ave. Nott ............. 161 E2
Joyce Cl. Nott .............. 161 E2
Jubilee Cl. Miss ............ 4 C4
Jubilee Dr. Lough ........... 220 A3
Jubilee Rd. Arn ............. 161 F3
Jubilee Rd. Ret ............. 39 E3
Jubilee Rd. S in A .......... 100 B2
Jubilee St. Mans ............ 158 C4
Jubilee St. N-on-T .......... 140 A4
Jubilee St. Nott ............ 173 F2
Jubilee Way N. Mans ......... 103 E3
Jubilee Way S. Mans ......... 103 D2
Judges St. Lough ............ 220 B2
Julian Cl. Ilk .............. 170 A3
Julian La. Shel ............. 164 B1
Julian Rd. W Brid ........... 174 A1
Julie Ave. Hean ............. 143 D1
Jumelles Dr. Calv ........... 148 B4
Junction Rd. Lo Ea .......... 194 A3
Juniper Cl. Nott ............ 184 B1
Juniper Ct. Greas ........... 158 B4
Juniper Gdns. Bing .......... 178 A2

Karen Rise. Arn ............. 148 A1
Katherine Dr. Bees .......... 182 C2
Kaye Rd. Mans ............... 101 E4
Kayes Wlk. Nott ............. 173 E2
Keats Ave. S in A ........... 100 A2
Keats Cl. Arn ............... 161 E4
Keats Cl. Kim ............... 159 D3
Keats Cl. Lo Ea ............. 193 D3
Keats Cres. Work ............ 36 A2
Keats Dr. Huck .............. 145 E3
Keats Rd. Bald .............. 140 A2
Kedleston Cl. Bees .......... 183 E3
Kedleston Cl. Lo Ea ......... 193 D3
Kedleston Dr. Ilk ........... 157 E2
Kedleston Rd. Work .......... 35 F3
Keel Dr. Bott ............... 181 D1
Keeling Cl. East ............ 144 A1
Keep The. E Lea ............. 205 F1
Keepers Cl. Bes Vil ......... 146 C2
Kegworth La. Lo Wh .......... 212 B3
Kegworth Rd. Goth ........... 204 C4
Kegworth Rd. K on S ......... 203 F3
Kegworth Rd. R on S ......... 203 F3
Keighton Hill. Nott ......... 172 B1
Keilder Dr. Bing ............ 177 E2
Kelfield Cl. Nott ........... 160 C3
Kelham Green. Nott .......... 173 F3
Kelham La. N-on-T ........... 124 B2
Kelham La. S Musk ........... 124 B3
Kelham Rd. Mans ............. 101 F4
Kelham Rd. N-on-T ........... 124 C1
Keller Ct. Wood ............. 53 D4
Kelling Cl. Nott ............ 161 D3
Kelsey Cl. Bees ............. 183 F2
Kelso Gdns. Nott ............ 173 D1
Kelstedge Dr. Mans .......... 103 D3
Kelstern Cl. Mans ........... 103 D4

Kelstern Cl. Nott ........... 160 B2
Kelvedon Gdns. Nott ......... 173 F3
Kelvin Cl. Staple ........... 182 B3
Kelvin Rd. Mans ............. 89 E2
Kelvin Rd. Nott ............. 174 A4
Kemmel Rd. Nott ............. 160 B3
Kempsey Cl. Nott ............ 160 C4
Kempson St. Rudd ............ 196 B3
Kempton Cl. Kim ............. 158 C4
Kempton Dr. Arn ............. 148 A1
Kempton Rd. Mans ............ 102 C4
Kendal Cl. Ann Wo ........... 130 A4
Kendal Cl. Huck ............. 145 F4
Kendal Cl. Work ............. 35 F4
Kendal Ct. W Brid ........... 186 A4
Kendal Dr. Bees ............. 183 E4
Kendal Rd. Cr Bi ............ 189 D2
Kendal Rd. Lo Ea ............ 182 A1
Kendale Ct. Nott ............ 161 F1
Kenia Cl. Carl .............. 174 B4
Kenilworth Ave. S in A ...... 101 D2
Kenilworth Cl. Bees ......... 184 A4
Kenilworth Ct. Nott ......... 173 D2
Kenilworth Dr. C in L ....... 25 F3
Kenilworth Rd. Bees ......... 184 A4
Kenilworth Rd. Nott ......... 173 D2
Kenmare Cres. Gain .......... 24 C3
Kenmore Cl. Mans ............ 101 F3
Kenmore Gdns. Nott .......... 173 E3
Kennedy Cl. Wale ............ 64 A1
Kennedy Ave. Lo Ea .......... 193 E3
Kennedy Ave. Mans ........... 88 B2
Kennedy Cl. Arn ............. 161 F4
Kennedy Ct. Work ............ 36 A2
Kennedy Dr. Staple .......... 170 C1
Kennedy Rise. Wale .......... 64 A1
Kennedy Wlk. Bald ........... 140 C2
Kennel Dr. Ba Mo ............ 28 B3
Kennel La. Ann Wo ........... 130 A1
Kennel La. Swine ............ 71 E1
Kennet Paddock. Mans ........ 88 B2
Kenneth Rd. Nott ............ 147 F1
Kennington Rd. Nott ......... 172 B3
Kenrick Rd. Carl ............ 162 A1
Kenrick St. Carl ............ 175 D4
Kensington Cl. Bees ......... 183 D1
Kensington Cl. Mans ......... 88 C3
Kensington Cl. S in A ....... 100 C1
Kensington Gdns. Nott ....... 161 E2
Kensington Gdns. Carl ....... 174 C4
Kensington Gdns. Ilk ........ 170 A4
Kenslow Ave. Nott ........... 172 C4
Kent Ave. Bees .............. 183 F2
Kent Ave. Sels .............. 128 A2
Kent Cl. Work ............... 36 A3
Kent Rd. Carl ............... 162 A1
Kent Rd. Greas .............. 158 B4
Kent St. Nott ............... 173 E3
Kentmere Cl. Gam ............ 186 B4
Kenton Ct. Nott ............. 173 E1
Kentwood Rd. Nott ........... 173 F2
Kenyon Rd. Nott ............. 172 B2
Keppel Ct. Ilk .............. 157 F2
Kersall Cl. Nott ............ 160 B3
Kersall Dr. Nott ............ 160 B3
Kersall Gdns. Huck .......... 146 A4
Kestral Rd. Mans ............ 101 F2
Kestrel Cl. Carl ............ 162 A1
Kestrel Mews. Work .......... 35 E4
Kestrel Rise. Eagle ......... 84 B1
Keswick Cl. Bees ............ 183 E4
Keswick Cl. Lo Ea ........... 182 A1
Keswick Cl. Nott ............ 173 F2
Keswick Rd. Work ............ 35 F4
Keswick St. Nott ............ 173 F2
Ketlock Hill La. N Le Ha .... 32 B1
Kett St. Nott ............... 160 A3
Kettlethorpe Rd. Kettl ...... 55 E3
Keverne Cl. Nott ............ 160 B1
Kevin Rd. Nott .............. 171 E1
Kew Cl. W Brid .............. 185 E2
Kew Gdns. Bald .............. 140 A2
Kexby Wlk. Gain ............. 24 C4
Key St. Nott ................ 173 F3
Keyes Cl. Matt .............. 19 F4
Keyes Ct. Matt .............. 19 F4
Keyes Rise. Matt ............ 19 F4
Keys Cl. Nott ............... 160 A4
Keyworth Cl. Mans ........... 101 F4
Keyworth Cl. Mans ........... 101 F4
Keyworth Dr. Mans ........... 89 E1
Keyworth Rd. Carl ........... 162 B2
Keyworth Rd. Widm ........... 208 B3
Keyworth Rd. Wys ............ 207 E3
Kibworth Cl. Nott ........... 160 C2
Kid La. Fir ................. 16 A3
Kiddier Ave. Arn ............ 162 A4
Kighill La. Raven ........... 132 A4
Kilbourn St. Nott ........... 173 E3
Kilbourne Rd. Arn ........... 148 A1
Kilburn Cl. Bees ............ 171 D1
Kilby Ave. Nott ............. 174 A3
Kildare Rd. Nott ............ 173 F4
Kildonan Cl. Nott ........... 159 E1
Killerton Green. Nott ....... 195 F4
Killerton Park Dr. W Brid ... 185 D2

Killisick Rd. Arn ........... 162 A4
Kilnbrook Ave. Arn .......... 148 A1
Kilnwood Cl. Nott ........... 174 A4
Kilsby Rd. Nott ............. 184 C1
Kilton Cl. Work ............. 36 A2
Kilton Cres. Work ........... 36 A2
Kilton Glade. Work .......... 36 A2
Kilton Hill. Work ........... 36 A3
Kilton Rd. Work ............. 36 A2
Kilton Terr. Work ........... 36 A2
Kilverton Cl. Nott .......... 172 B2
Kilvington Rd. Arn .......... 162 A4
Kimber Cl. Nott ............. 171 E3
Kimberley Cl. Kim ........... 158 C3
Kimberley Rd. Nott .......... 174 A2
Kimberley Rd. Nuth .......... 159 E3
Kimbolton Ave. Nott ......... 172 C2
King Charles St. Nott ....... 173 D2
King Edward Ave. Mans ....... 102 A2
King Edward Rd. Lough ....... 220 B2
King Edward St. Huck ........ 146 A3
King Edward St. Nott ........ 173 E3
King Edward St. Sand ........ 182 A3
King Edward St. Shireb ...... 72 C2
King Edward's Terr. Ret ..... 39 F3
King George Ave. Lough ...... 220 B1
King George Rd. Lough ....... 220 B1
King George V Ave. Mans . 102 C3
King John's Rd. N Clip ...... 90 A2
King Rd. Mar War ............ 74 A2
King St E. Gain ............. 24 B4
King St. Bees ............... 184 A3
King St. East ............... 143 F1
King St. Gain ............... 24 B4
King St. Ilk ................ 157 F1
King St. K-in-A ............. 115 D2
King St. Lo Ea .............. 193 E4
King St. Lough .............. 220 B2
King St. Mans ............... 102 B4
King St. Mar War ............ 73 E3
King St. Ne Br .............. 219 E4
King St. Nott ............... 173 E3
King St. Pinx ............... 113 E2
King St. S in A ............. 100 A2
King St. S in A ............. 100 C1
King St. S Norm ............. 113 D3
King St. South .............. 121 F1
King St. Tibs ............... 99 D4
King St. Whit ............... 45 E3
King St. Work ............... 35 F1
King's Meadow Rd. Nott ...... 173 D1
King's Pl. Nott ............. 173 E2
King's Rd. N-on-T ........... 124 C1
King's Wlk. Nott ............ 173 E3
Kingerby Cl. Gain ........... 24 C4
Kingfield Cl. Rain .......... 118 A4
Kingfisher Cl. Bald ......... 140 B3
Kingfisher Cl. Nott ......... 160 B2
Kingfisher Cl. Bees ......... 184 A3
Kingfisher Ct. Lough ........ 220 A1
Kingfisher Way. Lough ....... 220 A1
Kingfisher Wharf. Nott ...... 172 C1
Kingfisher Wlk. Work ........ 35 E4
Kingfishers Ct. W Brid ...... 186 B2
Kinglake Pl. Nott ........... 173 E1
Kingrove Ave. Bees .......... 183 E3
Kings Ave. Carl ............. 162 C1
Kings Cl. South ............. 121 F1
Kings Dr. Brin .............. 143 F4
Kings Lodge Dr. Mans ........ 101 F2
Kings Mill La. Mans ......... 101 F2
Kings Mill Rd E. S in A ..... 101 D3
Kings Mill Rd E. S in A ..... 114 C4
Kings Mill Way. Mans ........ 101 F2
Kings Moor. Nott ............ 160 C4
Kings Rd. Lo Ci ............. 211 E1
Kings Rd. Lo Ci ............. 211 E2
Kings Rd. Sand ............. 182 A3
Kings Wood Cl. Baw .......... 10 A4
Kingsbridge Ave. Carl ....... 162 B3
Kingsbridge Way. Bees ....... 183 E3
Kingsbury Dr. Nott .......... 172 A4
Kingsdale Cl. Lo Ea ......... 193 D3
Kingsdale. Work ............. 36 A4
Kingsdown Mount. Nott ....... 171 F1
Kingsford Ave. Nott ......... 172 C3
Kingsley Ave. Mans .......... 88 B3
Kingsley Cl. Mans ........... 88 B2
Kingsley Cres. Lo Ea ........ 193 D2
Kingsley St. Mans ........... 88 B3
Kingsley Dr. Carl ........... 175 D4
Kingsley Rd. Nott ........... 174 A2
Kingsley St. K-in-A ......... 115 D2
Kingsmead Ave. Staple ....... 170 B1
Kingsmead. Ret .............. 39 E2
Kingsmeadow. Rain ........... 118 B4
Kingsnorth Cl. N-on-T ....... 140 A4
Kingsthorpe Cl. Mans ........ 88 C1
Kingsthorpe Cl. Nott ........ 161 F1
Kingston Ave. Ilk .......... 170 A4
Kingston Cl. Work ........... 47 E4
Kingston Cl. Nott .......... 173 F2
Kingston Dr. Cotg .......... 187 F1
Kingston Dr. Oll ........... 77 D2
Kingston Rd. C in L ......... 25 F3
Kingston Rd. Mans .......... 102 B4

Kingston Rd. W Brid ......... 185
Kingston Rd. Work ........... 47
Kingsway Ave. Boug .......... 77
Kingsway Gdns. Huck ......... 145
Kingsway. Bald .............. 140
Kingsway. Ilk ............... 170
Kingsway. K-in-A ............ 115
Kingsway. Mans .............. 89
Kingsway. R on T ............ 175
Kingsway. Work .............. 35
Kingswell Rd. Arn ........... 161
Kingswood Cl. Fir ........... 16
Kingswood Cl. W Brid ........ 185
Kingswood Dr. K-in-A ........ 114
Kingswood Rd. Nott .......... 172
Kinlet Rd. Nott ............. 161
Kinoulton La. Kinou ......... 199
Kinoulton La. Owth .......... 199
Kinoulton Rd. Cr Bi ......... 188
Kinsdale Wlk. Nott .......... 184
Kipling Cl. Nott ............ 195
Kipling Cl. Work ............ 36
Kipling St. Mans ............ 102
Kippis St. Nott ............. 173
Kirby Cl. Blid .............. 118
Kirby Cl. East .............. 144
Kirby Dr. Kegw .............. 203
Kirby Rd. East .............. 144
Kirk Ave. Kegw .............. 203
Kirk Cl. Bees ............... 183
Kirk Dr. Boug ............... 77
Kirk Gate. N-on-T ........... 124
Kirk Hill. E Brid ........... 165
Kirk La. Rudd ............... 196
Kirk Ley Rd. E Lea .......... 214
Kirk Rd. Nott ............... 162
Kirk White Ct. Nott ......... 173
Kirkby Cl. South ............ 121
Kirkby Folly Rd. S in A ..... 101
Kirkby Gdns. Nott ........... 173
Kirkby House Dr. K-in-A ..... 114
Kirkby La. K-in-A ........... 114
Kirkby Rd. Raven ............ 116
Kirkby Rd. S in A ........... 100
Kirkdale Cl. Nott ........... 171
Kirkdale Gdns. Lo Ea ........ 193
Kirkdale Rd. Lo Ea .......... 193
Kirkdale Rd. Nott ........... 174
Kirke Cl. E Mark ............ 66
Kirke St. Ret ............... 39
Kirkewhite Ave. Lo Ea ....... 193
Kirkham Dr. Bees ............ 182
Kirkhill. Bing .............. 177
Kirkland Ave. Mans .......... 101
Kirkland Dr. Bees ........... 183
Kirksley Gdns. Arn .......... 162
Kirklington Rd. Bils ........ 105
Kirklington Rd. Bils ........ 106
Kirklington Rd. Eakr ........ 106
Kirklington Rd. Kirk ........ 106
Kirklington Rd. Rain ........ 104
Kirklington Rd. Ruff ........ 104
Kirkpatrick Dr. Work ........ 35
Kirkstead Cl. Pinx .......... 113
Kirkstead Gdns. Nott ........ 172
Kirkstead Rd. Pinx .......... 113
Kirkstead St. Nott .......... 172
Kirkstone Ct. Lo Ea ......... 182
Kirkstone Dr. Gam ........... 186
Kirtle Cl. Nott ............. 172
Kirton Ave. Lo Ea ........... 193
Kirton Cl. Mans ............. 101
Kirton Ct. Kirton ........... 78
Kirton Park. Kirton ......... 78
Kirton Rd. Egma ............. 79
Kitchener Dr. Mans .......... 102
Kitchener Terr. Scarc ....... 59
Kitson Ave. Sels ............ 128
Kiwi Cl. Huck ............... 145
Knapp Ave. East ............. 143
Knaton Rd. C in L ........... 25
Kneesall Cl. Mar War ........ 74
Kneesall Gr. Huck ........... 146
Kneeton Cl. Carl ............ 162
Kneeton Cl. Nott ............ 161
Kneeton Rd. E Brid ......... 165
Kneeton Vale. Nott .......... 161
Knight St. Carl ............. 174
Knight St. Carl ............. 175
Knight's Cl. Screv .......... 166
Knight's Ct. N-on-T ......... 140
Knighton Ave. Nott .......... 172
Knighton Rd. Arn ............ 161
Knights Cl. Nott ............ 160
Knights Cl. W Brid .......... 185
Knightsbridge Dr. Nuth ...... 159
Knightsbridge Dr. W Brid ... 185
Knightsbridge Gdns. Huck . 130
Knipton Cl. Bald ............ 140
Knole Rd. Nott .............. 171
Knoll Ave. Huck ............. 145
Knoll The. Mans ............. 101
Knoll The. Shireb ........... 72
Knott End. Lan .............. 16
Knott's Ct. Bald ........... 140 B2

owle Hill. Kim ............ 159 D3
owle La. Kim ............. 159 D3
owle Park. Kim .......... 159 D3
owles Wlk. Arn ........... 161 E4
os Cl. Nott ................ 184 B1
e View. Nott .............. 147 D1
ne St. Nott ................ 172 C3
ance Gdns. Nott ......... 185 D3
ray Rd. Calv .............. 148 C4
urnium Cl. Bald ......... 140 B3
urnum Ave. Gain ........ 15 E1
urnum Ave. K-in-A ..... 114 B2
urnum Ave. Keyw ...... 198 A1
urnum Avenue. Shireb .. 72 C3
urnum Cl. Hath .......... 213 D1
urnum Cl. S Norm ...... 113 D4
urnum Cl. Sand ......... 182 A4
urnum Cl. Work ......... 35 E1
urnum Gr. Bees ......... 184 A3
urnum Gr. Huck ........ 146 A3
urnum Gr. Mans ........ 88 A2
urnum Rd. Lan .......... 16 C2
urnum St. Nott .......... 173 E4
ce St. Nott ................ 172 B1
ceby Ct. Mans ........... 88 C2
cey Ave. Huck ........... 146 A3
cey Fields Rd. Hean .... 143 D1
cey Gn. Bald ............. 140 C2
dbrooke Cres. Nott ..... 160 B2
dy Bay Ave. W Brid .... 173 F1
dy Bay Bridge. Nott .... 173 F1
dy Bay Bridge. W Brid .. 173 F1
dy Bay Rd. W Brid ...... 174 A1
dy Well La. Head ........ 52 A4
dy Wlk. Work ............ 35 E4
dybank Rise. Arn ........ 162 B4
dybridge Cl. Bees ....... 183 F2
dybrook La. Mans ....... 101 F4
dybrook Pl. Mans ....... 101 F4
dycroft Ave. Huck ...... 146 A4
dylea Rd. Lo Ea ......... 193 D2
dysmith Rd. Nott ........ 174 A2
dysmock Gdns. Nott .... 173 E1
dywood La. West ........ 80 C3
ke Ave. Mans ............ 101 F4
ke Farm Rd. Mans ...... 103 F1
ke St. Nott ................ 172 C3
keland Ave. Huck ....... 146 B3
keside Ave. Lo Ea ...... 193 E3
keside Cres. Lo Ea ..... 193 E3
amartine St. Nott ....... 173 E3
amb Cl. N-on-T .......... 139 E4
amb Close Dr. Greas ... 144 A2
amb La. Fir ............... 16 B3
ambcroft Rd. Pinx ...... 113 E2
ambert Ct. Bees ......... 184 A4
ambert Gdns. Nott ...... 172 B4
ambert St. Nott .......... 172 C4
ambeth Rd. Bes Vil ..... 147 D1
ambie Cl. Nott ........... 172 B3
ambley Ave. Carl ....... 162 A2
ambley Ave. Mans ...... 102 C3
ambley Bridle Rd. Bu Jo .. 163 E3
ambley La. Bu Jo ....... 163 F3
ambley La. Carl ......... 162 C2
ambley Rd. Lowd ....... 150 A1
ambourne Cres. Lowd .. 150 C1
ambourne Gdns. Arn ... 162 A3
ambton Cl. Ilk ........... 157 F2
aming Gap La. N-on-W .. 198 C3
amins La. Bes Vil ....... 147 E2
ammas Cl. S in A ....... 100 C1
ammas Gdns. E Brid ... 165 E2
ammas La. E Brid ...... 165 E2
ammas Rd. S in A ...... 100 C1
amond Cl. Mans ........ 101 F3
amorna Gr. Nott ........ 185 D3
amp Wood Cl. Calv .... 148 C4
amplands. Cotg ......... 187 F2
anark Cl. Nott ........... 172 B2
ancaster Ave. Sand ..... 182 A2
ancaster Ave. Staple ... 182 C4
ancaster Cl. Tick ........ 8 A4
ancaster Dr. Baw ....... 9 F4
ancaster Rd. Bes Vil ... 146 C2
ancaster Rd. G on H ... 22 A4
ancaster Rd. Huck ..... 145 E2
ancaster Rd. Nott ...... 174 A4
ancaster Way. Work ... 159 E1
ancastrian Way. Work .. 36 A3
ancelot Dr. Greas ...... 145 D1
ancelyn Gdns. W Brid .. 185 E2
ancster Cres. Tick ...... 8 A4
anda Gr. Tux ............ 66 A2
andcroft Cres. Nott .... 161 D3
andcroft La. Su Bo ..... 204 B1
andmere Cl. Ship ....... 157 E2
andmere Gdns. Nott ... 161 F1
andmere La. Rudd ...... 185 F1
andmere La. W Brid ... 185 E2
andmere La. W Brid ... 186 A1

Landsdown Gr. Lo Ea ... 182 C1
Landsdowne Rd. Nott ... 160 C2
Landseer Cl. Nott ....... 172 C3
Landseer Cl. South ..... 136 B4
Landseer Rd. South .... 136 B4
Lane End. K-in-A ....... 115 D3
Lane The. Awsw ........ 158 B2
Lane The. Coth .......... 154 C2
Laneham Ave. Arn ...... 162 A4
Laneham Rd. D on T .... 54 A1
Laneham St. Ramp ..... 43 D1
Lanercost Mews. Work .. 35 F1
Lanesborough Ct. Lough ... 220 A1
Laneside Ave. Bees ..... 182 C1
Langar Cl. Nott ......... 161 E2
Langar La. Co Ba ....... 200 C4
Langar La. Harb ........ 202 A2
Langar Pl. Mans ........ 103 D4
Langar Rd. Bing ........ 177 F2
Langdale Cl. N-on-T .... 139 F2
Langdale Dr. Lo Ea ..... 193 D3
Langdale Dr. Tick ....... 8 A4
Langdale Gr. Bing ...... 177 D2
Langdale Rd. Nott ...... 174 B3
Langdale Rd. Work ..... 35 F4
Langdon Cl. Lo Ea ...... 182 A1
Langdown Cl. Nott ..... 160 A4
Langford La. Holme .... 111 D2
Langford Rd. Arn ....... 162 A4
Langford Rd. Mans ..... 101 F3
Langford St. Mans ...... 101 E3
Langford St. S in A ..... 100 C2
Langham Ave. Nott ..... 174 A3
Langham Dr. Bu Jo ..... 163 F3
Langham Pl. Mans ...... 101 F4
Langley Ave. Arn ....... 161 F3
Langley Ave. Ilk ........ 157 E3
Langley Cl. Mans ....... 87 F1
Langley Dr. Kegw ...... 203 E1
Langley Park. La Mi .... 143 D2
Langley St. Work ....... 35 F1
Langstrath Rd. Nott .... 184 C1
Langton Ave. K-in-A .... 114 B3
Langton Hollow. Sels ... 128 B3
Langton Rd. S in A ..... 100 C1
Langtree Gdns. Bing ... 177 F3
Langtry Gr. Nott ........ 161 D1
Langwell Dr. Mans ..... 89 E1
Langwith Dr. Scarc ..... 58 C1
Langwith Maltings. Scarc .. 72 C4
Langwith Rd. Cuck ..... 60 A1
Langwith Rd. Shireb ... 72 C3
Lansbury Ave. Oll ...... 77 E3
Lansbury Dr. Bils ....... 105 F4
Lansbury Dr. S Norm ... 113 D3
Lansbury Gdns. Mans .. 102 C4
Lansbury Rd. Bald ...... 140 B2
Lansbury Rd. Bils ....... 105 F4
Lansbury Rd. Edwin .... 76 A1
Lansbury Rd. S in A .... 100 C1
Lansdall Ave. Lea ....... 24 C2
Lansdown Cl. Bees ...... 183 D2
Lansdowne Ave. Mans .. 102 B1
Lansdowne Dr. Lough ... 220 A1
Lansdowne Dr. W Brid .. 185 E2
Lansic La. Hover ........ 151 E1
Lansing Cl. Nott ........ 195 F4
Lantern La. E Lea ....... 205 F1
Lanthwaite Cl. Nott .... 184 C1
Lanthwaite Rd. Nott ... 184 C1
Lapford Cl. Carl ........ 162 B3
Larch Ave. Mans ....... 88 A3
Larch Ave. Shireb ...... 72 B2
Larch Cl. Bes Vil ....... 161 E4
Larch Cl. Bing .......... 178 A2
Larch Cl. Huck ......... 146 A3
Larch Cres. Bees ....... 183 E4
Larch Cres. East ....... 143 F1
Larch Gdns. Nott ....... 160 A4
Larch Rd. Oll ........... 77 E3
Larch Way. Keyw ...... 198 A1
Larchdale Cl. S Norm ... 113 D2
Larchdene Ave. Nott ... 171 E2
Largs Cl. Nott .......... 146 C1
Lark Cl. Bees ........... 183 D3
Larkdale St. Nott ....... 173 D3
Larkfield Ave. Ann Wo .. 114 C1
Larkfield Rd. Kim ...... 159 D3
Larkhall Pl. Mans ...... 101 F3
Larklands Ave. Ilk ..... 170 A4
Larkspur Ave. Nott .... 147 F1
Larkspur Cl. Mans ..... 88 B1
Larkspur Cl. S Norm ... 113 D2
Larpit Green. Whit ..... 45 D3
Larwood Cres. Ann Wo .. 114 C1
Larwood Gr. Nott ...... 161 E2
Larwood. Work ......... 36 A3
Lascelles Ave. Carl ..... 162 B1
Latham St. Nott ........ 160 A4
Lathkill Ave. Ilk ........ 157 F3
Lathkill Cl. Nott ........ 160 A4
Lathkill Dr. Sels ........ 128 C4
Lathkilldale Cres. Lo Ea .. 193 D3
Latimer Cl. Nott ........ 160 B3
Latimer Dr. Bees ....... 171 D2
Laughton Ave. W Brid .. 185 E2
Laughton Cres. Huck ... 145 F2
Laughton Rd. Blyt ...... 15 E4

Laughton Rd. Mort ..... 15 E4
Launceston Cres. Nott .. 185 D2
Launder St. Nott ....... 173 E1
Launder St. Orst ....... 179 F4
Launds Ave. Sels ....... 128 B4
Laurel Ave. Keyw ...... 197 F1
Laurel Ave. Mans ...... 89 D1
Laurel Ave. Mans ...... 102 B3
Laurel Ave. Mar War ... 74 A4
Laurel Ave. Mist ....... 6 C2
Laurel Cl. Gain ......... 15 F1
Laurel Cl. Shireb ....... 72 B3
Laurel Cl. Wys ......... 207 E2
Laurel Cres. Kim ....... 159 D3
Laurel Cres. Lo Ea ..... 193 E3
Laurel Gr. K-in-A ...... 115 E3
Laurel Gr. S Norm ..... 113 D2
Laurel Rd. Carl ......... 174 B4
Laurie Ave. Nott ....... 173 D4
Laurie Cl. Nott ......... 173 D4
Lauriston Dr. Nott ..... 160 B2
Lavender Cl. Nott ...... 159 F1
Lavender Cres. Carl .... 162 B1
Lavender Gr. Bees ...... 184 A3
Lavender Wlk. Nott .... 173 E4
Lavenham Mews. Work .. 35 F1
Laver Cl. Arn ........... 162 A4
Laverick Rd. Sels ...... 128 A2
Lawdon Rd. Arn ........ 148 A1
Lawley Ave. Nott ...... 172 A1
Lawn La. Grim ......... 218 C1
Lawn La. S in A ........ 100 C1
Lawn Mill Rd. Kim ..... 158 C4
Lawn Rd. C in L ........ 25 F4
Lawn Rd. S in A ........ 101 D2
Lawns Rd. Ann Wo ..... 129 F4
Lawns The. Coll ........ 98 A1
Lawns The. What ....... 179 D2
Lawnwood Ave. Elk .... 50 A2
Lawnwood La. Elk ...... 50 A2
Lawrence Ave. Awsw ... 158 B2
Lawrence Ave. East .... 143 F1
Lawrence Ave. K-in-A .. 114 C3
Lawrence Ave. Mans ... 88 A2
Lawrence Cl. Cotg ...... 187 F2
Lawrence Cres. S in A .. 101 D2
Lawrence Dr. Brin ...... 143 E4
Lawrence Pl. N-on-T ... 125 D1
Lawrence St. Lo Ea ..... 193 E4
Lawrence St. N-on-T ... 125 D1
Lawrence St. Sand ..... 182 A4
Lawrence St. Staple .... 182 B3
Lawrence Way. Nott ... 173 D1
Lawson Ave. Lo Ea ..... 193 F4
Lawson Cl. W Dray .... 50 C1
Lawson St. Nott ........ 173 D3
Lawton Dr. Nott ........ 146 B1
Laxton Ave. S in A ..... 101 E1
Laxton Dr. Huck ....... 145 F3
Laxton Dr. Mar War .... 74 B4
Laxton Rd. Egma ...... 79 E2
Laxton Rd. Lax ........ 79 E2
Laycock Ave. G on H ... 12 C1
Layton Ave. Mans ..... 102 A4
Layton Burroughs. Mans .. 102 A4
Le Brun Sq. C in L ..... 25 F4
Le Page Ct. Nott ....... 172 A4
Lea Cl. Raven .......... 117 D1
Lea Ct. Work ........... 35 E1
Lea La. Sels ............ 128 C3
Lea Rd W. Gain ........ 24 B3
Lea Rd. Gain ........... 24 C3
Lea Rd. Mar War ....... 74 B2
Lea Rd. Raven .......... 117 D1
Lea Vale. S Norm ...... 113 D2
Leabrook Cl. Nott ...... 184 B2
Leabrook Gdns. Huck ... 146 B4
Leabrooks Ave. Mans .. 88 B3
Leabrooks Ave. S in A .. 101 E1
Leach Cl. D on T ....... 54 B1
Leachcroft Hill. South .. 136 A4
Leacroft Rd. Nott ...... 172 B4
Lead Hill. Work ........ 35 F1
Leadale Ave. Huck ..... 146 B4
Leadale Cres. Mans .... 88 C3
Leafield Green. Nott ... 184 C1
Leafield. Ret ........... 29 E1
Leafield. Ret ........... 39 E4
Leahurst Gdns. W Brid .. 186 A3
Leahurst Rd. W Brid ... 186 A3
Leake La. S on S ....... 214 B2
Leake Rd. Cost ......... 206 A1
Leake Rd. Goth ........ 205 E3
Leam Glen. Mans ...... 88 B1
Leamington Dr. Bees ... 183 E2
Leamington Dr. S in A .. 114 C4
Leamington Dr. S Norm . 113 D3
Leamington Hall. S in A .. 100 C1
Leander Cl. Nott ....... 185 D3
Leas Ave. Plea ......... 87 D3
Leas Rd. Mans ......... 88 B2
Leas The. Bulc ......... 164 A3
Leaway The. Shireb .... 72 B2
Lechlade Rd. Nott ...... 161 D3
Ledbury Vale. Nott ..... 172 A4
Lee Cres. Ilk ........... 170 A4

Lee La. Hean ........... 143 D1
Lee Rd. Bu Jo .......... 164 A3
Lee Rd. Calv ........... 148 B4
Leech Ct. Greas ........ 158 A4
Leeds Rd. Shire ........ 34 C4
Leeks Rd. South ....... 121 F1
Leeming Cl. Mar War .. 74 B3
Leeming La N. Mans ... 88 C3
Leeming La S. Mans ... 88 B1
Leeming La. Mar War .. 88 C4
Leeming Park. Mans ... 88 B2
Leeming St. Mans ...... 102 A4
Leen Cl. Bes Vil ........ 146 C2
Leen Cl. Huck .......... 146 B4
Leen Dr. Huck .......... 131 D1
Leen Gate. Nott ........ 172 C1
Leen Mills La. Huck .... 131 D1
Leen Pl. Nott ........... 172 C3
Leen Valley Dr. Shireb .. 72 C2
Lees Ave. Mans ........ 101 E4
Lees Barn Rd. R on T .. 175 E1
Lees Hill St. Nott ...... 173 F2
Lees La. S Norm ....... 113 D3
Lees Rd. Carl ........... 162 A1
Leeway Cl. Mans ....... 103 F1
Leeway Rd. Mans ...... 103 F1
Leeway Rd. South ...... 121 E1
Legion Dr. S in A ...... 100 B3
Leicester Rd. Lough .... 220 B1
Leicester St. Lo Ea ..... 193 F3
Leigh Cl. W Brid ....... 185 E3
Leigh Rd. Bees ......... 182 C2
Leighton St. Nott ...... 173 F3
Leiston Gdns. Nott ..... 161 D4
Leivers Ave. Arn ....... 161 F4
Lema Cl. Nott .......... 160 B4
Lemont Rd. Mans ...... 89 D1
Lemynton St. Lough .... 220 A2
Lendrum Ct. Bu Jo ..... 163 F2
Lennox St. Nott ........ 173 E3
Lenton Ave. Nott ...... 173 D2
Lenton Ave. Toll ....... 186 B1
Lenton Boulevard. Nott .. 172 C2
Lenton Cir. Toll ........ 186 B1
Lenton Ct. Nott ........ 172 C2
Lenton Hall Dr. Nott ... 172 B1
Lenton La. Nott ........ 184 C4
Lenton La. Nott ........ 185 D3
Lenton Manor. Nott .... 172 C2
Lenton Rd. Nott ........ 173 D2
Lenton St. Sand ........ 182 B4
Leonard Ave. Nott ..... 161 D1
Leonard St. Nott ....... 160 B3
Leopold St. Lo Ea ...... 193 E4
Leopold St. Lough ...... 220 A3
Leopold St. S in A ...... 100 C1
Leroy Wallace Ave. Nott . 172 C3
Lerwick Cl. Nott ....... 185 D1
Leslie Ave. Bees ....... 183 F3
Leslie Ave. Kim ........ 158 C3
Leslie Ave. Nott ....... 173 D4
Leslie Gr. Calv ......... 148 C4
Leslie Rd. Nott ........ 173 D4
Letchworth Cres. Bees .. 183 D4
Letcombe Rd. Nott ..... 184 C2
Letwell Ave. Let ....... 16 A1
Levels La. Blax ......... 1 A4
Levels La. Miss ........ 4 C2
Leverton Green. Nott ... 184 C1
Leverton Rd. Mans ..... 101 F4
Leverton Rd. Ret ...... 40 B4
Leverton Rd. S Le S .... 32 B2
Leverton Wlk. Arn ..... 162 A4
Levick Ct. Nott ........ 173 E1
Lewcote La. WeHa ..... 157 D1
Lewindon Ct. Arn ...... 161 F2
Lewis Cl. Nott ......... 173 E3
Lewis St. Gain ......... 24 B4
Lexington Ct. Tux ...... 65 F1
Lexington Gdns. Nott .. 161 E2
Lexington Gdns. Tux ... 65 F1
Ley Croft. Mans ....... 88 B3
Ley La. E Dray ......... 53 D2
Ley La. Mans ........... 88 B2
Leybourne Dr. Nott .... 160 C3
Leyland Cl. Bees ....... 182 C1
Leys La. G on H ........ 12 C1
Leys Rd. Rudd ......... 196 B3
Leys The. Lowd ........ 150 B1
Leys The. N-on-W ..... 197 F4
Leys The. Nott ......... 184 B1
Leyton Ave. S in A ..... 101 D3
Leyton Cres. Bees ...... 184 A3
Liber Cl. Mans ......... 102 C4
Library Rd. Nott ....... 172 B1
Lichfield Ave. Mans .... 102 B1
Lichfield Cl. Bees ...... 182 C1
Lichfield Cl. Mans ..... 102 B1
Lichfield Cl. Work ..... 36 A4
Lichfield La. Mans ..... 102 B1
Lichfield Rd. Nott ..... 174 A2
Lichfield Wlk. C in L ... 25 F4
Liddell Gr. Nott ....... 171 F1
Liddington St. Nott .... 160 C1
Lidget La. Ret ......... 40 A4
Lifton Ave. Ret ........ 29 F1
Lightfoot Cl. N-on-T ... 140 C4

Lilac Ave. Carl ......... 174 B4
Lilac Cl. Keyw ......... 198 A1
Lilac Cl. N-on-T ....... 139 F2
Lilac Cl. Nott .......... 159 F1
Lilac Cres. Bees ....... 184 A3
Lilac Gr. Baw .......... 9 F4
Lilac Gr. Bees ......... 184 A3
Lilac Gr. C in L ........ 25 F4
Lilac Gr. Glap ......... 86 A4
Lilac Gr. Mans ........ 89 E1
Lilac Gr. Mar War ..... 73 F4
Lilac Gr. S Norm ...... 113 D2
Lilac Gr. Shireb ....... 72 C3
Lilac Mews. Ilk ........ 157 E2
Lilac Rd. Huck ........ 146 A3
Lillee Ct. Work ........ 36 A3
Lilleker Rise. Nott ..... 147 F1
Lillington Rd. Nott .... 160 A4
Lily Ave. Carl ......... 175 D4
Lily Gr. Bees .......... 184 A3
Limb Cres. S in A ..... 100 C1
Lime Ave. Fir ......... 16 A3
Lime Ave. La Mi ...... 143 F1
Lime Ave. Lough ...... 220 B2
Lime Ave. S in A ...... 100 A2
Lime Ave. S in A ...... 100 C2
Lime Cl. Kim .......... 159 D3
Lime Cl. Pinx ......... 113 E2
Lime Cl. R on T ....... 175 F2
Lime Cres. Mar War ... 73 F4
Lime Gr Ave. Bees .... 183 F3
Lime Gr. Lo Ea ....... 193 E4
Lime Gr. Mans ........ 89 E1
Lime Gr. N-on-T ...... 139 E4
Lime Gr. Ret .......... 39 E4
Lime Gr. S Norm ..... 113 D3
Lime Gr. Sand ........ 182 A3
Lime Gr. Staple ....... 182 B3
Lime La. Arn .......... 147 F2
Lime St. K-in-A ....... 115 D3
Lime St. Mans ........ 102 B4
Lime St. Nott ......... 160 A4
Lime St. S in A ....... 101 D2
Lime Terr. Lo Ea ...... 193 E4
Lime Tree Ave. C in L .. 25 F4
Lime Tree Ave. Gain ... 15 E1
Lime Tree Ave. Glap ... 86 A4
Lime Tree Ave. K-in-A .. 114 C3
Lime Tree Ave. Mans ... 88 A3
Lime Tree Ave. Nott ... 160 B2
Lime Tree Ave. Ret .... 39 E4
Lime Tree Ave. S in A .. 100 B3
Lime Tree Cres. Baw ... 9 F4
Lime Tree Gdns. Lowd .. 150 C1
Lime Tree Pl. Mans .... 102 B3
Lime Tree Pl. Rain ..... 104 B1
Lime Tree Rd. Elk ..... 50 A2
Lime Tree Rd. Huck .... 146 A2
Lime Tree Rd. Oll ...... 77 E3
Limehurst Ave. Lough .. 220 A3
Limes Ave. Ne La ...... 59 D1
Limes Cres. Shireb ..... 72 B3
Limes Ct. S in A ....... 101 E1
Limes The. Beck ....... 14 A1
Limestone Terr. Mans .. 88 C2
Limetree Cl. Keyw ..... 197 F1
Limmen Gdns. Nott .... 173 F3
Limpenny St. Nott ..... 173 D3
Linby Ave. Huck ....... 146 A4
Linby Ave. Mans ...... 101 E3
Linby Cl. Carl ......... 162 C1
Linby Cl. Nott ......... 161 E3
Linby Gr. Huck ....... 146 A4
Linby La. Linby ....... 131 E2
Linby La. Papp ........ 131 E2
Linby Rd. Huck ....... 146 A4
Linby St. Nott ........ 160 B4
Linby Wlk. Huck ...... 146 A4
Lincoln Rd. Tux ....... 66 A2
Lincoln Ave. Sand ..... 182 A2
Lincoln Cir. Nott ...... 173 D2
Lincoln Cl. Staple ..... 170 C1
Lincoln Cl. Tibs ....... 99 D3
Lincoln Ct. Nott ...... 171 F4
Lincoln Dr. Mans ..... 88 B2
Lincoln Gr. R on T .... 175 F2
Lincoln Rd. Brox ..... 57 E2
Lincoln Rd. E Mark ... 66 A4
Lincoln Rd. Fent ..... 55 E3
Lincoln Rd. N-on-T ... 125 D2
Lincoln Rd. Sax ...... 57 E2
Lincoln Rd Bridge. N-on-T . 125 D1
Lincoln St. Gain ...... 15 E1
Lincoln St. N-on-T .... 125 D1
Lincoln St. Nott ...... 160 C2
Lincoln St. Tibs ...... 99 D3
Lincoln St. Work ..... 36 A1
Lincoln View. Work ... 36 A1
Lind Cl. Mans ........ 103 F1
Lindale Cl. Gam ...... 186 B3
Lindbridge Rd. Nott .. 159 F1
Linden Gr. Bees ...... 184 A3
Linden Ave. Bald ..... 140 A3
Linden Ave. Nott ..... 184 B1
Linden Ave. Tux ...... 66 A1

## Linden Gr. Carl

Linden Gr. Carl ............... 163  D1
Linden Gr. K-in-A ........... 114  B3
Linden Gr. Sand ............. 182  A4
Linden Gr. Shireb ............. 72  C2
Linden Gr. Staple ........... 182  C3
Linden Rd. Lough ........... 220  A3
Linden Rd. Mans ............ 102  C4
Linden St. Mans ............... 88  A1
Linden St. Nott .............. 173  E4
Linden St. Shireb ............. 72  C2
Linden Terr. Gain ............. 24  B4
Lindfield Cl. Nott ........... 160  A1
Lindfield Rd. Nott .......... 159  F1
Lindholme Way. S in A ... 100  C3
Lindhurst La. Mans ........ 102  C2
Lindisfarne Gdns. Bes Vil .. 147  D1
Lindley St. Greas ........... 144  A2
Lindley St. Mans ............ 102  A4
Lindley St. Sels ............. 128  B3
Lindley Terr. Nott .......... 172  C4
Lindley's La. K-in-A ....... 115  D2
Lindrick Cl. C in L ........... 25  F4
Lindrick Cl. Work ............. 36  A3
Lindrick Ct. Ret .............. 39  E1
Lindrick La. Tick ............... 8  A3
Lindrick Rd. K-in-A ........ 114  C4
Lindrick. Tick .................. 8  A3
Lindsay Ave. Ann Wo ..... 115  D1
Lindsay Ave. N-on-T ...... 139  F2
Lindsay Cl. Mans ........... 102  A3
Lindsey Dr. Mans ........... 103  D2
Lindsey Rd. Har ................. 9  D3
Lindum Gr. Nott ............. 173  F2
Lindum Mews. N-on-T .... 140  A4
Lindum Rd. Nott ............. 160  B2
Lindum St. N-on-T .......... 140  A4
Lindwall Ct. Work ............. 36  A3
Lindy Cl. Kinou .............. 199  F1
Linecroft La. Walker ......... 14  B4
Linette Cl. Nott .............. 161  D1
Linford. Bees ................. 171  D2
Ling Cres. Rudd .............. 196  B4
Ling Rd. Lough .............. 220  A1
Lingdale Cl. Lough ......... 220  A1
Lingfield Cl. Mans .......... 102  C3
Lingfield Ct. Nott ........... 171  E2
Lingford St. Huck ........... 146  A3
Lingford. Cotg ............... 188  A2
Lingforest Cl. Mans ........ 103  D3
Lingforest Rd. Mans ....... 103  D3
Lings La. Keyw .............. 207  F4
Lings View. Mar War ........ 74  B2
Lingwood Gr. Mans ........ 103  D4
Lingwood La. Lamb ........ 149  D2
Lingwood La. Woodb ...... 149  D2
Linkin Rd. Bees .............. 183  E3
Linkmel Rd. East ............ 143  E2
Links The. Mans ............. 103  D3
Linksfield Ct. W Brid ...... 185  E1
Linley Cl. Coll ................ 112  A4
Linmell St. Nott .............. 173  F3
Linnets Dr. Mans ............ 102  C4
Linnets The. Work ............ 35  E4
Linsdale Cl. Nott ............ 171  D3
Linsdale Gdns. Carl ........ 162  B2
Lintin Ave. Edwin ............. 75  F1
Linton Cl. Farn .............. 139  D3
Linton Cl. Mans ............. 103  D3
Linton Dr. Boug ............... 77  F3
Linton Rise. Nott ............ 174  A3
Linwood Cl. Gain ............. 24  C4
Linwood Cres. East ........ 144  A1
Linwood Cres. Raven ...... 116  C2
Linwood Ct. Mans ............ 88  C2
Lion Cl. Nott .................. 160  B1
Liquorice La. C in L .......... 26  A2
Lisle St. Lough .............. 220  A3
Lismore Cl. Nott ............. 172  C3
Lismore Ct. Mans ........... 101  E3
Lissington Rd. Gain .......... 24  C4
Lister Ct. Nott ............... 172  C1
Lister Gate. Nott ............ 173  E2
Listowel Cres. Nott ........ 195  F4
Litchen Cl. Ilk ............... 157  F1
Litchfield Cl. Lo Ea ....... 194  A4
Litchfield Rise. Nott ...... 147  F1
Little Acre. Mans ............. 88  C3
Little Barn Ct. Mans ...... 102  C3
Little Barn Gdns. Mans ... 102  C3
Little Barn La. Mans ....... 102  C3
Little Belt The. Gain ......... 15  E2
Little Breck. S Norm ....... 113  D2
Little Carter La. Mans .... 102  C4
Little Debdale La. Mans .... 87  F1
Little Hallam La. Ilk ....... 170  A3
Little Hayes. W Brid ....... 185  E2
Little Hollies. Mans ......... 89  D1
Little John Ave. Mar War ... 74  B1
Little John Cl. Boug .......... 77  E3
Little John Dr. Rain ........ 104  A1
Little John Wlk. Nott ...... 173  E4
Little La. Blyth ................ 18  A2
Little La. Calv ................ 148  B4
Little La. Coll ................ 111  F4
Little La. Edin ................ 120  B2
Little La. G on H .............. 12  C1
Little La. Kim ................ 158  C3
Little La. Mans ................ 87  D3

Little La. S in A ............... 99  F1
Little La. Shireb .............. 72  B2
Little La. Th Sa ................ 34  A3
Little La. Toll ................ 186  C2
Little Lunnon. B in F ....... 194  C3
Little Meadow. Cotg ....... 188  A1
Little Moor La. Lough ...... 220  B2
Little Oak Ave. Ann Wo ... 130  A4
Little Oakwood Dr. Nott .. 146  B1
Little Ox. Carl ................ 174  C2
Little Ricket La. Raven .... 116  B2
Little Tennis St S. Nott ... 174  A1
Little Tennis St. Nott ...... 174  A2
Little Top La. Lound .......... 20  B1
Little Wlk. E Stock ............. 7  E1
Littleborough Rd. S Le S ... 33  D2
Littlegreen Rd. Arn ......... 161  F3
Littleover Ave. Mans ...... 103  D3
Littlewood Gdns. Nott ..... 171  E3
Littlewood La. Mans ......... 88  A3
Littleworth. Mans .......... 102  B3
Litton Ave. S in A ........... 101  D3
Litton Cl. Arn ................ 161  F2
Litton Cl. Ilk ................. 157  F2
Litton Cl. Raven ............. 117  D2
Litton Rd. Mans ............... 88  C2
Littondale. Work .............. 36  A4
Liverpool St. Nott ........... 173  F3
Livingstone St. News ...... 130  C3
Llanberis Gr. Nott .......... 160  B1
Lloyd St. Nott ................ 161  E1
Loach Ct. Nott ............... 172  B3
Lobelia Cl. Nott .............. 173  E4
Lock Cl. Lo Ea ................ 193  E2
Lock La. Sand ................ 182  B2
Lockerbie St. Carl .......... 174  C3
Locksley La. Nott ........... 184  C2
Lockwood Cl. Bees ......... 184  B2
Lockwood Ct. Nott .......... 147  D1
Lodge Cl. Nott ............... 147  F1
Lodge Cl. Nott ............... 172  B4
Lodge Farm La. Nott ....... 147  F1
Lodge La. Elst ............... 153  E3
Lodge La. K-in-A ............ 115  E2
Lodge La. Screv ............. 166  B3
Lodge La. Tux .................. 66  A1
Lodge Rd. Greas ............ 158  A4
Lodge Rd. Lo Ea ............ 193  E3
Lodgefield La. Hover ....... 151  F1
Lodgewood Cl. Nott ........ 160  A3
Lodore Rd. Work .............. 35  F4
Logan St. Nott ............... 160  B3
Lois Ave. Nott ............... 172  C2
Lombard Cl. Nott ............ 172  C2
Lombard St. N-on-T ........ 139  F4
Lombard St. Orst ............ 180  A3
Lonan Cl. Mans ................ 89  D1
London La. W-on-W ........ 217  E4
London La. Wyme ........... 216  A2
London Rd. Bald ............. 140  B3
London Rd. Kegw ............ 203  E1
London Rd. Lo Wh .......... 212  C3
London Rd. N-on-T .......... 140  B3
London Rd. Nott ............. 173  E1
London Rd. Ret ................ 39  F3
London Rd. Ret ................ 40  A2
Long Acre. Huck ............. 145  E4
Long Brecks La. Blyth ....... 18  B1
Long Hill Rise. Huck ....... 145  F3
Long La. B in W .............. 141  F4
Long La. B-le-V .............. 192  C1
Long La. Bees ............... 183  F2
Long La. C in L ................ 25  F3
Long La. E Dray ............... 53  E2
Long La. Farn ................ 139  D3
Long La. Greas ............... 145  D1
Long La. Hick ................ 210  B3
Long La. Kegw ............... 203  E3
Long La. Redm ............... 192  C3
Long La. Ship ................ 157  E3
Long La. Ship ................ 157  F4
Long La. Shireb ............... 72  C2
Long La. Stat ................. 202  C2
Long Meadow Hill. Lowd ... 149  F1
Long Meadow Hill. Lowd ... 150  A1
Long Meadow. Farns ....... 120  A3
Long Meadow. Mans ......... 88  B3
Long Meadows. Ever ........ 11  D2
Long Row W. Nott ........... 173  E2
Long Row. K on S ........... 204  A2
Long Row. N-on-T ........... 140  A4
Long Row. Nott .............. 173  E2
Longacre. Arn ................ 161  F2
Longbeck Ave. Nott ........ 162  A1
Longcliff Hill. Ol Da ....... 218  C2
Longcroft View. Whit ........ 45  D3
Longdale La. Raven ........ 132  B4
Longdale Rd. Nott .......... 161  E3
Longdale. Mans ............... 88  C1
Longden Cl. Staple ......... 170  C1
Longden St. Nott ............ 173  F3
Longden Terr. Mar War ...... 74  B1
Longden Terr. S in A ....... 100  B3
Longfellow Dr. Bald ........ 140  B3
Longfellow Dr. Work .......... 36  A2
Longfellows Cl. Nott ....... 161  D4
Longfield La. Ilk ............ 170  A3

Longford Cres. Nott ....... 146  B1
Longford Wlk. Mans ....... 103  D3
Longhedge La. Alv .......... 180  C4
Longhedge La. Bott ........ 180  C2
Longhedge La. Bott ........ 180  C4
Longhedge La. Hawk ...... 167  F3
Longhedge La. Orst ........ 168  A1
Longhedge La. Plea ......... 86  C3
Longhill Rise. Ann Wo ..... 114  C1
Longholme Rd. Ret ........... 40  A4
Longhurst View. Whit ....... 45  D3
Longhurst. Work .............. 36  A3
Longland La. Farns ......... 119  E2
Longlands Cl. Bees ........ 184  A2
Longlands Rd. Bees ........ 184  A2
Longleat Cres. Bees ....... 183  E3
Longmead Cl. Nott ......... 161  E3
Longmead Dr. Fisk ......... 137  F2
Longmead Dr. Nott ......... 161  E3
Longmoor Ave. Lowd ...... 164  C4
Longmoor Gdns. Lo Ea ... 182  A1
Longmoor La. Aslo ......... 179  D4
Longmoor La. Sand ........ 182  A2
Longmoor La. Scarr ........ 179  D4
Longmoor Rd. Lo Ea ....... 182  A1
Longnor Wlk. Mans ........ 103  D3
Longore Sq. Nott ........... 172  B2
Longridge Rd. Arn .......... 161  F3
Longshaw Rd. Mans ....... 103  D3
Longster La. Mar War ....... 73  E2
Longstone Way. Mans .... 101  E3
Longue Dr. Calv ............. 148  B4
Longwall Ave. Nott ......... 173  D1
Longwood Ct. Nott ......... 160  C4
Longwood Rd. Pinx ........ 113  F1
Lonsdale Dr. Bees .......... 182  C1
Lonsdale La. Calv .......... 133  D3
Lonsdale Rd. Nott .......... 172  C3
Lord Haddon Rd. Ilk ....... 157  F1
Lord Nelson St. Nott ...... 173  F2
Lord St. Gain .................. 24  B4
Lord St. Mans ............... 102  A3
Lord St. Nott ................. 173  F2
Lordship La. Orst ........... 180  A3
Lorimer Ave. Carl ........... 162  C1
Lorne Cl. Nott ............... 173  E4
Lorne Gr. R on T ............ 175  F2
Lorne Wlk. Nott .............. 173  E4
Lortas Rd. Nott .............. 160  C1
Loscoe Gdns. Nott ......... 161  D1
Loscoe Mount Rd. Nott ... 161  E1
Loscoe Rd. Nott ............. 161  E1
Lothian Rd. Toll ............. 186  B1
Lothmore Ct. Nott .......... 173  D1
Lotus Cl. Nott ............... 173  F4
Loughan Cl. Nott ........... 180  A4
Loughborough Ave. Nott ... 173  F2
Loughborough Rd. Brad ... 196  C3
Loughborough Rd. Bunn ... 206  C4
Loughborough Rd. Cost ... 215  E3
Loughborough Rd. E Lea ... 214  C4
Loughborough Rd. Hath ... 213  D1
Loughborough Rd. Hoton ... 215  E1
Loughborough Rd. Lough ... 220  B1
Loughborough Rd. Remp ... 215  E3
Loughborough Rd. Rudd ... 196  C3
Loughborough Rd. W Brid ... 185  F3
Loughborugh Rd. Cotes ... 220  C3
Loughrigg Cl. Nott ......... 173  D1
Louis Ave. Bees ............. 183  F4
Louise Ave. Carl ............ 175  D4
Lound House Cl. S in A ... 100  C3
Lound House Rd. S in A ... 100  C3
Lound Low Rd. Lound ....... 29  E4
Louwil Ave. Mans ............ 88  C3
Love La. Gain .................. 15  E1
Loveden Cl. Bald ........... 140  B2
Lovell Cl. Nott ............... 159  F3
Lover's La. N-on-T .......... 125  D1
Low Field La. Aust ............ 3  E1
Low Holland La. S Le S ..... 32  C2
Low Moor Rd. K-in-A ...... 115  D3
Low Pavement. Nott ....... 173  E2
Low Rd. Best ................... 97  F3
Low Rd. S in A ............... 100  C4
Low St. Beck .................. 14  B1
Low St. C in L ................. 26  A3
Low St. Coll .................. 111  F4
Low St. E Dray ................ 53  D2
Low St. E Mark ................ 66  A4
Low st. Elst ................... 153  E3
Low St. G on H ................ 12  C1
Low St. Harby ................. 70  B1
Low St. N Whea ............... 31  E4
Low St. S in A ................ 100  C1
Low St. Torw ................... 19  D1
Low Wood La. Eagle ......... 98  C4
Low Wood Rd. Nott ........ 159  F3
Low Wood Rd. Nuth ........ 159  F3
Low's La. S-by-D ........... 170  A1
Lowater St. Carl ............ 174  A4
Lowcroft. Arn ................ 161  F2
Lowdam Rd. Epp ............ 150  A3
Lowdham La. Woodb ....... 149  F2
Lowdham Rd. Carl .......... 162  B2
Lowdham Rd. Gunt ......... 164  C4
Lowdham St. Nott .......... 173  F3

Lower Bagthorpe. Sels ... 128  C2
Lower Beauvale. Greas ... 144  A2
Lower Bloomsgrove Rd. Ilk  157  F1
Lower Brook St. Lo Ea ... 193  F4
Lower Cambridge St. Lough 220  A3
Lower Canaan. Rudd ...... 196  B4
Lower Chapel St. Ilk ....... 157  F1
Lower Clara Mount Rd. Hean 143  D1
Lower Ct. Bees ............... 184  A4
Lower Dunstead Rd. Ald ... 143  D2
Lower Dunstead Rd. La Mi  143  D2
Lower Eldon St. Nott ...... 173  F2
Lower Gladstone St. Lough  220  A3
Lower Granby St. Ilk ....... 157  F1
Lower Kirklington Rd. South 121  E1
Lower Middleton St. Coss .. 158  A1
Lower Orchard St. Staple ... 182  B4
Lower Park St. Staple ..... 182  B3
Lower Parliament St. Nott ... 173  E2
Lower Pasture La. N Whea . 31  F4
Lower Regent St. Bees ... 184  A3
Lower St. Bees ............... 184  A4
Lowes Wong. South ........ 136  B4
Loweswater Ct. Gam ...... 186  B4
Lowfield La. Bald ........... 140  B1
Lowfield. Ret ................... 29  E1
Lowlands Dr. Keyw ......... 197  F2
Lowther Sq. C in L ........... 25  F4
Lowther Way. Lough ...... 220  A1
Lowtown Cl. Work ............ 36  A1
Lowtown St. Work ............ 36  A1
Lowtown View. Work ........ 36  A1
Lucerne Cl. Nott ............ 185  D3
Lucknow Ave. Nott ......... 161  E1
Lucknow Ct. Nott ........... 173  A2
Lucknow Dr. Mans .......... 101  F3
Lucknow Dr. Nott ........... 161  E1
Lucknow Dr. S in A ......... 101  D2
Lucknow Rd. Mans ......... 101  A2
Ludborough Wlk. Mans ..... 88  C2
Ludford Cres. Gain .......... 24  C4
Ludford Rd. Nott ............ 160  B4
Ludgate Cl. Bes Vil ........ 147  D1
Ludgate Dr. E Brid ......... 165  E1
Ludham Ave. Nott .......... 160  A4
Ludlam Ave. Greas ......... 158  A4
Ludlow Cl. Bees ............. 171  E1
Ludlow Hill Rd. W Brid ... 185  F3
Lulworth Cl. W Brid ....... 185  E3
Lulworth Ct. Kim ............ 158  C4
Lumley Dr. Tick ................ 8  A4
Lune Cl. Bees ................ 183  F2
Lune Meadow. Mans ........ 88  C2
Lunn La. Coll ................ 111  F4
Lupin Cl. Nott ............... 173  E4
Luther Ave. S in A .......... 100  C1
Luther Cl. Nott .............. 173  F4
Luton Cl. Nott ............... 160  B1
Lutterell Way. W Brid ..... 186  B3
Lybster Mews. Nott ........ 173  D1
Lydney Park. W Brid ....... 185  E3
Lyle Cl. Kim .................. 158  C4
Lyme Park. W Brid ......... 185  D3
Lymington Gdns. Nott ..... 174  A3
Lymington Rd. Mans ...... 101  E3
Lymn Ave. Carl .............. 162  C1
Lyncombe Ct. Ret ............ 39  E2
Lyncombe Gdns. Keyw .... 197  F2
Lynd Cl. Sels ................ 129  D4
Lyndale Rd. Bees ........... 183  D4
Lynden Ave. Lo Ea ......... 193  E3
Lyndhurst Ave. Blid ....... 118  A3
Lyndhurst Gdns. W Brid .. 185  E2
Lyndhurst Rd. Nott ........ 173  F2
Lynds Cl. Edwin .............. 76  A1
Lyngs The. E Brid ........... 165  E1
Lynmouth Cres. Nott ...... 172  C4
Lynmouth Dr. Ship ......... 157  E2
Lynncroft. East .............. 144  A2
Lynnes Cl. Blid .............. 118  A2
Lynstead Dr. Huck ......... 145  E3
Lynton Gdns. Arn ........... 162  A4
Lynton Rd. Bees ............. 183  E3
Lyons Cl. Rudd .............. 196  A4
Lytham Dr. W Brid .......... 186  B2
Lytham Gdns. Nott ......... 147  D1
Lytham Rd. K-in-A .......... 114  C4
Lythe Cl. Nott ............... 185  D3
Lytton Cl. Nott .............. 173  F3

Mabel Ave. S in A ........... 101  D1
Mabel Gr. W Brid ........... 186  A4
Mabel St. Nott ............... 173  E1
Mable St. Rhod ................ 35  D2
Macaulay Cl. Bald .......... 140  B3
Macaulay Cl. Work ........... 36  B2
Macaulay Dr. Bald .......... 140  B3
Macaulay Gr. Arn ........... 159  D3
Mackinley Ave. Staple .... 170  C1
Mackleys La. N Musk ...... 110  C1
Mackworth Ct. Mans ...... 103  D3
Maclaren Gdns. Rudd ..... 196  B3
Maclean Rd. Carl ........... 174  B4
Macmillan Cl. Nott ......... 161  F1
Madryn Wlk. Nott .......... 161  D1
Mafeking St. Nott .......... 174  A2
Mag La. Elmt ................... 58  A3
Magdala Rd. Nott .......... 173  E4

## Main St. Re[c]

Magdalen Dr. E Brid ....... 165
Magdalene View. N-on-T ... 140
Magdalene Way. Huck .... 146
Magna Cl. Lowd ............. 150
Magnolia Cl. Nott .......... 159
Magnolia Ct. Bees .......... 171
Magnolia Gr. Huck ......... 146
Magnus Rd. Nott ........... 160
Magnus St. N-on-T ........ 140
Magpie Cl. Work .............. 35
Magpie La. N Le Ha ......... 32
Magson St. Nott ............ 173
Maid Marian Ave. Sels ... 129
Maid Marian Way. Nott ... 173
Maid Marion Ave. Bils .... 106
Maid Marion Way. Boug ... 77
Maid Marrion Dr. Edwin .... 76
Maida La. Oll .................. 77
Maiden La. Nott ............. 173
Maidens Dale. Arn .......... 161
Maidstone Dr. Nott ......... 171
Main Ave. Mans ............. 103
Main La. Shel ................ 164
Main Rd. Ald ................. 128
Main Rd. Ann Wo ........... 114
Main Rd. Carl ................ 162
Main Rd. Carl ................ 163
Main Rd. Cotg ............... 187
Main Rd. Kelh ............... 124
Main Rd. Kim ................ 159
Main Rd. Ne La ............... 59
Main Rd. Nott ................ 185
Main Rd. Ol Da .............. 218
Main Rd. Plum ............... 197
Main Rd. R on T ............. 175
Main Rd. Raven ............. 116
Main Rd. Raven ............. 117
Main Rd. Sels ............... 128
Main Rd. Sels ............... 128
Main Rd. Shel ............... 176
Main Rd. Upton ............. 122
Main St. Ann Wo ........... 129
Main St. Aslo ................ 179
Main St. Awsw .............. 158
Main St. Bald ................ 140
Main St. Bath ................ 110
Main St. Bleas .............. 152
Main St. Blid ................. 117
Main St. Blid ................. 118
Main St. Both ................. 63
Main St. Brad ................ 196
Main St. Brin ................. 128
Main St. Bu Jo .............. 163
Main St. Bunn ............... 206
Main St. Calv ................ 148
Main St. Caun ............... 109
Main St. Clar .................. 30
Main St. Codd ............... 126
Main St. Cost ................ 206
Main St. Cr Bu .............. 189
Main St. Crom ............... 110
Main St. Dry Do ............ 156
Main St. E Brid .............. 165
Main St. E Lea ............... 205
Main St. Eakr ................. 92
Main St. East ................ 143
Main St. East ................ 144
Main St. Edin ................ 120
Main St. Egma ................ 79
Main St. Farn ................ 139
Main St. Farns .............. 119
Main St. Fenton ............. 142
Main St. Fisk ................ 137
Main St. Flint ................ 167
Main St. Gam ................ 186
Main St. Gran ................ 191
Main St. Greas .............. 144
Main St. Gunt ................ 165
Main St. Har .................... 8
Main St. Harb ................ 202
Main St. Hayt .................. 30
Main St. Hick ................ 210
Main St. Hover .............. 151
Main St. Keyw ............... 197
Main St. Kim ................. 158
Main St. Kinou .............. 199
Main St. Kirton ............... 78
Main St. Lamb ............... 163
Main St. Lane ................. 54
Main St. Lax ................... 79
Main St. Linby ............... 131
Main St. Lo Ea .............. 193
Main St. Lo Wh ............. 212
Main St. Lowd ............... 150
Main St. Matt .................. 20
Main St. Morton ............ 137
Main St. N Le Ha ............ 32
Main St. N Musk ............ 110
Main St. N on S ............. 213
Main St. Newt ................. 99
Main St. Nott ................ 160
Main St. Old ................... 16
Main St. Oll .................... 77
Main St. Oss ................... 95
Main St. Oxt ................. 134
Main St. Papp ................ 131
Main St. Papp ................ 131
Main St. Redm ............... 192

241
ain St. S in A
Melbourne St. Sels

St. S in A 99 F2
St. S Musk 124 B4
St. S Norm 113 D3
St. S on S 214 B1
St. S on T 96 C4
n St. Scarc 59 D1
n St. Scarr 178 C4
n St. Shireb 72 B2
n St. Sibt 167 F4
n St. Stre 159 D1
n St. Su Bo 213 D2
n St. Su Bo 213 D4
n St. Swine 71 E1
n St. Tork 44 A1
n St. W Lea 204 C1
n St. W Sto 7 F1
n St. W-on-W 217 E4
n St. Wale 64 A1
n St. West 81 D2
n St. What 179 D2
n St. Woodb 149 E2
n St. Wys 207 E2
nside Cres. Sels 129 D1
tland Ave. Arn 161 F2
tland Rd. Arn 161 F2
or St. Nott 173 E3
bon Cl. Nott 173 F4
colm Cl. Nott 173 E4
don Cl. Bees 183 E2
ham Cl. Baw 9 F4
in Hill. Nott 173 E2
kin Ave. R on T 176 A2
lam Rd. Boug 77 E3
llard Cl. Nott 160 C2
llard Cl. Shireb 72 C2
llard Ct. Bees 184 A3
llard Gn. Bald 140 A3
llatratt Pl. Mans 88 A3
lling Wlk. Nott 161 F1
lmesbury Rd. Arn 162 A2
lt Cotts. Nott 160 C1
lt St. Goth 195 D1
ltby Cl. Nott 160 A1
ltby Rd. Arn 162 A2
ltby Rd. Mans 102 C3
ltby Rd. Old 16 C3
lthouse Cl. East 143 F1
lthouse Cotts. Scarc 72 C4
lthouse Rd. Whit 45 D3
lting Cl. Rudd 196 B3
ltings The. Blyth 18 A2
ltings The. Cr Bi 189 D2
ltkiln Cl. Oll 77 E1
ltkiln La. N-on-T 125 D1
ltkiln Rd. Fent 55 E3
ltmill La. Nott 173 E2
lton Rd. Nott 160 C1
ltsters The. N-on-T 139 E3
alvern Cl. Nott 161 F1
alvern Cres. W Brid 185 F3
alvern Gdns. Lo Ea 193 D4
alvern Rd. Nott 161 F1
alvern Rd. W Brid 185 F3
anby Ct. Mar War 74 B4
anchester St. Lo Ea 193 E3
andalay St. Nott 160 B2
andeen Gr. Mans 103 D2
anesty Cres. Nott 195 F4
angham La. Tick 8 A4
anifold Dr. Sels 128 C4
anifold Dr. Sels 129 D4
anifold Gdns. Nott 173 E1
anitoba Way. Sels 128 C4
anly Cl. Nott 160 C4
ann St. Nott 172 C4
anners Ave. Ilk 157 E1
anners Rd. Bald 140 B2
anners Rd. Ilk 157 F1
anners Rd. N-on-T 124 C1
anners St. Ilk 170 A3
anning St. Nott 173 E4
anning View. Ilk 157 F1
annion Cres. Lo Ea 193 D3
anns Leys. Cotg 187 F1
anor Ave. Bees 183 F2
anor Ave. Bees 183 F3
anor Ave. Staple 182 B4
anor Cl. Bleas 152 A4
anor Cl. Boug 77 F3
anor Cl. Cost 206 B1
anor Cl. Gams 50 C3
anor Cl. Lo Wh 212 A2
anor Cl. Miss 4 B2
anor Cl. Newt 99 D2
anor Cl. South 121 F1
anor Cl. W Brid 186 A2
anor Cl. Wale 64 A1
anor Cl. Work 35 E1
Manor Cres. Carl 174 C4
Manor Cres. K-in-A 115 D2
Manor Croft. Nott 160 C2
Manor Ct. Bees 183 D4
Manor Ct. Carl 174 C4
Manor Ct. Mar War 74 B3
Manor Dr. Morton 137 E2
Manor Farm Cl. Brad 196 C2
Manor Farm La. Nott 184 C1
Manor Fm Meadow. E Lea 205 F1
Manor Fm Rise. N Le Ha 32 B1
Manor Gr. Work 35 E1
Manor Green Wlk. Carl 174 C4
Manor House Cl. Lowd 150 B1
Manor House Ct. K-in-A 114 B2
Manor House La. Dry Do 156 B1
Manor House Rd. Lo Ea 193 F3
Manor La. Broad 71 D4
Manor La. Shel 164 B1
Manor La. What 179 D1
Manor Park. Rudd 196 B4
Manor Rd. B in F 194 C3
Manor Rd. Bing 177 F2
Manor Rd. Bott 181 E1
Manor Rd. Calv 148 C4
Manor Rd. Carl 174 C4
Manor Rd. Caun 109 D2
Manor Rd. Coll 112 A4
Manor Rd. E Lea 205 F2
Manor Rd. East 143 F1
Manor Rd. Ilk 157 F1
Manor Rd. Keyw 197 F2
Manor Rd. Mans 88 A2
Manor Rd. Mar War 74 B3
Manor Rd. Mort 15 D2
Manor Rd. S in A 100 C4
Manor Rd. Sax 57 D2
Manor Rise. E Brid 165 E2
Manor St. Nott 173 F2
Manor St. S in A 100 C1
Manorwood Rd. Cotg 187 F1
Manse Ave. Elmt 58 B4
Manse Cl. Elmt 58 B4
Mansell Cl. East 144 A1
Mansfield Gr. Nott 173 D3
Mansfield Ct. Nott 173 D4
Mansfield La. Calv 148 C4
Mansfield La. S in A 101 D3
Mansfield Rd. Ann Wo 130 A3
Mansfield Rd. Arn 132 A2
Mansfield Rd. Arn 161 E2
Mansfield Rd. Babw 38 B2
Mansfield Rd. Bes Vil 147 E3
Mansfield Rd. Blid 118 A3
Mansfield Rd. Blid 118 C4
Mansfield Rd. Brin 143 F2
Mansfield Rd. Cuck 60 A2
Mansfield Rd. East 143 F2
Mansfield Rd. Edin 120 B3
Mansfield Rd. Edwin 75 F1
Mansfield Rd. Edwin 76 A1
Mansfield Rd. Farns 119 E4
Mansfield Rd. Glap 86 B4
Mansfield Rd. Hean 143 D1
Mansfield Rd. Mans 88 B1
Mansfield Rd. Mar War 73 F1
Mansfield Rd. N Clip 90 A3
Mansfield Rd. Nott 161 E2
Mansfield Rd. Oll 76 C2
Mansfield Rd. Papp 132 A2
Mansfield Rd. Raven 116 C1
Mansfield Rd. Raven 116 C2
Mansfield Rd. Raven 132 A2
Mansfield Rd. S in A 100 C3
Mansfield Rd. S in A 101 D2
Mansfield Rd. S Norm 113 E3
Mansfield Rd. Sels 128 C4
Mansfield Rd. Sels 129 D2
Mansfield Rd. Tibs 99 D4
Mansfield Rd. Work 46 A4
Mansfield St. Nott 161 E1
Manthorpe Cres. Nott 161 F2
Manthorpe House. Bald 140 C2
Manthorpe Way. Bald 140 C2
Manton Cl. Rain 118 A4
Manton Cres. Nott 184 A4
Manton Cres. Work 36 A1
Manton Dale. Work 36 A1
Manton Villas. Work 36 B1
Manvers Cres. Edwin 75 F1
Manvers Ct. Nott 173 F2
Manvers Gr. R on T 175 F2
Manvers Rd. Ret 39 E3
Manvers Rd. W Brid 185 F3
Manvers St. Carl 175 D3
Manvers St. Mans 88 A2
Manvers St. Mans 102 A4
Manvers St. Mar War 73 D2
Manvers St. Mar War 74 A2
Manvers St. Nott 173 F2
Manvers St. Work 35 F2
Manvers View. Boug 77 F3
Manville Cl. Bees 171 D2
Manville Cl. Nott 172 B3
Maori Ave. Huck 145 E3
Maple Ave. Bees 184 A3
Maple Ave. Sand 182 A4
Maple Cl. E Lea 214 B4
Maple Cl. Gain 15 D2
Maple Cl. Keyw 198 A1
Maple Cl. Mans 88 C1
Maple Cl. R on T 175 F1
Maple Cl. Tux 66 A1
Maple Cres. K-in-A 114 C3
Maple Dr. Carl 163 D1
Maple Dr. Elk 50 A2
Maple Dr. Huck 145 F3
Maple Dr. Nuth 159 E3
Maple Dr. S Norm 113 D2
Maple Dr. Work 36 A4
Maple Gr. Baw 9 F4
Maple Gr. Glap 86 A4
Maple Gr. N-on-T 139 F2
Maplebeck Ave. Mar War 74 B4
Maplebeck Rd. Arn 162 A4
Maplebeck Rd. Caun 108 C3
Mapledene Cres. Nott 171 E2
Maples St. Nott 172 C4
Maplestead Ave. Nott 185 D3
Mapletoft Ave. Mans 88 A3
Mapleton Way. S in A 101 D2
Mapperley Cres. Nott 161 F1
Mapperley Hall Dr. Nott 161 E1
Mapperley Orch. Arn 162 B4
Mapperley Park Dr. Nott 173 E4
Mapperley Plains. Arn 162 B3
Mapperley Rd. Nott 173 E4
Mapperley Rise. Nott 161 F1
Mapperley Rise. Nott 161 F2
Mapperley St. Nott 161 E1
Mappleton Dr. Mans 103 D3
Mapplewells Cres. S in A 100 A1
Mapplewells Rd. S in A 100 B1
March Cl. Nott 160 C4
Marches Cl. Huck 145 F2
Marchwood Cl. Nott 172 B3
Margaret Ave. Lo Ea 182 C1
Margaret Ave. Sand 182 A2
Margaret Cres. Carl 162 C1
Margaret Pl. Bing 177 E3
Margaret's Ct. Bees 183 D4
Marhill Rd. Carl 174 C4
Marie Gdns. Huck 146 A3
Marina Ave. Bees 183 F3
Mariner Ct. Nott 160 A3
Marion Ave. Huck 131 E1
Marion Ave. K-in-A 115 D1
Marion Murdoch Ct. Carl 162 C1
Maris Cl. Nott 184 B1
Maris Dr. Bu Jo 163 F2
Marjorie St. Rhod 35 D2
Mark La. E Mark 65 F3
Mark St. Sand 182 B3
Market Cl. S Norm 113 D3
Market Cl. Shireb 72 C2
Market Pl. Bing 177 F2
Market Pl. Gain 24 B4
Market Pl. Huck 146 A4
Market Pl. Lo Ea 193 F4
Market Pl. Lough 220 A2
Market Pl. Mans 88 B2
Market Pl. Mans 102 A4
Market Pl. Nott 160 A4
Market Pl. Nott 160 B4
Market Pl. Oll 77 D2
Market Pl. Ret 39 F4
Market Pl. S in A 99 F2
Market Pl. S in A 100 C1
Market Pl. S Norm 113 D3
Market Pl. South 136 C4
Market Pl. Tick 8 A4
Market Pl. Tux 65 F2
Market Pl. Work 35 F1
Market Place. Kegw 203 E1
Market Side. Nott 160 A4
Market St. Bing 177 F2
Market St. Bott 181 D1
Market St. Gain 24 B4
Market St. Lough 220 A2
Market St. Mans 102 A4
Market St. Nott 173 E2
Market St. S in A 99 F2
Market St. S in A 100 C1
Market St. S Norm 113 D3
Market St. Shireb 72 C2
Market St. Work 35 F2
Markham Ave. N-on-T 125 D2
Markham Cres. Nott 161 E2
Markham Pl. Mans 101 E4
Markham Rd. Bees 171 E1
Markham Rd. Lan 16 C2
Markham Rd. Tux 65 F2
Markham St. News 130 B3
Markhams The. Oll 77 D2
Markland La. Elmt 58 A4
Marklew Cl. Blid 118 A3
Markwick Cl. N-on-T 140 B4
Marl Rd. R on T 176 A2
Marlborough Cl. N-on-T 139 E3
Marlborough Rd. Arn 161 F3
Marlborough Rd. Bees 183 F4
Marlborough Rd. K-in-A 115 D3
Marlborough Rd. Lo Ea 182 C1
Marlborough Rd. Mans 87 F1
Marlborough St. Gain 24 B4
Marldon Cl. Nott 171 E3
Marle Pit Hill. Su Bo 213 D4
Marlock Cl. Fisk 137 F2
Marlow Ave. Nott 160 C1
Marlow Rd. Gain 15 F1
Marlowe Dr. Bald 140 B2
Marlowe Gdns. Work 36 A2
Marlwood. Cotg 188 A1
Marmion Rd. Nott 174 A3
Marnham Dr. Nott 161 F1
Marnham Rd. Tux 66 B1
Marple Sq. Nott 173 E3
Marples Ave. Mans 88 C3
Marquis Ave. Bald 140 B2
Marquis Gdns. Ret 40 A2
Marquis Rd. Ne Br 219 D3
Marriots La. Blid 117 F2
Marriott Ave. Bees 183 D3
Marriott Ave. Mans 101 F4
Marriott Cl. Bees 183 D3
Marsh La. Farn 139 D3
Marsh La. Mist 7 E1
Marsh La. N Musk 110 C1
Marsh La. Saundby 23 E3
Marsh Rd. Walker 14 B3
Marsh's Paddock. Hick 210 B3
Marshall Ave. K-in-A 115 E2
Marshall Ct. Bald 140 C2
Marshall Dr. Bees 183 D4
Marshall Hill Dr. Carl 162 A1
Marshall Rd. Carl 162 A1
Marshall Rd. Cr Bi 189 D2
Marshall St. Hean 143 D1
Marshall St. Nott 161 E1
Marshall Terr. S in A 100 B3
Marston Ave. Mar War 74 B4
Marston Cl. Bald 140 B2
Marston Rd. Nott 174 A4
Martin Cl. Nott 160 A4
Martin Ct. Nott 160 A4
Martin La. Baw 9 F4
Martindale Cl. Gam 186 B4
Martins Hill. Carl 174 C4
Martlet Way. Work 47 D4
Marton Rd. Bees 183 E2
Marton Rd. N-on-T 140 A3
Marton Rd. Nott 146 B1
Martyn Ave. S in A 100 C1
Marvin Rd. Bees 183 F3
Marwood Cres. Carl 162 B1
Marwood Rd. Carl 162 B1
Mary Rd. East 144 A1
Mary St. K-in-A 115 D3
Mary St. Rhod 35 D2
Mary St. Scarc 59 D1
Maryfield Cl. Ret 29 F1
Maryland Ct. Staple 170 C1
Masefield Cres. Bald 140 B2
Masefield Pl. Work 36 A2
Mason St. S in A 101 D2
Masonic Pl. Nott 173 D3
Massey Cl. Bu Jo 163 F2
Massey Gdns. Nott 173 F3
Massey St. N-on-T 140 A4
Masson Ct. Nott 147 D1
Matlock Ave. Mans 102 A3
Matlock Ct. Nott 173 E3
Matlock St. Carl 174 C4
Mattersey Ct. Mans 88 A1
Mattersey Rd. Ever 11 E1
Mattersey Rd. Lound 20 A1
Mattersey Rd. Ran 19 E3
Mattersey Rd. Sutt 29 D4
Matthews Ct. Staple 170 C1
Mattingly Rd. Nott 160 A3
Mattley Ave. Ann Wo 115 D1
Maud St. Nott 161 D1
Maun Ave. K-in-A 115 D4
Maun Ave. Nott 172 B3
Maun Cl. Mans 101 F2
Maun Gn. N-on-T 125 D1
Maun Way. Mans 101 F2
Maundale Ave. S in A 101 D2
Maunleigh. Mans 88 C1
Maunside Ave. S in A 101 D1
Maunside. Mans 101 F2
Maurice Dr. Nott 161 F2
Mavis Ave. Raven 117 D1
Maws La. Kim 158 C4
Maxtoke Rd. Nott 173 D2
Maxwell Cl. Nott 172 C2
May Ave. Nott 171 F2
May Ct. Nott 161 D1
May Fair Pl. Tux 66 A1
May Lodge Dr. Ruff 91 F3
May St. Ilk 157 F2
Maycroft Gdns. Carl 174 A4
Mayes Rise. Bes Vil 146 C2
Mayfair Ave. Mans 102 B3
Mayfair Cl. Har 8 C2
Mayfair Ct. Nott 160 C1
Mayfair Gdns. Nott 160 C3
Mayfield Ave. Bu Jo 163 F3
Mayfield Ave. Gain 15 D2
Mayfield Cl. Mans 103 D3
Mayfield Ct. Nott 173 E1
Mayfield Dr. Lough 220 A1
Mayfield Dr. Staple 170 C1
Mayfield Gr. Lo Ea 182 C1
Mayfield Pl. S in A 100 B1
Mayfield Rd. Carl 174 A4
Mayfield St. K-in-A 114 B2
Mayfield Terr. Mar War 74 A2
Mayflower Ave. Scro 10 A1
Mayflower Cl. Baw 10 A4
Mayflower Cl. Lea 24 C2
Mayflower Cl. W Brid 186 A4
Mayflower Ct. Shireb 72 C2
Mayflower Rd. Greas 158 B4
Mayhall Ave. Mans 88 A2
Mayland Cl. Nott 171 E3
Mayo Rd. Nott 161 D1
Maypole Ct. Wellow 92 C4
Maypole Rd. Wellow 92 C4
Maypole Yd. Nott 173 E3
Maypole. Nott 184 C2
Mays Ave. Carl 174 B3
Mays Cl. Carl 174 B3
Mays La. Sax 57 E2
Maythorn Cl. W Brid 185 E2
Maythorn Gr. Edwin 76 A2
Maythorne Cl. Bald 140 B3
Maythorne Wlk. Nott 161 E4
Mcintosh Rd. Carl 162 B2
Meade Dr. Work 36 A4
Meadow Ave. Lough 220 A3
Meadow Ave. Mans 102 B3
Meadow Bank. Mans 88 C3
Meadow Cl. Aslo 179 D3
Meadow Cl. Farns 120 A3
Meadow Cl. Greas 143 F2
Meadow Cl. Huck 145 E3
Meadow Cl. K-in-A 114 C3
Meadow Cl. N Musk 110 C1
Meadow Cl. Nott 173 F1
Meadow Cl. Ret 29 F1
Meadow Cl. Tibs 99 D4
Meadow Cotts. Carl 174 C4
Meadow Cotts. Mans 88 B2
Meadow Ct. Nott 173 F1
Meadow Ct. S Norm 113 D2
Meadow Dr. Keyw 198 A2
Meadow Dr. Mist 6 C1
Meadow Dr. S in A 100 B2
Meadow Dr. Tick 8 B4
Meadow Dr. Work 35 E1
Meadow End. Goth 195 D1
Meadow End. R on T 176 B2
Meadow Gdns. Bees 183 F2
Meadow Gr. Newt 99 D2
Meadow Gr. Nott 173 F1
Meadow La Ind Est. Lough 220 A3
Meadow La. Bees 183 F2
Meadow La. Both 63 F4
Meadow La. Bu Jo 163 F2
Meadow La. Girt 82 C2
Meadow La. Lo Ea 193 F4
Meadow La. Lough 220 A4
Meadow La. N Sca 83 F1
Meadow La. Nott 173 F1
Meadow La. S Norm 113 D4
Meadow La. Sons 220 A4
Meadow La. West 81 D2
Meadow Pl. Mar War 74 A2
Meadow Rd. Awsw 158 B3
Meadow Rd. Bald 140 B2
Meadow Rd. Bees 184 A2
Meadow Rd. Blid 118 A3
Meadow Rd. Carl 174 C4
Meadow Rd. Work 35 E1
Meadow Rise. Nott 159 F3
Meadow Rise. Sax 57 D2
Meadow St. Ilk 157 F1
Meadow The. Ret 39 F3
Meadow View. South 121 F1
Meadow Way. Har 8 C3
Meadow Way. Kinou 199 F1
Meadowbank Way. East 143 E2
Meadows La. Hose 201 E1
Meadows The. Beck 23 D4
Meadows The. Farn 139 D3
Meadows The. S Whea 31 F4
Meadows The. Woodb 149 D2
Meadows Way. Nott 173 E1
Meadowsweet Hill. Bing 177 E2
Meadowvale Cres. Nott 184 C1
Medawar Cl. Nott 184 B1
Meden Ave. Mar War 74 B3
Meden Ave. Plea 86 C4
Meden Bank. Both 63 F4
Meden Bank. Mans 87 D3
Meden Bank. S in A 100 B3
Meden Cl. Mans 87 D3
Meden Cl. Nott 184 C2
Meden Cres. S in A 100 B2
Meden Gdns. Nott 172 B4
Meden Glen. Mar War 74 B3
Meden Rd. Mans 88 B2
Meden Sq. Mans 87 D3
Medina Dr. Toll 186 C1
Medway Cl. Bees 183 E3
Medway. Ret 29 E1
Meeks Rd. Arn 162 A4
Meer Rd. Bees 183 D3
Meering Ave. N-on-T 125 D2
Meering Cl. Coll 98 A1
Meerings The. S on T 81 F1
Meeting House Cl. E Lea 205 F1
Meetinghouse La. S Lev 42 A3
Melbourne Ct. Mans 103 D3
Melbourne Ct. Nott 160 B1
Melbourne Gr. Har 8 C2
Melbourne Rd. Nott 160 B1
Melbourne Rd. Staple 170 C1
Melbourne Rd. W Brid 174 A1
Melbourne St. Mans 88 B3
Melbourne St. Sels 129 D3

Melbury Rd. Arn ................. 162 A3
Melbury Rd. Nott ............... 171 E4
Meldreth Rd. Nott .............. 171 F4
Meldrum Cres. N-on-T ........ 139 F3
Melford Hall Dr. W Brid ..... 185 E2
Melford Rd. Nott ................ 171 E4
Melksham Rd. Nott ............ 161 E4
Mellish Rd. Lan .................. 16 C1
Mellors Rd. Mans .............. 101 E4
Mellors Rd. Nott ................ 147 F1
Mellors Rd. W Brid ............ 185 F3
Melrose Ave. Bees ............. 184 A3
Melrose Ave. Mans ............ 102 B3
Melrose Ave. Nott .............. 161 E2
Melrose Gdns. W Brid ........ 185 E2
Melrose Rd. Gain ............... 15 E1
Melrose St. Nott ................ 161 E2
Melrose Wlk. Work ............. 35 F1
Melton Ave. Plum .............. 197 F4
Melton Ct. Sand ................ 182 A3
Melton Gdns. W Brid ......... 186 A2
Melton Gr. W Brid ............. 185 F4
Melton La. Su Bo .............. 204 B1
Melton Rd. E Lea .............. 214 C3
Melton Rd. Hick ................ 209 E2
Melton Rd. Lo Cl ............... 211 D1
Melton Rd. N-on-W ........... 198 B2
Melton Rd. Remp ............... 215 E3
Melton Rd. S on S ............. 214 C3
Melton Rd. S-on-W ............ 198 B2
Melton Rd. Toll ................. 197 F4
Melton Rd. Up Br ............... 210 A1
Melton Rd. W Brid ............. 186 A2
Melton Rd. Widm ............... 208 C4
Melton Way. Mans ............. 101 F2
Melville Ct. Nott ................ 173 E4
Melville Gdns. Nott ............ 173 F3
Melville St. Nott ................ 173 E2
Melvyn Dr. Bing ................ 177 F2
Memorial Ave. Work ........... 35 F1
Mendip Cl. Lo Ea .............. 182 A1
Mendip Ct. C in L .............. 25 F4
Mendip Ct. Nott ................ 160 C4
Mensing Ave. Cotg ............ 187 F2
Mercer Rd. Gain ................ 15 D1
Merchant St. Nott .............. 160 A4
Merchant St. Shireb ........... 73 D2
Mercia Ave. Cr Bi .............. 189 D2
Mercia Cl. Work ................ 36 A4
Mercia Rd. N-on-T ............ 139 F3
Mercury Cl. Nott ............... 160 C3
Mere Ave. Calv ................. 148 C4
Mere Cl. Calv ................... 148 C4
Meredith Cl. Nott ............... 173 D1
Meredith Ct. Staple ........... 170 C1
Meregill Cl. Nott ............... 146 C1
Merevale Ave. Nott ............ 184 C2
Merevale Cl. Lowd ............. 150 C1
Meriac St. Nott ................. 160 C4
Meriden Ave. Nott ............. 184 A4
Merlin Cl. Nott .................. 184 C1
Merlin Dr. Huck ................ 145 F2
Merrick Dr. Work ............... 36 B2
Merrivale Ct. Nott .............. 173 E4
Merryvale Dr. Mans ........... 101 E3
Merryweather Cl. Edwin ...... 91 E4
Merryweather Cl. South ...... 121 F1
Mersey St. Nott ................ 160 A4
Merton Ave. Ret ............... 29 F1
Merton Cl. Arn .................. 148 A1
Merton Ct. Staple .............. 170 C1
Metcalf Cl. Bils ................. 105 F4
Metcalf Rd. Greas ............. 144 A2
Metcalfe Cl. South ............ 136 C4
Methuen St. Mans ............. 102 C3
Metro Ave. Newt ............... 99 D2
Mettham St. Nott ............... 172 C2
Mews La. Calv ................... 148 C4
Meynell Gr. Nott ............... 161 D1
Meynell Rd. Lo Ea ............. 193 E3
Meyrick Rd. N-on-T ........... 125 D1
Miall Ct. Nott ................... 172 C3
Micklebarrow Cl. South ...... 136 B4
Mickleborough Ave. Nott .... 174 A4
Mickleborough Way. W Brid 185 E2
Mickledale Cl. Bils ............ 105 F4
Mickledale La. Bils ............ 105 F4
Mickleden Cl. Nott ............. 173 D1
Mickledon Cl. Lo Ea .......... 193 D4
Middle Ave. Carl ............... 174 B4
Middle Furlong Gdns. Nott .. 173 D1
Middle Furlong Mews. Nott 173 D1
Middle Gate. N-on-T .......... 139 F4
Middle Hill. Nott ............... 173 E2
Middle Holme La. S on T .... 97 D4
Middle La. Bees ................ 183 F3
Middle La. Morton ............. 137 E2
Middle La. Ne Br ............... 219 E4
Middle Pavement. Nott ....... 173 E2
Middle St. B-le-V ............... 192 B1
Middle St. Bees ................. 183 F3
Middle St. Bees ................. 184 A3
Middle St. Hose ................ 211 F4
Middle St. Miss ................. 4 B1
Middle Wood La. Miss ........ 4 B3
Middlebeck Ave. Arn .......... 162 B4
Middlebeck Dr. Arn ............ 162 B4
Middlebridge Rd. G on H ..... 12 C2

Middlebrook Rd. Sels ........ 129 D2
Middledale Rd. Carl ........... 174 B3
Middlefell Way. Nott .......... 184 B1
Middlefield La. Gain .......... 24 C4
Middlefield Rd. N Whea ...... 31 F4
Middlegate Field Dr. Whit ... 45 D3
Middleton Bvd. Nott .......... 172 B2
Middleton Cl. Nuth ............ 159 E3
Middleton Cres. Bees ........ 171 F1
Middleton Ct. Mans ........... 103 D3
Middleton Ct. Oll .............. 77 E3
Middleton Pl. Lough .......... 220 A1
Middleton Rd. Ilk .............. 170 A3
Middleton Rd. Mans ........... 88 B3
Middleton Rd. N-on-T ........ 125 E2
Middleton St. Awsw .......... 158 A2
Middleton St. Bees ........... 183 F4
Middleton St. Coss ........... 158 A1
Middleton St. Nott ............ 172 C3
Midfield Rd. Ann Wo ......... 115 D1
Midhurst Cl. Bees ............. 183 D2
Midhurst Way. Nott ........... 184 C1
Midland Ave. Carl ............. 175 D4
Midland Ave. Nott ............. 172 C2
Midland Ave. Staple .......... 182 B3
Midland Cres. Carl ............ 174 C4
Midland Gr. Carl ............... 175 D4
Midland Rd. Carl ............... 174 C4
Midland Rd. East .............. 143 F1
Midland St. Lo Ea ............. 193 F4
Midway The. Nott .............. 184 C4
Midworth St. Mans ............ 102 A3
Mikado Rd. Lo Ea ............. 193 E3
Milburn Gr. Bing .............. 177 E2
Mildenhall Cres. Nott ........ 161 E4
Mile End Rd. Carl ............. 174 C3
Miles Yd. Lough ............... 220 A2
Milford Ave. Lo Ea ............ 182 A2
Milford Cl. Nott ................ 160 A4
Milford Cres. Mans ........... 101 E4
Milford Ct. Arn ................. 161 E3
Milford Dr. Ilk ................. 157 E2
Milford Dr. Nott ............... 174 B3
Milford Dr. Nott ............... 174 B4
Mill Baulk Rd. Walker ....... 14 A3
Mill Cl. N Le Ha ............... 32 B1
Mill Cl. S in A .................. 100 A2
Mill Cl. S on T ................. 96 C4
Mill Cres. Arn .................. 161 F4
Mill Cres. Whit ................ 45 D3
Mill Croft. S in A .............. 100 C1
Mill Field Cl. Bu Jo .......... 163 F2
Mill Field Cl. Harby .......... 70 B1
Mill Gate. E Brid .............. 165 E2
Mill Gate. N-on-T ............. 139 F4
Mill Gdns. Work ............... 35 E1
Mill Green. N-on-T ........... 140 A4
Mill Heyes. E Brid ............ 165 E2
Mill Hill. G on H .............. 12 B1
Mill La. Al Hu .................. 85 E4
Mill La. Ann Wo ............... 114 C1
Mill La. Arn ..................... 161 F4
Mill La. Aslo ................... 178 C4
Mill La. Caun .................. 109 D3
Mill La. Coss .................. 158 B1
Mill La. Cotg ................... 187 F2
Mill La. E Lea .................. 214 C4
Mill La. Eagle .................. 84 C2
Mill La. Edwin ................. 76 A1
Mill La. K-in-A ................. 114 C1
Mill La. Kegw .................. 203 E1
Mill La. Lamb .................. 163 D4
Mill La. Lo Cl .................. 211 E2
Mill La. Lo Wh ................. 212 B2
Mill La. Lough ................. 220 B3
Mill La. Mort ................... 15 E3
Mill La. N Clift ................. 68 C3
Mill La. N Le Ha ............... 42 A4
Mill La. N Musk ............... 110 C1
Mill La. N-on-T ................ 139 F4
Mill La. Nor on T .............. 81 E4
Mill La. Orst ................... 180 A4
Mill La. Pinx ................... 113 E1
Mill La. S in A ................. 100 A1
Mill La. S Lev .................. 42 B4
Mill La. Sand .................. 182 B3
Mill La. Sax .................... 57 D2
Mill La. Scarr .................. 178 C4
Mill La. Scro ................... 10 A2
Mill La. Upton ................. 137 F4
Mill La. W Dray ................ 51 D1
Mill La. W-on-W ............... 217 E4
Mill La. Wale ................... 63 F1
Mill La. Walker ................. 13 F2
Mill La. Whit ................... 45 D3
Mill Meadow View. Blyth ... 18 A2
Mill Rd. East ................... 144 A2
Mill Rd. Elst .................... 153 F2
Mill Rd. Hean .................. 157 D4
Mill Rd. Staple ................ 182 B4
Mill St. Ilk ...................... 157 F1
Mill St. Mans .................. 102 B3
Mill St. Nott .................... 160 B2
Mill St. S in A .................. 100 C1
Mill St. Work ................... 35 F2
Mill Wlk. Whit .................. 45 D3
Mill Yd. Bees ................... 183 F3

Mill Yd. Huck .................. 146 A4
Millash La. Whit ............... 45 D2
Millbank Cl. Ship .............. 157 E2
Millbank. Hean ................ 157 D4
Millbaulk La. Knee ............ 93 F4
Millbeck Ave. Nott ............ 171 E2
Millbeck Cl. Gam .............. 186 B3
Millbeck Cl. Nott .............. 184 B1
Milldale Cl. Nott ............... 171 E2
Milldale Rd. Farns ............ 120 A3
Milldale Rd. Lo Ea ............ 193 D3
Milldale Wlk. S in A ........... 100 B2
Miller Hives Cl. Cotg ......... 187 F2
Miller's La. Cost ............... 206 B1
Millers Bridge. Cotg .......... 187 F1
Millers Cl. Shel ................ 164 B1
Millers Ct. Nott ................ 172 C3
Millers Way. Ret .............. 39 E4
Millersdale Ave. Ilk .......... 157 F3
Millersdale Ave. Mans ....... 101 F2
Millfield Ave. Sax ............. 57 D2
Millfield Cl. Ret ............... 39 F2
Millfield Rd. Kim .............. 158 C4
Millfield Rd. Ilk ................ 170 A4
Millfield View. Work .......... 35 E1
Millicent Gr. W Brid .......... 185 F4
Millicent Rd. W Brid .......... 185 F4
Millingdon Ave. Nuth ........ 159 E2
Millman Way. Ret ............. 29 E1
Mills Dr. N-on-T ............... 139 E3
Millview Cl. Nott ............... 173 F2
Millview Ct. Nott ............... 173 F2
Millway. Mans .................. 88 B1
Milne Ave. Bir .................. 9 E2
Milne Dr. Bir .................... 9 E2
Milne Gr. Bir .................... 9 E2
Milne Rd. Bir ................... 9 E2
Milner Rd. Lo Ea .............. 193 E4
Milner Rd. Nott ................ 161 E1
Milner St. N-on-T ............. 140 A4
Milner St. S in A ............... 101 D3
Milnercroft Green. Ret ....... 29 E1
Milnercroft. Ret ............... 29 E1
Milnhay Rd. Hean ............. 143 E1
Milnhay Rd. La Mi ............ 143 E1
Milton Ave. Ilk ................. 157 F2
Milton Cl. S in A ............... 101 D2
Milton Cres. Bees ............. 183 E1
Milton Cres. Raven ........... 117 D1
Milton Ct. Arn .................. 162 A4
Milton Dr. Raven .............. 117 D1
Milton Dr. Work ............... 36 A2
Milton Rd. Gain ................ 15 F1
Milton Rd. Ilk .................. 157 F2
Milton Rd. W Mark ........... 65 D3
Milton Rise. Huck ............. 145 E3
Milton St. Bald ................. 140 B3
Milton St. Ilk ................... 157 F2
Milton St. K-in-A .............. 115 D3
Milton St. Lo Ea ............... 193 E4
Milton St. Mans ............... 102 A4
Milton St. Nott ................. 173 E3
Milton Wlk. Work .............. 36 A2
Milverton Rd. Nott ............ 161 E4
Mimosa Cl. Nott ............... 184 B1
Minerva St. Nott ............... 160 A4
Minster Cl. Huck .............. 146 A4
Minster Cl. K-in-A ............. 114 C3
Minster Gdns. East ........... 144 A1
Minster Rd. Mist ............... 6 C1
Minver Cres. Nott ............. 160 A1
Mirberry Mews. Nott ......... 172 C2
Mire La. Sutt ................... 28 C3
Misk Hollows. Huck .......... 145 F4
Misk View. East ............... 144 A1
Mission St. Nott ............... 161 F1
Misterton Ct. Mans ........... 88 A1
Mitchel Ave. Codd ............ 125 F1
Mitchell Ave. La Mi ........... 143 D2
Mitchell Cl. Nott ............... 160 A3
Mitchell St. Lo Ea ............. 193 F4
Mitchell Terr. Ilk .............. 170 A3
Mob La. W-on-W ............... 217 E4
Model Village. Elmt .......... 58 C4
Moffat Cl. Nott ................. 173 F4
Moira St. Lough ............... 220 A2
Mollington Sq. Nott .......... 160 A2
Mona Rd. W Brid .............. 174 A1
Mona St. Bees ................. 184 A3
Monarch Way. Lough ........ 220 A3
Monckton Rd. Bir .............. 9 E2
Monckton Rd. Ret ............. 39 E4
Monks Cl. Ilk ................... 170 A4
Monks Meadow. E Lea ....... 205 F1
Monksway. Nott ............... 185 D2
Monkton Cl. Ship ............. 157 E2
Monkton Dr. Nott .............. 171 F4
Monkton Dr. South ........... 121 F1
Monkwood Cl. Coll ........... 98 A1
Monmouth Cl. Nott ........... 171 D2
Monmouth Rd. Work .......... 36 A3
Monroe Wlk. Nott ............. 161 D4
Monsaldale Cl. Lo Ea ........ 193 D3
Monsall Ave. Ilk ............... 157 F3
Monsall St. Nott ............... 160 C1
Monsall St. Nott ............... 161 D1
Monsell Dr. Nott ............... 147 F1

Montague Rd. Huck ........... 146 A4
Montague St. Bees ............ 183 F4
Montague St. Mans ........... 102 C3
Montague St. Nott ............ 160 B4
Montfort Cres. Nott ........... 161 E2
Montfort St. Nott .............. 173 D3
Montgomery Rd. N-on-T .... 140 A3
Montgomery St. Nott ......... 173 D3
Montpelier Rd. Nott .......... 172 C1
Montrose Ct. Staple .......... 170 C1
Montrose Sq. Mans ........... 88 A3
Montrose. Work ................ 36 A3
Monyash Cl. Ilk ................ 157 F2
Moor Bridge. Nott ............ 146 B1
Moor Farm Inn La. Bees .... 171 D1
Moor La. Aslo .................. 178 B3
Moor La. Bees .................. 171 D2
Moor La. Best .................. 98 B3
Moor La. Bing .................. 177 F3
Moor La. Blyth ................. 18 B1
Moor La. Bunn ................. 206 B4
Moor La. Dry Do ............... 169 F3
Moor La. E Sto ................. 154 A3
Moor La. Epp ................... 149 E3
Moor La. Goth .................. 205 E4
Moor La. Lough ................ 220 B2
Moor La. Mans ................. 101 F3
Moor La. Morton ............... 137 E2
Moor La. N on S ............... 213 E2
Moor La. Rudd ................. 196 B3
Moor La. S Clift ............... 68 C1
Moor La. S Clift ............... 69 E2
Moor La. Scarc ................ 72 A4
Moor La. Scarr ................. 178 B3
Moor La. Stat ................... 202 C3
Moor La. Syer .................. 153 E2
Moor La. Thor .................. 69 E2
Moor La. Torw .................. 18 B1
Moor La. Woodb ............... 149 E3
Moor Rd. Brin .................. 143 F4
Moor Rd. Calv .................. 149 D4
Moor Rd. Coll .................. 98 A1
Moor Rd. Huck ................. 146 C3
Moor Rd. Nott .................. 159 E1
Moor St. Carl ................... 174 C4
Moor St. Carl ................... 175 D4
Moor St. Mans ................. 102 A3
Moor Top Rd. Har ............. 8 C3
Moorbridge Cotts. Nott ...... 146 B1
Moorbridge La. Staple ....... 170 B1
Moorbridge Rd. Bing ......... 177 F3
Moore Ave. Kegw ............. 203 E2
Moore Cl. E Lea ............... 205 F1
Moore Cl. W Brid .............. 174 A1
Moore Gate. Bees ............. 184 A3
Moore Rd. Carl ................ 162 A1
Moores Ave. Sand ............ 182 B4
Moorfield Cres. Sand ........ 182 A3
Moorfield Ct. Staple .......... 170 C1
Moorfield La. Scarc .......... 58 C2
Moorfield Pl. Mar War ....... 74 B3
Moorfields Ave. East ......... 143 F2
Moorgate Ave. Plea .......... 86 C4
Moorgate Park. Ret ........... 39 F4
Moorgate St. Nott ............. 173 D3
Moorgreen. Greas ............ 144 B2
Moorhaigh La. Mans ......... 87 D2
Moorhouse Rd. Lax .......... 80 B2
Moorhouse Rd. Nott .......... 171 F3
Moorhouse Rd. West ......... 80 B2
Moorings The. Nott ........... 172 C1
Moorland Ave. Staple ........ 182 B3
Moorland Ave. Walker ....... 13 F3
Moorland Cl. Mans ........... 101 F4
Moorland Cl. Walker ......... 13 F3
Moorland La. Mans ........... 101 F4
Moorland Way. Mans ........ 103 D3
Moorland Wlk. Walker ....... 13 F3
Moorsholm Dr. Nott .......... 171 E2
Moray Cl. Kim .................. 158 C4
Moray Sq. Mans ............... 101 E3
Morden Cl. Nott ............... 171 E4
Morden Rd. Greas ............ 158 B4
Moreland Ct. Carl ............. 174 B4
Moreland St. Nott ............. 173 F2
Moreland Terr. Nott .......... 173 F2
Morello Ave. Carl ............. 174 C4
Moreton Rd. Nott .............. 195 F4
Morgan Mews. Nott .......... 184 C1
Morgans Cl. Codd ............ 126 A1
Morkinshire Cres. Cotg ..... 187 F2
Morley Ave. Nott .............. 161 F1
Morley Ave. Ret ............... 29 E1
Morley Cl. Mans ............... 103 D3
Morley Cl. Nott ................ 173 F3
Morley Dr. Ilk .................. 157 E2
Morley Rd. Carl ................ 162 A1
Morley St. Arn ................. 161 F3
Morley St. Gain ................ 24 B4
Morley St. K-in-A ............. 115 D2
Morley St. Lough .............. 220 B3
Morley St. S in A .............. 100 A3
Morley St. S in A .............. 100 C2
Mornington Cl. Sand ......... 182 B3
Mornington Cres. Nuth ...... 159 E2
Morrell Bank. Nott ............ 160 B4
Morris Cl. Lough ............... 220 B1
Morris Rd. Nott ................ 159 E1

Morris St. Carl ................. 175
Morton Cl. Mans ............... 103
Morton Cl. Mort ................ 15
Morton Gdns. R on T ........ 176
Morton Rd. Gain ............... 15
Morton St. Mans ............... 87
Morton Terr. Gain ............. 15
Morval Rd. Nott ................ 171
Morven Ave. Huck ............ 146
Morven Ave. Mans ............ 88
Morven Ave. S in A ........... 100
Morven Rd. K-in-A ............ 115
Morven St. Elmt ............... 58
Morven Terr. Mar War ....... 74
Mosborough Rd. S in A ...... 100
Moseley Rd. Ann Wo ......... 130
Mosley St. Huck ............... 146
Mosley St. Nott ................ 172
Moss Cl. Bes Vil ............... 147
Moss Cl. E Brid ................ 165
Moss Rd. Huck ................. 145
Moss Rise. Carl ................ 162
Moss Side. Nott ............... 185
Mosscroft Ave. Nott .......... 184
Mossdale Rd. Mans ........... 161
Mossdale Rd. Nott ............ 161
Mosswood Cres. Nott ........ 145
Mottram Rd. Bees ............. 183
Moulton Cres. Bald ........... 140
Mount Ave. Work .............. 35
Mount Cl. Har ................... 8
Mount Cres. Mar War ........ 74
Mount Cres. S Norm .......... 113
Mount Ct. Bald ................. 140
Mount Hooton Rd. Nott ...... 173
Mount La. N-on-T ............. 140
Mount Milner. Mans .......... 102
Mount Pleasant Cl. Mart .... 44
Mount Pleasant. Carl ......... 174
Mount Pleasant. Ilk .......... 157
Mount Pleasant. Keyw ...... 198
Mount Pleasant. Keyw ...... 198
Mount Pleasant. Lowd ....... 150
Mount Pleasant. Mans ....... 102
Mount Pleasant. Nott ........ 160
Mount Pleasant. R on T ..... 175
Mount Pleasant. Ret .......... 39
Mount Pleasant. S in A ...... 100
Mount Rd. Bald ................ 140
Mount St. Mans ................ 88
Mount St. Nott ................. 160
Mount St. Staple .............. 182
Mount The. Bes Vil ........... 147
Mount The. Carl ............... 162
Mount The. Mans ............. 89
Mount The. Nott ............... 147
Mount The. Nott ............... 159
Mount The. Staple ............ 182
Mount View Cl. Mans ........ 102
Mountbatten Cl. Ilk ........... 157
Mountbatten Gr. Carl ........ 162
Mountfield Ave. Sand ........ 182
Mountfield Dr. Nott ........... 161
Mountsorrel Dr. W Brid ...... 186
Mowbray Ct. Nott ............. 173
Mowbray Gdns. W Brid ...... 185
Mowbray Rise. Arn ........... 161
Mowbray Str. Gain ............ 15
Mowlands Cl. S in A .......... 101
Moyra Dr. Arn .................. 161
Mozart Cl. Nott ................ 172
Muir Ave. Toll .................. 197
Muirfield Cl. K-in-A ........... 114
Muirfield Rd. Bes Vil ......... 147
Muirfield Way. Mans ......... 88
Muirfield. Work ................ 36
Mulberry Cl. W Brid .......... 185
Mulberry Cres. C in L ........ 25
Mulberry Gdns. Nott ......... 160
Mulberry Gr. Huck ............ 146
Mumby Cl. N-on-T ............ 125
Mundella Rd. Nott ............ 173
Mundy St. Ilk ................... 157
Munford Circ. Nott ............ 160
Munks Ave. Huck .............. 145
Munt's Hill. Greas ............ 144
Murby Cres. Nott .............. 160
Murden Way. Bees ............ 184
Muriel Rd. Bees ............... 183
Muriel St. Nott ................. 160
Murray St. Mans ............... 88
Muschamp Terr. Mar War .. 74
Mushill La. Wyme ............. 216
Muskham Ave. Ilk ............. 157
Muskham Ct. Mans ........... 88
Muskham La. Bath ............ 110
Muskham St. Nott ............. 173
Musters Cres. W Brid ........ 185
Musters Croft. Carl ........... 174
Musters Rd. Bing .............. 177
Musters Rd. News ............. 130
Musters Rd. Rudd ............. 196
Musters Rd. W Brid ........... 185
Musters Rd. W Brid ........... 185
Musters St. Shireb ............ 73
Musters Wlk. Nott ............. 160
Muston Cl. Nott ................ 161

| | | |
|---|---|---|
| ...ston La. Bott | 181 | E1 |
| ...tton La. Beck | 23 | D4 |
| ...ttonshire Hill. Gams | 50 | C3 |
| ...rnd The. Mans | 88 | C3 |
| ...rrtle Ave. Lo Ea | 193 | E3 |
| ...rrtle Ave. Nott | 173 | D4 |
| ...rrtle Ave. Staple | 182 | C3 |
| ...rrtle Cl. Shireb | 72 | B3 |
| ...rrtle Gr. Bees | 184 | A4 |
| ...rrtle Rd. Carl | 174 | B4 |
| ...rrtle St. Ret | 39 | E3 |
| ...rrtus Cl. Nott | 184 | B1 |
| ...abbs La. Huck | 145 | F3 |
| ...airn Cl. Arn | 148 | A1 |
| ...airn Cl. Farns | 119 | F3 |
| ...airn Mews. Carl | 174 | C4 |
| ...an Sampson Bank. Blax | 1 | B4 |
| ...ansen St. Nott | 160 | B3 |
| ...aomi Cres. Nott | 146 | B1 |
| ...aomi Ct. Nott | 146 | B1 |
| ...arrow La. Baw | 10 | A4 |
| ...arrow La. Greas | 145 | D2 |
| ...arrow La. Hath | 213 | D1 |
| ...arrow La. Wyme | 217 | D1 |
| ...aseby Cl. Nott | 160 | C2 |
| ...aseby Dr. Lo Ea | 193 | F2 |
| ...ash Cl. Work | 36 | B2 |
| ...athaniel Rd. Lo Ea | 193 | F3 |
| ...athans La. Ho Pi | 187 | D4 |
| ...avenby Wlk. Nott | 184 | C1 |
| ...avigation Way. Lough | 220 | A3 |
| ...avigation Yd. N-on-T | 139 | F4 |
| ...aworth Cl. Nott | 160 | C3 |
| ...aylor Ave. Goth | 195 | D1 |
| ...aylor Ave. Lough | 220 | B1 |
| ...eal Ct. La Mi | 143 | D2 |
| ...eale St. Lo Ea | 193 | F4 |
| ...ear Meadow. Lo Ea | 193 | F3 |
| ...earsby Dr. W Brid | 186 | A3 |
| ...eburn Ct. Nott | 172 | B4 |
| ...eedham Rd. Arn | 162 | A4 |
| ...eedham St. Bing | 177 | F2 |
| ...eedwood Ave. Staple | 170 | B1 |
| ...eeps Croft. Epp | 150 | A3 |
| ...eighwood Cl. Bees | 182 | C1 |
| ...ell Gwyn Cres. Bes Vil | 147 | E1 |
| ...elper Cres. Ilk | 170 | A3 |
| ...elson La. N Musk | 110 | C1 |
| ...elson Rd. Arn | 161 | F4 |
| ...elson Rd. Bald | 140 | A2 |
| ...elson Rd. Bees | 184 | A2 |
| ...elson Rd. Nott | 160 | B4 |
| ...elson St. Gain | 15 | E1 |
| ...elson St. Ilk | 157 | F2 |
| ...elson St. Lo Ea | 193 | E3 |
| ...elson St. Nott | 173 | E3 |
| ...elson St. Ret | 39 | F3 |
| ...ene Cl. Huck | 145 | F2 |
| ...ene Wlk. Work | 35 | F4 |
| ...esbitt St. S in A | 100 | C1 |
| ...esfield Ct. Ilk | 157 | F1 |
| ...esfield Rd. Ilk | 157 | F1 |
| ...eston Dr. Nott | 160 | B2 |
| ...ether Cl. Greas | 143 | F2 |
| ...ether Cl. Nott | 174 | A3 |
| ...ether Ct. Farns | 120 | A3 |
| ...ether St. Bees | 184 | A3 |
| ...ether St. Harb | 202 | A2 |
| Nether Thorpe Rd. Th Sa | 34 | A3 |
| Nethercross Dr. Mar War | 74 | B3 |
| Netherfield La. Budby | 61 | E1 |
| Netherfield La. Carl | 175 | D3 |
| Netherfield La. Mar War | 74 | B4 |
| Netherfield Rd. Lo Ea | 193 | E2 |
| Netherfield Rd. Sand | 182 | A2 |
| Nethergate. Nott | 184 | B1 |
| Netherholme Shop Cntre. Work | | |
| | 35 | F2 |
| Netherton Pl. Work | 36 | A1 |
| Netherton Rd. Work | 47 | D4 |
| Nettle Croft. Tick | 8 | B4 |
| Nettlecliff Wlk. Nott | 160 | C4 |
| Nevile Dr. Kinou | 200 | A1 |
| Neville Rd. Calv | 148 | C3 |
| Neville Sadler Ct. Bees | 184 | A4 |
| New Hill. Wale | 64 | A1 |
| New Brickyard La. Kegw | 203 | E1 |
| New Causeway. B-le-V | 192 | B1 |
| New Cl. Blid | 118 | A3 |
| New Cl. K-in-A | 115 | D3 |
| New Cottages. Cuck | 59 | F2 |
| New Cross St. S in A | 100 | C2 |
| New Derby Rd. East | 143 | E1 |
| New Eaton Rd. Staple | 182 | C2 |
| New England Way. Mans | 87 | E2 |
| New Fall St. S in A | 99 | F2 |
| New Farm La. Nuth | 159 | E3 |
| New Hill. Farns | 119 | F3 |
| New Holles Ct. Work | 35 | F1 |
| New Inn Wlk. Ret | 39 | F3 |
| New King St. Lough | 220 | B1 |
| New La. Blid | 117 | F3 |
| New La. Blid | 118 | A3 |
| New La. Girt | 83 | D2 |
| New La. Newt | 99 | E1 |
| New La. S in A | 100 | B3 |
| New La. Scarr | 178 | C3 |

| | | |
|---|---|---|
| New Linden St. Shireb | 73 | D2 |
| New Mill La. Mans | 88 | C2 |
| New Pl. Ret | 40 | A4 |
| New Rd. B in F | 194 | C3 |
| New Rd. Blid | 118 | A3 |
| New Rd. Bils | 105 | F3 |
| New Rd. Co Ba | 189 | E1 |
| New Rd. Fir | 16 | A3 |
| New Rd. Greas | 144 | C3 |
| New Rd. Hawk | 167 | E2 |
| New Rd. Morton | 137 | E3 |
| New Rd. Oxt | 134 | A2 |
| New Rd. R on T | 175 | F2 |
| New Rd. S in V | 169 | E2 |
| New Rd. Staple | 170 | B1 |
| New Rd. Tick | 8 | A4 |
| New Rd. Tith | 189 | E1 |
| New Rd. Tres | 42 | B2 |
| New Row. Carl | 174 | B4 |
| New Row. Sels | 128 | A3 |
| New St. Gain | 15 | E1 |
| New St. K-in-A | 115 | D2 |
| New St. Kegw | 203 | F2 |
| New St. Lo Ea | 193 | F4 |
| New St. Lough | 220 | A2 |
| New St. N-on-T | 140 | A4 |
| New St. Newt | 99 | D2 |
| New St. Nott | 173 | D4 |
| New St. Ret | 39 | F3 |
| New St. S in A | 99 | F2 |
| New St. S in A | 100 | C1 |
| New St. S Norm | 113 | D3 |
| New St. S Norm | 113 | E4 |
| New Terr. Plea | 86 | C3 |
| New Terr. Sand | 182 | A3 |
| New Tythe St. Lo Ea | 193 | F4 |
| New Vale Rd. Carl | 174 | C3 |
| Newall Dr. Matt | 11 | D1 |
| Newark Cl. Mans | 102 | C1 |
| Newark Cres. Nott | 173 | F2 |
| Newark Dr. Mans | 102 | C1 |
| Newark Rd. B in W | 141 | E3 |
| Newark Rd. Boug | 77 | E1 |
| Newark Rd. Caun | 109 | D2 |
| Newark Rd. Codd | 125 | F1 |
| Newark Rd. Eakr | 92 | C1 |
| Newark Rd. Fent | 55 | D4 |
| Newark Rd. Kirk | 120 | C4 |
| Newark Rd. Oll | 77 | D2 |
| Newark Rd. S in A | 101 | E1 |
| Newark Rd. South | 121 | F1 |
| Newark Rd. Stap | 127 | E4 |
| Newark Rd. Staple | 112 | C2 |
| Newark Rd. Tux | 65 | F1 |
| Newark Rd. Wellow | 77 | E1 |
| Newark St. Nott | 173 | F2 |
| Newark Way. Mans | 103 | D1 |
| Newbarn Cl. Shireb | 72 | B1 |
| Newberry Cl. Cr Bi | 189 | D2 |
| Newbery Ave. Lo Ea | 193 | F3 |
| Newbery Cl. Edwin | 76 | A1 |
| Newbold Way. Kinou | 199 | F1 |
| Newbound La. S in A | 86 | B1 |
| Newboundmill La. Plea | 87 | D3 |
| Newbury Cl. Arn | 162 | A2 |
| Newbury Ct. Nott | 173 | D4 |
| Newbury Mews. Work | 35 | F1 |
| Newcastle Ave. Bees | 183 | F3 |
| Newcastle Ave. Carl | 162 | C1 |
| Newcastle Ave. N-on-T | 140 | A3 |
| Newcastle Ave. Work | 35 | F1 |
| Newcastle Cir. Nott | 173 | D2 |
| Newcastle Dr. Nott | 173 | D3 |
| Newcastle St. Mans | 88 | A2 |
| Newcastle St. Mans | 102 | A4 |
| Newcastle St. Mar War | 74 | A2 |
| Newcastle St. Nott | 160 | B4 |
| Newcastle St. Nott | 173 | E3 |
| Newcastle St. S in A | 100 | A2 |
| Newcastle St. Tux | 65 | F1 |
| Newcastle St. Work | 35 | F1 |
| Newcombe Dr. Arn | 162 | B4 |
| Newdigate Rd. Kim | 159 | D4 |
| Newdigate St. Ilk | 170 | A3 |
| Newdigate St. Kim | 159 | D3 |
| Newdigate St. Nott | 173 | D3 |
| Newdigate Villas. Nott | 173 | D3 |
| Newfield La. Sibt | 167 | F3 |
| Newfield Rd. Nott | 161 | D2 |
| Newgate Cl. Carl | 174 | C4 |
| Newgate Ct. Nott | 172 | C2 |
| Newgate La. Mans | 102 | B4 |
| Newgate St. Bing | 177 | F3 |
| Newgate St. Work | 35 | F1 |
| Newgates La. S in A | 86 | C1 |
| Newhall Gr. W Brid | 173 | F1 |
| Newhall La. Edin | 120 | B1 |
| Newhall La. Halam | 120 | B1 |
| Newhaven Ave. Mans | 88 | A2 |
| Newholm Dr. Nott | 185 | D2 |
| Newings La. S Lev | 42 | C4 |
| Newington Rd. Aust | 10 | B4 |
| Newland Cl. Bees | 183 | D1 |
| Newland Cl. Nott | 172 | B3 |
| Newlands Ave. Boug | 77 | D2 |
| Newlands Cres. Newt | 99 | D2 |
| Newlands Dr. Carl | 162 | C1 |
| Newlands Dr. Mans | 89 | E1 |

| | | |
|---|---|---|
| Newlands Rd. Mans | 103 | D4 |
| Newlands. Gain | 15 | F1 |
| Newlands. Ret | 39 | E2 |
| Newlyn Dr. Nott | 172 | B4 |
| Newlyn Gdns. Nott | 172 | B4 |
| Newman Rd. Calv | 148 | C4 |
| Newmanleys Rd S. East | 157 | F4 |
| Newmanleys Rd. East | 157 | F4 |
| Newmarket Rd. Nott | 160 | A3 |
| Newmarket St. Mans | 102 | C3 |
| Newmarket Way. Bees | 182 | C1 |
| Newnham Rd. N-on-T | 125 | D1 |
| Newport Cres. Mans | 87 | F1 |
| Newport Dr. Nott | 160 | B1 |
| Newquay Ave. Nott | 172 | C4 |
| Newstead Ave. Carl | 162 | B1 |
| Newstead Ave. N-on-T | 125 | D1 |
| Newstead Ave. R on T | 176 | A2 |
| Newstead Cl. K-in-A | 115 | E3 |
| Newstead Cl. Sels | 129 | D4 |
| Newstead Dr. W Brid | 186 | A4 |
| Newstead Gr. Bing | 177 | E2 |
| Newstead Gr. Nott | 173 | D3 |
| Newstead Rd S. Ilk | 157 | E2 |
| Newstead Rd. Lo Ea | 182 | B2 |
| Newstead St. Mans | 101 | A4 |
| Newstead St. Nott | 161 | E2 |
| Newstead Terr. Huck | 146 | A4 |
| Newthorpe Comm. East | 144 | A1 |
| Newthorpe St. Nott | 173 | E1 |
| Newton Ave. Bing | 177 | E2 |
| Newton Ave. Bing | 177 | E3 |
| Newton Ave. R on T | 176 | A2 |
| Newton Cl. Arn | 162 | A3 |
| Newton Cl. Gain | 24 | C4 |
| Newton Cl. Lowd | 150 | C1 |
| Newton Cl. Work | 35 | E4 |
| Newton Dr. Staple | 182 | C3 |
| Newton Dr. W Brid | 185 | E2 |
| Newton Gdns. Bing | 177 | E3 |
| Newton Rd. Carl | 162 | C2 |
| Newton Rd. Newt | 99 | D2 |
| Newton St. Bees | 183 | F3 |
| Newton St. Mans | 102 | B3 |
| Newton St. N-on-T | 140 | A4 |
| Newton St. Nott | 172 | C1 |
| Newton St. Ret | 39 | F2 |
| Newton's La. Awsw | 158 | A2 |
| Newtondale Ave. Mans | 88 | C1 |
| Newtondale Cl. Nott | 160 | B1 |
| Newtonwood La. Tibs | 99 | D3 |
| Nicholas Pl. Tux | 66 | A2 |
| Nicholas Rd. Bees | 171 | E1 |
| Nicholson St. N-on-T | 140 | A4 |
| Nicholson's Row. Shireb | 72 | C2 |
| Nicker Hill. Keyw | 198 | A2 |
| Nicklaus Ct. Nott | 161 | D4 |
| Nidderdale. Nott | 171 | E2 |
| Nightingale Ave. Hath | 213 | D1 |
| Nightingale Ave. Plea | 87 | D2 |
| Nightingale Cl. Bald | 140 | C2 |
| Nightingale Cl. Nuth | 159 | E3 |
| Nightingale Cres. Sels | 129 | D3 |
| Nightingale Dr. Mans | 87 | F1 |
| Nightingale Gr. Work | 35 | E4 |
| Nightingale Way. Wood | 53 | D4 |
| Nine Acre Gdns. Nott | 159 | F4 |
| Nine Acres. Kegw | 203 | E1 |
| Nine Scores La. Fin | 1 | C4 |
| Ninth Ave. Mans | 103 | D4 |
| Nixon Rise. Huck | 145 | E3 |
| Noble La. Aslo | 179 | D3 |
| Noburn Cres. Nott | 160 | C2 |
| Noel St. Gain | 15 | E1 |
| Noel St. Kim | 159 | D3 |
| Noel St. Mans | 102 | A4 |
| Noel St. Nott | 172 | C4 |
| Nook The. Bees | 183 | F2 |
| Nook The. Bees | 184 | A4 |
| Nook The. Calv | 148 | C4 |
| Nook The. E Lea | 205 | F1 |
| Nook The. Nott | 171 | F2 |
| Nook The. Shireb | 72 | B2 |
| Nookin. E Mark | 66 | A3 |
| Norbett Cl. Bees | 183 | E2 |
| Norbett Ct. Arn | 148 | A1 |
| Norbett Rd. Arn | 148 | A1 |
| Norbreck Cl. Nott | 160 | A2 |
| Norbury Dr. Mans | 102 | C2 |
| Nordean Rd. Arn | 162 | A3 |
| Norfolk Ave. Bees | 183 | D1 |
| Norfolk Ave. Bir | 9 | D1 |
| Norfolk Cl. Huck | 145 | E3 |
| Norfolk Cl. Mar War | 74 | A2 |
| Norfolk Cl. Mans | 88 | C3 |
| Norfolk Dr. Bir | 9 | E2 |
| Norfolk Dr. Mans | 102 | A4 |
| Norfolk Pl. Arn | 162 | A3 |
| Norfolk Pl. Nott | 173 | E3 |
| Norfolk Rd. Bir | 9 | D1 |
| Norfolk Rd. Lo Ea | 182 | C1 |
| Norfolk St. Work | 35 | F1 |
| Norfolk Wlk. Sand | 182 | A3 |
| Norland Cl. Nott | 173 | F4 |
| Norman Ave. N-on-T | 125 | D2 |
| Norman Ave. S in A | 101 | D1 |
| Norman Cl. Bees | 183 | E3 |

| | | |
|---|---|---|
| Norman Cl. Nott | 173 | E3 |
| Norman Cres. Ilk | 157 | F2 |
| Norman Dr. East | 144 | A1 |
| Norman Dr. Huck | 145 | F2 |
| Norman Rd. Carl | 174 | A4 |
| Norman St. Carl | 175 | D3 |
| Norman St. Ilk | 157 | F2 |
| Norman St. Kim | 158 | C4 |
| Normanby Rd. Nott | 171 | E2 |
| Normanton Cl. Edwin | 75 | F2 |
| Normanton Dr. Mans | 102 | C4 |
| Normanton La. Bott | 181 | D3 |
| Normanton La. Keyw | 197 | F2 |
| Normanton La. S on S | 214 | A1 |
| Normanton Rd. South | 121 | F1 |
| Normanton Rd. South | 122 | A1 |
| Normanton Rd. Upton | 122 | A1 |
| Nornay Cl. Blyth | 18 | A2 |
| North Ave. Baw | 10 | A4 |
| North Ave. Rain | 104 | A1 |
| North Ave. Sand | 182 | A3 |
| North Carr Rd. Mist | 7 | E2 |
| North Carr Rd. W Sto | 7 | E2 |
| North Church St. Nott | 173 | E3 |
| North Circus St. Nott | 173 | D3 |
| North Cr. N Clip | 90 | A2 |
| North Cres. Bott | 181 | D1 |
| North Dr. Bald | 140 | C1 |
| North Dr. Bees | 183 | F3 |
| North Dr. Bils | 105 | F4 |
| North End. Farn | 138 | C3 |
| North Gate Pl. Nott | 160 | C1 |
| North Gate. N-on-T | 124 | C1 |
| North Gate. N-on-T | 125 | D1 |
| North Gate. Nott | 160 | C1 |
| North Gate. Tick | 8 | A4 |
| North Green. Calv | 133 | E1 |
| North Green. E Dray | 53 | D2 |
| North Hill Ave. Huck | 145 | F4 |
| North Hill Cres. Huck | 145 | F4 |
| North Leys Rd. N LeHa | 43 | E4 |
| North Marsh Rd. Gain | 15 | E1 |
| North Moor Dr. Walker | 13 | F3 |
| North Moor Rd. Walker | 13 | F3 |
| North Par. Gain | 24 | C4 |
| North Park. Mans | 102 | C2 |
| North Rd. Lo Ea | 193 | E3 |
| North Rd. Lough | 220 | A3 |
| North Rd. Nott | 173 | D2 |
| North Rd. Ret | 29 | D1 |
| North Rd. Rudd | 196 | A4 |
| North Rd. W Brid | 185 | F4 |
| North Scarle Rd. S Sca | 98 | C4 |
| North Sherwood St. Nott | 173 | E3 |
| North St. Ann Wo | 115 | D1 |
| North St. Bees | 183 | F3 |
| North St. East | 144 | B1 |
| North St. Gain | 15 | E1 |
| North St. Ilk | 157 | F1 |
| North St. Kim | 159 | D3 |
| North St. La Mi | 143 | D2 |
| North St. Mar War | 73 | E2 |
| North St. Mort | 15 | D2 |
| North St. Nott | 173 | F2 |
| North St. Pinx | 113 | E2 |
| North St. S in A | 100 | A2 |
| North St. S in A | 100 | C2 |
| North St. S Le S | 32 | B3 |
| North St. S Norm | 113 | D3 |
| North St. Scarc | 59 | D1 |
| North Warren Rd. Gain | 15 | D1 |
| North Way. C in L | 25 | F4 |
| North Wlk. Ret | 39 | E4 |
| Northall Ave. Nott | 160 | A3 |
| Northampton St. Nott | 173 | F3 |
| Northcliffe Ave. Carl | 162 | A1 |
| Northcote St. Lo Ea | 193 | F4 |
| Northcote Way. Nott | 160 | B3 |
| Northdale Rd. Nott | 174 | A4 |
| Northdown Dr. Bees | 183 | E2 |
| Northdown Rd. Nott | 172 | B3 |
| Northern Ct. Nott | 160 | B2 |
| Northern Dr. Staple | 170 | B2 |
| Northern Rd. N-on-T | 125 | D1 |
| Northern View. S in A | 100 | C2 |
| Northfield Ave. Ilk | 157 | F1 |
| Northfield Ave. Lo Ea | 193 | D2 |
| Northfield Ave. Mans | 87 | F2 |
| Northfield Ave. Mans | 88 | A2 |
| Northfield Ave. R on T | 176 | B2 |
| Northfield Cres. Bees | 183 | D2 |
| Northfield Dr. Mans | 102 | C3 |
| Northfield La. Mans | 87 | F2 |
| Northfield La. Mans | 88 | A3 |
| Northfield La. Tres | 42 | A2 |
| Northfield Park. Mans | 88 | A3 |
| Northfield Rd. Bees | 183 | D2 |
| Northfield Rd. N Le Ha | 33 | D1 |
| Northfield Way. Ret | 39 | E4 |
| Northfields Cl. S in A | 100 | C2 |
| Northfields. Lo Ea | 193 | D2 |
| Northgate St. Ilk | 157 | F1 |
| Northolme Ave. Nott | 160 | B4 |
| Northolme. Gain | 15 | E1 |
| Northolt Dr. Nuth | 159 | E2 |
| Northrowe. Ann Wo | 129 | F4 |
| Northside La. N Le Ha | 32 | C1 |
| Northside Wlk. Nott | 147 | F1 |

| | | |
|---|---|---|
| Northumberland Ave. C in L | 25 | F4 |
| Northumberland Cl. Nott | 173 | E3 |
| Northumbria Cl. Work | 36 | A3 |
| Northumbria Dr. Ret | 39 | E3 |
| Northwold Ave. W Brid | 185 | E3 |
| Northwood Ave. S in A | 100 | B2 |
| Northwood Cres. Nott | 161 | E3 |
| Northwood Rd. Nott | 161 | E3 |
| Northwood St. Staple | 182 | B4 |
| Northwood. Work | 36 | A3 |
| Norton La. Cuck | 60 | A2 |
| Norton Rd. Stap | 127 | F4 |
| Norton St. Nott | 172 | C3 |
| Norwell Ct. Mans | 88 | A1 |
| Norwell La. Crom | 110 | B4 |
| Norwell Rd. Caun | 109 | E3 |
| Norwich Cl. Mans | 88 | B3 |
| Norwich Gdns. Nott | 146 | A1 |
| Norwood Cl. S in A | 100 | A2 |
| Norwood Gdns. South | 121 | F1 |
| Norwood Rd. Nott | 172 | C3 |
| Nostell Mews. Work | 35 | F1 |
| Notintone St. Nott | 173 | F2 |
| Nottingham La. Ol Da | 218 | B3 |
| Nottingham Rd E. East | 144 | A1 |
| Nottingham Rd. Ann Wo | 115 | D1 |
| Nottingham Rd. Arn | 161 | F3 |
| Nottingham Rd. B in F | 195 | D2 |
| Nottingham Rd. Bees | 183 | D1 |
| Nottingham Rd. Bing | 177 | E2 |
| Nottingham Rd. Bott | 180 | C1 |
| Nottingham Rd. Bu Jo | 163 | E2 |
| Nottingham Rd. Bulc | 164 | A4 |
| Nottingham Rd. Cost | 206 | B1 |
| Nottingham Rd. Cr Bi | 188 | C2 |
| Nottingham Rd. East | 144 | A1 |
| Nottingham Rd. Goth | 195 | D1 |
| Nottingham Rd. Greas | 158 | B4 |
| Nottingham Rd. Huck | 146 | B2 |
| Nottingham Rd. Ilk | 170 | A3 |
| Nottingham Rd. K in A | 116 | B4 |
| Nottingham Rd. Kegw | 203 | E1 |
| Nottingham Rd. Keyw | 197 | F2 |
| Nottingham Rd. Kim | 159 | D3 |
| Nottingham Rd. Lamb | 148 | C1 |
| Nottingham Rd. Lo Ea | 193 | E2 |
| Nottingham Rd. Lough | 220 | B3 |
| Nottingham Rd. Lowd | 164 | A4 |
| Nottingham Rd. Mans | 102 | B2 |
| Nottingham Rd. Ne Br | 219 | F4 |
| Nottingham Rd. Nott | 160 | C1 |
| Nottingham Rd. Nott | 160 | C2 |
| Nottingham Rd. Nuth | 159 | F2 |
| Nottingham Rd. Oxt | 134 | A1 |
| Nottingham Rd. R on T | 175 | E1 |
| Nottingham Rd. Raven | 116 | C2 |
| Nottingham Rd. Sels | 129 | D3 |
| Nottingham Rd. South | 136 | B3 |
| Nottingham Rd. Staple | 170 | C3 |
| Nottingham Rd. Staple | 182 | C4 |
| Nottingham Rd. Thur | 151 | E3 |
| Nottingham Rd. Trow | 170 | C3 |
| Nuart Rd. Bees | 183 | F4 |
| Nugent Gdns. Nott | 173 | F3 |
| Nuncar Ct. Ann Wo | 115 | D1 |
| Nuncargate Rd. Ann Wo | 115 | D1 |
| Nunn Brook Rd. S in A | 99 | F1 |
| Nunn Brook Rise. S in A | 99 | F1 |
| Nunn Cl. S in A | 99 | F1 |
| Nurseries The. East | 144 | A1 |
| Nursery Ave. Bees | 183 | E3 |
| Nursery Ave. Farn | 139 | D3 |
| Nursery Ave. S in A | 100 | B1 |
| Nursery Cl. Huck | 146 | A2 |
| Nursery Cl. R on T | 176 | A2 |
| Nursery Cl. Sax | 57 | D2 |
| Nursery Ct. Mans | 102 | B4 |
| Nursery Ct. N-on-T | 125 | D1 |
| Nursery Dr. Carl | 174 | B4 |
| Nursery End. South | 121 | E1 |
| Nursery Gdns. S Norm | 113 | E2 |
| Nursery La. Nott | 160 | C2 |
| Nursery La. S on T | 96 | C4 |
| Nursery Rd. Arn | 162 | A4 |
| Nursery Rd. Bing | 178 | A3 |
| Nursery Rd. R on T | 176 | A2 |
| Nursery St. Mans | 102 | B4 |
| Nursury Gdns. Lowd | 150 | B1 |
| Nuthall Gdns. Nott | 172 | B4 |
| Nuthall Rd. Nott | 160 | B1 |
| | | |
| Oak Acres. Bees | 183 | D3 |
| Oak Ave. Ald | 143 | D3 |
| Oak Ave. Bing | 178 | A2 |
| Oak Ave. Blid | 118 | A2 |
| Oak Ave. Farn | 139 | D2 |
| Oak Ave. Mans | 102 | B4 |
| Oak Ave. Oll | 77 | E2 |
| Oak Ave. R on T | 175 | F2 |
| Oak Ave. Rain | 104 | B1 |
| Oak Ave. Sand | 182 | A4 |
| Oak Ave. Shireb | 72 | B2 |
| Oak Bank Cl. Mans | 102 | A4 |
| Oak Cl. Pinx | 113 | E2 |
| Oak Cl. Work | 35 | F1 |
| Oak Cres. E Lea | 214 | B4 |
| Oak Dr. Bald | 140 | B2 |
| Oak Dr. East | 143 | F1 |

## Oak Dr. Kim

Oak Dr. Kim ...................... 159  D3
Oak Flatt. Bees .................. 183  D3
Oak Gr. Huck .................... 146  A2
Oak Lodge Dr. Kim ............ 158  C4
Oak Rise. Bils ................... 105  F4
Oak St. K-in-A .................. 115  D3
Oak St. Nott ..................... 161  D1
Oak St. S in A ................... 100  B4
Oak Tree Ave. Edwin ......... 76  A1
Oak Tree Ave. Glap ........... 86  A4
Oak Tree Ave. R on T ........ 175  F2
Oak Tree Cl. Huck ............. 145  E2
Oak Tree Cl. Mans ............ 103  D4
Oak Tree Cl. W Brid .......... 186  A4
Oak Tree Cres. Mans ......... 88  A2
Oak Tree Dr. Carl .............. 163  D1
Oak Tree La. Mans ............ 103  D3
Oak Tree Rd. Baw ............. 9  F4
Oak Tree Rd. S in A ........... 101  D2
Oakdale Dr. Bees ............... 183  E2
Oakdale Rd. Arn ................ 162  A4
Oakdale Rd. Carl ............... 174  B3
Oakdale Rd. Nott .............. 174  B3
Oakdale Rd. S Norm .......... 113  D2
Oakenhall Ave. Huck ......... 146  B4
Oakfield Ave. Mar War ....... 74  A2
Oakfield Ave. S in A .......... 114  C4
Oakfield Cl. Mans ............. 102  C1
Oakfield Cl. Nott .............. 171  E2
Oakfield Dr. Sand .............. 182  A2
Oakfield La. Mar War ......... 74  A1
Oakfield Rd. Huck ............. 146  A3
Oakfield Rd. Nott .............. 171  E2
Oakfield Rd. Staple ........... 182  B4
Oakfield. Sax .................... 57  D2
Oakfields Rd. W Brid ......... 174  A1
Oakford Cl. Nott ............... 160  A1
Oakham Cl. Mans .............. 102  A2
Oakham Rd. W Brid ........... 185  E1
Oakham Way. Ilk ............... 157  F2
Oakhampton Cres. Carl ...... 162  B3
Oakholme Ave. Work ......... 35  F3
Oakholme Rise. Work ......... 35  F3
Oakington Cl. Nott ............ 161  D3
Oakland Ave. Lo Ea ........... 193  E3
Oakland Ave. S in A ........... 99  F1
Oakland Gr. Calv ............... 148  C4
Oakland Rd. Mans ............. 102  C4
Oakland St. Nott ............... 172  C4
Oakland Terr. Lo Ea ........... 193  E3
Oaklands Ave. Hean .......... 143  D1
Oaklands La. Ret ............... 40  A3
Oaklands The. S Norm ....... 113  D2
Oaklands. Coll .................. 112  A4
Oakleigh Ave. Carl ............ 162  B1
Oakleigh St. Nott .............. 160  B2
Oakley Dr. Lo Wh .............. 212  B1
Oakley Mews. Nott ............ 159  F3
Oakley's Rd W. Lo Ea ........ 193  E3
Oakley's Rd. Lo Ea ............ 193  F4
Oakmead Ave. Nott ........... 171  F4
Oakridge Cl. Mans ............ 88  C1
Oaks Ave. Elmt ................. 58  B4
Oaks Cl. Ran .................... 19  D3
Oaks Ind Est. Lough .......... 220  A3
Oaks La. Oxt ..................... 133  F4
Oaks La. Walker ................ 13  F2
Oaktree Dr. Bils ................ 106  A2
Oaktree Rd. Newt ............. 99  E1
Oakwood Dr. Nott ............. 172  B4
Oakwood Dr. Raven ........... 117  D1
Oakwood Gr. Edwin ........... 91  E4
Oakwood Rd. Mans ........... 103  D2
Oardale Rd. Mans ............. 101  F4
Oatfield La. New ............... 176  B3
Oban Rd. Bees .................. 183  E3
Occupation La. Fisk .......... 137  F3
Occupation La. K-in-A ....... 114  C3
Occupation La. W-on-W ..... 217  F3
Occupation Rd. Huck ........ 146  A3
Occupation Rd. Nott ......... 160  A3
Occupation Rd. Plea ......... 86  C4
Ochbrook Ct. Ilk ............... 157  F2
Ockerby St. Nott ............... 160  B3
Oddicroft La. S in A ........... 101  D1
Odesa Dr. Nott .................. 160  A2
Ogdon Ct. Nott ................. 173  F3
Ogle Dr. Nott .................... 173  D2
Ogle St. Huck ................... 146  A4
Old Bell La. C on T ............ 96  C2
Old Blyth Rd. Babw ........... 37  F4
Old Blyth Rd. Babw ........... 38  A3
Old Brickyard. Carl ............ 174  A4
Old Chapel La. K-in-A ........ 114  C3
Old Chapel La. Elst ........... 153  F3
Old Chapel La. Sels .......... 129  D2
Old Church St. Nott ........... 172  C1
Old Coach Rd. Nott ........... 171  F3
Old Coach Rd. Work .......... 47  F4
Old Dalby La. Ne Br .......... 219  D3
Old Derby Rd. East ........... 143  E2
Old Dr. Bees ..................... 183  F4
Old Engine Yd The. Remp . 215  F3
Old Epperstone Rd. Lowd .. 150  A2
Old Farm Rd. Nott ............. 160  C4
Old Forge Cl. Hath ............ 213  D1

Old Forge La. Gran ........... 191  E3
Old Forge Rd. Mist ............ 6  C1
Old Great North Rd. S on T . 96  C4
Old Hall Cl. Farn ............... 138  C2
Old Hall Cl. Mar War ......... 74  B3
Old Hall Dr. Nott .............. 161  E1
Old Hall Dr. Widm ............ 208  B3
Old Hall Gdns. Codd ......... 125  F1
Old Hall La. E Mark ........... 65  F4
Old Hall La. Norw .............. 110  A4
Old La. Rudd .................... 185  E1
Old Lenton Cl. Cr Bi .......... 189  D2
Old Lenton St. Nott ........... 173  E3
Old London Rd. Ba Mo ...... 28  B2
Old London Rd. Babw ........ 28  B2
Old London Rd. Babw ........ 38  C2
Old London Rd. Babw ........ 49  F4
Old Main Rd. Bulc ............. 164  A3
Old Main Rd. Cost ............. 206  B1
Old Manor Cl. Woodb ........ 149  E2
Old Manor Rd. Mans ......... 88  B2
Old Market Pl. Mans .......... 102  A4
Old Market Pl. S Norm ....... 113  D3
Old Market Sq. Nott .......... 173  E3
Old Melton Rd. Plum ......... 197  F4
Old Mill Cl. Bees ............... 183  D1
Old Mill Cl. Huck .............. 146  B2
Old Mill Cl. Nott ............... 172  C3
Old Mill Cres. N-on-T ........ 140  A4
Old Mill La. Bing .............. 177  F3
Old Mill La. Cuck .............. 60  A2
Old Mill La. Mans ............. 88  C1
Old Newark Rd. Mans ........ 102  C1
Old Park St. N on T ........... 203  F3
Old Parsonage La. Hoton .. 215  E1
Old Post Office St. Ever ..... 11  E2
Old Rd. S in A ................... 100  C3
Old Rectory Cl. E Lea ........ 205  F1
Old Rufford Rd. Calv ......... 133  E3
Old Rufford Rd. Edwin ....... 76  C1
Old Rufford Rd. Farns ........ 119  D3
Old Rufford Rd. Oll ........... 77  D2
Old Rufford Rd. Ruff ......... 91  E2
Old Rufford Rd. Ruff ......... 105  E2
Old School La. Plea .......... 87  D3
Old Sookholme La. Mar War 74  A2
Old St. Nott ...................... 173  E3
Old Storth La. S Norm ....... 113  D2
Old Terr. Plea ................... 86  C2
Old Tollerton Rd. Gam ....... 186  B4
Old Trent Rd. Beck ............ 14  C1
Old Way. Hath ................... 213  D1
Oldacres. Woodb .............. 149  E2
Oldbury Cl. Nott ............... 195  E4
Oldershaw Ave. Kegw ........ 203  E1
Oldershaw Rd. E Lea ......... 205  F1
Oldershaw Rd. E Lea ......... 214  C4
Oldknow St. Nott .............. 172  C4
Oldoak Rd. Nott ............... 185  D1
Olga Rd. Nott ................... 173  F3
Olive Ave. Lo Ea ............... 182  C1
Olive Ave. Shireb ............. 72  B3
Olive Gr. Bu Jo ................. 163  F3
Olive Gr. Mans ................. 103  D4
Oliver Cl. Hean ................. 143  D1
Oliver Cl. Nott .................. 173  D3
Oliver Ct. N-on-T .............. 140  A4
Oliver Rd. Lough ............... 220  A1
Oliver St. Nott .................. 173  D3
Ollerton Rd. Arn ............... 147  F3
Ollerton Rd. Budby ........... 61  E3
Ollerton Rd. Calv .............. 132  C1
Ollerton Rd. Edwin ........... 76  B2
Ollerton Rd. Gams ............ 50  C3
Ollerton Rd. Kelh ............. 124  A3
Ollerton Rd. Oll ................ 77  D2
Ollerton Rd. Oxt ............... 119  D1
Ollerton Rd. Ret ............... 39  F2
Ollerton Rd. S Musk .......... 124  A4
Ollerton Rd. Tux ............... 65  E1
Ollerton Rd. Tux ............... 78  C4
Ollerton Rd. Work ............. 47  D2
Olton Ave. Nott ................ 171  F1
Olympus Ct. Huck ............ 145  E2
Omberley Ave. S in A ........ 101  D3
Onchan Ave. Carl .............. 174  C3
Ontario Dr. Sels ............... 129  D4
Orange Cl. Shireb ............ 72  C3
Orange Croft. Tick ........... 8  A4
Orange Gdns. Nott ........... 173  E1
Orby Cl. Nott .................... 173  F3
Orby Wlk. Nott ................. 173  F3
Orchard Ave. Bing ............ 177  E2
Orchard Ave. Carl ............. 174  C4
Orchard Ave. N Le Ha ....... 42  B4
Orchard Ave. R on T .......... 175  F2
Orchard Cl. Bald .............. 140  A3
Orchard Cl. Bleas ............. 152  A4
Orchard Cl. Bu Jo ............. 163  F3
Orchard Cl. E Brid ............ 165  D3
Orchard Cl. E Lea ............. 214  B4
Orchard Cl. Gunt .............. 165  D3
Orchard Cl. Mort .............. 15  D3
Orchard Cl. N Le Ha .......... 42  B4
Orchard Cl. R on T ............ 175  F2
Orchard Cl. Ramp ............. 43  D1
Orchard Cl. Shireb ........... 72  C3

Orchard Cl. South ............. 121  E1
Orchard Cl. Su Bo ............. 213  E3
Orchard Cl. Toll ................ 186  B1
Orchard Cres. Bees ........... 183  E3
Orchard Cres. Glap ........... 86  A4
Orchard Cres. Tux ............. 65  F1
Orchard Ct. Carl ............... 162  B1
Orchard Ct. Huck .............. 146  A3
Orchard Ct. La Mi ............. 143  D2
Orchard Ct. Nott .............. 172  C4
Orchard Dr. Calv ............... 149  D4
Orchard Dr. Arn ................ 161  A3
Orchard La. Sax ................ 57  D2
Orchard Leigh. Ret ........... 39  E2
Orchard Rd. K-in-A ............ 114  C3
Orchard Rise. Lamb .......... 163  E4
Orchard St. East ............... 144  A1
Orchard St. Goth .............. 195  D1
Orchard St. Huck .............. 146  A3
Orchard St. Kim ............... 158  C3
Orchard St. La Mi ............. 143  D2
Orchard St. Lo Ea ............. 193  F4
Orchard St. Lough ............ 220  A2
Orchard St. Mans ............. 88  A1
Orchard St. Staple ............ 182  B4
Orchard The. S in A ........... 101  D2
Orchard View. Mans .......... 88  A2
Orchard Way. Bald ............ 140  B2
Orchard Way. Sand ........... 182  A2
Orchard Way. Wyme .......... 216  B2
Orchards The. Carl ............ 163  D1
Orchards The. Lowd .......... 164  C4
Orchards The. Oxt ............. 134  B2
Orchid Cl. Bald ................. 140  A3
Orchid Cl. K-in-A .............. 114  C4
Orchid Cl. W Brid ............. 185  E2
Orchid Dr. Farn ................ 139  D3
Ordsall Park Cl. Ret .......... 39  E3
Ordsall Park Dr. Ret .......... 39  E3
Ordsall Park Rd. Ret ......... 39  E3
Ordsall Rd. Ret ................. 39  E3
Orford Ave. Nott ............... 184  C2
Orford Ave. R on T ............ 175  F1
Orion Cl. Nott ................... 171  F4
Orion Dr. Nott ................... 171  F4
Orlando Dr. Carl ............... 174  C4
Orlock Wlk. Nott ............... 161  D3
Ormonde St. Ald .............. 143  D2
Ormonde Terr. Ald ............ 143  D2
Ormonde Terr. Nott .......... 161  E1
Ornsay Cl. Nott ................ 146  C1
Orpean Way. Bees ............ 182  C1
Orston Ave. Arn ................ 162  A4
Orston Ave. N-on-T ........... 139  F3
Orston Dr. Nott ................. 172  B2
Orston Green. Nott ........... 172  B2
Orston La. Bott ................. 180  C2
Orston Rd E. W Brid .......... 173  F1
Orston Rd W. W Brid .......... 173  F1
Orton Ave. Bees ............... 183  E3
Ortzen St. Nott ................. 172  C3
Orville Rd. Nott ................ 160  C3
Osberton Rd. Ret .............. 39  F3
Osberton View. Work ........ 36  A3
Osborne Ave. Nott ............ 161  E2
Osborne Cl. Sand ............. 182  A2
Osborne Gr. Nott .............. 161  E2
Osborne St. Nott .............. 172  C3
Osbourne St. Ann Wo ....... 129  F4
Osgood Rd. Arn ................ 162  B3
Osier Cl. Nott ................... 173  E1
Osman Cl. Nott ................. 173  D1
Osmaston St. Nott ............ 172  C2
Osmaston St. Sand ........... 182  B3
Osprey Cl. Nott ................ 184  B1
Ossington Cl. Mar War ...... 74  B4
Ossington Cl. Nott ............ 173  E3
Ossington Rd. Knee .......... 93  F3
Ossington Rd. Nott ........... 172  C3
Osterley Gr. Nott .............. 159  E1
Otter Ave. Sax .................. 57  D2
Oulton Cl. Arn .................. 161  F3
Oundle Dr. Ilk .................. 170  A4
Oundle Dr. Mans .............. 87  C1
Oundle Dr. Nott ................ 172  B2
Oursham St. S in A ............ 100  C1
Ouse Bridge Dr. Carl ......... 175  D4
Ousebridge Cres. Carl ....... 175  D4
Outgang La. Mans ............ 88  B2
Outgang La. Plea .............. 87  D3
Outgang La. Tres .............. 42  C2
Outgang Rd. Cott ............. 43  D2
Outram St. S in A .............. 100  C2
Oval Gdns. Nott ................ 172  B4
Oval The. Ret .................... 39  E2
Oval The. S in A ................ 100  B2
Oval The. Tick .................. 8  A4
Overdale Ave. S in A .......... 100  C4
Overdale Cl. Lo Ea ............ 193  D3
Overdale Rd. Nott ............. 160  B2
Overend Rd. Work ............. 35  F2
Overstone Cl. S in A .......... 100  C3
Overstrand Cl. Arn ............ 161  F3
Owday La. C in L ............... 25  E2
Owday La. Work ................ 25  E2
Owen Ave. Lo Ea ............... 194  A3
Owlston Cl. East ............... 143  F2
Owsthorpe Cl. Nott ........... 161  D4

Owston Ferry Rd. Haxey ..... 7  E4
Owston Rd. W Sto ............. 7  E2
Owthorpe Gr. Nott ............ 161  D1
Owthorpe La. Kinou .......... 199  F2
Owthorpe Rd. Co Ba ......... 200  A4
Owthorpe Rd. Cotg ........... 187  F1
Oxborough Rd. Arn ........... 161  E4
Oxbow Cl. Nott ................. 173  E1
Oxbury Rd. Greas ............. 158  C4
Oxclose La. Arn ................ 161  E4
Oxclose La. Mans ............. 88  A2
Oxcroft La. Elmt ............... 58  A4
Oxengate. Arn .................. 161  E3
Oxford Cl. Rain ................. 118  A4
Oxford Dr. Har .................. 8  C3
Oxford Rd. C in L .............. 25  F3
Oxford Rd. W Brid ............ 186  A4
Oxford St. Carl ................. 174  C4
Oxford St. East ................. 143  F1
Oxford St. K-in-A .............. 115  D2
Oxford St. Lo Ea ............... 193  E4
Oxford St. Lough .............. 220  A2
Oxford St. Mans ............... 88  B1
Oxford St. Nott ................. 173  D2
Oxford St. S in A ............... 100  B1
Oxpasture La. Elmt ........... 58  A3
Oxton Ave. Nott ............... 161  E2
Oxton By Pass. Oxt ........... 134  A2
Oxton Cl. Mans ................. 101  F4
Oxton Hill. Oxt ................. 134  C2
Oxton Rd. Arn .................. 148  A4
Oxton Rd. Calv ................. 133  E1
Oxton Rd. South .............. 135  E3
Ozier Holt. Carl ................ 174  C2

Pack Horse La. Lough ....... 220  A2
Packe St. Lough ............... 220  A2
Packington Hill. Kegw ....... 203  E1
Packman Dr. Rudd ............ 196  B4
Paddock Cl. Calv .............. 148  C4
Paddock Cl. Edwin ........... 76  A2
Paddock Cl. R on T ........... 175  F1
Paddock The. Bees ........... 183  E1
Paddock The. Bing ........... 177  F2
Paddock The. Coll ............ 112  A4
Paddock The. Gunt ........... 164  C3
Paddock The. K-in-A ......... 114  C2
Paddock The. Ret ............. 40  A2
Paddock The. S in A .......... 100  B3
Paddock The. Tick ............ 8  A4
Paddocks Cl. Elst ............. 153  F2
Paddocks Cl. Pinx ............ 113  E2
Paddocks The. Beck ......... 14  A1
Paddocks The. Bott .......... 181  D1
Paddocks The. Elst ........... 153  F2
Paddocks The. Hock ......... 122  A3
Paddocks The. Lound ....... 20  B1
Paddocks The. Mans ........ 88  C3
Paddocks The. N-on-T ...... 140  A4
Paddocks The. Sand ......... 182  A3
Paddocks The. Stap .......... 127  F4
Paddocks The. Su Bo ........ 213  D3
Paddocks The. W Brid ....... 186  A2
Paddocks The. Work ......... 36  A4
Paddocks View. Lo Ea ...... 193  D4
Paddy's La. Ol Da ............. 218  A1
Padge Rd. Bees ................ 184  A3
Padgham Ct. Nott ............ 161  D4
Padley Hill. Mans ............. 102  A3
Padleys La. Bu Jo ............. 163  F3
Padstow Rd. Nott ............. 160  C3
Pagdin Dr. Styr ................ 8  C3
Paget Cres. Rudd ............. 196  B4
Paget St. Lough ............... 220  A3
Paignton Cl. Nott ............. 160  A1
Palace View. South .......... 136  C4
Palatine St. Nott .............. 173  D2
Palin Gdns. R on T ........... 176  A2
Palin St. Nott ................... 172  C3
Paling Cres. S in A ............ 100  C2
Palm Court Ind Cntre. Nott . 160  C1
Palm St. Nott ................... 160  C1
Palm Wood Ct. Nott .......... 160  B3
Palmer Ave. Huck ............. 146  A4
Palmer Cres. Carl ............. 174  B4
Palmer Dr. Staple ............. 182  B3
Palmer Rd. Ret ................. 30  A1
Palmer Rd. S on T ............. 96  C4
Palmerston Gdns. Nott ...... 173  E3
Palmerston St. Sels .......... 128  B2
Palmwood Ct. Nott ........... 160  B3
Paper Mill La. Tick ........... 8  B4
Papplewick La. Huck ......... 146  B4
Paradise La. Ol Da ............ 218  C2
Park Ave E. Keyw .............. 197  F2
Park Ave E. Keyw .............. 197  F2
Park Ave W. Keyw ............. 197  E2
Park Ave. Ann Wo ............. 130  A4
Park Ave. Arn ................... 161  F3
Park Ave. Awsw ................ 158  A3
Park Ave. Blid .................. 118  A3
Park Ave. Bu Jo ................ 163  F2
Park Ave. Carl .................. 174  C4
Park Ave. East .................. 143  F2
Park Ave. Huck ................. 145  F4
Park Ave. Keyw ................ 197  F2
Park Ave. Kim .................. 159  D2

Park Ave. Lough ............... 220
Park Ave. Mans ................ 88
Park Ave. Mans ................ 102
Park Ave. Mist ................. 6
Park Ave. Nott ................. 173
Park Ave. Shireb .............. 72
Park Ave. W Brid .............. 185
Park Ave. Woodb .............. 149
Park Cl. Lea ..................... 24
Park Cl. Nott .................... 161
Park Cl. Pinx ................... 113
Park Cres. Greas .............. 143
Park Cres. Ilk ................... 170
Park Cres. N-on-T ............ 125
Park Cres. Nott ................ 171
Park Cres. Ret .................. 40
Park Ct. Lough ................. 220
Park Ct. Mans .................. 102
Park Dr. Blyth .................. 18
Park Dr. Huck .................. 146
Park Dr. Nott ................... 173
Park Dr. Sand .................. 182
Park Farm Cotts. Kettl ...... 55
Park Hall Gdns. Mans ....... 88
Park Hall Rd. Mans ........... 88
Park Hill Dr. Fir ............... 16
Park Hill. Awsw ................ 158
Park House Gates. Nott .... 161
Park La. Holb ................... 59
Park La. K-in-A ................ 114
Park La. Lamb .................. 163
Park La. Nott ................... 160
Park La. Owth ................. 199
Park La. Pinx ................... 113
Park La. Ret .................... 40
Park La. South ................. 136
Park La. Su Bo ................. 213
Park Mews. Mans ............. 88
Park Mews. Nott .............. 173
Park Pl. Work .................. 35
Park Ravine. Nott ............. 173
Park Rd E. Calv ................ 149
Park Rd N. Bees ............... 183
Park Rd. Arn .................... 161
Park Rd. Baw ................... 9
Park Rd. Bees .................. 183
Park Rd. Bees .................. 183
Park Rd. Bes Vil ............... 146
Park Rd. Calv ................... 148
Park Rd. Carl ................... 174
Park Rd. Huck .................. 145
Park Rd. Ilk ..................... 170
Park Rd. Keyw .................. 197
Park Rd. Lough ................ 220
Park Rd. Mans .................. 88
Park Rd. Nott ................... 172
Park Rd. R on T ................ 175
Park Rd. Shireb ................ 72
Park Springs Rd. Gain ...... 24
Park St. Bees ................... 183
Park St. K-in-A ................. 114
Park St. Lo Ea .................. 182
Park St. Lough ................. 220
Park St. Mans .................. 88
Park St. Nott .................... 172
Park St. S in A .................. 100
Park St. Staple ................ 182
Park Terr. Keyw ................ 197
Park Terr. Nott ................. 173
Park The. Cotg ................. 187
Park The. Mans ................ 102
Park The. N Musk ............. 110
Park The. N-on-T .............. 140
Park The. Nott .................. 173
Park View Way. Mans ....... 102
Park View. Bees ............... 183
Park View. Nott ................ 161
Parkcroft Rd. W Brid ........ 185
Parkdale Rd. Carl ............ 174
Parkdale Rd. Nott ............ 174
Parker Cl. Arn .................. 162
Parker St. Huck ................ 146
Parker St. N-on-T ............. 140
Parker's La. Mans ............ 88
Parkes Cl. Codd ............... 126
Parkham Rd. Kim ............. 158
Parkin Cl. Cr Bi ................ 189
Parkland Cl. Mans ............ 102
Parkland Ct. Nott ............. 184
Parklands Cl. Codd ........... 125
Parklands Dr. Lough ......... 220
Parkside Ave. Lo Ea ......... 193
Parkside Dr. Lo Ea ........... 193
Parkside Gdns. Nott ......... 171
Parkside Rd. Edwin .......... 75
Parkside Rise. Nott ........... 171
Parkside. Keyw ................ 197
Parkside. Nott .................. 171
Parkside. S in A ................ 100
Parkstone Ave. Mans ....... 103
Parkstone Cl. W Brid ........ 185
Parkview Rd. Nott ............ 161
Parkway Ct. Nott .............. 171
Parkway. Mans ................ 89
Parkway. N-on-T .............. 139
Parkway. S in A ................ 100

245
'arkway. Whit
Priory Ct. Carl

arkway. Whit 45 D3
arkwood Cres. Nott 161 F2
arkwood Ct. Nott 160 C3
arkyn Rd. Arn 161 E3
arkyns St. Rudd 196 B3
arliament Ct. N-on-T 139 F4
arliament Rd. Mans 101 F4
arliament St. N-on-T 139 F4
arliament St. S in A 100 C1
arliament Terr. Nott 173 D3
arliament Wlk. N-on-T 139 F4
arnell St. Gain 24 B4
arnham's Cl. Ne Br 219 E4
arr Gate. Bees 183 D3
arr La. Epp 150 A3
arry Way. Arn 162 A4
arsons Meadow. Carl 174 C2
aschall Rd. Ann Wo 115 D1
asteur Ct. Nott 172 C1
asture Cl. Carl 174 C2
asture Cl. S in A 100 B3
asture Cl. Work 35 E1
asture La. Hath 213 D1
asture La. Hose 211 F3
asture La. Lo Ea 194 A3
asture La. Newt 99 E1
asture La. Rudd 196 A4
asture La. Su Bo 213 D3
asture Rd. Gain 24 C4
asture Rd. Staple 170 B1
asture View. Gunt 165 D3
astures Ave. Nott 195 E4
astures The. Baw 10 A3
astures The. Calv 148 B4
astures The. Greas 158 B4
astures The. Mans 88 C3
Pastures The. Ramp 43 D1
Pastures The. Tux 65 F1
Patchills The. Mans 102 C4
Pateley Rd. Arn 162 A2
Paton Rd. Nott 160 C3
Patricia Dr. Arn 148 A1
Patrick Rd. W Brid 185 F4
Patterdale Rd. Arn 161 F3
Patterson Pl. Mans 102 B4
Patterson Rd. Nott 172 C4
Paul Ave. Mans 103 D3
Paulson's Dr. Mans 102 A4
Pavilion Cl. Nott 173 E1
Pavilion Cl. Gunt 164 C4
Pavilion Gdns. Plea 86 C4
Pavilion Rd. Bes Vil 147 D1
Pavilion Rd. Ilk 157 F3
Pavilion Rd. W Brid 173 F1
Paxton Gdns. Nott 173 F3
Paxtons Court. N-on-T 124 C1
Peach Ave. S Norm 113 D4
Peach Ave. Sels 128 C3
Peache Way. Bees 183 E4
Peachey St. Nott 173 E3
Peacock Cl. Gunt 165 D2
Peacock Cl. Rudd 196 A3
Peacock Cres. Nott 184 C1
Peacock Dr. Rain 118 B4
Peacock Pl. Ilk 157 E2
Peacock St. Mans 102 A3
Peafield La. Mans 88 C2
Peafield La. Mar War 89 D4
Peak The. Shireb 72 C2
Peakdale Cl. Lo Ea 193 D3
Peake's Croft. Baw 10 A4
Pear Tree Cl. Clar 30 B2
Pear Tree Ct. Nott 160 C2
Pear Tree Dr. Shireb 72 C3
Pearce Dr. Nott 172 A4
Pearl Ave. K-in-A 115 D2
Pearmain Dr. Nott 173 F4
Pearson Ave. Bees 183 D3
Pearson Cl. Bees 183 D3
Pearson St. Carl 175 D3
Pearson St. Nott 160 C1
Peartree La. S in A 86 A1
Peartree Orch. Rudd 196 B4
Peary Cl. Nott 160 C3
Peas Hill Rd. Nott 173 E3
Peatfield Rd. Staple 170 B1
Peck La. Nott 173 E2
Pecks Hill. Mans 102 C4
Pedmore Valley. Nott 161 D4
Peebles Rd. N-on-T 139 E3
Peel Ave. Ret 40 A2
Peel Ave. Tux 65 F1
Peel Cres. Mans 87 E1
Peel Dr. Lough 220 B2
Peel Rd. Mans 101 F4
Peel St. La Mi 143 D2
Peel St. Lo Ea 193 F4
Peel St. Nott 173 D3
Peel St. S in A 101 D2
Peel St. S Norm 113 D3
Peets Dr. N Musk 110 C1
Pelham Ave. Ilk 157 F1
Pelham Ave. Nott 173 D4
Pelham Cl. N-on-T 139 F4
Pelham Cres. Bees 184 A4
Pelham Cres. Nott 172 C2
Pelham Ct. Nott 173 D4
Pelham Gdns. N-on-T 139 F4
Pelham Rd. K-in-A 115 D3
Pelham Rd. Nott 173 D4
Pelham Rd. Ret 39 E3
Pelham St. Mans 102 B4
Pelham St. N-on-T 139 F4
Pelham St. Nott 173 E2
Pelham St. S in A 100 B1
Pelham St. Work 36 A1
Pelham Way. Mans 89 E2
Pemberton St. Nott 173 E2
Pemberton The. S Norm 113 D2
Pembleton Dr. Mans 87 E1
Pembrey Cl. Staple 170 B1
Pembridge Cl. Nott 160 B1
Pembroke Cres. Codd 125 E2
Pembroke Dr. C in L 25 F3
Pembroke Dr. Nott 161 E1
Pembroke Rd. Shire 34 C4
Pembury Rd. Nott 171 F3
Pen La. Widm 208 B2
Penarth Gdns. Nott 161 F2
Penarth Rise. Nott 161 F2
Pendeen Cl. Gain 15 F1
Pendennis Cl. Carl 163 D1
Pendine Cl. Nott 147 E1
Pendle Cres. Nott 161 F1
Pendock La. Brad 197 D1
Penfold Cl. Hath 213 D1
Penhale Dr. Huck 145 E3
Penhurst Cl. Nott 185 D2
Penllech Cl. Nott 161 D4
Penllech Wlk. Nott 161 D4
Penn Ave. Nott 172 C2
Penn La. Stat 202 C2
Penn St. S in A 100 C2
Pennant Rd. Nott 160 B1
Pennard Wlk. Nott 195 E4
Pennhome Ave. Nott 161 E1
Penniment La. Mans 87 D1
Pennine Cl. Bes Vil 147 D1
Pennine Cl. Lo Ea 182 A1
Pennine Cl. Lo Ea 193 E2
Pennine Cl. Newt 99 D2
Pennine Cl. S in A 99 F2
Pennine Dr. K-in-A 114 B2
Pennine Dr. Sels 128 C4
Pennington Wlk. Ret 40 A3
Penny Green. Whit 45 D3
Pennyfoot St. Nott 173 F2
Penrhyn Cl. Nott 173 E3
Penrhyn Cres. Bees 183 D2
Penrith Ave. R on T 176 A2
Penrith Cres. Nott 160 B1
Penrith Pl. Mans 101 E4
Penshore Cl. Nott 184 B1
Penswick Gr. Codd 125 F1
Pentland Ct. Mans 101 E3
Pentland Dr. Bes Vil 147 D1
Pentland Dr. C in L 25 F4
Pentland Gdns. Lo Ea 182 A1
Pentrich Wlk. Mans 103 D3
Pentwood Ave. Nott 147 F1
Penzance Pl. Mans 103 D4
Pepper Rd. Calv 148 C4
Pepper St. Nott 173 E2
Pepper St. S in A 101 D1
Peppercorn Gdns. Nott 172 B3
Peppers Dr. Kegw 203 D1
Percival Cl. S in A 100 C2
Percival Cres. S in A 100 C2
Percival Rd. Nott 161 E1
Percival St. Work 35 F3
Percy St. East 144 A1
Percy St. Nott 160 B2
Percy St. S in A 100 B1
Peregrine Ct. Work 35 E4
Perivale Cl. Nuth 159 E2
Perkin's La. Grim 219 D1
Perlethorpe Ave. Carl 162 C1
Perlethorpe Ave. Mans 88 A1
Perlethorpe Ave. Nott 173 F2
Perlethorpe Cl. Carl 162 C1
Perlethorpe Cl. Edwin 75 F2
Perlethorpe Cres. Carl 162 C1
Perlethorpe Dr. Carl 162 C1
Perlethorpe Dr. Huck 146 A4
Perlthorpe Ave. Mar War 74 B4
Perry Gdns. Nott 161 D2
Perry Gr. Bing 177 F2
Perry Rd. Nott 161 D2
Perth Cl. Mans 88 B3
Perth Dr. Staple 170 C1
Perth St. Nott 173 E3
Peterborough Rd. Coll 98 A1
Peters Cl. Arn 162 B3
Peters Cl. Greas 144 B1
Petersfield Cl. Mans 101 E4
Petersfield Cl. Nott 160 C4
Petersgate Cl. Lo Ea 182 A1
Petersgate. Lo Ea 182 A1
Petersham Mews. Nott 172 C2
Petersham Rd. Lo Ea 182 A1
Petersmiths Cres. Oll 77 E3
Petersmiths Dr. Oll 77 E3
Petworth Ave. Bees 182 C2
Petworth Dr. Nott 160 C2
Peveril Cres. Lo Ea 193 D3
Peveril Dr. Ilk 157 E1
Peveril Dr. Nott 173 D2
Peveril Dr. S in A 100 B1
Peveril Dr. W Brid 185 F2
Peveril Rd. Bees 184 A4
Peveril St. Huck 146 A4
Peveril St. Nott 172 C3
Pheasant Hill. Mans 88 A1
Philip Ave. East 144 A1
Philip Ave. K-in-A 115 D1
Philip Ave. Nuth 159 E3
Philip Gr. Carl 162 C1
Philip Rd. N-on-T 139 F3
Phoenix Ave. Carl 162 C1
Phoenix Cl. Nott 173 D1
Phoenix Ct. East 144 A1
Phoenix Ct. Nott 184 C4
Phoenix St. S in A 101 D2
Phyllis Cl. Huck 130 C1
Phyllis Gr. Lo Ea 193 F4
Piccadilly. Nott 160 B3
Pickard St. Mans 102 C4
Pickering Ave. East 143 F1
Pieris Dr. Nott 184 B1
Pierrepont Ave. Carl 162 C1
Pierrepont Rd. W Brid 174 A1
Pierson St. N-on-T 139 F3
Pilcher Gate. Nott 173 E2
Pilgrim Cl. Babw 38 C3
Pilgrim Cl. Raven 116 C1
Pilgrim Rise. Aust 3 E1
Pilgrim Way. Work 35 F1
Pilkington Rd. Carl 162 A1
Pilkington St. Nott 160 A4
Pillared House La. Gain 24 B4
Pimlico Ave. Bees 171 D2
Pinder St. Nott 173 E2
Pine Ave. La Mi 143 D2
Pine Ave. Oll 77 E2
Pine Cl. E Lea 214 B4
Pine Cl. Ever 11 E2
Pine Cl. K-in-A 114 C3
Pine Cl. Mans 88 B3
Pine Cl. N-on-T 125 D2
Pine Cl. Rain 103 F1
Pine Cl. Shireb 72 C3
Pine Hill Cl. Nott 146 C1
Pine Tree Cl. Work 35 F1
Pine Tree Wlk. East 143 E1
Pinehurst Ave. Huck 145 E3
Pines The. Gain 24 C3
Pineview Cl. Mans 102 C1
Pinewood Ave. Arn 148 A1
Pinewood Ave. Edwin 91 E4
Pinewood Cl. K-in-A 115 E3
Pinewood Cl. South 121 E1
Pinewood Dr. Mans 102 C2
Pinewood Gdns. Nott 195 E4
Pinfold Cl. Bott 181 D2
Pinfold Cl. Coll 98 A1
Pinfold Cl. Cotg 187 F2
Pinfold Cl. Kinou 199 F1
Pinfold Cl. Lound 20 B1
Pinfold Cl. Tick 8 A4
Pinfold Cl. Woodb 149 E2
Pinfold Cres. Woodb 149 E2
Pinfold Gate. Lough 220 A2
Pinfold Gdns. Lough 220 A2
Pinfold Jetty. Lough 220 B2
Pinfold La. Aver 123 F1
Pinfold La. Bald 140 B2
Pinfold La. Bott 181 D2
Pinfold La. Clar 40 C4
Pinfold La. Elst 153 E3
Pinfold La. Harb 202 B2
Pinfold La. Kinou 199 F1
Pinfold La. Shel 164 B1
Pinfold La. Staple 182 C4
Pinfold La. Styr 8 B1
Pinfold La. Tick 8 A4
Pinfold Place. Harb 202 B2
Pinfold Rd. Greas 144 B1
Pinfold The. Miss 4 A1
Pinfold. Bing 177 F2
Pingle Cl. Gain 24 C4
Pingle Cres. Nott 160 C4
Pingle The. Lo Ea 193 E4
Pingley Cl. Stay 138 B4
Pingley La. Stay 123 E1
Pingley La. Stay 138 B4
Pinxton Ct. Mans 103 D3
Pinxton Green. K in A 113 F2
Pinxton La. K-in-A 114 B2
Pinxton La. S in A 114 A4
Pinxton La. S Norm 113 E3
Pinxton Rd. K-in-A 114 B2
Piper Cl. Lo Wh 212 B1
Piper Dr. Lo Wh 212 B1
Piper La. Work 61 E4
Pippin Cl. Nott 173 F4
Pit La. Ship 157 D3
Pitcairn Cl. Nott 173 E1
Pithouse La. W Lea 204 C1
Pitt Hill. Scarc 58 C1
Pitt La. G on H 12 C2
Pl. South 136 B4
Pl. South 136 B4
Plains Farm Cl. Arn 162 B3
Plains Gr. Arn 162 A2
Plains Rd. Arn 162 A2
Plainspot Rd. Sels 128 C1
Plane Cl. Nott 159 F4
Plant La. Lo Ea 193 D2
Plantagenet Ct. Nott 173 E3
Plantagenet St. Nott 173 E3
Plantation Ave. E Mark 66 A4
Plantation Cl. Bes Vil 147 D1
Plantation Hill. Work 36 A2
Plantation La. Hod 27 D4
Plantation Rd. E Mark 66 A3
Plantation Rd. Keyw 197 E2
Plantation Rd. Nott 171 E2
Plantation Side. Nott 172 C4
Plantations The. Lo Ea 193 D4
Plants Yd. Work 35 F1
Platt La. Keyw 198 A3
Platt La. N-on-W 198 A3
Platt St. Pinx 113 E1
Platts The. N-on-T 139 F3
Player St. Nott 172 C3
Plaza Gdns. Nott 160 C2
Pleasant Pl. Kegw 203 E1
Pleasant Row. Nott 172 C4
Pleasley Rd. S in A 101 D3
Plot La. S Sca 98 C2
Plough La. Lowd 150 B1
Plough La. Nott 173 F2
Ploughman Ave. Woodb 149 E2
Plowman Ct. Staple 182 B3
Plowright Ct. Nott 173 E4
Plowright St. Nott 173 E4
Plum Tree Ave. Mans 89 D1
Plumb Rd. Huck 145 F4
Plummer La. Kegw 203 E1
Plumptre Cl. East 143 F1
Plumptre Pl. Nott 173 E2
Plumptre Sq. Nott 173 E2
Plumptre St. Nott 173 E2
Plumptre Way. East 143 F1
Plumptre. Ald 143 D3
Plumtree Gdns. Calv 148 C4
Plumtree Rd. Bir 9 E3
Plumtree Rd. Cotg 187 F2
Plungar Cl. Nott 172 A3
Plungar La. B-le-V 192 A1
Plungar Rd. Gran 191 E3
Plymouth Ave. Pinx 113 F1
Poacher's La. N Whea 31 E4
Pocklington Cres. Wint 125 E3
Pocklington Rd. Coll 98 A1
Podder La. Carl 162 B3
Point The. Nott 173 A2
Pollard Dr. Mans 102 B4
Pollard's La. South 136 C4
Polly Taylor' S Rd. H Marn 67 F1
Polperro Way. Huck 145 E3
Pond Hills La. Nott 147 F1
Pond St. K-in-A 115 D3
Pool Cl. Pinx 113 E1
Poole Meadow. Carl 174 C2
Popham Ct. Nott 173 E2
Popham St. Nott 173 E2
Poplar Ave. E Lea 214 B4
Poplar Ave. K-in-A 115 E3
Poplar Ave. Nott 161 D1
Poplar Ave. Sand 182 A4
Poplar Cl. Bing 178 A2
Poplar Cl. S on T 96 C4
Poplar Cl. Work 35 E1
Poplar Cres. Kim 159 D3
Poplar Dr. Glap 86 A4
Poplar Dr. Mans 87 D2
Poplar Gr. Mans 89 E1
Poplar Gr. Mar War 74 A3
Poplar Rd. S Norm 113 D4
Poplar St. Mans 88 B2
Poplar St. Nott 173 F2
Poplar St. Oll 77 E2
Poplar St. Ret 39 F3
Poplars Ave. Bu Jo 164 A3
Poplars Cl. Keyw 197 F2
Poplars The. Bees 183 F4
Poplars The. S in A 101 D2
Poplars The. W Brid 185 F4
Poplars The. Whit 45 D3
Porchester Cl. Huck 146 B4
Porchester Rd. Bing 177 E2
Porchester Rd. Carl 162 A1
Porlock Cl. Lo Ea 193 D4
Port Arthur Rd. Nott 174 A2
Portage Cl. R on T 175 F1
Porter Cl. Nott 195 E4
Portinscale Cl. W Brid 186 B3
Portland Cres. Mans 88 B2
Portland Cres. Staple 182 C3
Portland Ct Mews. Mans 88 B2
Portland Ct. Nott 161 D3
Portland Gdns. Huck 145 F4
Portland Grange. Huck 145 F4
Portland Hill. Nott 172 B1
Portland Meadows. Sutt 29 D3
Portland Park Cl. Huck 145 F4
Portland Pl. Sutt 29 D3
Portland Pl. Work 35 F2
Portland Rd. Bees 183 D1
Portland Rd. Carl 162 B1
Portland Rd. Greas 158 B4
Portland Rd. Huck 146 A3
Portland Rd. Ilk 157 F2
Portland Rd. Lo Ea 193 D2
Portland Rd. Nott 173 D3
Portland Rd. Ret 39 E3
Portland Rd. Scarc 59 D1
Portland Rd. Sels 129 D4
Portland Rd. Shireb 72 C2
Portland Rd. W Brid 185 F3
Portland St. Arn 161 F3
Portland St. Bees 184 A4
Portland St. K-in-A 115 D3
Portland St. Mans 88 B2
Portland St. Mans 102 A3
Portland St. Mar War 74 A2
Portland St. N-on-T 139 F4
Portland St. Plea 87 D4
Portland St. S in A 100 C1
Portland St. S in A 100 C1
Portland St. Work 35 F2
Portland Terr. Gain 24 B4
Portland Terr. Mar War 60 C1
Portland Terr. Scarc 59 D1
Portree Dr. Nott 146 C1
Post Office La. Plun 191 F1
Post Office La. Redm 192 C2
Post Office Rd. K-in-A 115 D3
Post Office Yd. Hover 151 E1
Postern St. Nott 173 D2
Posts The. Cr Bu 189 D3
Potter La. Wellow 92 B4
Potter St. S in A 101 D2
Potter St. Work 35 F1
Potters Ct. Bees 171 E1
Potters La. E Lea 214 C4
Potters Way. Ilk 170 A4
Poulter Cl. Nott 172 B4
Poulter St. Scarc 58 C1
Poulton Dr. Nott 173 F1
Poultry. Nott 173 E2
Powtrell Pl. Ilk 170 A3
Poynton St. Nott 173 D3
Poyser Cl. Nott 161 D1
Pratt Cl. Mans 87 E1
Prebends Cl. Farn 138 C2
Precinct Rd. K-in-A 115 D3
Precinct The. Cotg 187 F2
Premier Rd. Nott 173 D4
Prendwick Gdns. Nott 161 D4
Prest Ave. Mar War 74 C4
Preston Rd. Rain 118 A4
Prestwick Cl. Nott 159 E1
Prestwold Ave. Mans 89 D1
Prestwold Ave. Mans 103 D4
Prestwold La. Hoton 215 E1
Prestwood Dr. Nott 172 A4
Previn Gdns. Nott 173 F3
Priestgate. E Mark 65 F3
Priestsic Rd. S in A 100 C2
Primrose Ave. Farn 139 D3
Primrose Ave. N-on-T 125 D2
Primrose Ave. Sels 128 C1
Primrose Cl. K-in-A 114 C4
Primrose Cl. Nott 173 E4
Primrose Cres. Carl 174 C4
Primrose La. Kirton 78 B3
Primrose Rise. Greas 158 B4
Primrose St. Carl 174 C4
Primrose St. Gain 24 B4
Primrose St. Ilk 157 F2
Primrose Way. Work 36 A3
Primula Cl. Nott 184 B1
Prince Charles Rd. Work 35 E3
Prince Edward Cres. R on T 175 F1
Prince Of Wales St. Ret 39 F3
Prince St. Ilk 157 F2
Prince St. Lo Ea 193 E4
Prince William Rd. Lough 220 A3
Prince's St. N-on-T 139 F4
Princes Rd. Ne Br 219 D3
Princes St. Mans 102 A3
Princess Anne Rd. Work 35 F3
Princess Ave. Bees 184 A3
Princess Ave. Mans 103 D4
Princess Ave. Mar War 74 B2
Princess Ave. S Norm 113 D3
Princess Cl. Carl 162 C1
Princess Dr. Sand 182 A2
Princess St. East 143 F2
Princess St. K-in-A 114 B2
Princess St. Lo Ea 193 E4
Princess St. Lough 220 A2
Princess Wlk. Gain 15 F1
Prior Cl. S in A 101 D2
Prior Rd. Arn 161 E3
Priors Cl. Bing 178 A3
Priors The. Lowd 150 B1
Priorswell Rd. Work 35 F1
Priory Ave. Ann Wo 130 A4
Priory Ave. Raven 117 D1
Priory Ave. Toll 186 B1
Priory Cir. Toll 186 B1
Priory Cl. Bald 140 C2
Priory Cl. Blyth 18 A2
Priory Cl. Gain 24 C4
Priory Cl. Matt 20 A4
Priory Cres. Carl 162 C1
Priory Ct. Carl 162 C1

Priory La. Thur ............ 151 E4
Priory Mews. Nott ......... 172 C1
Priory Park. Thur .......... 151 E4
Priory Rd. Blid ............ 118 A3
Priory Rd. Carl ............ 162 C1
Priory Rd. East ........... 143 F1
Priory Rd. Huck ........... 145 F4
Priory Rd. Mans ............ 88 A2
Priory Rd. W Brid .......... 186 A4
Priory Sq. Mans ............ 88 A2
Priory St. Nott ........... 172 C1
Private Rd. Huck .......... 145 F4
Private Rd. Nott .......... 161 E1
Private Rd. South ......... 121 F1
Private Rd. Woodb ......... 149 E3
Private St. N-on-T ........ 140 A4
Privet Ave. K-in-A ........ 115 D3
Prize Cl. Nott ............ 184 B1
Procters Dr. Girt .......... 82 C1
Promenade The. K-in-A ..... 115 E3
Promenade. Nott ........... 173 E3
Prospect Cl. K-in-A ....... 115 D4
Prospect Ct. S in A ........ 99 F1
Prospect Dr. Shireb ........ 72 C2
Prospect Dr. Work .......... 35 F3
Prospect Pl. Nott ......... 172 C2
Prospect Pl. S in A ....... 100 C1
Prospect Prec. Work ........ 36 A3
Prospect Rd. Carl ......... 162 A1
Prospect Rd. Hean ......... 157 D4
Prospect St. Mans ......... 102 B3
Prospect St. Nott ......... 172 C3
Prospect Terr. Gain ........ 24 B4
Prospect Terr. Nott ....... 172 C3
Providence Pl. Ilk ........ 157 F1
Providence Rd. Sels ....... 128 A2
Prudhoe Ct. Nott .......... 173 E1
Pudding La. Hick .......... 210 B3
Pulborough Cl. Nott ....... 160 C2
Pullman Rd. Nott .......... 173 F2
Pump Hollow La. Mans ...... 103 D4
Pump Hollow Rd. Mans ...... 103 D4
Pump La. Fenton ........... 142 C1
Pump La. Wale ............. 64 A1
Purbeck Cl. Lo Ea ......... 193 D4
Purbeck Dr. W Brid ........ 185 E3
Purdy Meadow. Lo Ea ....... 193 D3
Pyatt St. Nott ............ 173 E1
Pye Ave. Mans ............. 101 E4
Pye Hill Rd. Sels ......... 128 A2
Pygall Ave. Goth .......... 195 D1
Pym St. Nott .............. 173 F3
Pym Wlk. Nott ............. 173 F3
Python Hill Rd. Rain ...... 104 A1

Quadrangle The. Blid ...... 118 A3
Quadrangle The. News ...... 130 B3
Quakefield Rd. E Mark ...... 66 A3
Quaker La. Farns .......... 119 F3
Quaker Way. Mans .......... 102 A4
Quantock Cl. Bes Vil ...... 147 D1
Quantock Gr. Bing ......... 177 E2
Quantock Rd. Lo Ea ........ 182 A1
Quarry Ave. Nott .......... 160 A3
Quarry Cl. Raven .......... 132 A4
Quarry Dr. K-in-A ......... 115 D2
Quarry Hill. S-by-D ....... 182 A4
Quarry La. Linby .......... 131 D2
Quarry La. Mans ........... 102 A3
Quarry Rd. Raven .......... 117 D1
Quarry Rd. Raven .......... 132 A4
Quarry Yard. S in A ....... 100 C1
Quarrydale Ave. S in A .... 100 C3
Quarrydale Dr. S in A ..... 100 C3
Quarrydale Rd. S in A ..... 100 C2
Quayside Cl. Nott ......... 173 E1
Queen Elizabeth Cres. Rhod 35 D2
Queen Elizabeth Rd. Bees . 183 D2
Queen St. Arn ............. 148 A1
Queen St. Bald ............ 140 C2
Queen St. Bott ............ 181 D1
Queen St. Coll ............. 98 A1
Queen St. Gain ............. 24 B4
Queen St. Huck ............ 145 F4
Queen St. K-in-A .......... 115 D2
Queen St. La Mi ........... 143 E2
Queen St. Lo Ea ........... 193 F4
Queen St. Lough ........... 220 B2
Queen St. Mans ............ 102 A4
Queen St. Mar War .......... 74 A3
Queen St. N-on-T .......... 139 F4
Queen St. Nott ............ 173 E3
Queen St. Pinx ............ 113 E2
Queen St. Ret .............. 39 E3
Queen St. S in A .......... 100 C2
Queen St. S Norm .......... 113 D3
Queen St. South ........... 121 E1
Queen St. Work ............. 35 F1
Queen's Ave. Carl ......... 162 C1
Queen's Bridge Rd. Nott .. 173 E2
Queen's Cres. Baw .......... 10 A4
Queen's Ct. Bing .......... 177 E3
Queen's Ct. Mans ........... 89 D1
Queen's Ct. N-on-T ........ 125 D1
Queen's Dr. Nott .......... 159 E3
Queen's Head Ct. N-on-T .. 139 F4
Queen's Rd. Lough ......... 220 B2

Queen's Rd. N-on-T ........ 125 D1
Queen's Rd. Nott .......... 173 E2
Queen's Rd R on T ......... 176 A2
Queen's Sq. East .......... 143 F1
Queen's Wlk. Ne La ......... 59 D1
Queen's Wlk. Nott ......... 173 D1
Queens Dr. Bees ........... 184 A3
Queens Ave. Ilk ........... 170 A3
Queens Bower Rd. Arn ...... 161 E4
Queens Bower Rd. Nott ..... 161 E4
Queens Cl. Whit ............ 45 E3
Queens Dr. Brin ........... 143 F4
Queens Dr. Nott ........... 185 D4
Queens Dr. Sand ........... 182 A2
Queens Rd E. Bees ......... 184 A4
Queens Rd N. East ......... 143 F1
Queens Rd S. East ......... 143 F1
Queens Rd W. Bees ......... 183 F2
Queens Rd. Bees ........... 184 A3
Queens Rd. C in L .......... 25 F4
Queens Rd. Kegw ........... 203 E1
Queens Rd. Whit ............ 45 E3
Queensberry St. Nott ...... 160 C2
Queensbury Ave. W Brid ... 185 E2
Queensway. Gain ............ 24 C4
Queensway. K-in-A ......... 115 D1
Queensway. Mans ............ 89 D1
Queensway. Ne Br .......... 219 E3
Queensway. Sax ............. 57 D2
Queensway. Skel ............ 71 F2
Queensway. Work ............ 35 F2
Querneby Ave. Nott ........ 161 F1
Querneby Rd. Nott ......... 161 F1
Quibell Rd. N-on-T ........ 140 A3
Quibell's La. N-on-T ...... 125 D2
Quines Hill Rd. Mans ....... 89 D1
Quinton Cl. Nott .......... 185 D3
Quorn Cl. Bees ............ 183 F2
Quorn Cl. Lough ........... 220 B1
Quorn Gr. Nott ............ 161 D2
Quorn Rd. Nott ............ 161 D1
Quorndon Cres. Lo Ea ...... 193 E3

Rabbithill La. Spal ........ 83 D3
Racecourse Rd. Mans ....... 102 C3
Rachel Cl. Gain ............ 15 E2
Radbourne Rd. Nott ........ 173 F2
Radbourne St. Mans ......... 88 C2
Radburn Ct. Staple ........ 170 C1
Radcliffe Gdns. Carl ...... 174 B4
Radcliffe Mount. W Brid .. 173 F1
Radcliffe Rd. Cr Bu ....... 189 D4
Radcliffe Rd. Gam ......... 186 B4
Radcliffe Rd. Ho Pi ....... 175 D1
Radcliffe Rd. W Brid ...... 186 A4
Radcliffe St. Nott ........ 173 E1
Radford Bridge Rd. Nott .. 172 B3
Radford Bvd. Nott ......... 172 C3
Radford Cres. Carl ........ 162 C1
Radford Ct. Nott .......... 172 C3
Radford Grove La. Nott .... 172 C3
Radford Rd. Nott .......... 172 C4
Radford St. Mans .......... 102 A3
Radford St. Work ........... 36 A1
Radley La. Halam .......... 135 E4
Radley Sq. Nott ........... 160 B3
Radmanthwaite Rd. Mans .... 87 E2
Radmoor Rd. Lough ......... 220 A2
Radnor Gr. Bing ........... 177 E2
Radnor Pl. Mans ............ 87 E2
Radstock Rd. Nott ......... 174 A4
Hadway Dr. Nott ........... 185 D3
Raeburn Dr. Bees .......... 182 C1
Ragdale Rd. Nott .......... 160 B4
Raglan Cl. Nott ........... 173 E4
Raglan Ct. N-on-T ......... 140 A4
Raglan Ct. Nott ........... 172 A1
Raglan Dr. Carl ........... 163 D1
Raglans Gdns. N-on-T ...... 140 A4
Raglan Rd. Ret ............. 40 A4
Raglan St. East ........... 144 A1
Raibank Gdns. Arn ......... 161 F3
Railway Ave. Elmt .......... 58 B4
Railway Cotts. Kim ........ 158 C3
Railway Terr. Lough ....... 220 B3
Raines Ave. Work ........... 35 F3
Raines Park Rd. Work ....... 35 F4
Rainham Gdns. Rudd ........ 196 B3
Rainworth Water Rd. Rain . 103 F1
Raithby Cl. Nott .......... 161 D3
Raleigh Cl. Ilk ........... 157 F2
Raleigh Ct. Nott .......... 184 B1
Raleigh Rd. Mans .......... 101 F4
Raleigh St. Nott .......... 173 D3
Ralf Cl. W Brid ........... 185 F2
Ramblers Cl. Carl ......... 174 C3
Ramper Rd. Beck ............ 23 E4
Ramper Rd. Let ............. 16 B2
Rampton Green Rd. Ramp .. 42 C1
Rampton La. S Lev ......... 42 B2
Rampton Rd. Lane ........... 54 A3
Rampton Rd. Tres .......... 42 C2
Ramsdale Ave. Calv ........ 148 B4
Ramsdale Cres. Nott ....... 161 E2
Ramsdale Rd. Carl ......... 162 C1
Ramsden Ave. Lan ........... 16 C1
Ramsden Cft. Rain ......... 104 A1
Ramsden Cres. C in L ....... 25 F4

Ramsey Cl. Mans ............ 89 D1
Ramsey Cl. Staple ......... 170 C1
Ramsey Ct. Nott ........... 161 D1
Ramsey Dr. Arn ............ 162 B3
Ranby Wlk. Nott ........... 173 F3
Rancliffe Ave. Keyw ....... 197 E2
Randal Gdns. Nott ......... 172 C4
Randal St. Nott ........... 172 C4
Randall Cl. N-on-T ........ 140 B4
Randall Way. Ret ........... 29 E1
Randol Cl. Mans ........... 101 E2
Ranelagh Gr. Nott ......... 172 A3
Ranmere Rd. Nott .......... 172 A4
Ranmoor Rd. Carl .......... 162 C1
Ranmore Cl. Bees .......... 171 D1
Rannoch Dr. Mans .......... 101 F3
Rannoch Rise. Nott ........ 147 F1
Rannock Gdns. Keyw ........ 197 F2
Ranskill Gdns. Nott ....... 161 D4
Ranskill Rd. Matt .......... 19 F3
Ransom Dr. Nott ........... 161 F1
Ransom Rd. Mans ........... 103 E2
Ransom Rd. Nott ........... 173 F4
Ransome Cl. N-on-T ........ 140 B4
Ratcliffe Gate. Mans ...... 102 B3
Ratcliffe La. Kegw ........ 203 E4
Ratcliffe Rd. Lough ....... 220 B3
Ratcliffe St. East ........ 143 F1
Rathgar Cl. Nott .......... 171 E2
Rathmines Cl. Nott ........ 172 C2
Rathvale Ct. Bees ......... 183 D2
Raven Ave. Nott ........... 161 D2
Ravencroft La. Beck ........ 14 A1
Ravendale Rd. Gain ......... 24 C4
Ravendale Rd. Gain ......... 24 C4
Ravenhill Cl. Bees ........ 183 D2
Ravens Ct. Nott ........... 161 D3
Ravenscourt. Work .......... 36 A3
Ravensdale Ave. Lo Ea ..... 182 A1
Ravensdale Ave. Mans ...... 102 B4
Ravensdale Dr. Nott ....... 171 E2
Ravensdale Rd. Mans ....... 102 C4
Ravensdene Ct. Nott ....... 173 A2
Ravensfleet Rd. E Stock .... 7 F2
Ravenshill Cl. Ran ......... 19 D2
Ravensmore Rd. Nott ....... 161 D1
Ravenswood Rd. Arn ........ 162 A4
Ravensworth Rd. Nott ...... 160 A4
Rawson St. Nott ........... 160 C1
Rawson St. Sels ........... 129 D3
Raylawn St. Mans .......... 103 D3
Raymede Cl. Nott .......... 160 C3
Raymede Dr. Nott .......... 160 C3
Raymond Cl. K-in-A ........ 114 C4
Raymond Dr. Bees .......... 178 A2
Raymoth La. Work ........... 35 F4
Rayner Ct. Nott ........... 172 C3
Raynford Ave. Bees ........ 183 E2
Raysmith Cl. South ........ 121 F1
Read Ave. Bees ............ 184 A3
Readman Rd. Bees .......... 183 D2
Rearsby Cl. Nott .......... 171 E3
Recreation Dr. Shireb ...... 72 C1
Recreation Rd. Ann Wo ..... 130 B4
Recreation Rd. Plea ........ 86 C4
Recreation Rd. Sand ....... 182 A2
Recreation Rd. Shireb ...... 72 C2
Recreation St. Lo Ea ...... 193 F4
Recreation St. Mans ....... 102 B4
Recreation St. Sels ....... 129 D3
Recreation Terr. Staple ... 182 B3
Recreation View. Shireb ... 72 C3
Rectory Ave. Gain .......... 15 E1
Rectory Ave. Nott ......... 171 F2
Rectory Dr. The. Carl ..... 162 C1
Rectory Gdns. Beck ......... 14 A1
Rectory Gdns. Kirton ....... 78 A3
Rectory Gdns. Nott ........ 171 F2
Rectory La. Bott .......... 181 D2
Rectory La. Clayp ......... 156 C2
Rectory La. Cotg .......... 187 F2
Rectory La. Gams ........... 50 C3
Rectory La. Lea ............ 24 C1
Rectory Pl. B in F ........ 194 C3
Rectory Pl. Lough ......... 220 A2
Rectory Rd. Carl .......... 174 C3
Rectory Rd. Lough ......... 220 A3
Rectory Rd. Mar War ........ 74 B4
Rectory Rd. Ret ............ 39 F4
Rectory Rd. Tres ........... 42 A2
Rectory Rd. W Brid ........ 185 F4
Rectory St. Beckin ........ 142 B4
Red Barn Cl. Newt .......... 99 D2
Red Causeway The. Harb .. 202 A1
Red La. Brin .............. 128 C1
Red La. C in L ............. 26 A1
Red La. Lowd .............. 150 B1
Red Lodge La. Kneet ....... 166 A4
Redbarn La. Newt ........... 99 D2
Redbourne Dr. Nott ........ 172 B3
Redbridge Dr. Nuth ........ 159 E2
Redcar Cl. Carl ........... 162 C1
Redcliffe Gdns. Nott ...... 173 E4
Redcliffe Rd. Mans ........ 102 B3
Redcliffe Rd. Nott ........ 173 E4
Redcliffe St. S in A ...... 101 D2

Redfield Rd. Nott ......... 184 C4
Redfield Way. Nott ........ 184 C4
Redforde Park Ave. Ret ..... 29 E1
Redforde Park Dr. Ret ...... 29 E1
Redforde Park Rd. Ret ...... 29 E1
Redgate Cl. Mans .......... 101 F4
Redgate St. Mans .......... 101 F4
Redgate St. Pinx .......... 113 E1
Redgates Ct. Calv ......... 148 B4
Redhill La. Both ........... 63 F4
Redhill Lodge Dr. Nott .... 147 E1
Redhill Rd. Arn ........... 161 F4
Redhill Rd. Nott .......... 147 F1
Redland Ave. Carl ......... 174 C4
Redland Cl. Bees .......... 183 E2
Redland Cl. Ilk ........... 157 F2
Redland Dr. Bees .......... 183 E2
Redland Gr. Carl .......... 174 C4
Redman Cl. Gain ............ 15 F1
Redmays Dr. Bulc .......... 164 A3
Redmile La. Kegw .......... 192 B2
Redmile La. Redm .......... 192 B2
Redmile Rd. Nott .......... 160 B1
Redoubt St. Nott .......... 172 C3
Redruth Cl. Nott .......... 171 E1
Redruth Dr. Mans .......... 103 D1
Redthorn Way. Clayp ....... 156 C3
Redwood Ave. Nott ......... 171 E2
Redwood Cres. Bees ........ 184 A3
Redwood Ct. Huck .......... 145 F4
Redwood. W Brid ........... 185 E3
Reedham Wlk. Nott ......... 161 D4
Reedman Rd. Lo Ea ......... 193 D2
Rees Gdns. Nott ........... 147 D1
Rees Row. Wood ............. 42 A1
Reform St. Ann Wo ......... 129 F4
Reform St. S in A ......... 100 C1
Regatta Way. Gam .......... 186 B4
Regency Ct. Bees .......... 184 A4
Regent St. Bees ........... 184 A4
Regent St. K-in-A ......... 114 C2
Regent St. Kim ............ 158 C3
Regent St. La Mi .......... 143 D2
Regent St. Lo Ea .......... 193 E4
Regent St. Lough .......... 220 A2
Regent St. Mans ........... 102 A4
Regent St. Nott ........... 161 D1
Regent St. Nott ........... 173 D2
Regent St. S in A ......... 100 B1
Regent St. Staple ......... 182 B3
Regents Cl. Coll .......... 112 A4
Regina Cl. R on T ......... 175 F3
Regina Cres. Raven ........ 116 C1
Reigate Cl. Bees .......... 183 F1
Reigate Dr. Bees .......... 183 F1
Reigate Rd. Nott .......... 160 C1
Reindeer St. Mans ......... 102 C3
Rempstone Dr. Nott ........ 160 B3
Rempstone Rd. E Lea ....... 214 C4
Rempstone Rd. Hoton ....... 215 E1
Rempstone Rd. N on S ...... 214 A3
Rempstone Rd. Wyme ........ 216 A2
Renals Way. Calv .......... 148 C4
Renfrew Ct. Mans ........... 88 C2
Renfrew Dr. Nott .......... 171 F2
Repton Ct. Mans ............ 88 C2
Repton Dr. Ilk ............ 170 A4
Repton Rd. Nott ........... 160 B3
Repton Rd. W Brid ......... 185 F3
Reston Cl. Mans ........... 103 D3
Retford Gate. N Le Ha ...... 41 F4
Retford Rd. Babw ........... 37 E2
Retford Rd. Blyth .......... 18 A1
Retford Rd. Boug ........... 77 F4
Retford Rd. E Dray ......... 52 C2
Retford Rd. Matt ........... 20 B3
Retford Rd. N Le Ha ........ 41 F4
Retford Rd. N Le Ha ........ 42 A4
Retford Rd. N Whea ......... 31 E4
Retford Rd. Nott .......... 161 D2
Retford Rd. Ramp ........... 42 B1
Retford Rd. S Lev .......... 42 A4
Retford Rd. Wood ........... 42 B1
Retford Rd. Work ........... 36 B1
Retford Rd. Work ........... 37 E2
Revelstoke Ave. Nott ...... 146 B1
Revelstoke Way. Nott ...... 146 C1
Revesby Gdns. Nott ........ 172 B4
Revesby Rd. Arn ........... 161 F3
Revill Cres. Staple ....... 182 C4
Revill Ct. K-in-A ......... 114 C4
Reydon Dr. Nott ........... 160 B1
Reynolds Dr. Nott ......... 171 F3
Rhodes Wlk. Mans .......... 101 F3
Rhyl Cres. Carl ........... 162 C1
Ribble St. Nott ........... 172 B3
Ribblesdale Ct. Bees ...... 183 D2
Ribblesdale Rd. Lo Ea ..... 193 D2
Ribblesdale Rd. Nott ...... 161 E3
Ribblesdale. Work .......... 36 A4
Riber Cl. Ann Wo .......... 115 D1
Riber Cl. Lo Ea ........... 193 D2
Richard St. Ret ............ 40 A3
Richards Cl. Cr Bi ........ 189 D2
Richardson Cl. Nott ....... 184 B1
Richborough Pl. Nott ...... 171 F1
Richey Cl. Arn ............ 162 A4
Richmond Ave. Calv ........ 149 D4

Richmond Ave. East ........ 144 A
Richmond Ave. Ilk ......... 157 F
Richmond Ave. Lo Ea ....... 193 D
Richmond Ave. Nott ........ 173 D
Richmond Ave. Sand ........ 182 A
Richmond Cl. Bald ......... 140 A
Richmond Dr. Bees ......... 183 F
Richmond Dr. Mans .......... 88 B
Richmond Dr. Nott ......... 161 E
Richmond Dr. R on T ....... 175 F
Richmond Gdns. Nott ....... 147 F
Richmond Rd. C in L ........ 25 F
Richmond Rd. Gain .......... 24 C
Richmond Rd. K-in-A ....... 115 E
Richmond Rd. Ret ........... 30 A
Richmond Rd. W Brid ....... 173 F
Richmond Rd. Work .......... 36 A
Richmond St. Mans ......... 102 C
Richmond Terr. R on T ..... 175 F
Rick St. Nott ............. 173 E
Ricket La. Blid ........... 117 E
Ricket La. Raven .......... 116 C
Ricket La. Raven .......... 117 E
Ricklow Ct. Nott .......... 161 D
Riddell Ave. Lan ........... 16 C
Ridding Terr. Nott ........ 173 E
Ridge Cl. S in A .......... 100 B
Ridge Hill. Lowd .......... 150 B
Ridge La. R on T .......... 176 A
Ridgeway Cl. Farns ........ 119 F
Ridgeway La. Mar War ....... 74 A
Ridgeway St. Nott ......... 173 F
Ridgeway Terr. Mar War .... 74 A
Ridgeway The. Farns ....... 120 A
Ridgeway Wlk. Nott ........ 161 D
Ridgeway. Hean ............ 157 D
Ridgeway. Nott ............ 161 D
Ridgeway. South ........... 121 E
Ridgeway. Work ............. 36 A
Ridgewood Dr. Bees ........ 183 E
Ridgwood Gr. Raven ........ 117 D
Ridgmont Walk. Nott ....... 195 E
Ridgway Cl. W Brid ........ 186 B
Riding or Ridding La. Aust ... 3 D
Ridings The. Bulc ......... 164 A
Ridings The. E Brid ....... 165 E
Ridings The. Keyw ......... 198 A
Ridings The. Mans .......... 88 C
Ridsdale Rd. Nott ......... 161 E
Rifle St. Nott ............ 172 C
Rigg La. Raven ............ 132 C
Rigley Ave. Ilk ........... 157 F
Rigley Dr. Nott ........... 160 C
Riley Ave. S in A ......... 100 B
Riley Cl. S in A .......... 100 B
Ring Leas. Cotg ........... 188 A
Ringrose Cl. N-on-T ....... 140 B
Ringstead Cl. W Brid ...... 185 E
Ringstead Wlk. Nott ....... 161 D
Ringwood Ave. Mans ........ 102 B
Ringwood Cres. Nott ....... 172 B
Ringwood Rd. Bing ......... 177 E
Ringwood. Work ............. 36 A
Ripon Rd. Nott ............ 174 A
Rise Park Rd. Nott ........ 146 C
Rise The. Nott ............ 161 E
Riseborough Wlk. Nott ..... 146 B
Risegate. Cotg ............ 187 F
Riseholme Ave. Nott ....... 171 E
Riseholme Rd. Gain ......... 24 C
Risley Ct. Ilk ............ 157 F
Risley Dr. Nott ........... 173 D
Riste's Pl. Nott .......... 173 E
Ritson Cl. Nott ........... 173 E
River Cl. Ret .............. 29 F
River La. Miss .............. 4 B
River La. Ret .............. 39 F
River Rd. Carl ............ 174 C
River View. Ald ........... 128 A
River View. Mar War ........ 74 A
River View. Nott .......... 173 E
River View. Ret ............ 39 F
Riverdale Rd. Bees ........ 183 E
Rivergreen Cl. Bees ....... 171 E
Rivergreen Cres. Bees ..... 171 E
Rivergreen. Nott .......... 184 C
Rivermead. Cotg ........... 188 A
Rivermead. N-on-T ......... 139 F
Riverside Cl. Bott ........ 181 D
Riverside Rd. Cuck ......... 60 A
Riverside Rd. Bees ........ 184 A
Riverside Rd. N-on-T ...... 139 E
Riverside Way. Mans ........ 88 B
Riverside Way. Nott ....... 173 D
Riverside. South .......... 121 F
Riverside. What ........... 179 D
Riverview Cotts. Miss ...... 4 B
Riverway Gdns. Nott ....... 173 E
Rivington Rd. Bees ........ 182 C
Road No 1. Carl ........... 174 C
Road No 2. Carl ........... 174 C
Road No 3. Carl ........... 175 D
Road No 4. Carl ........... 175 D
Road No 5. Carl ........... 175 E
Road No 7. Carl ........... 174 C
Road No 8. Carl ........... 174 C
Robbie Burns Rd. Nott ..... 161 E4
Robert Ave. Mans .......... 101 F3

247
Robert's La. Huck
Salterford La. Calv

obert's La. Huck 145 F4
oberts Ave. S in A 99 F1
oberts Cl. D on T 54 A1
oberts Cl. Kegw 203 E1
oberts St. Ilk 170 A3
oberts St. Nott 173 F2
oberts Yd. Bees 184 A4
obey Cl. Mans 89 D1
obey Dr. East 143 F2
obin Down Cl. Mans 102 B1
obin Down La. Mans 102 B1
obin Gr. Raven 117 D1
obin Hood Ave. Edwin 91 E4
obin Hood Ave. Mar War 74 B1
obin Hood Cl. East 143 F1
obin Hood Dr. Huck 145 F3
obin Hood Ind Est. Nott 173 F3
obin Hood Rd. Ann Wo 130 A4
obin Hood Rd. Bes Vil 147 E1
obin Hood Rd. Blid 118 A3
obin Hood St. Nott 173 F3
obin Hood Terr. Nott 173 E3
obin Hood Terr. Raven 117 D2
obin Hood Way. Nott 173 D1
obin's Wood Rd. Nott 172 A4
obina Dr. Greas 158 B4
obinet Rd. Bees 183 F3
obinettes La. Coss 158 B1
obinia Ct. W Brid 186 A3
obins Ct. N-on-T 140 A4
obinson Cl. N-on-T 140 C4
obinson Dr. Work 35 F1
obinson Gdns. Nott 184 B1
obinson Rd. Carl 162 A1
Roche Cl. Arn 162 B4
Rochester Ave. Carl 175 D4
Rochester Cl. Work 36 A4
Rochester Ct. Nott 159 F3
Rochester Rd. Rain 118 A4
Rochester Wlk. Nott 184 C1
Rochford Ct. W Brid 186 B2
Rock Ct. Mans 102 B4
Rock Ct. Nott 160 B2
Rock Dr. Nott 173 D2
Rock Hill. Mans 102 B3
Rock St. Mans 102 B3
Rock St. Nott 160 A4
Rock Valley. Mans 102 B4
Rockford Ct. Staple 170 C1
Rockford Rd. Nott 160 C2
Rockingham Gr. Bing 177 E2
Rocklands The. Shireb 72 C2
Rockley Ave. East 144 A1
Rockley Ave. R on T 175 F2
Rockley Cl. Huck 145 E3
Rockley Way. Shireb 72 C2
Rockleys View. Lowd 150 A1
Rockwood Cl. Blid 118 A3
Rockwood Wlk. Huck 145 F3
Rodel Ct. Nott 173 E3
Roden St. Nott 173 F3
Roderick Ave. Ann Wo 115 D1
Roderick St. Nott 160 B2
Rodney Rd. W Brid 186 A3
Rodney Way. Ilk 157 F2
Rodwell Cl. Nott 172 B3
Roe Hill. Woodb 149 E3
Roebuck Dr. Mans 102 A2
Roecliffe. W Brid 185 F2
Roehampton Dr. Staple 170 B1
Roes La. Calv 149 D4
Roewood La. Wink 107 F1
Roger Cl. S in A 100 C3
Roker Cl. Nott 160 A1
Rolaine Cl. Mans 88 B2
Roland Ave. Nott 185 D4
Roland Ave. Nuth 159 F2
Rolleston Cl. Huck 145 E3
Rolleston Cres. Greas 144 C1
Rolleston Cres. Greas 158 C4
Rolleston Dr. Arn 162 A4
Rolleston Dr. Greas 158 B4
Rolleston Dr. Nott 172 C2
Roman Bank La. Ran 18 C3
Roman Bank. Mans 88 B2
Roman Dr. Nott 160 C2
Romans Ct. Nott 160 C1
Romilay Cl. Nott 172 A1
Romney Ave. Nott 171 E1
Rona Cl. Mans 101 F3
Rona Ct. Nott 160 C3
Ronald St. Nott 172 C3
Rook's La. Mist 6 C1
Rookery Gdns. Arn 161 F4
Rookery La. S in A 114 A4
Rookery The. Mans 102 A4
Rookwood Cl. Bees 183 F3
Rookwood Cres. Huck 145 E3
Rooley Ave. S in A 100 B2
Rooley Dr. S in A 100 B2
Roosa Cl. Nott 159 F3
Roosevelt Ave. Lo Ea 193 E3
Roosevelt Rd. S in A 101 D2
Rooth St. Mans 102 A3
Rope Wlk. E Lea 205 E1
Ropery Rd. Gain 15 E1
Ropewalk The. Ilk 158 A1
Ropewalk The. N-on-T 140 A4
Ropewalk The. Nott 173 D2
Ropewalk The. South 121 F1
Ropewalk. Kegw 203 E1
Ropework Seedbed Cntr. Ilk158 A1
Ropsley Cres. W Brid 186 A4
Roscoe Ave. Nott 147 F1
Rose Ash La. Nott 161 D4
Rose Ave. Ilk 157 F1
Rose Ave. Ret 40 A2
Rose Cl. Nott 173 E4
Rose Cottage Dr. S in A 99 F1
Rose Cotts. Bu Jo 163 F3
Rose Ct. Lo Ea 182 A1
Rose Farm Dr. S on T 96 C4
Rose Gr. Bees 184 A3
Rose Gr. Keyw 197 F2
Rose Hill. Keyw 197 F2
Rose La. Mans 88 B2
Rose Lea. Ret 39 E2
Rosebank Dr. Arn 148 A1
Roseberry Ave. W Brid 173 F1
Roseberry Gdns. Huck 146 B3
Roseberry St. K-in-A 115 E2
Rosebery Hill. Mans 102 B3
Rosebery St. Nott 160 C2
Rosecroft Dr. Nott 161 E3
Rosedale Cl. Lo Ea 193 D3
Rosedale Dr. Nott 171 D2
Rosedale La. Raven 116 C2
Rosedale Rd. Nott 174 B3
Rosedale. Work 36 A4
Rosegarth Wlk. Nott 160 B2
Rosegrove Ave. Nott 147 F1
Rosehill Cl. Sax 57 D2
Roseleigh Ave. Carl 162 A1
Rosemary Ave. Mans 102 A4
Rosemary Cl. Nott 159 F1
Rosemary St. Mans 102 A4
Rosemont Cl. S in A 100 C3
Roseneath Ave. Nott 146 C1
Rosetta Rd. Nott 160 C1
Rosewall Ct. Arn 162 A4
Roseway. Gain 15 E1
Rosewood Cl. N-on-T 125 D1
Rosewood Cl. S Norm 113 D4
Rosewood Cres. Hean 143 D1
Rosewood Dr. K-in-A 115 E3
Rosewood Gdns. Nott 159 F4
Rosewood Gdns. W Brid 185 E2
Roslyn Ave. Carl 162 C1
Ross Cl. Codd 126 A1
Ross Cl. Lowd 150 C1
Ross La. Lamb 163 E4
Rossell Dr. Staple 182 C3
Rossendale. Ilk 157 F2
Rossetti Gdns. Work 36 B2
Rossington Rd. Nott 173 F3
Rosslyn Dr. Huck 146 B4
Rosslyn Dr. Nott 160 A1
Rosthwaite Cl. W Brid 186 B3
Rothbury Ave. Staple 170 B1
Rothbury Gr. Bing 177 E3
Rotherham Baulk. C in L 25 E4
Rotherham Baulk. Let 25 E4
Rotherham Rd. Plea 86 C4
Rothley Ave. Nott 173 F3
Rothwell Cl. Gain 24 C4
Rothwell Cl. Nott 185 D2
Roughs Wood La. Huck 145 E2
Roulstone Cres. E Lea 205 F2
Roundhill Cl. S in A 101 E1
Roundwood Rd. Arn 161 E4
Row The. Orst 179 F3
Rowan Ave. Hath 213 D1
Rowan Ave. Raven 117 D1
Rowan Ave. Staple 170 C1
Rowan Cl. Calv 148 B4
Rowan Cl. Mans 88 B1
Rowan Cres. Work 35 F1
Rowan Croft. S in A 99 F2
Rowan Ct. Kim 159 D3
Rowan Dr. K-in-A 114 C3
Rowan Dr. Keyw 198 A1
Rowan Dr. Nott 185 D2
Rowan Dr. Sels 128 B4
Rowan Dr. Shireb 72 B3
Rowan Gdns. Nott 159 F4
Rowan Way. Bald 140 A3
Rowan Wlk. Carl 174 A4
Rowe Gdns. Nott 160 B3
Rowland Ave. Carl 162 A1
Rowland Mews. Nott 173 F4
Rowsley Ave. Lo Ea 193 D3
Rowston Cl. Gain 15 E1
Rowthorne La. Al Hu 86 A4
Rowthorne La. Glap 86 A4
Roxton Ct. Kim 158 C4
Roy Ave. Bees 184 A2
Royal Ave. Lo Ea 182 B1
Royal Cres. Work 35 F3
Royal Mews. Bees 183 E2
Royal Oak Ct. Edwin 76 A1
Royal Oak Dr. Sels 129 D4
Royal Way. Lough 220 A3
Royce Ave. Huck 145 F2
Royds Cres. Rhod 35 D3
Royland Rd. Lough 220 A2
Royston Cl. Nott 173 D1
Ruddington Ct. Mans 103 D1
Ruddington La. Nott 185 D3
Ruddington Rd. Mans 103 D1
Rudge Cl. Nott 171 F3
Ruffles Ave. Arn 162 A3
Rufford Ave. Bees 183 D4
Rufford Ave. Carl 162 B1
Rufford Ave. Mans 102 B4
Rufford Ave. Mar War 74 C4
Rufford Ave. N-on-T 139 F4
Rufford Ave. Oll 77 E2
Rufford Ave. Rain 104 B1
Rufford Ave. Ret 39 E2
Rufford Cl. Bils 106 A2
Rufford Cl. Huck 146 B3
Rufford Cl. S in A 100 C3
Rufford Dr. Mans 88 C2
Rufford Gr. Bing 177 E2
Rufford La. Oll 92 A4
Rufford La. Ruff 91 F4
Rufford Rd. Edwin 91 E4
Rufford Rd. Lo Ea 193 D2
Rufford Rd. Nott 161 E2
Rufford Rd. Rudd 196 B4
Rufford St. Work 47 D4
Rufford Way. W Brid 186 A3
Rufford Wlk. Nott 160 A4
Ruffs Dr. Huck 145 F3
Rugby Cl. Nott 160 C4
Rugby Rd. Rain 118 A4
Rugeley Ave. Lo Ea 194 A4
Ruislip Cl. Kim 158 C4
Runcie Cl. Cotg 187 F1
Runnymede Ct. Nott 173 D3
Runswick Dr. Arn 161 F4
Runswick Dr. Nott 172 A3
Runton Dr. Nott 160 C2
Rupert Cres. N-on-T 139 F4
Rupert Rd. Bing 177 E2
Rupert St. Ilk 158 A1
Rush Leys. Lo Ea 193 E3
Rushcliffe Ave. Carl 174 B4
Rushcliffe Ave. R on T 175 F2
Rushcliffe Ct. Nott 160 B3
Rushcliffe Gr. E Lea 205 F2
Rushcliffe Rd. Huck 145 F3
Rushcliffe Rise. Nott 161 E3
Rushes The. Goth 195 D1
Rushes The. Lough 220 A2
Rushes The. Mans 88 B3
Rushey Cl. Work 36 A1
Rushford Dr. Nott 171 E2
Rushmere Wlk. Arn 161 F3
Rushpool Ave. Mans 88 B2
Rushton Gdns. Nott 173 F4
Rushworth Ave. W Brid 185 F4
Rushworth Cl. Nott 173 F4
Rushy Cl. Nott 171 E3
Ruskin Ave. Bees 183 E2
Ruskin Ave. Lo Ea 193 D3
Ruskin Rd. Mans 87 E1
Ruskin St. Gain 24 B3
Russell Ave. Bald 140 A2
Russell Ave. Har 8 C2
Russell Ave. Nott 171 F2
Russell Cres. Nott 171 F2
Russell Dr. Nott 171 F2
Russell Pl. Nott 173 D3
Russell Rd. Nott 172 C4
Russell St. Lo Ea 182 B1
Russell St. Lough 220 B2
Russell St. Nott 173 D3
Russell St. S in A 100 C2
Russet Ave. Carl 174 C4
Russet Gr. Baw 10 A4
Russey Cl. Lowd 150 C1
Russley Rd. Bees 183 D4
Ruth Dr. Arn 148 A1
Rutherford Ave. Mans 102 C2
Ruthwell Gdns. Bes Vil 147 D1
Rutland Ave. Bees 183 D1
Rutland Ave. N-on-T 140 A3
Rutland Cl. Mar War 74 A2
Rutland Cres. Har 8 C3
Rutland Dr. Har 8 B2
Rutland Dr. Har 8 C3
Rutland Gr. Staple 182 B3
Rutland La. Bott 181 D1
Rutland Rd. Bing 177 F3
Rutland Rd. Carl 162 B2
Rutland Rd. Ret 40 A2
Rutland Rd. Sels 128 B2
Rutland Rd. W Brid 186 A4
Rutland St. Ilk 157 F1
Rutland St. Lough 220 B2
Rutland St. Mans 102 B3
Rutland St. Nott 173 D2
Rutland Terr. Ilk 157 F1
Rutland. K-in-A 115 E3
Rydal Dr. Huck 145 F4
Rydal Ave. Lo Ea 182 A1
Rydal Dr. Bees 183 E4
Rydal Dr. Work 35 F4
Rydal Gdns. W Brid 186 A3
Rydal Gr. Nott 160 C2
Rydale Rd. Nott 161 E3
Ryder St. Nott 160 B2
Rye Croft. Tick 8 A4
Rye St. Nott 160 C1
Ryecroft St. Staple 182 C4
Ryehill Cl. Nott 173 E1
Ryehill St. Nott 173 E1
Ryeholme Cl. E Lea 205 F2
Ryeland Gdns. Nott 173 E1
Ryemere Cl. East 143 F1
Rylands Cl. Bees 184 A2
Ryton Cl. Blyth 18 A1
Ryton Ct. Nott 173 E1
Ryton Fields. Blyth 18 A1
Ryton Pl. Work 35 F2
Ryton Sq. Nott 160 A1
Ryton St. Work 35 F2

Sacheverall Ave. Pinx 113 E2
Saddlers Cl. Mans 88 C1
Saddleworth Ct. Nott 173 E3
Sadler St. Mans 101 F4
Saffron Gdns. Nott 173 D1
St Agnes Cl. Nott 171 E4
St Aidan's Ct. Nott 160 C2
St Albans Ct. Bes Vil 147 D1
St Albans Mews. Nott 160 B3
St Albans Rd. Arn 161 F4
St Albans Rd. Bes Vil 146 C2
St Albans Rd. Nott 160 B4
St Albans St. Nott 161 E2
St Andrew Cl. Goth 195 D1
St Andrew St. Mans 102 B3
St Andrew's Cl. Huck 146 A4
St Andrew's Rd. Nott 173 E4
St Andrew's Rise. Kegw 203 E1
St Andrews Cl. Nott 160 B4
St Andrews Cres. S in A 100 C3
St Andrews Ct. Nott 160 B4
St Andrews Dr. Sax 56 C2
St Andrews St. K-in-A 115 D3
St Andrews St. S in A 100 C3
St Ann's Gdns. Nott 173 F4
St Ann's Hill Rd. Nott 173 E4
St Ann's Hill. Nott 173 E4
St Ann's St. Nott 173 E3
St Ann's Valley. Nott 173 F4
St Ann's Way. Nott 173 E3
St Ann's Way. Shelt 168 B3
St Ann's Well Rd. Nott 173 F3
St Anne's La. Su Bo 213 D3
St Annes Cl. Work 35 E2
St Annes Dr. Work 35 E1
St Annes Mews. Work 35 E2
St Annes View. Work 35 E2
St Annes Way. Work 35 E2
St Anthony Ct. Nott 172 C1
St Augustines Cl. Nott 161 D1
St Austell Dr. Nott 185 D3
St Austins Ct. Carl 174 C4
St Austins Dr. Carl 174 C4
St Bartholomew's Rd. Nott 173 F4
St Botolphs Cl. Sax 57 D3
St Catherine St. Mans 102 B3
St Catherines Cl. N-on-T 139 F4
St Catherines St. R on T 175 F1
St Cecilia Gdns. Nott 173 E3
St Chad's Rd. Nott 173 F3
St Christopher St. Nott 173 F2
St Clare's Gate. N-on-T 140 A3
St Cuthbert St. Work 35 F1
St Cuthbert's Rd. Nott 173 F3
St David's Cl. Work 36 A3
St Edmund's Ave. Mans 88 B2
St Edwin's Dr. Edwin 76 A1
St Ervan Rd. Nott 185 D3
St George's Ct. Huck 146 A4
St George's Dr. Nott 173 E1
St Giles Way. Cr Bi 189 D2
St Giles' Way. Bald 140 C2
St Helen's Cres. Bu Jo 163 F2
St Helen's Cres. Trow 170 B2
St Helen's Dr. Sels 128 B4
St Helen's Gr. Bu Jo 163 F2
St Helen's La. Halam 120 C1
St Helen's Rd. Ret 40 A2
St Helen's Rd. W Brid 185 F3
St Helen's St. Nott 173 D3
St Helens Ave. Pinx 113 E2
St Jame's Terr. Nott 173 D2
St James Ave. Ilk 170 A4
St James Ct. Sand 182 A2
St James' Dr. Brin 143 E4
St James's Ct. Huck 146 A4
St James's St. Staple 182 B3
St James's Terr. Staple 182 B3
St John St. Mans 102 A4
St John St. Ret 39 F4
St John's Ave. K-in-A 115 D2
St John's Cl. Brin 128 B1
St John's Cres. Huck 146 B3
St John's Dr. Clar 30 B2
St John's Pl. Mans 102 A4
St John's Rd. Ilk 170 A4
St John's Rd. Rudd 196 B4
St John's St. Lo Ea 193 E4
St John's Terr. Gain 24 B4
St Johns Ct. Carl 174 B4
St Jude's Ave. Nott 161 F1
St Judes Way. Rain 104 A1
St Lawrence Bvd. R on T 175 F1
St Leonard's Ct. N-on-T 124 C1
St Leonard's Dr. Nott 171 F2
St Leonard's. Tick 8 A4
St Leven Cl. Nott 171 E4
St Luke's Cl. W Brid 186 A3
St Luke's St. Nott 173 F3
St Luke's Way. St Ba 175 F4
St Lukes Way. Wood 53 D4
St Margaret St. Mans 102 B3
St Margarets Ave. Nott 172 B4
St Mark's La. N-on-T 139 F4
St Mark's Pl. N-on-T 139 F4
St Marks St. Nott 173 E3
St Martin's Ave. Baw 9 F4
St Martin's Cl. Fir 16 A3
St Martin's Cl. Nott 171 F4
St Martin's Rd. Nott 171 F4
St Martin's Wlk. Whit 45 E3
St Martins Cl. Blyth 18 A1
St Martins Rd. N Le Ha 42 B4
St Mary's Rd. S in A 100 B2
St Mary's Ave. Carl 162 C1
St Mary's Cl. Bott 181 D2
St Mary's Cl. Lough 220 A2
St Mary's Cl. Lowd 150 B1
St Mary's Cl. Nott 147 F1
St Mary's Cres. E Lea 205 F2
St Mary's Cres. Rudd 196 B4
St Mary's Cres. Tick 8 A4
St Mary's Ct. S in A 100 B2
St Mary's Dr. Edwin 76 A1
St Mary's Gate. Nott 173 E2
St Mary's Gate. Tick 8 A4
St Mary's Gdns. N-on-T 139 F3
St Mary's La. Bott 181 D1
St Mary's Mews. Tick 8 A4
St Mary's Pl. Nott 173 E2
St Mary's Rd. Tick 8 A4
St Mary's Way. Huck 146 A4
St Mary's Wlk. Sels 128 A2
St Marys Cl. Bees 183 E1
St Marys Rd. Bing 177 F3
St Matthias Rd. Nott 173 F3
St Mawes Ave. Nott 185 D3
St Mellion Way. K-in-A 114 C4
St Michael's Ave. Carl 162 C1
St Michael's Cl. Halam 120 C1
St Michael's Dr. S Norm 113 D4
St Michael's Green. Ret 39 E4
St Michael's Sq. Bees 183 D4
St Michael's St. S in A 101 D2
St Michaels Ave. Nott 171 E4
St Nicholas Cl. Arn 161 F4
St Nicholas St. Nott 173 E2
St Patrick's Rd. Huck 145 F4
St Patrick's Rd. Nuth 159 E3
St Patrick's Rd. Nuth 159 E3
St Paul's Ave. Nott 172 C4
St Paul's Rd. Gain 15 D2
St Paul's St. Nott 172 B3
St Peter's Ave. Mar War 74 A3
St Peter's Church Wlk. Nott 173 E2
St Peter's Cres. Rudd 196 B4
St Peter's Gate. Nott 173 E2
St Peter's La. Clay 21 E3
St Peter's St. Nott 172 C3
St Peter's Way. Mans 102 B3
St Peters Ave. Hath 213 D1
St Peters Cl. E Stock 7 F1
St Peters Cl. Farn 138 C2
St Peters Cl. Oll 77 D2
St Peters Dr. Rain 104 A1
St Saviour's Cl. Ret 40 A4
St Saviour's Gdns. Nott 173 E1
St Stephen's Ave. Nott 173 F2
St Stephen's Rd. Nott 173 F2
St Stephen's Rd. Ret 40 A2
St Thomas' Ave. K-in-A 115 D2
St Vincent Cl. Lo Ea 193 F3
St Wilfreds Cl. N Musk 110 C1
St Wilfrid's Sq. Calv 148 C4
St Wilfrids Dr. K-in-A 114 B3
Salamander Cl. Carl 162 B1
Salcey Dr. Staple 170 B1
Salcombe Circus. Nott 147 E1
Salcombe Cres. Rudd 196 B4
Salcombe Dr. Nott 147 E1
Salcombe Gr. Baw 9 F4
Salcombe Rd. Nott 160 C2
Salford Gdns. Nott 173 E3
Saliisbury St. Lough 220 B2
Salisbury Ave. E Lea 205 F1
Salisbury Cl. Mans 88 B2
Salisbury Rd. Gain 15 E1
Salisbury Rd. Mans 101 F4
Salisbury Rd. N-on-T 139 F3
Salisbury Sq. Nott 172 C2
Salisbury St. Bees 184 A4
Salisbury St. Lo Ea 193 F4
Salisbury St. Nott 172 C2
Sallie Bank La. Kettl 55 D2
Salmon Cl. Nott 159 F4
Salmon La. Ann Wo 129 E4
Salop St. Arn 161 E4
Salt Hill. Fir 16 A3
Saltburn Rd. Nott 172 A3
Salterford Ave. Calv 148 C4
Salterford La. Calv 133 E3

Salterford Rd. Huck ............ 145 F3
Saltford Cl. Carl ................. 162 C1
Salthouse Ct. Bees ............ 184 A4
Salthouse La. Bees ............ 184 A4
Saltney Way. Nott ............. 185 D2
Salvin Cl. Cr Bi ................. 189 D2
Sampson Dr. Ann Wo ......... 130 A4
Sampson's La. Mans ........... 87 D2
Samson Ct. Rudd ............... 196 A4
Samuel Cl. Mans ................ 101 F4
Sand La. Best .................... 97 F4
Sand La. Sax ..................... 70 C4
Sand La. Spal .................... 83 D4
Sand La. Tork ................... 44 B1
Sand Pit La. Lo Cl ............ 211 E2
Sandalwood Cl. Mans ........ 103 D2
Sandalwood Dr. K-in-A ....... 115 E3
Sandays Cl. Nott .............. 173 E1
Sandby Ct. Bees ............... 183 E3
Sanders Ave. Mans ........... 102 C4
Sanderson's Bank. Miss ....... 2 A2
Sanderson's Bank. Wroot ..... 2 A2
Sandfield La. Kirton ........... 78 A3
Sandfield Rd. Ann Wo ........ 129 F4
Sandfield Rd. Arn .............. 161 F3
Sandfield Rd. Bees ........... 182 C1
Sandfield Way. N-on-T ....... 139 E3
Sandford Ave. Lo Ea .......... 193 F4
Sandford Rd. Carl .............. 162 A2
Sandford Rd. Nott ............. 172 C2
Sandgate Ave. Mans ........... 88 B2
Sandgate Rd. Mans ............. 88 B2
Sandgate. Bees ................. 171 E1
Sandhill Rd. Farn .............. 139 D3
Sandhill Rd. Sels .............. 129 D2
Sandhill St. Work ............... 35 F2
Sandhurst Ave. Mans ......... 102 B2
Sandhurst Dr. Rudd ........... 196 A3
Sandhurst Rd. Nott ........... 146 B1
Sandiacre Rd. Staple ......... 182 B3
Sandmartins. Work ............. 35 E4
Sandon St. Nott ................ 161 D1
Sandown Rd. Bees ............ 182 C1
Sandown Rd. Mans ........... 103 D2
Sandown Rd. S in A ........... 101 D2
Sandringham Ave. W Brid .. 185 F4
Sandringham Cres. Nott .... 171 E3
Sandringham Cres. Work ..... 35 F3
Sandringham Ct. Har ............ 9 D3
Sandringham Ct. Mans ........ 88 A3
Sandringham Dr. Bees ....... 171 E1
Sandringham Dr. Mans ........ 88 A3
Sandringham Pl. Huck ....... 146 A4
Sandringham Rd. Mans ....... 88 C3
Sandringham Rd. Nott ....... 173 F2
Sandringham Rd. Ret .......... 29 E1
Sandringham Rd. Sand ...... 182 A2
Sandrock Rd. Har ................ 8 C3
Sands The. Lo Cl .............. 211 E2
Sandsfield La. Gain ............ 24 B3
Sandsfield La. Gain ............ 24 B4
Sandside. Cotg ................. 187 F1
Sandwich Cl. K-in-A .......... 114 C4
Sandwood Cl. Newt ............ 99 D2
Sandy La. Bees ................ 171 E1
Sandy La. Edwin ................ 91 D4
Sandy La. Gams ................. 50 C2
Sandy La. Ho Pi ............... 175 D1
Sandy La. Huck ................ 146 A4
Sandy La. Mans ................ 102 B4
Sandy La. Mar War ............. 74 A3
Sandy La. Oxt .................. 134 B2
Sandy La. Raven .............. 117 D2
Sandy La. Work .................. 35 E2
Sandycliffe Cl. Mans .......... 88 C1
Sandyford Cl. Nott ............ 160 B2
Sandymount East. Har .......... 9 D2
Sandymount West. Har ......... 9 D3
Sandymount. Har ................. 9 D3
Sanger Cl. Nott ................ 195 E4
Sanger Gdns. Nott ............ 195 E4
Sankey Dr. Nott ............... 160 A4
Santon Cl. Mans ................ 89 D1
Santon Rd. Mans ............... 89 D1
Sapele Cl. Carl ................. 163 D1
Sapphire Dr. K-in-A .......... 115 E2
Saracen Cl. Gain ................ 24 C3
Saracen's Head Yd. N-on-T 139 F4
Sargent Gdns. Nott ........... 173 F3
Sartfield Rd. Mans ............. 89 D1
Saskatoon Cl. R on T ........ 175 F1
Saucers The. Scarr ........... 178 C4
Saunby Cl. Arn ................. 162 A4
Saundby Ave. Mans ............ 87 E1
Saundby Rd. Saundby ......... 23 E2
Savage's Rd. Rudd ........... 196 B4
Savages Row. Rudd .......... 196 B4
Saversick La. South .......... 136 A4
Savile Rd. Bils ................. 105 F3
Savile St. Ret .................... 39 E4
Saville Cl. Staple ............. 182 C4
Saville Rd. Arn ................. 161 F3
Saville Rd. S in A ............. 100 C3
Saville St. Blid ................. 118 A3
Saville Way. Mar War .......... 74 A2
Saw Pit La. Tibs ................ 99 D3
Sawley Dr. Mans .............. 103 D2

Sawyers Cl. N-on-T .......... 140 A4
Saxby Dr. Mans ................ 103 D2
Saxelby Gdns. Nott .......... 160 A4
Saxilby Rd. Skel ................ 71 F4
Saxon Green. Nott ............ 172 C2
Saxon Way. Cotg ............. 188 A1
Saxon Way. Har .................. 8 C2
Saxondale Dr. Nott ........... 160 C3
Saxton Cl. Bees ............... 184 A3
Saxton Cl. Work ................ 35 E1
Scafell Way. Nott ............. 195 E4
Scalby Cl. East ................ 143 E1
Scalford Dr. Nott .............. 172 B2
Scampton Way. Gain .......... 24 C4
Scarborough Rd. Bils ........ 105 F3
Scarborough St. Nott ........ 173 E3
Scarbrough Cl. Tick ............. 8 A4
Scarcliffe Ct. S in A .......... 100 C2
Scarcliffe La. Scarc ........... 72 B4
Scarcliffe St. Mans ........... 102 B4
Scarcliffe Terr. Scarc .......... 59 D1
Scargill Ave. East ............. 144 A1
Scargill Cl. East ............... 144 A1
Scargill Wlk. East ............. 143 F2
Scarle La. Eagle ................ 84 B2
Scarrington Ct. Mans ........ 103 D1
Scarrington Rd. W Brid ..... 173 F1
Sceptre St. Nott ............... 161 E1
School Ave. Huck .............. 145 E2
School Cl. Nott ................ 173 E1
School Green. E Lea .......... 205 F1
School Hill. Ann Wo .......... 130 A4
School House La. Walker ...... 13 F3
School La. Beckin ............. 142 B4
School La. Bees ............... 183 E2
School La. Bing ................ 177 F3
School La. Caun ............... 109 D2
School La. Clayp .............. 156 C4
School La. Co Ba .............. 200 B4
School La. Cuck ................ 60 A2
School La. E Sto ............... 153 E4
School La. Farn ................ 139 D2
School La. Halam .............. 121 D2
School La. Harb ................ 202 A2
School La. Knee ................. 93 F3
School La. Lo Cl ............... 211 E2
School La. Mans ................ 88 B2
School La. N Sca ................ 83 E1
School La. Norw ............... 110 A4
School La. Oll ................... 77 D2
School La. Remp ............... 215 E3
School La. S Norm ............ 113 D2
School La. What ............... 179 D2
School Rd. Lan .................. 16 C2
School Rd. Sels ................ 129 D2
School Rd. Sels ................ 129 D4
School St. K-in-A .............. 115 D3
School St. Lough .............. 220 A2
School Wlk. Baw ................ 10 A4
School Wlk. Bes Vil .......... 146 C2
Schrimshire's Rd. S Le S ..... 32 A1
Science Rd. Nott .............. 172 B1
Scot La. Baw ..................... 10 A4
Scotholme Ave. Nott ......... 172 C4
Scotland Bank. Cotg ......... 187 F2
Scotland Rd. Nott ............ 160 C2
Scotsdale Wlk. Nott ......... 161 F1
Scotswood Rd. Mans .......... 88 A3
Scott Ave. Bees ............... 184 A3
Scott Cl. Nott .................. 159 F3
Scott Cl. Work ................... 36 B2
Scott St. Gain ................... 15 E1
Scott St. Scarc .................. 59 D1
Scotton Sq. Ret ................. 29 E1
Scotts Way. Ann Wo ......... 115 D1
Scratta La. Whit ................ 34 B1
Scrimshire La. Cotg .......... 187 F2
Script Dr. Nott ................. 160 C2
Scrivelsby Gdns. Bees ...... 183 E2
Scrooby Dr. Bir .................... 9 E2
Scrooby Rd. Har .................. 8 C2
Seaburn Rd. Bees ............ 182 C1
Seaford Ave. Nott ............. 172 A3
Seaford Way. Ilk .............. 157 F3
Seaforth Sq. Mans ........... 101 E3
Seagrave Ave. Ann Wo ..... 115 D1
Seagrave Rd. Nott ............ 159 E1
Seamer Rd. Kim ............... 158 C4
Searby Rd. S in A ............. 101 E1
Searby Rd. S in A ............. 101 E1
Searwood Ave. K-in-A ....... 114 C4
Seatoller Cl. W Brid ......... 186 B3
Seaton Cres. Nott ............ 160 A1
Second Ave. Carl ............. 162 C1
Second Ave. Carl ............. 174 B4
Second Ave. Edwin ............ 76 A1
Second Ave. Mans ............. 89 D1
Second Ave. Mans ........... 103 F1
Second Ave. N Clip ............ 90 A2
Sedgebrook Cl. Nott ......... 160 B2
Sedgebrook St. Mans ......... 88 C2
Sedgeley Rd. Toll ............. 186 B1
Sedgewood Gr. Nott ......... 184 C2
Sedgley Ave. Nott ............ 173 F3
Sedgwick St. La Mi ........... 143 D2
Sedgwick St. Sels ............ 128 A2
Sedley Ave. Nuth .............. 159 E3
Seely Ave. Calv ............... 148 C4

Seely Rd. Nott ................ 173 D3
Sefton Ave. Staple ........... 182 C4
Sefton Dr. Nott ................ 161 E1
Selbourne Ct. Lough ........ 220 B1
Selbourne St. Lough ........ 220 B2
Selby Cl. Bees ................. 182 C2
Selby La. Keyw ................ 197 F1
Selby Rd. W Brid ............. 185 F3
Selhurst Ct. Nott ............. 172 C4
Selhurst St. Nott ............. 172 C4
Selkirk Way. Nott ............. 161 E1
Sellars Ave. Rudd ............ 196 B3
Seller's Wood Dr W. Nott .. 159 F4
Seller's Wood Dr. Nott ..... 160 A4
Selsey Ct. Ret ................... 29 E1
Selside Ct. Bees ............... 183 D2
Selston Dr. Nott ............... 172 B2
Selston Rd. Sels .............. 128 A3
Selwyn Cl. Nott ............... 160 C3
Selwyn St. Mans .............. 102 C3
Sennen Ct. Ret .................. 29 F1
Serlby Rd. East ................ 144 A2
Serlby Rise. Nott .............. 173 F3
Seven Hills. N-on-T .......... 125 D2
Seven Oaks Cres. Bees ..... 171 E1
Seven Oaks Rd. S-by-D ..... 170 A1
Seventh Ave. Mans .......... 103 D4
Seventh Ave. N Clip ........... 89 F1
Severals. Staple ............... 182 C4
Severn St. Nott ............... 160 A4
Seward St. Lough ............ 220 A2
Seymour Rd. East ............ 143 F1
Seymour Rd. Huck ........... 145 F3
Seymour Rd. W Brid ........ 186 A4
Seymour St. Nott ............. 173 F3
Shackleton Cl. Nott ......... 159 F4
Shacklock Cl. Bes Vil ....... 147 D1
Shadwell Gr. R on T ......... 175 F2
Shady La. Bees ................ 183 E1
Shaftesbury Ave. Bu Jo .... 164 A3
Shaftesbury Ave. Lo Ea .... 193 E3
Shaftesbury Ave. Mans ...... 87 F1
Shaftesbury Ave. Sand ..... 182 A3
Shaftesbury St. Nott ........ 161 D1
Shakespear St. Gain .......... 24 B3
Shakespeare Ave. Mans ..... 88 A2
Shakespeare Cl. Carl ........ 174 C3
Shakespeare Rd. Awsw .... 158 B3
Shakespeare St. Bald ....... 140 A3
Shakespeare St. Lo Ea ..... 182 B1
Shakespeare St. Lough .... 220 A2
Shakespeare St. Nott ....... 173 E3
Shakespeare St. Work ........ 36 A1
Shakespeare Villas. Nott .. 173 E3
Shaldon Cl. Nott .............. 146 C1
Shandwick Cl. Arn ............ 148 A1
Shanklin Dr. Staple .......... 182 B4
Shanwell Cl. Nott ............ 159 E1
Shardlow Way. Mans ........ 103 D2
Sharnford Way. Bees ....... 171 D2
Sharp Cl. Lo Ea ............... 193 E3
Sharphill Rd. W Brid ........ 186 A2
Sharpley Dr. E Lea ........... 205 F2
Sharrard Ct. Sels ............. 129 D1
Sharrat Ct. Mans ............. 103 D1
Shaw Cres. Huck .............. 145 F2
Shaw Rd. G on H ............... 12 C2
Shaw St E. Ilk ................. 170 A3
Shaw St W. Ilk ................ 170 A3
Shaw St. Mans ................ 102 C4
Shaw St. Rudd ................. 196 B3
Shaw St. Work ................... 35 F2
Sheaf Pl. Work ................... 35 F4
Shearing Cl. Carl ............. 163 D1
Shearing Hill. Carl ........... 163 D1
Sheepbridge La. Mans ...... 101 F3
Sheepfold La. Rudd .......... 196 B3
Sheepwalk La. Raven ....... 116 C1
Sheepwash La. S in A ....... 101 D1
Sheepwash La. Tick ............ 8 C4
Sheffield Rd. Blyth ............ 18 A2
Sheldon Cl. Lo Ea ............ 182 A2
Sheldrake Rd. N-on-T ....... 140 B4
Shelford Ave. K-in-A ........ 114 B3
Shelford Cl. Bees ............. 183 E2
Shelford Cl. R on T ........... 176 A2
Shelford Cres. Bu Jo ........ 164 A3
Shelford Dr. Bing ............. 177 E2
Shelford Hill. Mans .......... 101 F3
Shelford Hill. Shel ............ 176 B4
Shelford Rd. Carl ............. 162 B2
Shelford Rd. R on T .......... 176 A3
Shelford Rise. Nott .......... 174 A3
Shellburne Cl. Nott .......... 160 C4
Shelley Ave. Mans ............. 88 A2
Shelley Cl. Nott ............... 184 C2
Shelley Cl. Bald ............... 140 B2
Shelley Cl. Huck .............. 145 E3
Shelley Cl. Kim ................ 159 D3
Shelley Rd. Arn ................ 161 E4
Shelley St. Work ................ 36 A2
Shelthorpe Ave. Lough ..... 220 A1
Shelthorpe Rd. Lough ...... 220 A1
Shelton Ave. Huck ........... 146 B2
Shelton Cl. N-on-T ........... 139 F3
Shelton Cl. Mans ............... 87 F1
Shelton Gdns. Rudd ......... 196 A4

Shelton Rd. Mans ............ 103 D1
Shelton St. Nott .............. 173 E3
Shenfield Gdns. Nott ....... 146 B1
Shepard Cl. Nott .............. 159 F3
Shepherd Walk. Kegw ...... 203 E1
Shepherd's Ave. Work ........ 36 A3
Shepherd's Cl. Su Bo ....... 213 E3
Shepherds Cl. Nott .......... 172 A4
Shepherds Oak. S in A ..... 100 C3
Shepherds Wood Dr. Nott . 172 B4
Shepshed Rd. Hath .......... 212 C1
Shepton Cl. Ship .............. 157 E2
Shepton Cres. Nott .......... 160 A1
Sheraton Dr. Nott ............ 171 F2
Sherborne Rd. Nott .......... 160 A1
Sherborne Rd. W Brid ...... 185 F3
Sherbrook Ave. Arn .......... 161 E3
Sherbrook Cl. Calv ........... 148 C4
Sherbrook Rd. Arn ........... 161 E3
Sherbrook Terr. Arn .......... 161 E3
Sherbrooke Rd. Nott ........ 161 D1
Sheridan Cl. Nott ............. 173 E3
Sheridan Ct. Staple .......... 170 C1
Sheriffs Way. Nott ........... 173 E1
Sheringham Cl. Arn .......... 161 F3
Sheringham Dr. Mans ....... 102 B3
Sherriff's Lea. Bees ......... 182 C1
Sherrington Cl. Nott ........ 195 E4
Sherview Ave. Mans ......... 103 D4
Sherwin Cl. Nott .............. 173 E3
Sherwin Rd. Nott ............. 172 C2
Sherwin Rd. Staple .......... 170 C1
Sherwin Wlk. Nott ........... 173 E3
Sherwood Ave. Blid .......... 118 B3
Sherwood Ave. Calv ......... 148 B4
Sherwood Ave. Edwin ........ 76 A1
Sherwood Ave. N-on-T ..... 140 A4
Sherwood Ave. Nott ......... 161 E2
Sherwood Ave. Pinx ......... 113 E2
Sherwood Ave. Shireb ....... 72 C2
Sherwood Cl. Mans .......... 102 C4
Sherwood Cres. Blyth ........ 18 A1
Sherwood Dr. Oll ............... 77 E2
Sherwood Dr. Shireb .......... 72 C2
Sherwood Gr. Bing ........... 177 E2
Sherwood Gr. Calv ........... 148 C4
Sherwood Hall Gdns. Mans 102 C4
Sherwood Hall Rd. Mans .. 102 C4
Sherwood Lodge Dr. Arn .. 132 B1
Sherwood Pl. Ann Wo ...... 115 D1
Sherwood Pl. N Clip ........... 90 A2
Sherwood Rd. Har .............. 8 C3
Sherwood Rd. Rain .......... 104 A1
Sherwood Rd. Ret .............. 39 F2
Sherwood Rd. S in A ......... 100 C1
Sherwood Rise. Ann Wo ... 115 D1
Sherwood Rise. East ........ 144 A1
Sherwood Rise. Mans ........ 88 C2
Sherwood Rise. Nott ........ 173 D4
Sherwood St. Ann Wo ...... 130 A4
Sherwood St. Huck .......... 146 B3
Sherwood St. K-in-A ........ 115 D3
Sherwood St. Mans ........... 88 A1
Sherwood St. Mans .......... 102 A3
Sherwood St. Mar War ....... 74 A2
Sherwood St. Newt ............ 99 D2
Sherwood St. S in A ........... 99 F2
Sherwood Vale. Nott ........ 161 F2
Sherwood Way. Sels ........ 129 D4
Shetland Cl. Mans ............. 88 C1
Shipley Ct. Ilk ................. 157 E1
Shipley Rd. Nott .............. 159 F1
Shipley Rise. Carl ............ 174 C4
Shipstone St. Ilk ............. 170 A3
Shipstone St. Nott ........... 172 C4
Shipstones Yd. Nott ......... 160 B4
Shirburn Ave. Mans ......... 102 B4
Shire La. Clayp ................ 156 A4
Shirebrooke Cl. Nott ........ 160 B2
Shireoaks Ct. Mans ......... 103 D1
Shireoaks Comm. Shire ...... 34 C4
Shireoaks Comm. Work ...... 35 D4
Shireoaks Rd. Rhod ........... 35 D3
Shireoaks Rd. Shire .......... 34 C3
Shireoaks Row. Shire ......... 34 C4
Shires The. Mans ............... 88 C1
Shirland Dr. Mans ............ 103 D2
Shirley Dr. Arn ................ 162 A4
Shirley Rd. Nott .............. 173 E4
Shirley St. Lo Ea ............. 193 D2
Shoreswood Cl. Nott ........ 161 D4
Short Hill. Nott ............... 173 E2
Short St. Mar War ............. 74 A2
Short St. S in A ............... 101 D2
Short Wheatley La. Coll ... 112 A3
Shortcross Ave. Arn ......... 161 F2
Shortwood Ave. Huck ....... 145 F3
Shortwood Cl. Nott .......... 173 E2
Shortwood La. Omp ........... 93 E4
Shorwell Rd. Nott ............ 174 B4
Shoulder Of Mutton Hill. Ann Wo
...................................115 D1
Shrewsbury Rd. Bir ............. 9 D2
Shrewsbury Rd. Nott ........ 161 D1
Shrewsbury Rd. Work ......... 36 A1
Shrewsbury View. Ret ........ 29 E1
Shrimpton Ct. Rudd ......... 196 B3

Shropshire Ave. Sels ........ 128 E
Sibcy La. Bald ................. 140 B
Sibson Dr. Kegw .............. 203 D
Sibson Wlk. Nott ............. 147 F
Sibthorpe St. Mans .......... 102 A
Siddalls Dr. S in A ........... 100 A
Side La. Eakr .................. 106 C
Side Ley. Kegw ................ 203 E
Side Row. N-on-T ............. 140 A
Sidings Rd. K-in-A ........... 115 E
Sidings The. Sax ............... 57 E
Sidlaw Rise. Bes Vil ........ 147 D
Sidmouth Cl. Keyw .......... 197 D
Sidney Rd. Bees .............. 183 F
Sidney St. Kim ................ 158 C
Sidney St. Lo Ea .............. 193 E
Silbury Cl. Nott ............... 195 E
Silk St. S in A ................. 100 C
Silken Holme. S Norm ...... 113 D
Silver St. Gain .................. 24 B
Silver St. Grass ................. 81 F
Silver St. N Clift ............... 68 C
Silver St. Ret ................... 39 E
Silverdale Ave. Mans ......... 88 A
Silverdale Cl. Ret .............. 29 E
Silverdale Rd. Nott .......... 160 C
Silverdale. Staple ............ 182 C
Silverhill Cotts. S in A ...... 100 A
Silverhill La. S in A ........... 99 F
Silverwood Ave. Raven .... 117 D
Silverwood Rd. Bees ........ 183 F
Silverwood Rd. Bott ........ 181 D
Silvey Ave. South ............ 121 E
Sime St. Work .................. 35 F
Simkin Ave. Carl ............. 162 A
Simon Cl. Wood ................ 42 A
Simone Gdns. Nott .......... 184 C
Simons Ct. Bees .............. 171 E
Simpson Cl. Bald ............. 140 C
Simpson Rd. Mans ........... 101 E
Singleton Ave. Mans ....... 102 C
Sisley Ave. Staple ........... 182 C
Sitwell Cl. Work ................ 36 A
Sitwell Rd. Work ............... 36 B
Six Hills La. Grim ............ 219 D
Sixth Ave. Edwin ............... 76 A
Sixth Ave. Mans .............. 103 D
Sixth Ave. N Clip .............. 89 F
Skeavington's La. Ilk ....... 157 F
Skegby La. Mans ............. 101 E
Skegby Mount. Mans ....... 101 F
Skegby Rd. Ann Wo ........ 129 F
Skegby Rd. S in A ........... 100 A
Skegby Rd. S in A ........... 101 D
Skegby Road. Nor on T ..... 81 E
Skerry Hill. Mans ............ 102 C
Skerry La. Bott ............... 181 F
Sketchley Ct. Nott ........... 160 A
Sketchley St. Nott ........... 173 F
Skipton Circus. Nott ........ 174 A
Skipton Cl. Ship .............. 157 E
Skirbeck Dr. Sax ............... 57 D
Skithorne Rise. Lowd ...... 164 B
Slack Wlk. Work ................ 35 F
Slack's La. Kneet ............ 152 A
Slade Cl. S Norm ............. 113 D
Slade Rd. Bees ................ 183 D
Slaidburn Ave. Nott ......... 185 D
Slake La. S Musk ............. 124 C
Slant La. Mans .................. 88 A
Slant The. Shireb .............. 72 B
Slater St. S in A .............. 100 C
Slaughter House La. N-on-T 124 C
Sleaford Rd. B in W ......... 126 B
Sleaford Rd. Beckin ......... 142 B
Sleaford Rd. Codd ........... 126 B
Sleaford Rd. N-on-T ........ 125 D
Sleights La. Pinx ............. 113 E
Sloan Dr. Bees ................ 171 D
Sloane Ct. W Brid ........... 185 E
Slowthorne Gdns. Arn ..... 161 E
Small Gate. Mans ............. 88 C
Smalls Croft. Woodb ........ 149 E
Smalley Cl. Sels .............. 129 D
Smeath La. Ret ................. 30 A
Smeath Rd. Ret ................. 30 A
Smeath Rd. Sels .............. 129 D
Smedley Ave. Ilk ............. 170 A
Smedley Cl. Nott ............. 160 A
Smedley's Ave. Sand ....... 182 A
Smeeton St. Hean ............ 143 D
Smite Cl. What ................ 179 F
Smite La. Orst ................. 179 F
Smite La. Thoro .............. 179 F
Smith Dr. La Mi ............... 143 D
Smith Sq. Har ................... 8 C
Smith St. Bald ................ 140 B
Smith St. Mans ............... 102 C
Smith St. N-on-T ............. 140 A
Smithfield Ave. Trow ....... 170 B
Smiths Cl. Cr Bi .............. 189 D
Smithson Cl. Bald ........... 140 B
Smithson Dr. Nott ........... 171 F
Smithurst Rd. Greas ........ 158 A
Smithy Cl. Nott ............... 184 B
Smithy Cres. Arn ............. 161 E
Smithy La. Lo Wh ............ 212 A
Smithy Row. Nott ............ 173 E

| | | |
|---|---|---|
| Smithy View. Calv | 148 | C4 |
| Snaefell Ave. Mans | 89 | D1 |
| Snape La. Styr | 9 | D1 |
| Snape Nook Ct. Nott | 159 | F4 |
| Snape Wood Rd. Nott | 159 | F4 |
| Snead Ct. Nott | 147 | D1 |
| Sneinton Bvd. Nott | 173 | F2 |
| Sneinton Dale. Nott | 174 | A3 |
| Sneinton Hermitage. Nott | 173 | F2 |
| Sneinton Hollows. Nott | 173 | F2 |
| Snell Cl. S on T | 81 | F1 |
| Snipe Park Rd. Bir | 9 | D2 |
| Snowdon Rd. Coll | 112 | A4 |
| Soar La. N on S | 213 | E2 |
| Soar La. Su Bo | 212 | C4 |
| Soarbank Cl. Kim | 158 | C4 |
| Sobers Gdns. Arn | 162 | A3 |
| Softwood Cl. Nott | 159 | F4 |
| Soloman Rd. Coss | 158 | A1 |
| Solway Cl. Bees | 183 | F3 |
| Sophie Rd. Nott | 172 | C3 |
| Somerby Ct. Bees | 171 | D2 |
| Somerby Rd. Gain | 15 | F1 |
| Somersall St. Mans | 101 | F4 |
| Somersby Ct. Mans | 103 | D3 |
| Somersby Rd. Arn | 162 | A3 |
| Somerset Cl. Lo Ea | 194 | A4 |
| Somerton Ave. Nott | 185 | D2 |
| Sookholme Cl. Shireb | 72 | C2 |
| Sookholme Dr. Mar War | 74 | A2 |
| Sookholme La. Mar War | 73 | F3 |
| Sookholme Rd. Mar War | 73 | F1 |
| Sookholme Rd. Shireb | 72 | C2 |
| Sopwith Rd. Nott | 172 | C3 |
| Soss La. Mist | 7 | D1 |
| Sotheby Ave. S in A | 101 | E1 |
| Soudan Dr. Nott | 173 | D1 |
| Sough Rd. S Norm | 113 | D4 |
| South Ave. Baw | 10 | A4 |
| South Ave. R on T | 176 | A2 |
| South Ave. Rain | 104 | A1 |
| South Ave. Shireb | 72 | C2 |
| South Ave. Work | 36 | A1 |
| South Cres. Bott | 181 | D1 |
| South Cres. N Clip | 90 | A2 |
| South Croft. Ashkh | 51 | F1 |
| South Devon Ave. Carl | 162 | A1 |
| South Dr. Bald | 140 | C1 |
| South Dr. Bils | 105 | F4 |
| South End. Coll | 111 | F4 |
| South La. Nor on T | 81 | F3 |
| South Moor Rd. Walker | 13 | F3 |
| South Par. Baw | 10 | A3 |
| South Par. Gain | 24 | C4 |
| South Par. Nott | 173 | E2 |
| South Par. Work | 36 | A2 |
| South Parade. Sax | 57 | D2 |
| South Rd. Bees | 184 | A2 |
| South Rd. Nott | 173 | D2 |
| South Rd. W Brid | 185 | F3 |
| South Ridge Dr. Mans | 102 | B2 |
| South Scarle La. N Sca | 83 | E1 |
| South Scarle Rd. Coll | 98 | A1 |
| South Sherwood St. Nott | 173 | E3 |
| South Snape Cl. Nott | 159 | F4 |
| South St. Bole | 23 | F1 |
| South St. East | 143 | F1 |
| South St. Greas | 158 | B4 |
| South St. Huck | 146 | A4 |
| South St. Lo Ea | 193 | F4 |
| South St. Lough | 220 | A2 |
| South St. Mort | 15 | D2 |
| South St. Nor on T | 81 | F3 |
| South St. Ret | 39 | F3 |
| South St. S Norm | 113 | D3 |
| South View Dr. Clar | 30 | B2 |
| South View Rd. Carl | 162 | B1 |
| South View. Aust | 3 | E1 |
| South View. Whit | 45 | D3 |
| South View. Work | 35 | F3 |
| Southampton St. Nott | 173 | F3 |
| Southbreck Rise. Work | 36 | A1 |
| Southchurch Dr. Nott | 184 | C1 |
| Southcliffe Rd. Carl | 174 | B4 |
| Southdale Dr. Carl | 174 | B4 |
| Southdale Rd. Carl | 174 | B4 |
| Southdene. Work | 36 | A3 |
| Southend Ave. N-on-T | 139 | F4 |
| Southern Wood. Work | 46 | C4 |
| Southey St. Nott | 173 | D3 |
| Southfall Cl. Ran | 19 | D3 |
| Southfield Dr. S Norm | 113 | E3 |
| Southfield La. Whit | 45 | D3 |
| Southfield Rd. Nott | 172 | B3 |
| Southfield. Bald | 140 | C2 |
| Southfields Ave. Pinx | 113 | E2 |
| Southfields Cl. Ann Wo | 114 | C1 |
| Southfields Rise. N Le Ha | 42 | B4 |
| Southfields. Lo Ea | 193 | F4 |
| Southgate Rd. Mar War | 74 | B3 |
| Southglade Rd. Nott | 160 | C3 |
| Southgore La. N Le Ha | 42 | B4 |
| Southgreen Cl. Mans | 102 | C1 |
| Southgreen Hill. Mans | 102 | C1 |
| Southlands Ave. Mort | 15 | D2 |
| Southlands Gdns. Mort | 15 | D2 |
| Southlea Rd. Carl | 174 | B4 |

| | | |
|---|---|---|
| Southmoor La. Ne on T | 69 | D4 |
| Southmoor Rd. Work | 36 | A1 |
| Southolme. Gain | 24 | B4 |
| Southpark Ave. Mans | 102 | C1 |
| Southport Terr. Nott | 172 | C4 |
| Southside. Arn | 162 | B4 |
| Southview Gdns. Raven | 117 | D1 |
| Southwark St. Nott | 160 | C2 |
| Southwell Cl. E Lea | 205 | F1 |
| Southwell Cl. K-in-A | 115 | D3 |
| Southwell La. K-in-A | 114 | C3 |
| Southwell Rd E. Mans | 103 | F1 |
| Southwell Rd E. Rain | 118 | A4 |
| Southwell Rd W. Mans | 102 | C3 |
| Southwell Rd. Edin | 120 | A3 |
| Southwell Rd. Farns | 120 | A3 |
| Southwell Rd. Gona | 150 | C1 |
| Southwell Rd. Kirk | 120 | C4 |
| Southwell Rd. Lowd | 150 | C1 |
| Southwell Rd. Nott | 173 | E2 |
| Southwell Rd. Oxt | 134 | B2 |
| Southwell Rd. Thur | 151 | E4 |
| Southwold Dr. Nott | 172 | B3 |
| Southwood Ave. S in A | 100 | B2 |
| Sowter Ave. S in A | 100 | C2 |
| Spa Cl. S in A | 114 | C4 |
| Spa La. Orst | 180 | A4 |
| Spa Rd. Ret | 39 | F3 |
| Spafford Cl. Mart | 44 | B4 |
| Spalding Rd. Nott | 173 | F3 |
| Spalford La. N Sca | 83 | E2 |
| Spalford Rd. N Sca | 83 | F3 |
| Spang La. S in A | 99 | F2 |
| Spaniel Row. Nott | 173 | E2 |
| Sparken Cl. Work | 46 | C4 |
| Sparken Dale. Work | 46 | C4 |
| Sparrow Hill. Lough | 220 | A2 |
| Sparrow La. H Marn | 68 | A1 |
| Spean Ct. Nott | 172 | A3 |
| Spean Dr. Nott | 172 | A4 |
| Speedwell Pl. Work | 35 | F2 |
| Spencer Ave. Carl | 162 | B3 |
| Spencer Ave. Sand | 182 | A3 |
| Spencer Cl. Rudd | 196 | A4 |
| Spencer Cres. Staple | 182 | C4 |
| Spencer Dr. Nuth | 159 | E3 |
| Spencer St. Mans | 102 | A3 |
| Sperry Cl. Sels | 128 | C3 |
| Spey Cl. Huck | 145 | E2 |
| Spindle Gdns. Nott | 160 | A4 |
| Spindle View. Calv | 148 | C3 |
| Spinney Cl. Cotg | 187 | F1 |
| Spinney Cl. K-in-A | 114 | C3 |
| Spinney Cl. Mans | 88 | C3 |
| Spinney Cl. N-on-T | 139 | F3 |
| Spinney Cl. W Brid | 186 | B2 |
| Spinney Cres. Bees | 182 | C2 |
| Spinney Dr. Lo Ea | 182 | B1 |
| Spinney Rd. Bing | 177 | E2 |
| Spinney Rd. Keyw | 197 | F2 |
| Spinney Rd. Lo Ea | 182 | B1 |
| Spinney Rise. Bees | 182 | C2 |
| Spinney The. Arn | 161 | F2 |
| Spinney The. Bes Vil | 146 | C3 |
| Spinney The. Bulc | 164 | A3 |
| Spinney The. Elst | 153 | E3 |
| Spinney The. Shireb | 72 | B2 |
| Spinney The. Wint | 125 | E3 |
| Spinney Way. Nott | 185 | D2 |
| Spinneymead. Ran | 19 | D3 |
| Spinningdale. Arn | 162 | A4 |
| Spital Hill. Gain | 15 | F1 |
| Spital Hill. Ret | 39 | F4 |
| Spital Rd. Blyth | 18 | A1 |
| Spital Terr. Gain | 15 | E1 |
| Spitalfields. Blyth | 18 | A1 |
| Spondon St. Nott | 161 | E1 |
| Sporton Cl. S Norm | 113 | D4 |
| Sporton La. S Norm | 113 | D4 |
| Spright Cl. Wint | 125 | E3 |
| Spring Cl. Kim | 159 | D4 |
| Spring Ct. Farns | 119 | F4 |
| Spring Dale Gdns. Staple | 170 | B2 |
| Spring Dr. Bald | 140 | C1 |
| Spring Garden Terr. Ilk | 157 | F1 |
| Spring Gdns. Baw | 10 | A4 |
| Spring Gdns. Gain | 24 | B4 |
| Spring Gdns. N-on-T | 139 | F4 |
| Spring Green. Nott | 195 | F4 |
| Spring Hill. Kim | 158 | C3 |
| Spring Hill. Mans | 88 | A2 |
| Spring Hill. South | 136 | C4 |
| Spring Hill. Whit | 45 | D3 |
| Spring La. Bald | 140 | C1 |
| Spring La. Bald | 140 | C2 |
| Spring La. Carl | 162 | C3 |
| Spring La. Elmt | 58 | A4 |
| Spring La. Farns | 119 | F4 |
| Spring La. Flint | 166 | C4 |
| Spring La. Lamb | 163 | D3 |
| Spring La. Lo Wh | 212 | B1 |
| Spring La. S Le S | 32 | B2 |
| Spring La. Shire | 34 | C3 |
| Spring Meadow. Cotg | 188 | A2 |
| Spring Moor. Nott | 174 | B3 |
| Spring Rd. Nott | 160 | B4 |
| Spring Rd. S in A | 100 | C1 |
| Spring St. Huck | 146 | A4 |

| | | |
|---|---|---|
| Spring St. Whit | 45 | D3 |
| Spring Terr. Nuth | 159 | E3 |
| Spring The. Lo Ea | 193 | E3 |
| Spring Wlk. Work | 35 | F1 |
| Springdale La. E Brid | 165 | F1 |
| Springfield Ave. East | 144 | A1 |
| Springfield Ave. Lo Ea | 193 | F4 |
| Springfield Ave. Sand | 182 | A2 |
| Springfield Ave. Shireb | 72 | C3 |
| Springfield Cl. Cr Bi | 189 | D2 |
| Springfield Cl. Gain | 24 | C3 |
| Springfield Cl. Mans | 103 | D3 |
| Springfield Ct. Staple | 170 | C1 |
| Springfield Dr. Nott | 159 | F3 |
| Springfield Gdn. Ilk | 157 | F1 |
| Springfield Rd. Huck | 145 | E3 |
| Springfield Rd. Nott | 147 | F1 |
| Springfield Rd. Ret | 39 | F4 |
| Springfield Rd. South | 121 | E1 |
| Springfield St. Nott | 160 | C1 |
| Springfield Way. K-in-A | 115 | E3 |
| Springfield Way. K-in-A | 115 | E3 |
| Springfield. Kegw | 203 | D1 |
| Springfields. W Brid | 185 | E3 |
| Springhead Ct. Nott | 160 | A3 |
| Springhill Cl. Nott | 146 | A1 |
| Springland Farm Cotts. Nuth | 159 | E3 |
| Springs Rd. Miss | 4 | B3 |
| Springthorpe Rd. Gain | 24 | C4 |
| Springwood Gdns. Nott | 161 | F2 |
| Springwood View Cl. S in A | 100 | B2 |
| Spruce Ave. Sels | 128 | B3 |
| Spruce Gdns. Nott | 160 | A4 |
| Spruce Gr. Huck | 146 | A3 |
| Spruce Gr. K-in-A | 115 | E3 |
| Sprydon Walk. Nott | 195 | F4 |
| Spur Cres. Work | 47 | D4 |
| Square The. Bees | 183 | F3 |
| Square The. Bes Vil | 146 | C2 |
| Square The. Bott | 181 | D2 |
| Square The. Cost | 206 | B1 |
| Square The. Goth | 195 | D1 |
| Square The. Keyw | 197 | F1 |
| Square The. Nott | 171 | F2 |
| Square The. Rain | 104 | A1 |
| Square The. Ret | 39 | F4 |
| Squires Ave. Nott | 160 | A4 |
| Squires Cl. Cr Bi | 189 | D2 |
| Squires Croft. N Clip | 90 | B3 |
| Squires La. N Clip | 90 | A3 |
| Squires Way. W Brid | 185 | E3 |
| Stable Cl. Work | 36 | A4 |
| Stacey Ave. Nott | 160 | C4 |
| Stacey Rd. Mans | 87 | E1 |
| Stafford Ave. Bald | 140 | B2 |
| Stafford Ave. Nott | 160 | A3 |
| Stafford Ct. Nott | 159 | F3 |
| Stafford St. Lo Ea | 193 | F4 |
| Stafford St. Mans | 101 | F4 |
| Staffords Acre. Kegw | 203 | E1 |
| Stagsden Cres. Nott | 171 | E3 |
| Staindale Dr. Nott | 160 | B1 |
| Stainforth St. Mans | 88 | B1 |
| Stainmore Gr. Bing | 177 | E2 |
| Stainsborough Rd. Huck | 145 | E3 |
| Stainsby Dr. Mans | 103 | D4 |
| Stamford Cl. Lo Ea | 193 | F2 |
| Stamford Ct. Nott | 161 | D4 |
| Stamford Rd. W Brid | 186 | A3 |
| Stamford St. Awsw | 158 | B2 |
| Stamford St. Greas | 144 | B1 |
| Stamford St. Ilk | 157 | F1 |
| Stamper Cres. S in A | 100 | C3 |
| Stanage Ct. Mans | 103 | D3 |
| Stancliffe Ave. Nott | 160 | B4 |
| Standard Hill. Nott | 173 | D2 |
| Standhill Ave. Carl | 174 | A4 |
| Standhill Rd. Carl | 174 | A4 |
| Stanesby Rise. Nott | 184 | C1 |
| Stanford Gdns. R on T | 175 | F2 |
| Stanford Hill. Lough | 220 | A3 |
| Stanford La. Cotes | 220 | B4 |
| Stanford St. N on S | 213 | F1 |
| Stanford St. Nott | 173 | E2 |
| Stanhome Dr. W Brid | 185 | E2 |
| Stanhome Sq. W Brid | 185 | E2 |
| Stanhope Ave. N-on-T | 125 | E2 |
| Stanhope Cl. Wale | 64 | A1 |
| Stanhope Cres. Arn | 161 | F4 |
| Stanhope Cres. St Ba | 175 | F4 |
| Stanhope Rd. Arn | 161 | F4 |
| Stanhope Rd. Carl | 162 | B2 |
| Stanhope St. Ilk | 170 | A3 |
| Stanhope St. Lo Ea | 193 | E4 |
| Stanhope St. Nott | 173 | E2 |
| Stanhope Way. Bing | 177 | F2 |
| Stanley Ave. Nott | 173 | D4 |
| Stanley Cl. Raven | 117 | D2 |
| Stanley Dr. Bees | 171 | D1 |
| Stanley La. S in A | 85 | E1 |
| Stanley Pl. Nott | 173 | D3 |
| Stanley Rd. Carl | 162 | A1 |
| Stanley Rd. Mans | 89 | D1 |
| Stanley Rd. Mans | 102 | A2 |
| Stanley Rd. Nott | 173 | D4 |
| Stanley Rd. W Brid | 185 | F3 |
| Stanley St. Gain | 24 | B3 |
| Stanley St. Lo Ea | 193 | F4 |

| | | |
|---|---|---|
| Stanley St. Lough | 220 | A1 |
| Stanley St. N-on-T | 125 | D1 |
| Stanley St. Ret | 40 | A2 |
| Stanley St. Work | 35 | F3 |
| Stanley Terr. N-on-T | 140 | A4 |
| Stanmore Cl. Nott | 159 | F2 |
| Stanmore Gdns. Arn | 161 | F3 |
| Stansfield St. Nott | 172 | C3 |
| Stanstead Ave. Nott | 146 | B1 |
| Stanstead Ave. Toll | 186 | B1 |
| Stanthorne Cl. Nott | 185 | D2 |
| Stanton Cres. S in A | 100 | B2 |
| Stanton Gate. S-by-D | 170 | B1 |
| Stanton La. S-on-W | 198 | A1 |
| Stanton Pl. Mans | 102 | A3 |
| Stanton Pl. Plea | 86 | C4 |
| Stanton Rd. Sand | 182 | A4 |
| Stanton St. Plea | 86 | C4 |
| Stanway Cl. Nott | 174 | B3 |
| Stanwick Cl. Nott | 171 | F4 |
| Staple La. Bald | 140 | B1 |
| Stapleford La. Bees | 182 | C2 |
| Stapleford La. Codd | 126 | B2 |
| Stapleford La. Coll | 112 | B1 |
| Stapleford Rd. Staple | 170 | B2 |
| Stapleford Rd. Trow | 170 | B2 |
| Staplehurst Dr. Nott | 161 | D2 |
| Staples St. Nott | 161 | F1 |
| Stapleton Rd. Ilk | 157 | F2 |
| Starch Cl. E Lea | 205 | F1 |
| Starch La. Sand | 182 | B4 |
| Starr Ave. S in A | 100 | C1 |
| Starth Wood Rd. Huck | 145 | E2 |
| Statham St. Work | 36 | A3 |
| Stathern La. Harb | 202 | A1 |
| Stathern Rd. Harb | 202 | B2 |
| Stathern Wlk. Nott | 161 | D4 |
| Station Ave. Carl | 163 | D1 |
| Station Ave. Ran | 19 | D3 |
| Station Cl. Coll | 112 | A4 |
| Station Cl. Ilk | 157 | F1 |
| Station Hill. Mans | 88 | A2 |
| Station La. Bald | 128 | A2 |
| Station La. Edwin | 76 | A1 |
| Station La. Farns | 119 | F4 |
| Station La. Ol Da | 218 | C2 |
| Station Rd. Awsw | 158 | B3 |
| Station Rd. Ba Mo | 28 | C3 |
| Station Rd. Baw | 10 | A4 |
| Station Rd. Beck | 23 | E4 |
| Station Rd. Bees | 184 | A3 |
| Station Rd. Bleas | 151 | F4 |
| Station Rd. Bott | 181 | E2 |
| Station Rd. Bu Jo | 163 | F2 |
| Station Rd. Carl | 174 | C4 |
| Station Rd. Coll | 112 | A4 |
| Station Rd. E Lea | 205 | E1 |
| Station Rd. Edin | 120 | C3 |
| Station Rd. Fisk | 137 | F2 |
| Station Rd. Harby | 70 | C2 |
| Station Rd. Hean | 143 | D1 |
| Station Rd. Huck | 146 | A4 |
| Station Rd. Ilk | 157 | F1 |
| Station Rd. K on S | 203 | F1 |
| Station Rd. K on S | 204 | A2 |
| Station Rd. Kegw | 203 | F1 |
| Station Rd. Keyw | 197 | F2 |
| Station Rd. Kim | 158 | C3 |
| Station Rd. La Mi | 143 | D1 |
| Station Rd. Lo Ea | 193 | F4 |
| Station Rd. Lowd | 150 | C1 |
| Station Rd. Mans | 102 | A3 |
| Station Rd. Miss | 4 | A2 |
| Station Rd. Mist | 7 | D1 |
| Station Rd. N Clip | 89 | F1 |
| Station Rd. News | 130 | C3 |
| Station Rd. Nott | 160 | B3 |
| Station Rd. Oll | 77 | D2 |
| Station Rd. Plum | 197 | F3 |
| Station Rd. Rain | 118 | A4 |
| Station Rd. Ran | 19 | D2 |
| Station Rd. Ret | 39 | F3 |
| Station Rd. Roll | 138 | A3 |
| Station Rd. S in A | 101 | D1 |
| Station Rd. S Le S | 32 | B3 |
| Station Rd. S Lev | 42 | B4 |
| Station Rd. S on T | 96 | C4 |
| Station Rd. Sand | 182 | B3 |
| Station Rd. Scro | 10 | A1 |
| Station Rd. Sels | 113 | F1 |
| Station Rd. Shireb | 72 | C3 |
| Station Rd. South | 121 | F1 |
| Station Rd. Sutt | 28 | C3 |
| Station Rd. Thur | 151 | E3 |
| Station Rd. Tork | 44 | A2 |
| Station Rd. Up Br | 218 | B4 |
| Station Rd. Walker | 14 | A3 |
| Station Rd. Whit | 45 | D3 |
| Station Rd. Widm | 208 | C3 |
| Station St. Bing | 177 | F3 |
| Station St. Coss | 158 | A1 |
| Station St. K-in-A | 115 | D3 |
| Station St. Lo Ea | 193 | F4 |
| Station St. Mans | 88 | A2 |
| Station St. Mans | 102 | A3 |
| Station St. Mist | 7 | D1 |
| Station St. Nott | 173 | E2 |
| Station St. S in A | 100 | C1 |

| | | |
|---|---|---|
| Station Terr. Huck | 146 | A4 |
| Station Terr. R on T | 175 | F2 |
| Station View. Shireb | 72 | C2 |
| Station Yd. S in A | 100 | C4 |
| Staunton Dr. Nott | 161 | E2 |
| Staunton Rd. N-on-T | 139 | F3 |
| Staveley Ct. Lough | 220 | A3 |
| Staverton Rd. Nott | 171 | F4 |
| Staythorpe Rd. Aver | 123 | F1 |
| Staythorpe Rd. Roll | 138 | B4 |
| Staythorpe Rd. Stay | 138 | B4 |
| Steadfold Cl. Nott | 160 | A3 |
| Steads Cl. Carl | 174 | C4 |
| Stedman Ave. Arn | 162 | A2 |
| Steeles Way. Lamb | 163 | D4 |
| Steeple Row. Lough | 220 | A2 |
| Steetley La. Shire | 35 | D2 |
| Steetley La. Whit | 34 | C2 |
| Steetley La. Work | 34 | C2 |
| Steinbeck Rd. Carl | 174 | B4 |
| Stella Ave. Toll | 197 | E4 |
| Stella Gr. Toll | 197 | E4 |
| Stella St. Mans | 102 | A3 |
| Stenton Cl. South | 121 | F1 |
| Stepnall Hts. Boug | 77 | F3 |
| Stepney Ct. Nott | 159 | F1 |
| Sterndale Rd. Lo Ea | 193 | D3 |
| Sternthorpe Cl. S on T | 81 | F1 |
| Steven Cl. Bees | 182 | C2 |
| Stevenholme Cres. Nott | 161 | D3 |
| Stevens Rd. Sand | 182 | A3 |
| Stevenson Cres. S in A | 100 | C1 |
| Stevenson Gdns. Rudd | 196 | B3 |
| Stewart Cl. C in L | 25 | F3 |
| Stewart Rd. C in L | 25 | F3 |
| Stewarton Cl. Arn | 148 | A1 |
| Stiles Rd. Arn | 162 | B3 |
| Stinsford Cl. Nott | 161 | E4 |
| Stinting La. Mans | 88 | C1 |
| Stinting La. Shireb | 72 | B1 |
| Stirling Ave. Baw | 10 | A4 |
| Stirling Ave. Mans | 101 | F3 |
| Stirling Cl. Gain | 15 | F1 |
| Stirling Dr. C in L | 25 | F3 |
| Stirling Gr. Kim | 158 | C4 |
| Stirling Grove. Nott | 195 | F4 |
| Stirling Rd. Ret | 39 | E3 |
| Stock Well. Nott | 160 | A3 |
| Stockdale Cl. Bes Vil | 147 | D1 |
| Stockhill Circus. Nott | 160 | B1 |
| Stockhill La. Nott | 160 | B2 |
| Stocking La. Ashkh | 51 | F2 |
| Stocking La. E Lea | 205 | E2 |
| Stocks Rd. Kim | 158 | C4 |
| Stockton St. Nott | 160 | A4 |
| Stockwell La. Carl | 175 | E4 |
| Stockwell La. Cr Bi | 189 | D2 |
| Stockwell The. Wyme | 216 | B2 |
| Stockwith Rd. Haxey | 7 | E4 |
| Stockwith Rd. Mist | 7 | E1 |
| Stockwith Rd. Walk | 14 | A4 |
| Stockwith Rd. Walker | 14 | A4 |
| Stodman Mews. N-on-T | 139 | F4 |
| Stodman St. N-on-T | 139 | F4 |
| Stoke Ave. N-on-T | 139 | F2 |
| Stoke Ferry La. Shel | 164 | A1 |
| Stoke La. Bu Jo | 163 | F1 |
| Stoke La. Carl | 175 | E4 |
| Stoke La. St Ba | 163 | F1 |
| Stoke La. St Ba | 175 | E4 |
| Stolle Cl. Arn | 162 | B4 |
| Stone Bridge Rd. Nott | 173 | F3 |
| Stone Cres. Mans | 101 | E4 |
| Stone Cross La. Mans | 102 | A4 |
| Stone La. N Whea | 31 | E4 |
| Stone Meadows. Lo Ea | 193 | F3 |
| Stoneacre. Nott | 161 | D4 |
| Stonebridge Ct Ind Est. Nott | 173 | F3 |
| Stonebridge Dr. E Lea | 205 | F1 |
| Stonebridge La. Mar War | 74 | A2 |
| Stonebridge Rd. Mar War | 74 | A2 |
| Stonechurch View. Ann Wo | 130 | A4 |
| Stonehaven Cl. Arn | 148 | A1 |
| Stonehill Cl. Ran | 19 | D3 |
| Stonehills. Kegw | 203 | E1 |
| Stoneleigh Cl. Bees | 183 | E3 |
| Stoneleigh St. Nott | 173 | D3 |
| Stonemasons Mews. K-in-A | 115 | D3 |
| Stonepit Cl. Nott | 161 | F1 |
| Stoney Bank. Lowd | 150 | B1 |
| Stoney Houghton Gdns. Nott | 159 | F4 |
| Stoney La. Brin | 143 | E3 |
| Stoney La. Sels | 128 | C4 |
| Stoney La. Trow | 170 | A3 |
| Stoney St. Bees | 183 | F4 |
| Stoney St. Nott | 173 | E2 |
| Stoney St. S in A | 101 | D2 |
| Stoneycroft Rd. Nott | 160 | C3 |
| Stoneyford Rd. S in A | 100 | C2 |
| Stonish Hill. Eakr | 92 | B1 |
| Storcroft Rd. Ret | 40 | A3 |
| Storey Ave. Carl | 162 | C1 |
| Stormont Cl. S Norm | 113 | D2 |
| Stornoway Cl. Bees | 184 | A3 |
| Stort Sq. Mans | 88 | B1 |
| Storth Ave. Huck | 146 | A3 |
| Storth La. S Norm | 113 | D2 |
| Storthfield Way. S Norm | 113 | D2 |

250

Story Gdns. Huck
Tom Wass Rd. S in A

Story Gdns. Huck 146 B3
Stotfield Rd. Nott 171 D3
Stourdale Cl. Lo Ea 193 D3
Stow Ct. Mans 88 C2
Stow Park Rd. Mart 44 B4
Stowe Ave. W Brid 185 E3
Strafford St. Gain 24 B3
Straight Mile. Babw 38 B3
Strand The. Bees 183 F1
Stranraer Cl. Mans 88 B3
Stratford Cl. Carl 174 C3
Stratford Cres. Ret 39 E3
Stratford Rd. W Brid 185 F4
Stratford St. Ilk 157 F2
Strathavon Rd. C in L 25 F3
Strathglen Cl. Kim 158 C4
Strathmore Cl. Huck 145 F3
Strathmore Ct. Har 9 D3
Strathmore Dr. C in L 25 F3
Strathmore Rd. Arn 148 A1
Straw's La. E Brid 165 E2
Strawberry Bank. S in A 99 F2
Strawberry Hall La. N-on-T 125 D1
Strawberry Rd. Ret 40 A3
Street Lane Rd. N Le Ha 42 C4
Strelley La. Stre 171 D4
Strelley Rd. Nott 159 F1
Strelley St. Nott 160 A4
Stripe Rd. 8 B4
Stripes View. Calv 148 C3
Strome Cl. Nott 173 E1
Strome Ct. Nott 173 E1
Stroud Ct. Bott 181 D2
Stroud's Cl. Hose 211 F4
Stuart Ave. Boug 77 E3
Stuart Ave. Mans 102 C4
Stuart Cl. Arn 162 A4
Stuart St. Mans 102 C4
Stuart St. S in A 100 C1
Stubbin's La. South 136 B3
Stubbing La. Work 35 E2
Stubbins Wood La. Shireb 72 C3
Stubbins Wood. Shireb 72 C3
Stubton Rd. Clayp 156 C3
Studland Way. W Brid 185 E3
Sturgate Wlk. Gain 24 C4
Sturgeon Ave. Nott 184 C2
Sturton Rd. N Le Ha 32 B1
Sturton Rd. S Whea 31 F4
Sturton Rd. Saundby 23 E2
Sturton Rd. Sax 57 D4
Sturton St. Nott 173 D4
Styring St. Bees 183 F3
Styrrup La. Malt 8 A1
Styrrup La. Styr 8 A1
Styrrup Rd. Har 8 B1
Styrrup Rd. Styr 8 C2
Sudbury Ave. Ilk 170 A4
Sudbury Ave. Sand 182 A3
Sudbury Ct. Mans 103 D3
Sudbury Mews. East 143 F1
Suez St. Nott 160 C1
Suff La. Pinx 113 E2
Suffolk Ave. Bees 184 B2
Suffolk Ave. Bir 9 E2
Suffolk Ave. Huck 145 E3
Suffolk Gr. Bir 9 E2
Suffolk Rd. Bir 9 E2
Sulby Cl. Mans 89 D1
Sullivan Cl. Nott 174 A3
Sumburgh Rd. Nott 185 D1
Summer Hill. Gain 15 F1
Summer Leys La. Nott 173 E2
Summer Way. R on T 175 F2
Summer's Rd. N-on-T 125 D1
Summercourt Dr. Raven 116 C2
Summerfield Rd. K-in-A 114 C4
Summerfields Way. Ship 157 E2
Summergangs La. Gain 24 B3
Summerwood La. Nott 195 F4
Summit Cl. K-in-A 115 D3
Summit Dr. Shireb 72 C2
Sunbeam St. What 179 D2
Sunbourne Ct. Nott 173 D3
Sunbury Gdns. Arn 148 A1
Sunderland Gr. Nott 159 E1
Sunderland Pl. Tick 8 A4
Sunderland St. Tick 8 A4
Sunfield Ave. Work 36 A2
Sunlea Cres. Staple 182 C3
Sunnindale Dr. Toll 186 C1
Sunningdale Av. Hean 157 D4
Sunningdale Cl. K-in-A 114 C4
Sunningdale Dr. Woodb 149 E3
Sunningdale Rd. Nott 160 C3
Sunningdale. Ret 39 E1
Sunninghill Dr. Nott 184 C2
Sunninghill Rise. Arn 148 A1
Sunny Bank. Mans 102 B2
Sunny Bank. Tibs 99 D3
Sunny Bank. Work 36 A2
Sunnydale Rd. Nott 174 A4
Sunnymede. Work 36 A3
Sunnyside Rd. Bees 183 F4
Sunnyside. Whit 45 D3
Sunnyside. Work 35 F3
Sunridge Ct. Nott 173 E4

Sunrise Ave. Nott 160 C3
Surbiton Sq. Nott 160 A2
Surfleet Cl. Nott 171 E2
Surgery La. Blid 118 A2
Surgey's La. Arn 148 A1
Surrey Dr. Mans 101 F4
Susan Cl. Huck 131 D1
Susan Dr. Nott 160 B2
Sussex Way. Sand 182 A3
Sutherland Cl. C in L 25 F4
Sutherland Dr. W Brid 186 A2
Sutherland Rd. Nott 174 A4
Suthers Rd. Kegw 203 E1
Sutton Cl. S in A 101 D3
Sutton Cl. Su Bo 213 E3
Sutton Ct. East 143 F1
Sutton Gdns. Rudd 196 B3
Sutton La. Babw 29 D1
Sutton La. Gran 191 E3
Sutton Middle La. K-in-A 114 C3
Sutton Passeys Cres. Nott 172 A2
Sutton Rd. Beckin 142 C3
Sutton Rd. K-in-A 114 C3
Sutton Rd. Kegw 203 E1
Sutton Rd. Mans 101 F3
Sutton Rd. Nott 147 F1
Sutton Rd. S in A 100 C3
Swab's La. Co Ba 199 F4
Swab's La. Cr Bi 188 C1
Swain's Ave. Nott 174 A3
Swaledale Cl. Nott 160 B1
Swaledale. Work 36 A4
Swales Cl. Ret 39 E4
Swallow Ct. Mist 7 D1
Swallow Gdns. Carl 162 A1
Swallow Gr. Work 35 E4
Swallow Wlk. Hath 213 D1
Swallows Dr. Stat 202 C2
Swan Ct. Su Bo 213 D3
Swan Ct. Work 35 E4
Swan La. Mans 88 A2
Swan Meadow. Carl 174 C2
Swan St. Baw 10 A3
Swan St. Lough 220 A2
Swann Yd. S in A 99 F2
Swansdowne Dr. Nott 184 C1
Swanson Ave. S in A 99 F2
Swanwick Ave. Shireb 72 C2
Sweeney Cl. Nott 161 D4
Sweet Leys Dr. E Lea 205 F2
Sweet Leys Rd. Nott 173 E1
Swenson Ave. Nott 172 C2
Swift Ct. East 143 F1
Swift's Cl. Wyme 216 B2
Swigert Cl. Nott 159 F3
Swildon Wlk. Nott 160 C4
Swinburne Cl. Bald 140 B3
Swinburne St. Nott 173 F3
Swinburne Way. Arn 161 E4
Swinderby Rd. Coll 112 A4
Swinderby Rd. Eagle 83 F1
Swinderby Rd. Eagle 84 B1
Swinderby Rd. N Sca 83 F1
Swinderby Rd. S Sca 98 C3
Swindon Cl. Greas 158 B4
Swinecote Rd. Edwin 76 A2
Swiney La. Bees 183 D1
Swinfen Broun. Mans 102 B2
Swingate. Kim 159 D3
Swinnow Rd. Bir 9 E2
Swinscoe Gdns. Nott 160 C4
Swinstead Ct. Nott 171 F3
Swinton Copse. Boug 77 F3
Swinton Rise. Raven 117 D1
Swish La. Ruff 105 F4
Swithland Dr. W Brid 185 F2
Swynford Cl. Kettl 55 D2
Sycamore Ave. Glap 86 A4
Sycamore Ave. K-in-A 114 C3
Sycamore Cl. Bing 178 A2
Sycamore Cl. Hawt 139 E2
Sycamore Cl. Huck 145 F3
Sycamore Cl. Pinx 113 E2
Sycamore Cl. R on T 175 F1
Sycamore Cl. Rain 104 A1
Sycamore Cl. Sels 128 B4
Sycamore Cl. Work 35 F1
Sycamore Cres. Baw 9 F4
Sycamore Cres. Sand 182 A4
Sycamore Cres. Bees 184 A4
Sycamore Dr. Codd 125 F1
Sycamore Dr. Gain 15 F1
Sycamore Dr. Ilk 170 A4
Sycamore Gr. Mans 102 C3
Sycamore La. Bleas 152 A4
Sycamore Pl. Nott 173 E4
Sycamore Rd. Awsw 158 B3
Sycamore Rd. C in L 25 F4
Sycamore Rd. E Lea 214 B4
Sycamore Rd. Lo Ea 193 E3
Sycamore Rd. Mans 88 A3
Sycamore Rd. Oll 77 E2
Sycamore Rise. Nott 160 B4
Sycamore St. Mar War 74 A3
Sycamores The. East 143 F1
Sycamores The. S Norm 113 D3
Sydenham Ct. Nott 172 C1

Syderstone Wlk. Arn 161 F3
Sydney Cl. Mans 88 B3
Sydney Gr. R on T 175 F2
Sydney Rd. Nott 172 A3
Sydney St. N-on-T 125 D1
Sydney Terr. N-on-T 140 A4
Syerston Rd. Mans 103 D1
Syke Rd. Nott 160 C4
Sykes La. Bald 140 B2
Sykes La. Sax 56 C3
Sylvan Cres. S in A 101 D3
Sylvester St. Mans 101 F3
Synge Cl. Nott 195 E4
Sywell Cl. S in A 100 C3

Taft Ave. Sand 182 A3
Taft Leys Rd. E Lea 205 F2
Talbot Cl. R on T 175 F2
Talbot Dr. Staple 170 B1
Talbot Rd. Bir 9 D2
Talbot Rd. Work 36 A1
Talbot St. Mans 102 A2
Talbot St. Nott 173 D3
Talbot St. Pinx 113 E1
Tall Gables. D on T 54 B1
Tamarix Cl. Carl 163 D1
Tambling Cl. Arn 162 A3
Tame Cl. Nott 184 C2
Tamworth Gr. Nott 184 C1
Tamworth Rd. Lo Ea 193 E3
Tangmere Cres. Nott 159 F1
Tanner's La. Hath 213 D1
Tanyard. Egma 79 F3
Tarbert Cl. Nott 173 D1
Target St. Nott 172 C3
Tatham's La. Ilk 157 F1
Tattersall Wlk. Mans 88 C2
Tattershall Dr. Bees 184 A4
Tattershall Dr. Nott 173 D2
Taunton Rd. W Brid 185 F3
Taupo Dr. Huck 145 E3
Tavern Ave. Nott 160 B1
Tavistock Ave. Nott 161 E1
Tavistock Cl. Huck 145 E3
Tavistock Dr. Nott 161 E1
Tavistock Rd. W Brid 185 F3
Taylor Cl. Nott 174 A2
Taylor Cres. S in A 100 C1
Taylor Cres. Staple 182 C4
Taylor St. Ilk 157 F1
Taylor's Cl. Mans 102 C4
Teague Pl. Work 35 E2
Teak Cl. Nott 173 E4
Teal Cl. Shireb 72 B2
Teal Ct. Work 35 E4
Teal Wharf. Nott 173 D1
Tealby Cl. Nott 159 F4
Tealby Wlk. Mans 88 C2
Technology Dr. Bees 184 A3
Tedburn Dr. Mans 103 D1
Teesbrook Dr. Nott 171 D2
Teesdale Ct. Bees 183 D2
Teesdale Rd. Lo Ea 193 D3
Teesdale Rd. Nott 161 D1
Teignmouth Ave. Mans 102 C3
Telford Dr. Greas 144 A2
Telford Dr. N-on-T 125 E2
Temperance La. Coll 111 F4
Templar Rd. Bees 184 A3
Temple Cres. Nuth 159 E2
Temple Dr. Nuth 159 F2
Templemans Way. South 136 C4
Templemen Cl. Rudd 196 A4
Templeoak Dr. Nott 171 E2
Tenbury Cres. Nott 160 B1
Tenby Gr. Work 36 A1
Tene Cl. Nott 147 F1
Tenman La. Car Co 166 A1
Tennis Court Ind Est. Nott 174 A2
Tennis Dr. Nott 173 D2
Tennyson Ave. Carl 162 C1
Tennyson Ave. Mans 88 B1
Tennyson Ct. Huck 145 E3
Tennyson Dr. Bees 183 E1
Tennyson Dr. Work 36 B2
Tennyson Rd. Arn 161 F2
Tennyson Rd. Bald 140 B2
Tennyson Sq. Awsw 158 B2
Tennyson St. Gain 15 E1
Tennyson St. Ilk 157 F2
Tennyson St. K-in-A 115 D2
Tennyson St. Mans 102 A4
Tennyson St. Nott 173 D3
Tenter Cl. Lo Ea 193 E3
Tenter Cl. Nott 160 C4
Tenzing Wlk. Bald 140 C2
Terrace La. Plea 86 C3
Terrace Rd. Mans 102 B4
Terrace St. Nott 172 C4
Terrian Cres. W Brid 185 F4
Terry Ave. N-on-T 125 D2
Terton Rd. Nott 146 C1
Terton Rd. Nott 160 C4
Tetford Wlk. Mans 88 C2
Tetney Wlk. Nott 172 A3
Tettenbury Rd. Nott 160 C2
Teversal Ave. Mans 87 D2

Teversal Ave. Nott 172 C2
Tevery Cl. Staple 182 C4
Teviot Rd. Nott 160 C3
Tewkesbury Ave. Mans 88 B2
Tewkesbury Cl. W Brid 186 A3
Tewkesbury Dr. Kim 158 C4
Tewkesbury Dr. Nott 160 C2
Tewkesbury Rd. Lo Ea 193 F3
Thackeray St. Work 36 A3
Thackeray's La. Arn 161 F3
Thackeray St. Nott 172 C3
Thames St. Nott 160 A4
Thane Rd. Nott 184 C3
Thaxted Cl. Nott 171 E3
Theaker Ave. Gain 15 F1
Theaker La. Scaf 10 B3
Theatre Sq. Nott 173 E3
Thelda Ave. Keyw 197 F2
Theresa Ct. Bald 140 B2
Thetford Cl. Arn 162 A3
Thickley Cl. Shireb 72 C2
Thieveves Bank. Work 35 F4
Thievesdale La. Work 36 A4
Third Ave. Carl 162 C1
Third Ave. Carl 174 A4
Third Ave. Mans 89 D1
Third Ave. Mans 103 F1
Third Ave. N Clip 89 F2
Thirlbeck. Cotg 188 A1
Thirlmere Cl. Lo Ea 182 A1
Thirlmere Cl. Nott 173 F4
Thirlmere Rd. Lo Ea 182 A1
Thirston Cl. Nott 159 F4
Thistle Cl. Greas 158 B4
Thistle Green Cl. Hean 143 D1
Thistledown Rd. Nott 195 F4
Thomas Ave. R on T 176 B2
Thomas Cl. Nott 173 E3
Thomas Cl. W Brid 185 E2
Thomas Parkyn Cl. Bunn 206 C2
Thomas Rd. Kegw 203 E1
Thomas St. Ret 39 F3
Thompson Ave. Har 8 C2
Thompson Cl. Bees 183 E2
Thompson Cres. S in A 100 C1
Thompson Gdns. Nott 147 D1
Thompson St. La Mi 143 D2
Thonock Cl. Sax 56 C2
Thonock Hill. Gain 15 E2
Thonock Rd. Thon 15 F3
Thor Gdns. Nott 146 C1
Thoresby Ave. Carl 162 B1
Thoresby Ave. Edwin 76 A1
Thoresby Ave. K-in-A 115 E2
Thoresby Ave. N-on-T 140 A3
Thoresby Ave. Nott 173 E4
Thoresby Ave. Shireb 72 C2
Thoresby Cl. Har 9 D3
Thoresby Cl. Mar War 74 B4
Thoresby Cl. R on T 176 A2
Thoresby Cres. S in A 100 B3
Thoresby Ct. Hello 173 A2
Thoresby Dale. Huck 146 A4
Thoresby Glade. Bils 106 A3
Thoresby Rd. Bees 171 E1
Thoresby Rd. Bing 177 E2
Thoresby Rd. Lo Ea 193 E3
Thoresby Rd. Mans 88 A2
Thoresby Rd. Rain 103 F1
Thoresby Rd. Nott 173 F2
Thoresby St. Mans 102 A4
Thoresby St. S in A 101 D2
Thorn Ave. Mans 87 F1
Thorn Bank. Haxey 2 B4
Thorn Bank. Wroot 2 B4
Thorn Dr. Greas 158 B4
Thorn Gr. Huck 146 A2
Thorn Tree Gdns. Greas 143 F2
Thornbury Dr. Mans 101 E4
Thornbury Hill La. Malt 16 B4
Thornbury Way. Nott 160 C4
Thorncliffe Rd. Nott 173 E4
Thorncliffe Rise. Nott 173 E4
Thorndale Rd. Nott 160 B1
Thorndike Cl. Bees 184 A2
Thorndike Way. Gain 24 C4
Thorne Rd. Baw 10 A4
Thorner Cl. Nott 160 C3
Thorney Abbey Rd. Blid 118 A3
Thorney Ct. Mans 103 D1
Thorney Hill. Nott 173 F4
Thorneywood Ave. Ann Wo 129 F2
Thorneywood Mount. Nott 173 F4
Thorneywood Rd. Lo Ea 193 F4
Thornham Cres. Ann Wo 129 F2
Thornhill Cl. Bees 171 D1
Thornhill Dr. Boug 77 F3
Thornhill La. N Le Ha 33 E1
Thornhill La. S Le S 33 E1
Thornhill Rd. Har 8 C2
Thornley St. Nott 172 C4
Thornton Ave. Nott 147 F1
Thornton Cl. Mans 103 D3
Thornton Cl. Nott 171 F2
Thornton Dale. Work 36 A4
Thornton Rd. Coll 112 A4
Thornton St. Gain 24 B4
Thornton S. in A 100 C1

Thorntons Cl. Cotg 188 A4
Thorold Cl. Nott 184 C
Thoroton Ave. Bald 140 B
Thoroton St. Nott 173 D
Thoroughfare La. Langf 125 D
Thorpe Cl. Codd 126 A
Thorpe Cl. N-on-T 139 F
Thorpe Cl. Nott 161 C
Thorpe Cl. Staple 182 B
Thorpe Cres. Carl 162 A
Thorpe La. Eagle 84 C
Thorpe La. Shire 34 B
Thorpe Lea. Gunt 165 D
Thorpe Leys. Lo Ea 193 E
Thorpe Rd. Greas 143 F
Thorpe Rd. Mans 103 D
Thorpe Rd. Matt 20 A
Thorpe St. Head 52 B
Thorpe St. Ilk 157 F
Thorpelands Ave. Mans 88 C
Thrapston Ave. Nott 147 F
Three Leys La. S Le S 32 B
Three Tuns Rd. East 144 A
Thrumpton Ave. Lo Ea 194 A
Thrumpton Cl. Ret 39 F
Thrumpton Dr. Nott 173 D
Thrumpton Lanes. Ret 39 F
Thurgarton Ave. Nott 173 F
Thurgarton La. Hover 151 F
Thurgarton St. Nott 173 F
Thurland St. Nott 173 E
Thurlby Cl. Cr Bi 189 D
Thurlby Ct. Mans 88 C
Thurlby La. S-on-W 198 B
Thurlby La. Widm 208 B
Thurlby Rd. Gain 24 C
Thurlestone Dr. Carl 162 B
Thurley Wlk. Mans 103 D
Thurloe Ct. W Brid 185 E
Thurman Dr. Cotg 187 F
Thurman St. Ilk 170 A
Thurman St. Nott 172 C
Thursby Rd. Nott 184 C
Thymus Wlk. Nott 184 B
Thyra Ct. Nott 161 F
Thyra Gr. Bees 184 A
Thyra Gr. S in A 161 F
Tibshelf Rd. S in A 100 A
Tickhill Rd. Baw 9 F
Tickhill Rd. Har 8 C
Tideswell Cl. Raven 117 D
Tideswell Ct. Mans 102 A
Tidworth Cl. Nott 172 A
Tilbury Rise. Nott 160 A
Tilbury Rise. Nott 160 A
Till Bridge La. Mart 44 C
Tiln Ct. Ret 29 F
Tiln La. Ret 29 F
Tilstock Ct. Greas 159 D
Timothy Rd. Lax 79 E
Tindale Bank Rd. Haxey 6 B
Tinker La. Ba Mo 27 F
Tinker's La. Best 97 F
Tinsley Cl. Clayp 156 C
Tinsley Rd. East 143 E
Tintagel Green. Nott 184 C
Tintern Dr. Nott 160 C
Tip Tree Cl. Kim 158 C
Tippett Ct. Nott 173 F
Tippings La. Farns 119 F
Tiree Cl. Staple 170 B
Tishbite St. Nott 160 A
Tissington Ave. Mar War 74 B
Tissington Cl. Nott 173 D
Tissington Rd. Nott 173 D
Titchfield Ave. Mans 88 B
Titchfield Ave. S in A 100 C
Titchfield St. Huck 146 A
Titchfield St. Mans 102 A
Titchfield St. Mar War 74 A
Titchfield Terr. Huck 146 A
Tithby Ct. Mans 103 D
Tithby Dr. Nott 161 E
Tithby Rd. Bing 177 F
Tithby Rd. Tith 189 E
Tithe Barn Ct. N-on-T 125 D
Tithe Gdns. Bes Vil 147 D
Tithe La. Calv 148 C
Tithes La. Tick 8 A
Tiverton Cl. Huck 145 E
Tiverton Cl. Nott 160 A
Toad La. Elst 153 F
Toad La. Epp 150 A
Toad La. Lax 79 D
Tobias Cl. Nott 160 C
Todd Cl. Nott 195 E
Todd Ct. Nott 195 E
Toft Cl. Cotg 187 F
Toft Rd. Bees 183 D
Tokenhouse Yd. Nott 173 E
Toll Bar Ave. Bott 181 D
Tollerton Gn. Nott 160 B
Tollerton Rd. Toll 186 C
Tollhouse Hill. Nott 173 D
Tolney La. N-on-T 139 F
Tom Otter's La. Harby 70 C
Tom Otter's La. Sax 70 C
Tom Wass Rd. S in A 114 C4

Tomlinson Ave. Goth ......... 195 D1
on La. Lowd ........................ 150 B1
onbridge Mount. Nott ........ 171 E1
ooley St. Gain .................... 24 B4
oothill La. Mans ................ 102 B4
oothill Rd. Lough .............. 220 A3
oothill Rd. Mans ............... 102 A4
op Green. Up Br ............... 210 A1
op La. Mans ....................... 87 D1
op Pasture La. N Whea ..... 31 F4
op Rd. Blid ....................... 118 A1
op Rd. Miss ....................... 4 B2
op Rd. Rudd ..................... 196 B3
op Rd. Thor ....................... 69 F3
op Row. N-on-T ............... 140 B4
op Row. Sels .................... 128 A3
op Sandy La. Mar War ..... 74 B2
op St. Ashkh .................... 51 F1
op St. Baw ........................ 10 A4
op St. E Dray .................... 53 D2
op St. Elst ........................ 153 E2
op St. N Whea ................... 31 E4
op St. Rain ....................... 104 A1
op Valley Dr. Nott ............ 160 C4
op Valley Way. Nott .......... 160 C4
opyard La. Hayt ................ 30 B3
or La. Oll .......................... 77 D2
orbay Cres. Nott .............. 161 D3
orkard Dr. Nott ................ 160 C4
orksey Ave. Sax ............... 56 C2
orksey Ferry Rd. Ramp ..... 43 E1
orksey Mews. Ret .............. 39 E1
orksey St. Ramp ............... 43 D1
orksey Wlk. Mans .............. 88 C2
orr St. Gain ....................... 24 B4
orvill Dr. Nott .................. 171 F3
oston Dr. Nott .................. 172 B2
otland Dr. Nott ................ 160 B1
otland Rd. Bees ............... 171 E2
otley Cl. Nott ................... 146 B1
otnes Cl. Huck ................ 145 E4
otnes Rd. Nott ................. 174 A3
oton Cl. Nott .................... 160 B3
oton La. Bees .................. 182 C3
oton La. Staple ................ 182 C3
ottle Gdns. Nott .............. 172 B3
Tow Ct. Farn ..................... 139 D2
Towe's Mount. Carl .......... 174 C4
Tower Cres. Kim ............... 159 D2
Tower St. Gain ................... 15 E1
Towle St. Lo Ea ............... 193 D2
Towlsons Croft. Nott ........ 160 B2
Town Ct. Nott ................... 161 D4
Town End La. Flint ........... 167 D4
Town La. Newt .................. 99 D2
Town St. Askh ................... 52 A2
Town St. Bees .................. 183 D4
Town St. Clay .................... 21 E3
Town St. Clayp ................. 156 B4
Town St. Cott .................... 43 E3
Town St. Grass .................. 81 F2
Town St. Hawk .................. 167 E2
Town St. Lound .................. 20 B1
Town St. Pinx ................... 113 F2
Town St. S Lev ................... 42 B4
Town St. Sand .................. 182 A3
Town St. Sutt ..................... 28 C3
Town St. Tres .................... 42 A2
Town View. Kim ................ 158 C4
Townroe Dr. Mans ............ 101 E4
Townsend Ct. Nott ........... 147 D1
Townside Cl. Lo Ea ........... 193 D2
Townside La. Tres .............. 42 B2
Townside Rd. N Le Ha ....... 32 B1
Towson Ave. La Mi ........... 143 E1
Tracy Cl. Bees .................. 171 F1
Trafalgar Cl. Nott ............. 172 C3
Trafalgar Rd. Bees ........... 184 A2
Trafalgar Rd. Lo Ea .......... 193 E3
Trafalgar Sq. Lo Ea .......... 193 F4
Traffic St. Nott .................. 173 E2
Trafford Gdns. Nott .......... 172 B4
Tranby Gdns. Nott ............ 171 F2
Tranker La. Work ............... 35 D3
Travell's Hill. N on S ........ 214 A4
Travers Rd. Sand .............. 182 A3
Treegarth Sq. Nott ........... 147 D1
Trefan Gdns. Nott ............ 161 D4
Trelawn Cl. Nott ............... 161 E1
Tremayne Rd. Nott ........... 171 E3
Trenchard Ave. Codd ........ 125 F1
Trenchard Cl. New ............ 177 E4
Trenchham Gdns. Bu Jo ... 163 E2
Trent Ave. Rudd ............... 196 B4
Trent Bvd. W Brid ............. 174 A1
Trent Cl. N Musk ............... 110 C4
Trent Cl. Nott ................... 173 F2
Trent Cres. Bees .............. 183 F3
Trent Dr. Huck .................. 145 E2
Trent Gdns. Bu Jo ............ 164 A2
Trent La. Best .................... 97 F3
Trent La. Bu Jo ................. 164 B2
Trent La. E Brid ................ 165 D2
Trent La. Girt .................... 82 C1
Trent La. Kelh ................... 124 A3
Trent La. Lo Ea ................ 193 F3
Trent La. N Clift ................. 68 C3
Trent La. N-on-T .............. 125 D1

Trent La. Nott ............ 174 A2
Trent La. S Clift ............ 68 B1
Trent Port Rd. Mart ......... 44 A4
Trent Rd. Bees ............ 184 A2
Trent Rd. Mart ............. 44 B4
Trent Rd. Nott ............. 173 F2
Trent South Ind Park. Nott .174 A2
Trent St. Gain ............. 24 B4
Trent St. Lo Ea ............ 193 F4
Trent St. Nott ............. 173 E2
Trent St. Ret .............. 40 A3
Trent St. Work ............. 35 F2
Trent Vale Rd. Bees ....... 184 A2
Trent View Gdns. R on T .. 176 A3
Trent Way. N-on-T ......... 125 D1
Trent Wlk. Mans ........... 88 C2
Trentdale Rd. Carl ......... 174 B3
Trentham Dr. Nott ......... 172 B4
Trentham Gdns. Nott ...... 172 B4
Trenton Cl. Bees .......... 171 D1
Trenton Dr. Lo Ea ......... 194 A4
Trentside N. W Brid ....... 173 F1
Trentside. Gunt ........... 165 D2
Trentview Ct. Nott ........ 173 F1
Tressall Cl. Ilk ............ 170 A4
Treswell Ct. Mans ......... 103 D1
Treswell Rd. Ramp ......... 42 C1
Treswell Rd. S Lev ......... 42 B3
Trevelyan Rd. W Brid ...... 173 F1
Trevino Gdns. Nott ........ 147 D1
Trevone Ave. Staple ....... 182 C3
Trevor Rd. Bees ........... 183 F3
Trevor Rd. W Brid ......... 186 A3
Trevose Gdns. Nott ....... 161 E2
Treyford Cl. Nott .......... 185 D2
Triangle The. Ilk ........... 170 A3
Tricornia Dr. Nott ......... 160 A2
Tring Vale. Nott ........... 161 D2
Trinity Cl. Ilk ............. 157 F2
Trinity Cres. E Mark ....... 66 A4
Trinity Cres. Lamb ......... 163 E4
Trinity Cres. Wyme ........ 216 A2
Trinity Rd. N-on-T ......... 140 A2
Trinity Rd. Ret ............ 29 E1
Trinity Rd. South .......... 136 B4
Trinity Sq. Nott ............ 173 E3
Trinity St. Gain ............ 24 B4
Trinity St. Lough .......... 220 B2
Trinity Wlk. Nott .......... 173 E3
Trinstead Way. Nott ....... 161 E4
Triumph Cl. Eakr .......... 106 C4
Triumph Rd. Eakr .......... 106 C4
Triumph Rd. Nott ......... 172 B2
Trivett Sq. Nott ........... 173 E2
Troon Cl. Kim ............. 158 C4
Trough La. Greas .......... 158 C4
Trough Rd. Greas ......... 159 D4
Troutbeck Cres. Bees ..... 183 E4
Troutbeck. Cotg .......... 188 A2
Trowell Ave. Ilk ........... 170 A3
Trowell Ave. Nott ......... 171 D3
Trowell Gr. Lo Ea ......... 182 B1
Trowell Gr. Staple ......... 170 C2
Trowell La. Su Bo ......... 213 F4
Trowell Park Dr. Staple ... 170 B1
Trowell Rd. Nott .......... 171 E3
Trowell Rd. Staple ........ 170 B1
True Lovers Wlk. Lough ... 220 A2
Trueman Ct. Work .......... 36 A3
Trueman Gdns. Arn ........ 162 A3
Trueman St. Ilk ........... 157 F2
Truman Cl. Nott ........... 173 E3
Truman Dr. Huck .......... 146 A3
Truman St. Coss .......... 158 A1
Truman St. Kim ........... 158 B4
Truman's Rd. Nott ........ 173 E1
Truro Cl. E Lea ........... 205 F1
Truro Cres. Nott .......... 172 C4
Trusley Wlk. Mans ........ 88 C2
Tryst The. N-on-T ......... 125 D1
Tuckers Cl. Lough ........ 220 B1
Tudor Ave. Mans .......... 102 C4
Tudor Cl. Carl ............ 174 C3
Tudor Cl. Lo Ea ........... 182 C1
Tudor Cres. Rain .......... 118 A4
Tudor Ct. Arn ............. 162 A3
Tudor Ct. Huck ........... 145 E3
Tudor Dr. Mans ........... 102 B2
Tudor Dr. Mort ............ 15 D2
Tudor Gr. Nott ............ 173 D3
Tudor Rd. W Brid ......... 185 F4
Tudor Sq. W Brid ......... 185 F4
Tudor St. S in A .......... 100 C1
Tudsbury Terr. S in A ..... 101 D2
Tudwal Cl. Nott ........... 161 D4
Tudwal Wlk. Nott ......... 161 D4
Tulip Ave. Nott ........... 173 E4
Tulip Rd. Awsw .......... 158 A3
Tunnel Rd. Nott .......... 173 D2
Tunnel Rd. Ret ........... 39 F3
Tunstall Cres. Nott ....... 160 A1
Tunstall Dr. Nott ......... 160 C2
Tunstall Rd. Arn ......... 161 F2
Turnberry Ave. K-in-A ... 114 C4
Turnberry Cl. Bees ....... 183 E3
Turnberry Ct. W Brid ..... 186 B2

Turnberry Rd. Nott ......... 160 B3
Turnberry. Work ............ 36 A3
Turner Ave. La Mi .......... 143 D2
Turner Ave. Lough ......... 220 A1
Turner Cl. Staple .......... 182 C3
Turner Dr. Greas .......... 158 B4
Turner Dr. Work ............ 35 F2
Turner Rd. Lo Ea .......... 193 E2
Turner St. Work ............ 35 F2
Turner St. Huck ........... 146 A4
Turners Croft. N Le Ha ... 42 B4
Turney St. Nott ............ 173 E1
Turneys Ct. Nott .......... 173 F1
Turnpike La. Nott .......... 184 A4
Turnstone Wharf. Nott ... 172 C1
Turpin Ave. Carl ........... 162 B2
Turpin Cl. Gain ............ 15 F1
Turton Cl. La Mi ............ 143 D2
Turvey La. Lo Wh .......... 212 B1
Tuxford Ave. Mans ........ 103 D1
Tuxford Cl. Mans ........... 103 D1
Tuxford Rd. Boug .......... 77 F3
Tuxford Rd. E Mark ......... 65 F3
Tuxford Rd. Egma ........... 79 F4
Tuxford Rd. Nor on T ...... 81 E3
Tuxford Rd. Wale ........... 64 B1
Tuxford Rd. West ........... 81 E3
Tuxford Wlk. Nott .......... 173 F3
Twells Cl. Nott ............. 173 F4
Twentylands Dr. E Lea .... 205 E1
Twin Oaks Dr. S in A ....... 100 B1
Twitchell The. Bees ....... 183 F2
Twitchell The. N-on-T ..... 139 F3
Twitchell The. S in A ....... 100 C1
Two Acres. Blyth ........... 18 A1
Twycross Rd. Nott ......... 161 D4
Twyford Gdns. Nott ........ 184 C2
Twyford La. Elk ............ 50 B2
Tyburn Cl. Bes Vil ......... 147 D1
Tylden Rd. Rhod ........... 35 D3
Tylden Way. Rhod ......... 35 D3
Tyne Gdns. Huck ......... 145 E2
Tynedale Cl. Lo Ea ........ 193 D3
Tynedale Cl. Nott .......... 160 B1

Ulldale Ct. Bees ........... 183 D2
Ullswater Cl. Carl ......... 162 C1
Ullswater Cres. Bees ...... 183 E4
Ullswater Dr. Huck ........ 145 F4
Ulster Rd. Gain ........... 15 E1
Underwood Ave. Torw ..... 19 D2
Underwood Gdns. Work ... 35 E2
Union Rd. Nott ............ 173 E3
Union St. Bees ............ 184 A3
Union St. Bing ............ 177 F2
Union St. Lo Ea ........... 193 F4
Union St. Lough .......... 220 A2
Union St. Mans ........... 102 A4
Union St. Ret ............. 39 F4
Union St. S in A ........... 100 C1
Union St. Sels ............ 129 D4
Unity Cres. Carl ........... 162 B1
Unity Rd. K-in-A .......... 115 D4
University Bvd. Nott ....... 184 B4
Unwin Rd. S in A ........... 101 D2
Unwin St. S in A ........... 100 A2
Uplands Ct. Nott .......... 171 F3
Upminster Dr. Nott ........ 147 F1
Upper Canaan. Rudd ...... 196 B4
Upper College St. Nott ... 173 D3
Upper Dunstead Rd. Ald .. 143 D2
Upper Eldon St. Nott ...... 173 F2
Upper Mexborough Rd. Sels129 D4
Upper Orchard St. Staple . 182 C3
Upper Parliament St. Nott .. 173 E3
Upper Row. D on T ......... 54 A1
Upper Wellington St. Lo Ea 182 B1
Uppingham Cres. W Brid .. 185 E3
Uppingham Gdns. Nott ... 173 E1
Upton Dr. Nott ............ 161 E3
Upton Hill. Askh .......... 52 A2
Upton Mount. Mans ....... 87 F1
Upton Rd. Askh ........... 52 A2
Upton Rd. South .......... 136 C4
Upton Rd. Upton .......... 122 A1
Upton Wlk. Gain .......... 24 C4
Urban Rd. K-in-A .......... 115 D3
Utile Gdns. Nott .......... 160 A4

Vale Ave. Mar War ........ 74 A2
Vale Cl. Aslo .............. 179 D2
Vale Cl. East .............. 144 A1
Vale Cl. Mans ............. 102 C2
Vale Cres N. Nott ......... 172 B3
Vale Cres S. Nott ......... 172 B3
Vale Dr. Shireb ........... 72 C1
Vale Gdns. Carl ........... 174 B3
Vale Rd. Carl ............. 174 C3
Vale Rd. Mans ............ 88 A2
Vale The. Ilk ............. 157 F2
Valentine Ave. Sels ....... 128 C4
Valeside Gdns. Carl ....... 174 C3
Valetta Rd. Arn ........... 162 A4
Valiant Rd. Codd .......... 125 F1
Vallance St. Mans ........ 88 A2
Valley App. Bils .......... 105 F4
Valley Dr. East ........... 144 A1
Valley Farm Ct. Nott ...... 161 D4

Valley Gdns. W Brid ....... 186 B3
Valley La. Dry Do .......... 169 E4
Valley Prospect. N-on-T ... 139 E3
Valley Rd. Bees ........... 183 D3
Valley Rd. Bils ............ 105 F4
Valley Rd. Carl ............ 162 A1
Valley Rd. Kim ............ 158 B4
Valley Rd. Nott ........... 161 D2
Valley Rd. R on T .......... 176 A3
Valley Rd. Shireb .......... 72 C3
Valley Rd. W Brid ......... 186 A3
Valley Rd. Work ............ 35 F3
Valley View. Codd ......... 126 A1
Valmont Ave. Mans ........ 103 D3
Valmont Rd. Bees ......... 183 D4
Valmont Rd. Nott .......... 161 D2
Vancouver Ave. R on T .... 175 F1
Vanessa Dr. Gain .......... 15 E2
Vanguard Rd. Lo Ea ....... 193 E3
Varden Ave. Nott .......... 172 A1
Varney Rd. Nott ........... 184 C2
Vaughan Ave. Bott ........ 181 E1
Vaughan Ave. Huck ........ 131 E1
Vaughan Pl. Shireb ........ 72 C3
Vaughan Rd. Bees ......... 183 D2
Vellus Ct. S in A ........... 101 D1
Ventnor Rise. Nott ........ 160 C2
Venus Cl. Nott ............ 160 C3
Vera Cres. Rain ........... 118 A4
Verbena Cl. Nott .......... 173 E4
Verder Gr. Nott ........... 160 C4
Vere Ave. S in A ........... 100 C3
Vere St. Nott ............. 160 A4
Verne Cl. Carl ............ 174 B4
Verney St. Plea ........... 86 C4
Verney Way. Plea .......... 86 C4
Vernon Ave. Bees ......... 183 F3
Vernon Ave. Carl .......... 162 C1
Vernon Ave. N-on-T ....... 140 A4
Vernon Ave. Nott .......... 160 C2
Vernon Ave. Raven ........ 116 C1
Vernon Ave. Ret ........... 40 A2
Vernon Cres. Raven ....... 117 D1
Vernon Ct. Nuth .......... 159 F2
Vernon Ct. Shireb ......... 73 D2
Vernon Dr. Nuth .......... 159 F2
Vernon Park Dr. Nott ...... 160 C2
Vernon Rd. K-in-A ......... 114 C3
Vernon Rd. Nott ........... 160 C2
Vernon St. Ilk ............ 157 F2
Vernon St. N-on-T ......... 140 A4
Vernon St. Nott ........... 173 D3
Vernon St. Shireb ......... 73 D2
Vernon St. Work ........... 36 A1
Verona Ct. Mans .......... 103 D2
Veronica Dr. Carl ......... 162 B1
Veronica Dr. Greas ........ 158 B4
Veronica Wlk. Nott ........ 184 B1
Veronne Dr. S in A ........ 101 F4
Vesper Ct. Mans .......... 102 C4
Vessey Cl. Bald .......... 140 B2
Vessey Rd. Work .......... 35 F4
Vexation La. Edwin ....... 91 F4
Vicar La. Miss ............ 4 B2
Vicar La. Tibs ............ 99 D3
Vicar's La. Ramp ......... 43 D1
Vicar's Wlk. Work ......... 35 F1
Vicarage Cl. Nott ......... 173 E3
Vicarage Ave. Ilk ......... 157 E2
Vicarage Ave. N Le Ha .... 42 B4
Vicarage Cl. Coll ......... 98 A1
Vicarage Cl. N Le Ha ...... 42 B4
Vicarage Cl. Shireb ....... 72 C2
Vicarage Cl. S in A ........ 100 C1
Vicarage Dr. Bu Jo ........ 163 F2
Vicarage Dr. Hayt ......... 30 B3
Vicarage Green. W Brid ... 186 A2
Vicarage La. Beck ......... 14 B1
Vicarage La. Farns ........ 119 F3
Vicarage La. Kneet ........ 151 F1
Vicarage La. N Musk ...... 110 B2
Vicarage La. R on T ....... 175 F2
Vicarage La. Rudd ......... 196 B4
Vicarage Rd. Nott ......... 160 C2
Vicarage Rd. South ....... 136 B4
Vicarage St. Bees ......... 183 F3
Vicarage St. Ilk .......... 157 E2
Vicarage Way. Ann Wo .... 129 F4
Vicarage Wlk. N Le Ha .... 42 B4
Vickers St. Hello ......... 173 A2
Vickers St. Mar War ....... 74 A2
Victor Cres. Sand ......... 182 B2
Victor Terr. Nott ......... 161 E1
Victoria Ave. Lowd ....... 150 C1
Victoria Ave. Lowd ....... 164 C4
Victoria Ave. Nott ........ 173 F2
Victoria Centre. Nott ..... 173 E3
Victoria Cl. Boug ......... 77 F3
Victoria Cl. Gain ......... 24 C3
Victoria Cl. Nott .......... 147 F1
Victoria Cres. Nott ....... 161 E1
Victoria Ct. Ilk ........... 157 F1
Victoria Ct. Mans ......... 103 A3
Victoria Emb. Nott ........ 185 E4
Victoria Gdns. Greas ...... 145 D1
Victoria Gdns. N-on-T ..... 140 A4
Victoria Park. Carl ........ 175 D3

Victoria Rd. Bing ......... 178 A3
Victoria Rd. Bunn ......... 196 C1
Victoria Rd. Carl .......... 175 D3
Victoria Rd. K-in-A ........ 114 C3
Victoria Rd. Nott .......... 161 D2
Victoria Rd. Pinx ......... 113 E2
Victoria Rd. Ret .......... 39 F3
Victoria Rd. Sand ......... 182 A3
Victoria Rd. Sels ......... 129 D4
Victoria Rd. W Brid ....... 185 F4
Victoria Rd. Work ......... 35 F1
Victoria Sq. Work ......... 35 F2
Victoria St. Carl .......... 162 C1
Victoria St. Huck ......... 146 A4
Victoria St. Ilk ........... 157 F2
Victoria St. Ilk ........... 157 F2
Victoria St. Kim .......... 159 D3
Victoria St. La Mi ......... 143 E2
Victoria St. Lo Ea ........ 193 D3
Victoria St. Lough ........ 220 A2
Victoria St. Mar War ...... 74 A3
Victoria St. N-on-T ....... 139 F4
Victoria St. Nott .......... 173 E2
Victoria St. R on T ........ 175 F2
Victoria St. S in A ......... 100 B3
Victoria St. S in A ......... 100 C1
Victoria St. S Norm ....... 113 D3
Victoria St. Sels ......... 128 A2
Victoria St. Sels ......... 129 D4
Victoria St. Shireb ........ 72 C2
Victoria St. Staple ........ 182 B4
Victoria Terr. Tibs ......... 99 D4
Victory Cl. Lo Ea ......... 193 E3
Victory Cl. Mans .......... 89 D1
Victory Dr. Mans .......... 88 C1
Victory Rd. Bees ......... 184 A2
Villa Rd. Keyw ............ 197 C2
Villa Rd. Nott ............ 173 E4
Villa St. Bees ............ 183 F4
Village Cl. Farn .......... 139 D3
Village Cl. W Brid ........ 186 A2
Village Farm Cl. W Lea ... 204 C1
Village Rd. N on S ........ 213 E1
Village Rd. Nott .......... 184 B1
Village St. Owth ......... 199 F4
Village St. W Brid ........ 186 A2
Village Way. Farn ........ 139 D3
Villiers Rd. Arn .......... 161 E2
Villiers Rd. Mans ........ 102 C4
Villiers Rd. W Brid ....... 186 A3
Vincent Ave. Bees ....... 183 F3
Vincent Gdns. Nott ...... 172 C4
Vine Cres. Sand ......... 182 A3
Vine Rd. Tick ............ 8 B4
Vine Terr. Huck .......... 146 A4
Vine Tree Terr. Hoton .... 215 E1
Vine Way. N-on-T ........ 140 A4
Vines Cross. Nott ........ 171 F1
Violet Ave. East ......... 144 A1
Violet Cl. Nott .......... 160 B2
Violet Hill. Mans ........ 103 D4
Violet Rd. Carl .......... 162 B1
Violet Rd. W Brid ........ 186 A3
Vista The. Staple ........ 182 C3
Vivian Ave. Nott ........ 173 D4
Voca Ct. Work .......... 36 A3
Vulcan Cl. Nott ......... 160 C2
Vulcan Pl. Work ........ 35 F2
Vyse Dr. Lo Ea ......... 193 E3

W End Cl. Bott .......... 181 D2
W Furlong. Cotg ........ 188 A1
W Leake La. K on S ..... 204 B3
W Leake Rd. E Lea ...... 205 E1
W Wlk. Nott ............ 173 F2
Waddington Dr. W Brid .. 185 E2
Wade Ave. Ilk .......... 170 A4
Wadham Rd. Arn ........ 161 F3
Wadhurst Gdns. Nott .... 173 E3
Wadhurst Gr. Nott ...... 171 E1
Wadnal La. West ........ 80 C2
Wadsworth Rd. Staple ... 182 C4
Wagstaff La. Sels ....... 128 B3
Wain Ct. Work .......... 36 A4
Waingrove. Nott ........ 185 D2
Wainwright Ave. Mans .. 101 E4
Wakefield Ave. R on T ... 176 A2
Wakeling Cl. South ...... 136 C4
Walbrook Cl. Nott ....... 160 A2
Walcot Green. Nott ...... 184 B1
Walcote Dr. W Brid ...... 185 E2
Waldeck Rd. Nott ....... 161 D1
Waldemar Gr. Bees ...... 184 A3
Waldron Cl. Nott ........ 173 E1
Walesby Cl. Mans ....... 103 D2
Walesby Dr. K-in-A ...... 115 E3
Walesby La. Oll ......... 77 E3
Walford Cl. Bott ........ 181 D1
Walgrave Wlk. Nott ...... 161 D4
Walk Mill Dr. Huck ...... 131 D1
Walk The. Gain ......... 24 C4
Walkden St. Mans ....... 102 A4
Walker Cl. N-on-T ....... 140 A4
Walker St. East ......... 144 A2
Walker St. Nott ......... 173 F2
Walkeringham Rd. Beck .. 14 A2
Walkeringham Rd. G on H . 13 D2
Walkerith Rd. E Stock ... 14 B4

Walkerith Rd. Mort .............. 15 D3
Walkerith Rd. Walk ............. 14 C3
Walkers Ave. Brin ............. 143 F3
Walkers Cl. Bing .............. 177 F2
Walkers Cl. Mans .............. 89 D1
Walkers Yd. R on T ............ 175 F2
Wall St. Gain .................. 24 B4
Wallace Ave. Carl ............ 174 C4
Wallace Rd. Lough ............ 220 A1
Wallace St. Goth .............. 195 D1
Wallan St. Nott ............... 172 C3
Wallet St. Carl ............... 175 D4
Wallett Ave. Bees ............ 183 F4
Wallingwells La. Wall .......... 25 D3
Wallis Rd. Mans .............. 102 B4
Wallis St. Nott ............... 160 C2
Walnut Ave. Shire ............. 34 C4
Walnut Ave. Tick ............... 8 A4
Walnut Cl. Aslo .............. 178 C3
Walnut Cl. Ilk ............... 170 A4
Walnut Dr. Bees .............. 183 D4
Walnut Dr. Calv .............. 148 C4
Walnut Gr. E Brid ............ 165 E1
Walnut Gr. R on T ............ 175 F2
Walnut Paddock. Harb ......... 202 A2
Walnut Rd. Bott .............. 181 D1
Walnut Tree Gdns. Nott ....... 159 F4
Walnut Tree Green. Mans ...... 89 E1
Walnut Tree La. E Brid ....... 165 E1
Walsham Cl. Bees ............. 183 E1
Walsingham Rd. Arn ........... 162 A3
Walter St. Nott .............. 173 D3
Walters Cres. Sels ........... 128 B3
Waltham Cl. Bald ............. 140 B2
Waltham Cl. W Brid ........... 186 A3
Waltham La. Harb ............. 202 A1
Waltham La. Lo Cl ............ 211 F1
Waltham Rd. Raven ............ 117 D1
Walton Ave. Nott ............. 173 F3
Walton Ave. Nott ............. 173 F3
Walton Cl. Mans .............. 103 D4
Walton Cres. Carl ............ 174 C4
Walton Dr. Keyw .............. 197 F2
Walton Dr. S in A ............ 114 B4
Walton Rd. Arn ............... 148 A1
Walton St. Lo Ea ............. 182 B1
Walton St. S in A ............ 101 D2
Walton's La. N Musk .......... 110 C2
Wands Cl. South .............. 136 B4
Wansbeck Cl. Nott ............ 173 D3
Wanstead Way. Work ........... 146 C1
Wapping La. Mart .............. 44 B4
Warburton St. N-on-T ......... 125 D1
Ward Ave. Huck ............... 130 C1
Ward Pl. Mans ................ 101 F3
Ward St. Nott ................ 172 C4
Ward's End. Lough ............ 220 A2
Wardle Gr. Arn ............... 162 A4
Wardlow Rd. Ilk .............. 157 F2
Wareham Cl. Nott ............. 160 A2
Wareham Cl. W Brid ........... 185 E3
Warkton Cl. Bees ............. 183 E3
Warnadene Rd. S in A ......... 114 C4
Warner Pl. Lough ............. 220 B2
Warner St. Nott .............. 172 C3
Warrands Cl. South ........... 136 B4
Warren Ave Ext. Staple ....... 182 B4
Warren Ave. Ann Wo ........... 130 B4
Warren Ave. Nott ............. 161 D1
Warren Ave. Staple ........... 182 B4
Warren Cl. Gain ............... 15 D1
Warren Ct. S in A ............ 100 A1
Warren Ct. Staple ............ 182 B4
Warren La. Kegw .............. 203 D2
Warren Rd. Ann Wo ............ 115 D1
Warren Rd. Huck .............. 145 E3
Warren The. Cotg ............. 187 F1
Warrender Cl. Bees ........... 171 E1
Warrener Gr. Nott ............ 160 C4
Warrenhill Cl. Arn ........... 161 E4
Warrington Rd. Nott .......... 160 B4
Warser Gate. Nott ............ 173 E2
Warsop La. Rain .............. 117 F4
Warsop Rd. Mans ............... 88 B2
Warton Ave. Nott ............. 173 F4
Warwick Ave. Arn ............. 161 F3
Warwick Ave. Bees ............ 183 F4
Warwick Ave. C in L ........... 25 E1
Warwick Cl. K-in-A ........... 115 E3
Warwick Dr. Mans ............. 102 C4
Warwick Dr. Ship ............. 157 E2
Warwick Gdns. Cotg ........... 187 F1
Warwick Rd. Bald ............. 140 B2
Warwick Rd. Lo Ea ............ 193 A4
Warwick Rd. Nott ............. 161 E1
Wash Pit La. Co Ba ........... 200 B4
Washdyke La. Huck ............ 145 F4
Washington Dr. Staple ........ 170 C1
Washington St. Gain ........... 24 B3
Wasnidge Cl. Nott ............ 173 E3
Wasnidge Wlk. Nott ........... 173 E3
Watchwood Gr. Calv ........... 148 C4
Watcombe Cir. Nott ........... 161 E1
Watcombe Rd. Nott ............ 161 E1
Watendlath Cl. W Brid ........ 186 B3
Water La. C in L .............. 26 A3
Water La. Lo Cl .............. 211 F2
Water La. Mans ................ 87 D2

Water La. N-on-T ............. 124 C1
Water La. Oxt ................ 134 A2
Water La. R on T ............. 175 F2
Water La. Ret ................. 39 F4
Water La. Shel ............... 164 B1
Water La. Tick ................. 8 A3
Water Meadows. Work ........... 35 E1
Water Orton Cl. Bees ......... 182 C2
Waterdown Rd. Nott ........... 184 B1
Waterford St. Nott ........... 160 C2
Waterfurrows La. Shel ........ 164 B1
Waterhouse La. Carl .......... 163 D1
Waterloo Cl. S Norm .......... 113 E4
Waterloo Cres. Nott .......... 173 D3
Waterloo La. Trow ............ 170 C3
Waterloo Prom. Nott .......... 173 D3
Waterloo Rd. Bees ............ 184 A3
Waterloo Rd. Nott ............ 173 D3
Watermeadow Cl. Mans .......... 88 B3
Watermeadows The. Lo Ea ...... 193 D4
Waterside Cl. Lough .......... 220 A3
Waterside Cl. Sand ........... 182 A2
Waterside Gdns. Nott ......... 172 C1
Waterslack Rd. Bir ............. 9 D2
Waterson Ave. Mans ........... 102 C2
Waterson Cl. Mans ............ 103 D2
Waterway St W. Nott .......... 173 E1
Waterway St. Nott ............ 173 E1
Waterway The. Sand ........... 182 B2
Waterworks St. Gain ........... 24 B3
Watford St. Nott ............. 160 A1
Watkin St. Nott .............. 173 E3
Watkins La. S Le S ............ 32 B3
Watnall Cres. Mans ........... 101 F4
Watnall Rd. Huck ............. 145 F2
Watnall Rd. Kim .............. 158 C4
Watnall Rd. Nuth ............. 159 E3
Watson Ave. Mans ............. 102 B4
Watson Ave. Nott ............. 174 A3
Watson Rd. Work ............... 35 F1
Watson St. Mar War ............ 74 A2
Watson's La. Harb ............ 202 A2
Wavell Cres. Matt ............. 11 D1
Waveney Cl. Arn .............. 162 A3
Waverley Ave. Bees ........... 184 A4
Waverley Ave. Carl ........... 163 D1
Waverley Pl. Work ............. 47 D4
Waverley Rd. Mans ............ 102 A2
Waverley St. Lo Ea ........... 193 F4
Waverley St. Nott ............ 173 D3
Waverley St. Tibs ............. 99 D4
Waverley Way. Work ............ 47 D4
Waverly Cl. K-in-A ........... 115 E3
Wayford Wlk. Nott ............ 160 A4
Wayne Cl. Nott ............... 184 C1
Weardale Rd. Nott ............ 161 D1
Wearmouth Gdns. Bes Vil ...... 147 D1
Weaver La. Ann Wo ............ 129 F2
Weavers Cl. E Lea ............ 205 F2
Weavers The. N-on-T .......... 139 E3
Weaverthorpe Rd. Arn ......... 162 A3
Webb Rd. Nott ................ 172 A4
Webster Ave. East ............ 143 F1
Webster Cl. Rain ............. 104 A1
Weedon Cl. Nott .............. 174 A3
Weekday Cross. Nott .......... 173 E2
Weetman Ave. Mar War .......... 74 A3
Weetman Gdns. Nott ........... 161 D4
Weighbridge Rd. Mans ......... 102 B3
Weightman Dr. Greas .......... 158 A4
Welbank Cl. Bees ............. 183 D2
Wolbeck Ave. Carl ............ 162 B1
Welbeck Ave. N-on-T .......... 125 D1
Welbeck Cl. Nott ............. 173 E3
Welbeck Cl. S in A ........... 100 C3
Welbeck Dr. Edwin ............. 75 F1
Welbeck Gdns. Arn ............ 162 A2
Welbeck Gdns. Bees ........... 182 C2
Welbeck Gr. Bing ............. 177 E2
Welbeck Pl. Tux ............... 66 A2
Welbeck Rd. Har ............... 9 D3
Welbeck Rd. Lo Ea ............ 182 B2
Welbeck Rd. Mans .............. 88 B2
Welbeck Rd. R on T ........... 176 A2
Welbeck Rd. Ret ............... 39 F2
Welbeck Rd. W Brid ........... 185 F4
Welbeck Sq. S in A ........... 100 B3
Welbeck St. Elmt ............. 58 C4
Welbeck St. K-in-A ........... 115 E3
Welbeck St. Mans ............. 102 A4
Welbeck St. Mar War ........... 74 A2
Welbeck St. S in A ........... 100 C1
Welbeck St. Whit .............. 45 D3
Welbeck St. Work .............. 35 F2
Welbeck Wlk. Nott ............ 173 E3
Welby Ave. Nott .............. 172 C2
Welch Ave. Staple ............ 182 C4
Welfare Cl. Shireb ............ 72 C2
Welfitt Gr. Ne La ............. 59 D1
Welham Cres. Arn ............. 162 A4
Welham Gr. Ret ................ 40 A4
Welham Rd. Clar ............... 40 A4
Welham Rd. Ret ................ 40 A4
Well Fen La. Clayp ........... 156 B4
Well La. Up Br ............... 210 A1
Welland Cl. N-on-T ........... 125 D1
Welland Cl. Work .............. 35 F4

Wellesley Cres. Nott ......... 159 E1
Wellin Cl. W Brid ............ 186 A2
Wellin Ct. W Brid ............ 186 A2
Wellin La. W Brid ............ 186 A2
Wellington Cir. Nott ......... 173 D2
Wellington Cl. Mar War ........ 74 A2
Wellington Cres. W Brid ...... 185 F4
Wellington Gr. Baw ............. 9 F4
Wellington Pl. East .......... 143 F1
Wellington Rd. Bu Jo ......... 164 A3
Wellington Rd. N-on-T ........ 140 A4
Wellington Sq. Nott .......... 173 D3
Wellington Sq. Ret ............ 39 F4
Wellington St. East .......... 143 F2
Wellington St. Gain ........... 24 B4
Wellington St. Lo Ea ......... 182 B1
Wellington St. Lough ......... 220 B2
Wellington St. Nott .......... 173 E3
Wellington St. Ret ............ 39 F4
Wellington St. Staple ........ 182 B3
Wellington Villas. Nott ...... 173 D3
Wellow Cl. Mans .............. 101 E4
Wellow Green. Oll ............. 77 E1
Wellow Rd. Eakr ............... 92 C1
Wellow Rd. Oll ................ 77 E1
Wells Cl. Mans ................ 88 B2
Wells Gdns. Nott ............. 173 F4
Wells La. Cott ................ 43 E3
Wells Road The. Nott ......... 161 F1
Wellspring Dale. Staple ...... 182 C3
Welshcroft Cl. K-in-A ........ 115 D4
Welstead Ave. Nott ........... 160 A4
Welton Gdns. Nott ............ 160 A4
Welwyn Ave. Mans .............. 88 C2
Welwyn Rd. Nott .............. 171 F3
Wembley Gdns. Bees ........... 171 D1
Wembley Rd. Arn .............. 162 A3
Wembley Rd. Lan ............... 16 C2
Wembley St. Gain .............. 24 B4
Wemyss Gdns. Nott ............ 172 B2
Wendling Gdns. Nott .......... 161 D4
Wendover Dr. Nott ............ 160 A1
Wenham La. S in A ............. 99 F2
Wenlock Cl. Greas ............ 158 B4
Wensley Rd. Arn .............. 161 F3
Wensleydale Cl. Mans .......... 88 C1
Wensleydale Cl. Nott ......... 160 B1
Wensleydale Rd. Lo Ea ........ 193 D3
Wensleydale. Work ............. 36 A4
Wensor Ave. Nott ............. 183 F4
Wentbridge Dr. Mans .......... 103 D2
Wentworth Cnr. N-on-T ........ 139 F3
Wentworth Croft. Hean ........ 143 D2
Wentworth Ct. Kim ............ 158 C3
Wentworth Green. Ret .......... 39 E2
Wentworth Rd. Bees ........... 183 E3
Wentworth Rd. K-in-A ......... 114 C4
Wentworth Rd. Nott ........... 161 D1
Wentworth St. Coss ........... 158 A1
Wentworth Way. W Brid ........ 186 B2
Wesley Cl. Bald .............. 140 B2
Wesley Cl. Hath .............. 213 D1
Wesley Gr. Nott .............. 161 D1
Wesley Pl. Staple ............ 182 C4
Wesley Rd. Ret ................ 39 F4
Wesley St. Ann Wo ............ 130 A4
Wesley St. Ilk ............... 157 F2
Wesley St. La Mi ............. 143 E2
Wesley St. Nott .............. 161 D1
Wesley Way. Rudd ............. 196 B3
Wesleyan Chpl Wlk. Staple .... 182 B4
Wessex Cl. Work ............... 36 A3
Wessex Rd. Work ............... 36 A3
West Ave. K-in-A ............. 115 E2
West Ave. Sand ............... 182 A3
West Ave. Staple ............. 182 C4
West Ave. W Brid ............. 185 F4
West Bank Ave. Mans .......... 102 A4
West Bank Lea. Mans ........... 88 A1
West Bank Link. Mans .......... 88 A1
West Bank Mews. Kegw ......... 203 E1
West Bank Wynd. Mans ......... 102 A4
West Bank. Sax ................ 56 C1
West Brook La. Coll .......... 112 A3
West Carr Rd. Ret ............. 39 E3
West Cl. Keyw ................ 197 F1
West Cres. Bees .............. 184 A2
West Cres. K-in-A ............ 115 E2
West Ct. Ret .................. 39 E4
West Dr. Edwin ................ 76 A1
West Dr. Nott ................ 184 A4
West End Arc. Nott ........... 173 D3
West End St. Staple .......... 182 B3
West End. Bees ............... 183 F3
West End. Calv ............... 148 B4
West End. Lo Cl .............. 211 E2
West End. Lo Wh .............. 212 A2
West End. Pinx ............... 113 E2
West End. S in A ............. 100 C1
West Furlong. Ret ............. 39 E4
West Gate. Lo Ea ............. 193 F4
West Gate. Mans .............. 102 A4
West Gate. Tick ............... 8 A3
West Grove Rd. Ret ............ 39 F3
West Hill Dr. Mans ........... 102 A4
West Hill Park. Mans .......... 88 A2

West Hill Rd. Ret ............. 39 E2
West Hill Way. Mans .......... 102 A4
West Hill. Mans .............. 102 A4
West Hill. S in A ............ 100 B3
West La. Edwin ................ 76 A1
West La. Girt ................. 82 C1
West Moor Rd. Walker .......... 13 F3
West Moor. Nott .............. 174 B2
West Park Pl. Ret ............. 39 E3
West St. Arn ................. 161 F4
West St. Har .................. 9 D3
West St. Huck ................ 146 A4
West St. Kim ................. 159 D2
West St. La Mi ............... 143 D2
West St. Mar War .............. 73 A2
West St. Miss .................. 4 A1
West St. Mort ................. 15 D2
West St. Nott ................ 173 F2
West St. Ret .................. 39 F3
West St. Scarc ................ 59 D2
West St. Work ................. 35 F1
West Terr. Huck .............. 146 A4
West Terr. Ilk ............... 157 F1
West Thorpe. W-on-W .......... 217 E4
West View. C in L ............. 25 F4
West View. W Brid ............ 185 E3
West Wells La. G on H ......... 12 C1
West Wlk. Ret ................. 39 E4
West Wood Estate. Baw .......... 9 F3
Westbourne Cl. Ret ............ 40 A3
Westbourne Cl. S in A ........ 100 B2
Westbourne Rd. S in A ........ 100 B2
Westbourne Rd. Sels .......... 128 B2
Westbourne View. S in A ...... 100 B2
Westbrecks La. S Lev .......... 43 D3
Westbrook Ave. Raven ......... 116 C2
Westbury Cl. Bees ............ 183 E2
Westbury Rd. Nott ............ 161 D1
Westby La. Awsw .............. 158 B2
Westby La. Kim ............... 158 B2
Westcliffe Ave. Carl ......... 162 B2
Westcliffe Ave. R on T ....... 176 A2
Westcroft Dr. Sax ............. 57 D3
Westcross Ave. Staple ........ 182 C4
Westdale Ave. S in A ......... 101 D3
Westdale Cl. Lo Ea ........... 193 D3
Westdale Cres. Carl .......... 162 C1
Westdale La East. Carl ....... 162 B1
Westdale La West. Carl ....... 162 A2
Westdale Rd. Mans ............. 88 A1
Westdale Rd. Sels ............ 128 B2
Westerdale. Work .............. 36 A4
Westerfield Way. Nott ........ 185 D3
Westerham Cl. Nott ........... 171 E4
Westerham Rd. Rudd ........... 196 A3
Westerlands. Staple .......... 182 C3
Western Ave. Bing ............ 177 E3
Western Ave. K-in-A .......... 115 D2
Western Ave. Mans ............ 101 F3
Western Ave. Sax .............. 56 C2
Western Bvd. Nott ............ 172 B4
Western Dr. Bald ............. 140 C1
Western Fields. Rudd ......... 196 A3
Western Gdns. Nott ........... 172 B4
Western St. Nott ............. 173 E3
Western Terr. Nott ........... 173 D2
Western Wlk. Baw .............. 10 A4
Westfield Cl. Mans ........... 101 F4
Westfield Dr. Mans ........... 101 F4
Westfield Dr. Work ............ 36 A3
Westfield La. Coll ........... 111 F4
Westfield La. Mans ........... 101 F4
Westfield La. Mans ........... 102 A4
Westfield Rd. Ann Wo ......... 115 D1
Westfield Rd. Bing ........... 177 E2
Westfield Rd. Ret ............. 39 E3
Westfield Way. Farn .......... 139 D2
Westfields La. Woodb ......... 149 D2
Westgate St. Nott ............ 173 F3
Westgate View. Work ........... 35 F1
Westgate. South .............. 136 B4
Westgate. Work ................ 35 F1
Westhay Ct. Nott ............. 172 B3
Westholme Gdns. Nott ......... 172 B3
Westhorpe Ave. Nott .......... 173 F3
Westhorpe Dr. Lo Ea .......... 193 E4
Westhorpe Market Pl. South ... 136 B4
Westland Ave. Huck ........... 145 E2
Westland Dr. Pinx ............ 113 E2
Westleigh Rd. Nott ........... 159 F1
Westleigh. Mans ............... 88 B3
Westminster Ave. K-in-A ...... 115 E3
Westminster Ave. Staple ...... 182 B3
Westminster Cl. Nott ......... 173 F4
Westminster Cl. Work .......... 36 A4
Westmoore Cl. Carl ........... 162 A2
Westmoreland Ct. Nott ........ 161 D1
Westmorland Ct. Bir ........... 9 E2
Westmorland Dr. C in L ........ 25 F4
Westmorland Way. Sels ........ 128 A2
Weston Ave. Nott ............. 173 D4
Weston Cl. Arn ............... 161 F2
Weston Cl. S in A ............ 115 E4
Weston La. Nor on T ........... 81 E3
Weston Rd. Egma .............. 80 A3
Weston St. Hean .............. 157 D4

Westray Cl. Bees ............. 171 D
Westview Ct. Carl ............ 174 C
Westville Dr. Huck ........... 145 F
Westville Gdns. Nott ......... 173 E
Westward Ave. Bees ........... 184 A
Westway. Cotg ................ 187 F
Westway. Work ................. 36 A
Westwick Rd. Nott ............ 171 E
Westwick St. Ilk ............. 170 A
Westwood Rd. Nott ............ 173 F
Wetherby Cl. Kim ............. 158 C
Wetherby Cl. Nott ............ 160 A
Wetherlam Cl. Nott ........... 173 E
Wetsyke La. Bald ............. 140 C
Whaddon Ct. Lough ............ 220 B
Whaley Common. Scarc .......... 58 B
Whaley Rd. Scarc .............. 58 C
Wharf La. R on T ............. 175 C
Wharf Rd. Mist ................. 6 C
Wharf Rd. Nott ............... 173 D
Wharf Rd. Pinx ............... 113 E
Wharf Rd. Ret ................. 39 F
Wharf Rd. S in A ............. 100 B
Wharf St. Baw ................. 10 A
Wharfdale Rd. Lo Ea .......... 193 D
Wharfedale. Nott ............. 171 D
Wharfedale. Work .............. 36 A
Wharmby Ave. Mans ............. 87 E
Wharncliffe Rd. Ilk .......... 157 F
Wharncliffe Rd. Lough ........ 220 B
Wharncliffe Rd. Ret ........... 39 F
Wharton Ct. Mans ............. 103 D
Wharton St. Ret ............... 40 A
Whatton Rd. Hath ............. 212 C
Whatton Rd. Kegw ............. 203 E
Whatton Rd. Kegw ............. 212 B
Whatton Rise. Nott ........... 161 E
Wheat Cl. Nott ............... 171 E
Wheat Croft. Work ............. 36 A
Wheatacre Rd. Nott ........... 184 C
Wheatcroft View. W Brid ...... 186 B
Wheatfield Cres. Mans ......... 88 C
Wheatfield Dr. Tick ........... 8 A
Wheatfield Way. S in A ....... 100 A
Wheatfields Rd. Nott ......... 174 A
Wheatgrass Hill. Hock ........ 122 B
Wheatgrass Rd. Bees .......... 183 D
Wheatland Dr. Lough .......... 220 B
Wheatley Ave. K-in-A ......... 114 C
Wheatley Cl. Mans ............. 88 C
Wheatley Dr. Carl ............ 174 B
Wheatley Gr. Bees ............ 183 F
Wheatley La. Coll ............ 112 A
Wheatley Rd. Clay ............. 21 F
Wheatley Rd. S Le S ........... 32 A
Wheatsheaf Ct. Bu Jo ......... 163 F
Wheeldale Cl. Nott ........... 171 D
Wheeldon St. Gain ............. 24 B
Wheeler Ave. East ............ 144 A
Wheeler Gate. Nott ........... 173 E
Wheeler Gate. Sels ........... 129 D
Wheldon Ave. Carl ............ 162 B
Whernside Rd. Arn ............ 161 F
Whetstone Cl. Nuth ........... 159 E
Whickham Cl. Nott ............ 173 E
Whilton Cl. S in A ........... 101 D
Whimsey Park. Carl ........... 174 C
Whinbush La. Calv ............ 133 F
Whinfell Cl. Nott ............ 184 C
Whinleys Rd. Clar ............. 31 D
Whinney Bank. Mans ............ 88 B
Whinney Hill. Mans ............ 88 B
Whinney La. Boug .............. 77 E
Whinney Moor Cl. Ret .......... 39 F
Whinney Moor La. Ret .......... 39 F
Whinney Moor Way. Ret ......... 39 F
Whiston Cl. Nott ............. 161 D
Whitaker Cl. Ret .............. 29 E
Whitbread St. Nott ........... 172 C
Whitburn Rd. Bees ............ 182 C
Whitby Cl. Nott .............. 171 D
Whitby Cres. Arn ............. 162 A
Whitby Rd. East .............. 144 A
Whitby Rd. Har ................. 9 D
Whitchurch Cl. Nott .......... 160 C
Whitcombe Gdns. Nott ......... 147 D
White Ave. Lan ................ 16 C
White Furrows. Cotg .......... 187 F
White Hart La. Coll .......... 112 A
White Hart St. Mans .......... 102 A
White Hart Yd. Work ........... 35 F
White House Rd. Bir ........... 9 E
White Lodge Gdns. Nott ....... 171 E
White Rd. Nott ............... 160 C
White's Ave. Nott ............ 174 A
White's Wood La. Gain ......... 24 C
Whitebeam Gdns. Nott ......... 159 F
Whitechapel St. Nott ......... 160 B
Whitegate Vale. Nott ......... 184 B
Whitehall Ct. Ret ............. 39 F
Whitehall Gdns. Ret ........... 39 F
Whitehall Rd. Ret ............. 39 F
Whitehead Dr. Brin ........... 143 E
Whitehead La. S in A ......... 100 C
Whitehouse Ave. Lough ........ 220 B
Whitelands. Cotg ............. 188 A
Whitely Cl. Staple ........... 182 C
Whitemoor Ave. Nott ......... 172 B4

| | | |
|---|---|---|
| Whitemoor Ct. Nott | 172 | B4 |
| Whitemoor La. Coll | 112 | A2 |
| Whitemoor Rd. Nott | 160 | B1 |
| Whitemoss Cl. Nott | 171 | F2 |
| Whitestone Cl. Mans | 103 | D2 |
| Whitestub La. Kirk | 106 | C3 |
| Whitewater La. Oll | 63 | D1 |
| Whitewater Rd. Oll | 77 | E3 |
| Whitewates La. Blyth | 18 | A2 |
| Whitfield Cl. Nott | 185 | D3 |
| Whitfield St. N-on-T | 140 | A4 |
| Whiting Ave. Bees | 182 | C1 |
| Whitsun Dale. Work | 36 | A4 |
| Whittaker Rd. Bees | 183 | D2 |
| Whittaker Rd. Rain | 118 | A4 |
| Whittier Rd. Nott | 174 | A2 |
| Whittingham Ct. Carl | 162 | A2 |
| Whittingham Rd. Carl | 162 | A2 |
| Whittle Cl. N-on-T | 125 | D1 |
| Whitton Cl. Nott | 147 | D1 |
| Whitton Cl. Ran | 19 | D2 |
| Whitwell Cl. Nott | 159 | F1 |
| Whitwell Rd. Nott | 159 | F1 |
| Whitwell Rd. Th Sa | 34 | A2 |
| Whitworth Dr. Bu Jo | 163 | E1 |
| Whitworth Dr. R on T | 175 | F1 |
| Whitworth Rise. Nott | 160 | C4 |
| Whomsley Cl. N-on-T | 140 | B4 |
| Whyburn La. Huck | 145 | E4 |
| Whyburn St. Huck | 146 | B3 |
| Whyston Ct. Huck | 145 | E3 |
| Wichnor Cl. Nott | 184 | C2 |
| Wickens Wlk. Nott | 173 | F3 |
| Wickersley Dr. K-in-A | 114 | C3 |
| Wickstead Cl. Nott | 161 | F2 |
| Widdowson Cl. Nott | 159 | F4 |
| Wide La. Hath | 213 | D1 |
| Wide La. Wyme | 217 | E2 |
| Wide St. Hath | 213 | D1 |
| Widecombe La. Nott | 195 | E4 |
| Widmerpool La. W-on-W | 217 | E4 |
| Widmerpool Rd. Wys | 207 | F2 |
| Widmerpool St. Pinx | 113 | E1 |
| Wighay Rd. Huck | 131 | D1 |
| Wighay Rd. Linby | 131 | D1 |
| Wigley Cl. Nott | 173 | F3 |
| Wigsley Rd. Harby | 70 | B1 |
| Wigsley Rd. N Sca | 83 | E3 |
| Wigthorpe La. C in L | 26 | A2 |
| Wigthorpe La. C in L | 26 | A3 |
| Wigwam Gr. Huck | 146 | B4 |
| Wigwam La. Huck | 146 | B4 |
| Wilberforce Rd. Mans | 87 | E1 |
| Wilcox Ave. Mans | 88 | A3 |
| Wilcox Dr. Sels | 129 | D1 |
| Wild Hill. S in A | 99 | F4 |
| Wilde Cres. Sels | 129 | D3 |
| Wildman St. Nott | 173 | D3 |
| Wildman Villas. Beck | 14 | A1 |
| Wilford Cl. N-on-T | 140 | A4 |
| Wilford Cres E. Nott | 173 | E1 |
| Wilford Cres W. Nott | 173 | E1 |
| Wilford Cres. Rudd | 196 | B4 |
| Wilford Gr. Nott | 173 | E1 |
| Wilford Gr. Nott | 185 | E4 |
| Wilford La. Nott | 185 | E4 |
| Wilford La. W Brid | 185 | E4 |
| Wilford Rd. Mans | 103 | D2 |
| Wilford Rd. Nott | 173 | D1 |
| Wilford Rd. Nott | 173 | E2 |
| Wilford Rd. Rudd | 185 | E1 |
| Wilford Rd. W. Bald | 140 | B2 |
| Wilfred Gr. W Brid | 185 | F2 |
| Wilhallow La. Sels | 128 | C1 |
| Wilkins Gdns. Nott | 184 | B1 |
| Wilkinson Ave. Bees | 183 | F3 |
| Wilkinson Cl. Plea | 87 | D3 |
| Wilkinson St. Nott | 172 | C4 |
| Willand Cl. Ret | 29 | F1 |
| Willaston Cl. Nott | 160 | B2 |
| Willbert Rd. Arn | 148 | A1 |
| Willerby Rd. Arn | 162 | A3 |
| Willersley Dr. Nott | 173 | E1 |
| Willesden Green. Nuth | 159 | E2 |
| Willetts Ct. S in A | 100 | C1 |
| Willey La. Greas | 144 | A4 |
| William Ave. East | 143 | F1 |
| William Bradford Cl. Aust | 3 | E1 |
| William Cl. Carl | 175 | D4 |
| William Old Ct. Nott | 172 | A3 |
| William Rd. Staple | 182 | B4 |
| William Rd. W Brid | 185 | F4 |
| William St. Huck | 146 | A4 |
| William St. Lo Ea | 182 | B1 |
| William St. Lough | 220 | A2 |
| William St. N-on-T | 140 | A4 |
| William St. Sax | 57 | D2 |
| Williams St. Lan | 16 | C2 |
| Williams St. Bees | 183 | D2 |
| Williamson St. Mans | 101 | F4 |
| Willingham Rd. Lea | 24 | C1 |
| Willis Rd. Nott | 184 | C1 |
| Willoughby Ave. Lo Ea | 182 | B2 |
| Willoughby Ave. Nott | 172 | C2 |
| Willoughby Cl. Nott | 184 | A4 |
| Willoughby Ct. Mans | 103 | D1 |
| Willoughby Ct. Nott | 172 | C2 |
| Willoughby Rd. W Brid | 185 | F3 |
| Willoughby Rd. Widm | 208 | B2 |
| Willoughby St. Bees | 184 | A3 |
| Willoughby St. Coss | 158 | A1 |
| Willoughby St. Gain | 24 | B4 |
| Willoughby St. Nott | 172 | C2 |
| Willow Ave. C in L | 25 | F4 |
| Willow Ave. Carl | 175 | D4 |
| Willow Ave. Huck | 145 | E2 |
| Willow Ave. K-in-A | 114 | C3 |
| Willow Ave. Lo Ea | 182 | B1 |
| Willow Ave. Mans | 89 | D1 |
| Willow Ave. Mist | 6 | C1 |
| Willow Ave. Shireb | 72 | B3 |
| Willow Ave. Staple | 182 | B3 |
| Willow Brook. Keyw | 198 | A1 |
| Willow Cl. Bu Jo | 163 | F3 |
| Willow Cl. E Lea | 214 | B4 |
| Willow Cl. Gain | 15 | D2 |
| Willow Cl. R on T | 175 | F1 |
| Willow Cl. S Norm | 113 | D3 |
| Willow Cl. Sax | 57 | D2 |
| Willow Cl. Sels | 129 | D4 |
| Willow Cl. Work | 35 | F1 |
| Willow Cres. Carl | 163 | D1 |
| Willow Cres. Lamb | 163 | E4 |
| Willow Cres. S in A | 100 | B2 |
| Willow Cres. Sels | 129 | D1 |
| Willow Dr. N Musk | 110 | C1 |
| Willow Hill Cl. Nott | 160 | A3 |
| Willow Holt. Lowd | 150 | C1 |
| Willow Holt. Ret | 39 | F2 |
| Willow Ind Est. Nott | 160 | B4 |
| Willow La. Carl | 163 | D1 |
| Willow Pool La. Su Bo | 213 | E3 |
| Willow Rd. Bald | 140 | B3 |
| Willow Rd. Bing | 178 | A2 |
| Willow Rd. Carl | 175 | D4 |
| Willow Rd. Nott | 172 | C1 |
| Willow Rd. W Brid | 185 | F2 |
| Willow Rise. Sand | 182 | A3 |
| Willow Tree Cl. Mans | 89 | E1 |
| Willow Wong. Bu Jo | 163 | F3 |
| Willowbridge La. S in A | 100 | B1 |
| Willowbrook Cl. Nott | 173 | E1 |
| Willows The. Farn | 139 | D2 |
| Willows The. Nott | 172 | A4 |
| Willwell Dr. W Brid | 185 | E2 |
| Wilmington Cl. Lough | 220 | B1 |
| Wilmington Gdns. Nott | 161 | E3 |
| Wilmot La. Bees | 183 | F3 |
| Wilmot St. Ilk | 157 | F1 |
| Wilmot St. Lo Ea | 193 | D3 |
| Wilne Ave. Lo Ea | 193 | D2 |
| Wilne Rd. Lo Ea | 193 | D2 |
| Wilsic Rd. Tick | 8 | A4 |
| Wilson Ave. K-in-A | 114 | C3 |
| Wilson Cl. Arn | 162 | A3 |
| Wilson Cl. Matt | 11 | D1 |
| Wilson Rd. East | 143 | F1 |
| Wilson St. Gain | 15 | D1 |
| Wilson St. Mans | 87 | E1 |
| Wilson St. N-on-T | 124 | C1 |
| Wilson St. Pinx | 113 | E2 |
| Wilson's La. Morton | 137 | F2 |
| Wilsthorpe Rd. Lo Ea | 193 | D3 |
| Wilsthorpe Rd. Lo Ea | 193 | D4 |
| Wilton Ave. Lough | 220 | B1 |
| Wilton Pl. Ilk | 157 | F1 |
| Wilton Rd. Nott | 172 | C3 |
| Wilton St. Nott | 160 | C2 |
| Wilton Terr. Nott | 160 | C2 |
| Wiltshire Ave. Sels | 128 | A2 |
| Wimbishthorpe Cl. Bott | 181 | D2 |
| Wimbledon Rd. Nott | 161 | D2 |
| Wimborne Cl. W Brid | 185 | E3 |
| Wimpole Rd. Bees | 171 | E1 |
| Winborne Cl. Mans | 101 | E1 |
| Winchester Ave. Bees | 183 | F4 |
| Winchester Cl. E Lea | 205 | F1 |
| Winchester Cl. Mans | 103 | D2 |
| Winchester Cl. Work | 36 | A4 |
| Winchester Cres. Ilk | 170 | A4 |
| Winchester Ct. Nott | 161 | F2 |
| Winchester Dr. Mans | 88 | B2 |
| Winchester St. Nott | 161 | E1 |
| Winchester Terr. Nott | 161 | E2 |
| Winchilsea Ave. N-on-T | 140 | A4 |
| Windermere Ave. Har | 8 | C2 |
| Windermere Cl. Carl | 162 | C1 |
| Windermere Cl. Work | 35 | E4 |
| Windermere Gdns. Lo Ea | 182 | A1 |
| Windermere Rd. Bees | 183 | E4 |
| Windermere Rd. Huck | 145 | F4 |
| Windermere Rd. Lo Ea | 182 | A1 |
| Windermere Rd. Nott | 173 | D4 |
| Windley Dr. Ilk | 157 | E2 |
| Windmill Ave. Huck | 146 | A3 |
| Windmill Cl. Nott | 173 | F3 |
| Windmill Ct. Keyw | 197 | F1 |
| Windmill Gr. Huck | 146 | A3 |
| Windmill Hill. Oxt | 134 | B3 |
| Windmill La. Mans | 102 | B4 |
| Windmill La. Nott | 173 | F3 |
| Windmill La. Work | 47 | D4 |
| Windmill Rd. Lough | 220 | B2 |
| Windmill Way. Kegw | 203 | D1 |
| Windrush Cl. Bees | 171 | E1 |
| Windsmoor Rd. Brin | 143 | E4 |
| Windsor Ave. N-on-T | 139 | F3 |
| Windsor Ave. S in A | 100 | A2 |
| Windsor Cl. Coll | 112 | A4 |
| Windsor Cl. G on H | 12 | C1 |
| Windsor Cl. Huck | 146 | A4 |
| Windsor Cl. Trow | 170 | A3 |
| Windsor Cres. Arn | 162 | A3 |
| Windsor Cres. Staple | 182 | C4 |
| Windsor Ct. Bing | 177 | E2 |
| Windsor Ct. Har | 9 | D3 |
| Windsor Ct. Sand | 182 | A2 |
| Windsor Dr. Mar War | 74 | A2 |
| Windsor Gdns. C in L | 25 | F3 |
| Windsor Gdns. Mans | 102 | B3 |
| Windsor Rd. C in L | 25 | F3 |
| Windsor Rd. Mans | 102 | B3 |
| Windsor Rd. N-on-T | 139 | F3 |
| Windsor Rd. Ret | 29 | E1 |
| Windsor Rd. Sels | 129 | D4 |
| Windsor Rd. Work | 35 | E4 |
| Windsor St. Bees | 184 | A3 |
| Windsor St. Staple | 182 | C4 |
| Windy Ridge. Mar War | 74 | B2 |
| Windyridge. Ever | 11 | E2 |
| Wing Alley. Nott | 173 | E2 |
| Wingate Cl. Nott | 171 | F3 |
| Wingbourne Wlk. Nott | 146 | B1 |
| Wingfield Ave. Work | 36 | A3 |
| Wingfield Dr. Ilk | 157 | E2 |
| Wingfield Dr. Nott | 172 | A1 |
| Wingfield Rd. Mans | 103 | D2 |
| Wings Dr. Huck | 145 | E2 |
| Winifred Cres. Bu Jo | 163 | F2 |
| Winifred St. Huck | 146 | A3 |
| Winifred St. Rhod | 35 | D2 |
| Winkburn La. Hock | 121 | F4 |
| Winkburn Rd. Mans | 101 | F4 |
| Winnery Cl. Tick | 8 | A4 |
| Winrow Gdns. Nott | 160 | B2 |
| Winscale Ave. Nott | 161 | D4 |
| Winscale Gdns. Nott | 161 | D4 |
| Winscombe Mount. Nott | 195 | F4 |
| Winsford Cl. Nott | 160 | A1 |
| Winster Ave. Carl | 162 | B1 |
| Winster Ave. Raven | 117 | D2 |
| Winster Cl. Nott | 171 | F1 |
| Winston Cl. Carl | 162 | B3 |
| Winston Cl. N-on-T | 139 | F3 |
| Winston Dr. Elst | 153 | F2 |
| Winston Gr. Ret | 30 | A1 |
| Winston Green. Matt | 19 | F4 |
| Winter Closes. Sels | 128 | C1 |
| Winterbourne Dr. Staple | 170 | C1 |
| Wintern Ct. Gain | 24 | B3 |
| Winterton Cl. Arn | 161 | F3 |
| Winterton Rise. Nott | 161 | D4 |
| Winthorpe Rd. Arn | 162 | A4 |
| Winthorpe Rd. N-on-T | 125 | D2 |
| Winthorpe St. Mans | 101 | E3 |
| Wintringham Cres. Arn | 162 | A3 |
| Wire La. Newt | 99 | D2 |
| Wisa Terr. Nott | 161 | E2 |
| Wiseton Rd. Clay | 21 | E3 |
| Wishford Ave. Nott | 172 | C2 |
| Wisley Cl. W Brid | 185 | E3 |
| Wistow Cl. Nott | 172 | C4 |
| Witch La. S on T | 96 | C4 |
| Witham Cl. N-on-T | 125 | D1 |
| Withern Rd. Nott | 159 | F1 |
| Witney Cl. Nott | 160 | C4 |
| Wiverton Rd. Nott | 173 | D4 |
| Woburn Ave. K-in-A | 115 | E3 |
| Woburn Croft. Sand | 182 | A2 |
| Woburn La. Mans | 87 | E2 |
| Woburn Pl. Mans | 87 | E2 |
| Woburn Rd. Mans | 87 | E2 |
| Woburn Rise. Arn | 162 | A3 |
| Wodehouse Ave. Goth | 195 | D1 |
| Wolds Dr. Keyw | 197 | F2 |
| Wolds La. Clip | 197 | E1 |
| Wolds Rise. Keyw | 197 | F2 |
| Wolfit Ave. Bald | 140 | C3 |
| Wollacombe Cl. Carl | 162 | B3 |
| Wollaton Ave. Carl | 162 | C1 |
| Wollaton Cres. Bees | 183 | F4 |
| Wollaton Ct. Nott | 160 | C3 |
| Wollaton Hall Dr. Nott | 172 | B2 |
| Wollaton Paddocks. Nott | 171 | E2 |
| Wollaton Rd. Bees | 183 | F4 |
| Wollaton Rd. K-in-A | 115 | E3 |
| Wollaton Rd. Nott | 172 | B3 |
| Wollaton Rise. Nott | 171 | F1 |
| Wollaton St. Nott | 173 | D3 |
| Wollaton Vale. Nott | 171 | F1 |
| Wolseley Ct. S in A | 100 | C2 |
| Wolsey Ave. Nott | 172 | C3 |
| Wolsey Dr. K-in-A | 115 | D4 |
| Wolsey N-on-T | 125 | D2 |
| Wolsey Way. Lough | 220 | B2 |
| Wong La. Tick | 8 | A4 |
| Wood Ave. Elmt | 58 | B4 |
| Wood Ave. Sand | 182 | A3 |
| Wood Cl. Mans | 102 | C4 |
| Wood End Dr. Raven | 117 | D1 |
| Wood Gate. Lough | 220 | A2 |
| Wood Gr. Calv | 148 | C4 |
| Wood Hill. Ol Da | 218 | C2 |
| Wood La. B-le-V | 192 | B1 |
| Wood La. Beck | 23 | D4 |
| Wood La. Carl | 163 | D1 |
| Wood La. Egma | 79 | F3 |
| Wood La. Elmt | 58 | B4 |
| Wood La. Elmt | 58 | B4 |
| Wood La. G on H | 12 | C2 |
| Wood La. Goth | 204 | C4 |
| Wood La. Huck | 145 | F4 |
| Wood La. Kers | 94 | A1 |
| Wood La. Mar War | 73 | F4 |
| Wood La. N Whea | 22 | B1 |
| Wood La. Plea | 72 | C1 |
| Wood La. S Sca | 98 | C3 |
| Wood La. Shireb | 72 | C1 |
| Wood La. Tres | 41 | F2 |
| Wood Link. Nott | 159 | F4 |
| Wood Nook Cl. Sels | 128 | C3 |
| Wood St. Arn | 161 | F4 |
| Wood St. East | 143 | F2 |
| Wood St. Ilk | 157 | F1 |
| Wood St. Mans | 102 | A4 |
| Wood St. Mar War | 74 | A3 |
| Wood St. N-on-T | 140 | A4 |
| Wood St. Nott | 173 | D3 |
| Wood View Bsns Cntre. Nott | 147 | D1 |
| Wood View. W Brid | 186 | A2 |
| Wood's La. Flint | 153 | D1 |
| Woodbank Dr. Nott | 171 | E1 |
| Woodbeck Rise. Ret | 39 | E4 |
| Woodborough La. Arn | 148 | B2 |
| Woodborough Rd. Mans | 87 | F1 |
| Woodborough Rd. Nott | 161 | F1 |
| Woodbridge Ave. Nott | 184 | C2 |
| Woodchurch Rd. Bes Vil | 147 | D1 |
| Woodcoates Rd. Darl | 67 | D3 |
| Wooden Beck Hill. Walker | 13 | E2 |
| Woodfield Rd. Gain | 15 | F1 |
| Woodfield Rd. Nott | 159 | F1 |
| Woodfield Rd. Pinx | 113 | E2 |
| Woodford Cl. Nott | 146 | C1 |
| Woodford Rd. Arn | 162 | A3 |
| Woodford Rd. Huck | 146 | A3 |
| Woodgate Cl. Cotg | 187 | F2 |
| Woodgate La. Beckin | 142 | C4 |
| Woodgate La. Cotg | 187 | E2 |
| Woodgate Rd. E Lea | 214 | B4 |
| Woodhall Cl. K-in-A | 114 | C4 |
| Woodhall Cl. Mans | 102 | C4 |
| Woodhall Cres. Sax | 56 | C2 |
| Woodhall Gdns. Mans | 102 | C4 |
| Woodhall Green. Ret | 39 | E1 |
| Woodhall Rd. Nott | 172 | A3 |
| Woodhead Cl. Edwin | 76 | A1 |
| Woodhedge Dr. Nott | 174 | A4 |
| Woodhill Rd. Coll | 99 | F2 |
| Woodhouse La. C in L | 26 | A4 |
| Woodhouse La. Hod | 17 | D1 |
| Woodhouse La. S in A | 101 | D1 |
| Woodhouse Pl. Tux | 66 | A1 |
| Woodhouse Rd. Mans | 102 | A4 |
| Woodhouse St. Nott | 173 | F3 |
| Woodhouse Way. Nott | 159 | E2 |
| Woodhouse Way. Nuth | 159 | E2 |
| Woodkirk Rd. Nott | 184 | C1 |
| Woodlake Gdns. Nott | 173 | F4 |
| Woodland Ave. Gain | 15 | D2 |
| Woodland Ave. Ilk | 157 | E2 |
| Woodland Ave. S in A | 99 | F2 |
| Woodland Ave. Work | 36 | A1 |
| Woodland Cl. Cotg | 187 | F1 |
| Woodland Cl. Farns | 120 | A3 |
| Woodland Cl. N Clip | 90 | A2 |
| Woodland Cl. R on T | 176 | A2 |
| Woodland Cres. Mans | 102 | C2 |
| Woodland Dr. Mans | 102 | C2 |
| Woodland Dr. Nott | 161 | E1 |
| Woodland Dr. Nuth | 159 | F2 |
| Woodland Dr. South | 121 | E1 |
| Woodland Dr. Work | 35 | F3 |
| Woodland Gr. Arn | 161 | E2 |
| Woodland Gr. Bees | 183 | E3 |
| Woodland Gr. Carl | 174 | C3 |
| Woodland Gr. Mans | 88 | B2 |
| Woodland Gr. Mar War | 74 | A3 |
| Woodland Rd. Mans | 102 | C4 |
| Woodland Rd. W Brid | 173 | F1 |
| Woodland Rise. Raven | 117 | D1 |
| Woodland View. Scarc | 59 | D2 |
| Woodland View. South | 136 | B4 |
| Woodland Walk. K-in-A | 115 | E3 |
| Woodland Way. East | 143 | F1 |
| Woodlands Cl. N-on-T | 139 | F3 |
| Woodlands Cl. Wyme | 216 | B2 |
| Woodlands Dr. Lough | 220 | A1 |
| Woodlands Farm Cl. Huck | 145 | E2 |
| Woodlands Gr. Huck | 145 | E2 |
| Woodlands The. Blyth | 18 | A3 |
| Woodlands The. Mans | 88 | A1 |
| Woodlands The. Nott | 160 | B3 |
| Woodlands The. Scarc | 59 | D2 |
| Woodlands. Wint | 125 | D4 |
| Woodley Sq. Nott | 146 | B1 |
| Woodley St. Rudd | 196 | B4 |
| Woodmill Ave. Gain | 15 | F1 |
| Woods Hill. S in A | 100 | C1 |
| Woods La. Calv | 148 | C4 |
| Woods Terr. Gain | 15 | E1 |
| Woodsend. Bu Jo | 163 | F2 |
| Woodsetts La. Work | 25 | D1 |
| Woodsford Gr. Nott | 184 | C1 |
| Woodside Ave. Kim | 159 | D3 |
| Woodside Ave. Mans | 102 | B2 |
| Woodside Ave. R on T | 176 | A2 |
| Woodside Cres. Ilk | 157 | E3 |
| Woodside Cres. Lo Ea | 193 | D4 |
| Woodside Dr. Arn | 161 | E4 |
| Woodside Rd. Bees | 183 | D2 |
| Woodside Rd. Bu Jo | 163 | E2 |
| Woodside Rd. Nott | 183 | F4 |
| Woodside Rd. R on T | 176 | A2 |
| Woodside Rd. Raven | 116 | C2 |
| Woodside Rd. Sand | 182 | A3 |
| Woodside Rd. Shire | 34 | C4 |
| Woodside Rd. Shireb | 72 | C3 |
| Woodside View. Har | 9 | D2 |
| Woodside. East | 143 | F2 |
| Woodside. Farns | 120 | A3 |
| Woodside. Ret | 39 | E4 |
| Woodside. S in A | 100 | C4 |
| Woodstock Ave. Nott | 172 | C3 |
| Woodstock Cl. N-on-T | 140 | B4 |
| Woodstock Rd. Bees | 182 | C2 |
| Woodstock St. Huck | 146 | A3 |
| Woodston Wlk. Arn | 148 | A1 |
| Woodthorpe Ave. Nott | 161 | F2 |
| Woodthorpe Ave. Lough | 220 | A1 |
| Woodthorpe Ct. Nott | 161 | F2 |
| Woodthorpe Dr. Arn | 161 | F2 |
| Woodthorpe Gdns. Nott | 161 | F2 |
| Woodthorpe Rd. Lough | 220 | A1 |
| Woodthorpe Rd. Nott | 161 | F2 |
| Woodview Ct. Nott | 174 | B3 |
| Woodview Gdns. Mans | 89 | E1 |
| Woodview. Cotg | 188 | A1 |
| Woodville Cl. Bees | 183 | E3 |
| Woodville Dr. Nott | 161 | E2 |
| Woodville Rd. Nott | 161 | E1 |
| Woodward St. Nott | 173 | E1 |
| Woodyard La. Nott | 172 | A3 |
| Woollaton St. Huck | 146 | A4 |
| Woolmer Rd. Nott | 173 | E1 |
| Woolpack La. Nott | 173 | E2 |
| Woolpack St. Ret | 39 | F4 |
| Woolsington Cl. Nott | 159 | E1 |
| Woolsthorpe Cl. Nott | 172 | A3 |
| Wootton Cl. Nott | 171 | E4 |
| Worcester Ave. Mans | 88 | B3 |
| Worcester Cl. Lowd | 150 | C1 |
| Worcester Cl. Work | 36 | A4 |
| Worcester Gdns. Arn | 161 | F3 |
| Worcester Mews. Mans | 88 | B3 |
| Worcester Rd. Arn | 161 | F3 |
| Wordsworth Ave. Huck | 145 | E3 |
| Wordsworth Ave. Mans | 88 | A2 |
| Wordsworth Ave. S in A | 100 | A2 |
| Wordsworth Dr. Bald | 140 | B3 |
| Wordsworth Rd. Arn | 161 | E4 |
| Wordsworth Rd. Awsw | 158 | B3 |
| Wordsworth Rd. Nott | 172 | C3 |
| Wordsworth Rd. W Brid | 185 | F3 |
| Worksop Rd. Babw | 49 | E4 |
| Worksop Rd. Blyth | 18 | A1 |
| Worksop Rd. Budby | 76 | B3 |
| Worksop Rd. Cuck | 60 | A2 |
| Worksop Rd. Edwin | 76 | B3 |
| Worksop Rd. Elk | 49 | E4 |
| Worksop Rd. Oll | 76 | B3 |
| Worksop Rd. Whit | 45 | D4 |
| Worksop Rd. Woods | 25 | D1 |
| Worrall Ave. Arn | 161 | F4 |
| Worrall Ave. Lo Ea | 182 | C1 |
| Worth St. Carl | 174 | C4 |
| Worthington Rd. Bald | 140 | C2 |
| Wortley Cl. Ilk | 170 | A4 |
| Wortley Ave. Staple | 170 | B2 |
| Wortley Hall Cl. Nott | 172 | B1 |
| Worwood Dr. W Brid | 185 | E2 |
| Wossock La. W Lea | 204 | C2 |
| Woulds Field. Cotg | 187 | F1 |
| Wray Cl. Nott | 173 | F3 |
| Wren Ct. Work | 35 | E4 |
| Wrenthorpe Vale. Nott | 184 | C1 |
| Wrenthorpe Vale. Nott | 195 | F4 |
| Wright St. Carl | 175 | D4 |
| Wright St. N-on-T | 140 | A4 |
| Wright Wilson St. Ret | 39 | F3 |
| Wrights Orch. Keyw | 197 | F1 |
| Wrightson Cl. S in A | 101 | D2 |
| Wroot Rd. Fin | 1 | A3 |
| Wroughton Ct. East | 144 | A1 |
| Wroxham Dr. Nott | 171 | E1 |
| Wycar Rd. Bils | 106 | A2 |
| Wychwood Dr. Staple | 170 | B1 |
| Wychwood Rd. Bing | 177 | E2 |
| Wycliffe Gr. Nott | 161 | F1 |
| Wycliffe St. Nott | 160 | C1 |
| Wycombe Cl. Nott | 195 | E4 |
| Wye Gdns. Nott | 172 | B3 |
| Wyggeston Rd. Bott | 181 | D2 |
| Wyke La. Farn | 138 | C3 |

# Wykeham Rd. Arn

Zulla Rd. No

Wykeham Rd. Arn ............. 162 A3
Wykes Ave. Carl ................ 162 C1
Wymeswold Rd. Hoton ...... 215 F1
Wymeswold Rd. Remp ...... 215 F3
Wymeswold Rd. Wys ........ 207 E1
Wymondham Cl. Arn ......... 162 A3
Wynbreck Dr. Keyw .......... 197 F2
Wyndale Dr. Mans ............ 103 D3
Wyndham Ct. Bees ........... 183 D2
Wyndham Mews. Nott ....... 173 D4
Wyndings The. Arn ........... 161 F2
Wynhill Ct. Bing ................ 177 E3
Wynlea Dr. Old .................... 16 C3
Wynndale Dr. Nott ............. 161 D2
Wynwood Cl. Bees ............ 183 D1
Wynwood Rd. Bees ........... 183 D1
Wyrale Dr. Nott ................ 159 F1

Wysall Cl. Mans ................... 87 F1
Wysall La. Keyw ................ 207 E4
Wysall La. Wyme .............. 216 B3
Wysall Rd. Bunn ............... 197 D1
Wysall Rd. Bunn ............... 207 D4
Wysall Rd. Cost ................ 206 C1
Wysall Rd. Remp .............. 215 F3
Wysall Rd. Widrn ,............. 208 A2
Wyton Cl. Nott .................. 161 D3
Wyvelle Cres. Kegw ......... 203 E2
Wyvern Ave. Lo Ea ........... 193 E3
Wyvern Cl. Greas ............. 158 A4
Wyville Cl. Nott ................. 172 C3

Yalding Dr. Nott ................ 171 E2
Yalding Gdns. Nott ........... 171 E2
Yarwell Cl. Nott ................ 174 B4

Yates Gdns. Nott ............... 161 D4
Yatesbury Cres. Nott ......... 171 F4
Yeoman Ave. Bes Vil ........ 146 C2
Yeomans Ct. Nott .............. 173 D2
Yeovil Ct. Mans ................ 103 D1
Yew Cl. E Lea ................... 214 B4
Yew Cl. Nott ..................... 161 E1
Yew Tree Ave. K-in-A ........ 114 C3
Yew Tree Ave. Nott ........... 161 E1
Yew Tree Cl. Oll .................. 77 E3
Yew Tree Cl. R on T .......... 175 E2
Yew Tree Dr. Baw ................. 9 F4
Yew Tree Dr. S in A ............. 99 F1
Yew Tree Dr. Shireb ........... 72 B3
Yew Tree La. Carl .............. 163 D1
Yew Tree La. Nott .............. 184 B1
Yew Tree Rd. Elk ................ 50 A2

Yew Tree Rd. Huck ........... 146 A2
Yew Tree Rd. Oll ................. 77 E3
Yewdale Cl. Nott ............... 195 E4
Yonge Cl. R on T .............. 175 F1
York Ave. Bees ................. 183 F2
York Ave. Sand ................. 182 A2
York Ave. Sels .................. 128 A2
York Cl. Carl ..................... 162 C1
York Cl. E Lea .................. 205 E1
York Dr. Nott .................... 159 E1
York Pl. Shire ..................... 34 C4
York Rd. Har ....................... 9 D2
York Rd. Lo Ea ................. 182 B1
York Rd. Lough ................. 220 A2
York Rd. Shireb .................. 72 C2
York Rd. Tick ....................... 8 A4
York St. Carl ..................... 175 D4

York St. E Mark ................. 65 F
York St. Mans ................... 102 A
York St. Nott .................... 173 B
York St. S in A .................. 100 C
York Terr. Mar War ............ 74 A
York Terr. Mist .................... 7 B
York Terr. Pinx .................. 113 B
Yorke Dr. N-on-T .............. 125 D
Yorke St. Huck ................. 146 A
Yorke St. Mans ................... 88 A
Young Cl. Nott .................. 159 F
Young Cres. S in A ........... 101 D
Yvonne Cres. Carl ............ 174 C

Zouch Rd. N on S ............. 213 D
Zulla Rd. Nott ................... 173 E
Zulu Rd. Nott .................... 160 C

# ORDNANCE SURVEY
# STREET ATLASES

**The Ordnance Survey / Philip's County Street Atlases provide unique and definitive mapping of entire counties**

## Counties available

- ◆ Berkshire
- ◆ Buckinghamshire
- ◆ East Essex
- ◆ West Essex
- ◆ North Hampshire
- ◆ South Hampshire
- ◆ Hertfordshire
- ◆ East Kent
- ◆ West Kent
- ◆ Nottinghamshire
- ◆ Oxfordshire
- ◆ Surrey
- ◆ East Sussex
- ◆ West Sussex
- ◆ Warwickshire

*The County Street Atlases are revised and updated on a regular basis and new titles are added to the series. Many counties are now available in full-size hardback and softback editions as well as handy pocket-size versions.*

*The series is available from all good bookshops or by mail order direct from the publisher. However, the order form opposite may not reflect the complete range of titles available so it is advisable to check by telephone before placing your order. Payment can be made by credit card or cheque/postal order in the following ways:*

## By phone

*Phone your order through on our special Credit Card Hotline on 0933 410511. Speak to our customer service team during office hours (9am to 5pm) or leave a message on the answering machine, quoting CSA94, your full credit card number plus expiry date and your full name and address*

## By post

*Simply fill out the order form opposite (you may photocopy it) and send it to:*
*Cash Sales Department, Reed Book Services, PO Box 5, Rushden, Northants, NN10 6YX*

# STREET ATLASES

**CSA94**

| | Hardback | | Softback | | Pocket | | | |
|---|---|---|---|---|---|---|---|---|
| | QUANTITY | TOTAL | QUANTITY | TOTAL | QUANTITY | TOTAL | | |
| | **£12.99** | | **£8.99** | | **£4.99** | | | |
| **East Essex** | | £ | | £ | | £ | | £ |
| | ISBN 0-540-05848-3 | | ISBN 0-540-05866-1 | | ISBN 0-540-05850-5 | | | |
| **West Essex** | | £ | | £ | | £ | | £ |
| | ISBN 0-540-05849-1 | | ISBN 0-540-05867-X | | ISBN 0-540-05851-3 | | | |
| **North Hampshire** | | £ | | £ | | £ | | £ |
| | ISBN 0-540-05852-1 | | ISBN 0-540-05853-X | | ISBN 0-540-05854-8 | | | |
| **South Hampshire** | | £ | | £ | | £ | | £ |
| | ISBN 0-540-05855-6 | | ISBN 0-540-05856-4 | | ISBN 0-540-05857-2 | | | |
| **Nottinghamshire** | | £ | | £ | | £ | | £ |
| | ISBN 0-540-05858-0 | | ISBN 0-540-05859-9 | | ISBN 0-540-05860-2 | | | |
| **East Sussex** | | £ | | £ | | £ | | £ |
| | ISBN 0-540-05875-0 | | ISBN 0-540-05874-2 | | ISBN 0-540-05873-4 | | | |
| **West Sussex** | | £ | | £ | | £ | | £ |
| | ISBN 0-540-05876-9 | | ISBN 0-540-05877-7 | | ISBN 0-540-05878-5 | | | |
| | **£10.99** | | | | **£4.99** | | | |
| **Berkshire** | | £ | | | | £ | | £ |
| | ISBN 0-540-05738-X | | | | ISBN 0-540-05835-1 | | | |
| **Buckinghamshire** | | £ | | | | £ | | £ |
| | ISBN 0-540-05660-X | | | | ISBN 0-540-05711-8 | | | |
| **Hertfordshire** | | £ | | | | £ | | £ |
| | ISBN 0-540-05720-7 | | | | ISBN 0-540-05840-8 | | | |
| **East Kent** | | £ | | | | | | £ |
| | ISBN 0-540-05661-8 | | | | | | | |
| **West Kent** | | £ | | | | | | £ |
| | ISBN 0-540-05662-6 | | | | | | | |
| **Oxfordshire** | | £ | | | | | | £ |
| | ISBN 0-540-05665-0 | | | | | | | |
| **Warwickshire** | | £ | | | | | | £ |
| | ISBN 0-540-05642-1 | | | | | | | |
| | **£10.99** | | | | **£3.99** | | | |
| **Surrey** | | £ | | | | £ | | £ |
| | ISBN 0-540-05694-4 | | | | ISBN 0-540-05708-8 | | | |

Name _____

Address _____

Postcode _____

I enclose a cheque/postal order for £ _____ made payable to **Reed Book Services** or please debit my ◄ *Access*
◄ *American Express*
◄ *Visa*
*account by*
£ _____

Account number ◯◯◯◯◯ ◯◯◯◯◯ ◯◯◯◯◯ ◯◯◯◯◯

Expiry date ◯◯ ◯◯

Signature _____

◯ Please tick this box if you do not wish your name to be used by other carefully selected organisations that may wish to send you information about other products and services

◆ *Free postage and packing* ◆ *All available titles will normally be dispatched within 5 working days of receipt of order, but please allow up to 28 days for delivery.*

Registered office: Michelin House, 81 Fulham Road, London SW3 6RB. Registered in England No 1974080

John Beal   0115 9879458

0971 121 586

11.30

Gedling

FRITHS ENTERPRISE

LIGHTS.